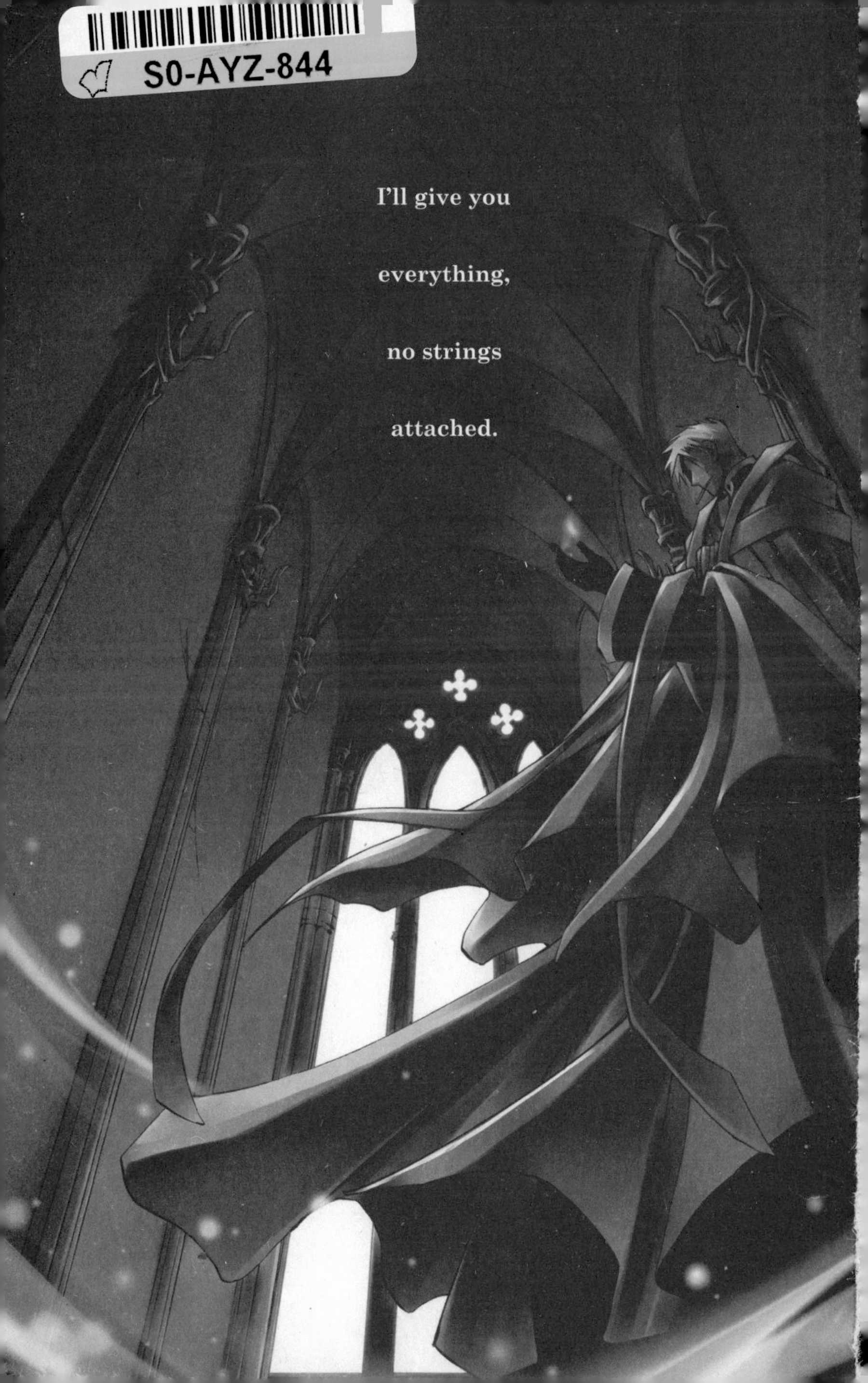
I'll give you
everything,
no strings
attached.

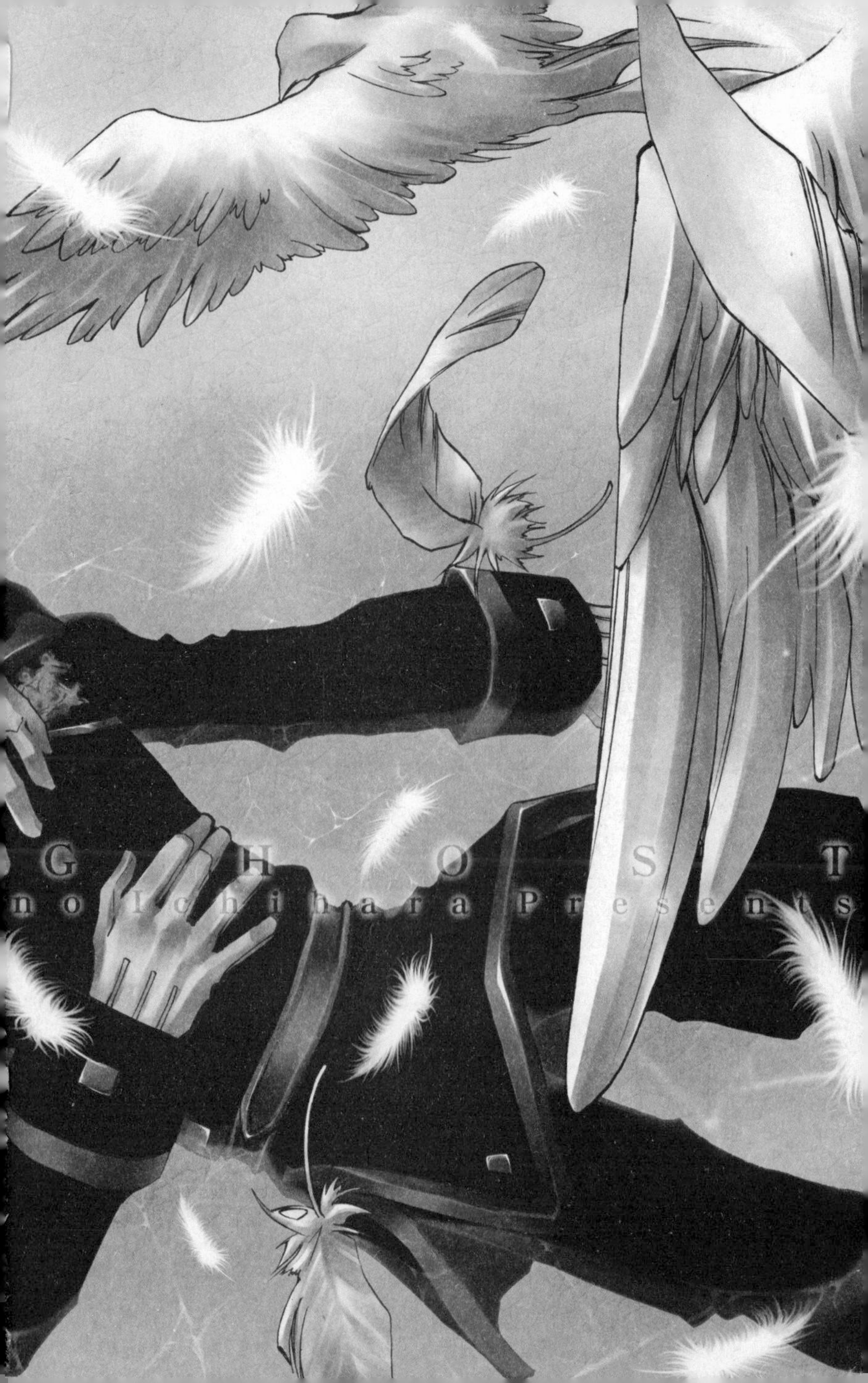
GHOST
noIchihara Presents

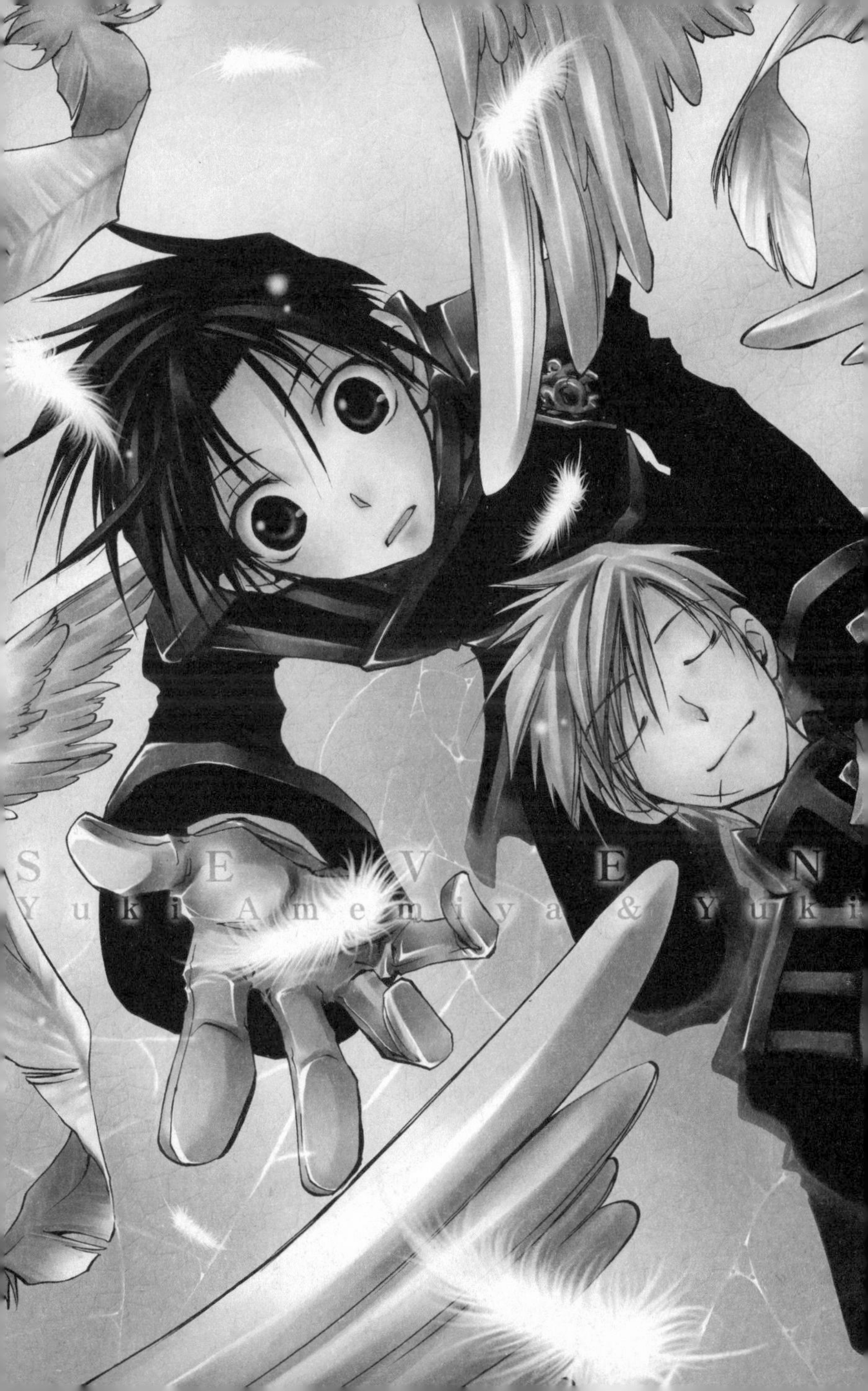
S E V E N
Yuki Amemiya & Yuki

C O N T E N T S

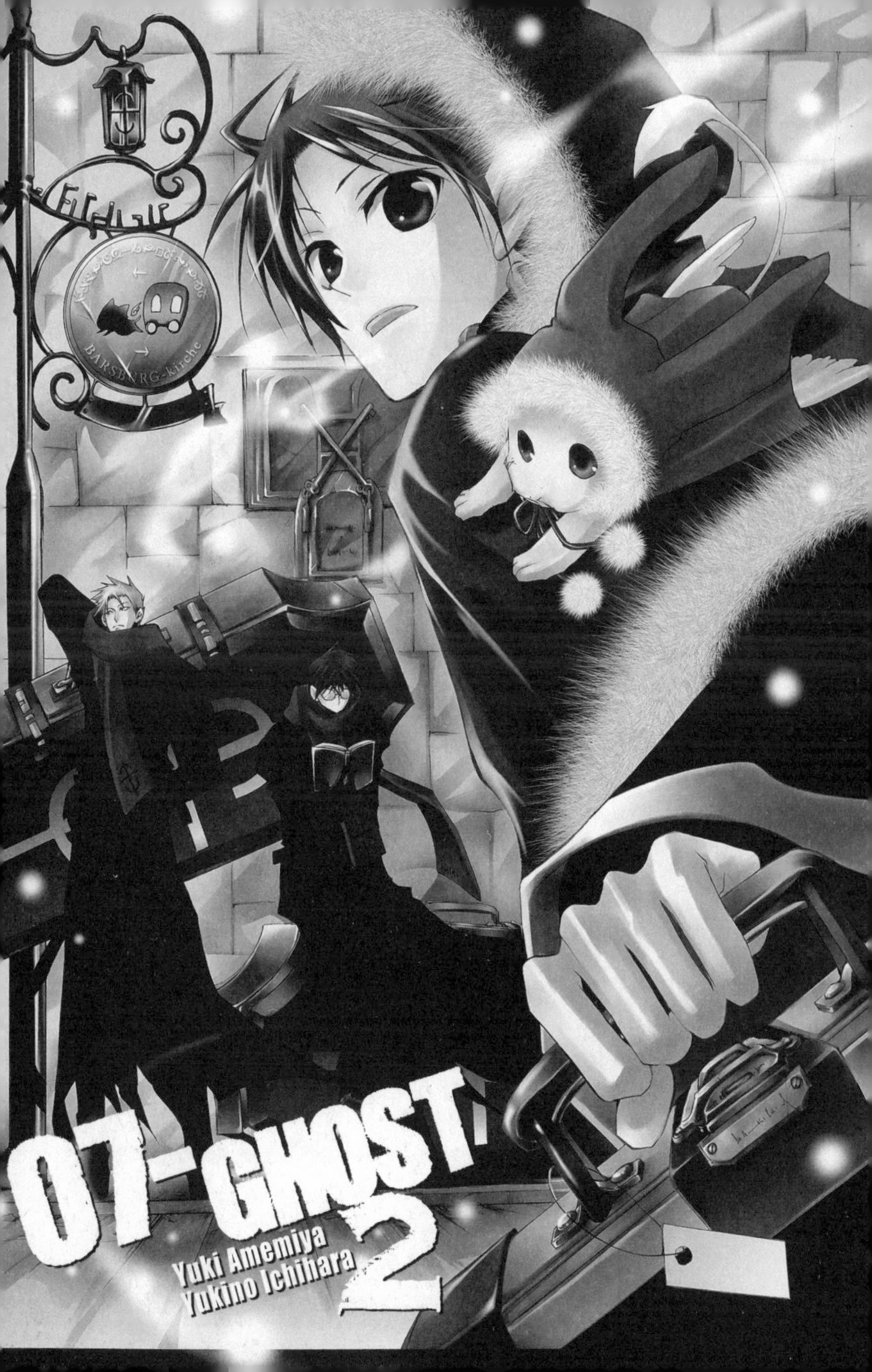
BARSBURG-kirche
07-GHOST
2
Yuki Amemiya
Yukino Ichihara

07 GHOST

Characters

One thousand years ago, two equally powerful nations coexisted. One was the Barsburg Empire, protected by the Eye of Raphael. The other was the Raggs Kingdom, protected by the Eye of Mikael. Now that the Raggs Kingdom has been destroyed, things have changed...

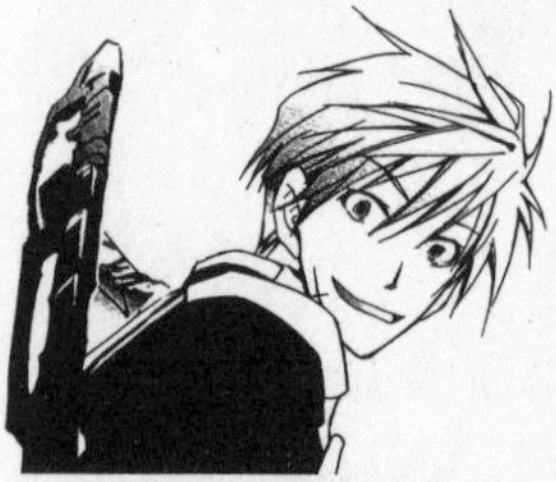

Mikage

Teito's best friend. He helped Teito escape the military academy.

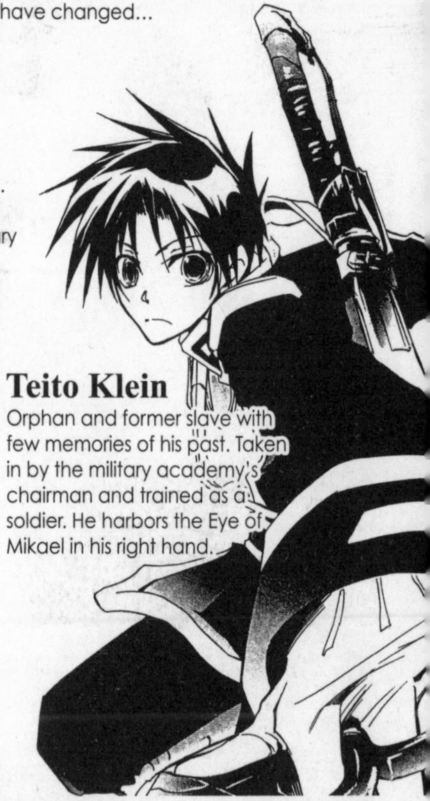

Teito Klein

Orphan and former slave with few memories of his past. Taken in by the military academy's chairman and trained as a soldier. He harbors the Eye of Mikael in his right hand.

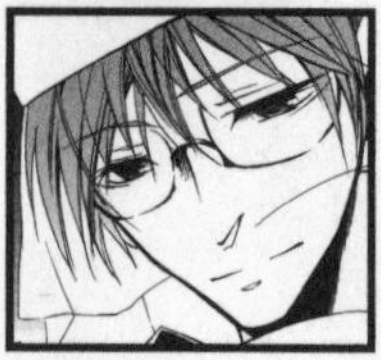

Castor

Bishop who can manipulate puppets. Along with Frau, he shelters Teito.

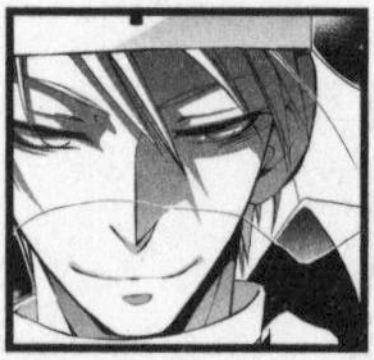

Frau

Bishop who saved Teito when he was fleeing from the academy.

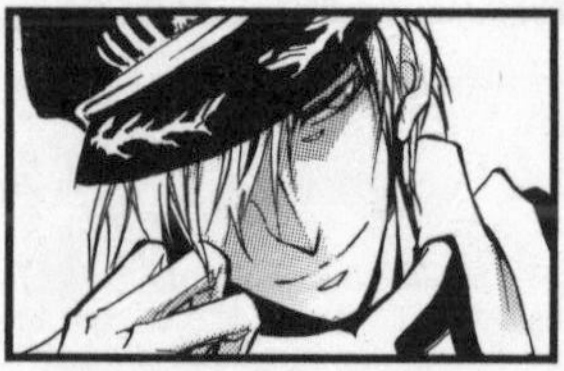

Ayanami

Imperial Army's Chief of Staff. Murderer of the King of Raggs?

Story

Teito is a student at the Barsburg Empire's military academy until the day he discovers his father was the king of Raggs, the ruler of a kingdom the Barsburg Empire destroyed. Teito runs away and is given sanctuary by the Barsburg Church's bishops. His best friend Mikage soon joins him, but the reunion sours when Mikage, possessed by another, attacks Teito.

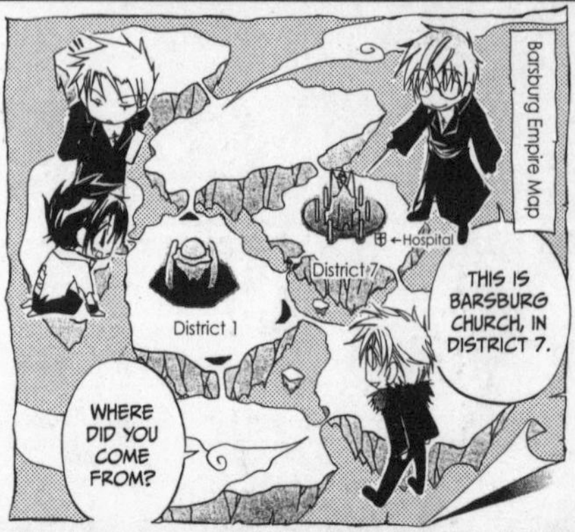

Barsburg Empire Map
←Hospital
District 7
District 1
THIS IS BARSBURG CHURCH, IN DISTRICT 7.
WHERE DID YOU COME FROM?

Kapitel.6 "Awakening"

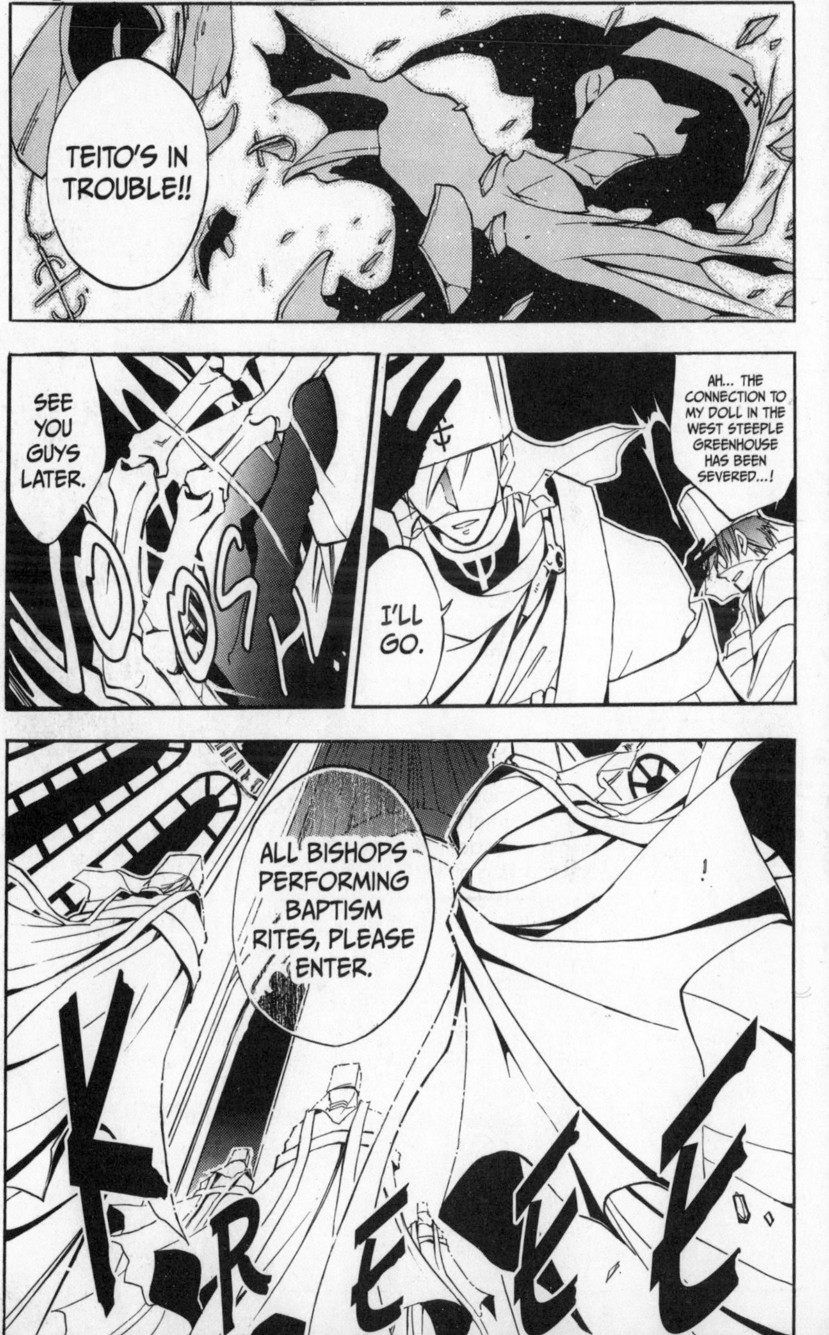
TEITO'S IN TROUBLE!!
AH... THE CONNECTION TO MY DOLL IN THE WEST STEEPLE GREENHOUSE HAS BEEN SEVERED...!
I'LL GO.
SEE YOU GUYS LATER.
ALL BISHOPS PERFORMING BAPTISM RITES, PLEASE ENTER.

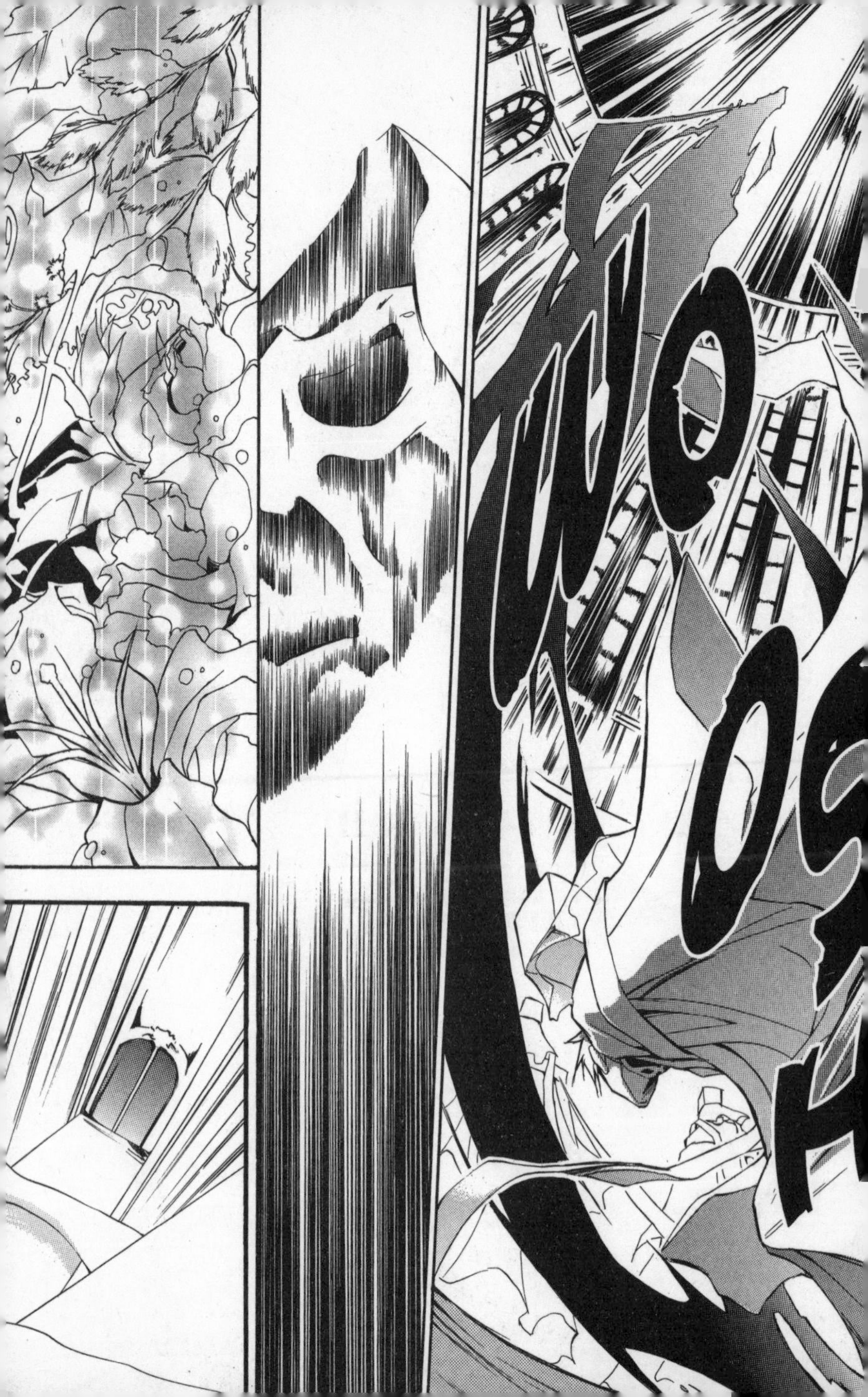
WHOOSH

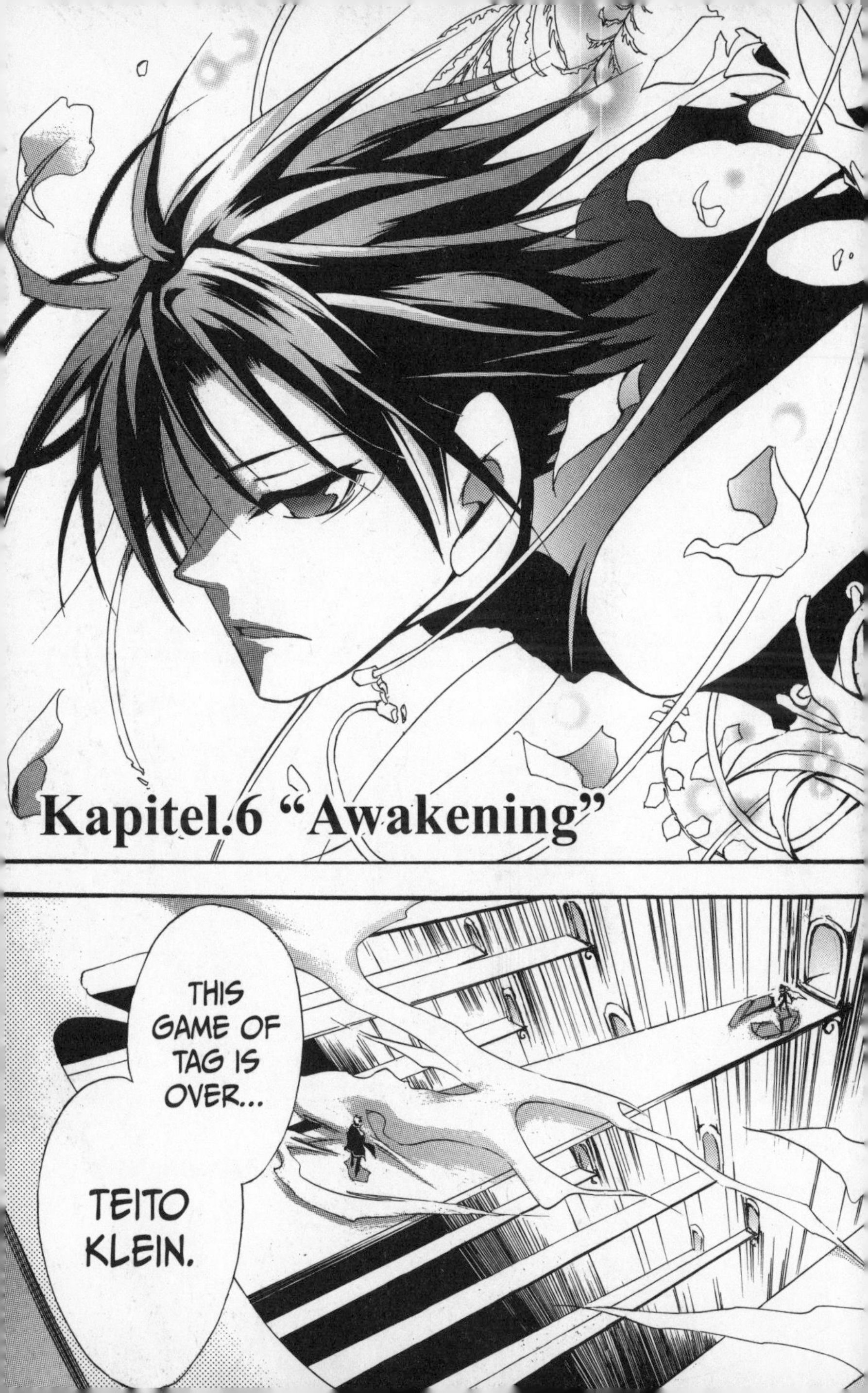
Kapitel.6 “Awakening”
THIS GAME OF TAG IS OVER...
TEITO KLEIN.

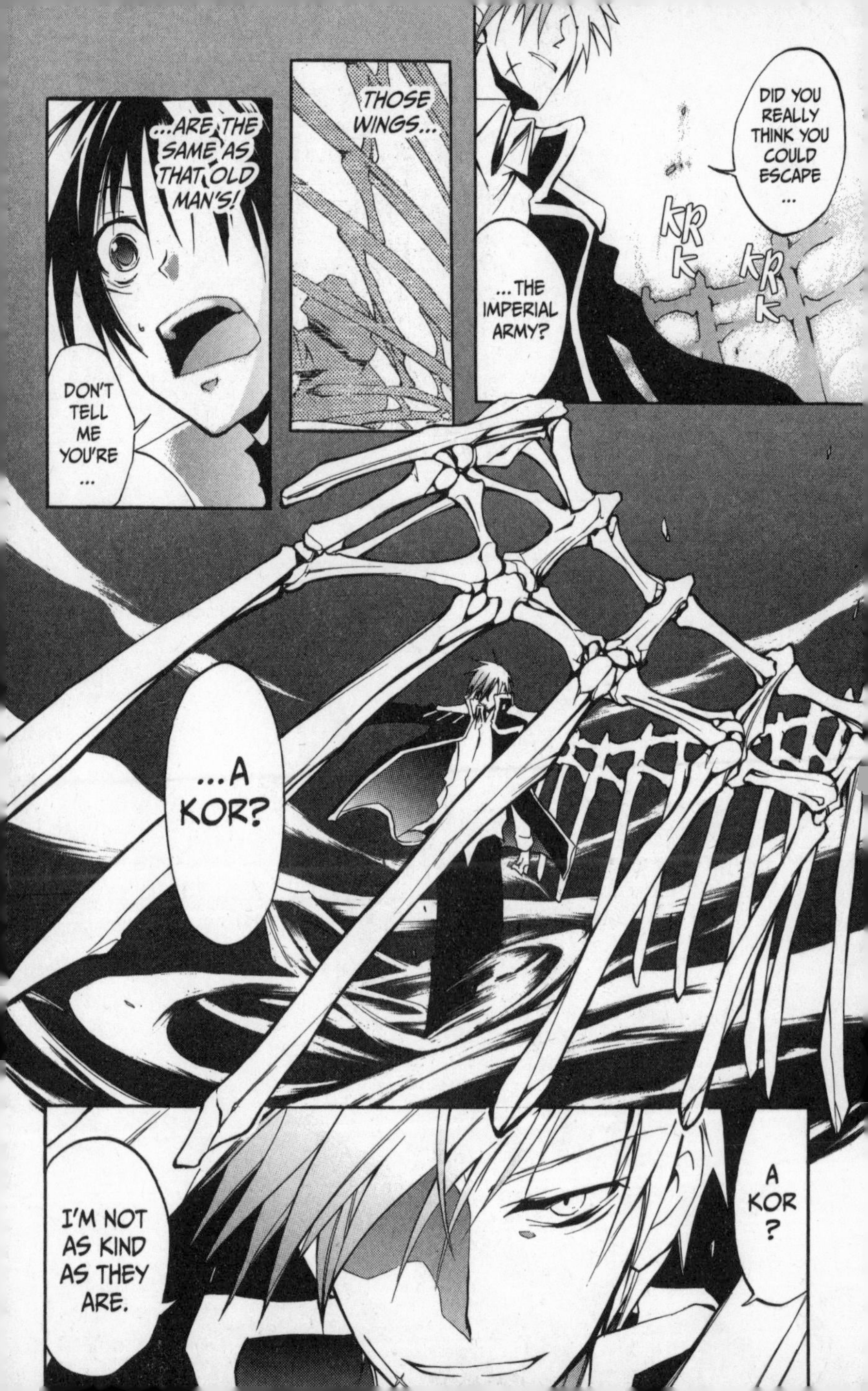
DID YOU REALLY THINK YOU COULD ESCAPE ...
KRK
KRK
...THE IMPERIAL ARMY?
THOSE WINGS...
...ARE THE SAME AS THAT OLD MAN'S!
DON'T TELL ME YOU'RE ...
...A KOR?
A KOR?
I'M NOT AS KIND AS THEY ARE.

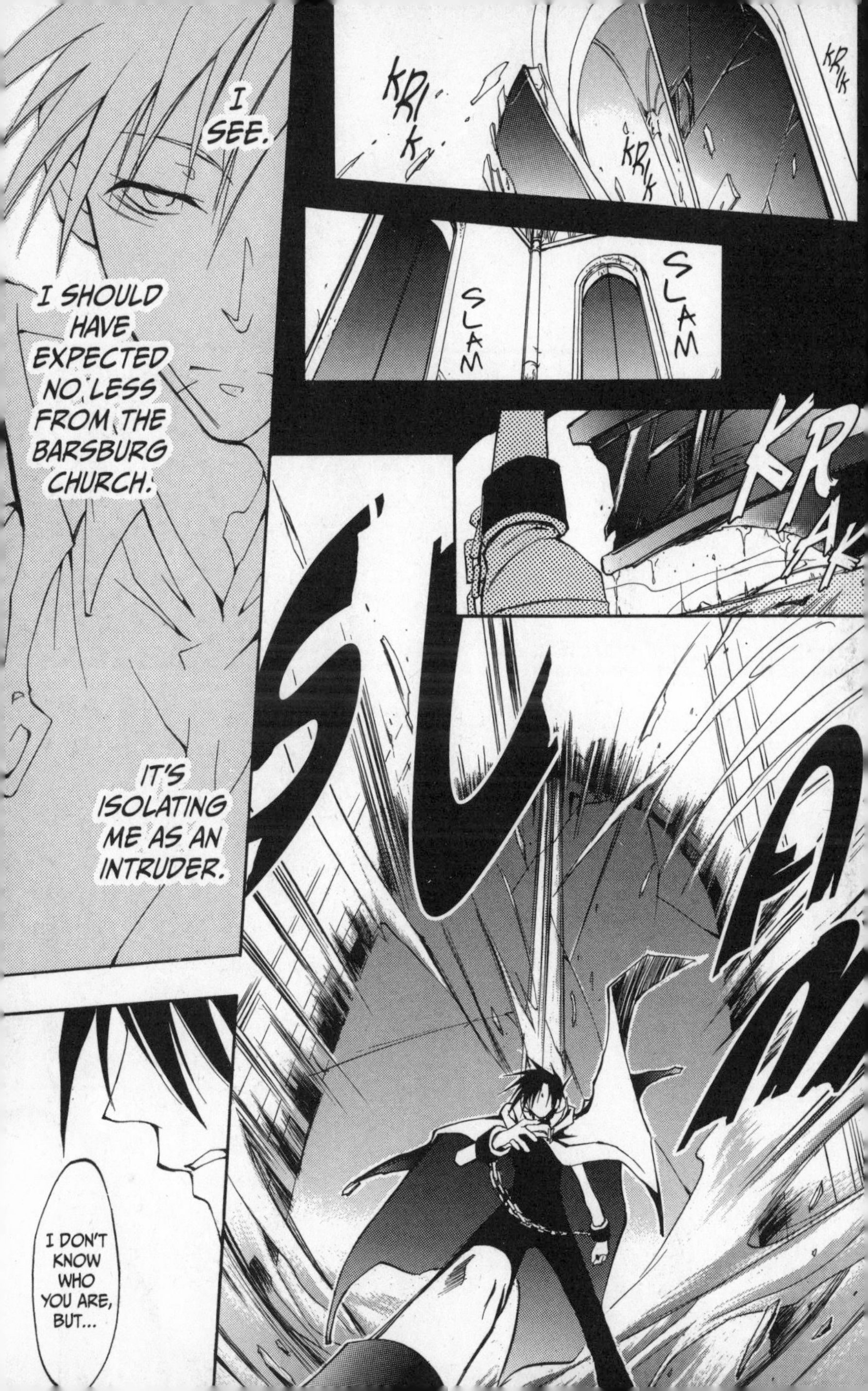
KRIK
KRIK
KRIK
SLAM
SLAM
KRAK
I SEE.
I SHOULD HAVE EXPECTED NO LESS FROM THE BARSBURG CHURCH.
IT'S ISOLATING ME AS AN INTRUDER.
SLAM
I DON'T KNOW WHO YOU ARE, BUT...

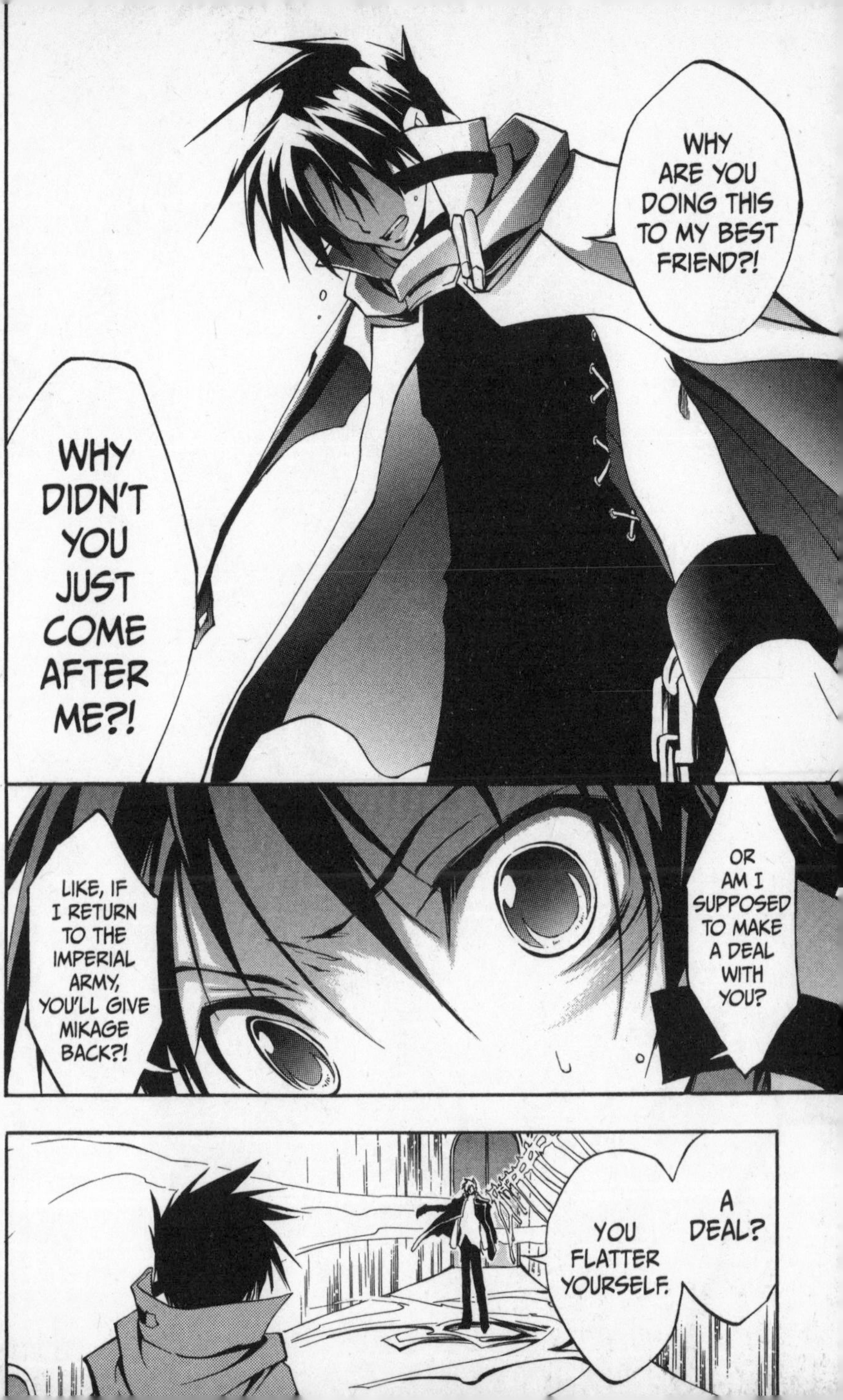
WHY ARE YOU DOING THIS TO MY BEST FRIEND?!
WHY DIDN'T YOU JUST COME AFTER ME?!
OR AM I SUPPOSED TO MAKE A DEAL WITH YOU?
LIKE, IF I RETURN TO THE IMPERIAL ARMY, YOU'LL GIVE MIKAGE BACK?!
A DEAL?
YOU FLATTER YOURSELF.

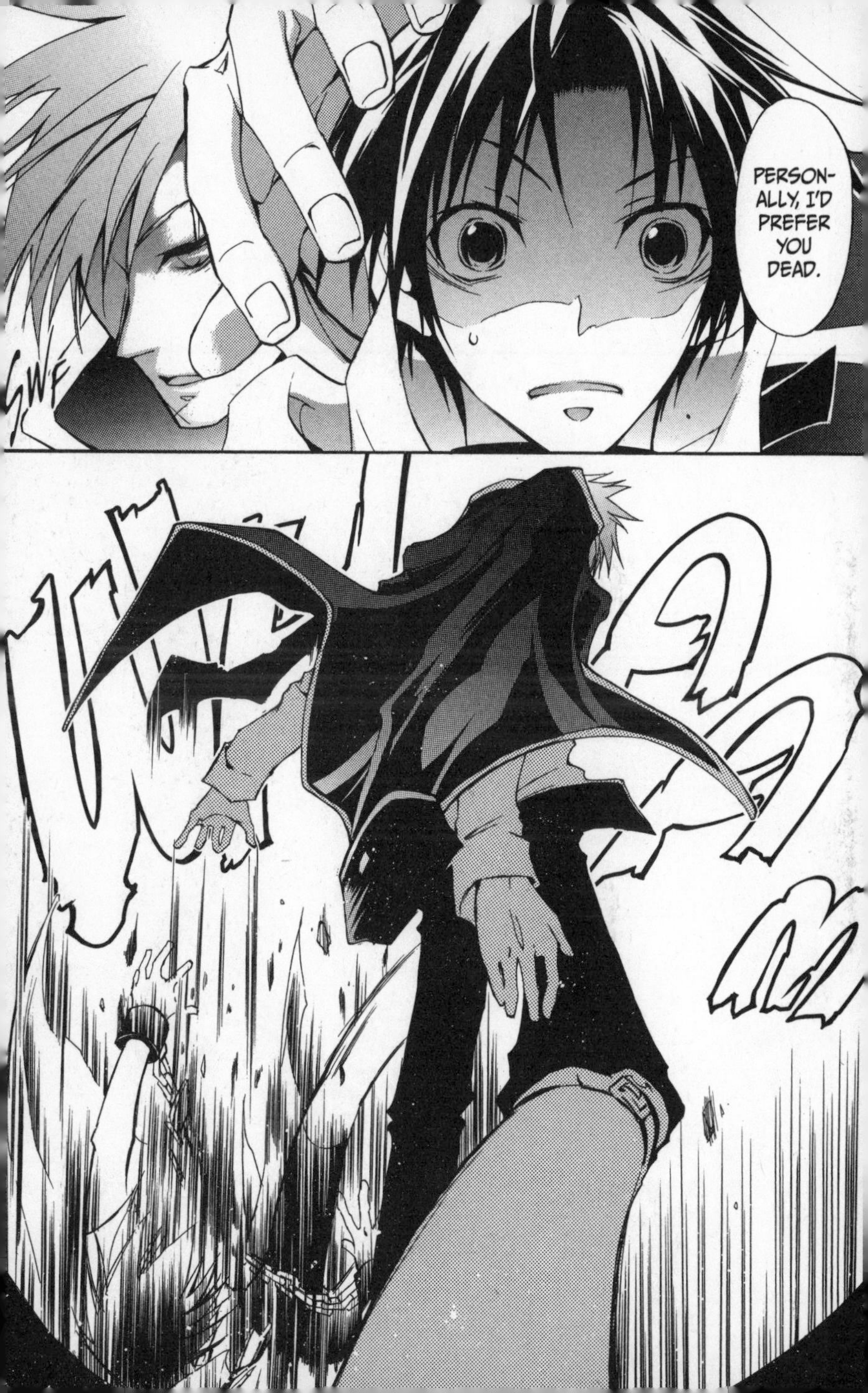
PERSON-ALLY, I'D PREFER YOU DEAD.
SWF

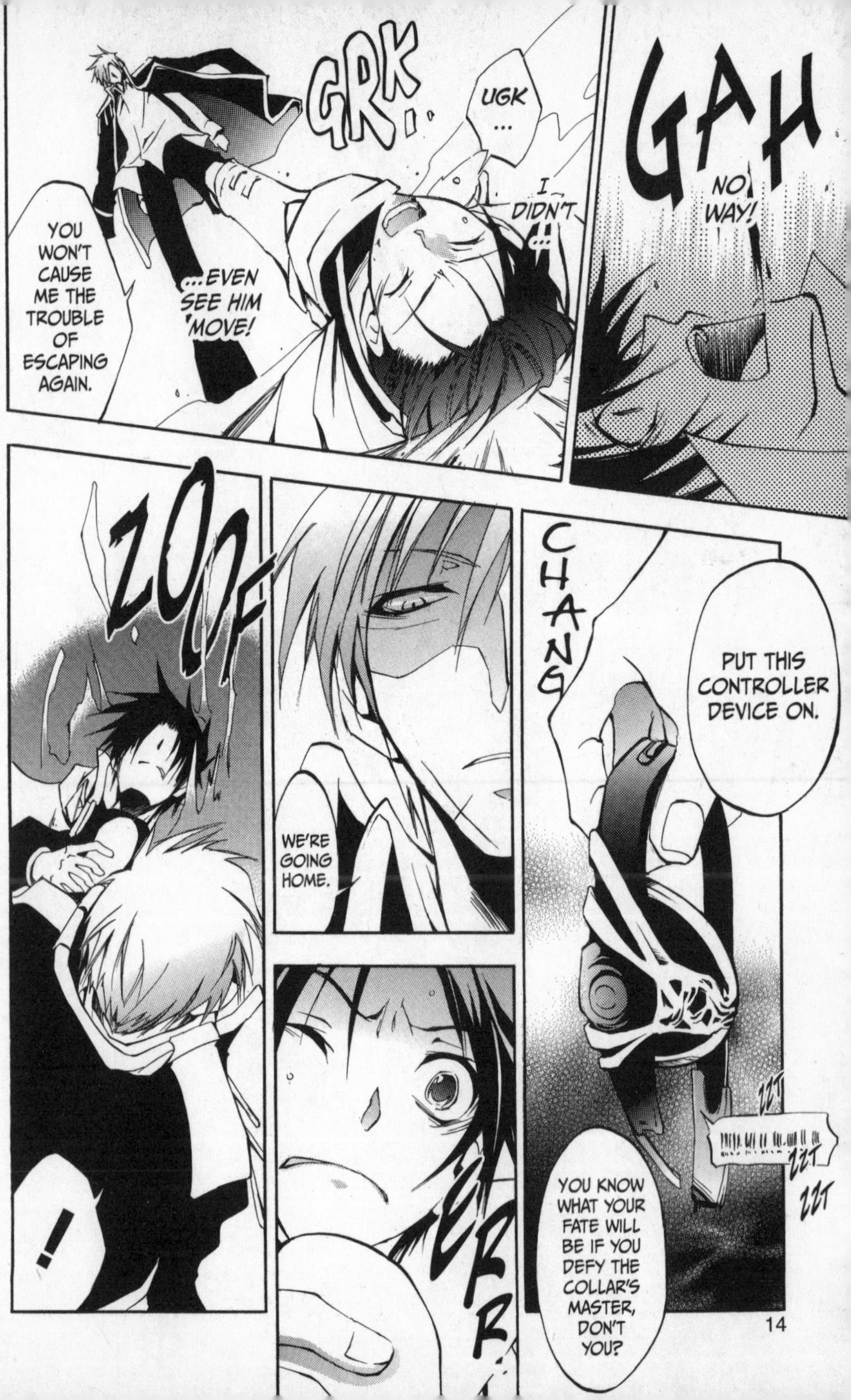
GAH
NO WAY!
UGK ...
I DIDN'T ...
GRK
...EVEN SEE HIM MOVE!
YOU WON'T CAUSE ME THE TROUBLE OF ESCAPING AGAIN.
CHANG
PUT THIS CONTROLLER DEVICE ON.
ZZT
ZZT
ZZT
YOU KNOW WHAT YOUR FATE WILL BE IF YOU DEFY THE COLLAR'S MASTER, DON'T YOU?
WE'RE GOING HOME.
ERR
ZOOF
!

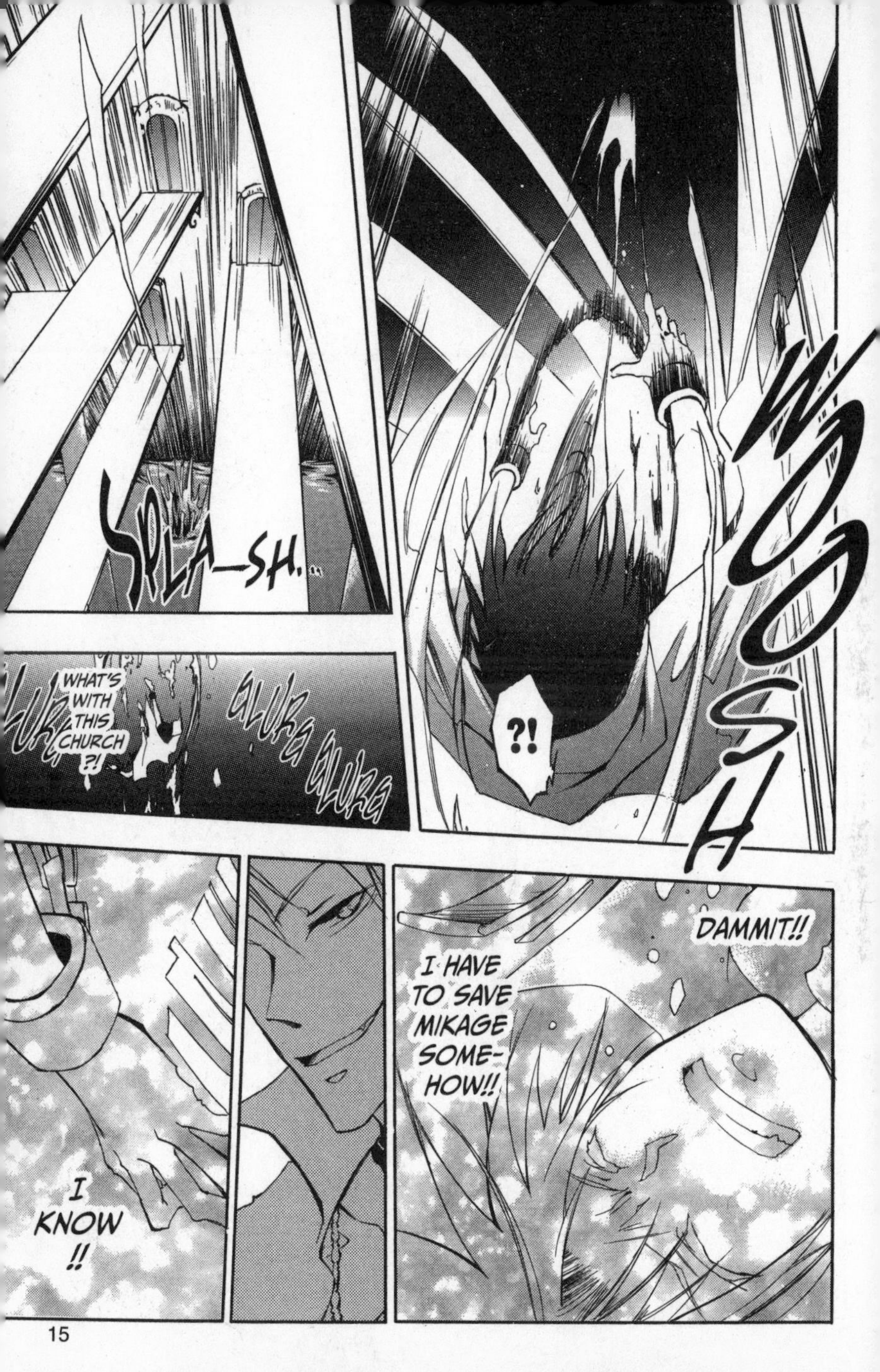
?!
WOOSH
SPLA-SH...
WHAT'S WITH THIS CHURCH ?!
DAMMIT!!
I HAVE TO SAVE MIKAGE SOME-HOW!!
I KNOW !!

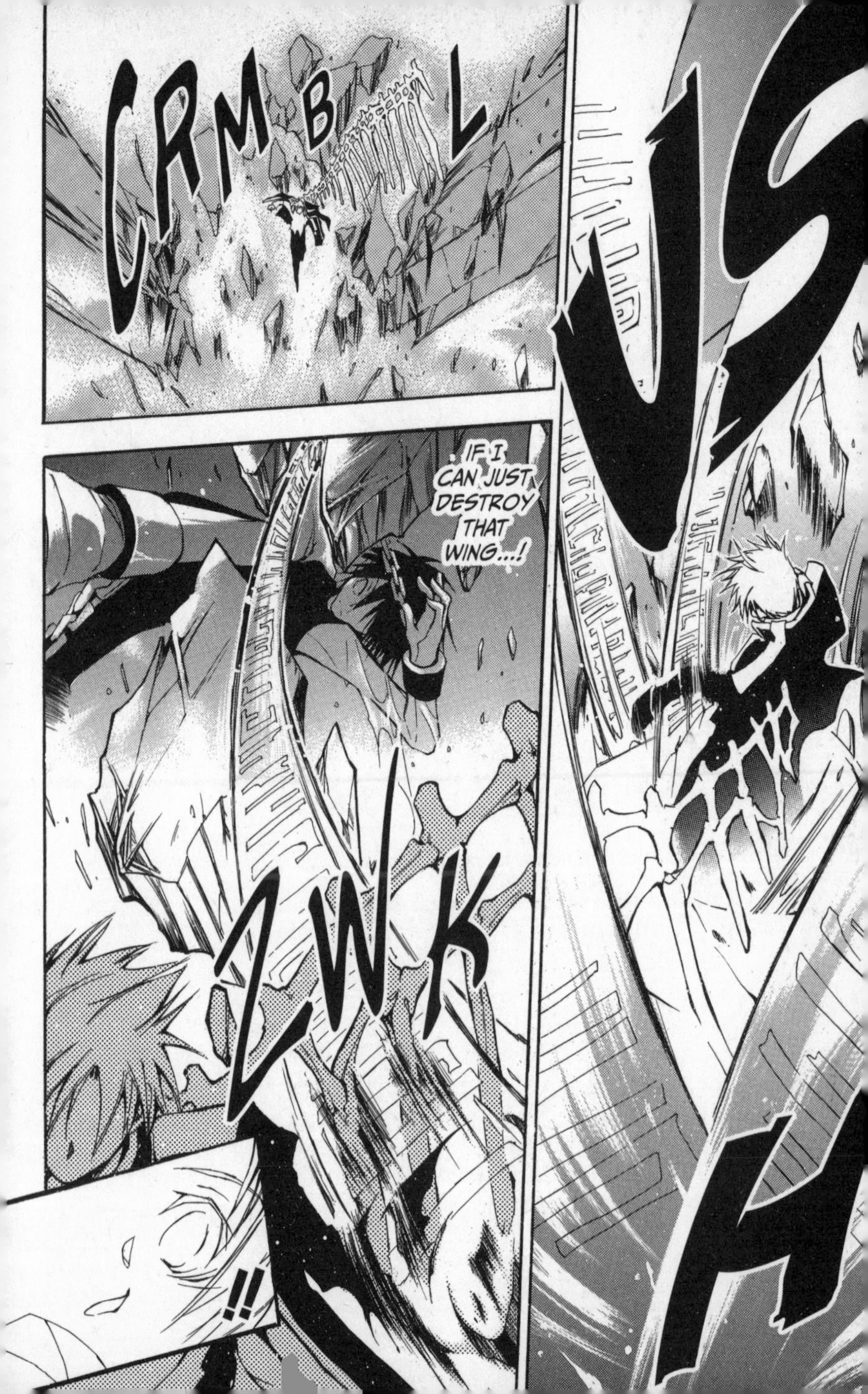
CRMBL
IF I CAN JUST DESTROY THAT WING...!
ZWK
!!

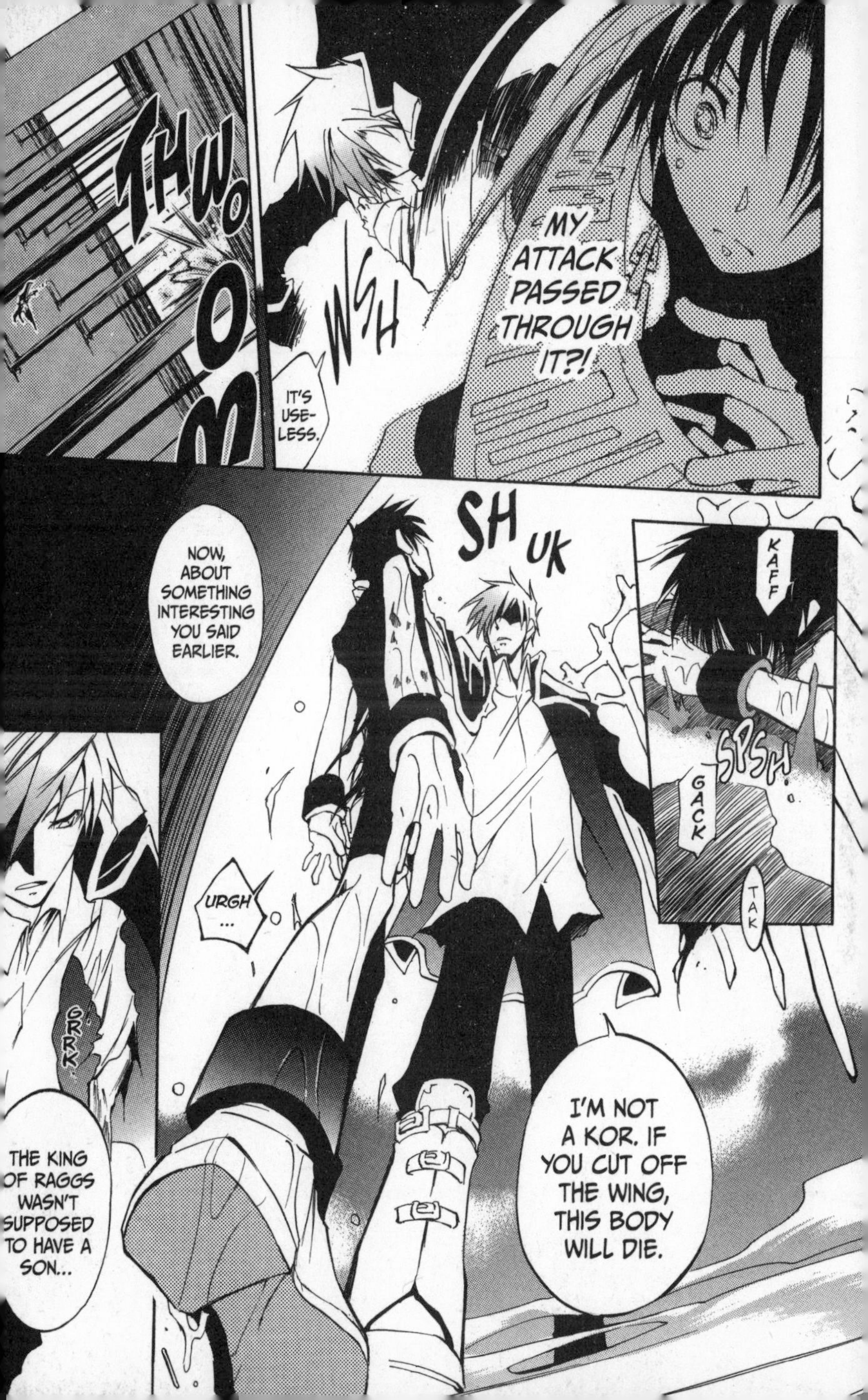
MY ATTACK PASSED THROUGH IT?!
WSH
IT'S USE-LESS.
THWOOM
KAFF
SPSH
GACK
TAK
SH UK
NOW, ABOUT SOMETHING INTERESTING YOU SAID EARLIER.
URGH...
I'M NOT A KOR. IF YOU CUT OFF THE WING, THIS BODY WILL DIE.
GRRK
THE KING OF RAGGS WASN'T SUPPOSED TO HAVE A SON...

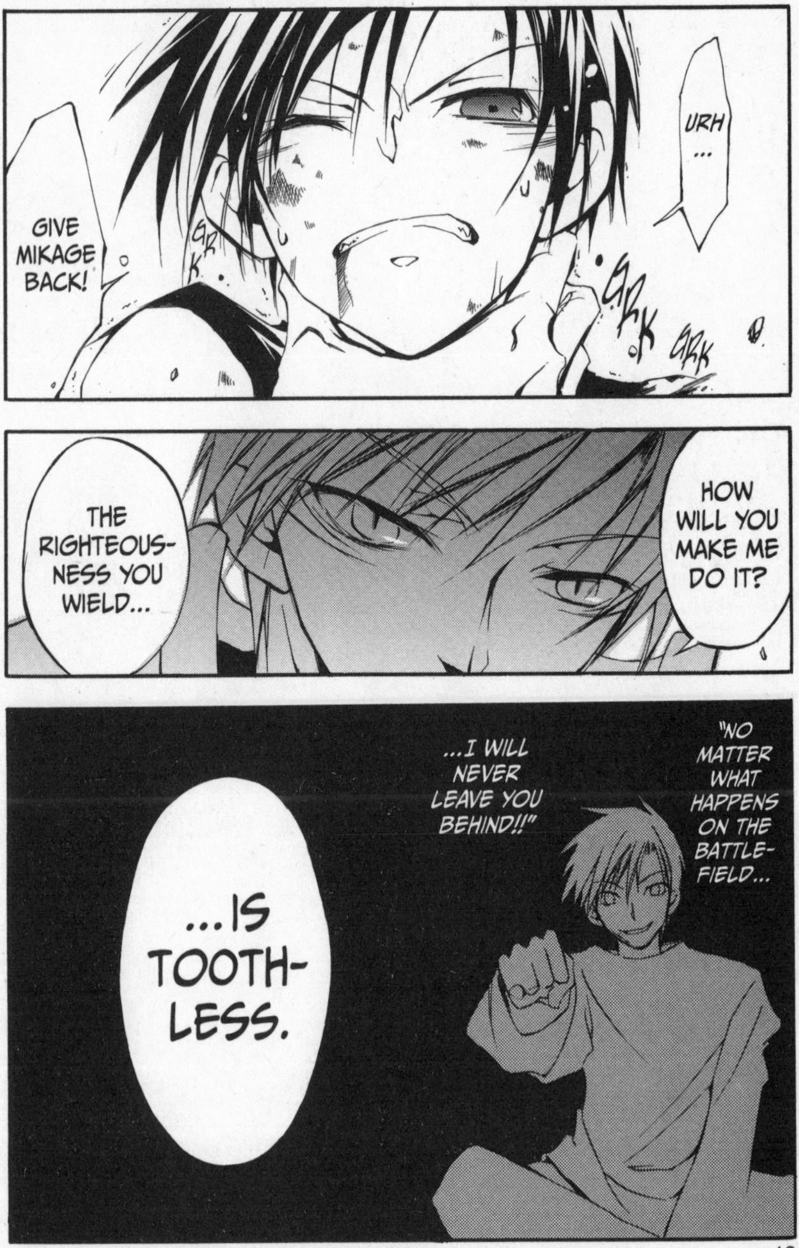
URH ...
GRK
GRK
GRK
GIVE MIKAGE BACK!
HOW WILL YOU MAKE ME DO IT?
THE RIGHTEOUSNESS YOU WIELD...
"NO MATTER WHAT HAPPENS ON THE BATTLEFIELD...
...I WILL NEVER LEAVE YOU BEHIND!!"
...IS TOOTHLESS.

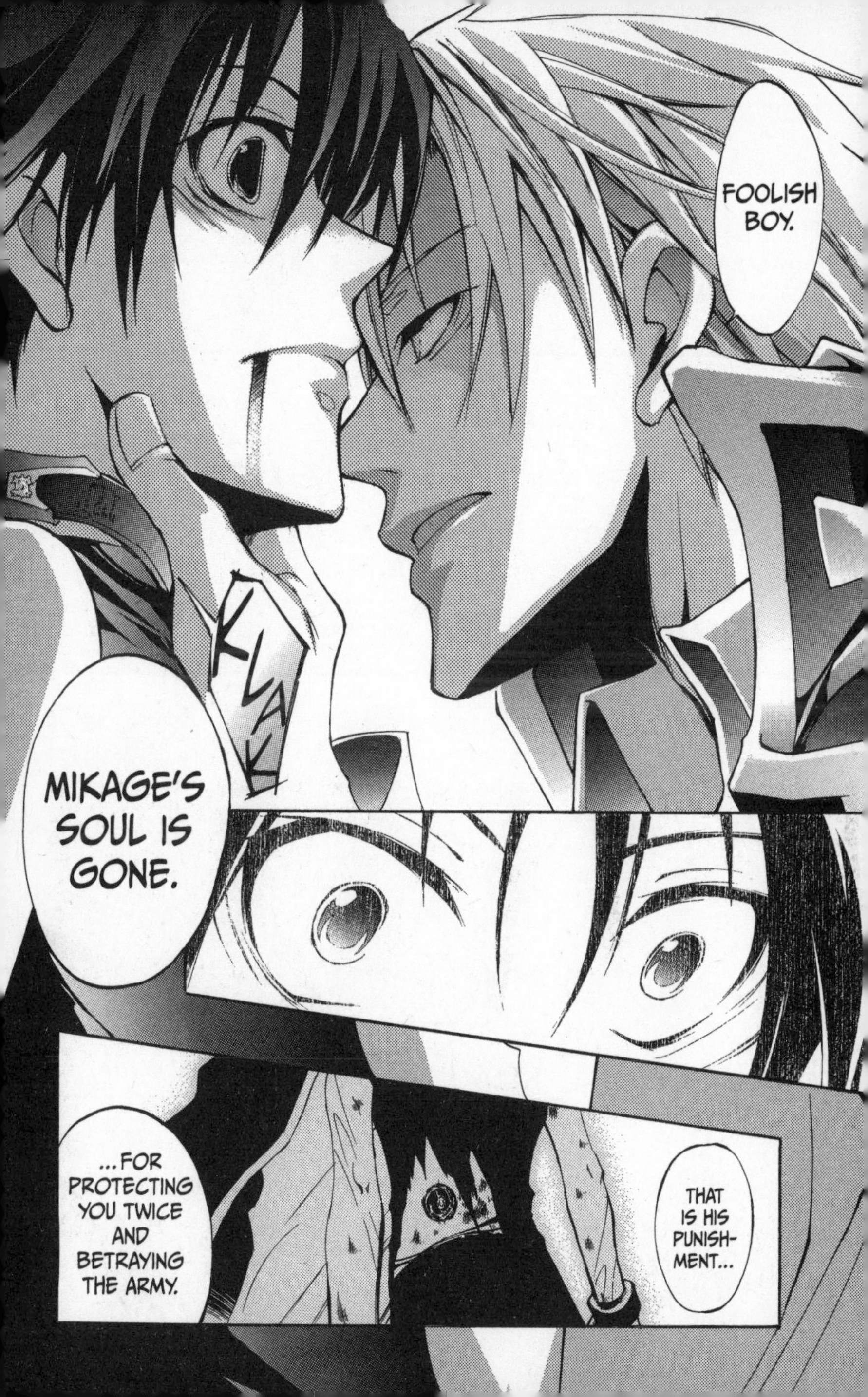
FOOLISH BOY.
KLAK
MIKAGE'S SOUL IS GONE.
THAT IS HIS PUNISHMENT...
...FOR PROTECTING YOU TWICE AND BETRAYING THE ARMY.

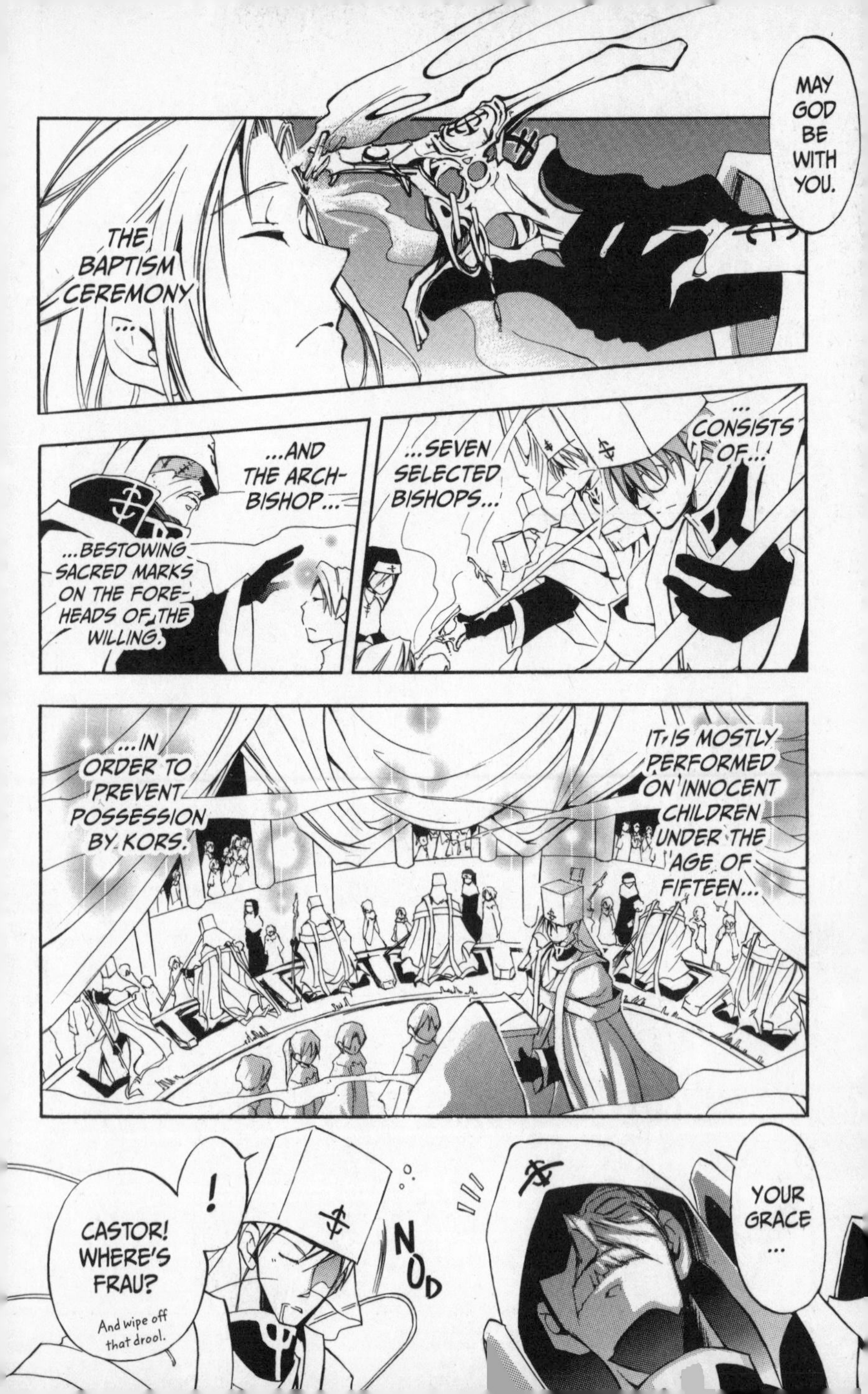
MAY GOD BE WITH YOU.
THE BAPTISM CEREMONY ...
... CONSISTS OF...
...SEVEN SELECTED BISHOPS...
...AND THE ARCH-BISHOP...
...BESTOWING SACRED MARKS ON THE FORE-HEADS OF THE WILLING.
IT IS MOSTLY PERFORMED ON INNOCENT CHILDREN UNDER THE AGE OF FIFTEEN...
...IN ORDER TO PREVENT POSSESSION BY KORS.
YOUR GRACE ...
NOD
!
CASTOR! WHERE'S FRAU?
And wipe off that drool.

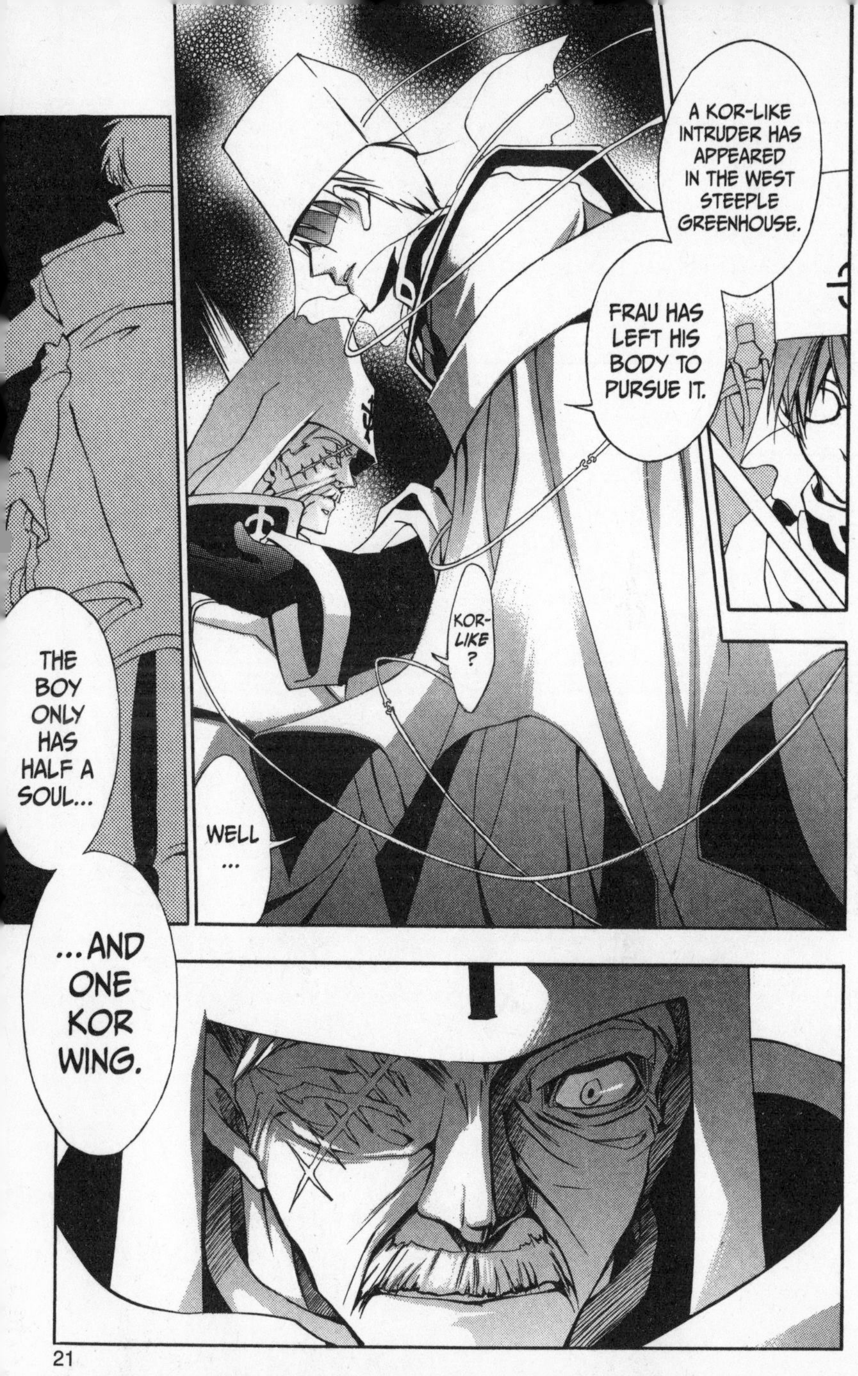
A KOR-LIKE INTRUDER HAS APPEARED IN THE WEST STEEPLE GREENHOUSE.
FRAU HAS LEFT HIS BODY TO PURSUE IT.
KOR-LIKE?
WELL...
THE BOY ONLY HAS HALF A SOUL...
...AND ONE KOR WING.

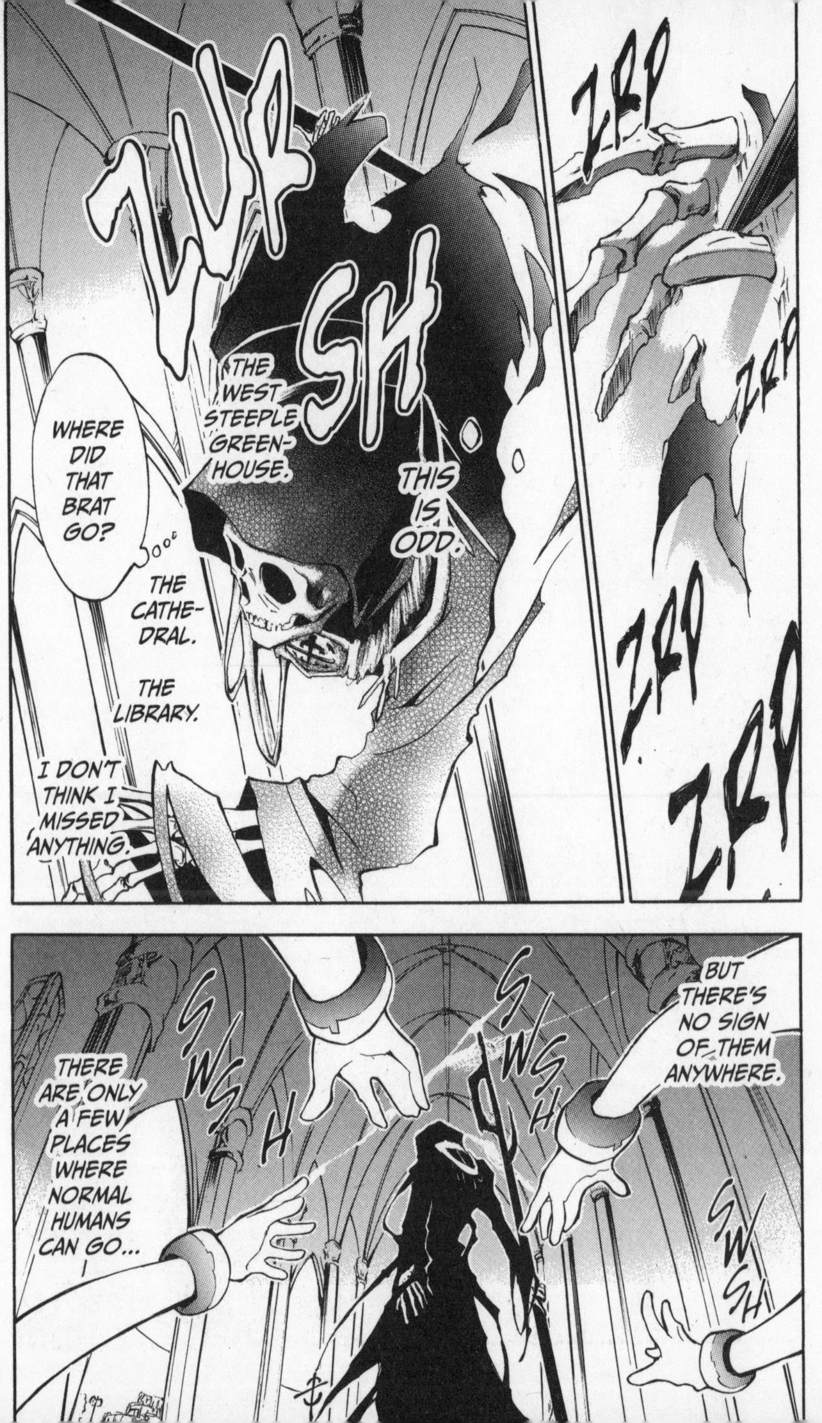
ZRP
ZRP
ZRP
ZRP
ZRP
ZUPSH
WHERE DID THAT BRAT GO?
THE WEST STEEPLE GREENHOUSE.
THIS IS ODD.
THE CATHEDRAL.
THE LIBRARY.
I DON'T THINK I MISSED ANYTHING.
SWSH
SWSH
SWSH
THERE ARE ONLY A FEW PLACES WHERE NORMAL HUMANS CAN GO...
BUT THERE'S NO SIGN OF THEM ANYWHERE.

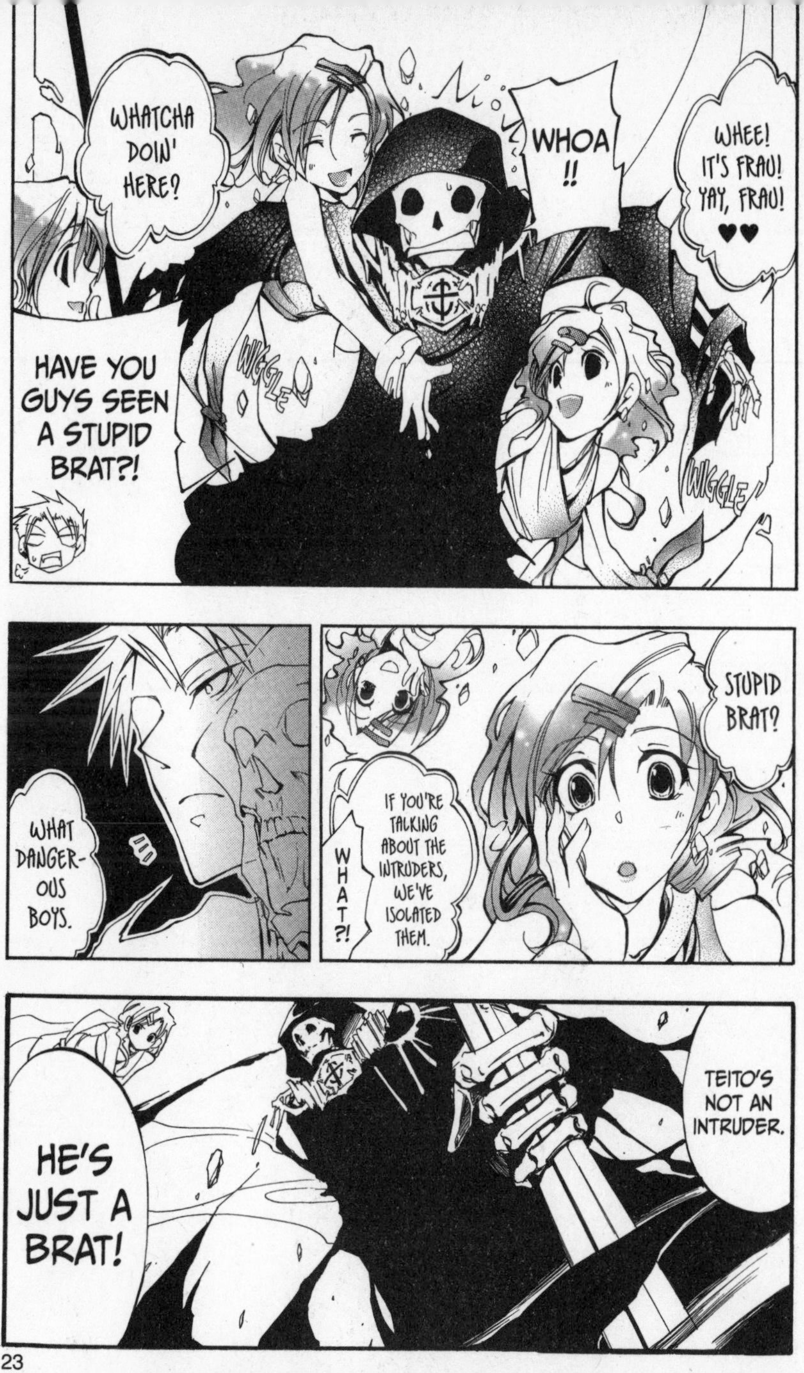
WHEE! IT'S FRAU! YAY, FRAU! ♥♥
WHOA !!
WIGGLE
WHATCHA DOIN' HERE?
WIGGLE
HAVE YOU GUYS SEEN A STUPID BRAT?!
STUPID BRAT?
IF YOU'RE TALKING ABOUT THE INTRUDERS, WE'VE ISOLATED THEM.
WHAT?!
...
WHAT DANGER-OUS BOYS.
TEITO'S NOT AN INTRUDER.
HE'S JUST A BRAT!

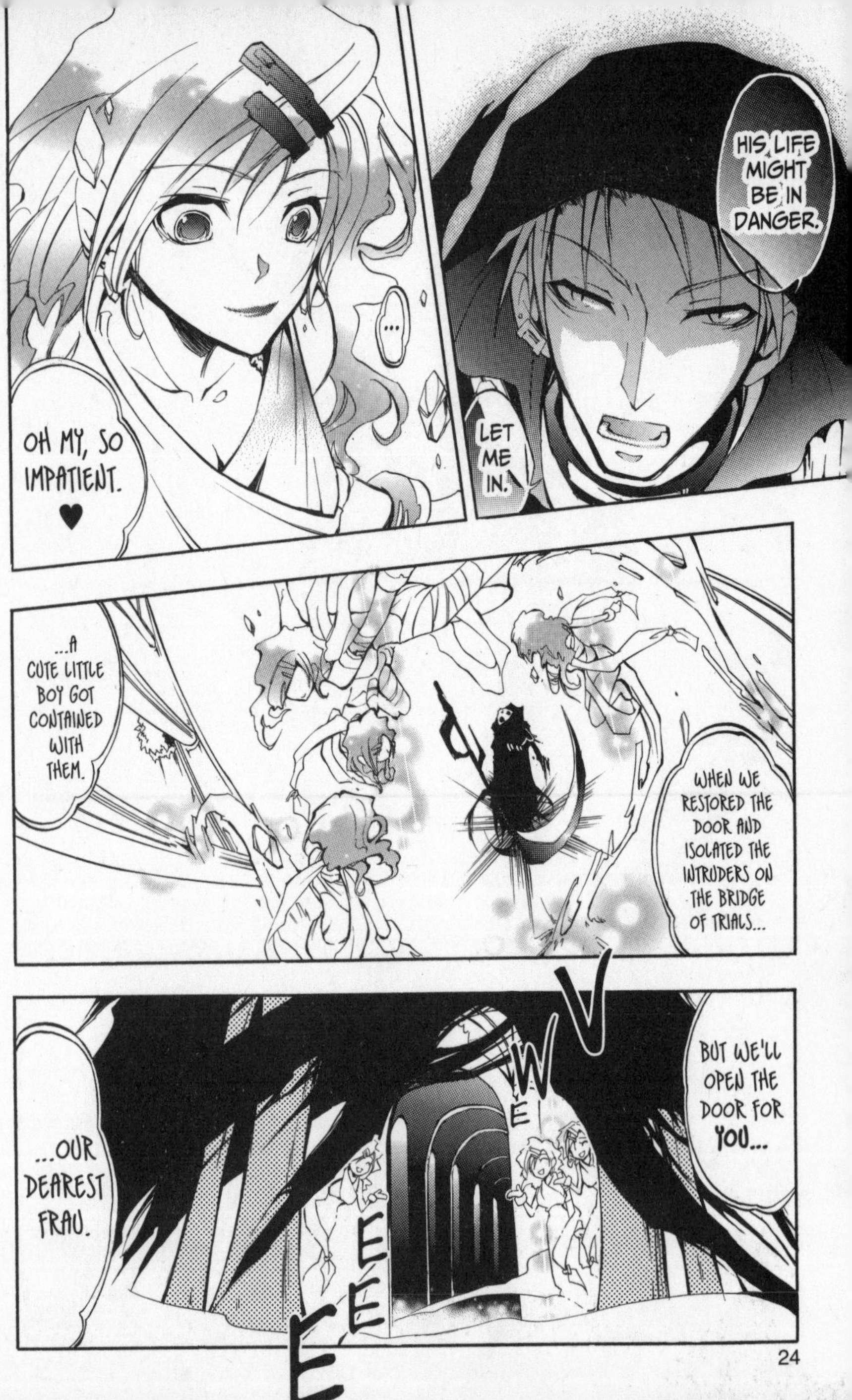

HIS LIFE MIGHT BE IN DANGER.
LET ME IN.
...
OH MY, SO IMPATIENT. ♥
WHEN WE RESTORED THE DOOR AND ISOLATED THE INTRUDERS ON THE BRIDGE OF TRIALS...
...A CUTE LITTLE BOY GOT CONTAINED WITH THEM.
BUT WE'LL OPEN THE DOOR FOR YOU...
VWEEEE
...OUR DEAREST FRAU.

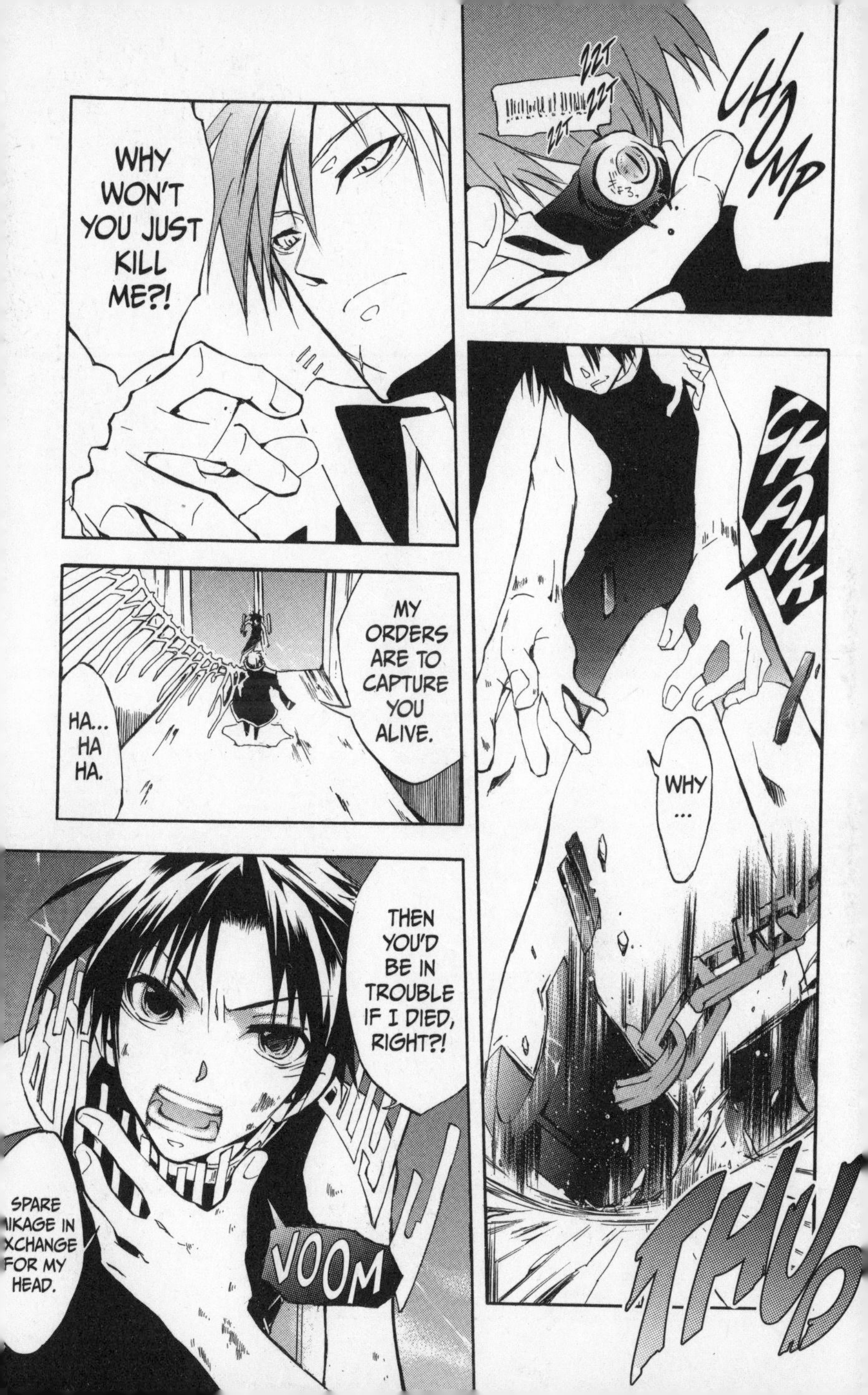
ZZT ZZT ZZT
CHOMP
CHANK
WHY...
THUD
WHY WON'T YOU JUST KILL ME?!
MY ORDERS ARE TO CAPTURE YOU ALIVE.
HA... HA HA.
THEN YOU'D BE IN TROUBLE IF I DIED, RIGHT?!
VOOM
SPARE IKAGE IN XCHANGE FOR MY HEAD.

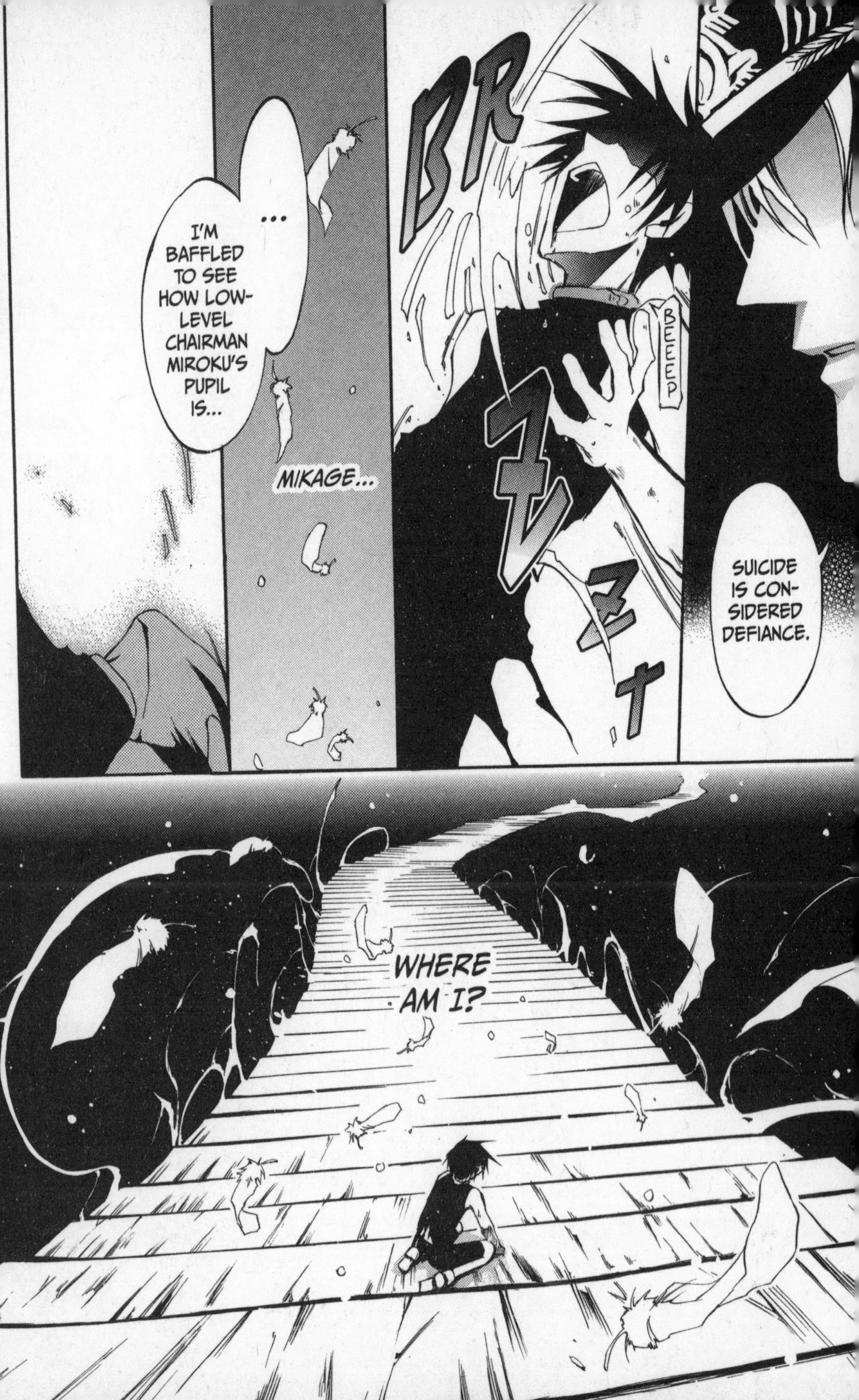
SUICIDE IS CON-SIDERED DEFIANCE.
BEEEP
BRZZT
...
MIKAGE...
I'M BAFFLED TO SEE HOW LOW-LEVEL CHAIRMAN MIROKU'S PUPIL IS...
WHERE AM I?

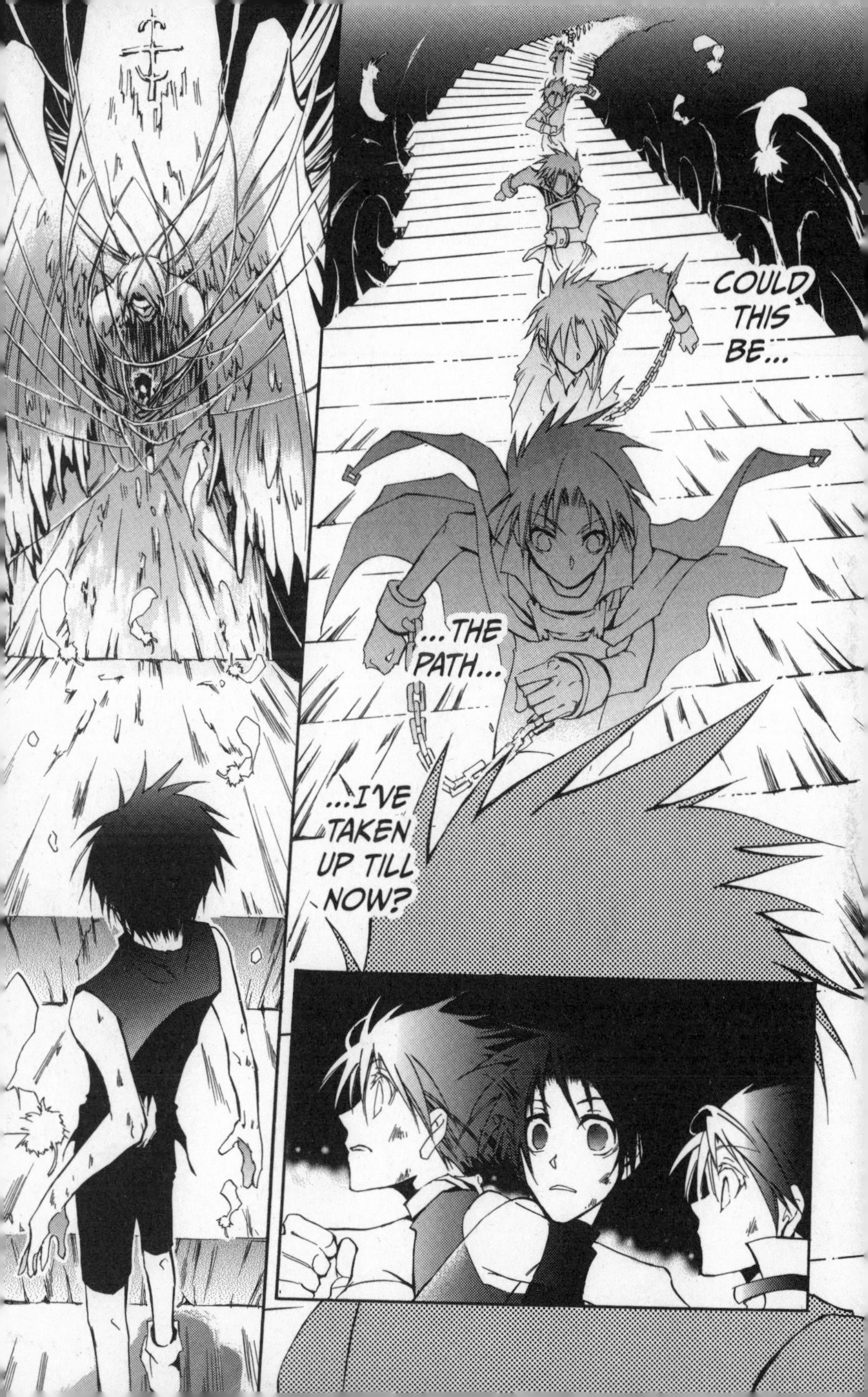

COULD THIS BE...
...THE PATH...
...I'VE TAKEN UP TILL NOW?

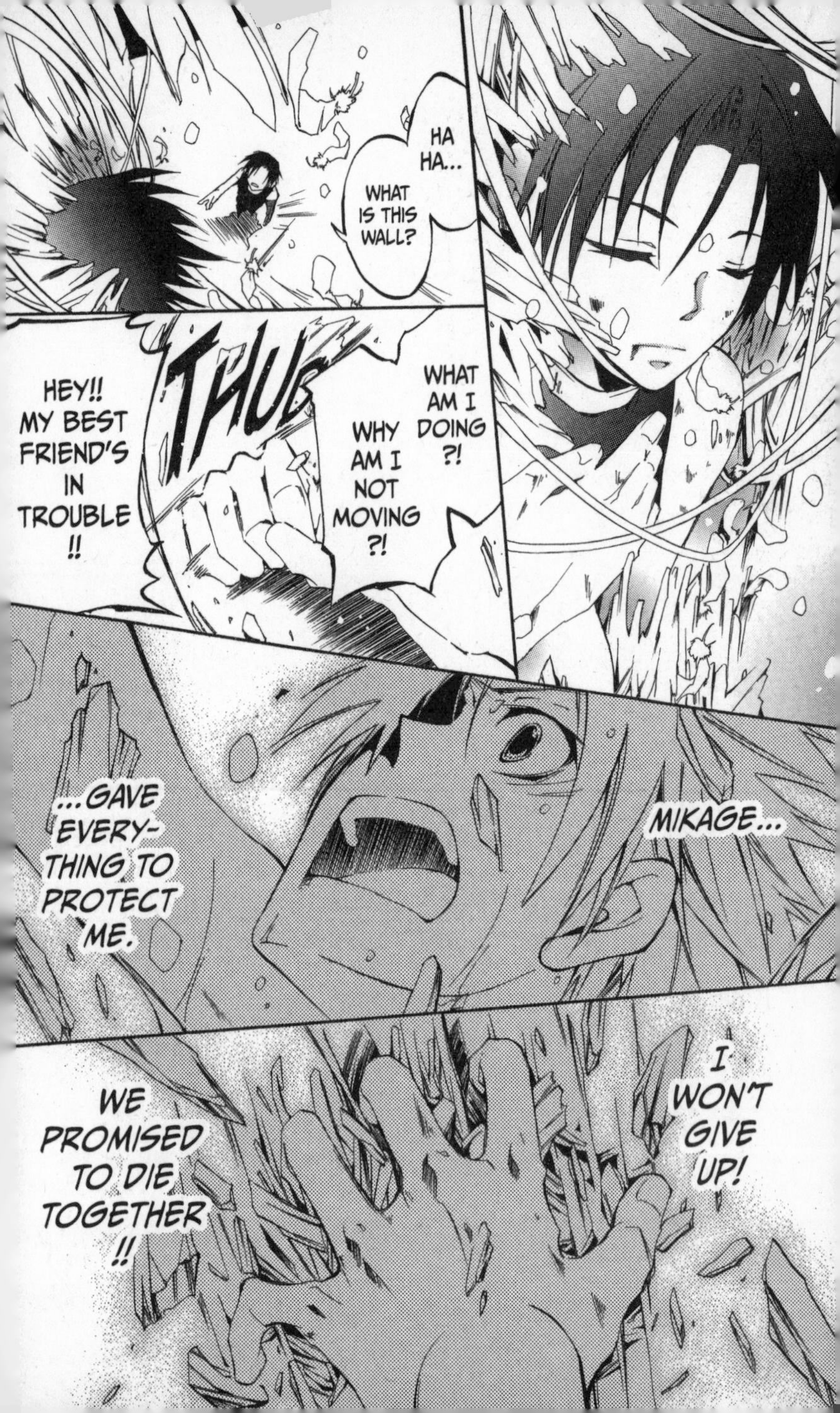
HA HA...
WHAT IS THIS WALL?
WHAT AM I DOING ?!
WHY AM I NOT MOVING ?!
THUD
HEY!! MY BEST FRIEND'S IN TROUBLE !!
MIKAGE...
...GAVE EVERY-THING TO PROTECT ME.
I WON'T GIVE UP!
WE PROMISED TO DIE TOGETHER !!

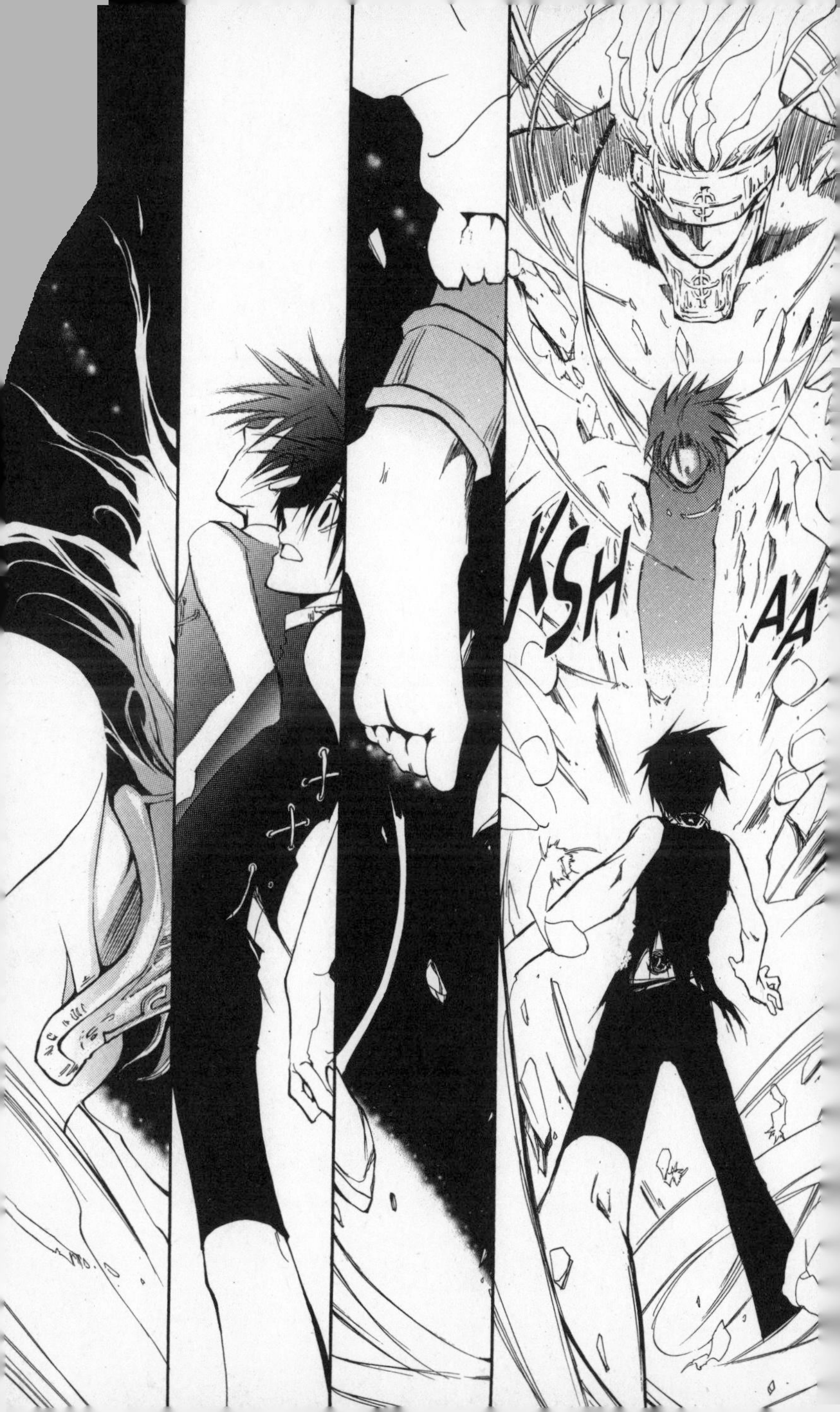
KSH
AA

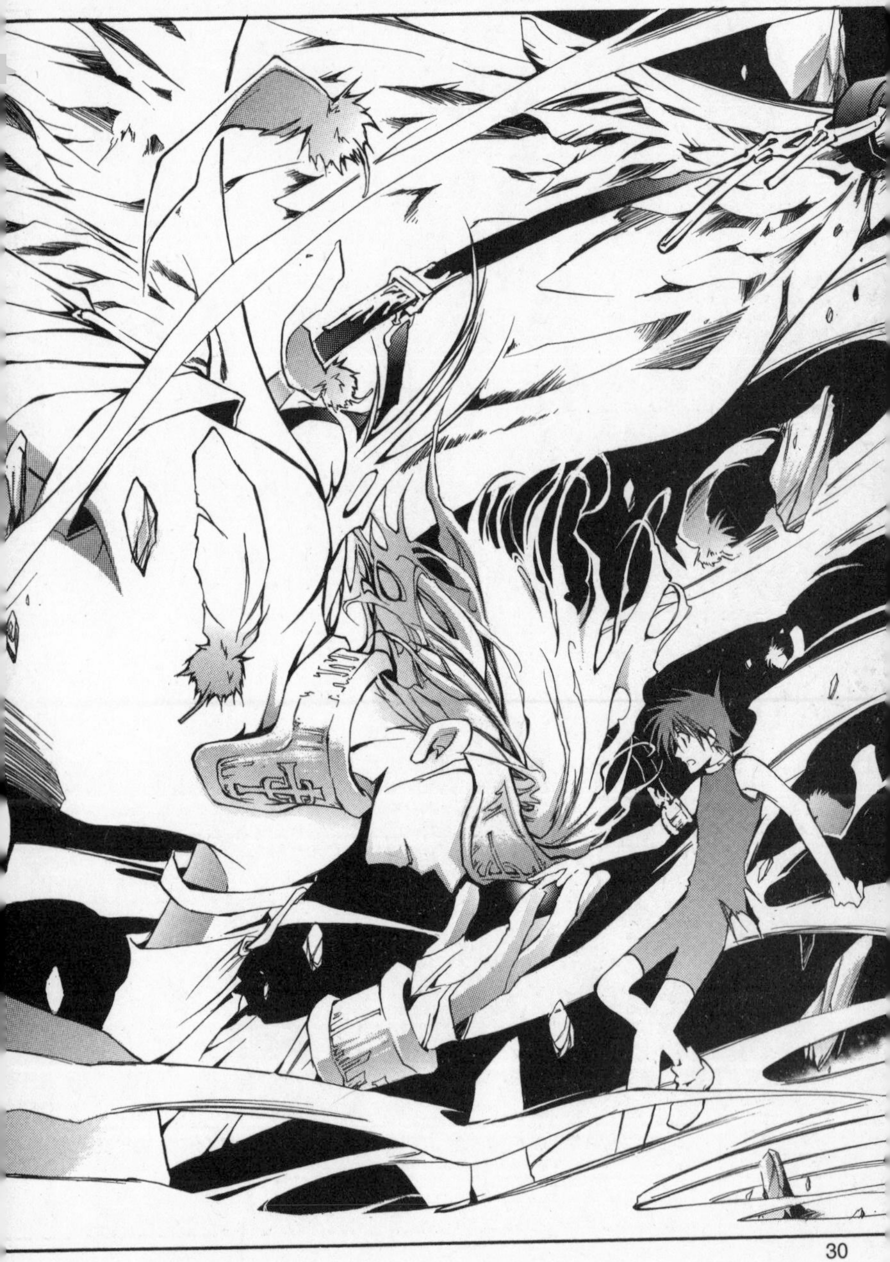

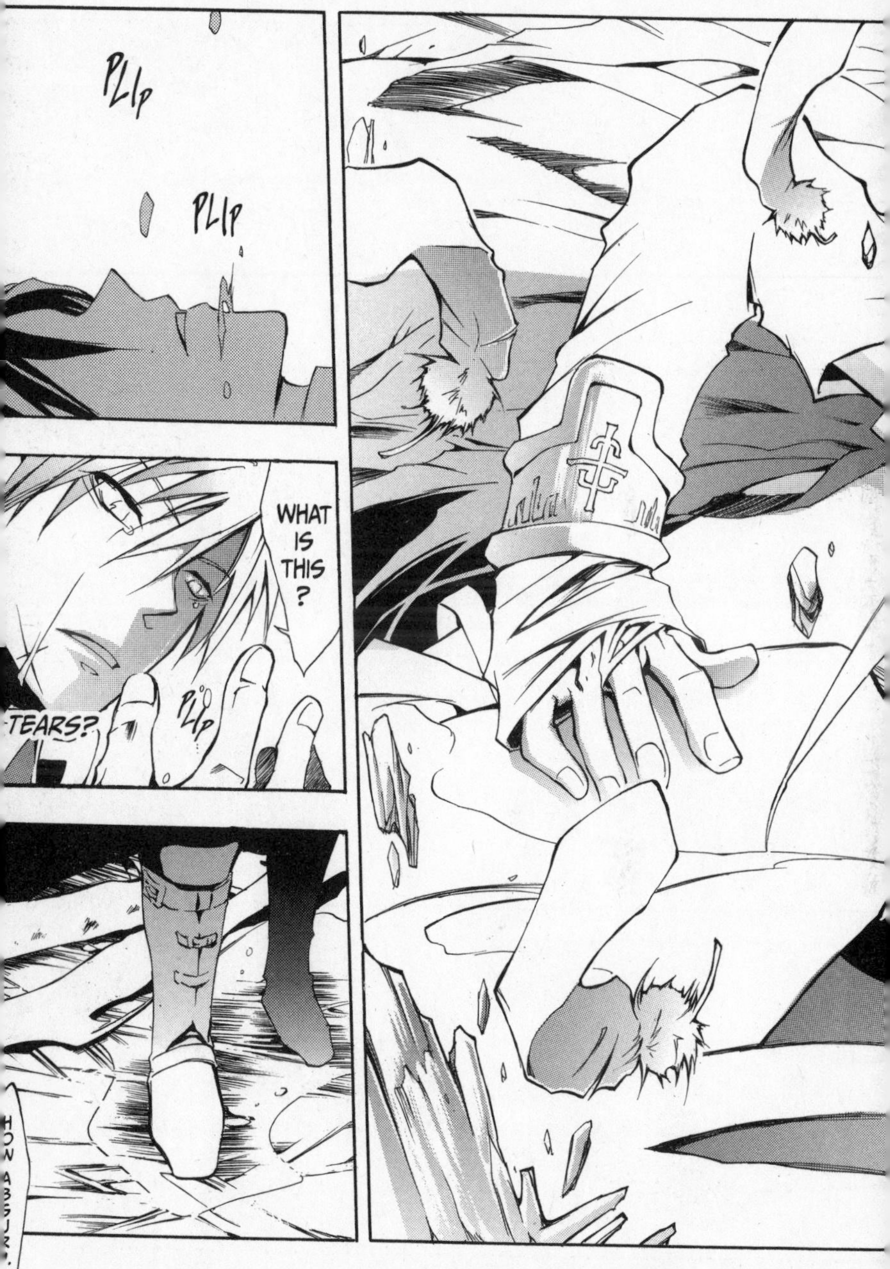
PLIP
PLIP
WHAT IS THIS?
TEARS?
PLIP
HOW ABSURD...

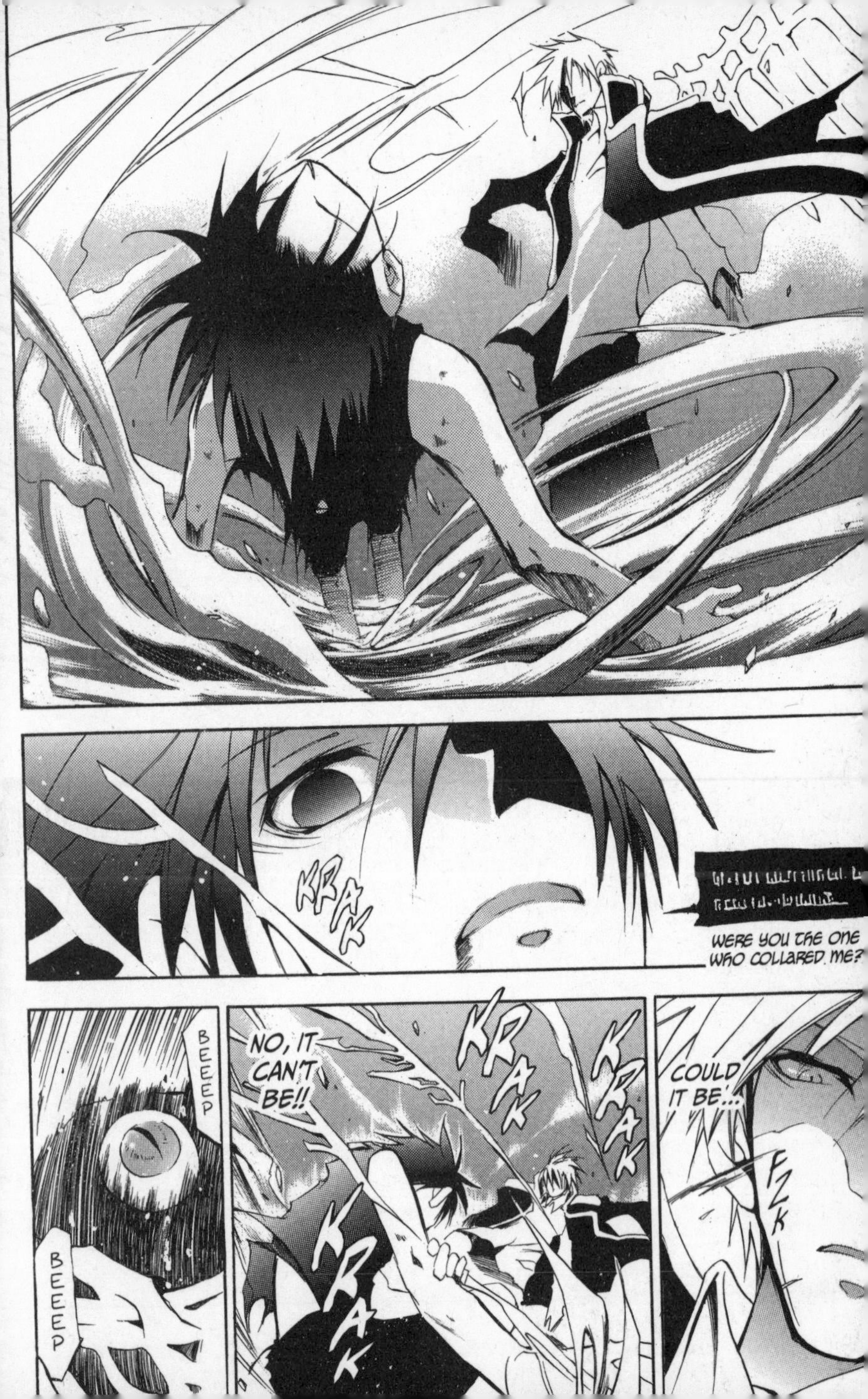
WERE YOU THE ONE WHO COLLARED ME?
KRAK
COULD IT BE...
FZK
KRAK
KRAK
NO, IT CAN'T BE!!
KRAK
BEEEP
BEEEP

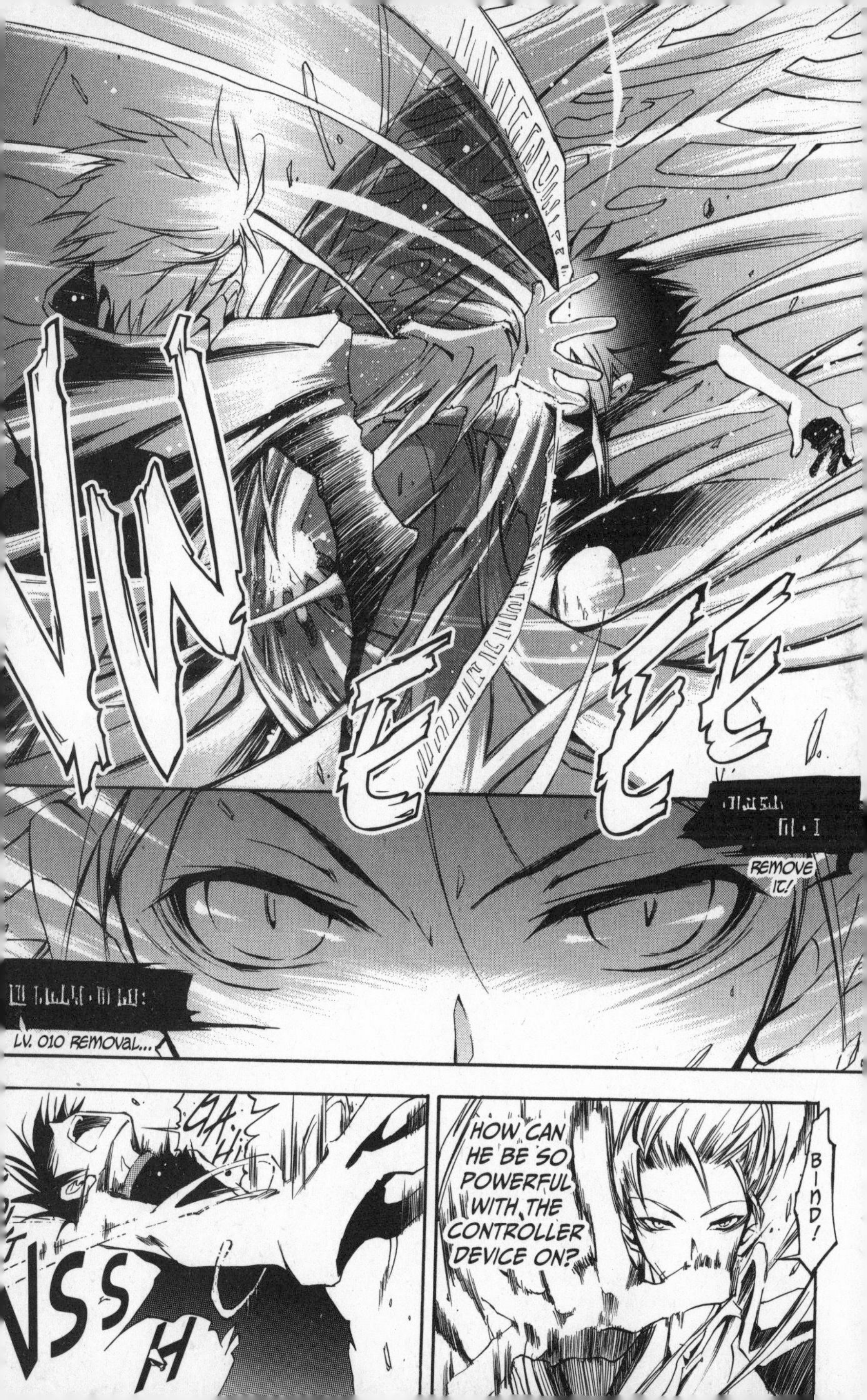
REMOVE IT!
LV. 010 REMOVAL...
BIND!
HOW CAN HE BE SO POWERFUL WITH THE CONTROLLER DEVICE ON?

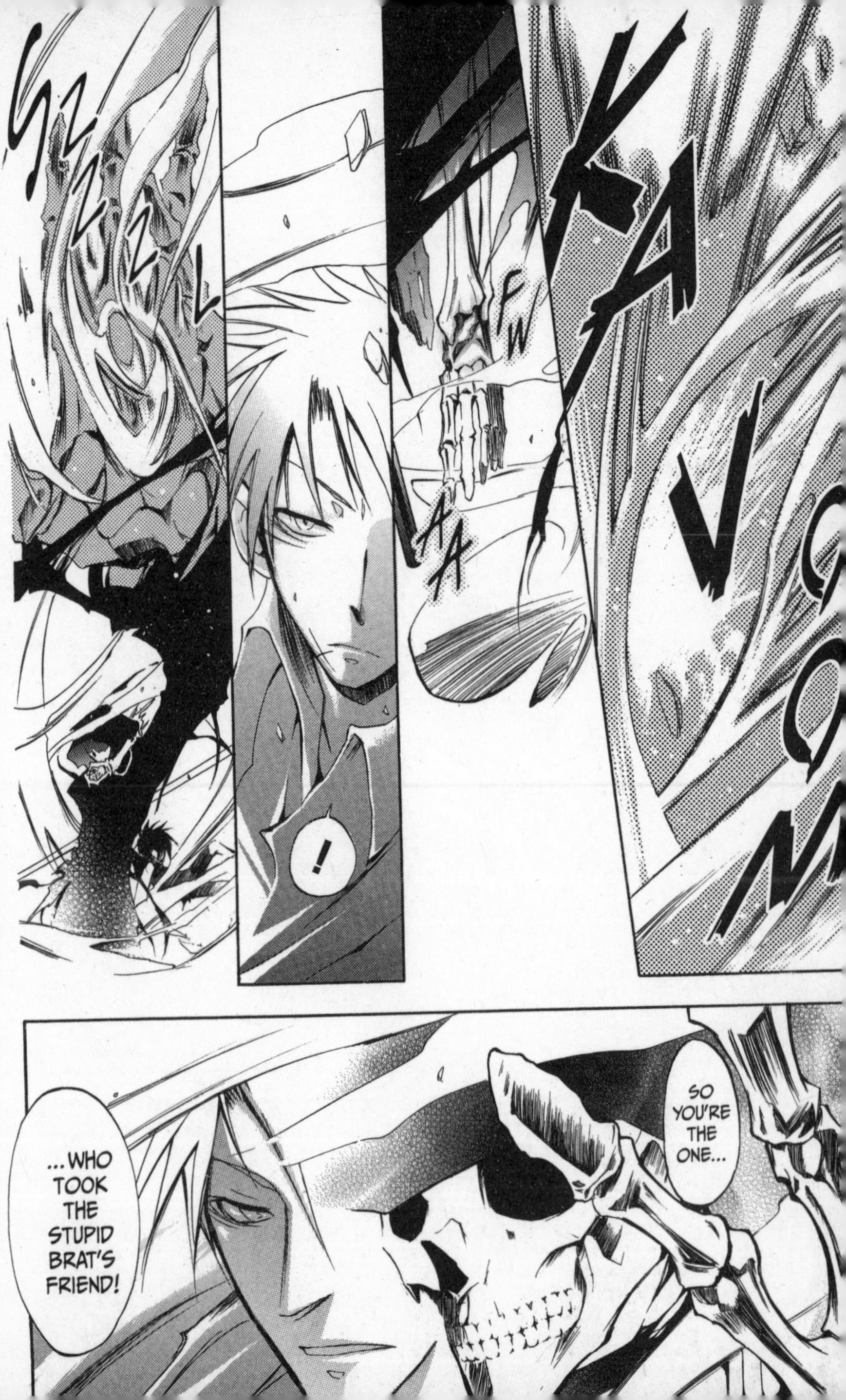
KAVOOM
FWAA
!
SZZZL
SO YOU'RE THE ONE...
...WHO TOOK THE STUPID BRAT'S FRIEND!

Kapitel.7 “Metempsychosis”

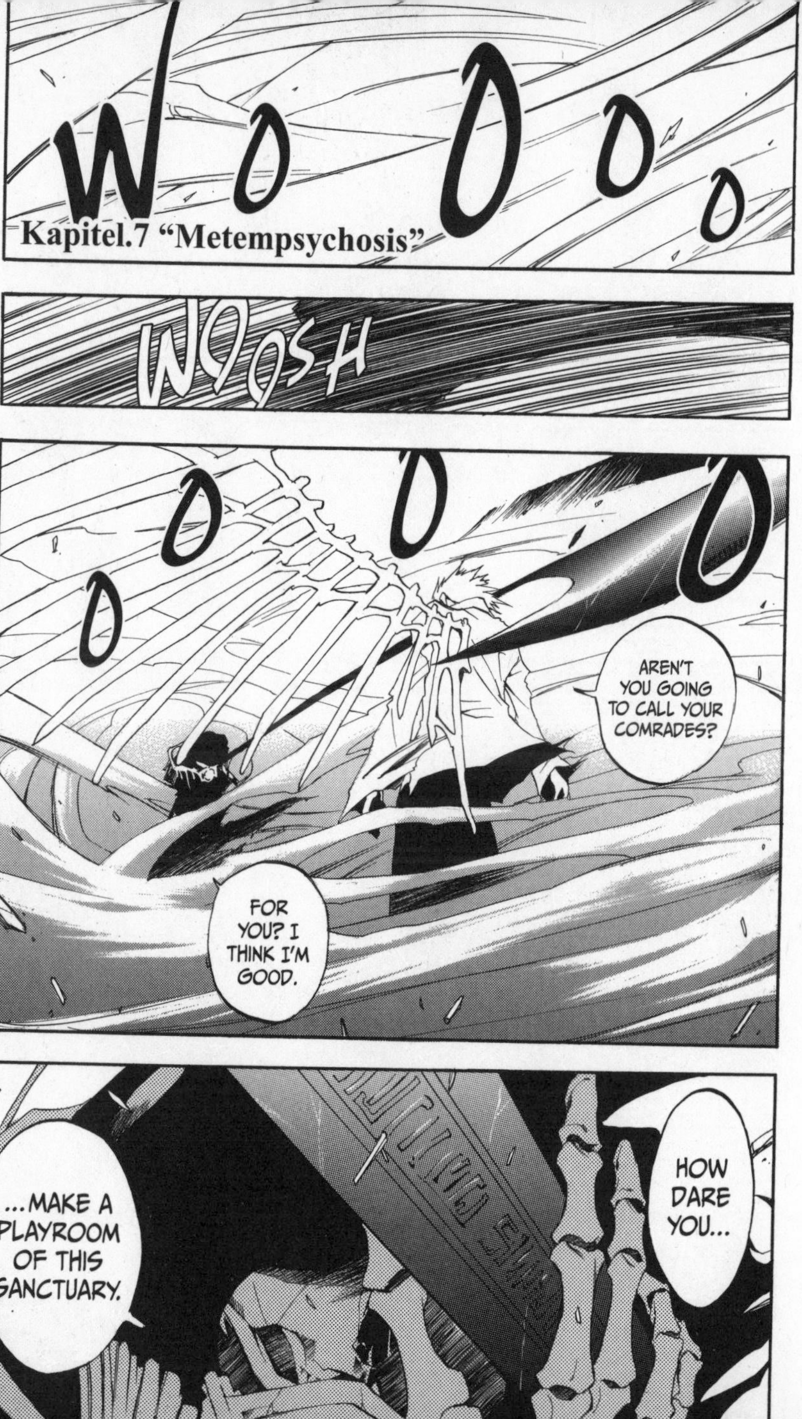
WOOOOO
WOOSH
OOOO
AREN'T YOU GOING TO CALL YOUR COMRADES?
FOR YOU? I THINK I'M GOOD.
HOW DARE YOU...
...MAKE A PLAYROOM OF THIS SANCTUARY.

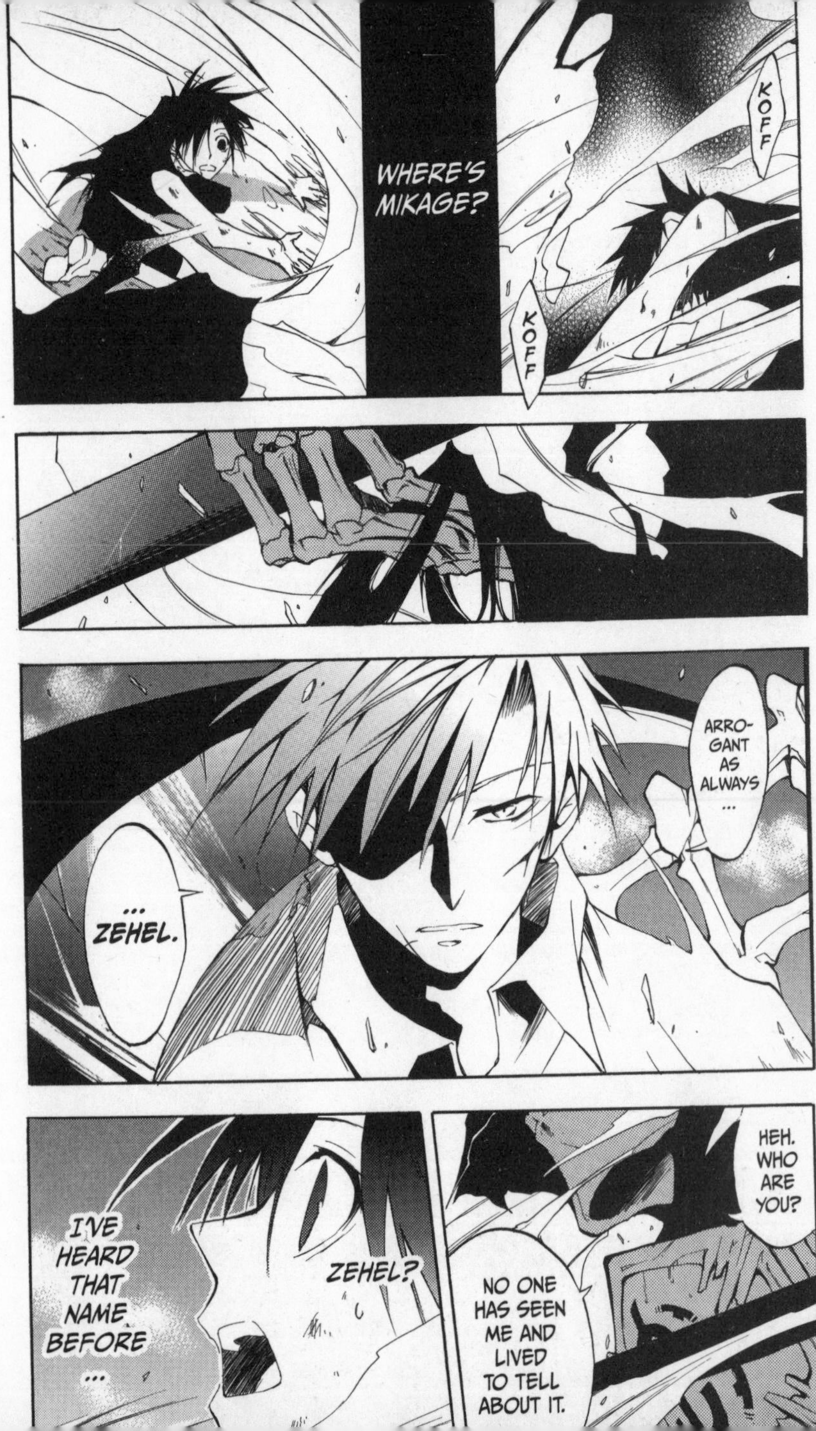
KOFF
KOFF
WHERE'S MIKAGE?
ARRO-GANT AS ALWAYS ...
... ZEHEL.
HEH. WHO ARE YOU?
NO ONE HAS SEEN ME AND LIVED TO TELL ABOUT IT.
ZEHEL?
I'VE HEARD THAT NAME BEFORE ...

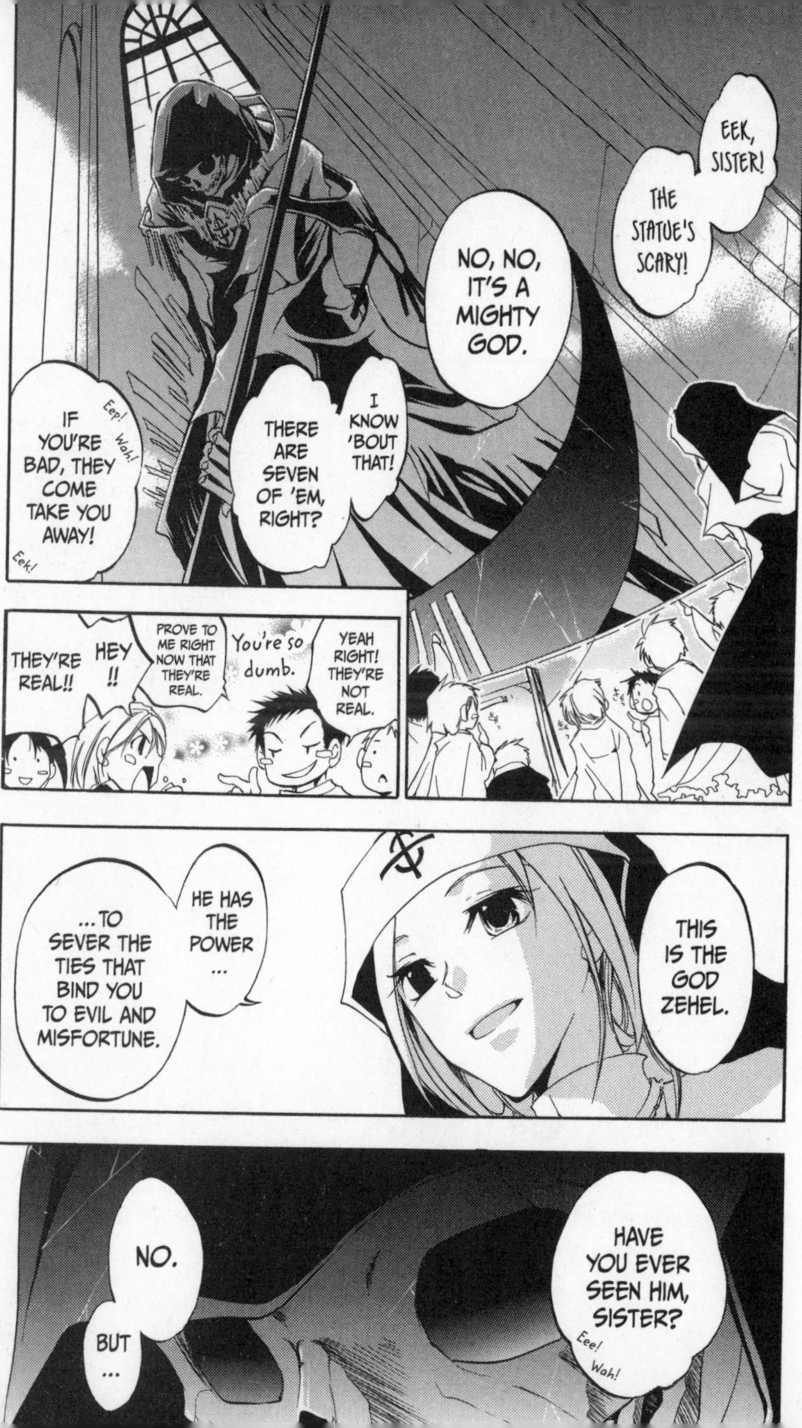
EEK, SISTER!
THE STATUE'S SCARY!
NO, NO, IT'S A MIGHTY GOD.
I KNOW 'BOUT THAT!
THERE ARE SEVEN OF 'EM, RIGHT?
IF YOU'RE BAD, THEY COME TAKE YOU AWAY!
Eep!
Wah!
Eek!
YEAH RIGHT! THEY'RE NOT REAL.
You're so dumb.
PROVE TO ME RIGHT NOW THAT THEY'RE REAL.
HEY !!
THEY'RE REAL!!
THIS IS THE GOD ZEHEL.
HE HAS THE POWER ...
...TO SEVER THE TIES THAT BIND YOU TO EVIL AND MISFORTUNE.
HAVE YOU EVER SEEN HIM, SISTER?
Eee!
Wah!
NO.
BUT ...

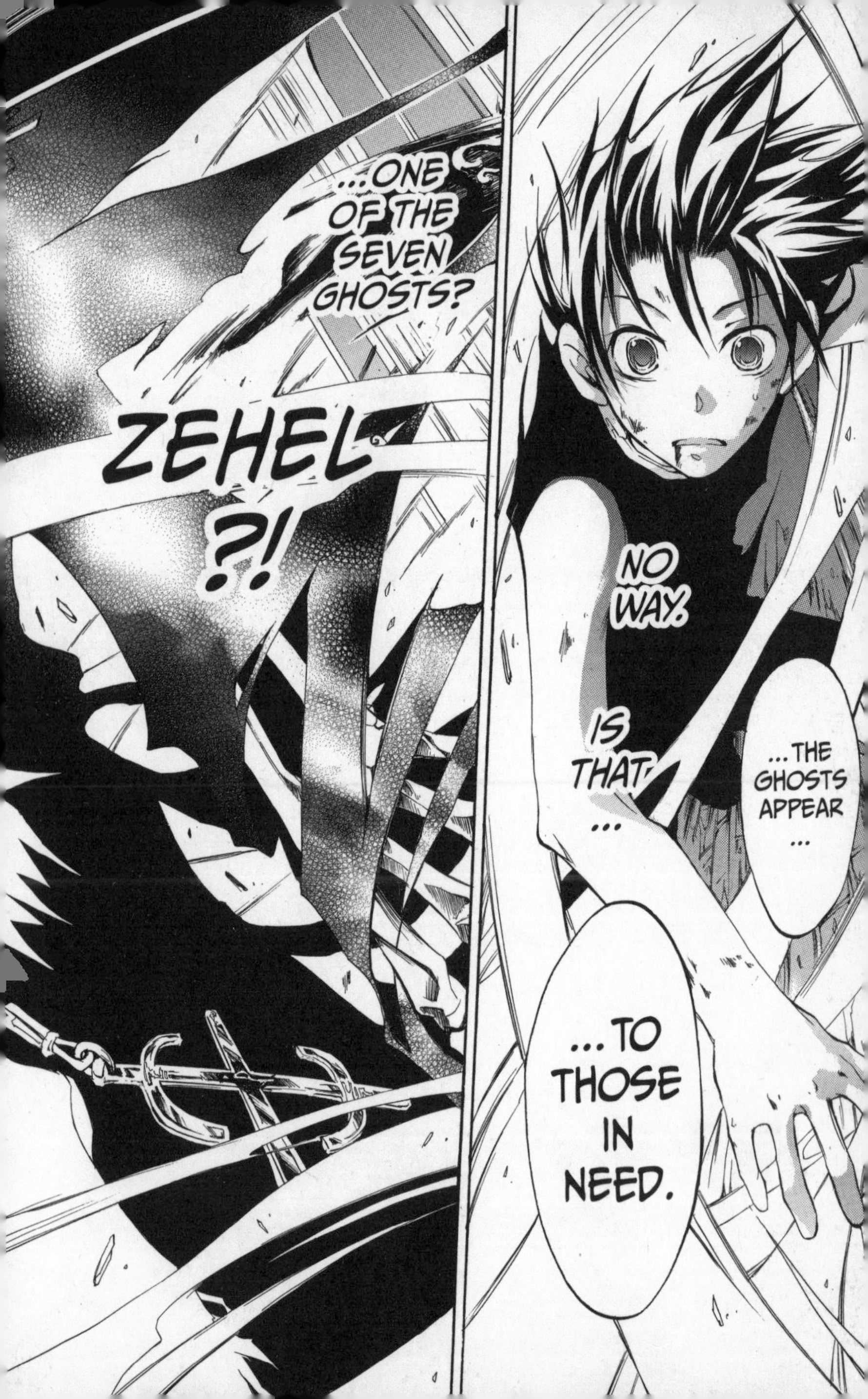
NO WAY.
...THE GHOSTS APPEAR...
...TO THOSE IN NEED.
IS THAT...
...ONE OF THE SEVEN GHOSTS?
ZEHEL ?!

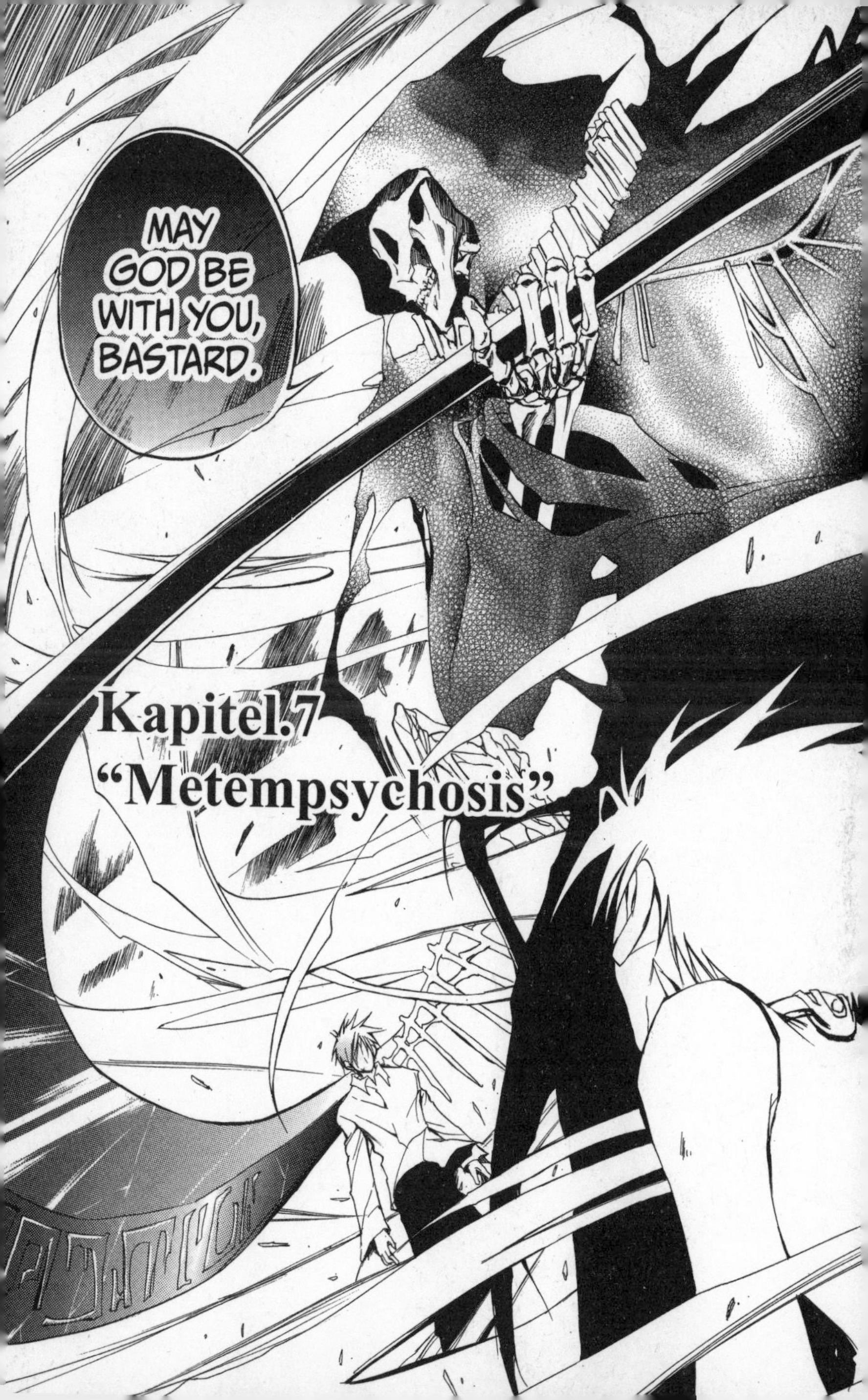
MAY GOD BE WITH YOU, BASTARD.
Kapitel.7
“Metempsychosis”

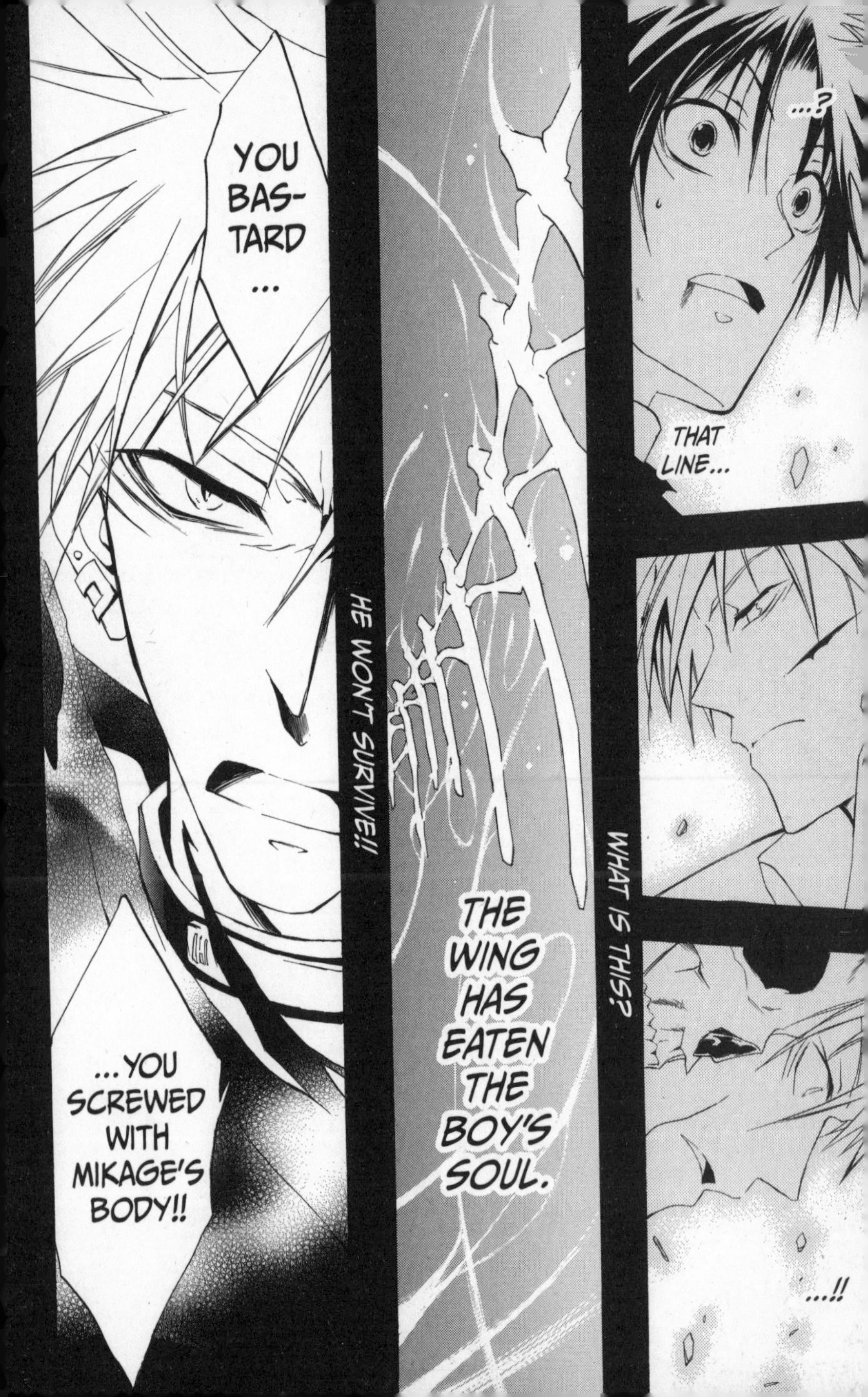
...?
THAT LINE...
WHAT IS THIS?
...!!
THE WING HAS EATEN THE BOY'S SOUL.
HE WON'T SURVIVE!!
YOU BASTARD...
...YOU SCREWED WITH MIKAGE'S BODY!!

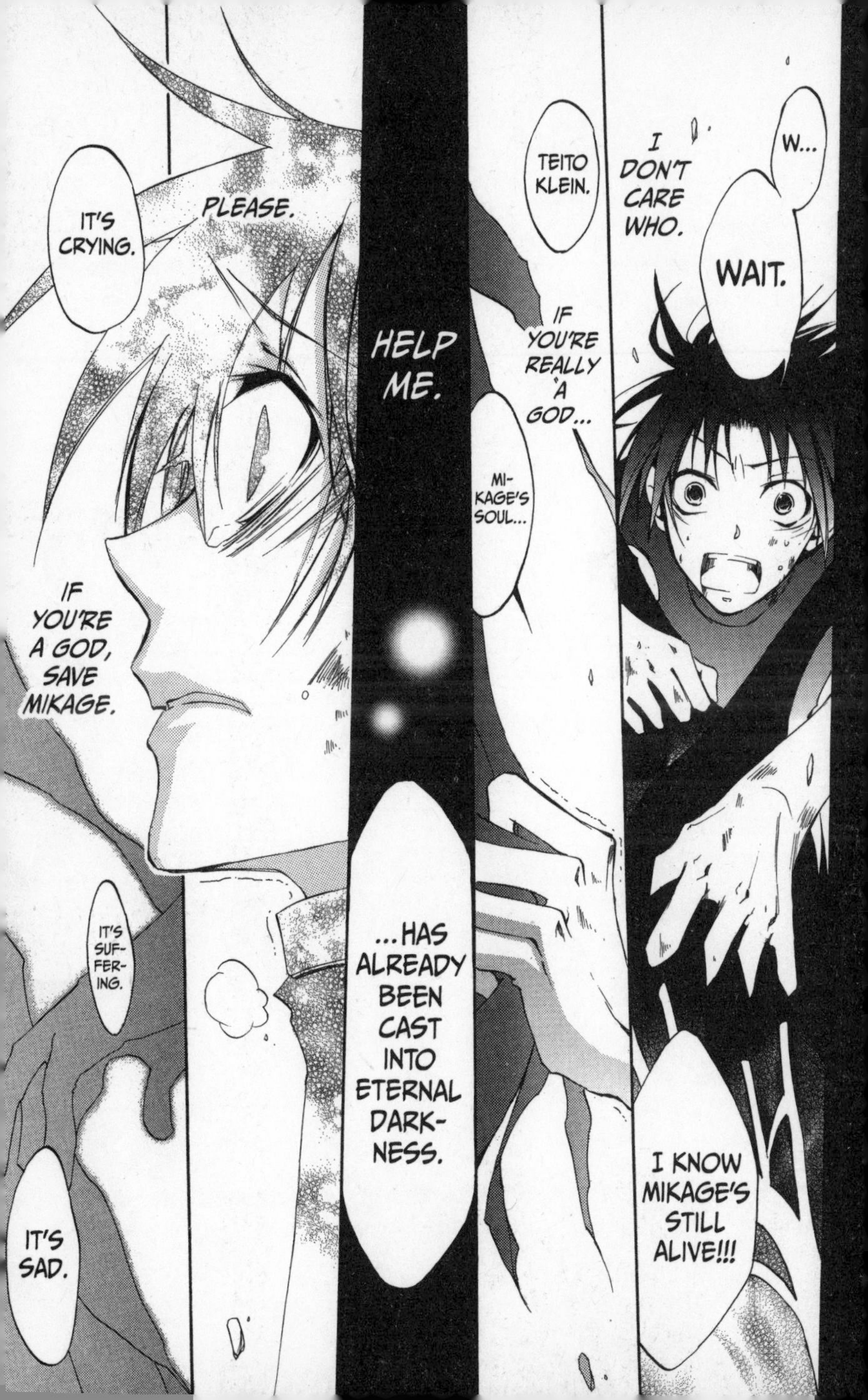
W...
WAIT.
I DON'T CARE WHO.
I KNOW MIKAGE'S STILL ALIVE!!!
TEITO KLEIN.
IF YOU'RE REALLY A GOD...
MI-KAGE'S SOUL...
HELP ME.
...HAS ALREADY BEEN CAST INTO ETERNAL DARK-NESS.
PLEASE.
IT'S CRYING.
IF YOU'RE A GOD, SAVE MIKAGE.
IT'S SUF-FER-ING.
IT'S SAD.

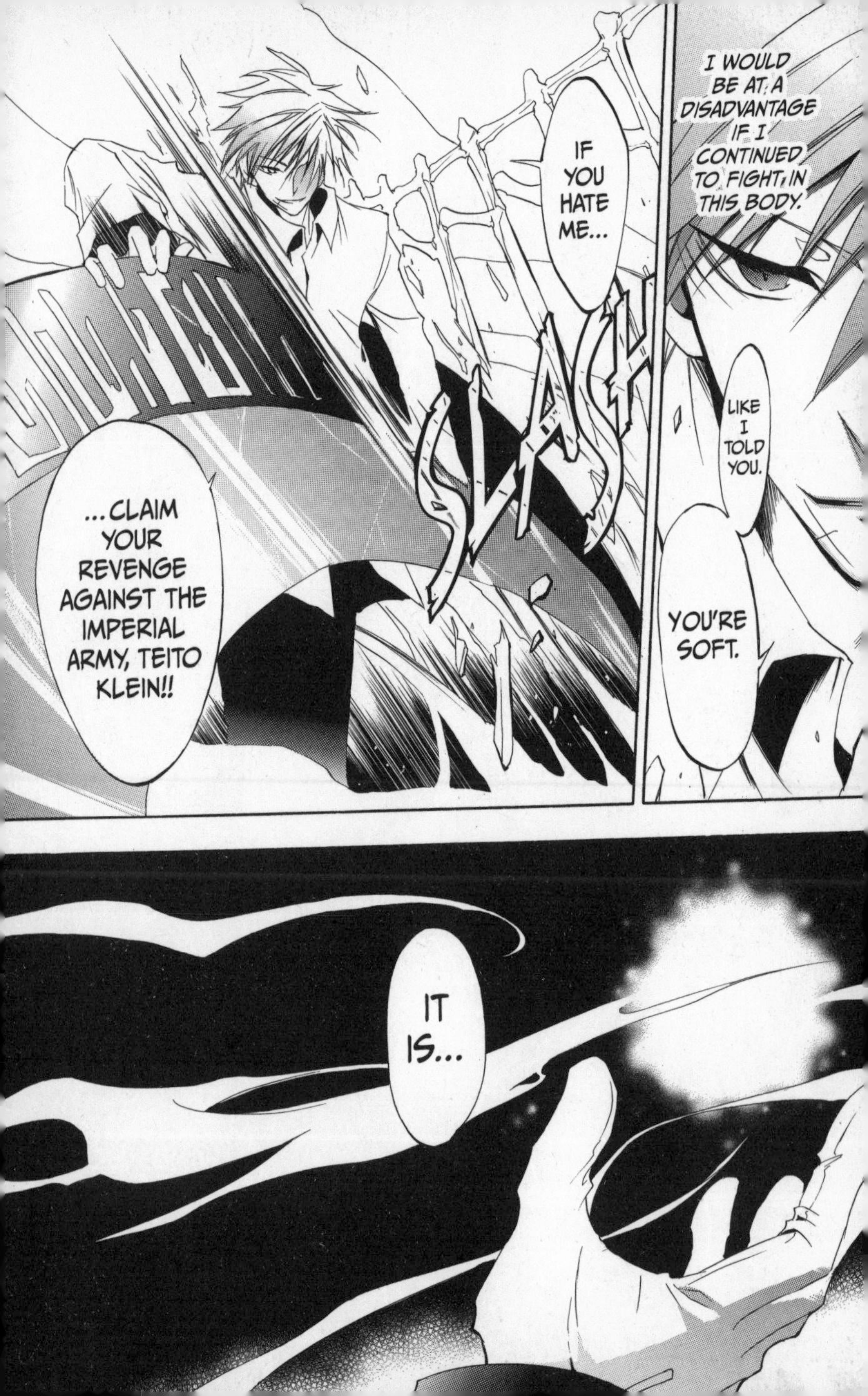
I WOULD BE AT A DISADVANTAGE IF I CONTINUED TO FIGHT IN THIS BODY.
LIKE I TOLD YOU.
YOU'RE SOFT.
IF YOU HATE ME...
SLASH
...CLAIM YOUR REVENGE AGAINST THE IMPERIAL ARMY, TEITO KLEIN!!
IT IS...

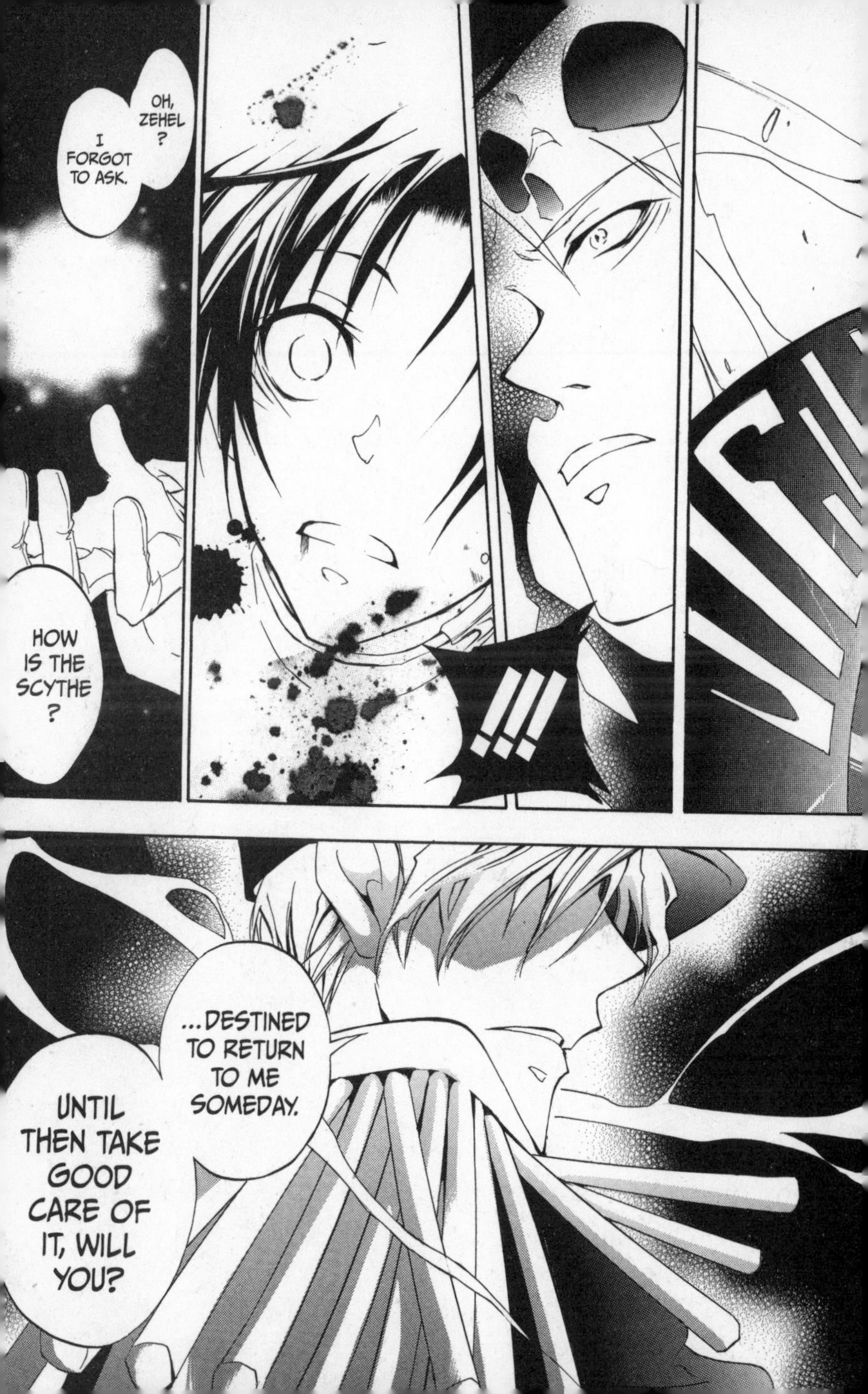
OH, ZEHEL?
I FORGOT TO ASK.
HOW IS THE SCYTHE?
...DESTINED TO RETURN TO ME SOMEDAY.
UNTIL THEN TAKE GOOD CARE OF IT, WILL YOU?

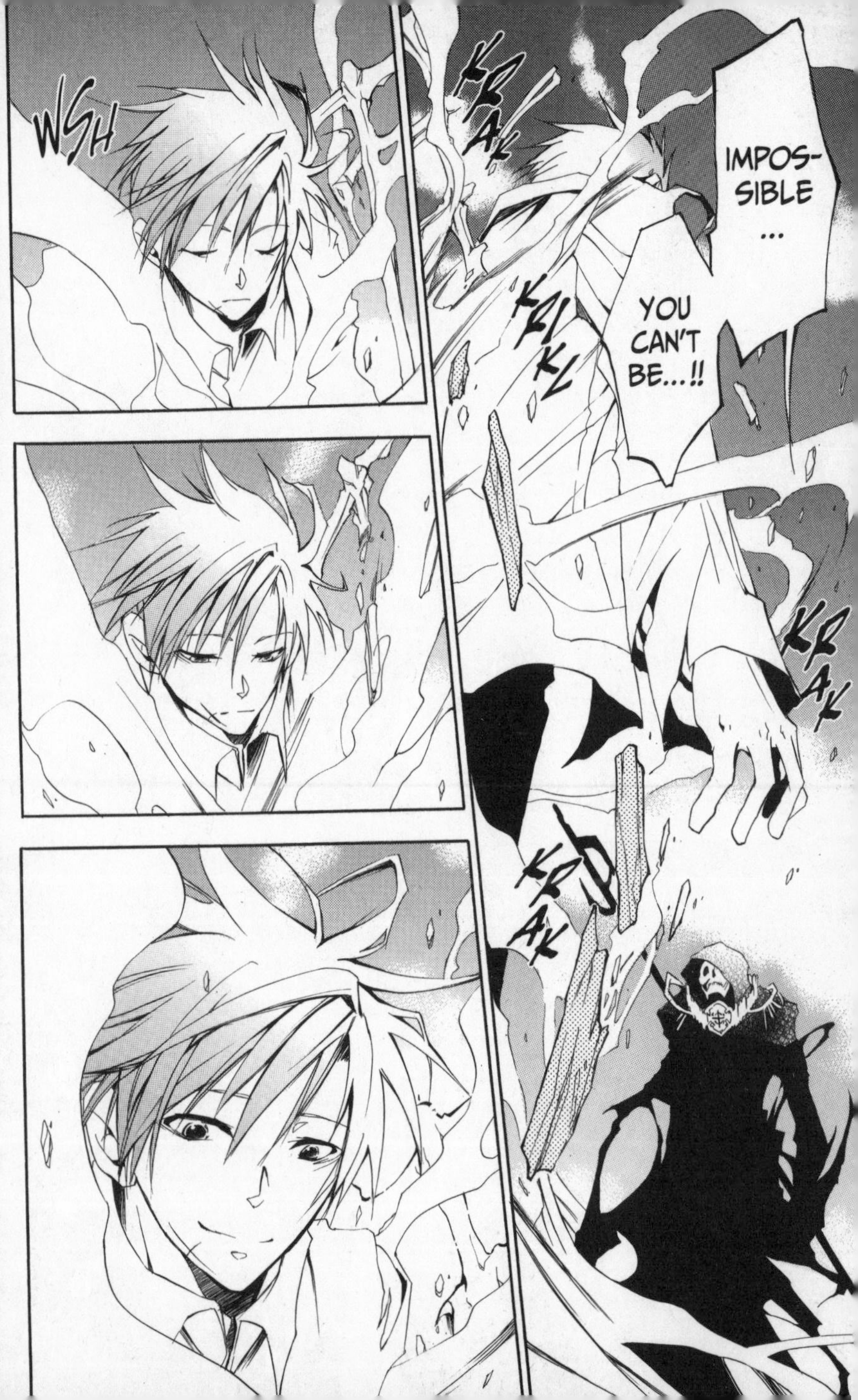
KRAK
IMPOS-SIBLE ...
YOU CAN'T BE...!!
KRAK
KRAK
WSH

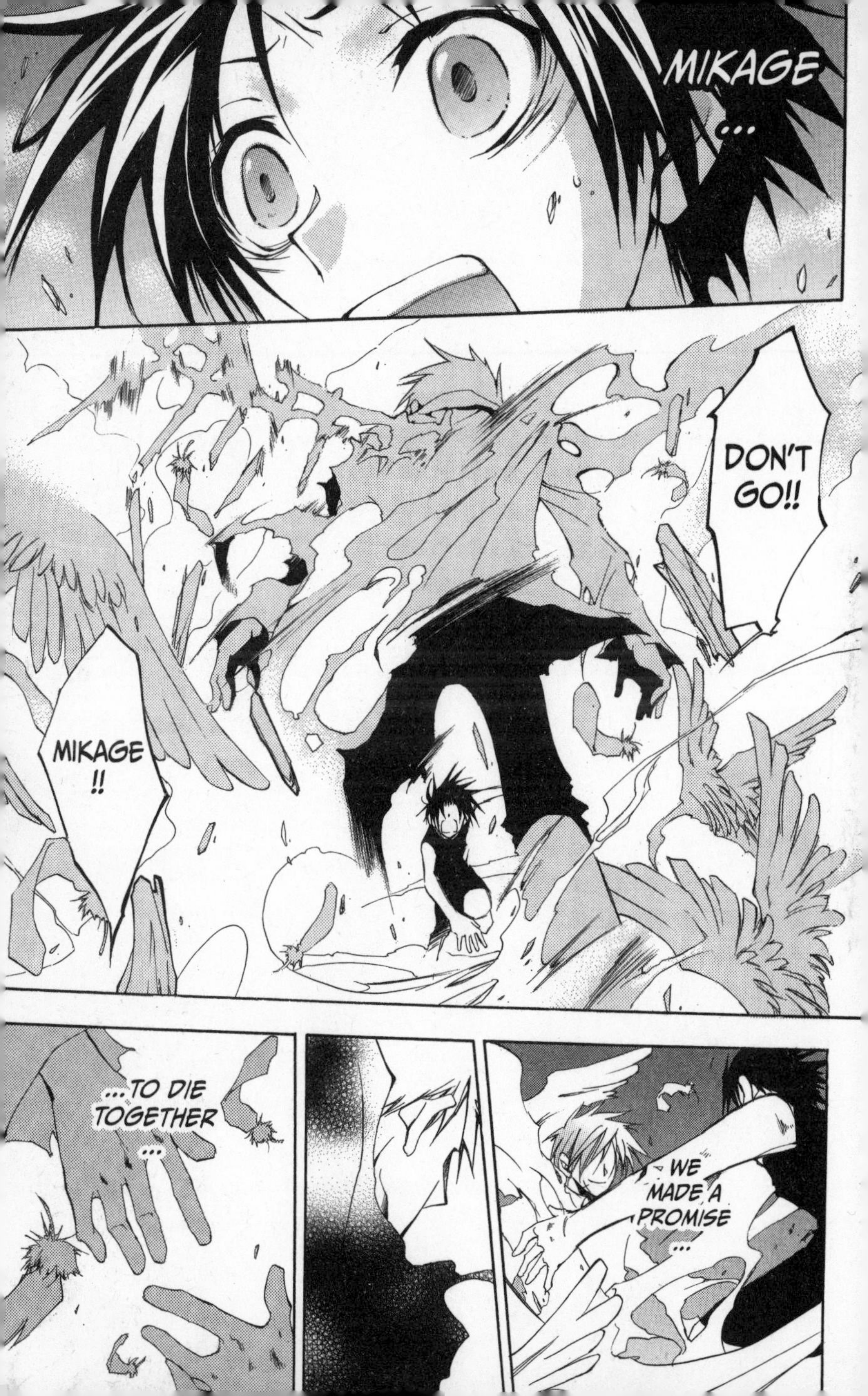
MIKAGE ...
DON'T GO!!
MIKAGE !!
WE MADE A PROMISE ...
...TO DIE TOGETHER ...

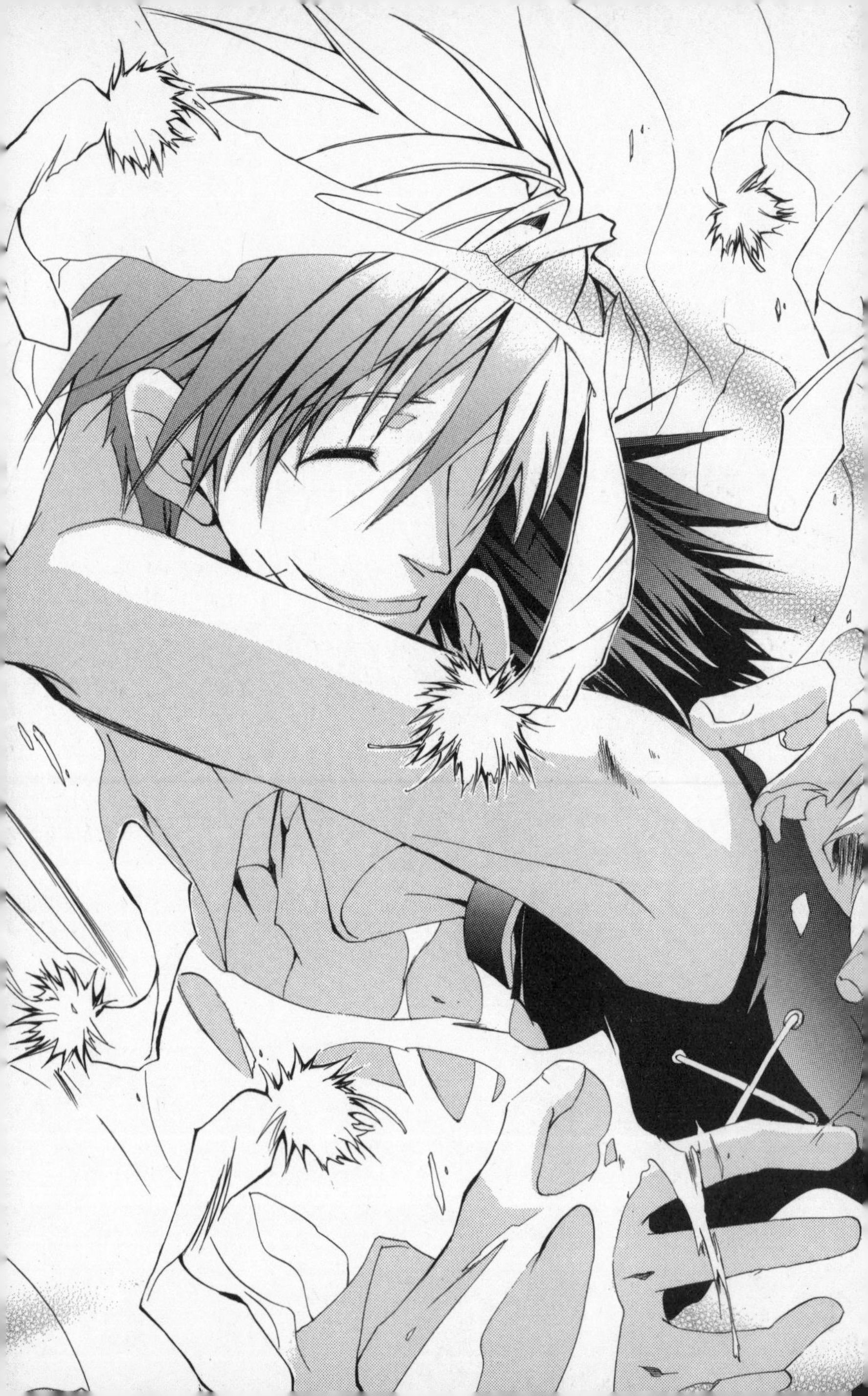

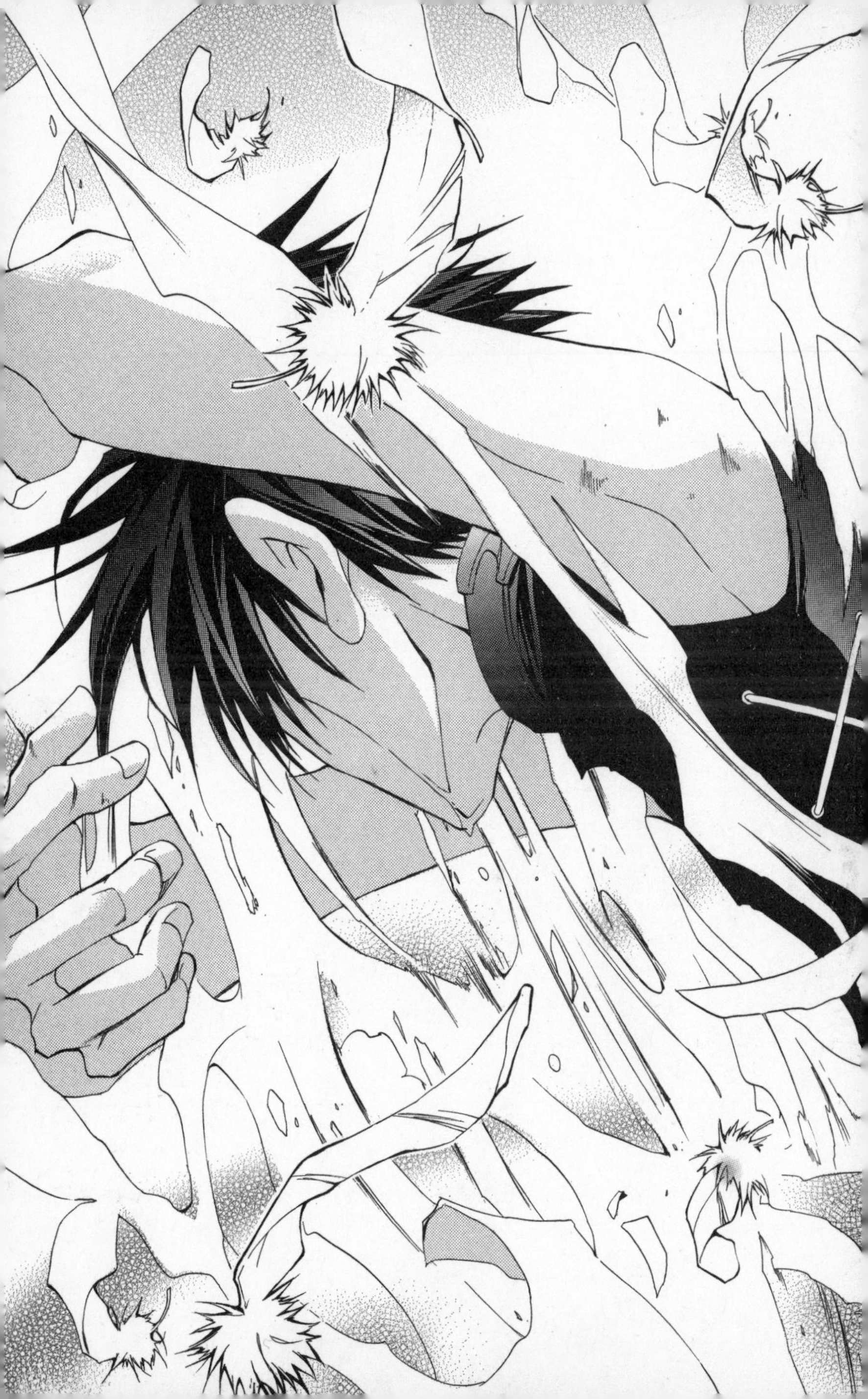

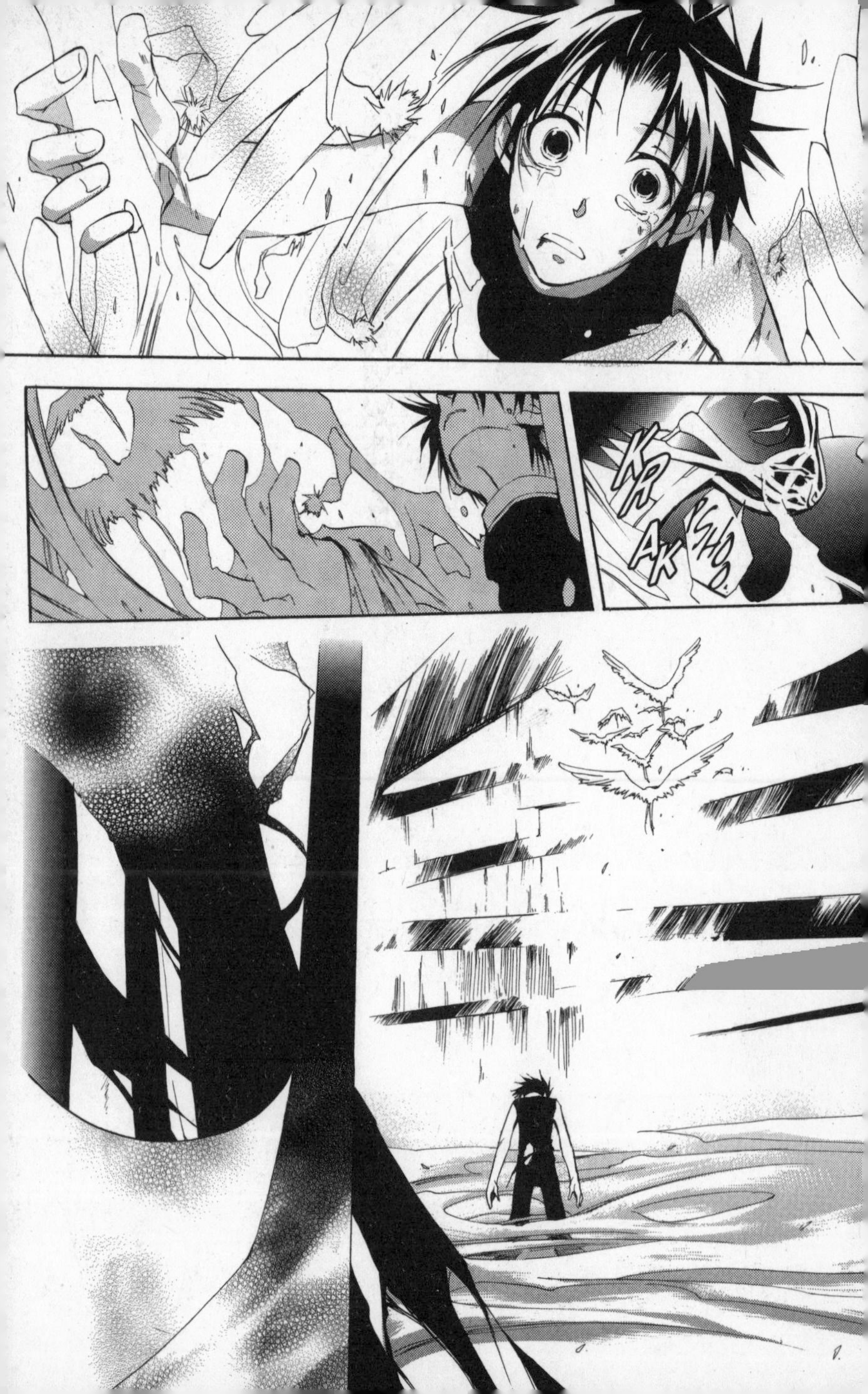
KRRAK
SHOO

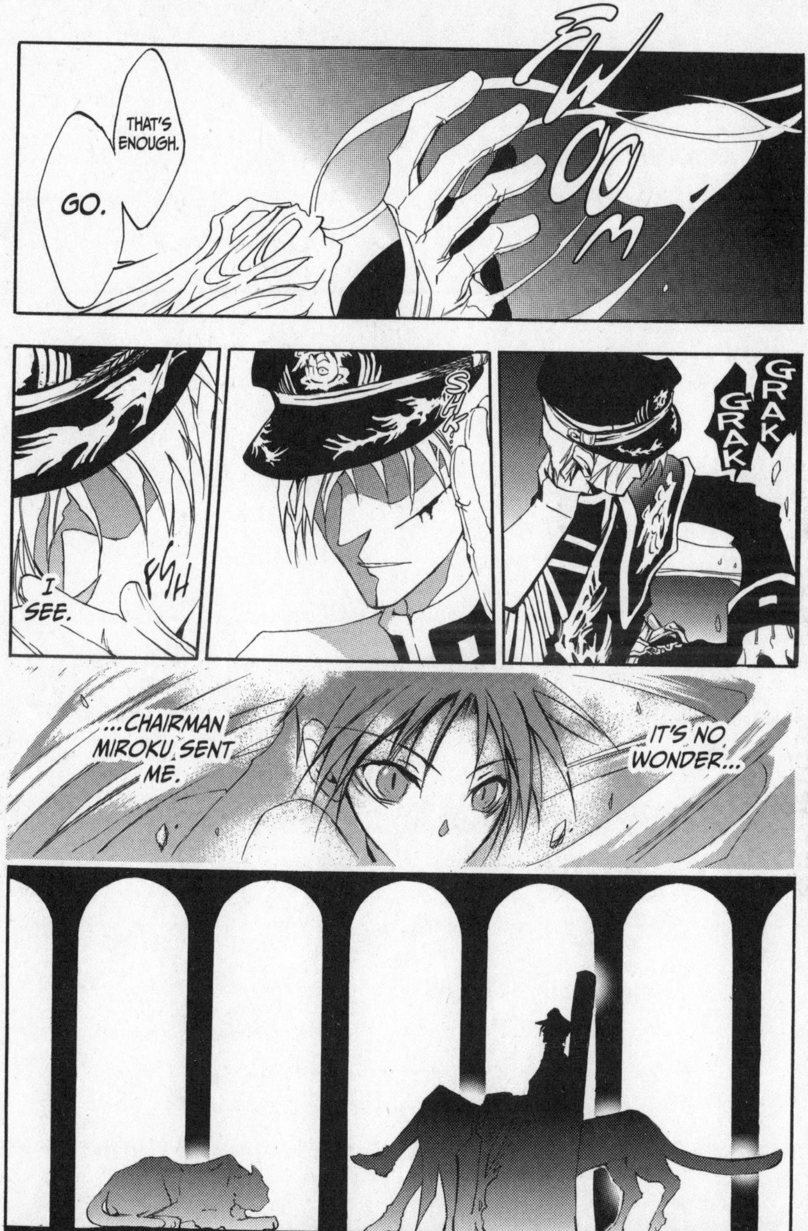
FWOOM
THAT'S ENOUGH.
GO.
GRAK GRAK
SHK!
FSH
I SEE.
IT'S NO WONDER...
...CHAIRMAN MIROKU SENT ME.

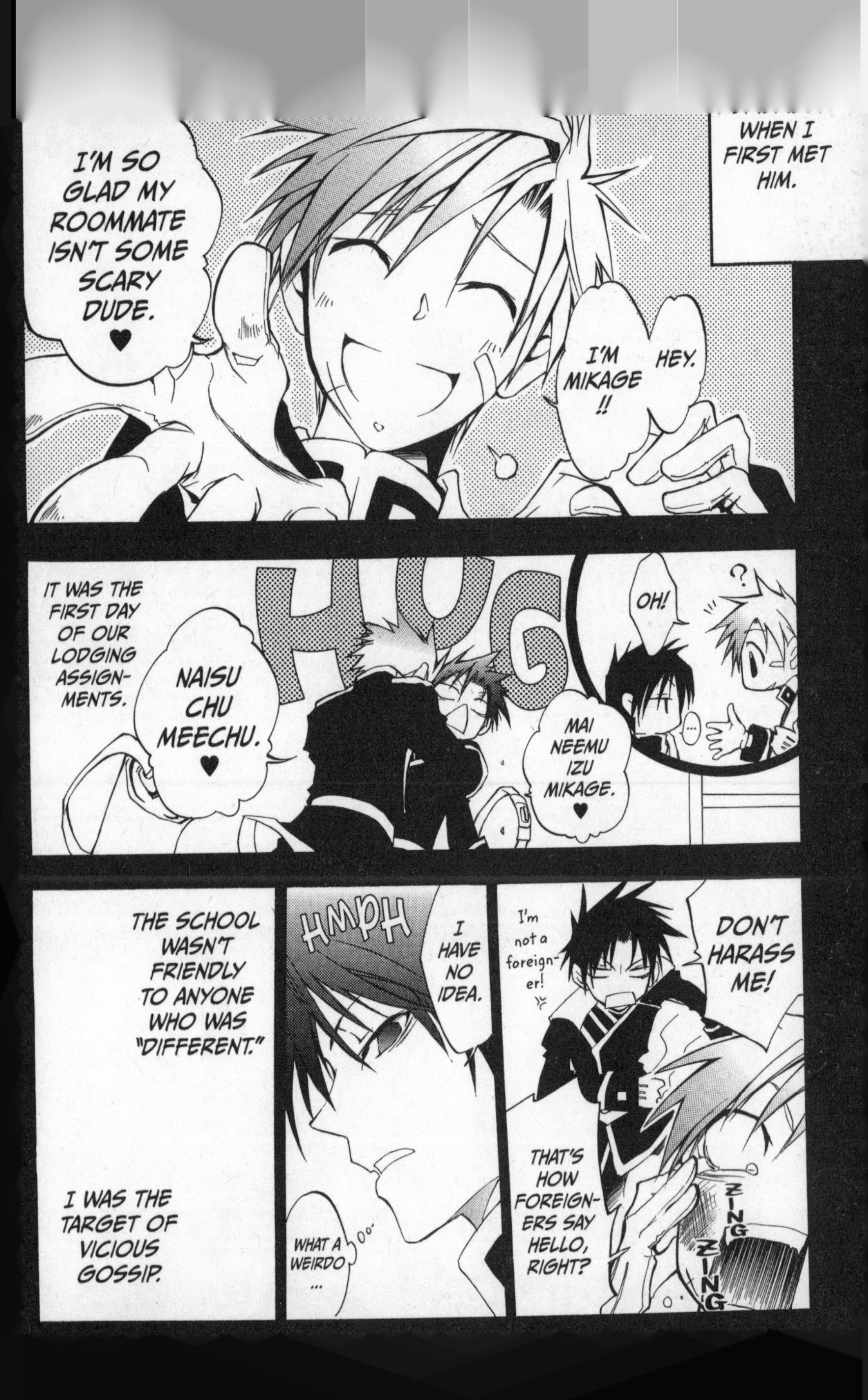
WHEN I FIRST MET HIM.
HEY. I'M MIKAGE!!
I'M SO GLAD MY ROOMMATE ISN'T SOME SCARY DUDE. ♥
?
OH!
...
MAI NEEMU IZU MIKAGE. ♥
HUG
NAISU CHU MEECHU. ♥
IT WAS THE FIRST DAY OF OUR LODGING ASSIGN-MENTS.
DON'T HARASS ME!
I'm not a foreign-er!
THAT'S HOW FOREIGN-ERS SAY HELLO, RIGHT?
ZING ZING ZING
I HAVE NO IDEA.
HMPH
WHAT A WEIRDO...
THE SCHOOL WASN'T FRIENDLY TO ANYONE WHO WAS "DIFFERENT."
I WAS THE TARGET OF VICIOUS GOSSIP.

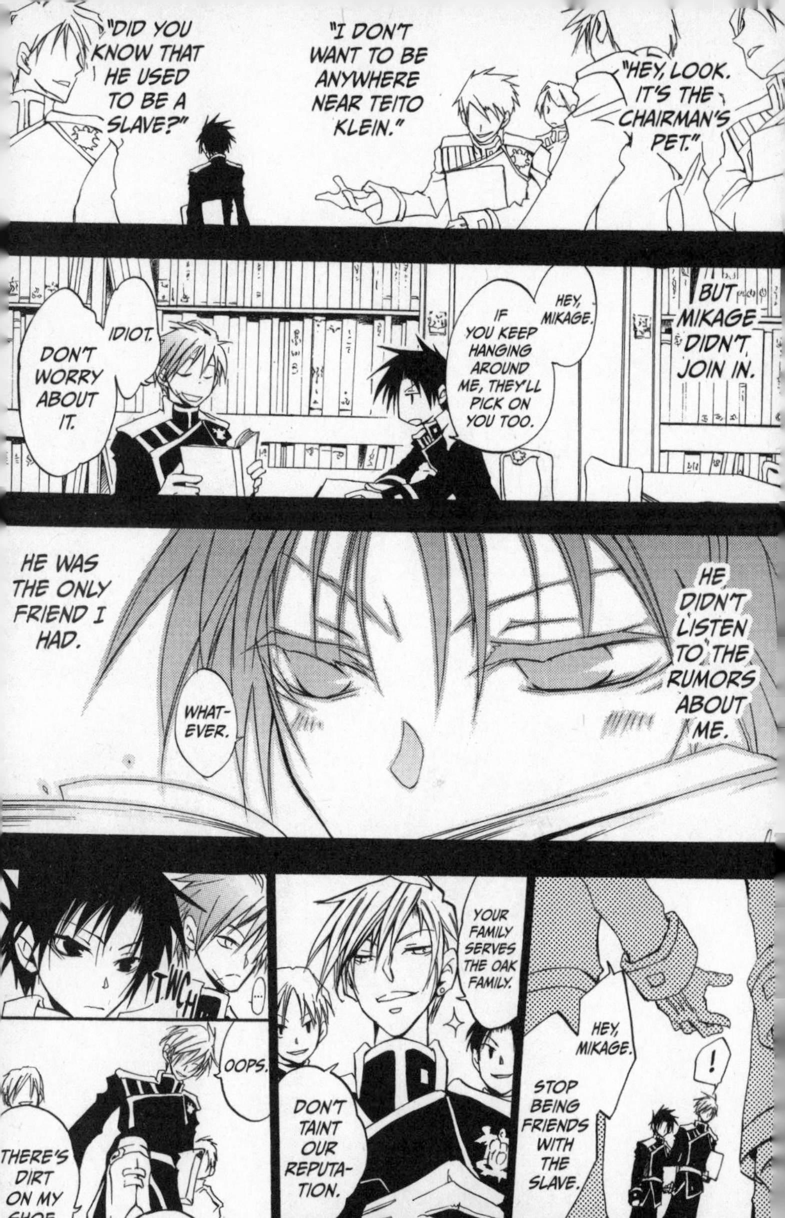
"HEY, LOOK. IT'S THE CHAIRMAN'S PET."
"I DON'T WANT TO BE ANYWHERE NEAR TEITO KLEIN."
"DID YOU KNOW THAT HE USED TO BE A SLAVE?"
BUT MIKAGE DIDN'T JOIN IN.
HEY, MIKAGE.
IF YOU KEEP HANGING AROUND ME, THEY'LL PICK ON YOU TOO.
IDIOT.
DON'T WORRY ABOUT IT.
HE DIDN'T LISTEN TO THE RUMORS ABOUT ME.
WHAT-EVER.
HE WAS THE ONLY FRIEND I HAD.
HEY, MIKAGE.
!
STOP BEING FRIENDS WITH THE SLAVE.
YOUR FAMILY SERVES THE OAK FAMILY.
DON'T TAINT OUR REPUTA-TION.
TWCH
...
OOPS.
THERE'S DIRT ON MY SHOE.

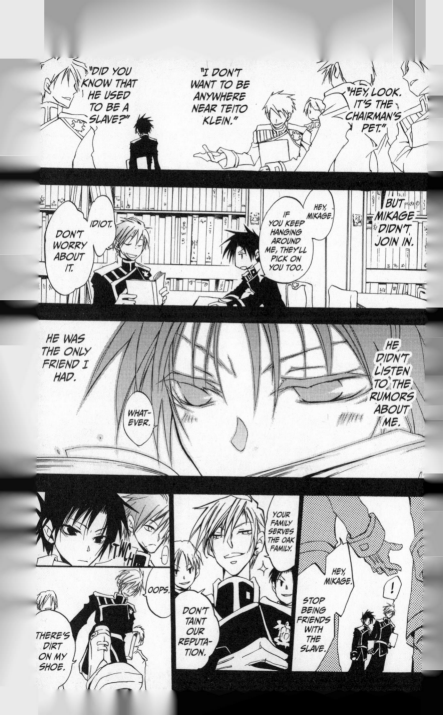

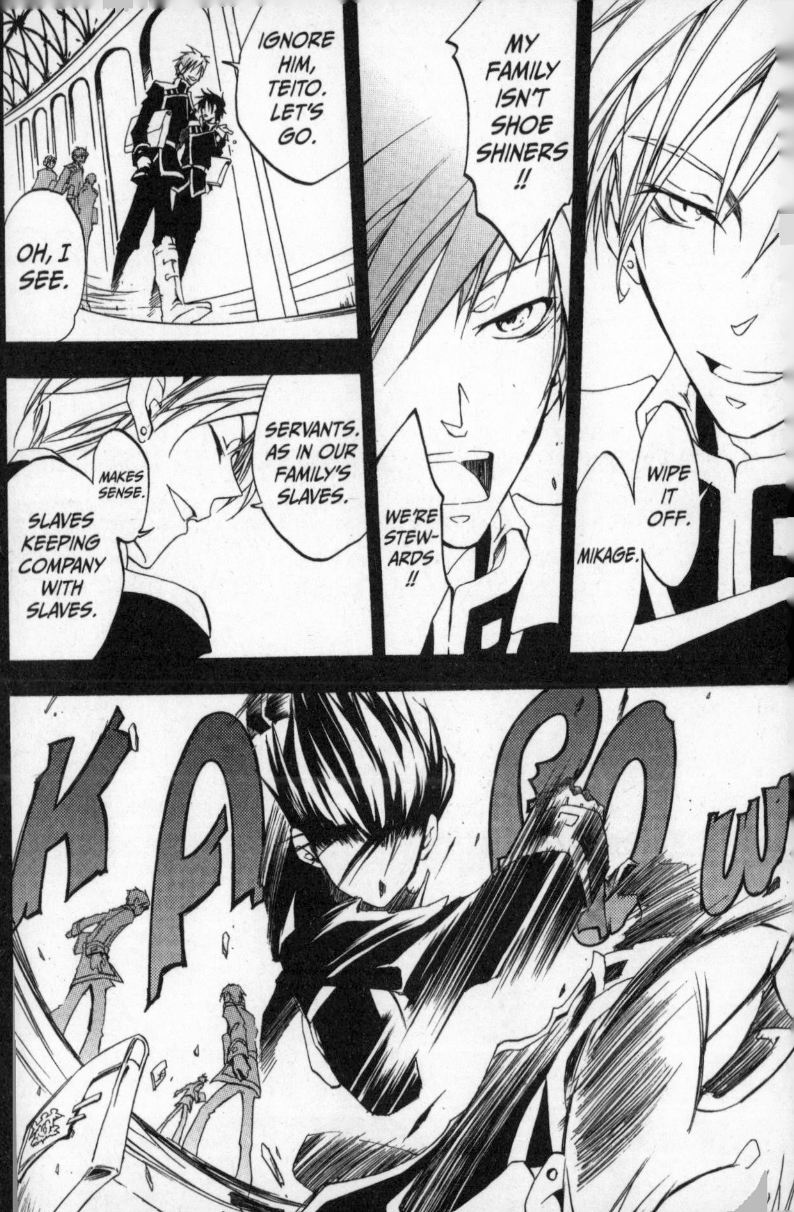
WIPE IT OFF.
MIKAGE.
MY FAMILY ISN'T SHOE SHINERS !!
WE'RE STEWARDS !!
IGNORE HIM, TEITO. LET'S GO.
OH, I SEE.
SERVANTS. AS IN OUR FAMILY'S SLAVES.
MAKES SENSE.
SLAVES KEEPING COMPANY WITH SLAVES.
KAPOW

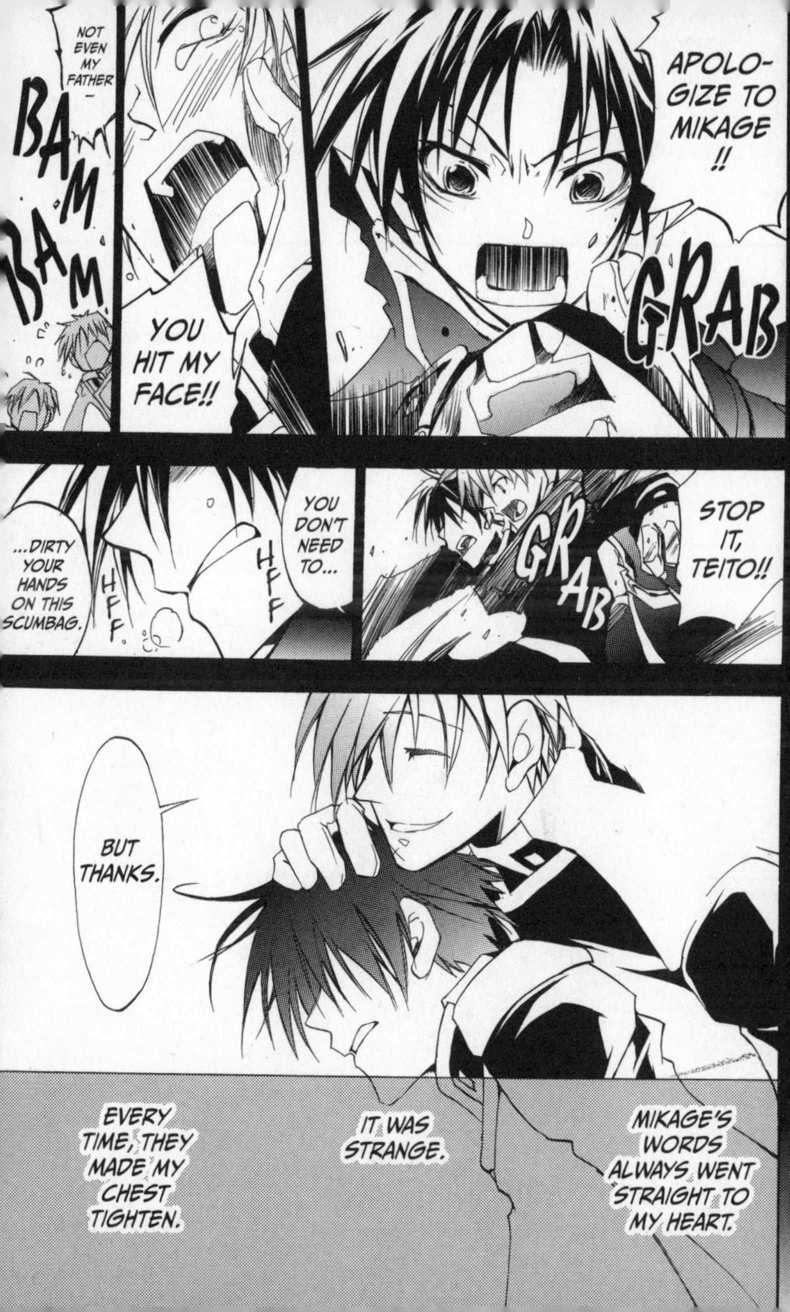

APOLOGIZE TO MIKAGE!!
GRAB
YOU HIT MY FACE!!
NOT EVEN MY FATHER—
BAM BAM
STOP IT, TEITO!!
GRAB
YOU DON'T NEED TO...
...DIRTY YOUR HANDS ON THIS SCUMBAG.
HFF HFF
BUT THANKS.
MIKAGE'S WORDS ALWAYS WENT STRAIGHT TO MY HEART.
IT WAS STRANGE.
EVERY TIME, THEY MADE MY CHEST TIGHTEN.

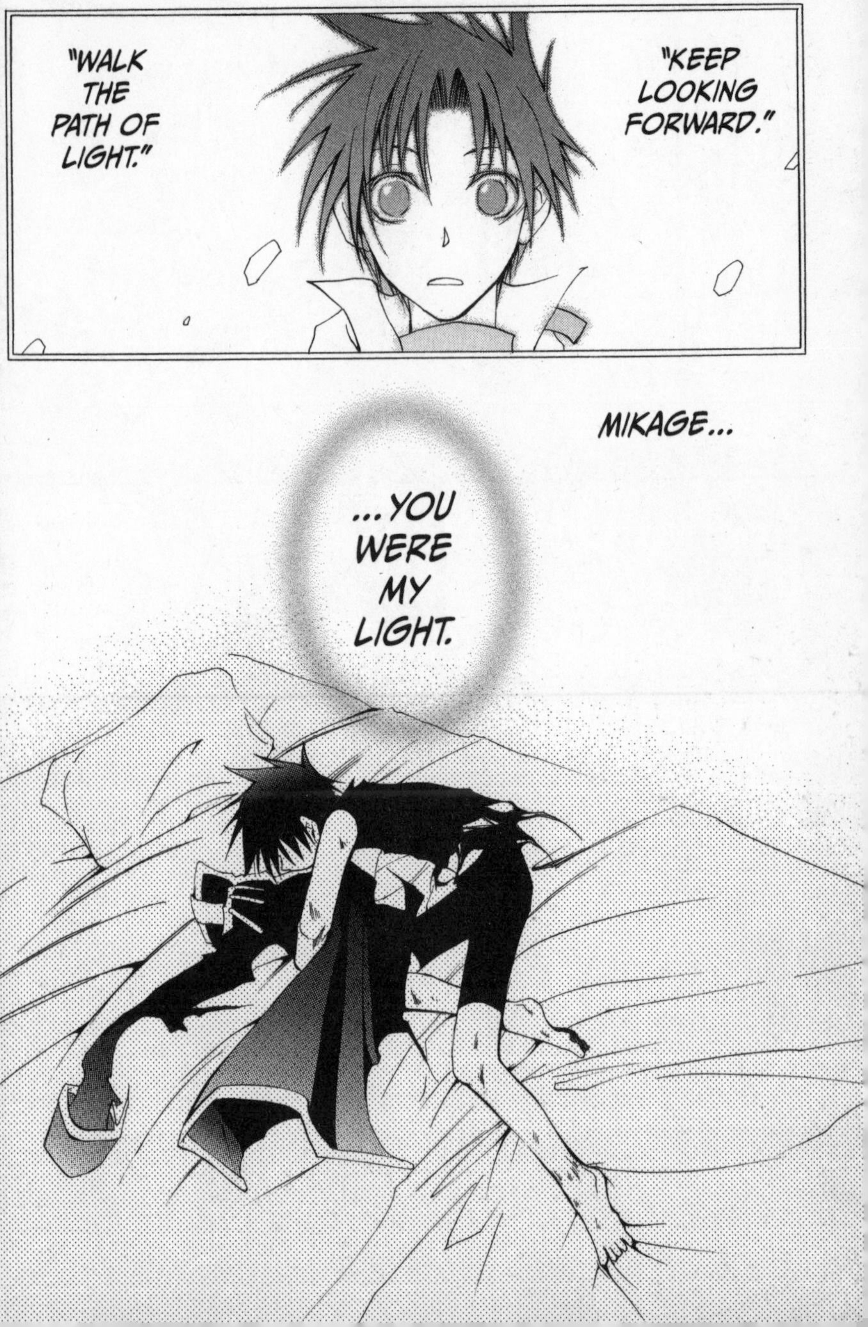
"KEEP LOOKING FORWARD."
"WALK THE PATH OF LIGHT."
MIKAGE...
...YOU WERE MY LIGHT.

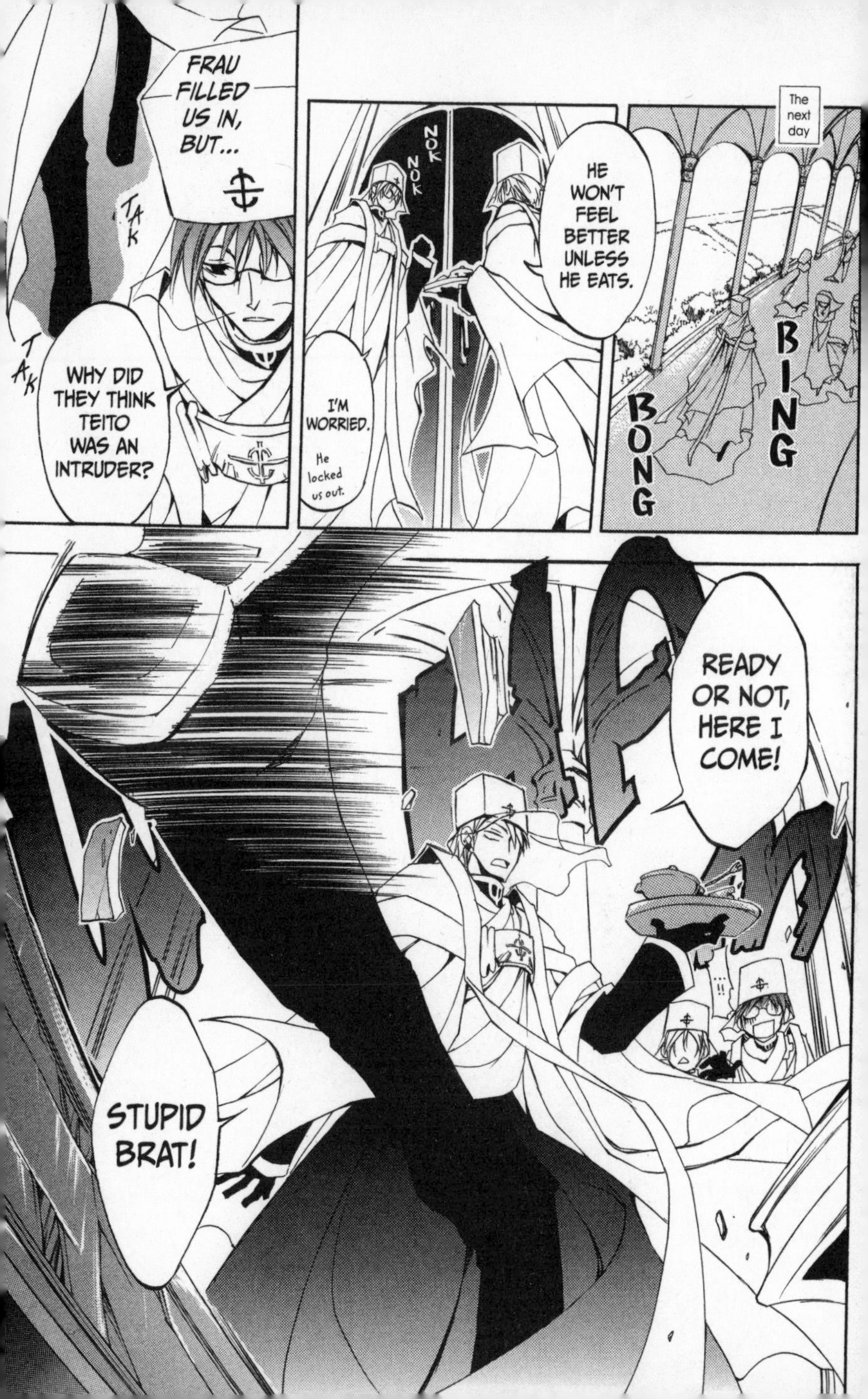
The next day
BING
BONG
NOK NOK
HE WON'T FEEL BETTER UNLESS HE EATS.
I'M WORRIED.
He locked us out.
FRAU FILLED US IN, BUT...
TAK TAK
WHY DID THEY THINK TEITO WAS AN INTRUDER?
READY OR NOT, HERE I COME!
...!!
STUPID BRAT!

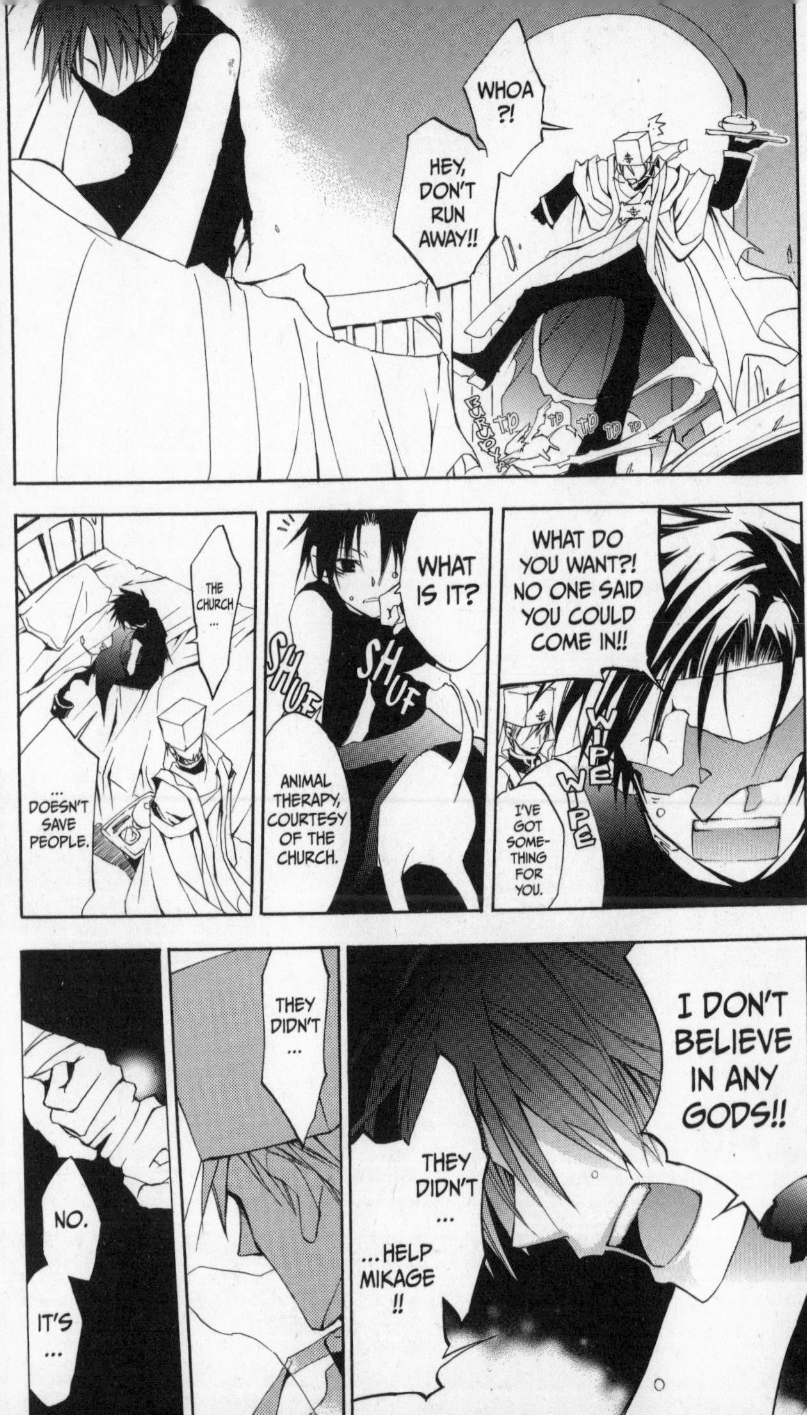
WHOA ?!
HEY, DON'T RUN AWAY!!
TIP TIP TIP TIP TIP
WHAT DO YOU WANT?! NO ONE SAID YOU COULD COME IN!!
WIPE WIPE
I'VE GOT SOMETHING FOR YOU.
WHAT IS IT?
SHUF SHUF
ANIMAL THERAPY, COURTESY OF THE CHURCH.
THE CHURCH ...
... DOESN'T SAVE PEOPLE.
I DON'T BELIEVE IN ANY GODS!!
THEY DIDN'T ...
...HELP MIKAGE !!
THEY DIDN'T ...
NO.
IT'S ...

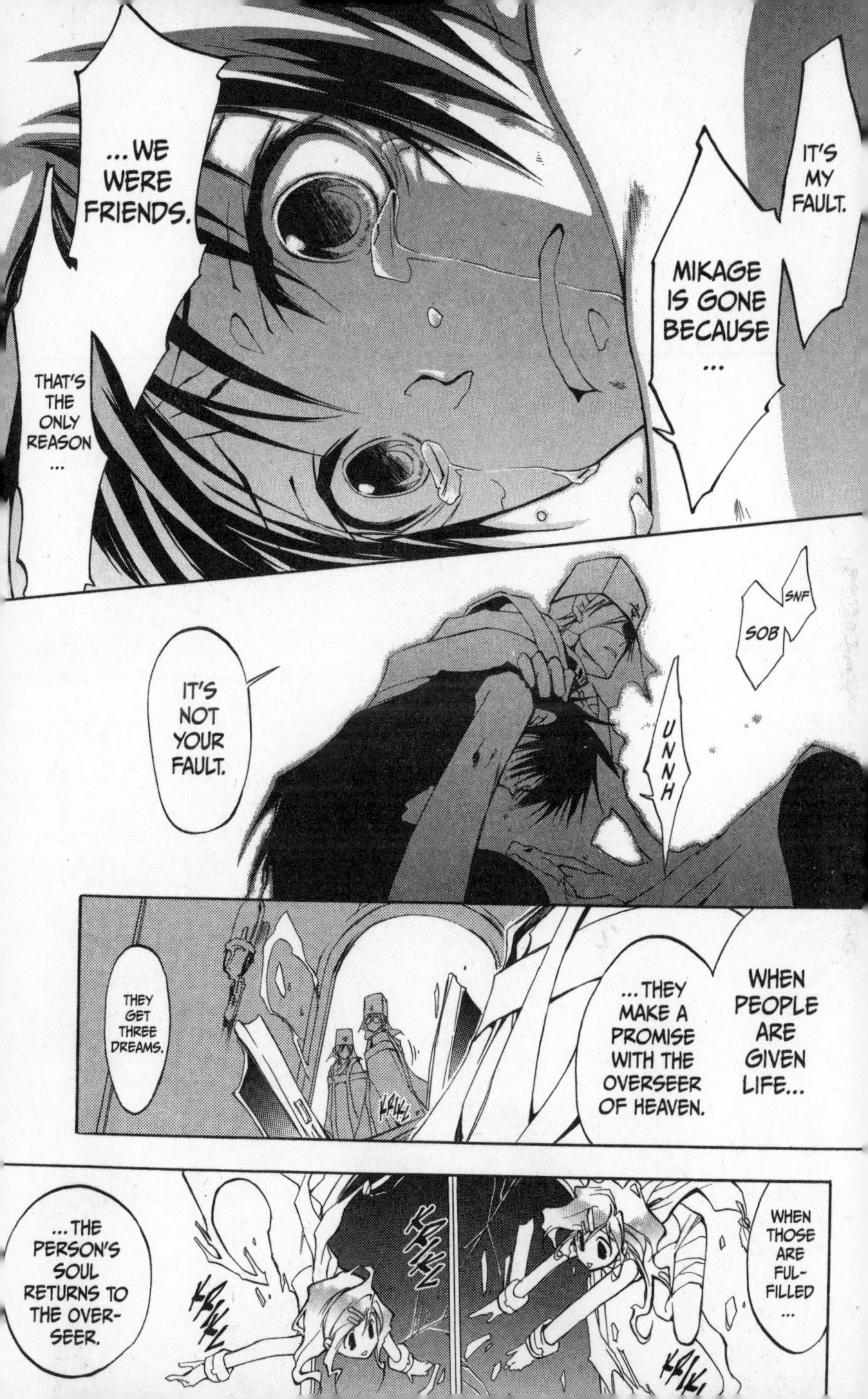
IT'S MY FAULT.
MIKAGE IS GONE BECAUSE ...
...WE WERE FRIENDS.
THAT'S THE ONLY REASON ...
SNF
SOB
UNNH
IT'S NOT YOUR FAULT.
WHEN PEOPLE ARE GIVEN LIFE...
...THEY MAKE A PROMISE WITH THE OVERSEER OF HEAVEN.
THEY GET THREE DREAMS.
WHEN THOSE ARE FUL-FILLED ...
...THE PERSON'S SOUL RETURNS TO THE OVER-SEER.

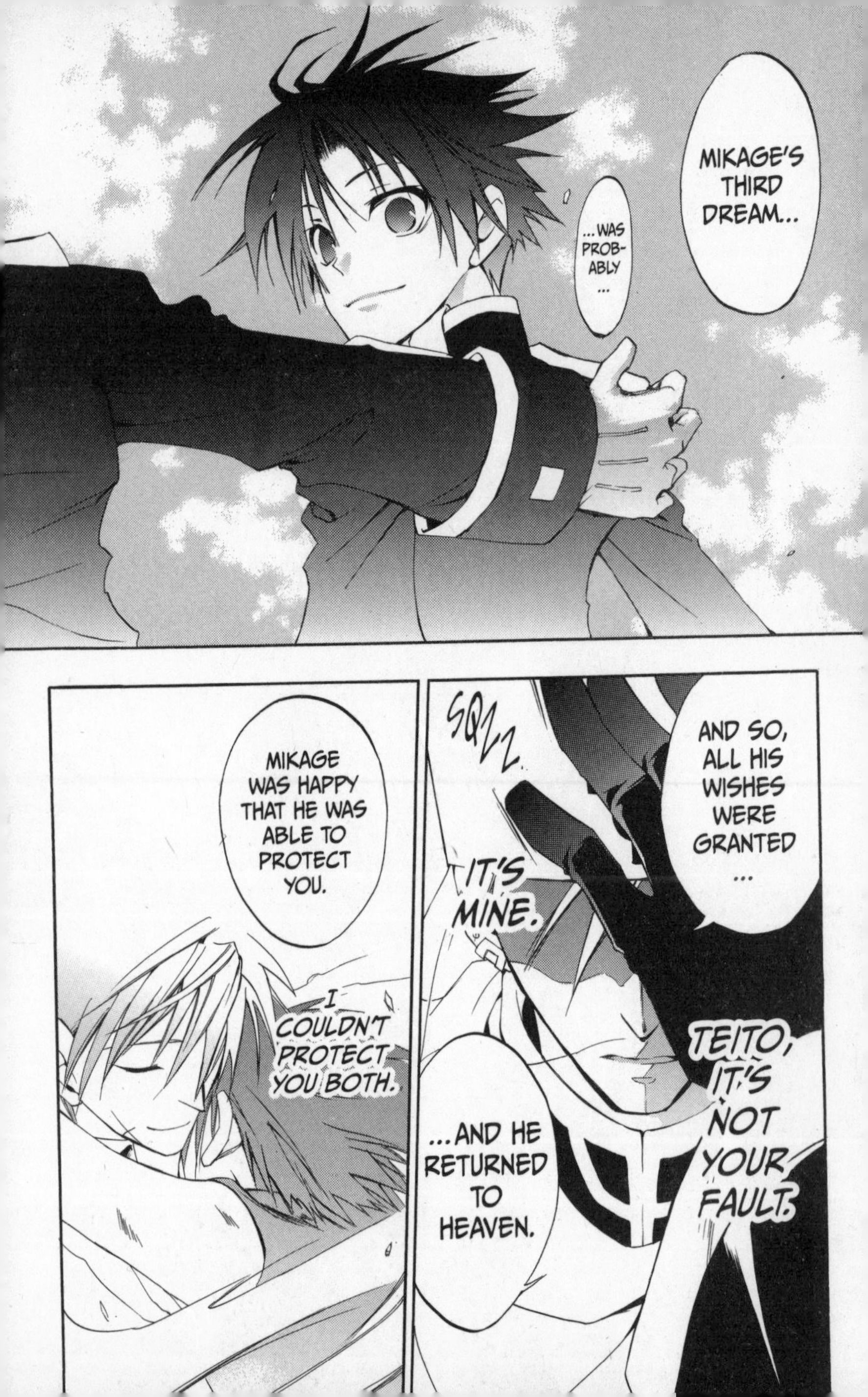
MIKAGE'S THIRD DREAM...
...WAS PROB-ABLY ...
AND SO, ALL HIS WISHES WERE GRANTED ...
SQZZ
IT'S MINE.
TEITO, IT'S NOT YOUR FAULT.
...AND HE RETURNED TO HEAVEN.
MIKAGE WAS HAPPY THAT HE WAS ABLE TO PROTECT YOU.
I COULDN'T PROTECT YOU BOTH.

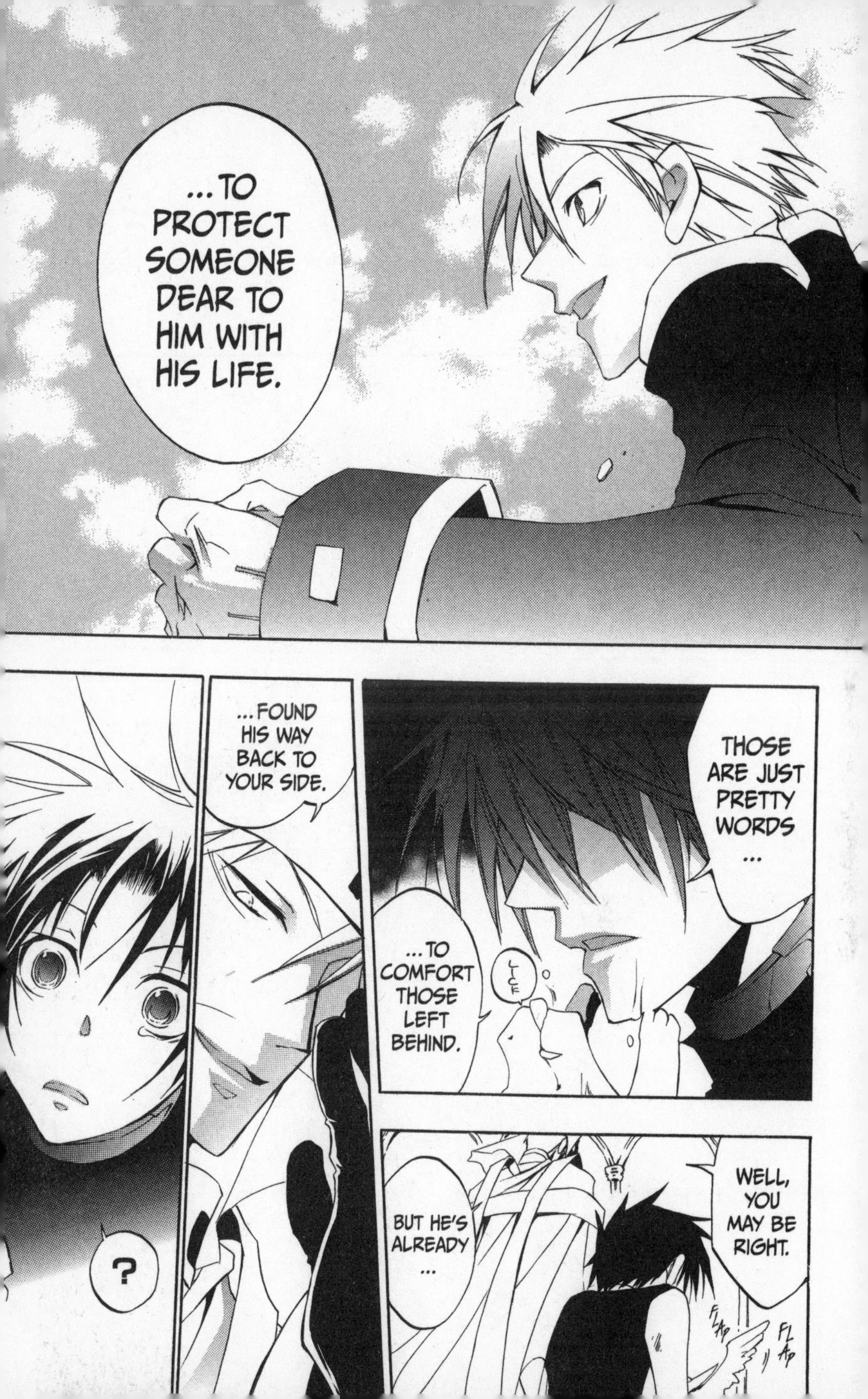
...TO PROTECT SOMEONE DEAR TO HIM WITH HIS LIFE.
THOSE ARE JUST PRETTY WORDS ...
...TO COMFORT THOSE LEFT BEHIND.
LICK
WELL, YOU MAY BE RIGHT.
BUT HE'S ALREADY ...
FLAP
FLAP
...FOUND HIS WAY BACK TO YOUR SIDE.
?

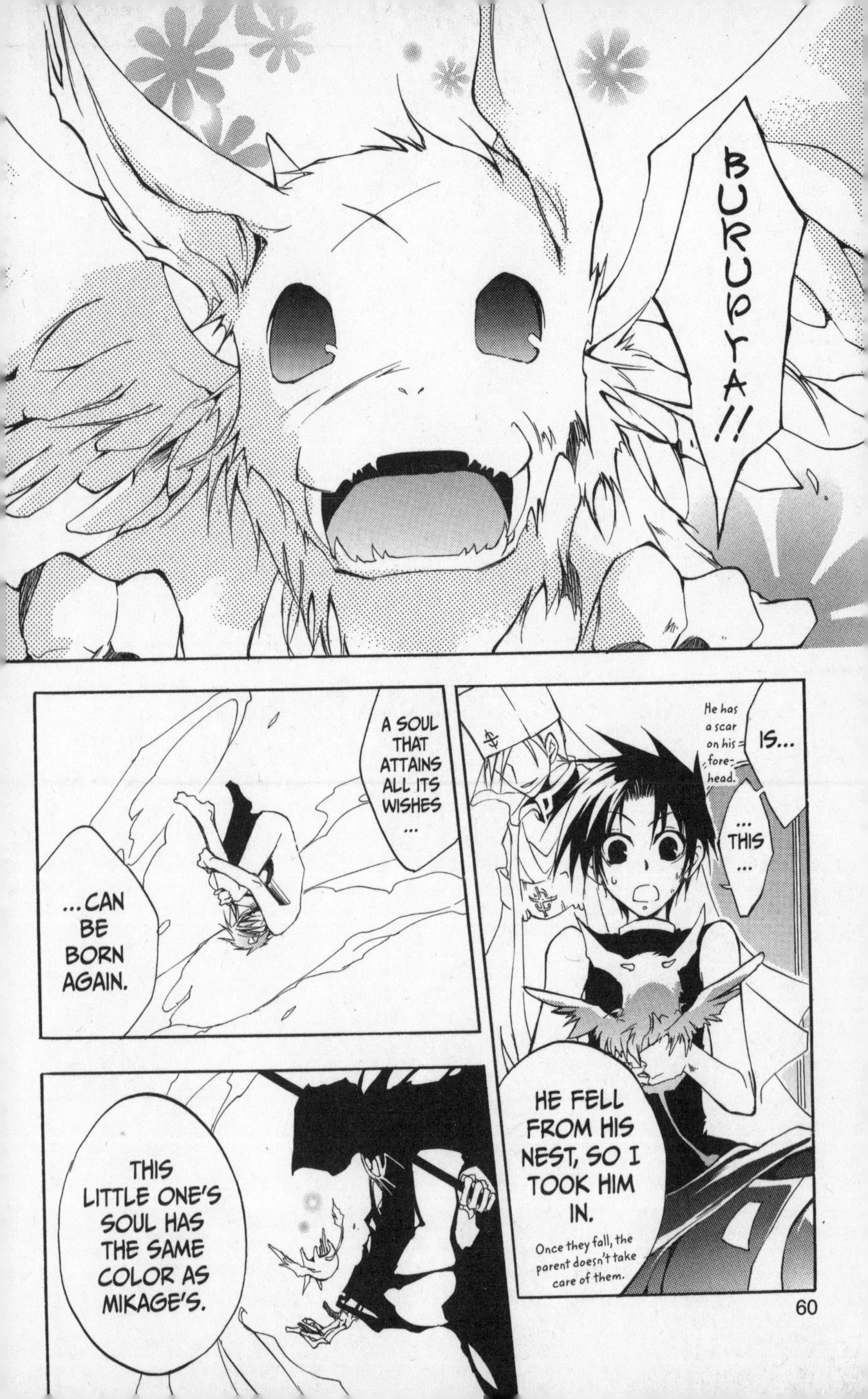
BURUPYA!!
IS...
He has a scar on his forehead.
...THIS...
HE FELL FROM HIS NEST, SO I TOOK HIM IN.
Once they fall, the parent doesn't take care of them.
A SOUL THAT ATTAINS ALL ITS WISHES...
...CAN BE BORN AGAIN.
THIS LITTLE ONE'S SOUL HAS THE SAME COLOR AS MIKAGE'S.

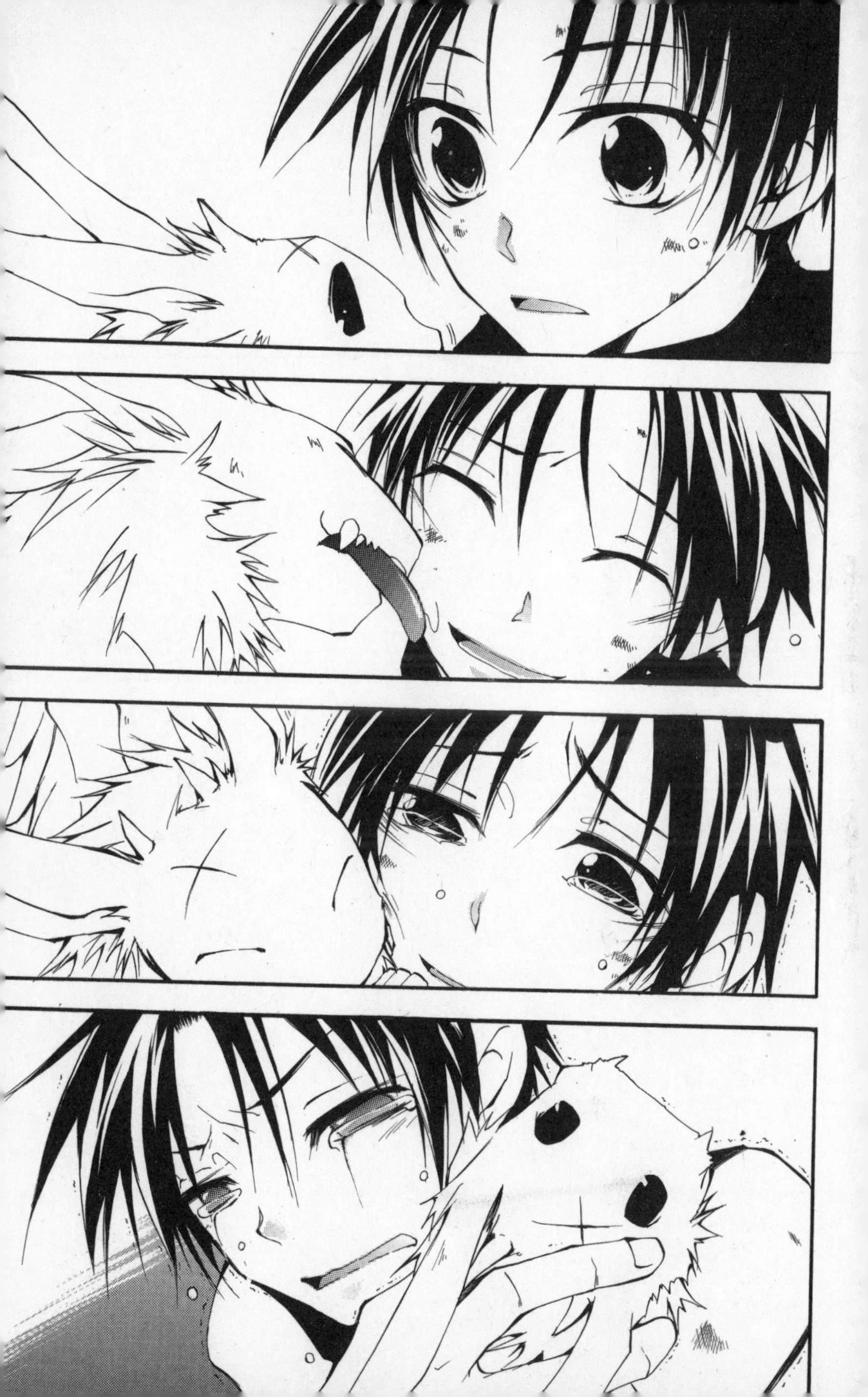

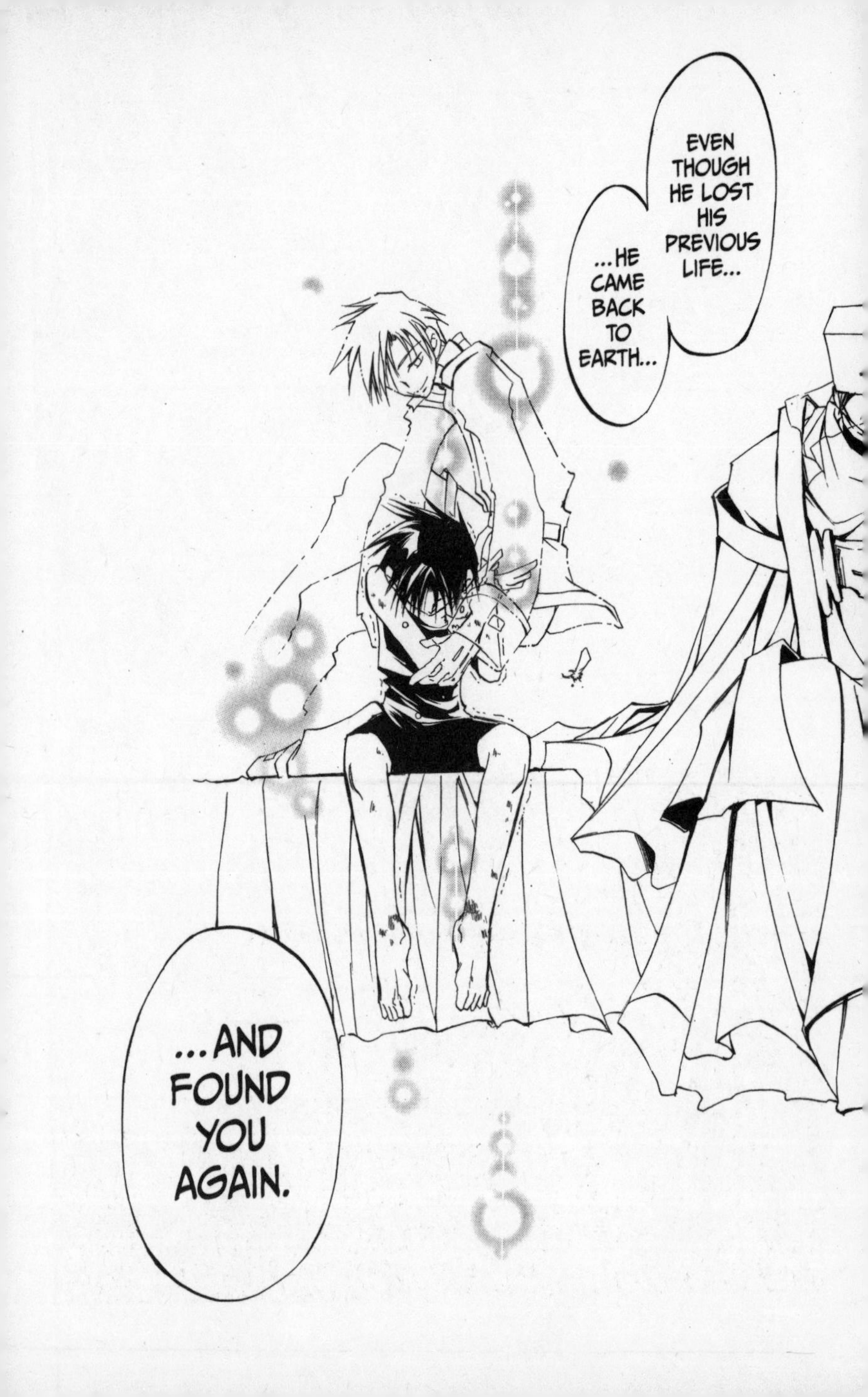
EVEN THOUGH HE LOST HIS PREVIOUS LIFE...
...HE CAME BACK TO EARTH...
...AND FOUND YOU AGAIN.

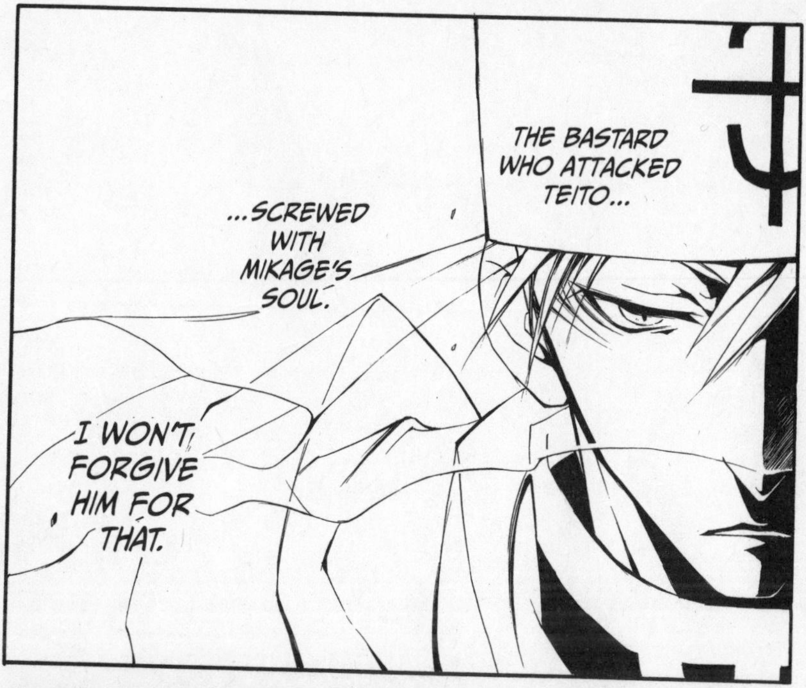
THE BASTARD WHO ATTACKED TEITO...
...SCREWED WITH MIKAGE'S SOUL.
I WON'T FORGIVE HIM FOR THAT.

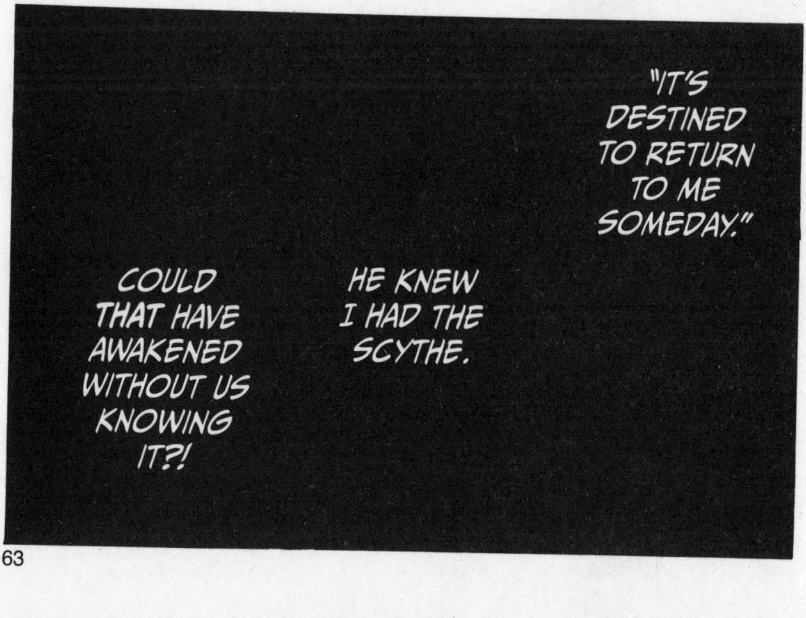
"IT'S DESTINED TO RETURN TO ME SOMEDAY."
HE KNEW I HAD THE SCYTHE.
COULD THAT HAVE AWAKENED WITHOUT US KNOWING IT?!

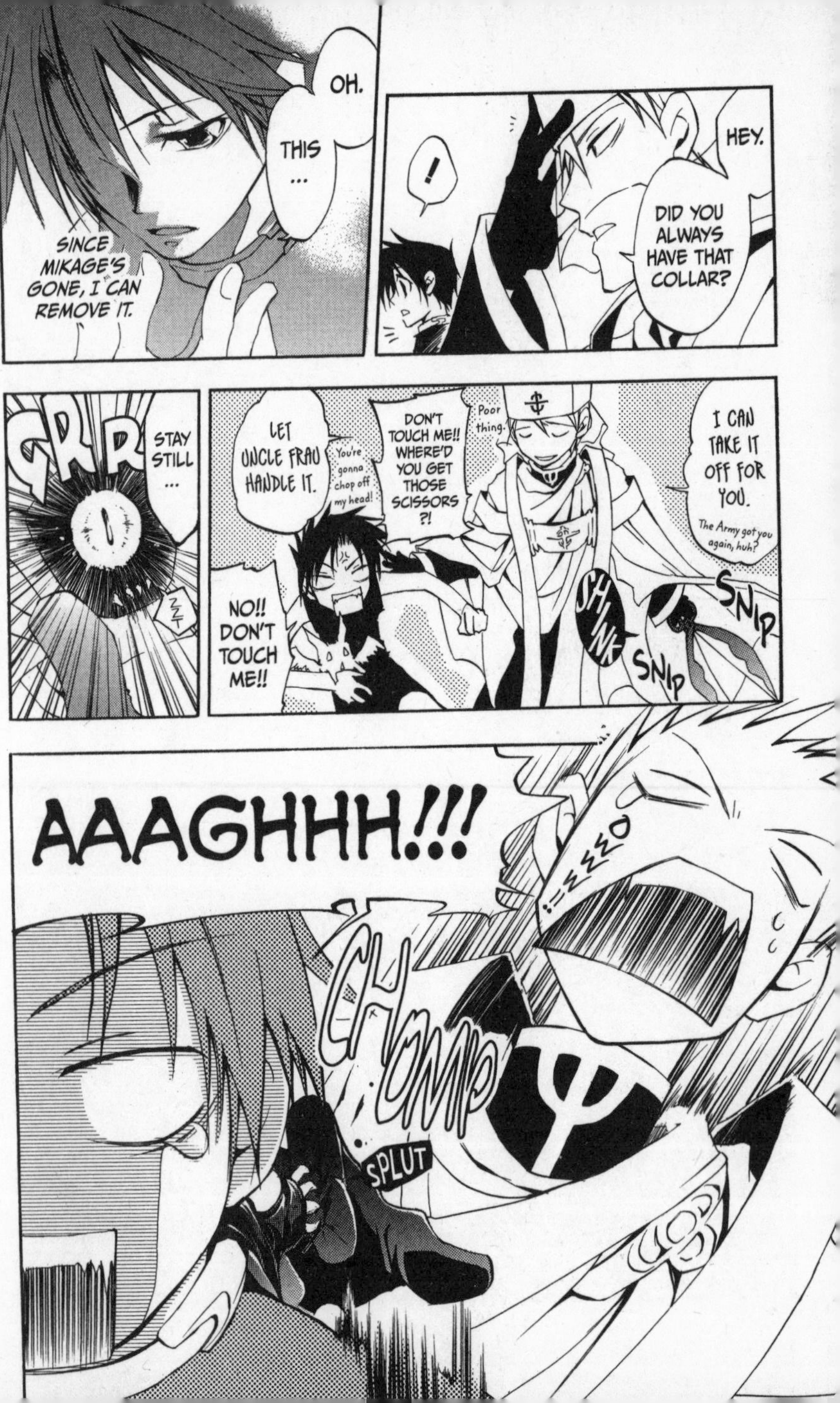
HEY.
!
DID YOU ALWAYS HAVE THAT COLLAR?
OH.
THIS ...
SINCE MIKAGE'S GONE, I CAN REMOVE IT.
I CAN TAKE IT OFF FOR YOU.
The Army got you again, huh?
Poor thing.
DON'T TOUCH ME!! WHERE'D YOU GET THOSE SCISSORS?!
LET UNCLE FRAU HANDLE IT.
You're gonna chop off my head!
SHINK
SNIP
SNIP
NO!! DON'T TOUCH ME!!
GRR
STAY STILL ...
ZZT
AAAGHHH!!!
CHOMP
SPLUT

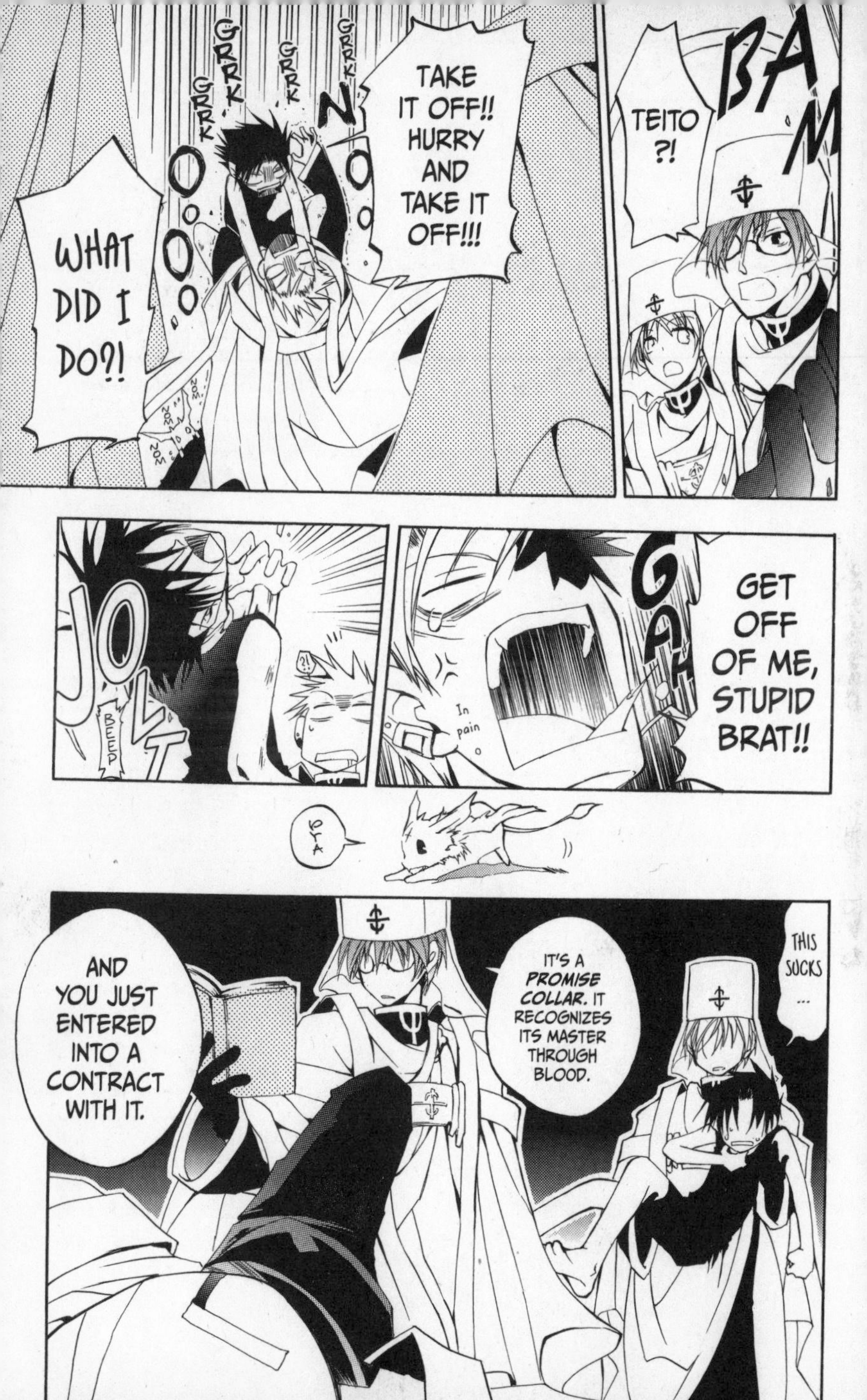
BAM
TEITO ?!
TAKE IT OFF!! HURRY AND TAKE IT OFF!!!
GRRK GRRK GRRK GRRK
NOOOOOOO
WHAT DID I DO?!
NOM NOM NOM NOM
GAH
GET OFF OF ME, STUPID BRAT!!
In pain
JOLT
BEEP
?!
THIS SUCKS ...
IT'S A PROMISE COLLAR. IT RECOGNIZES ITS MASTER THROUGH BLOOD.
AND YOU JUST ENTERED INTO A CONTRACT WITH IT.

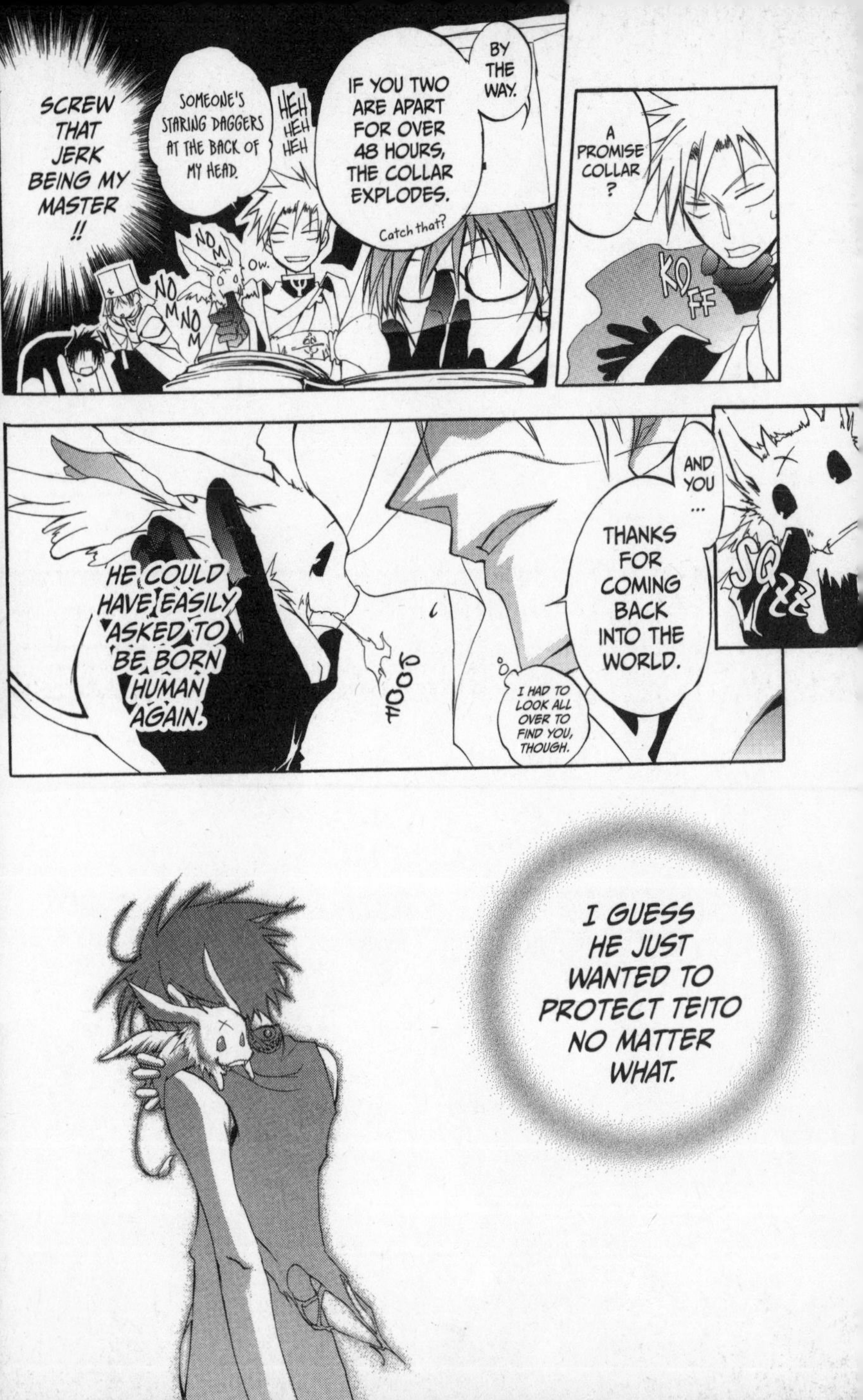
A PROMISE COLLAR?
KOFF
BY THE WAY.
IF YOU TWO ARE APART FOR OVER 48 HOURS, THE COLLAR EXPLODES.
Catch that?
HEH HEH HEH
SOMEONE'S STARING DAGGERS AT THE BACK OF MY HEAD.
SCREW THAT JERK BEING MY MASTER!!
NOM NOM NOM NOM
Ow.
SQZZ
AND YOU...
THANKS FOR COMING BACK INTO THE WORLD.
I HAD TO LOOK ALL OVER TO FIND YOU, THOUGH.
FOOF
HE COULD HAVE EASILY ASKED TO BE BORN HUMAN AGAIN.
I GUESS HE JUST WANTED TO PROTECT TEITO NO MATTER WHAT.

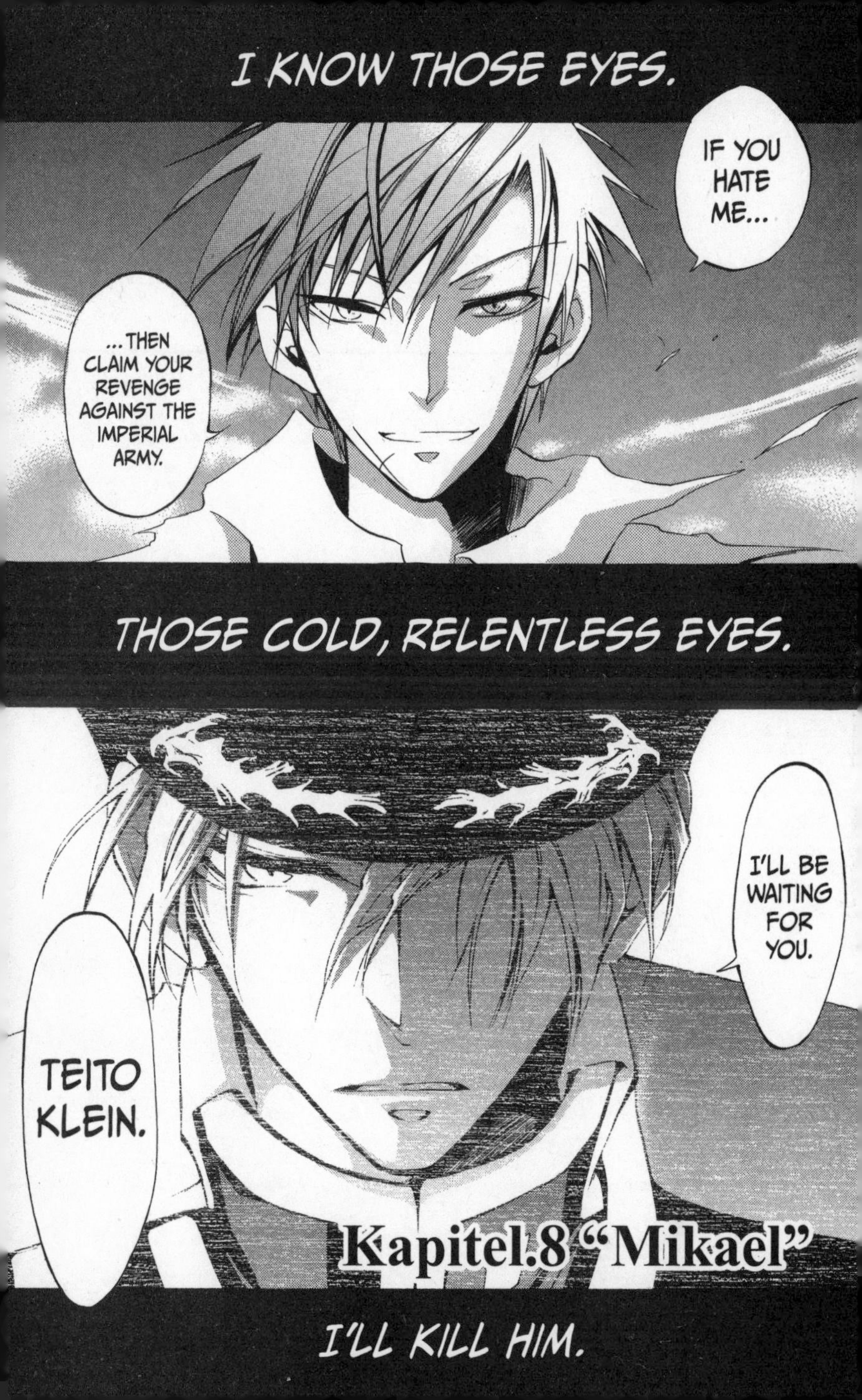
I KNOW THOSE EYES.
IF YOU HATE ME...
...THEN CLAIM YOUR REVENGE AGAINST THE IMPERIAL ARMY.
THOSE COLD, RELENTLESS EYES.
I'LL BE WAITING FOR YOU.
TEITO KLEIN.
Kapitel.8 “Mikael”
I'LL KILL HIM.

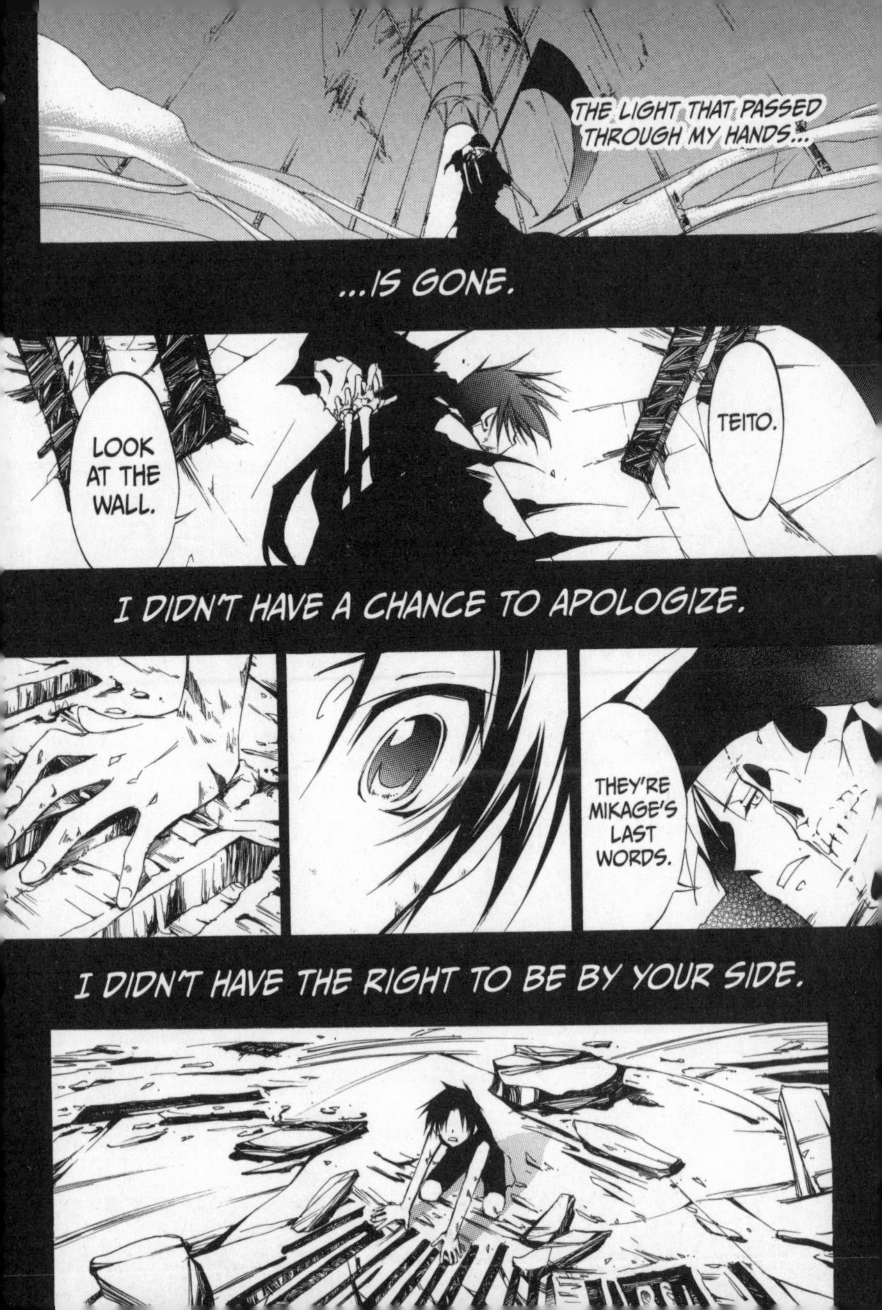
THE LIGHT THAT PASSED THROUGH MY HANDS...
...IS GONE.
TEITO.
LOOK AT THE WALL.
I DIDN'T HAVE A CHANCE TO APOLOGIZE.
THEY'RE MIKAGE'S LAST WORDS.
I DIDN'T HAVE THE RIGHT TO BE BY YOUR SIDE.

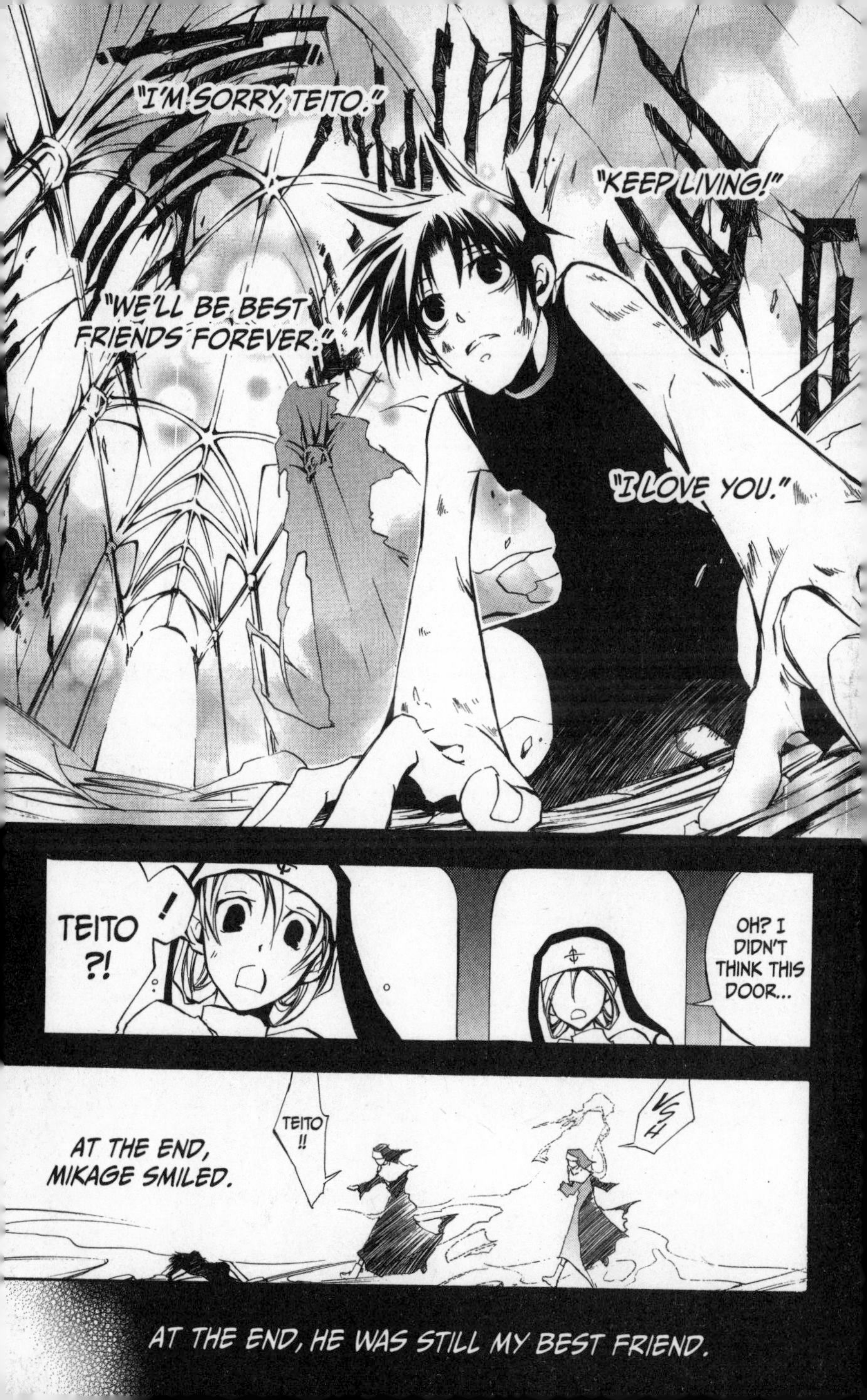
"KEEP LIVING!"
"I LOVE YOU."
"I'M SORRY, TEITO."
"WE'LL BE BEST FRIENDS FOREVER."
OH? I DIDN'T THINK THIS DOOR...
!
TEITO ?!
TEITO !!
AT THE END, MIKAGE SMILED.
AT THE END, HE WAS STILL MY BEST FRIEND.

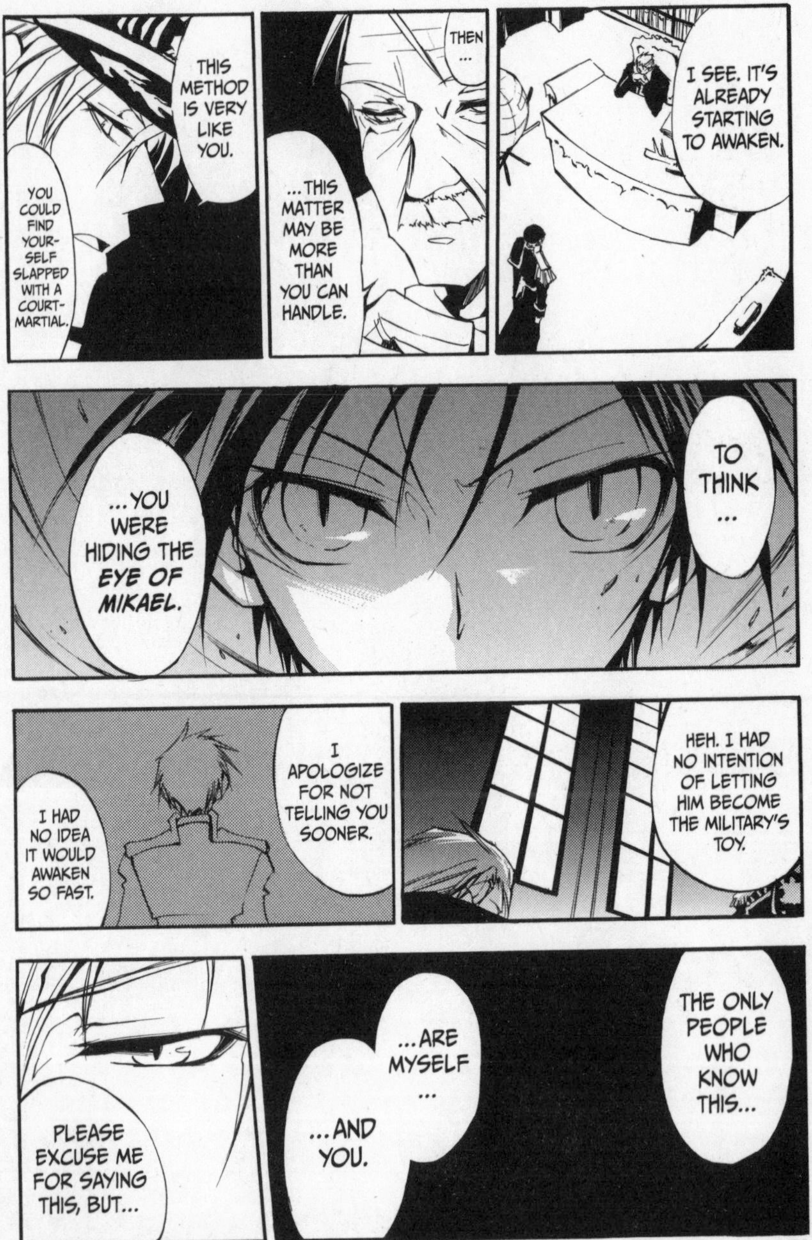
I SEE. IT'S ALREADY STARTING TO AWAKEN.
THEN ...
...THIS MATTER MAY BE MORE THAN YOU CAN HANDLE.
THIS METHOD IS VERY LIKE YOU.
YOU COULD FIND YOUR-SELF SLAPPED WITH A COURT-MARTIAL.
TO THINK ...
...YOU WERE HIDING THE *EYE OF MIKAEL.*
HEH. I HAD NO INTENTION OF LETTING HIM BECOME THE MILITARY'S TOY.
I APOLOGIZE FOR NOT TELLING YOU SOONER.
I HAD NO IDEA IT WOULD AWAKEN SO FAST.
THE ONLY PEOPLE WHO KNOW THIS...
...ARE MYSELF ...
...AND YOU.
PLEASE EXCUSE ME FOR SAYING THIS, BUT...

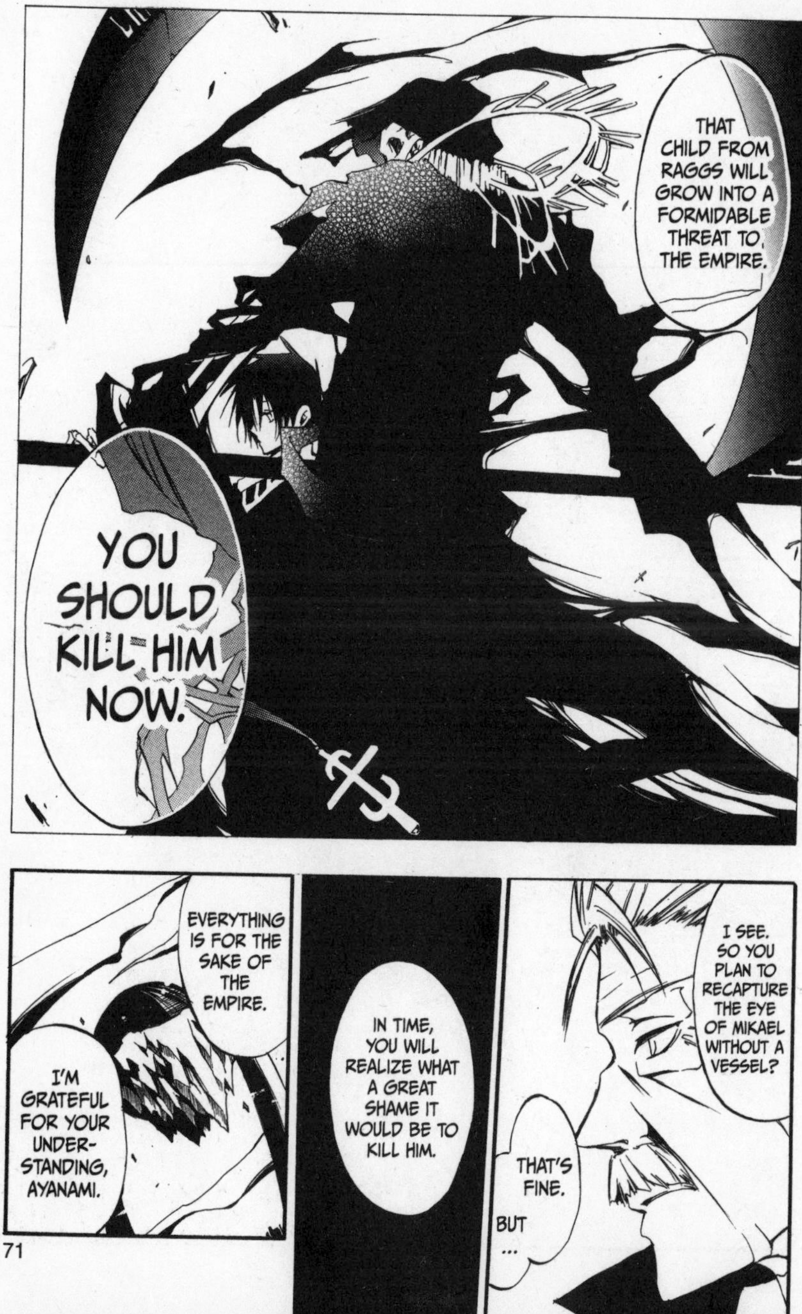
THAT CHILD FROM RAGGS WILL GROW INTO A FORMIDABLE THREAT TO THE EMPIRE.
YOU SHOULD KILL HIM NOW.
I SEE. SO YOU PLAN TO RECAPTURE THE EYE OF MIKAEL WITHOUT A VESSEL?
THAT'S FINE.
BUT ...
IN TIME, YOU WILL REALIZE WHAT A GREAT SHAME IT WOULD BE TO KILL HIM.
EVERYTHING IS FOR THE SAKE OF THE EMPIRE.
I'M GRATEFUL FOR YOUR UNDER-STANDING, AYANAMI.

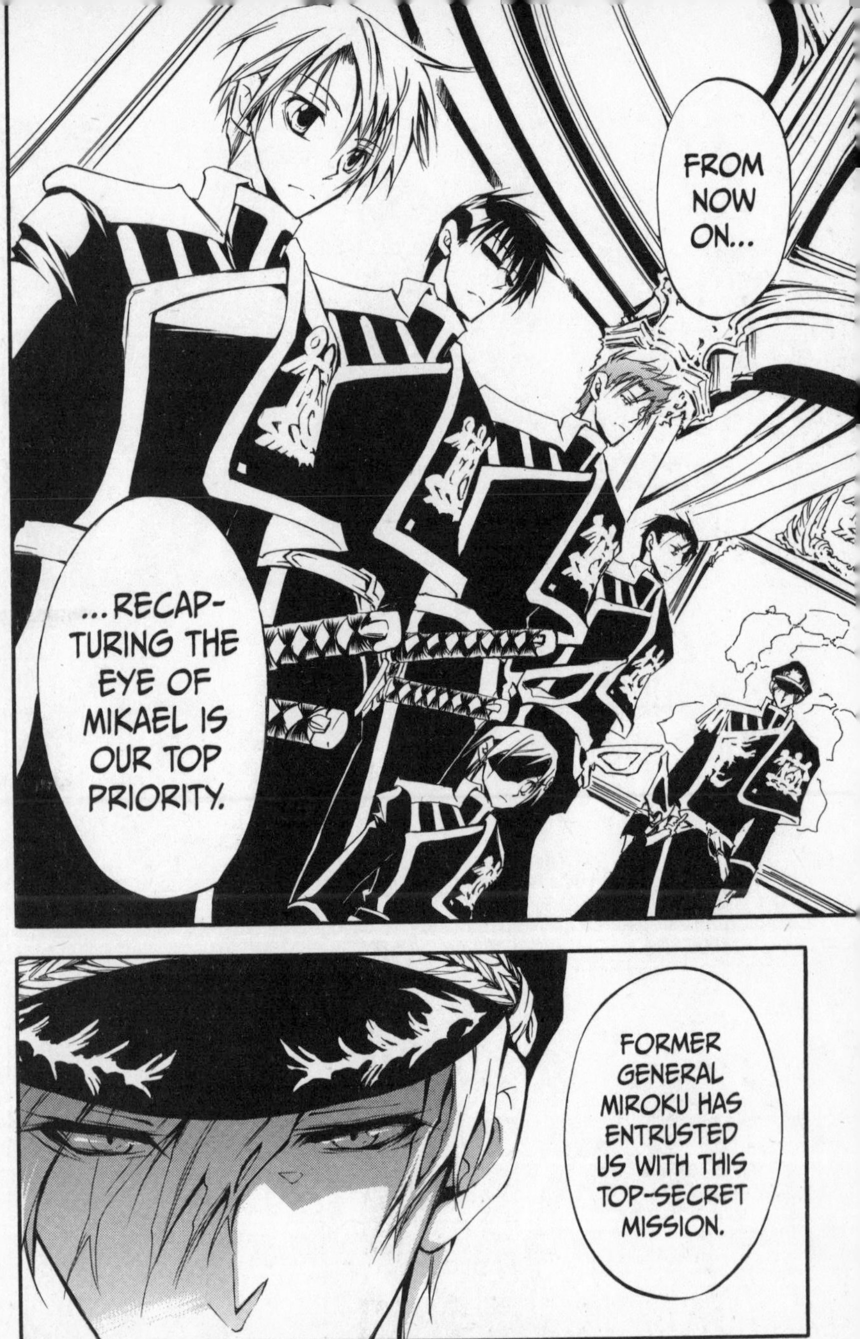
FROM NOW ON...
...RECAPTURING THE EYE OF MIKAEL IS OUR TOP PRIORITY.
FORMER GENERAL MIROKU HAS ENTRUSTED US WITH THIS TOP-SECRET MISSION.

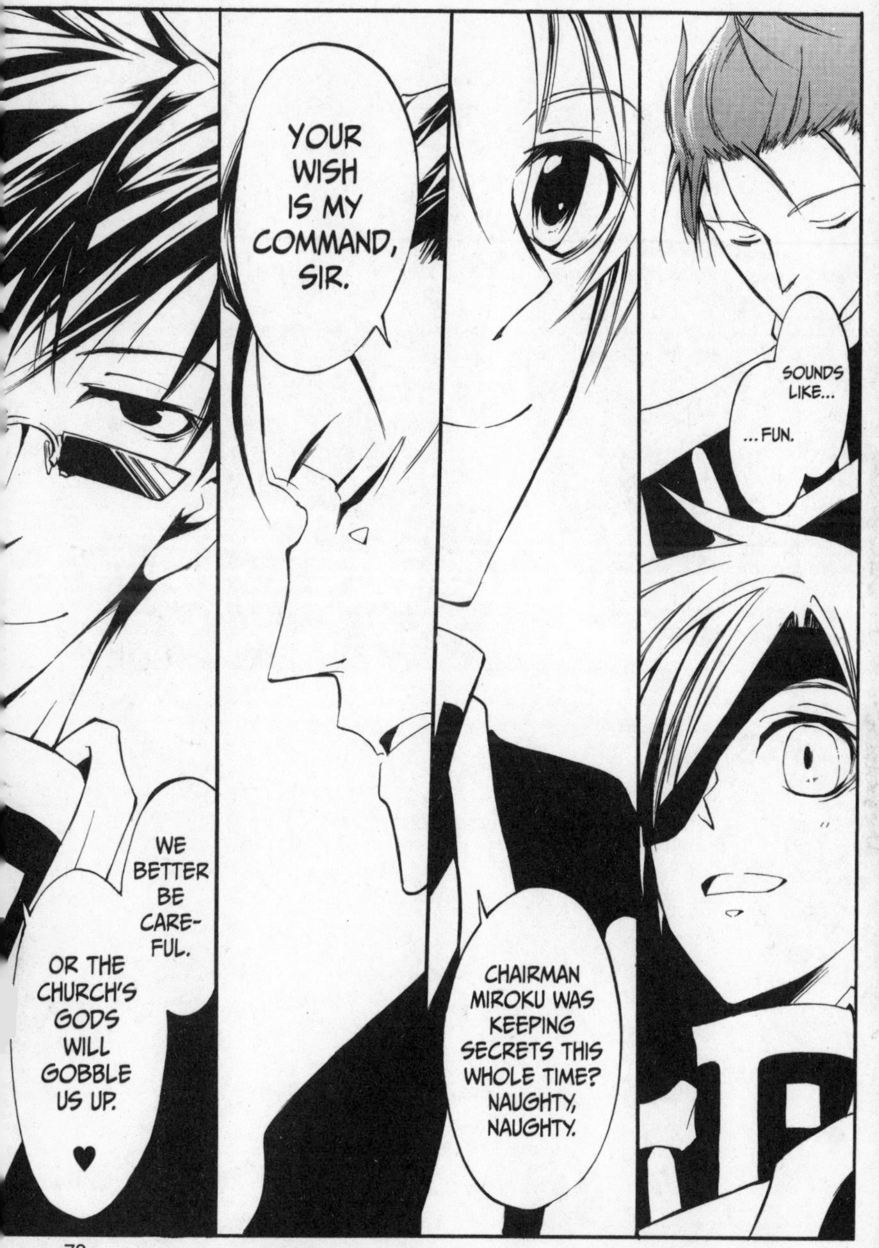
SOUNDS LIKE...
...FUN.
CHAIRMAN MIROKU WAS KEEPING SECRETS THIS WHOLE TIME? NAUGHTY, NAUGHTY.
YOUR WISH IS MY COMMAND, SIR.
WE BETTER BE CARE-FUL.
OR THE CHURCH'S GODS WILL GOBBLE US UP. ♥

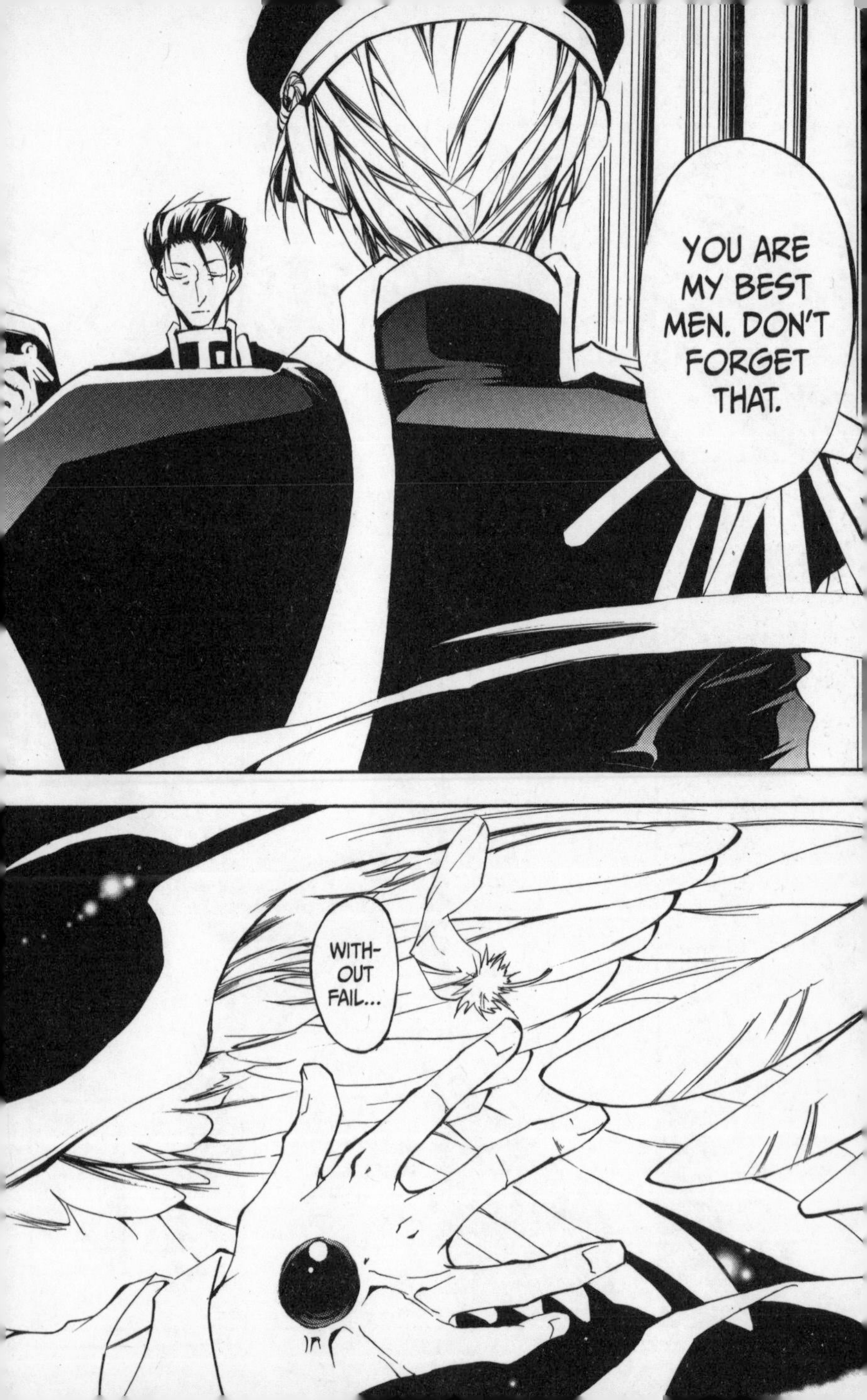
YOU ARE MY BEST MEN. DON'T FORGET THAT.
WITH-OUT FAIL...

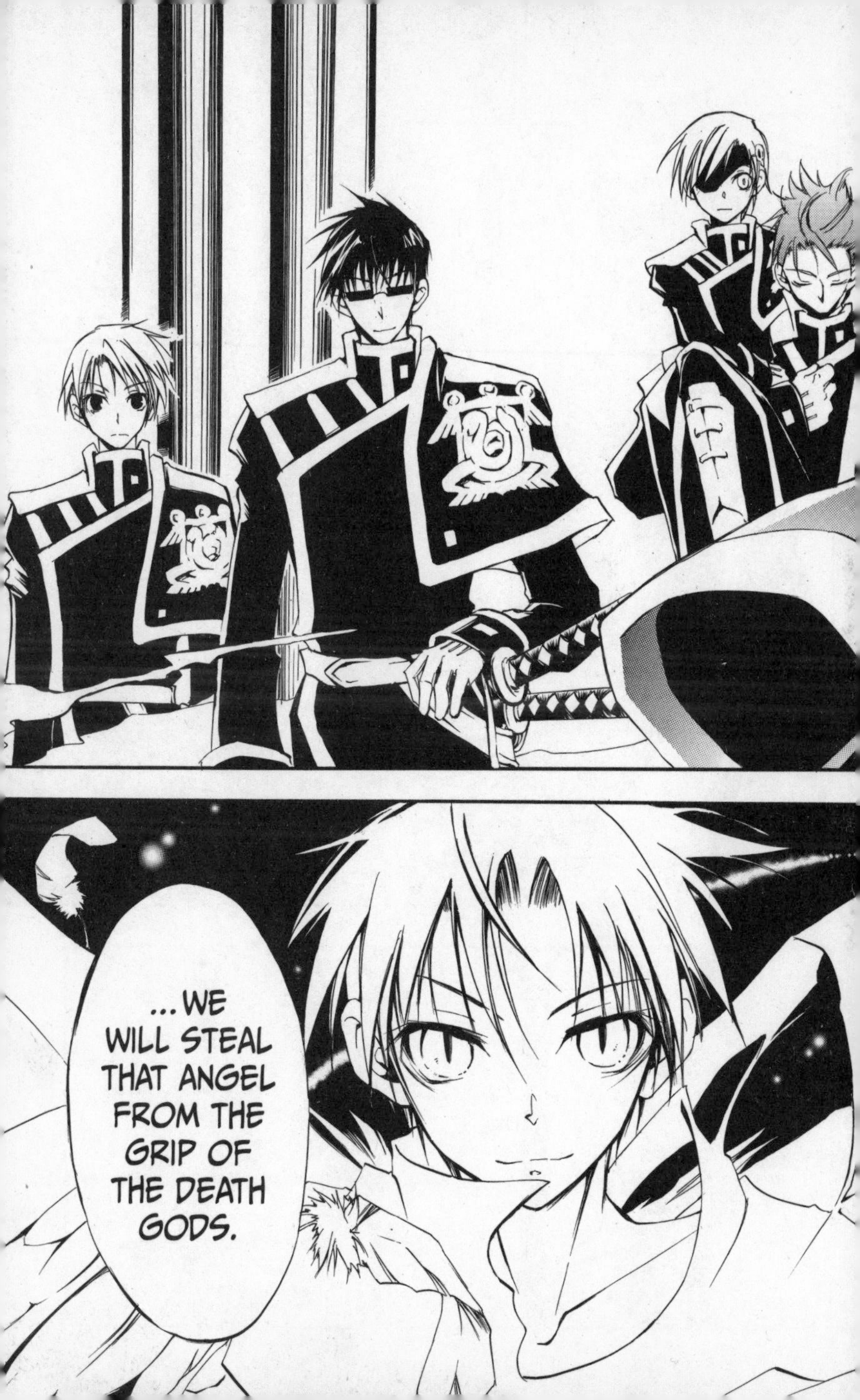
...WE WILL STEAL THAT ANGEL FROM THE GRIP OF THE DEATH GODS.

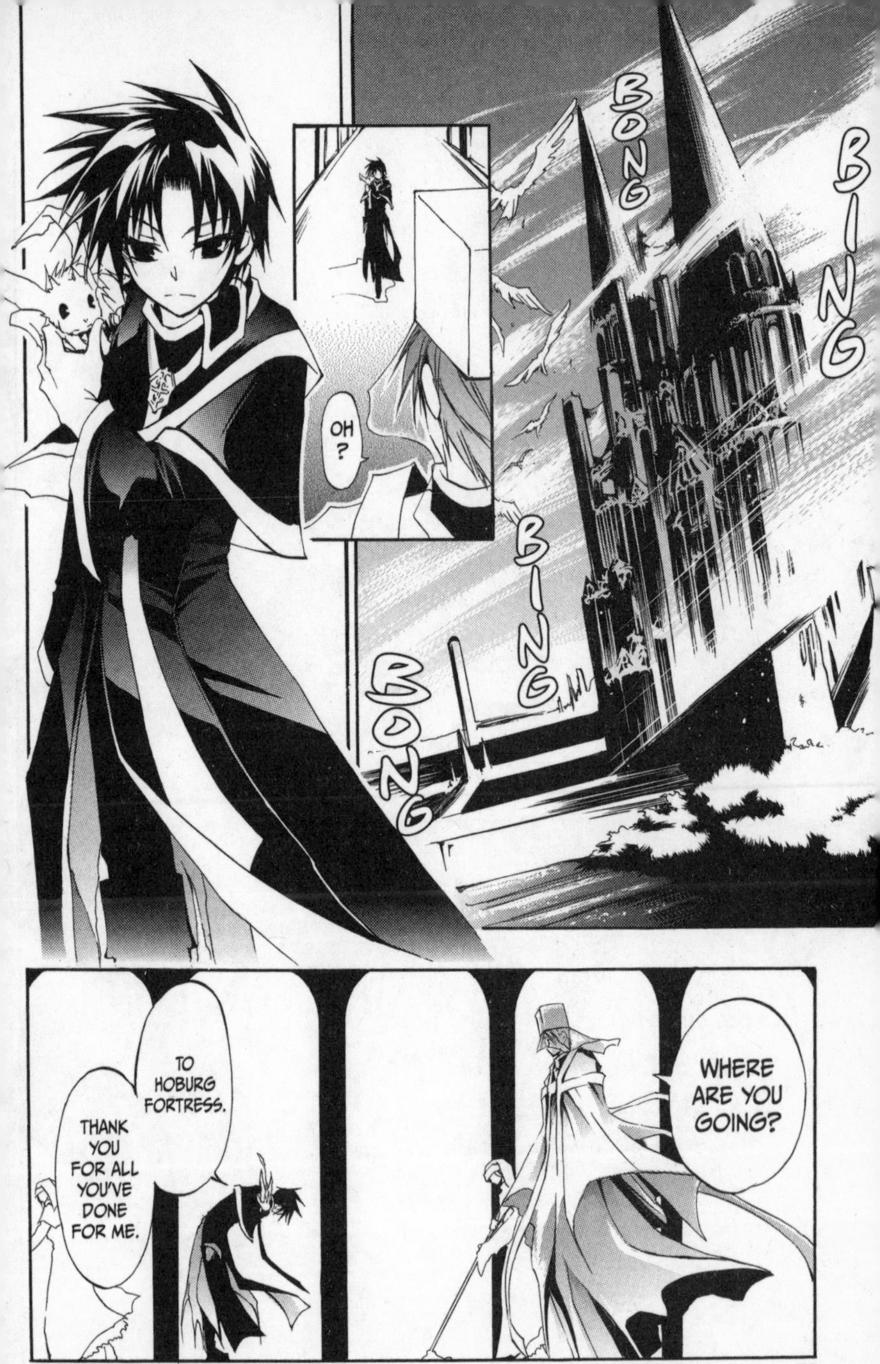
BING
BONG
BING
BONG
OH ?
WHERE ARE YOU GOING?
TO HOBURG FORTRESS.
THANK YOU FOR ALL YOU'VE DONE FOR ME.

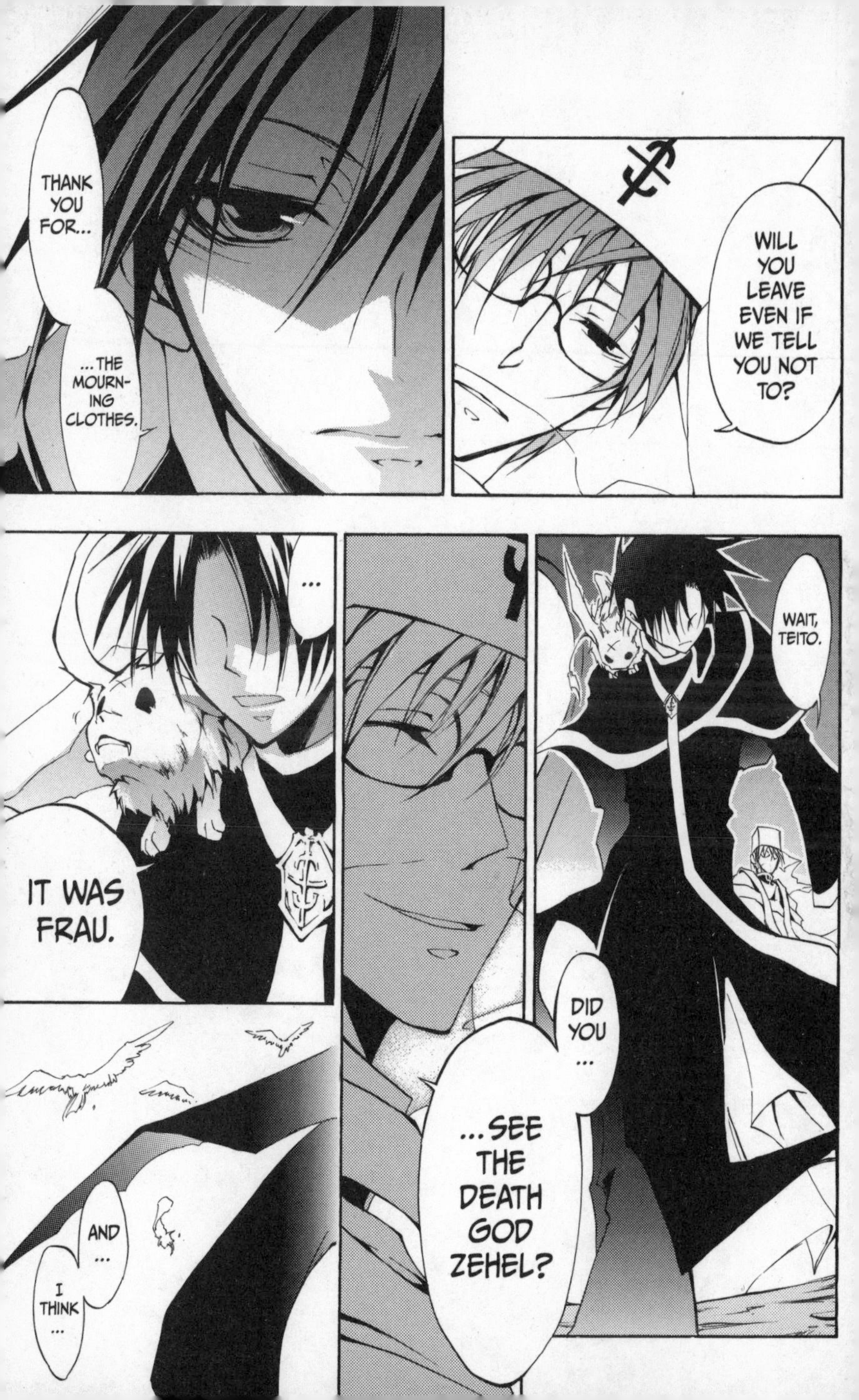
WILL YOU LEAVE EVEN IF WE TELL YOU NOT TO?
THANK YOU FOR...
...THE MOURNING-ING CLOTHES.
WAIT, TEITO.
DID YOU ...
...SEE THE DEATH GOD ZEHEL?
...
IT WAS FRAU.
AND ...
I THINK ...

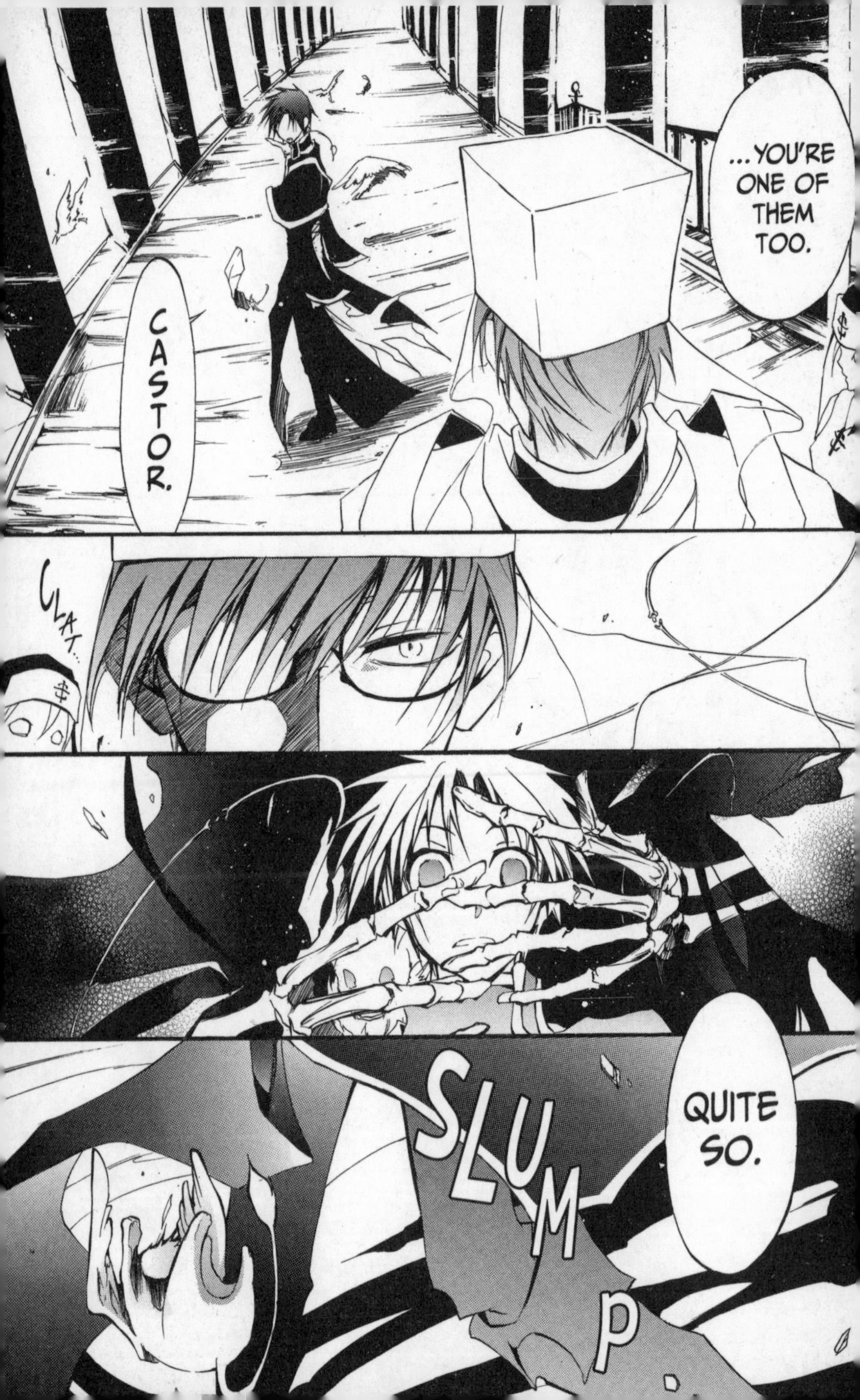
...YOU'RE ONE OF THEM TOO.
CASTOR.
CLAT...
QUITE SO.
SLUMP

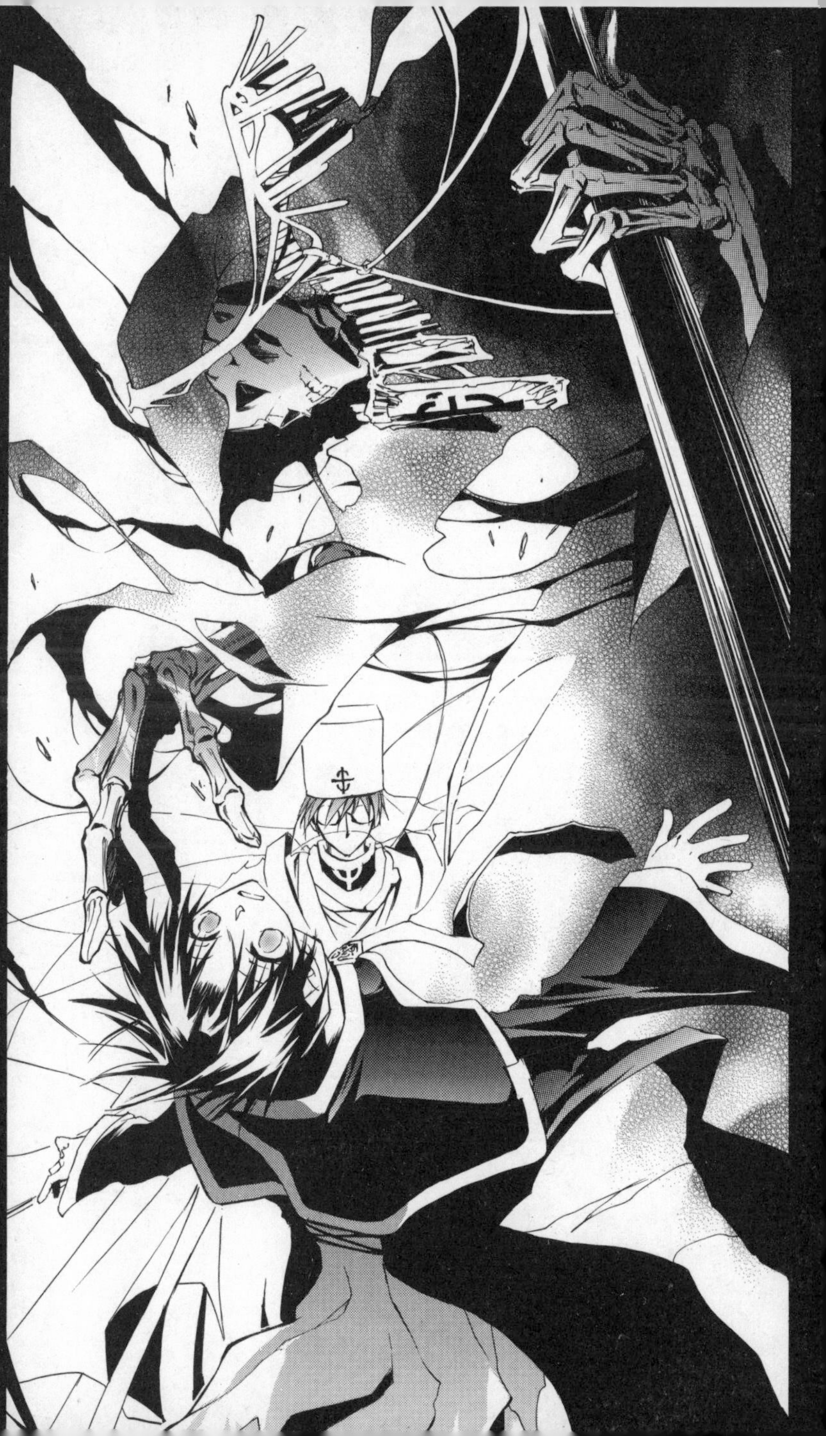

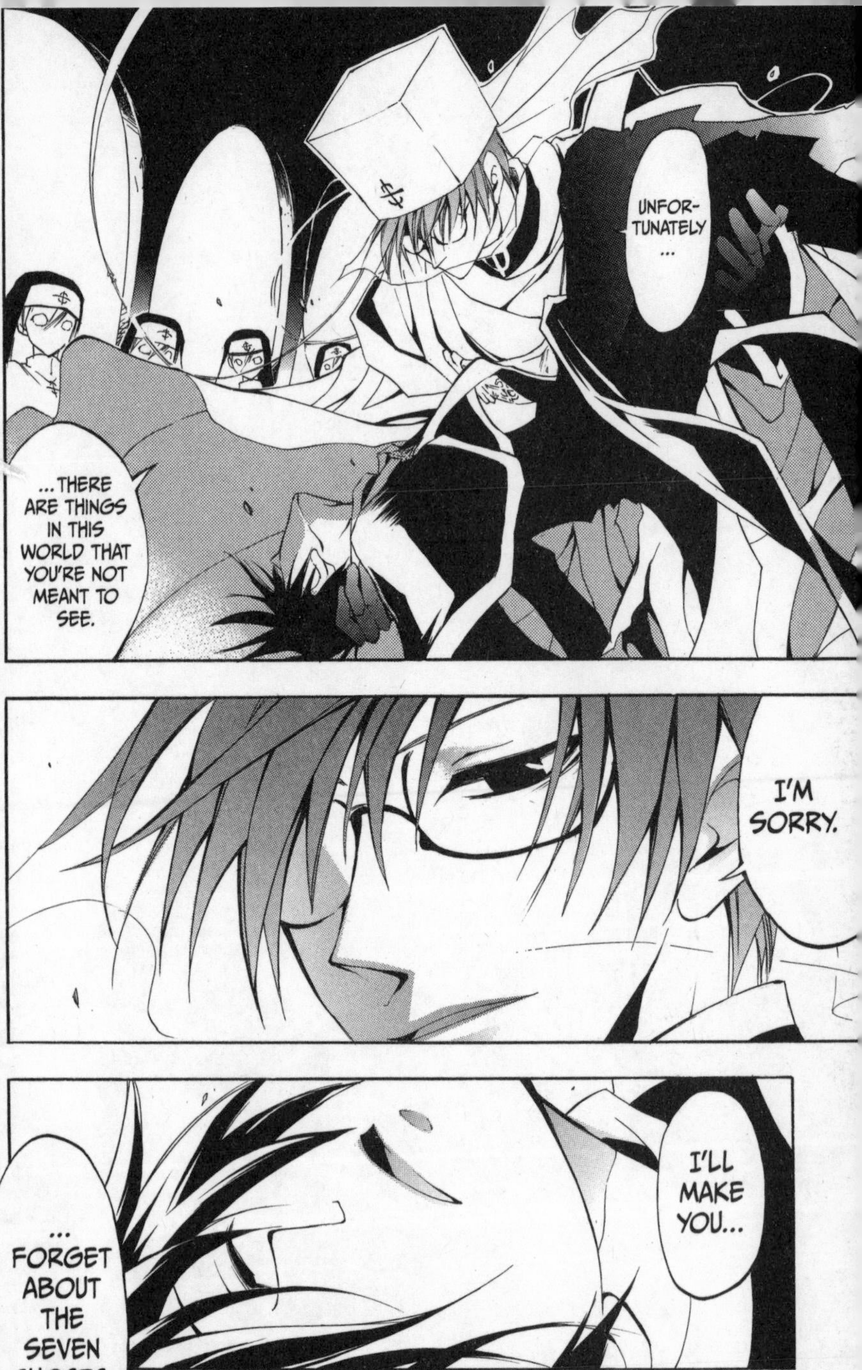
UNFOR-TUNATELY...
...THERE ARE THINGS IN THIS WORLD THAT YOU'RE NOT MEANT TO SEE.
I'M SORRY.
I'LL MAKE YOU...
...FORGET ABOUT THE SEVEN GHOSTS.

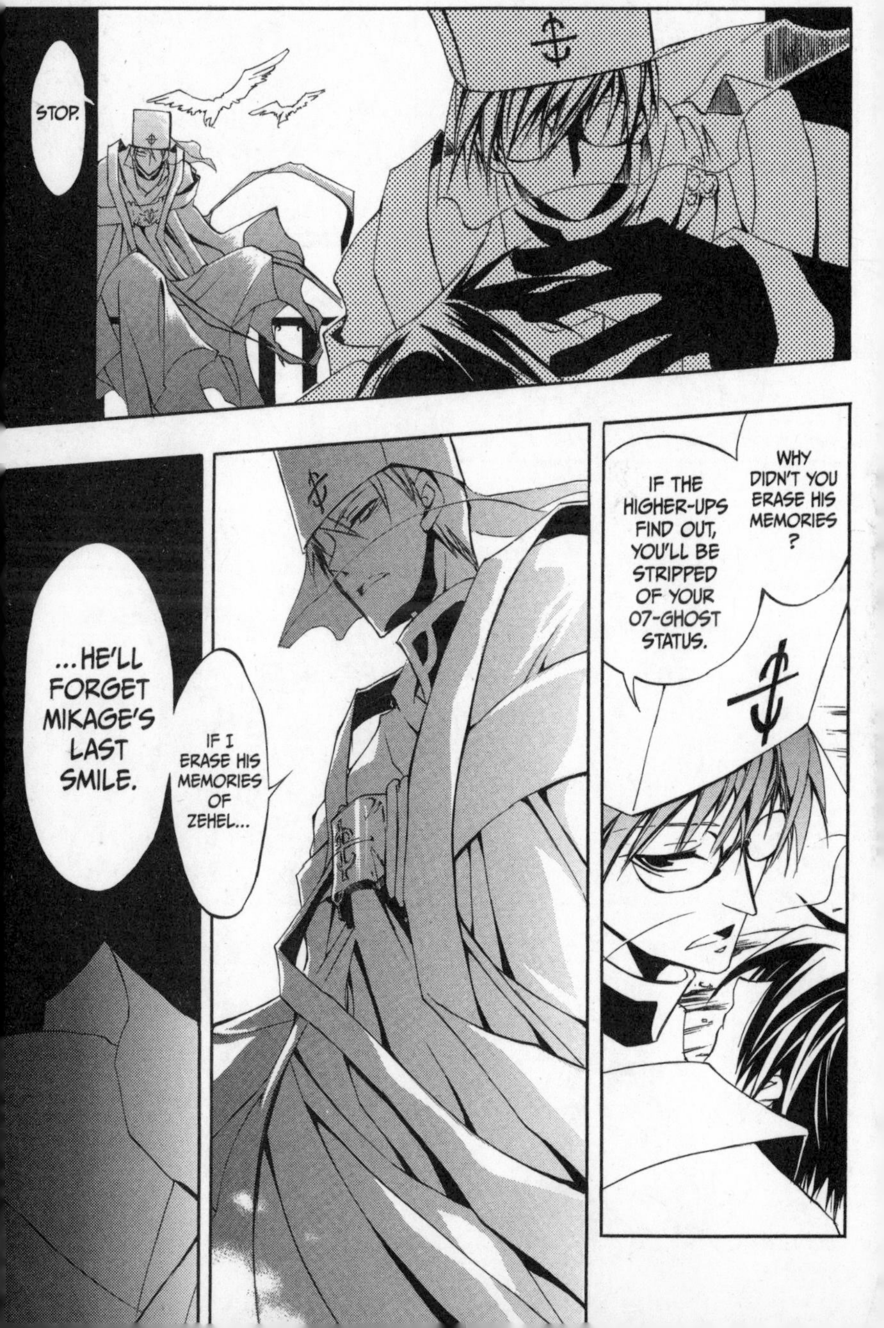
STOP.
WHY DIDN'T YOU ERASE HIS MEMORIES?
IF THE HIGHER-UPS FIND OUT, YOU'LL BE STRIPPED OF YOUR 07-GHOST STATUS.
IF I ERASE HIS MEMORIES OF ZEHEL...
...HE'LL FORGET MIKAGE'S LAST SMILE.

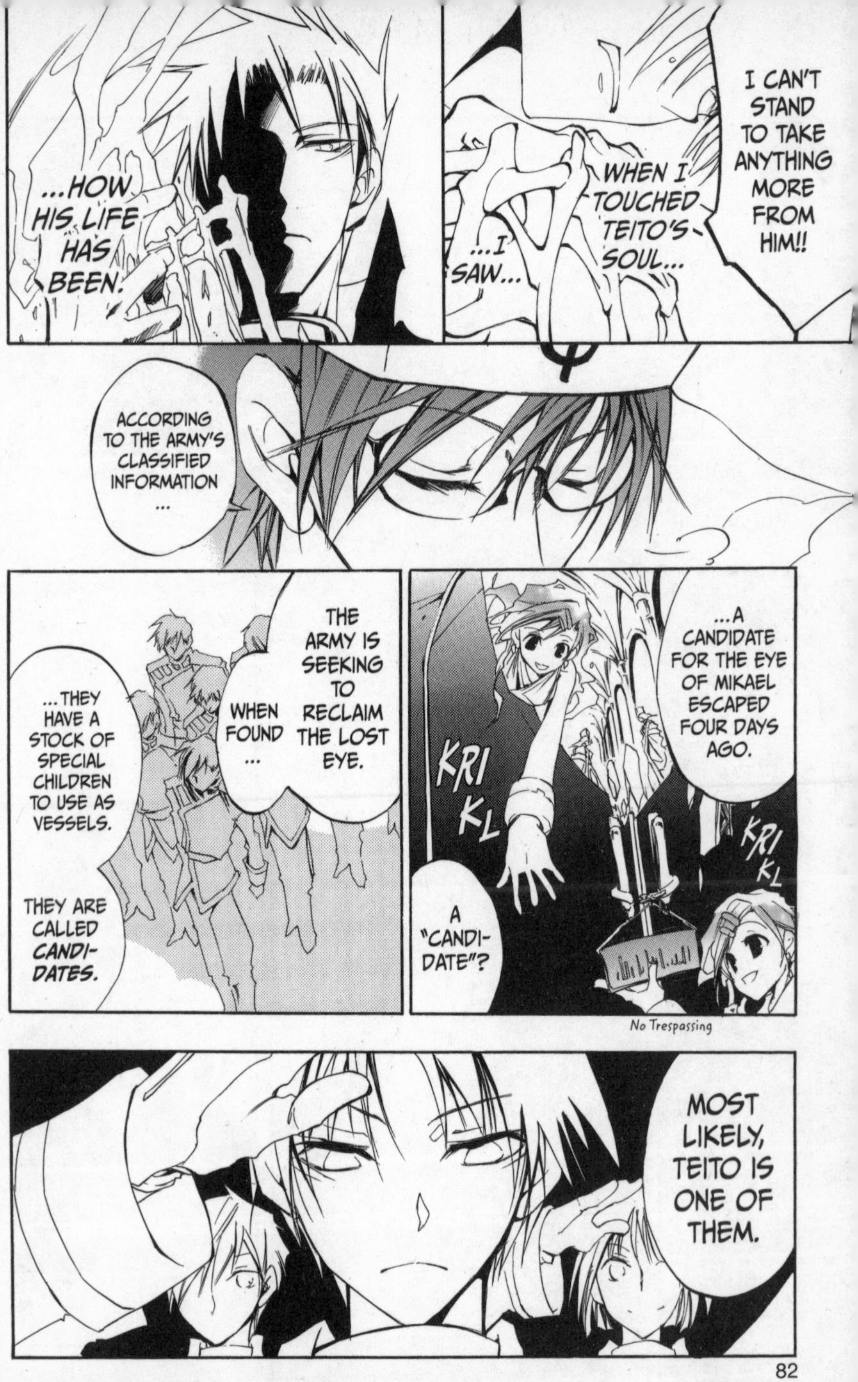
I CAN'T STAND TO TAKE ANYTHING MORE FROM HIM!!
WHEN I TOUCHED TEITO'S SOUL...
...I SAW...
...HOW HIS LIFE HAS BEEN.
ACCORDING TO THE ARMY'S CLASSIFIED INFORMATION ...
...A CANDIDATE FOR THE EYE OF MIKAEL ESCAPED FOUR DAYS AGO.
KRIKL
KRIKL
A "CANDIDATE"?
THE ARMY IS SEEKING TO RECLAIM THE LOST EYE.
WHEN FOUND ...
...THEY HAVE A STOCK OF SPECIAL CHILDREN TO USE AS VESSELS.
THEY ARE CALLED CANDIDATES.
MOST LIKELY, TEITO IS ONE OF THEM.
No Trespassing

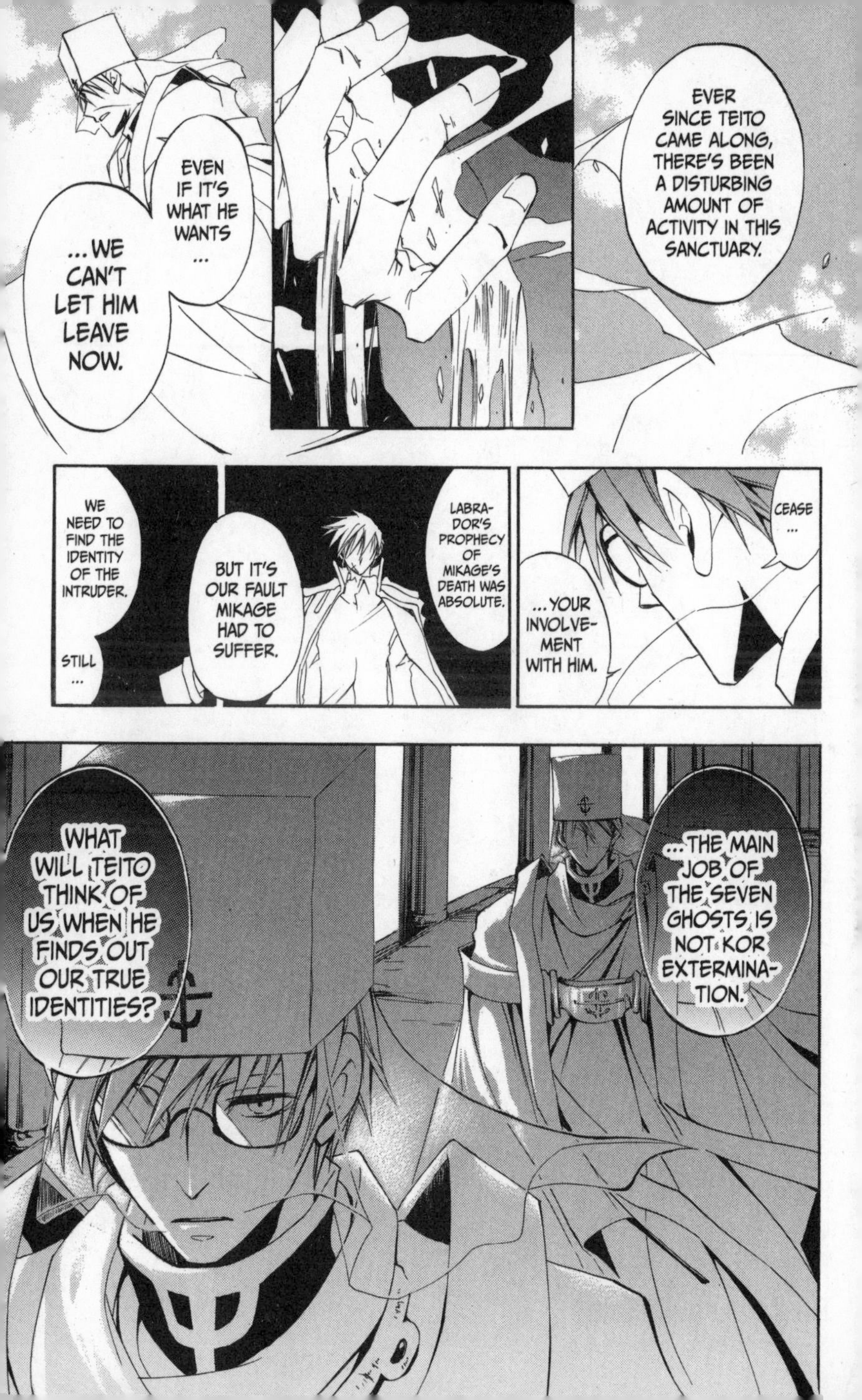
EVER SINCE TEITO CAME ALONG, THERE'S BEEN A DISTURBING AMOUNT OF ACTIVITY IN THIS SANCTUARY.
EVEN IF IT'S WHAT HE WANTS ...
...WE CAN'T LET HIM LEAVE NOW.
CEASE ...
...YOUR INVOLVEMENT WITH HIM.
LABRADOR'S PROPHECY OF MIKAGE'S DEATH WAS ABSOLUTE.
BUT IT'S OUR FAULT MIKAGE HAD TO SUFFER.
WE NEED TO FIND THE IDENTITY OF THE INTRUDER.
STILL ...
...THE MAIN JOB OF THE SEVEN GHOSTS IS NOT KOR EXTERMINATION.
WHAT WILL TEITO THINK OF US WHEN HE FINDS OUT OUR TRUE IDENTITIES?

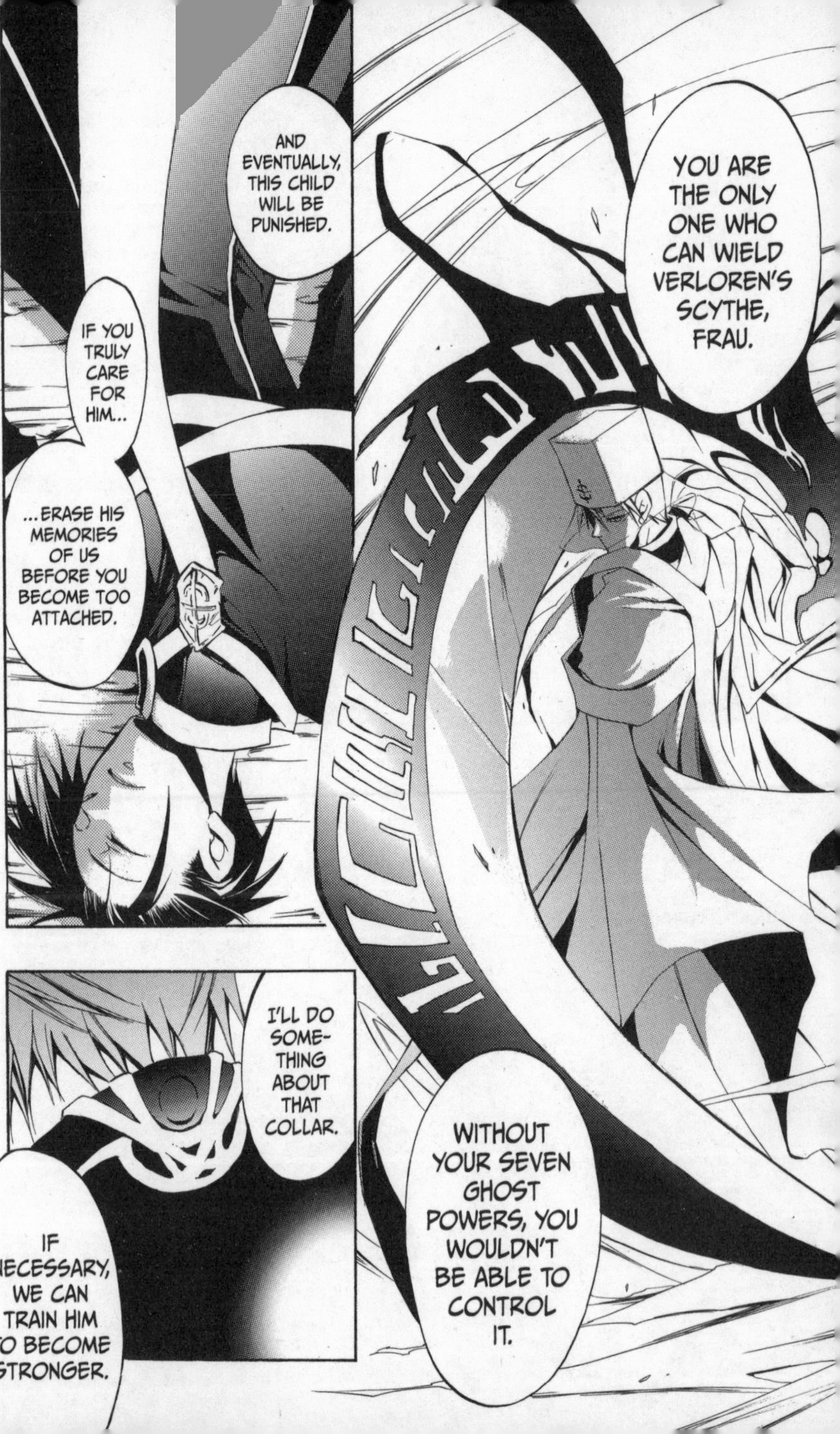
YOU ARE THE ONLY ONE WHO CAN WIELD VERLOREN'S SCYTHE, FRAU.
WITHOUT YOUR SEVEN GHOST POWERS, YOU WOULDN'T BE ABLE TO CONTROL IT.
AND EVENTUALLY, THIS CHILD WILL BE PUNISHED.
IF YOU TRULY CARE FOR HIM...
...ERASE HIS MEMORIES OF US BEFORE YOU BECOME TOO ATTACHED.
I'LL DO SOME-THING ABOUT THAT COLLAR.
IF NECESSARY, WE CAN TRAIN HIM TO BECOME STRONGER.

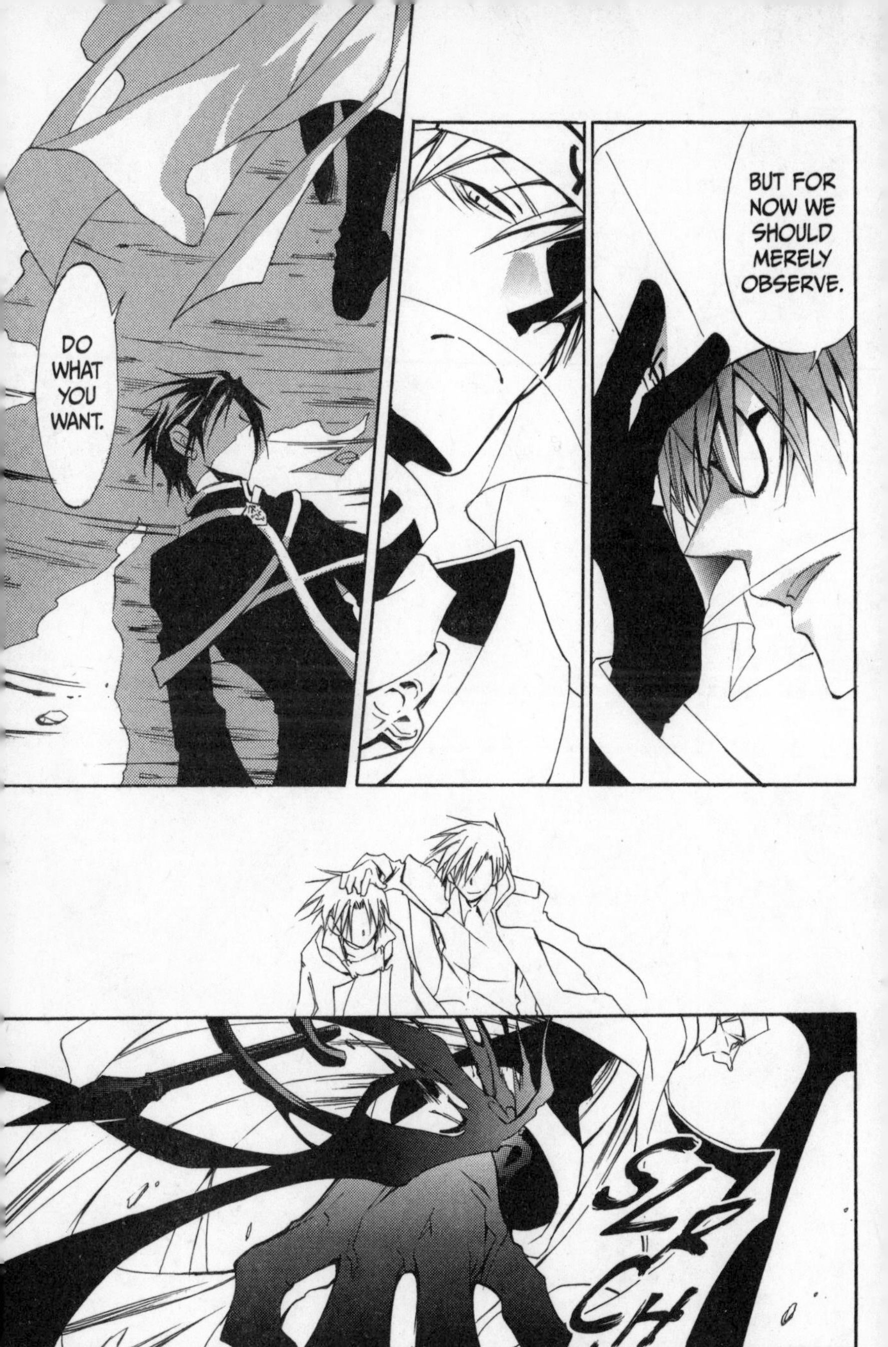
BUT FOR NOW WE SHOULD MERELY OBSERVE.
DO WHAT YOU WANT.

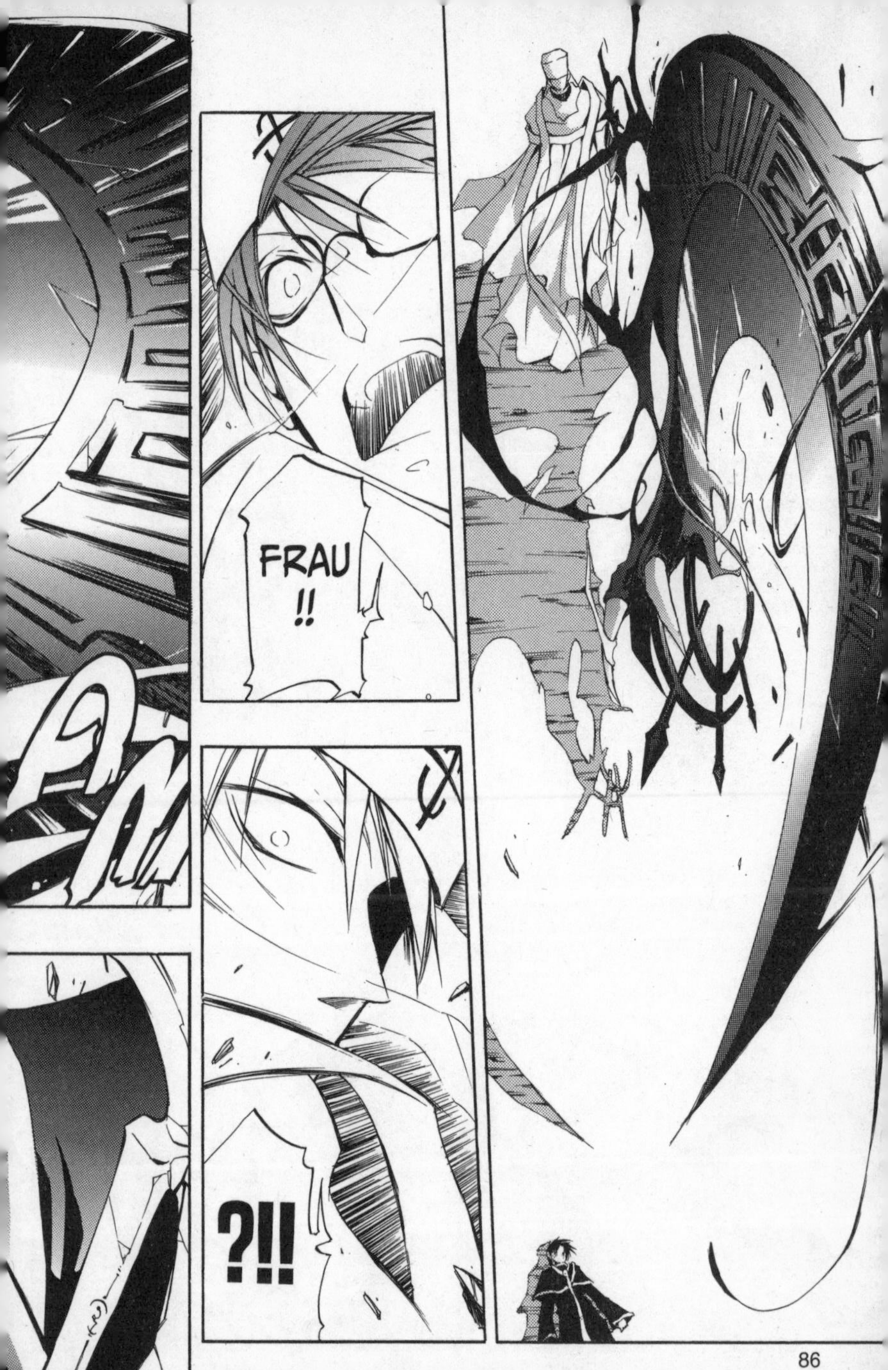
FRAU !!
?!!

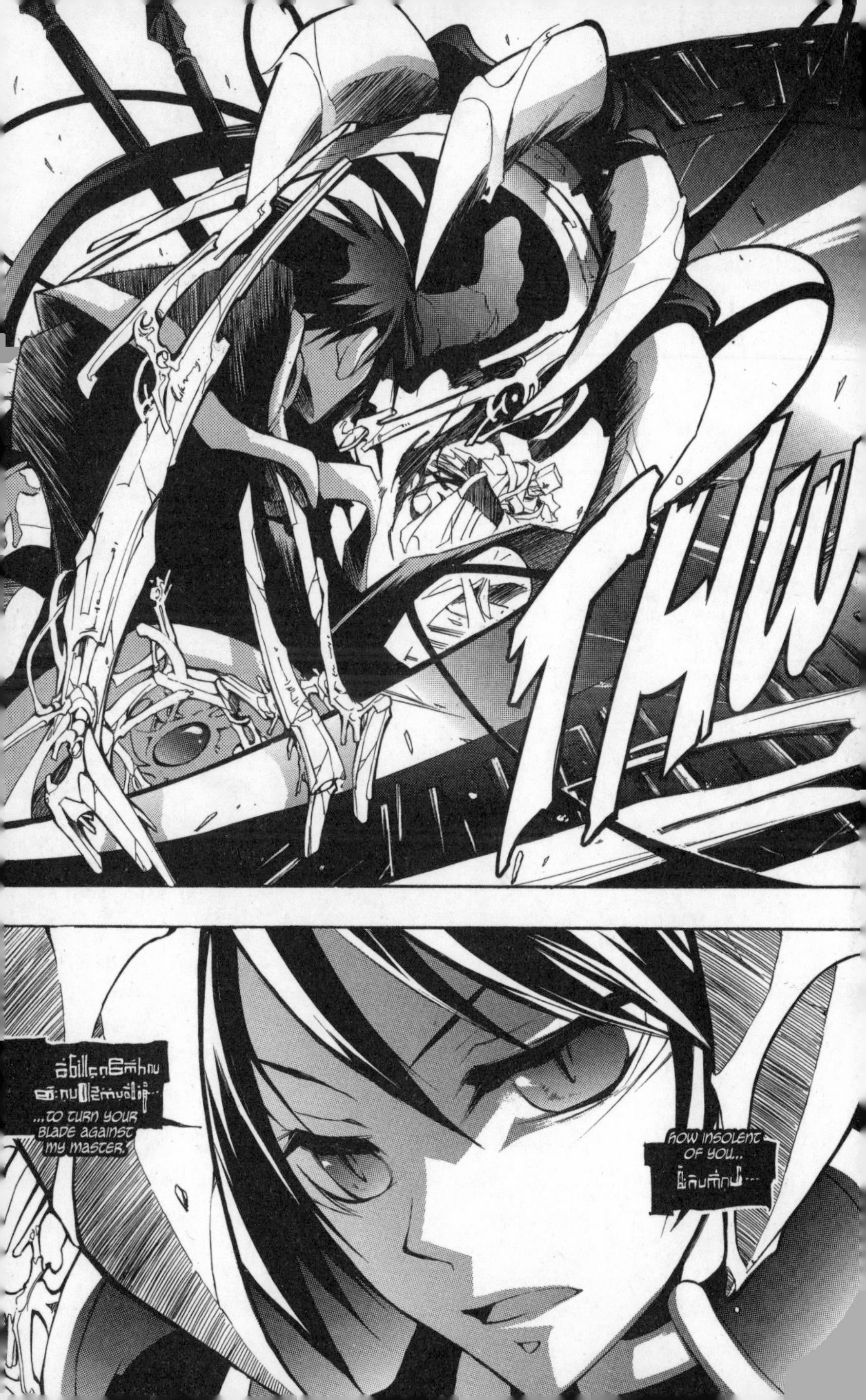
THU
HOW INSOLENT OF YOU...
...TO TURN YOUR BLADE AGAINST MY MASTER.

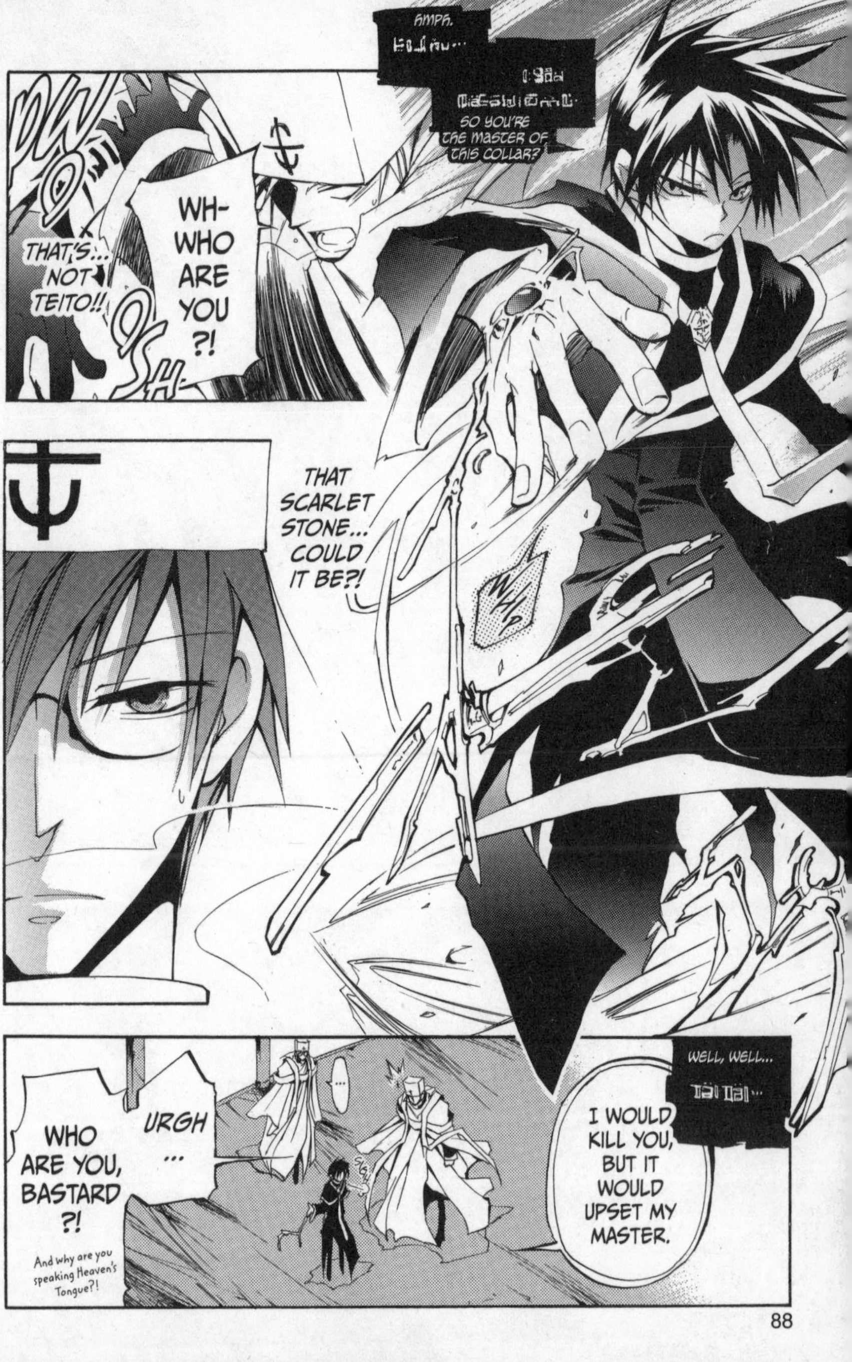
HMPH.
SO YOU'RE THE MASTER OF THIS COLLAR?
WH-WHO ARE YOU?!
THAT'S... NOT TEITO!!
THAT SCARLET STONE... COULD IT BE?!
WELL, WELL...
I WOULD KILL YOU, BUT IT WOULD UPSET MY MASTER.
...
URGH...
WHO ARE YOU, BASTARD?!
And why are you speaking Heaven's Tongue?!

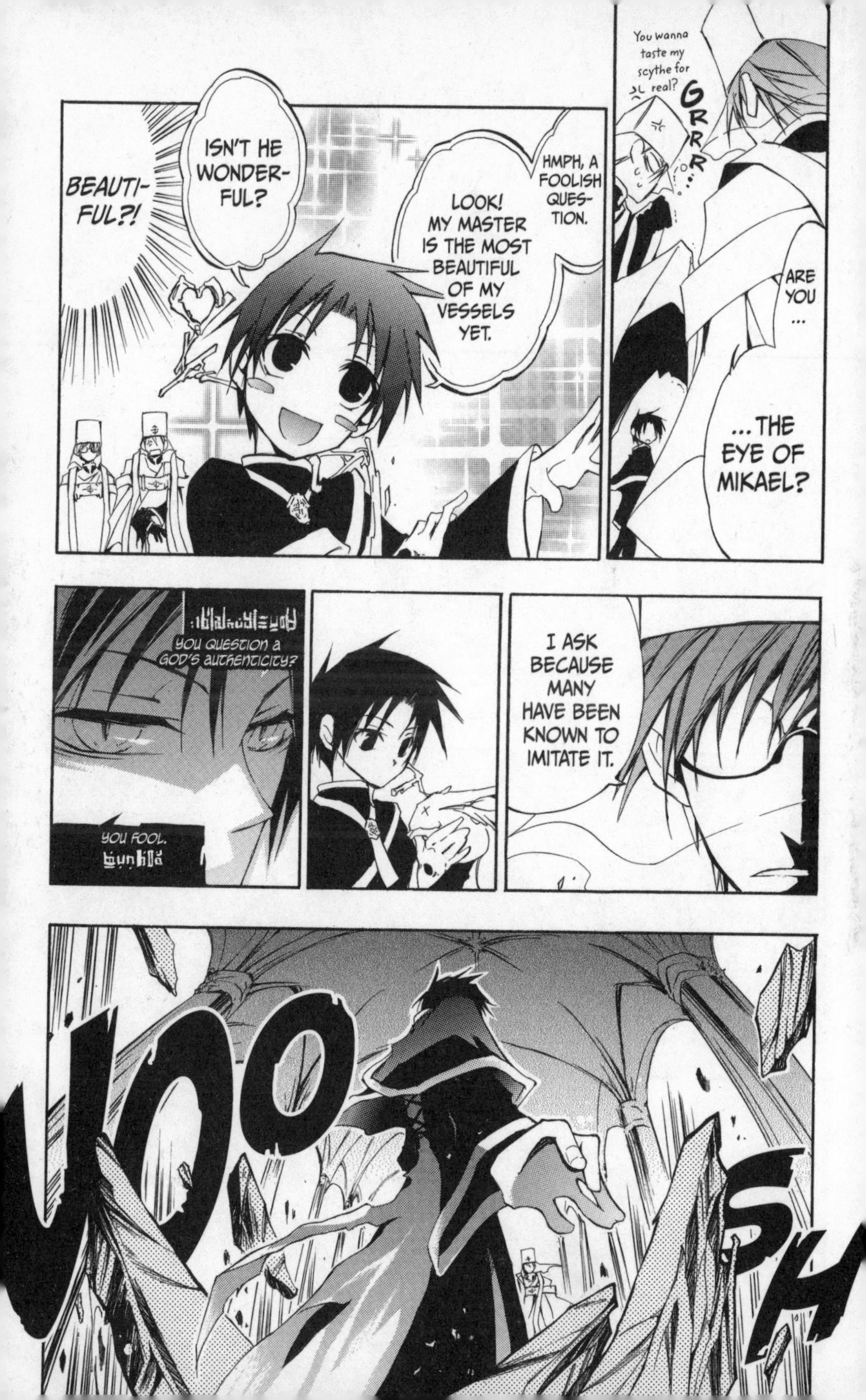

ARE YOU ...
...THE EYE OF MIKAEL?
You wanna taste my scythe for real?
GRRR
HMPH, A FOOLISH QUESTION.
LOOK! MY MASTER IS THE MOST BEAUTIFUL OF MY VESSELS YET.
ISN'T HE WONDERFUL?
BEAUTIFUL?!
I ASK BECAUSE MANY HAVE BEEN KNOWN TO IMITATE IT.
YOU QUESTION A GOD'S AUTHENTICITY?
YOU FOOL.

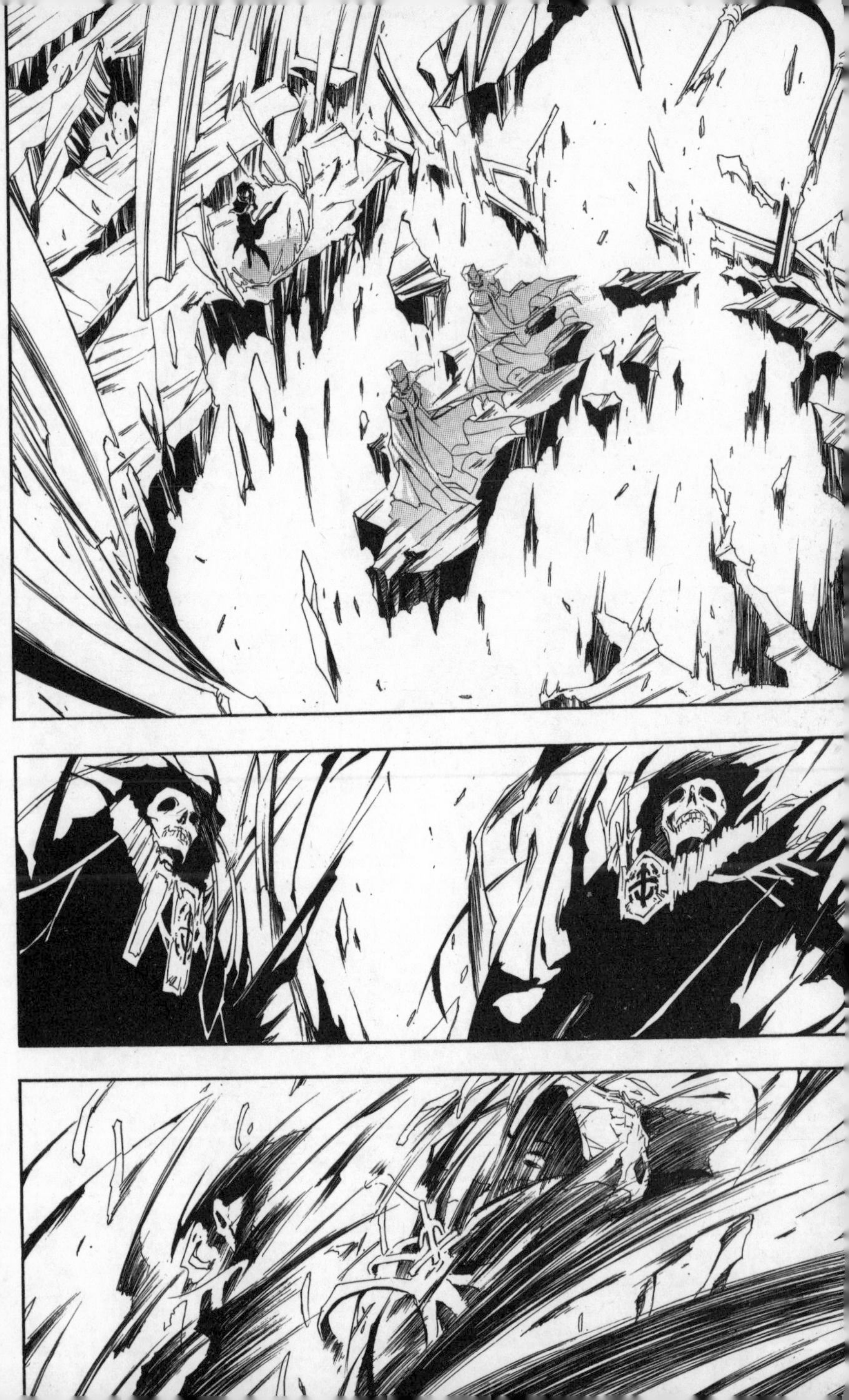

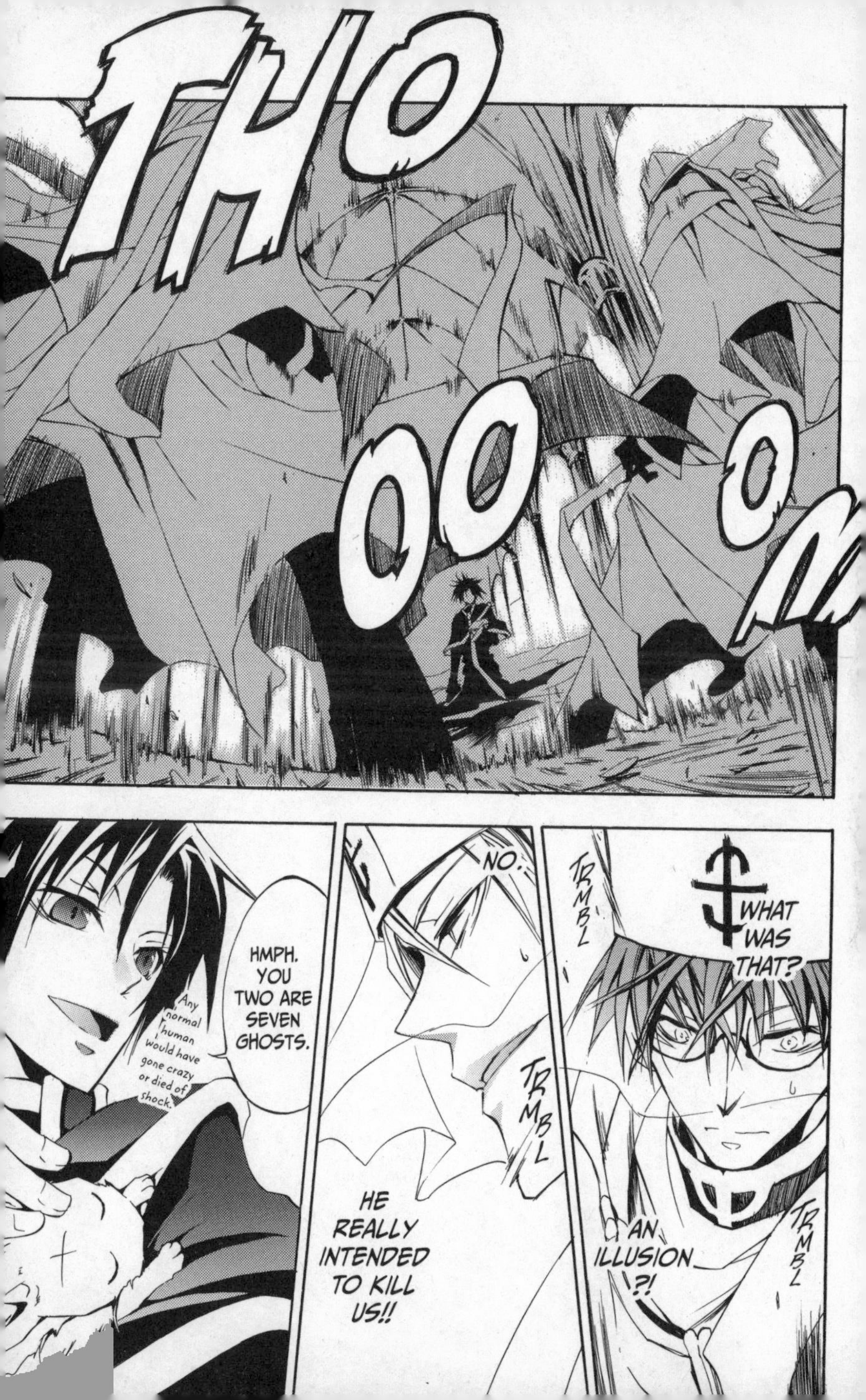
THOOOON
TRMBL
WHAT WAS THAT?
AN ILLUSION?!
TRMBL
NO..
TRMBL
HE REALLY INTENDED TO KILL US!!
HMPH. YOU TWO ARE SEVEN GHOSTS.
Any normal human would have gone crazy or died of shock.

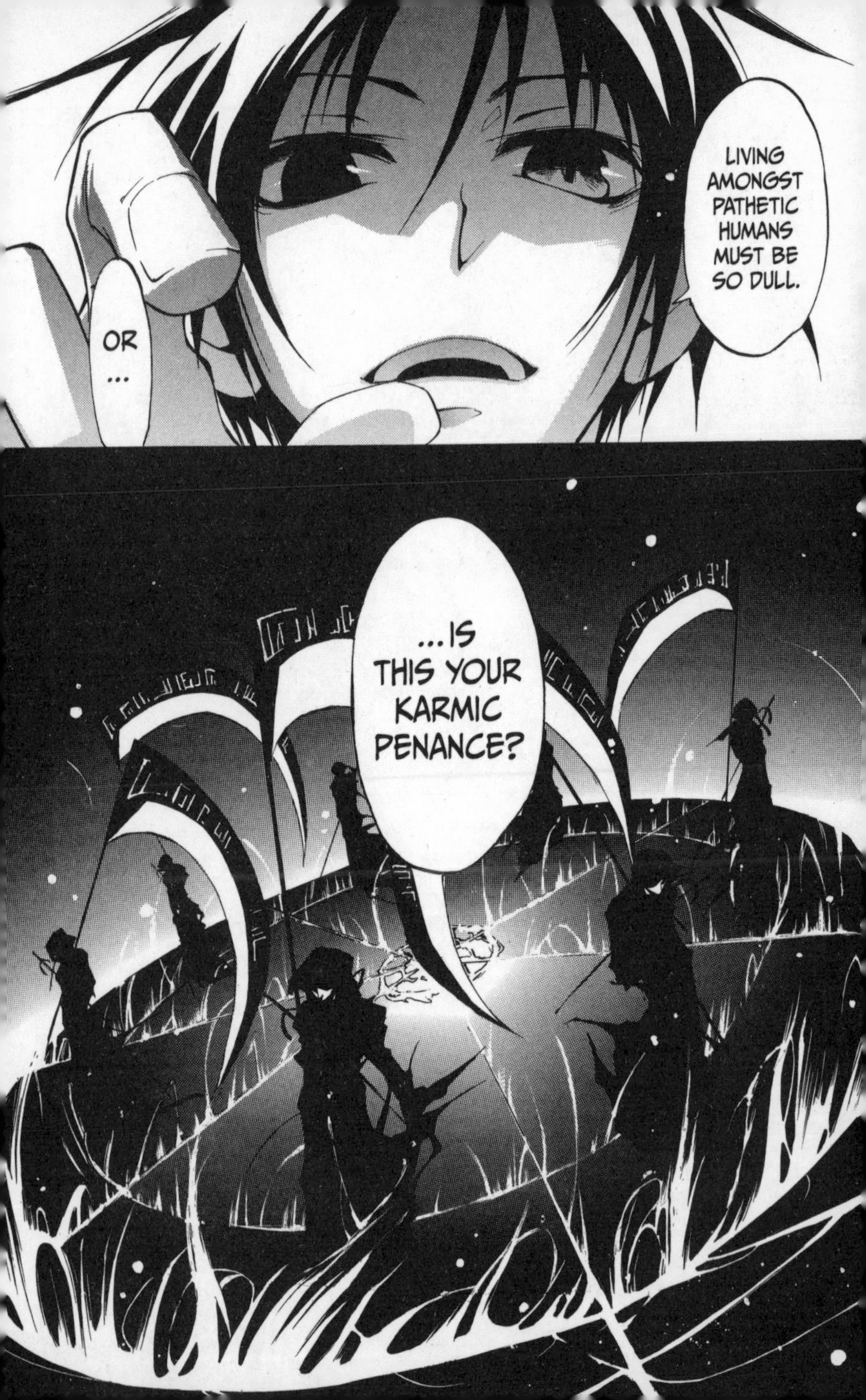
LIVING AMONGST PATHETIC HUMANS MUST BE SO DULL.
OR ...
...IS THIS YOUR KARMIC PENANCE?

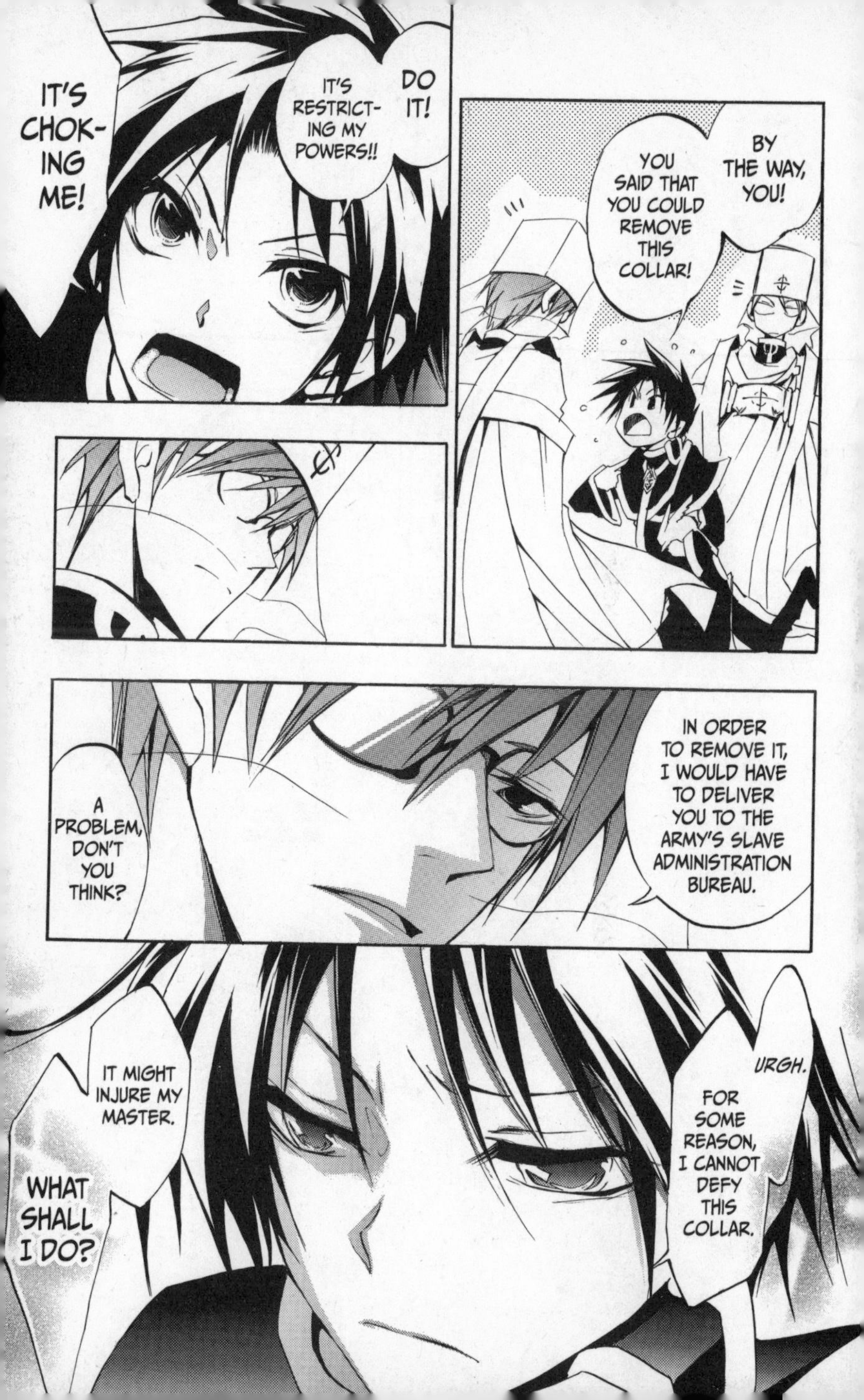
BY THE WAY, YOU!
YOU SAID THAT YOU COULD REMOVE THIS COLLAR!
DO IT!
IT'S RESTRICTING MY POWERS!!
IT'S CHOKING ME!
IN ORDER TO REMOVE IT, I WOULD HAVE TO DELIVER YOU TO THE ARMY'S SLAVE ADMINISTRATION BUREAU.
A PROBLEM, DON'T YOU THINK?
URGH.
FOR SOME REASON, I CANNOT DEFY THIS COLLAR.
IT MIGHT INJURE MY MASTER.
WHAT SHALL I DO?

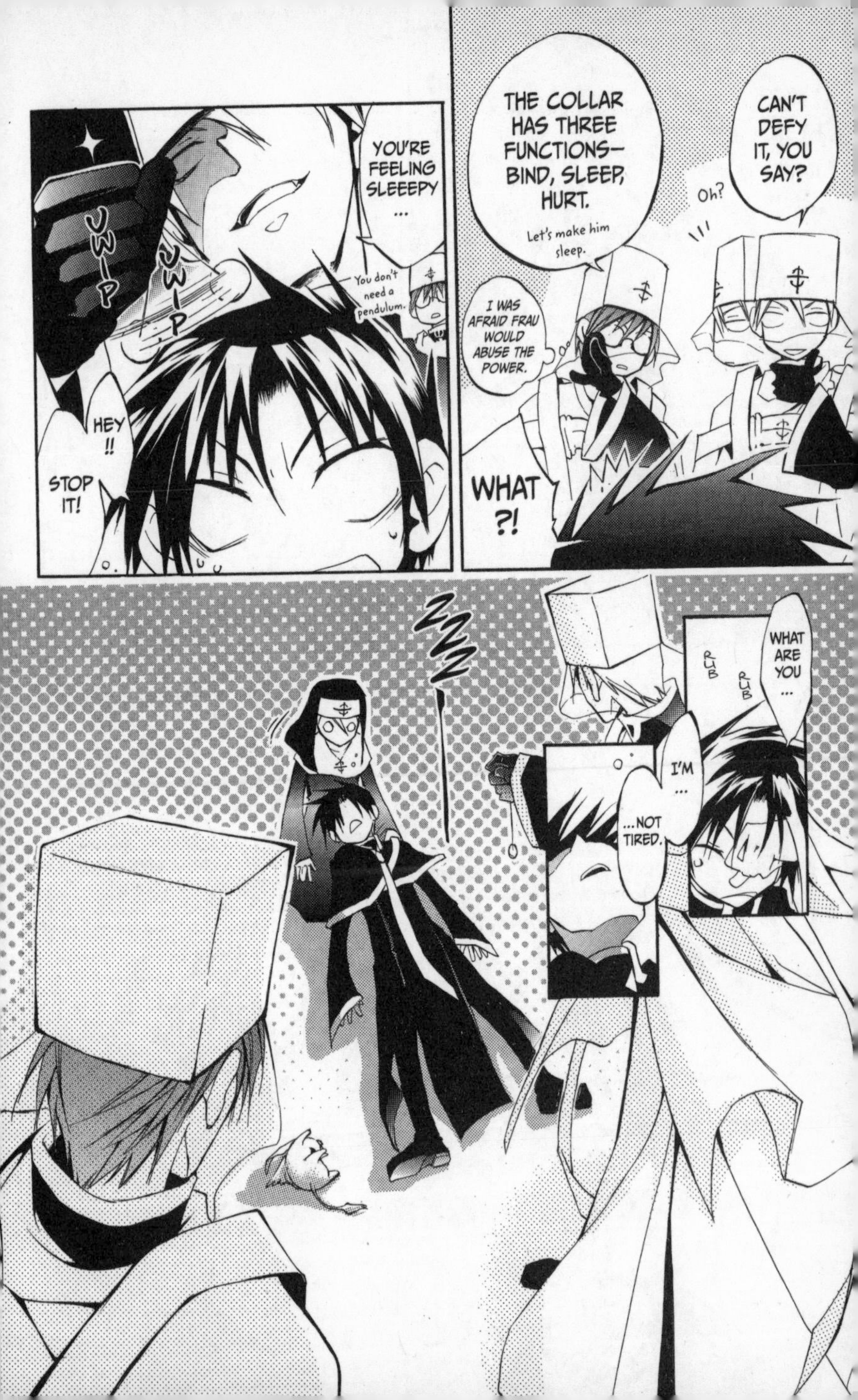
CAN'T DEFY IT, YOU SAY?
Oh?
THE COLLAR HAS THREE FUNCTIONS— BIND, SLEEP, HURT.
Let's make him sleep.
I WAS AFRAID FRAU WOULD ABUSE THE POWER.
WHAT ?!
YOU'RE FEELING SLEEEPY ...
You don't need a pendulum.
JWIP
JWIP
HEY !!
STOP IT!
WHAT ARE YOU ...
RUB
RUB
I'M ...
...NOT TIRED.
ZZZ

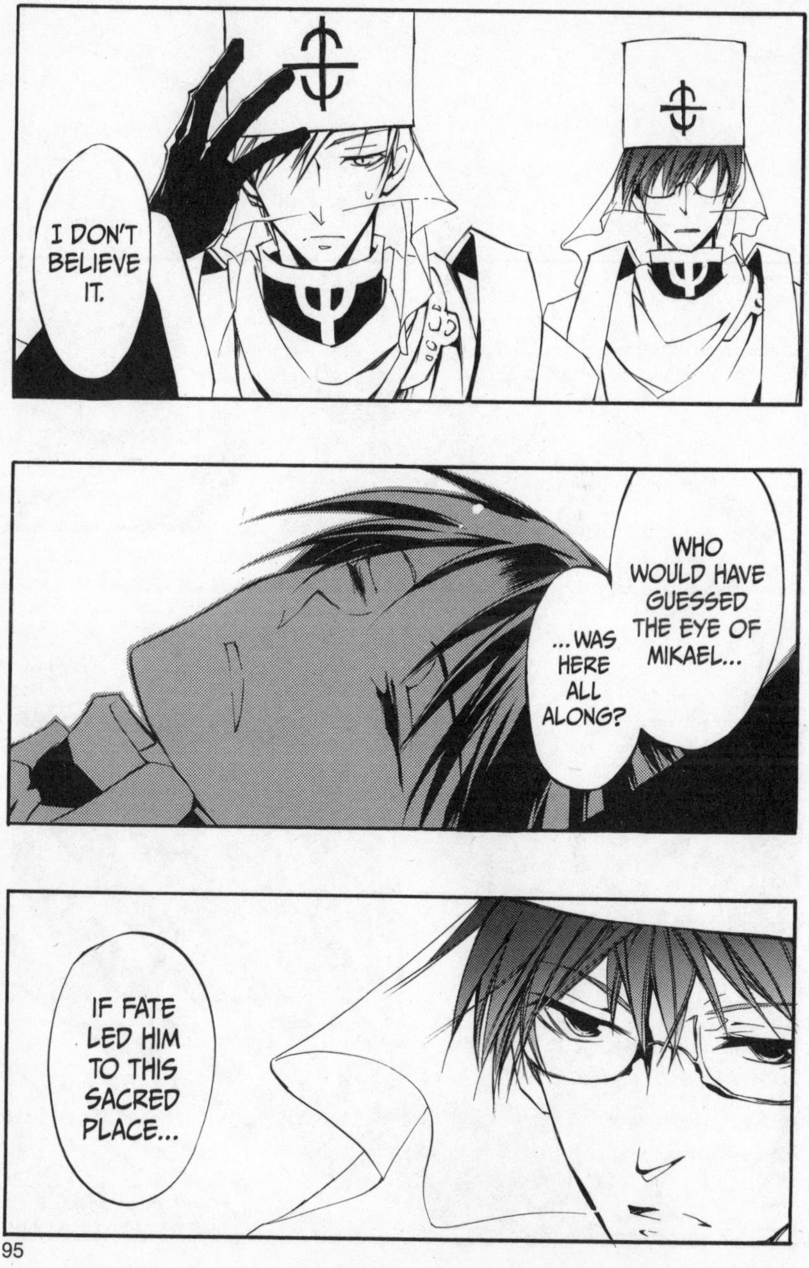
I DON'T BELIEVE IT.
WHO WOULD HAVE GUESSED THE EYE OF MIKAEL...
...WAS HERE ALL ALONG?
IF FATE LED HIM TO THIS SACRED PLACE...

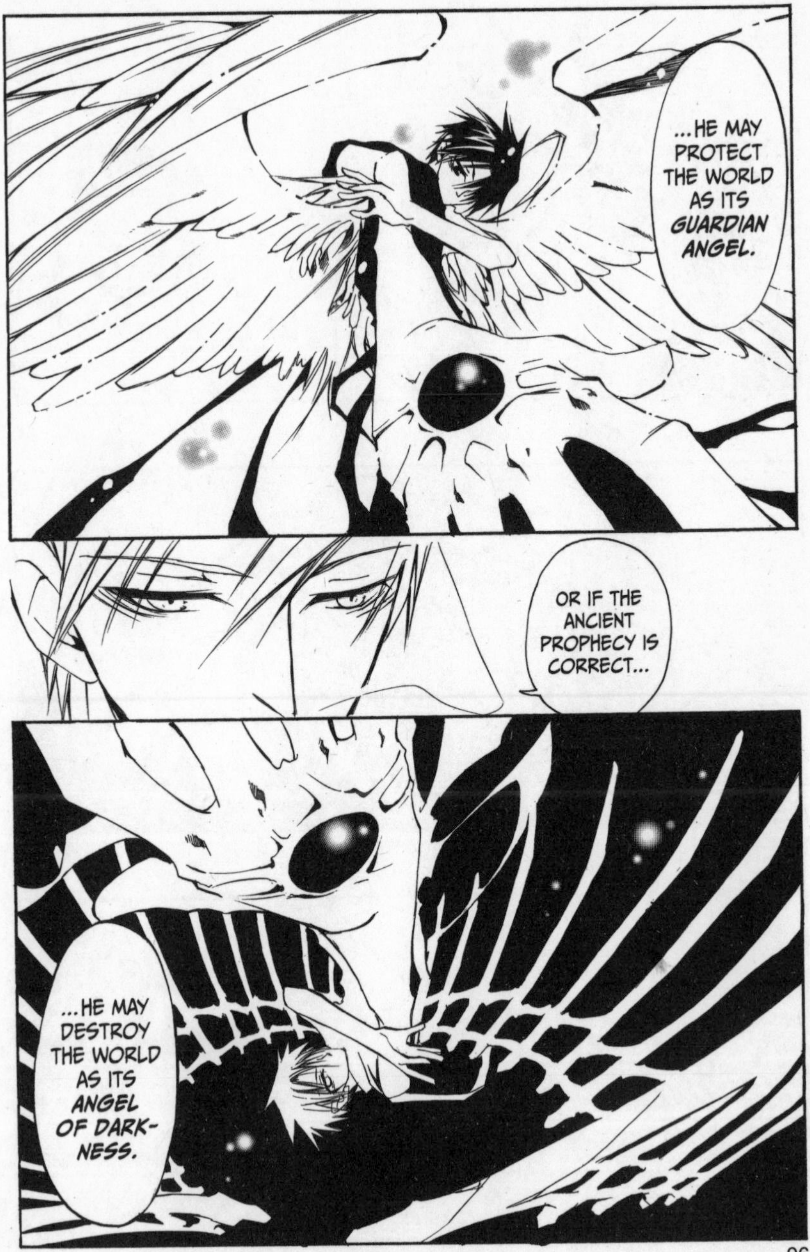
...HE MAY PROTECT THE WORLD AS ITS *GUARDIAN ANGEL.*
OR IF THE ANCIENT PROPHECY IS CORRECT...
...HE MAY DESTROY THE WORLD AS ITS *ANGEL OF DARK-NESS.*

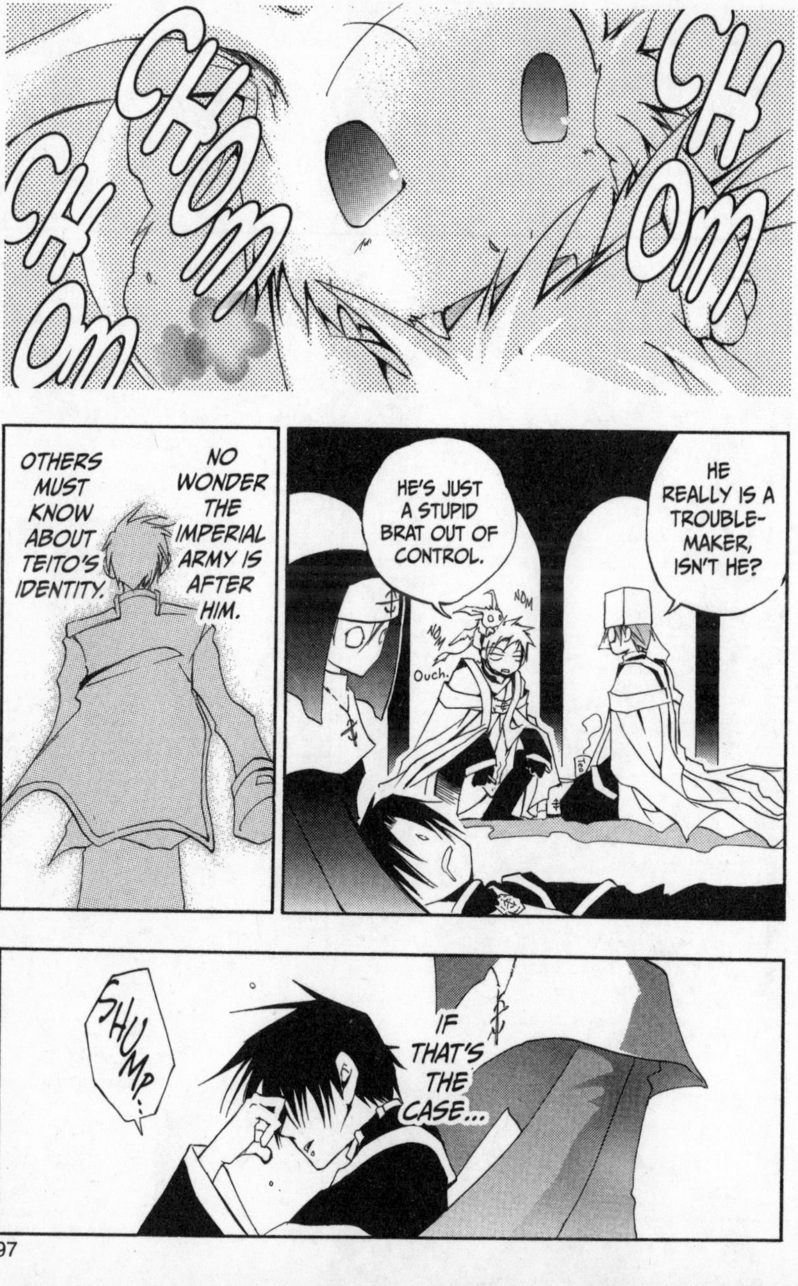
CHOM
CHOM CHOM
HE REALLY IS A TROUBLE-MAKER, ISN'T HE?
HE'S JUST A STUPID BRAT OUT OF CONTROL.
NOM NOM
Ouch.
NO WONDER THE IMPERIAL ARMY IS AFTER HIM.
OTHERS MUST KNOW ABOUT TEITO'S IDENTITY.
IF THAT'S THE CASE...
SHUMP...

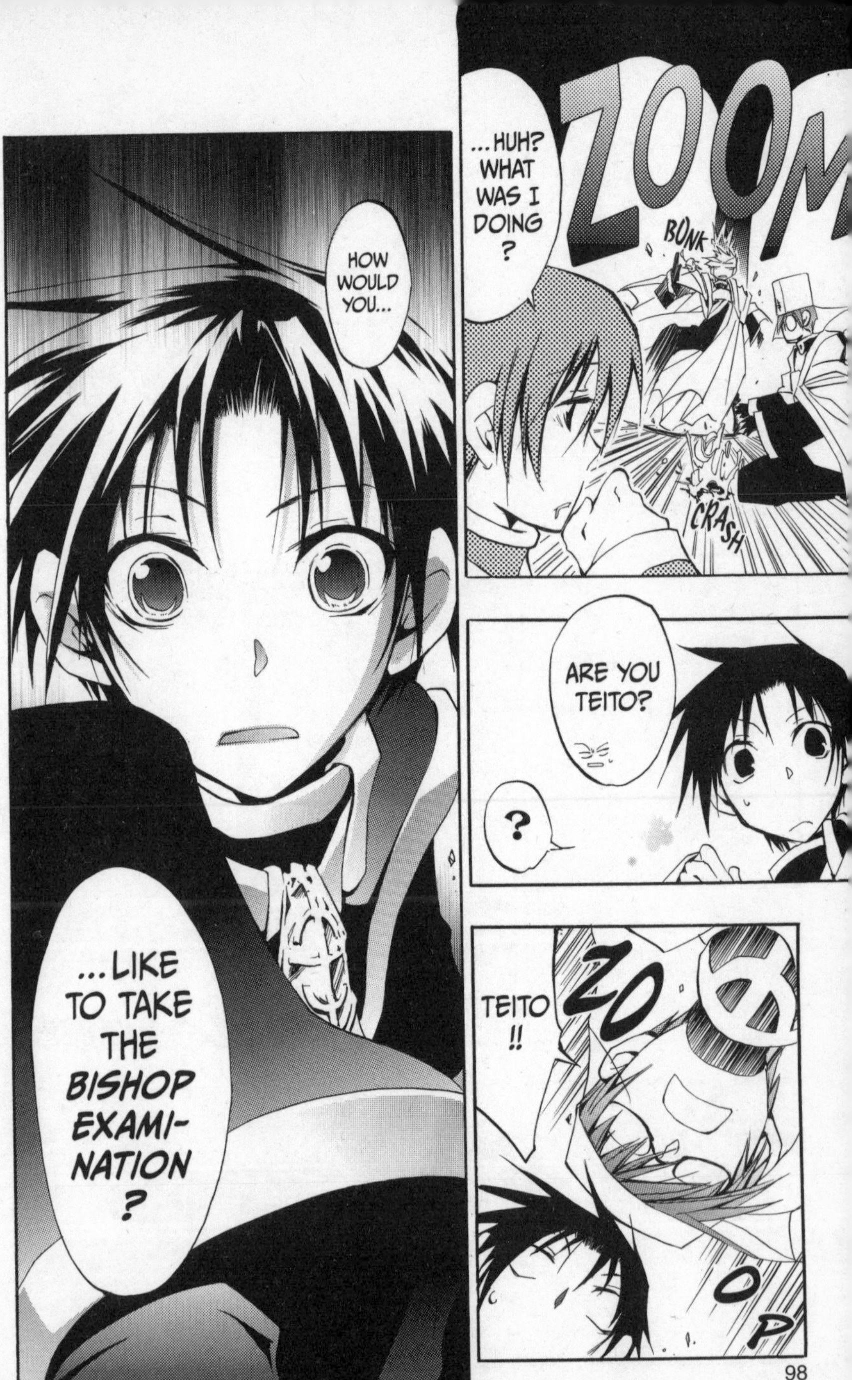
...HUH? WHAT WAS I DOING?
ZOOM
BONK
CRASH
ARE YOU TEITO?
?
TEITO!!
ZOOP
HOW WOULD YOU...
...LIKE TO TAKE THE BISHOP EXAMINATION?

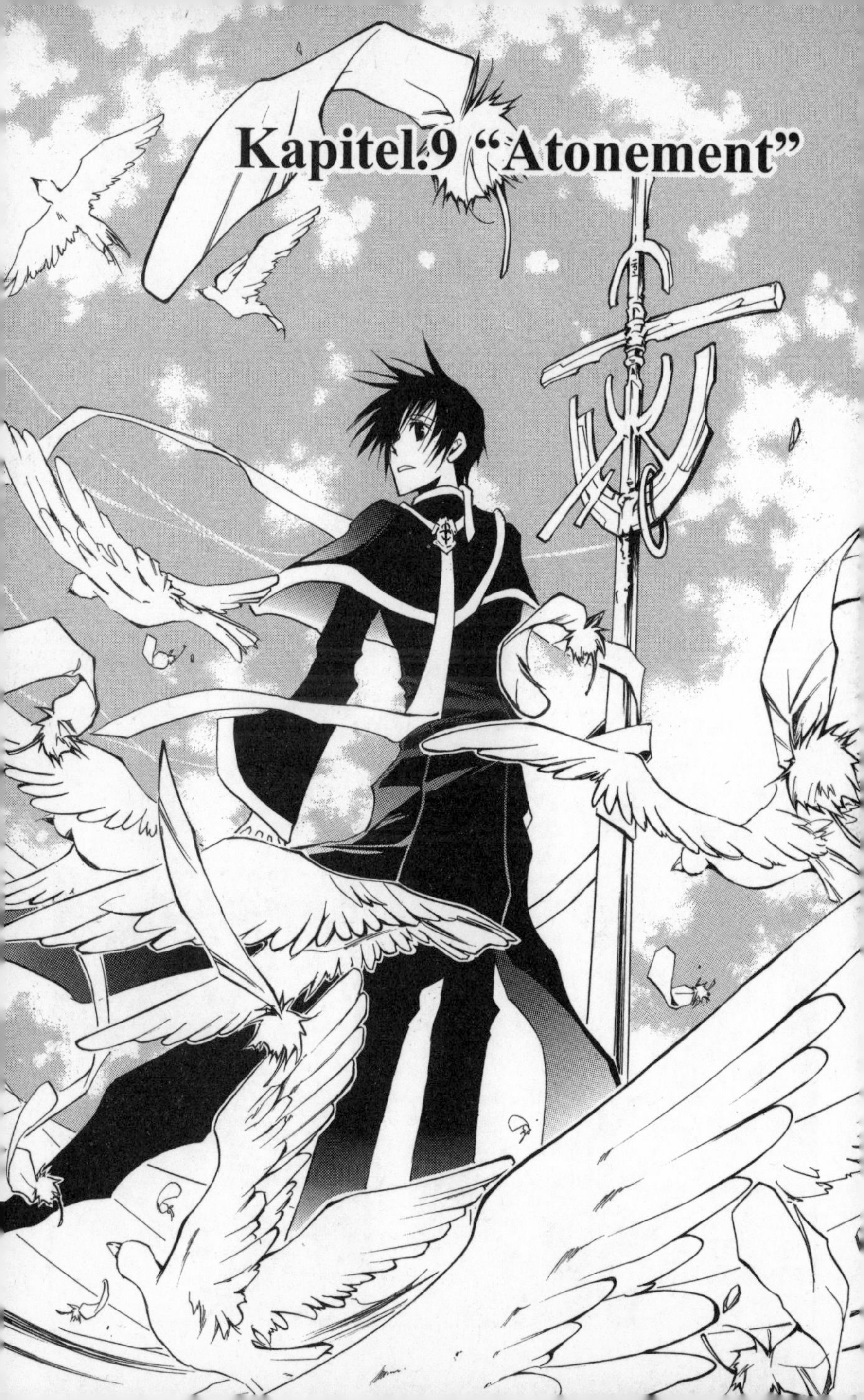
Kapitel.9 "Atonement"

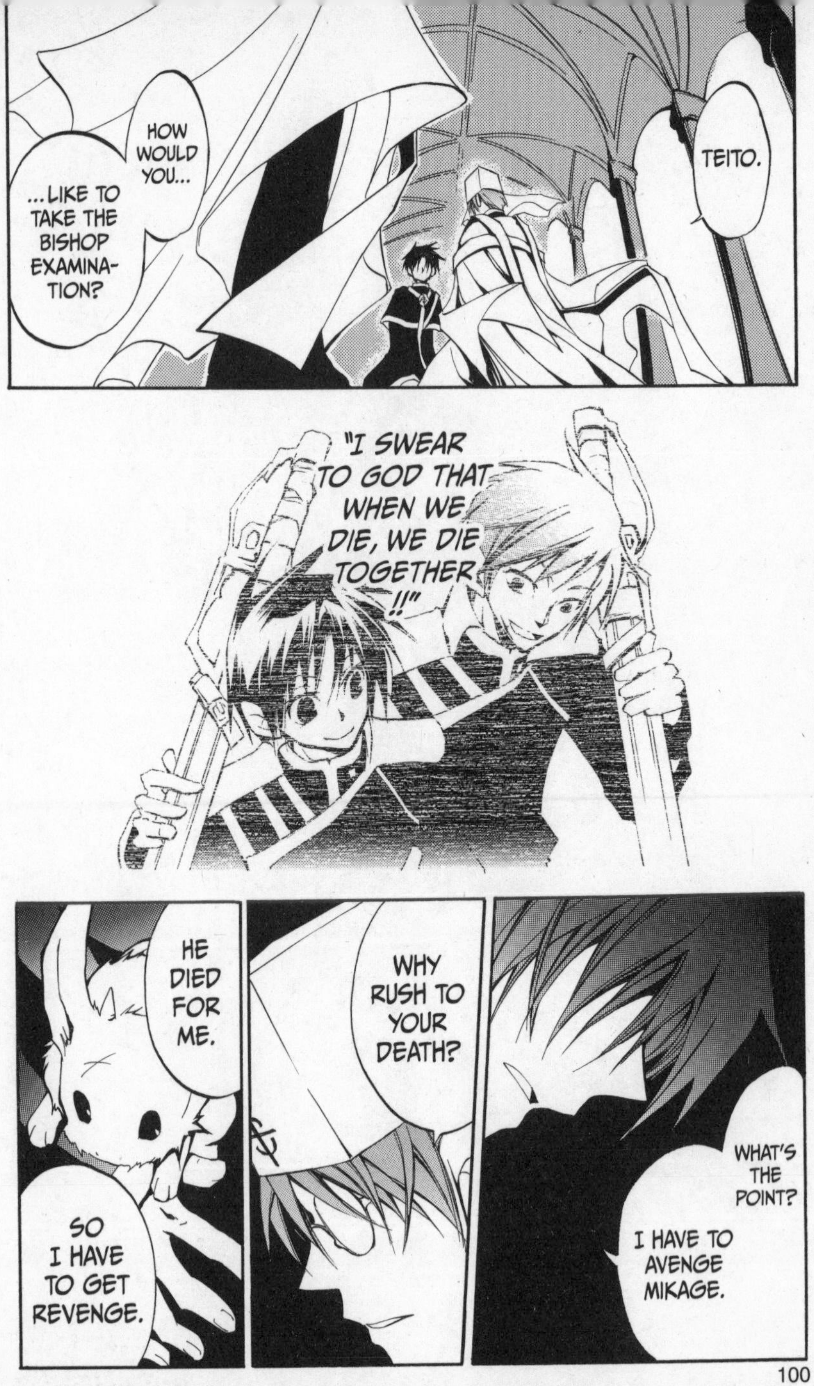
TEITO.
HOW WOULD YOU...
...LIKE TO TAKE THE BISHOP EXAMINA-TION?
"I SWEAR TO GOD THAT WHEN WE DIE, WE DIE TOGETHER!!"
WHAT'S THE POINT?
I HAVE TO AVENGE MIKAGE.
WHY RUSH TO YOUR DEATH?
HE DIED FOR ME.
SO I HAVE TO GET REVENGE.

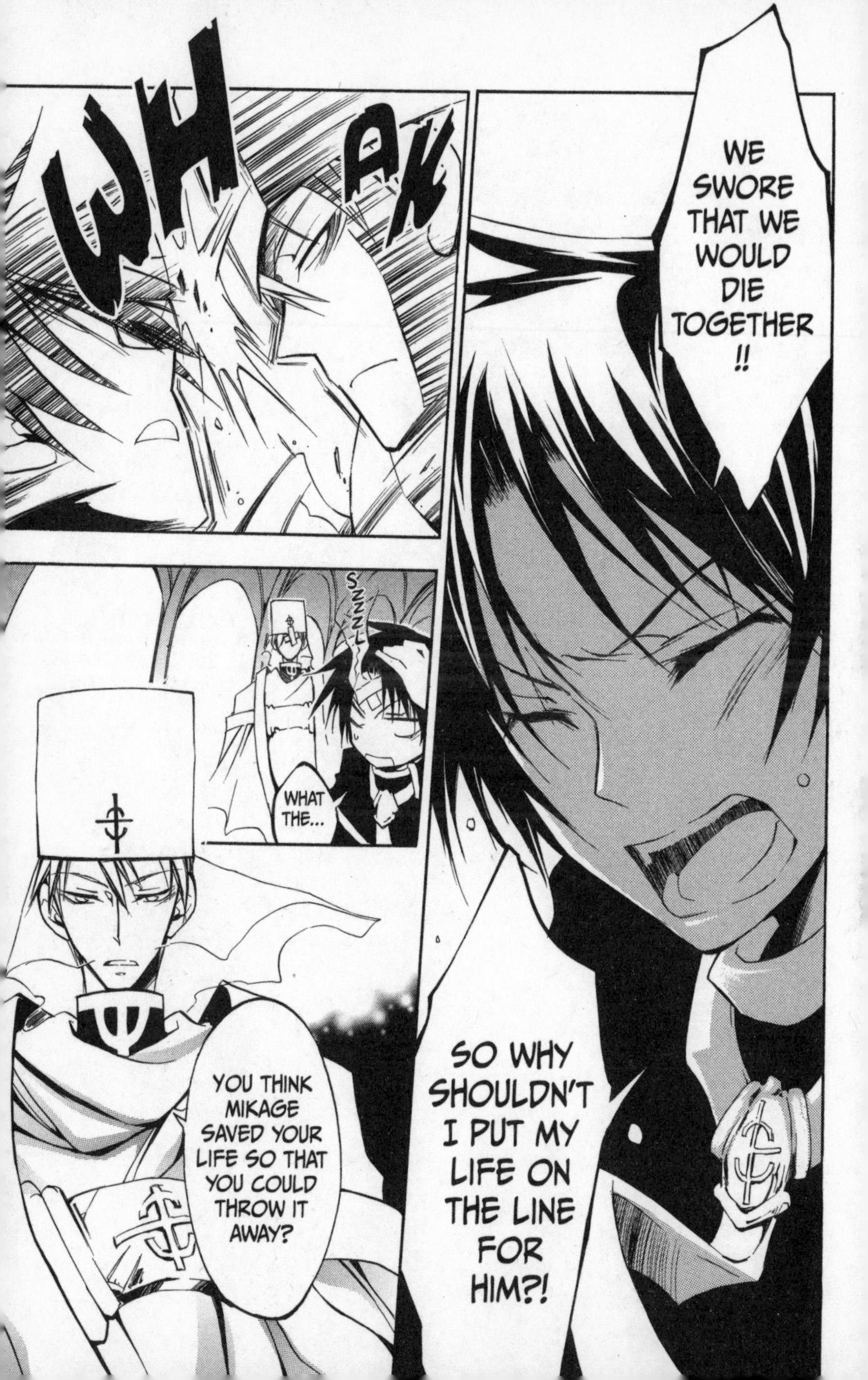
WE SWORE THAT WE WOULD DIE TOGETHER !!
SO WHY SHOULDN'T I PUT MY LIFE ON THE LINE FOR HIM?!
WHAK
SZZZL
WHAT THE...
YOU THINK MIKAGE SAVED YOUR LIFE SO THAT YOU COULD THROW IT AWAY?

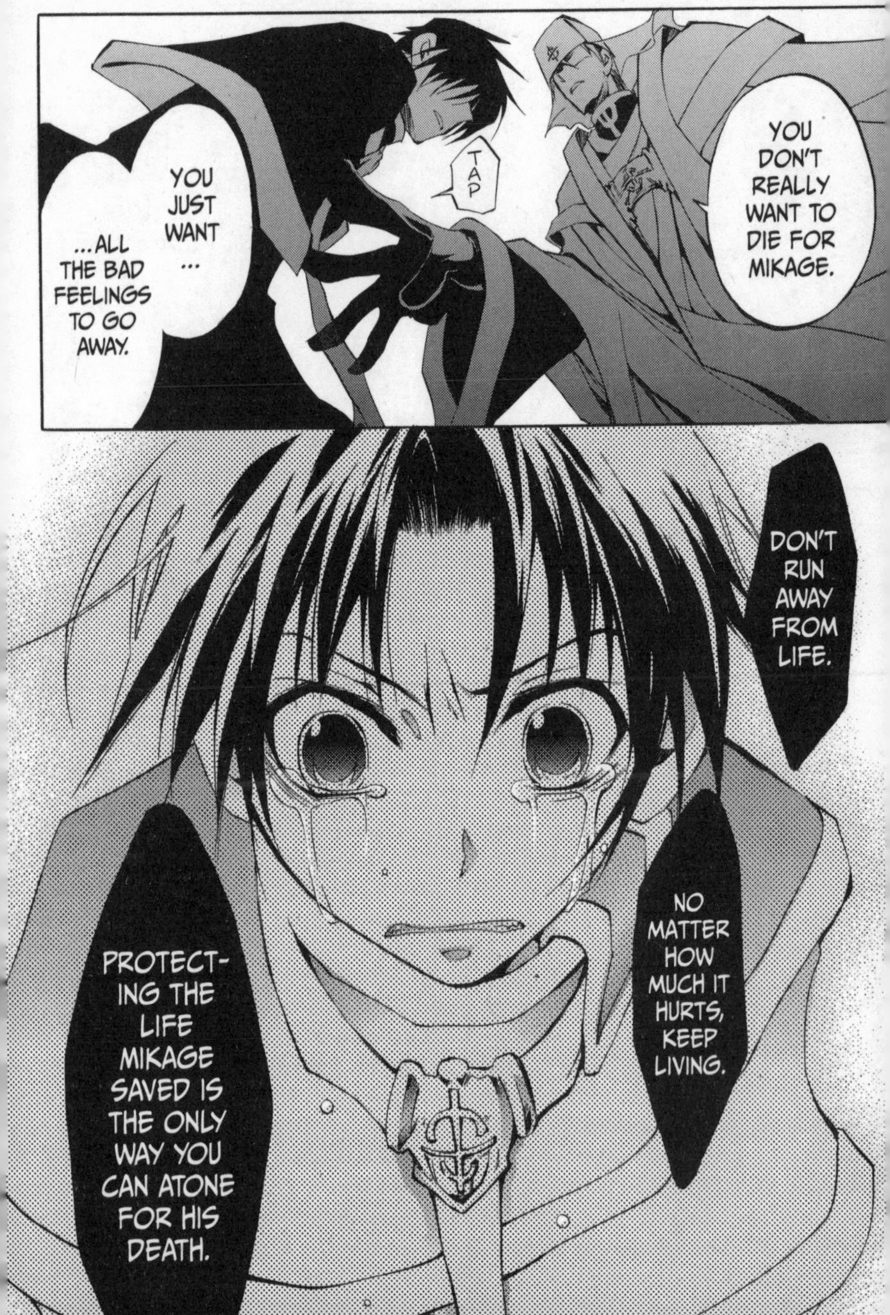
YOU DON'T REALLY WANT TO DIE FOR MIKAGE.
TAP
YOU JUST WANT ...
...ALL THE BAD FEELINGS TO GO AWAY.
DON'T RUN AWAY FROM LIFE.
NO MATTER HOW MUCH IT HURTS, KEEP LIVING.
PROTECT-ING THE LIFE MIKAGE SAVED IS THE ONLY WAY YOU CAN ATONE FOR HIS DEATH.

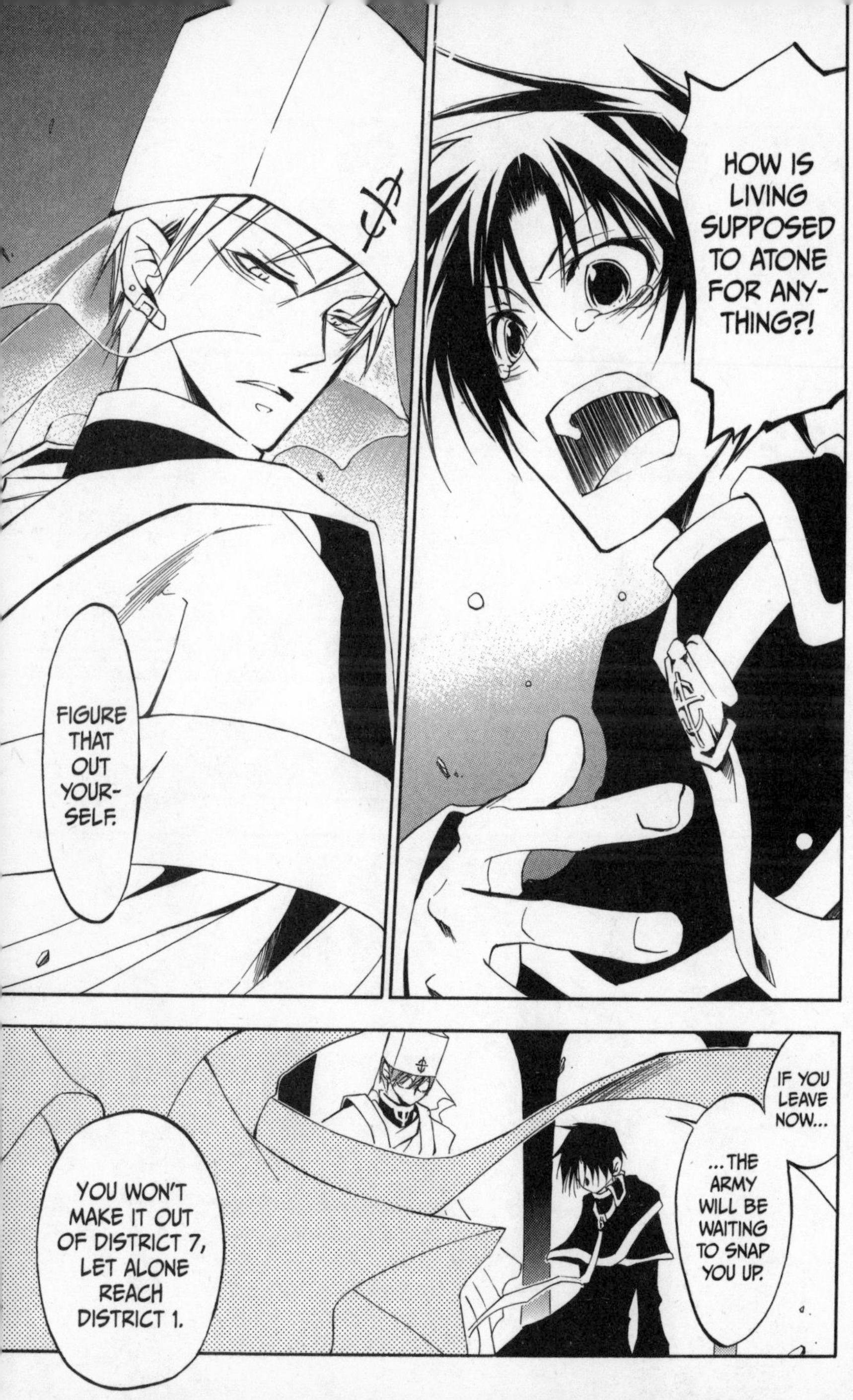
HOW IS LIVING SUPPOSED TO ATONE FOR ANY-THING?!
FIGURE THAT OUT YOUR-SELF.
IF YOU LEAVE NOW...
...THE ARMY WILL BE WAITING TO SNAP YOU UP.
YOU WON'T MAKE IT OUT OF DISTRICT 7, LET ALONE REACH DISTRICT 1.

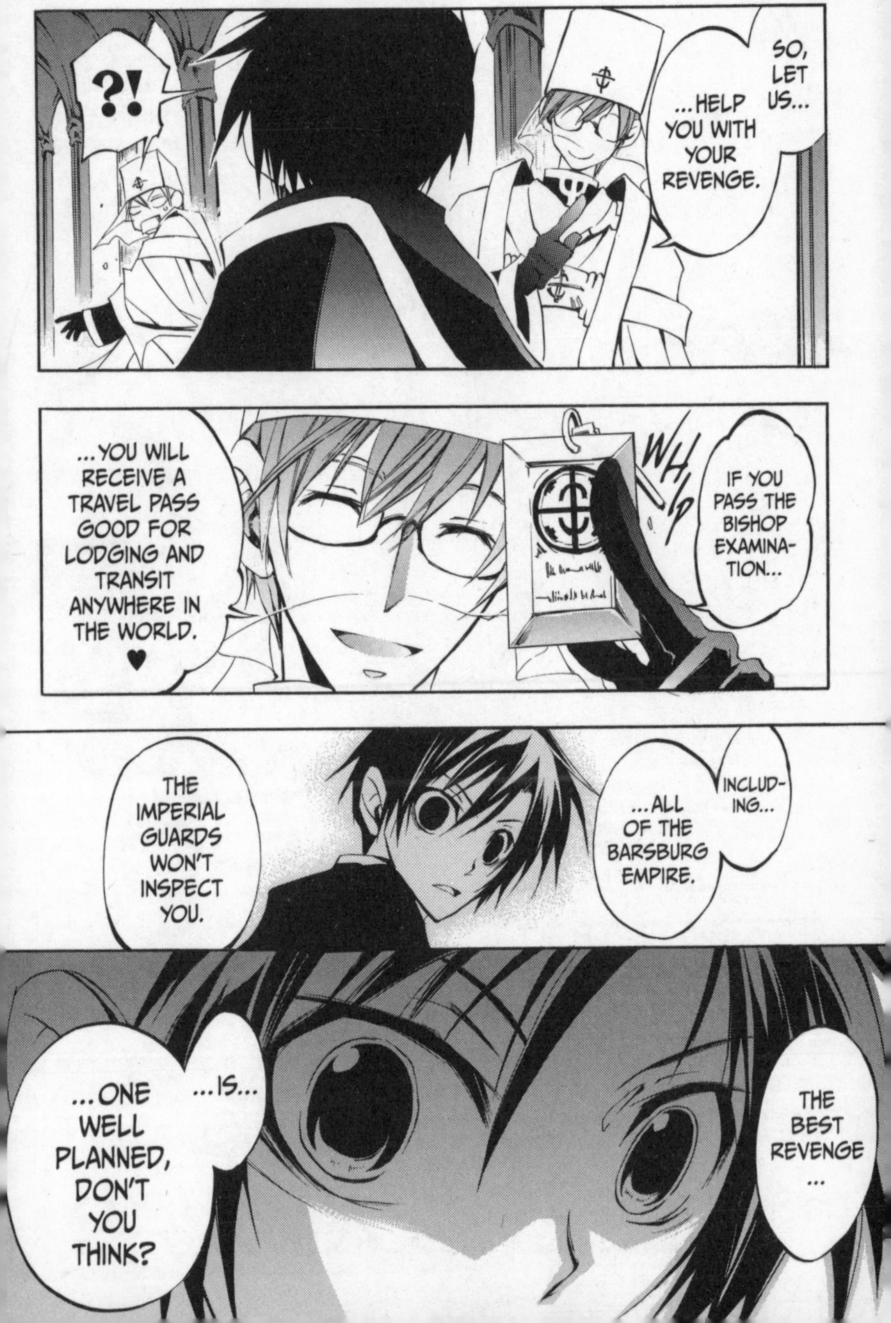
SO, LET US...
...HELP YOU WITH YOUR REVENGE.
?!
IF YOU PASS THE BISHOP EXAMINA-TION...
WHIP
...YOU WILL RECEIVE A TRAVEL PASS GOOD FOR LODGING AND TRANSIT ANYWHERE IN THE WORLD. ♥
INCLUD-ING...
...ALL OF THE BARSBURG EMPIRE.
THE IMPERIAL GUARDS WON'T INSPECT YOU.
THE BEST REVENGE ...
...IS...
...ONE WELL PLANNED, DON'T YOU THINK?

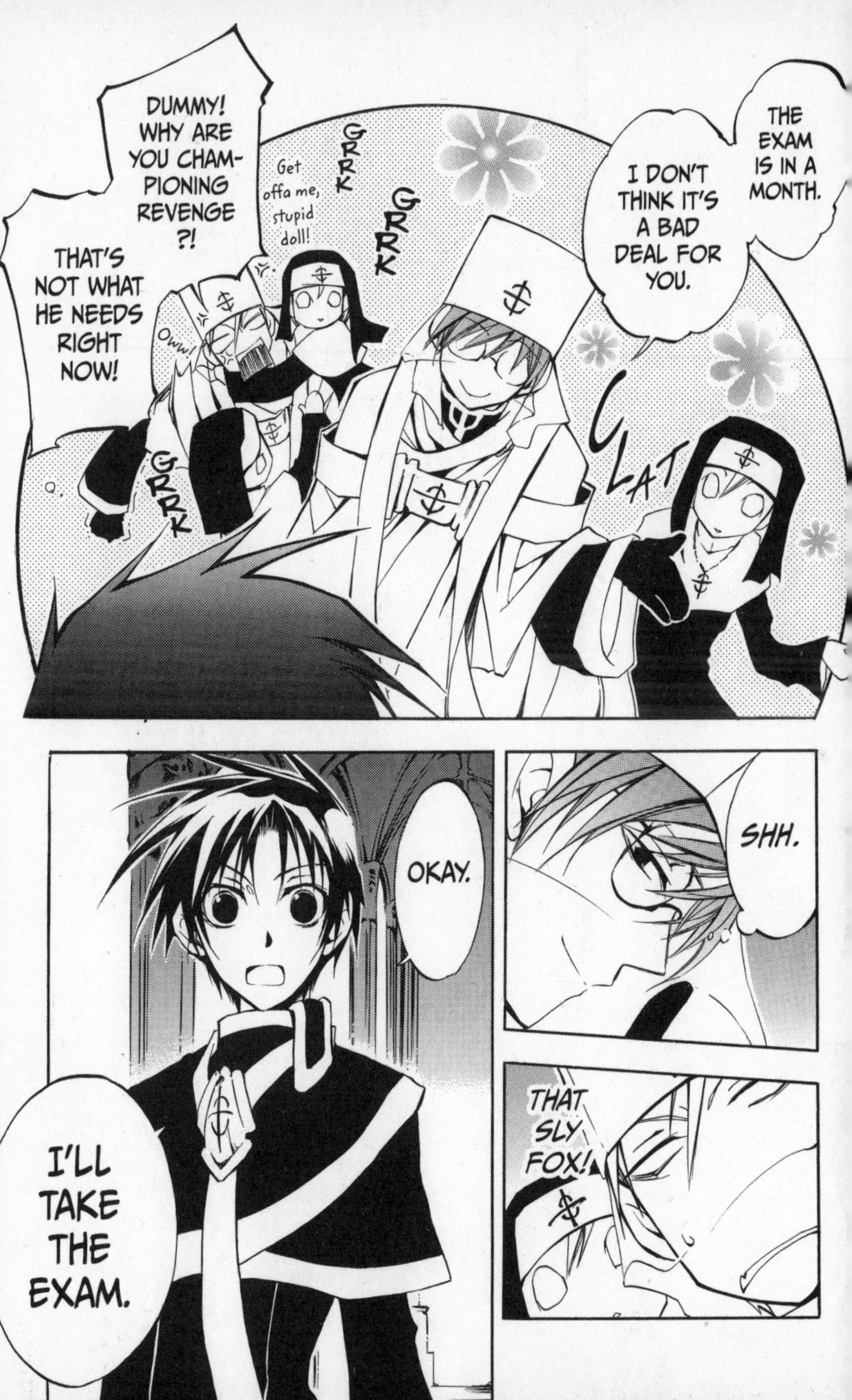
THE EXAM IS IN A MONTH.
I DON'T THINK IT'S A BAD DEAL FOR YOU.
CLAT
GRRK
GRRK
Get offa me, stupid doll!
DUMMY! WHY ARE YOU CHAMPIONING REVENGE ?!
THAT'S NOT WHAT HE NEEDS RIGHT NOW!
Oww!
GRRK
SHH.
THAT SLY FOX!
OKAY.
I'LL TAKE THE EXAM.

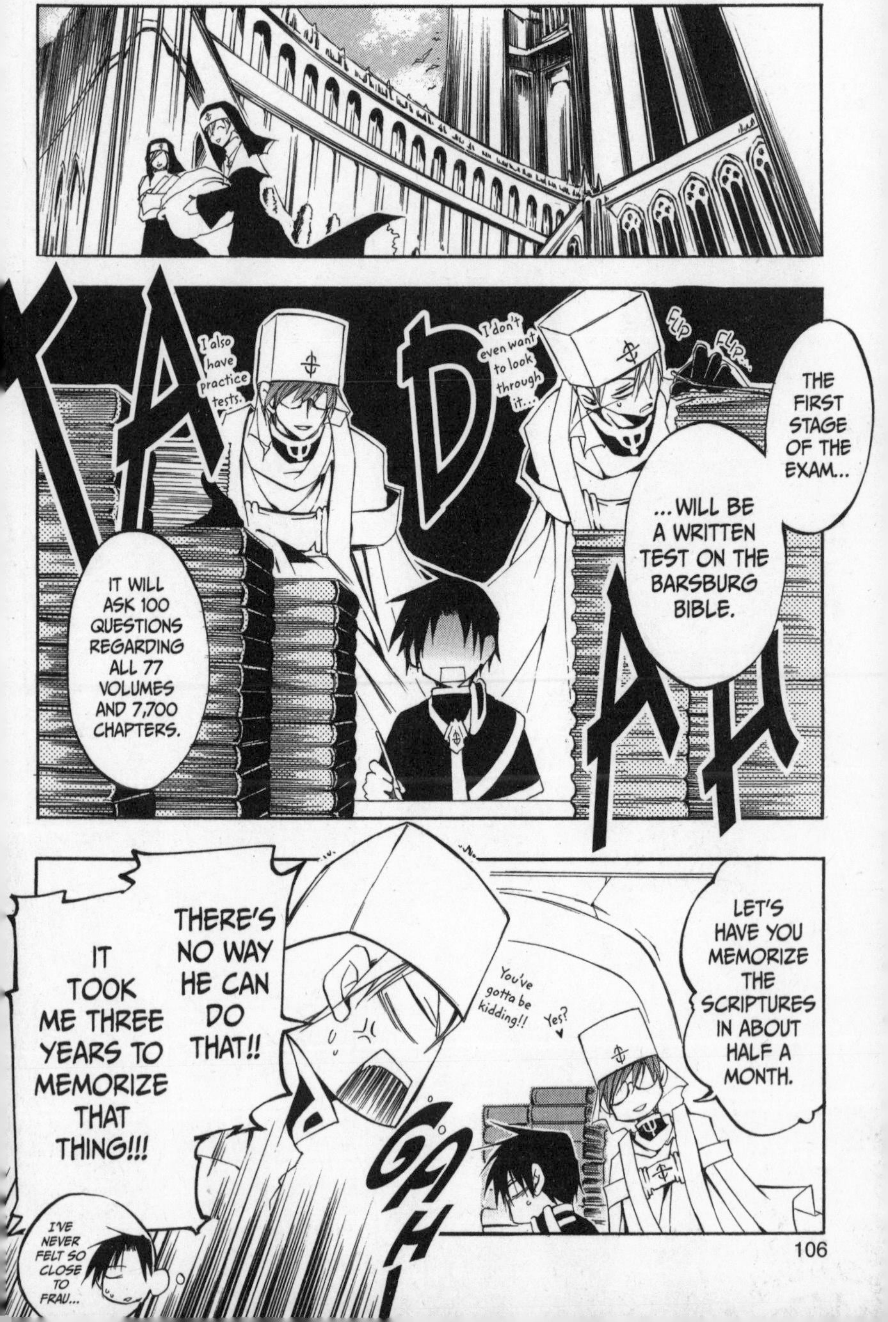
THE FIRST STAGE OF THE EXAM...
...WILL BE A WRITTEN TEST ON THE BARSBURG BIBLE.
Flip
Flip...
I don't even want to look through it...
I also have practice tests.
IT WILL ASK 100 QUESTIONS REGARDING ALL 77 VOLUMES AND 7,700 CHAPTERS.
LET'S HAVE YOU MEMORIZE THE SCRIPTURES IN ABOUT HALF A MONTH.
Yes?
You've gotta be kidding!!
THERE'S NO WAY HE CAN DO THAT!!
IT TOOK ME THREE YEARS TO MEMORIZE THAT THING!!!
I'VE NEVER FELT SO CLOSE TO FRAU...

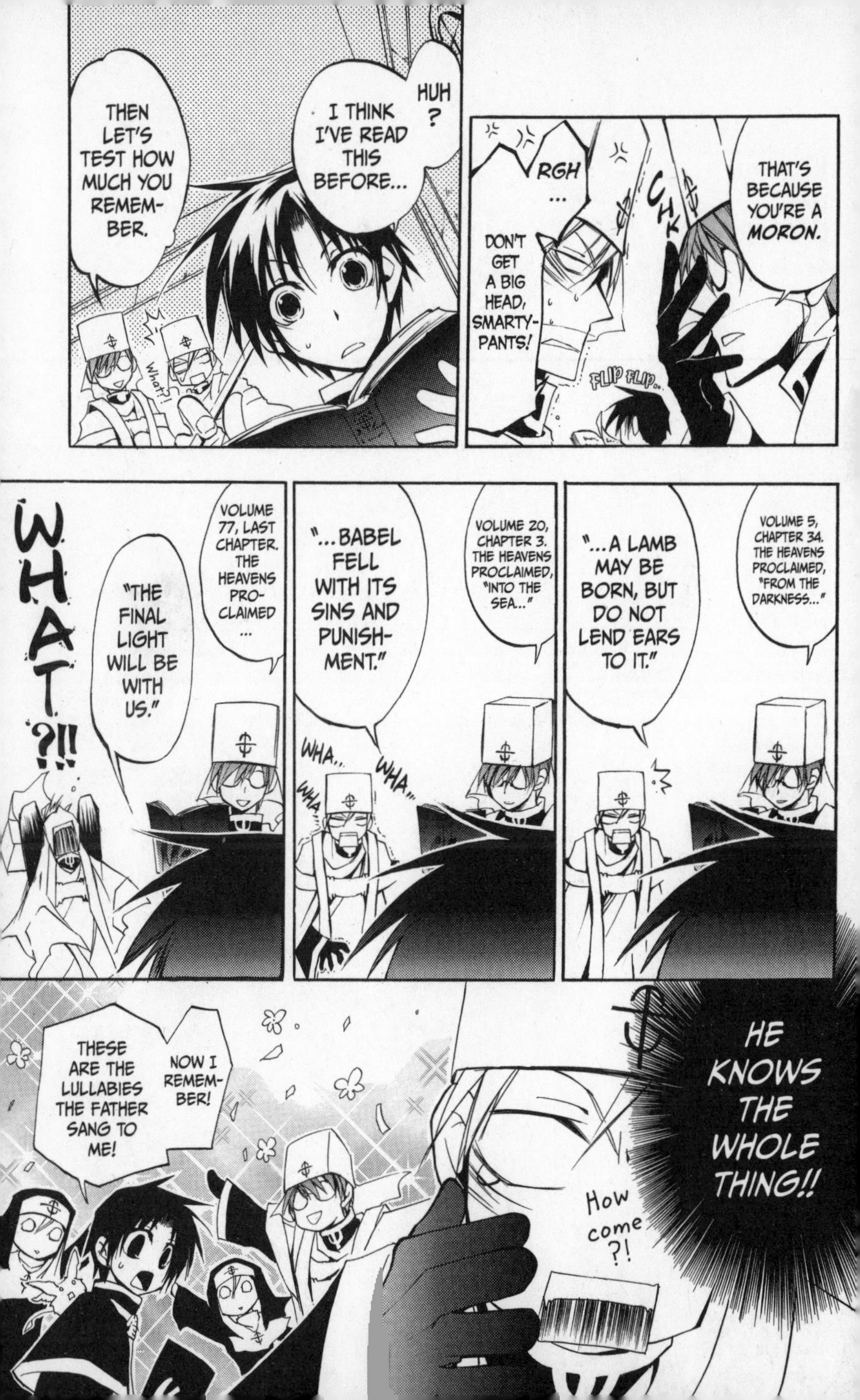
THAT'S BECAUSE YOU'RE A MORON.
CHK
RGH ...
DON'T GET A BIG HEAD, SMARTY-PANTS!
FLIP FLIP..
HUH ?
I THINK I'VE READ THIS BEFORE...
THEN LET'S TEST HOW MUCH YOU REMEMBER.
What?!
VOLUME 5, CHAPTER 34. THE HEAVENS PROCLAIMED, "FROM THE DARKNESS..."
"...A LAMB MAY BE BORN, BUT DO NOT LEND EARS TO IT."
VOLUME 20, CHAPTER 3. THE HEAVENS PROCLAIMED, "INTO THE SEA..."
"...BABEL FELL WITH ITS SINS AND PUNISHMENT."
WHA..
WHA..
WHA
VOLUME 77, LAST CHAPTER. THE HEAVENS PROCLAIMED ...
"THE FINAL LIGHT WILL BE WITH US."
WHAT ?!!
HE KNOWS THE WHOLE THING!!
How come ?!
NOW I REMEMBER!
THESE ARE THE LULLABIES THE FATHER SANG TO ME!

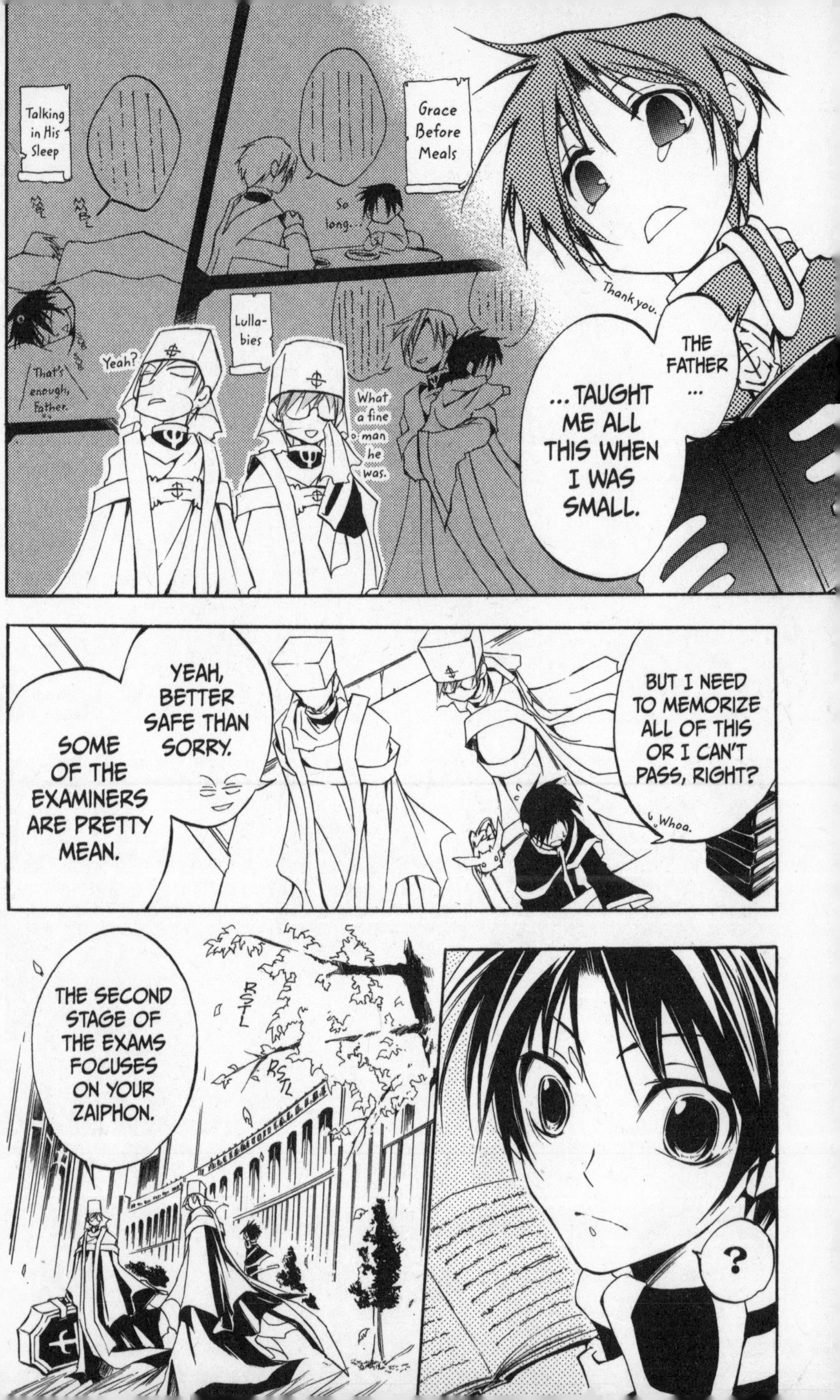
Thank you.
THE FATHER ...
...TAUGHT ME ALL THIS WHEN I WAS SMALL.
Grace Before Meals
So long...
Talking in His Sleep
Lullabies
What a fine man he was.
Yeah?
That's enough, Father.
BUT I NEED TO MEMORIZE ALL OF THIS OR I CAN'T PASS, RIGHT?
Whoa.
YEAH, BETTER SAFE THAN SORRY.
SOME OF THE EXAMINERS ARE PRETTY MEAN.
?
THE SECOND STAGE OF THE EXAMS FOCUSES ON YOUR ZAIPHON.
RSTL
RSTL

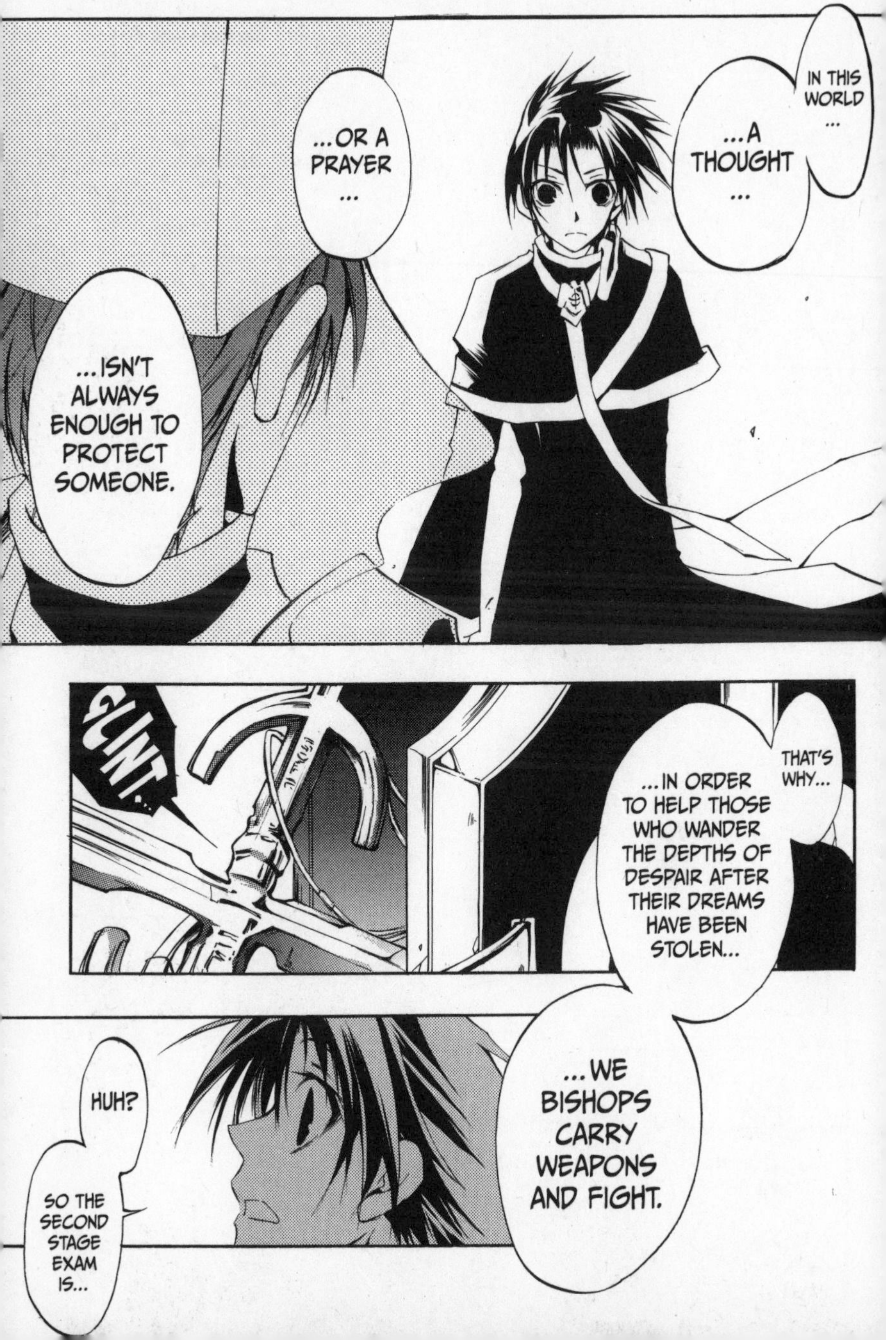
IN THIS WORLD ...
...A THOUGHT ...
...OR A PRAYER ...
...ISN'T ALWAYS ENOUGH TO PROTECT SOMEONE.
THAT'S WHY...
...IN ORDER TO HELP THOSE WHO WANDER THE DEPTHS OF DESPAIR AFTER THEIR DREAMS HAVE BEEN STOLEN...
GLINT...
...WE BISHOPS CARRY WEAPONS AND FIGHT.
HUH?
SO THE SECOND STAGE EXAM IS...

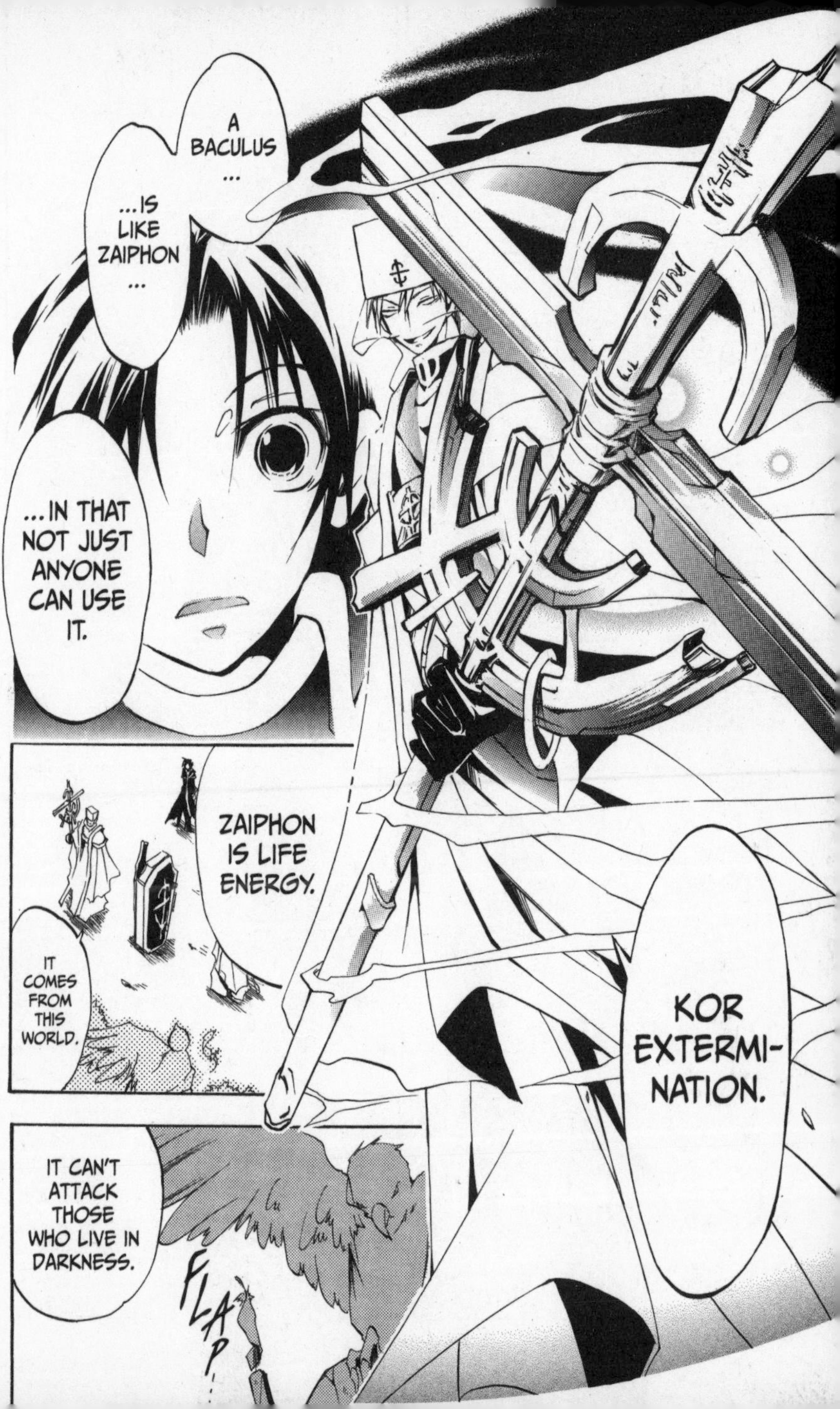
A BACULUS...
...IS LIKE ZAIPHON...
...IN THAT NOT JUST ANYONE CAN USE IT.
KOR EXTERMI-NATION.
ZAIPHON IS LIFE ENERGY.
IT COMES FROM THIS WORLD.
IT CAN'T ATTACK THOSE WHO LIVE IN DARKNESS.
FLAP

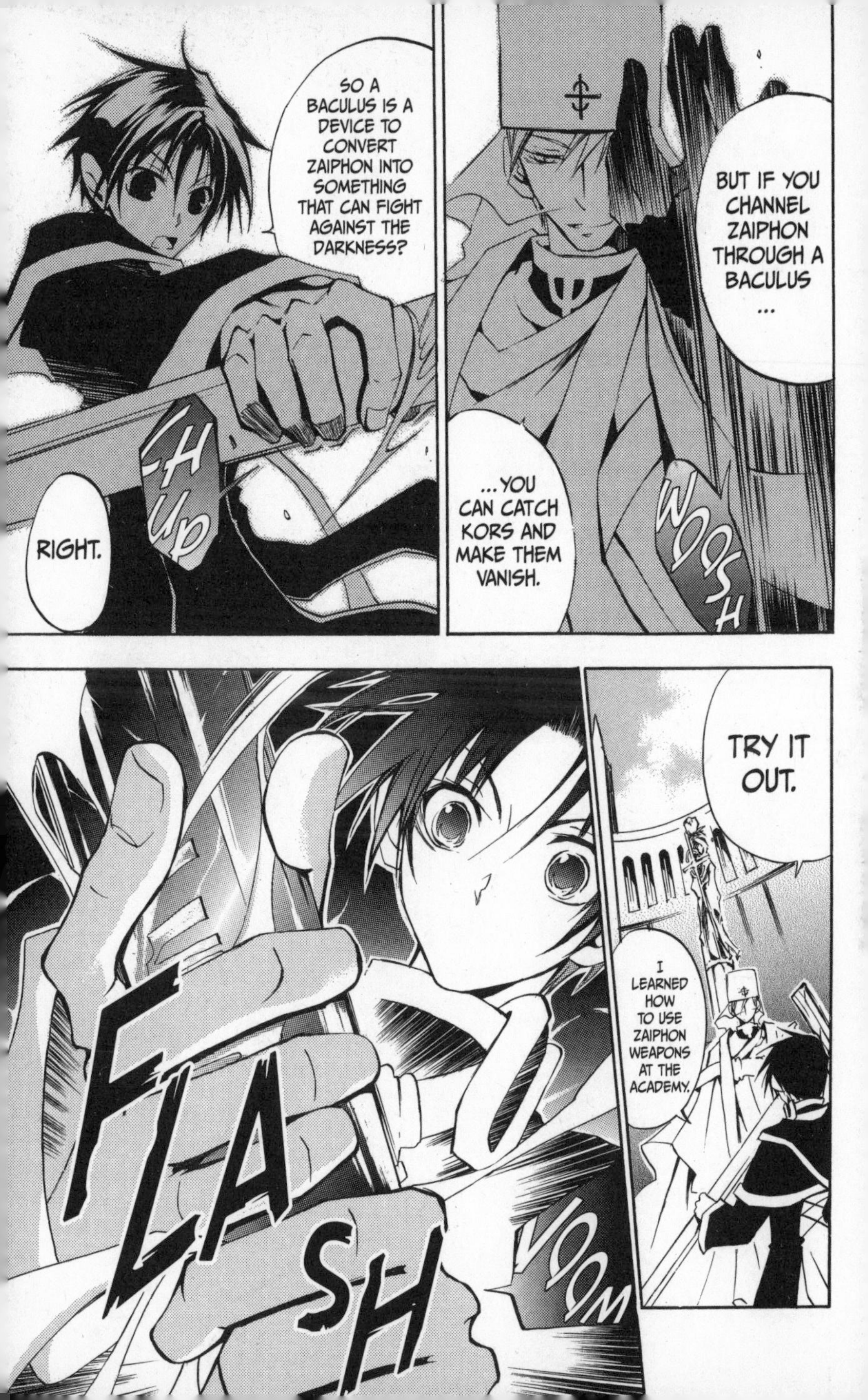
BUT IF YOU CHANNEL ZAIPHON THROUGH A BACULUS ...
...YOU CAN CATCH KORS AND MAKE THEM VANISH.
WOOSH
SO A BACULUS IS A DEVICE TO CONVERT ZAIPHON INTO SOMETHING THAT CAN FIGHT AGAINST THE DARKNESS?
CHUP
RIGHT.
TRY IT OUT.
I LEARNED HOW TO USE ZAIPHON WEAPONS AT THE ACADEMY.
FLASH
VOOM

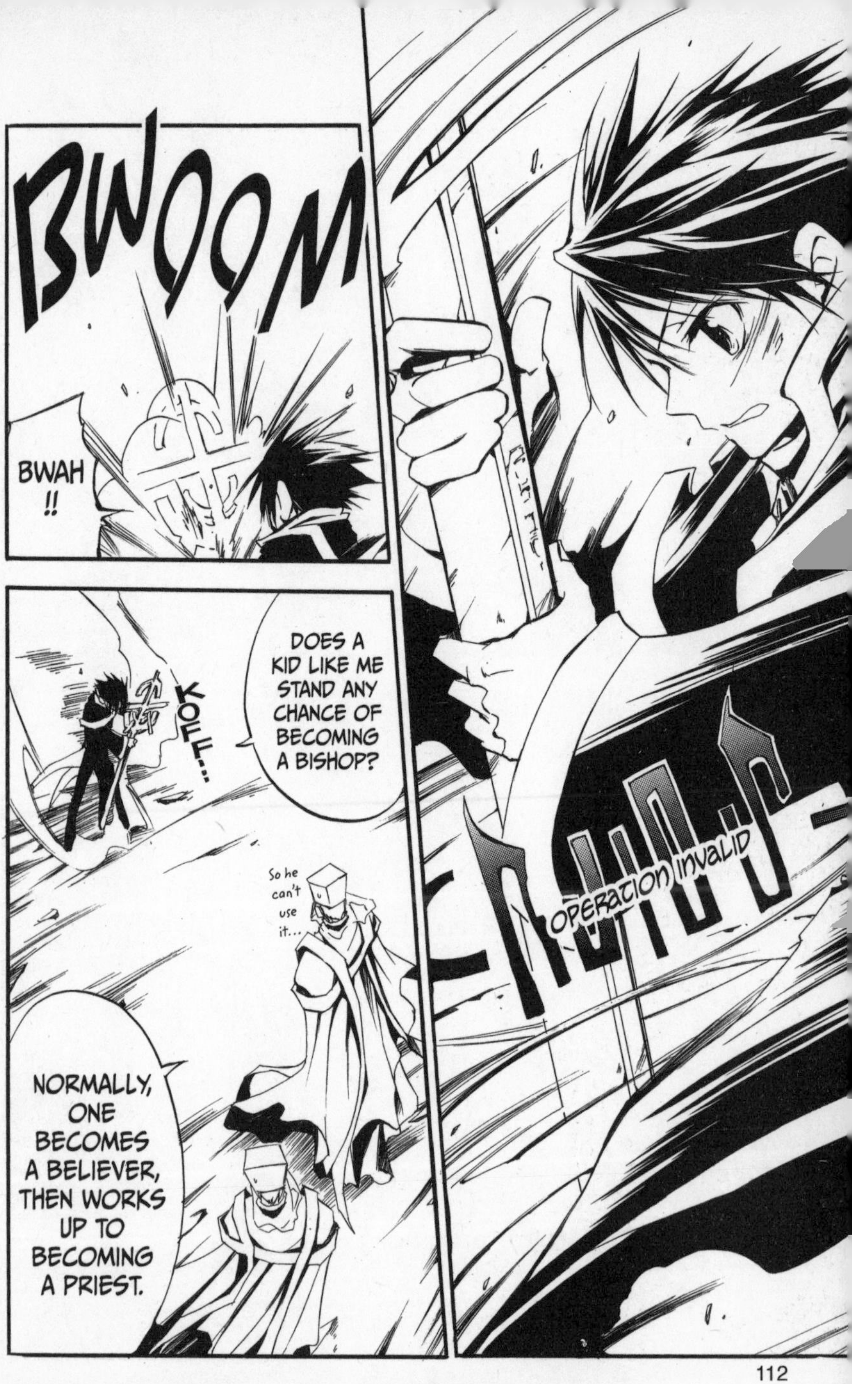
OPERATION INVALID
BWOOM
BWAH!!
DOES A KID LIKE ME STAND ANY CHANCE OF BECOMING A BISHOP?
KOFF...
So he can't use it...
NORMALLY, ONE BECOMES A BELIEVER, THEN WORKS UP TO BECOMING A PRIEST.

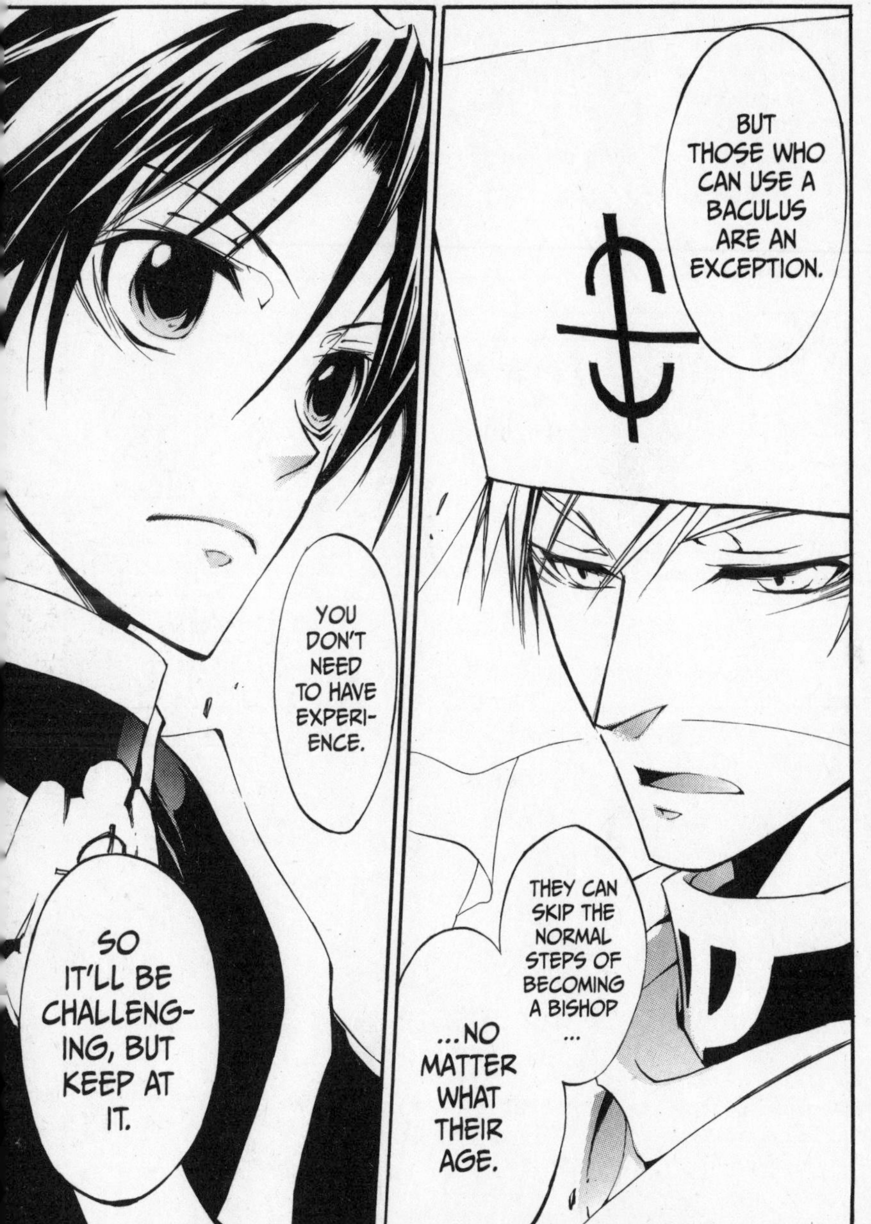
BUT THOSE WHO CAN USE A BACULUS ARE AN EXCEPTION.
THEY CAN SKIP THE NORMAL STEPS OF BECOMING A BISHOP ...
...NO MATTER WHAT THEIR AGE.
YOU DON'T NEED TO HAVE EXPERI-ENCE.
SO IT'LL BE CHALLENG-ING, BUT KEEP AT IT.

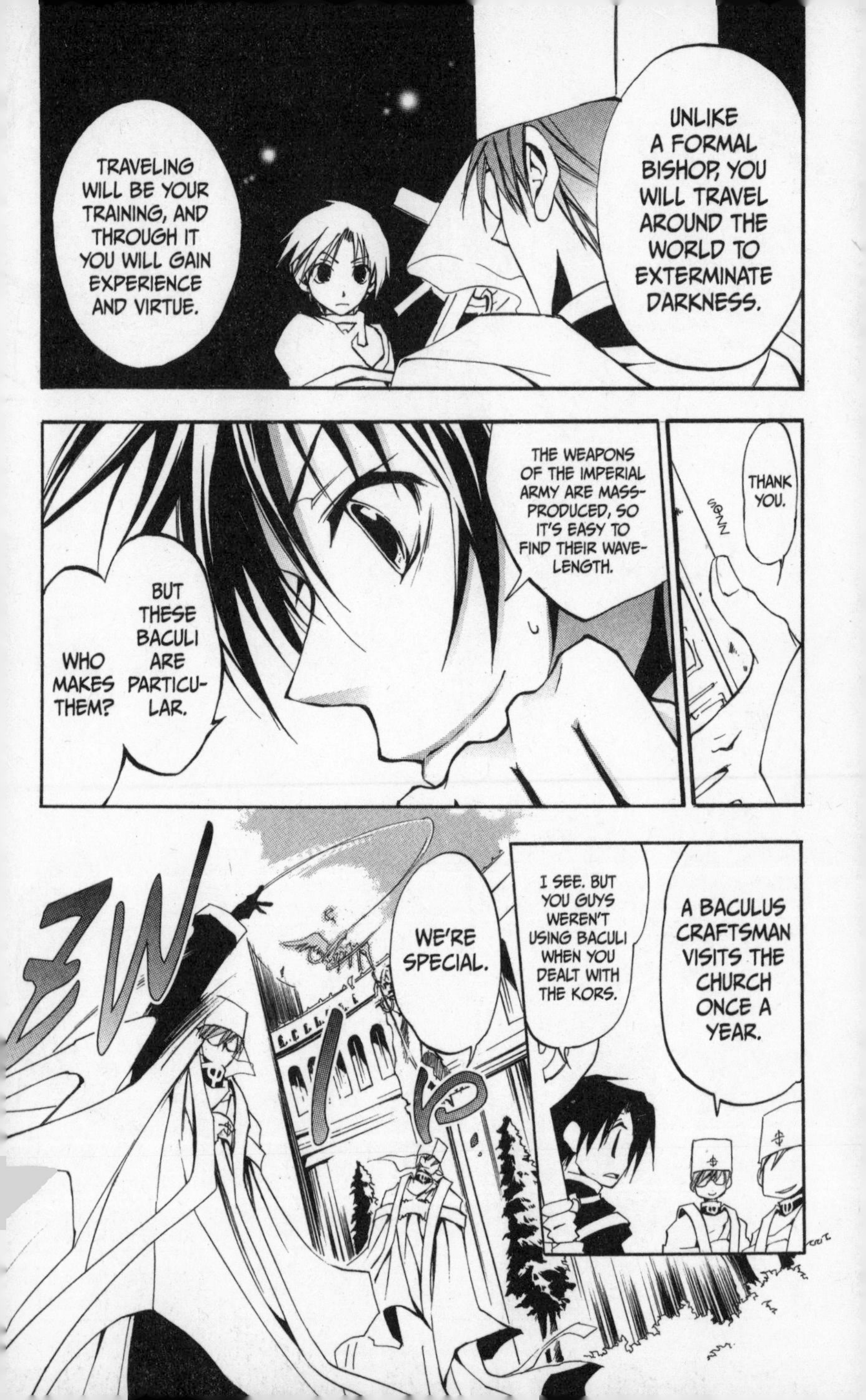
UNLIKE A FORMAL BISHOP, YOU WILL TRAVEL AROUND THE WORLD TO EXTERMINATE DARKNESS.
TRAVELING WILL BE YOUR TRAINING, AND THROUGH IT YOU WILL GAIN EXPERIENCE AND VIRTUE.
THANK YOU.
THE WEAPONS OF THE IMPERIAL ARMY ARE MASS-PRODUCED, SO IT'S EASY TO FIND THEIR WAVE-LENGTH.
BUT THESE BACULI ARE PARTICU-LAR.
WHO MAKES THEM?
A BACULUS CRAFTSMAN VISITS THE CHURCH ONCE A YEAR.
I SEE. BUT YOU GUYS WEREN'T USING BACULI WHEN YOU DEALT WITH THE KORS.
WE'RE SPECIAL.

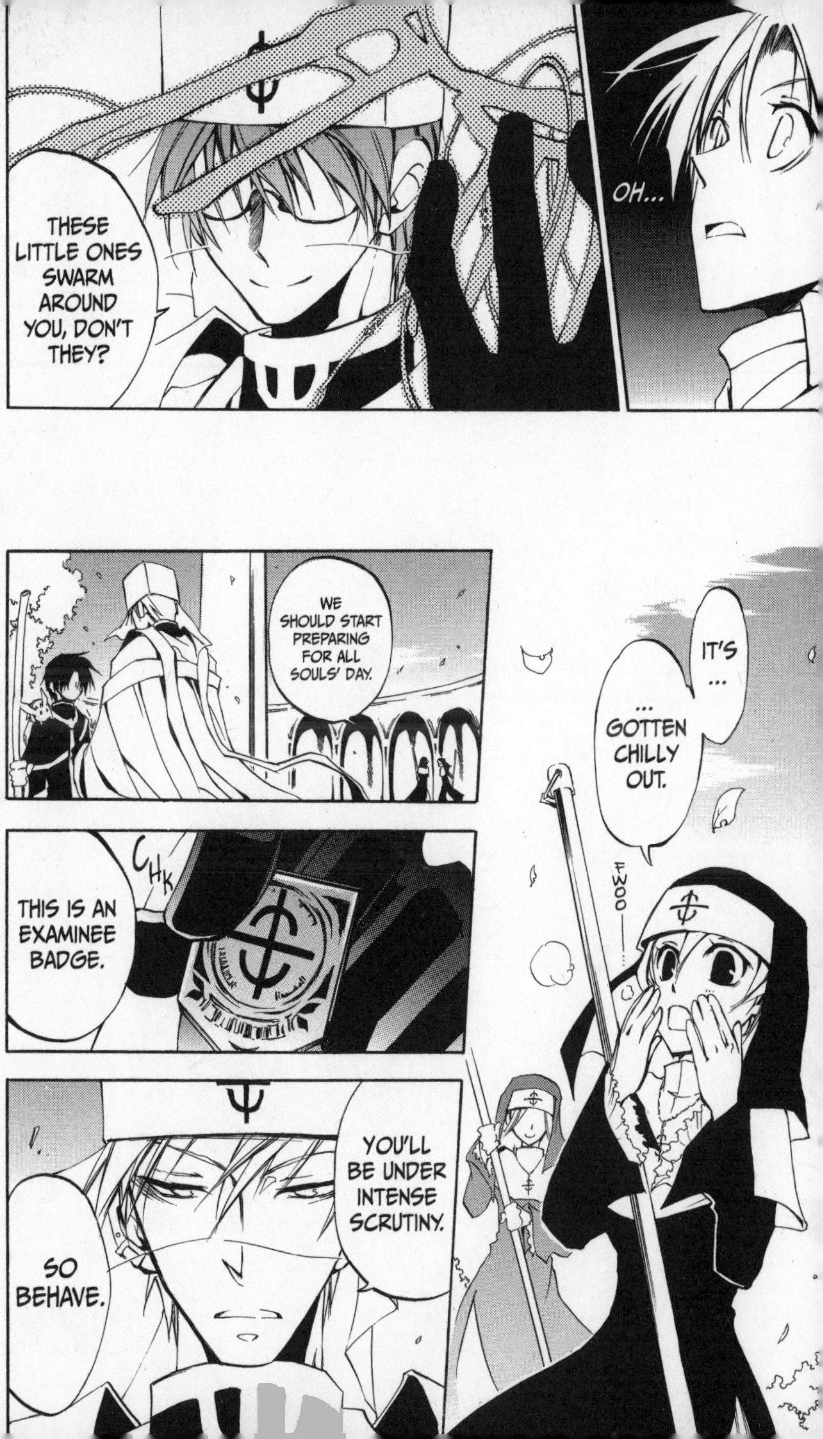
OH...
THESE LITTLE ONES SWARM AROUND YOU, DON'T THEY?
IT'S ...
... GOTTEN CHILLY OUT.
FWOO——
WE SHOULD START PREPARING FOR ALL SOULS' DAY.
CHK
THIS IS AN EXAMINEE BADGE.
YOU'LL BE UNDER INTENSE SCRUTINY.
SO BEHAVE.

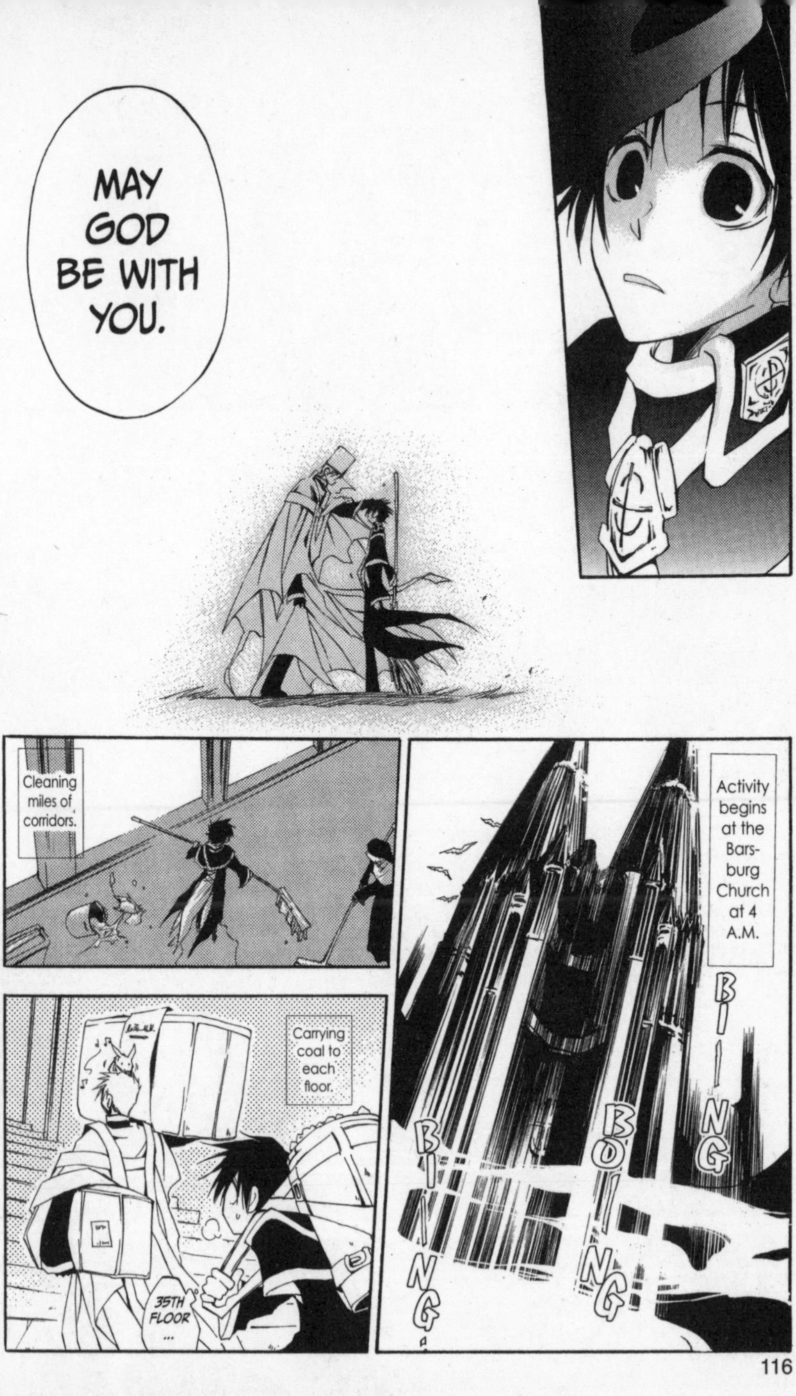
MAY GOD BE WITH YOU.
Activity begins at the Barsburg Church at 4 A.M.
BIING
BOING
BIING
Cleaning miles of corridors.
Carrying coal to each floor.
35TH FLOOR ...

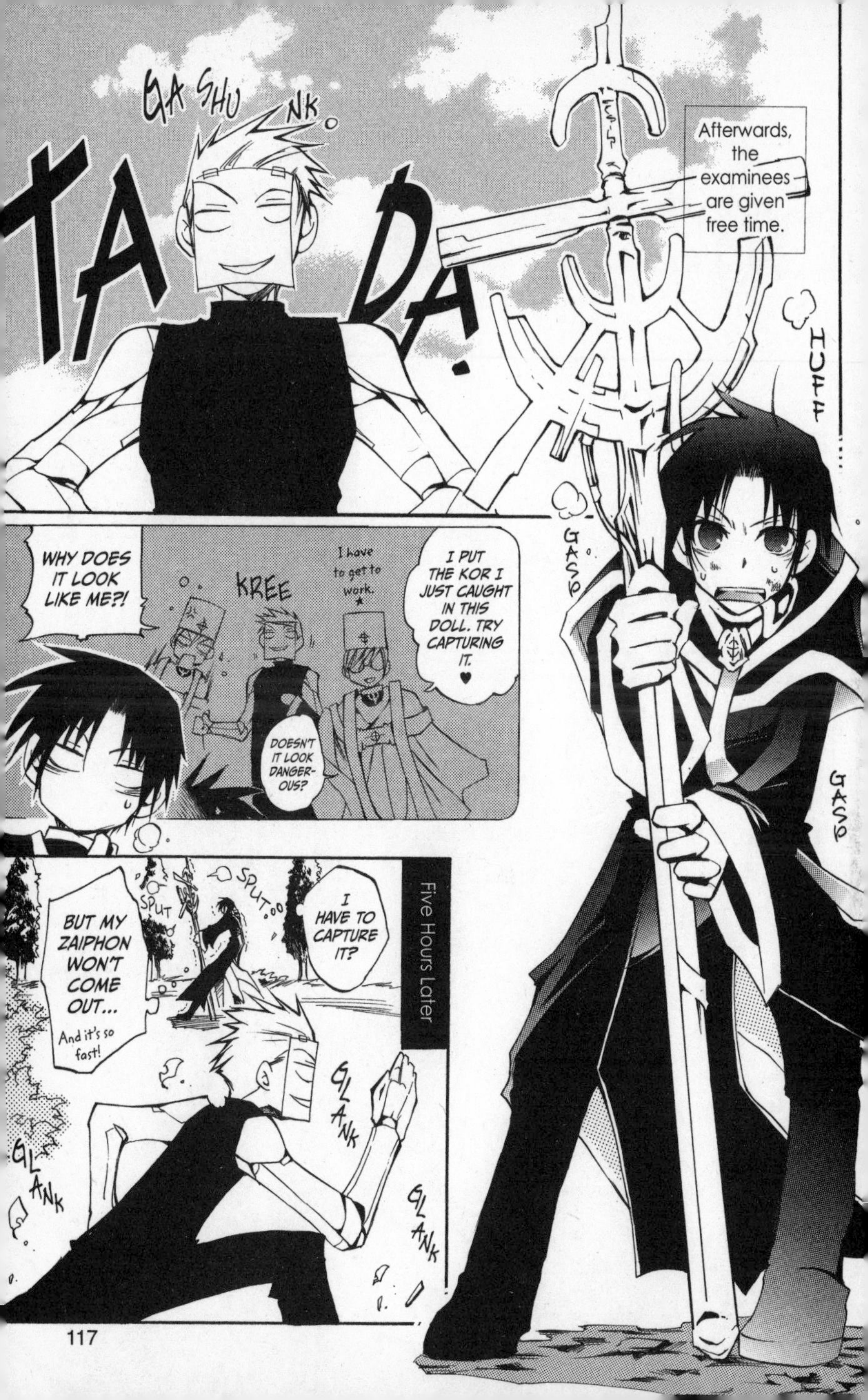

Afterwards, the examinees are given free time.
GASHUNK.
TA DA.
HUFF
GASP
GASP
I PUT THE KOR I JUST CAUGHT IN THIS DOLL. TRY CAPTURING IT. ♥
I have to get to work. ★
KREE
WHY DOES IT LOOK LIKE ME?!
DOESN'T IT LOOK DANGEROUS?
Five Hours Later
I HAVE TO CAPTURE IT?
SPUT
SPUT
BUT MY ZAIPHON WON'T COME OUT...
And it's so fast!
GLANK
GLANK
GLANK

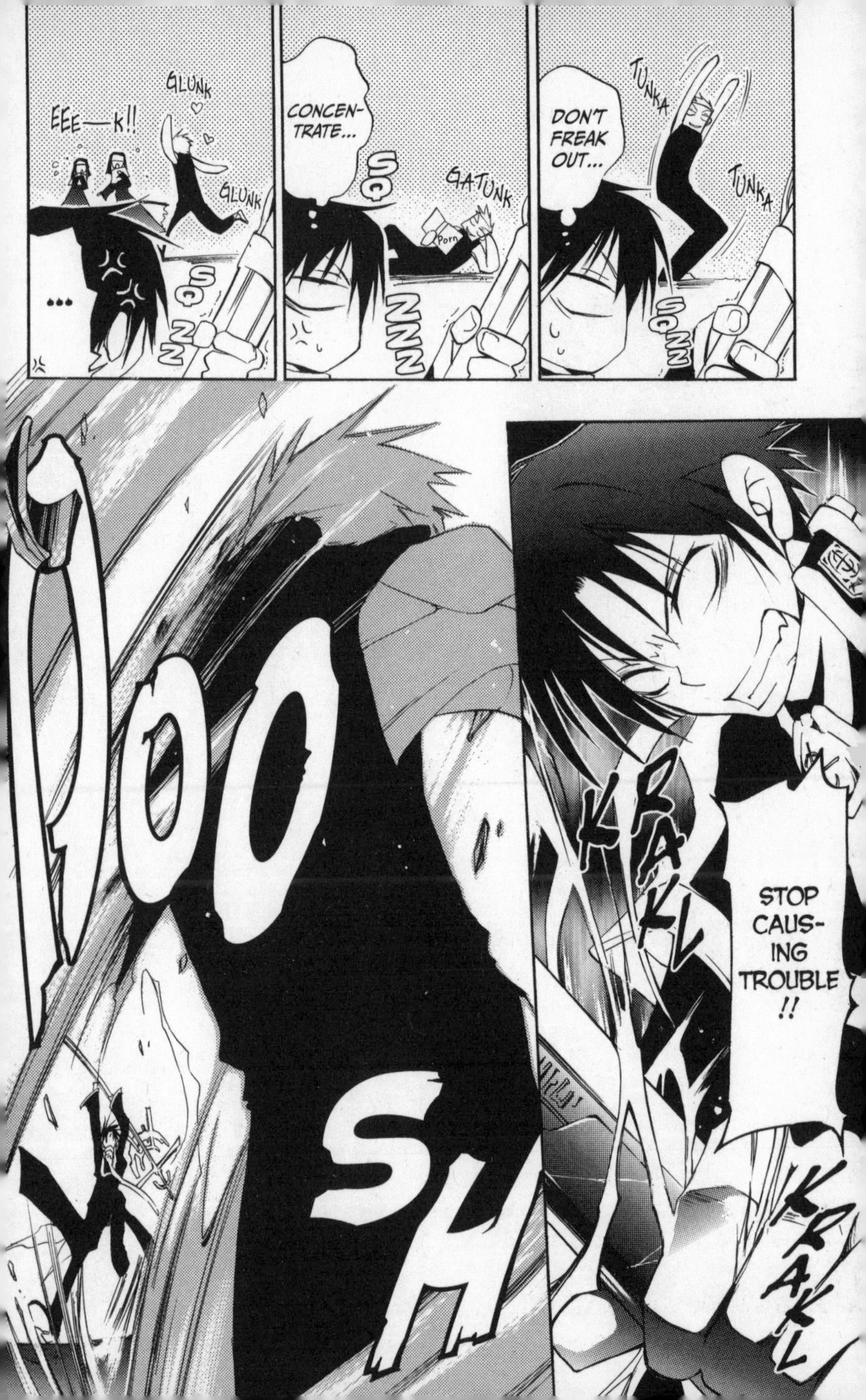
TUNKA
DON'T FREAK OUT...
TUNKA
SQZZ
CONCEN-TRATE...
SQ
GATUNK
Porn
ZZZ
GLUNK
EEE—K!!
GLUNK
SQZZ
...
KRAKL
STOP CAUS-ING TROUBLE!!
KRAKL
DOO
SH

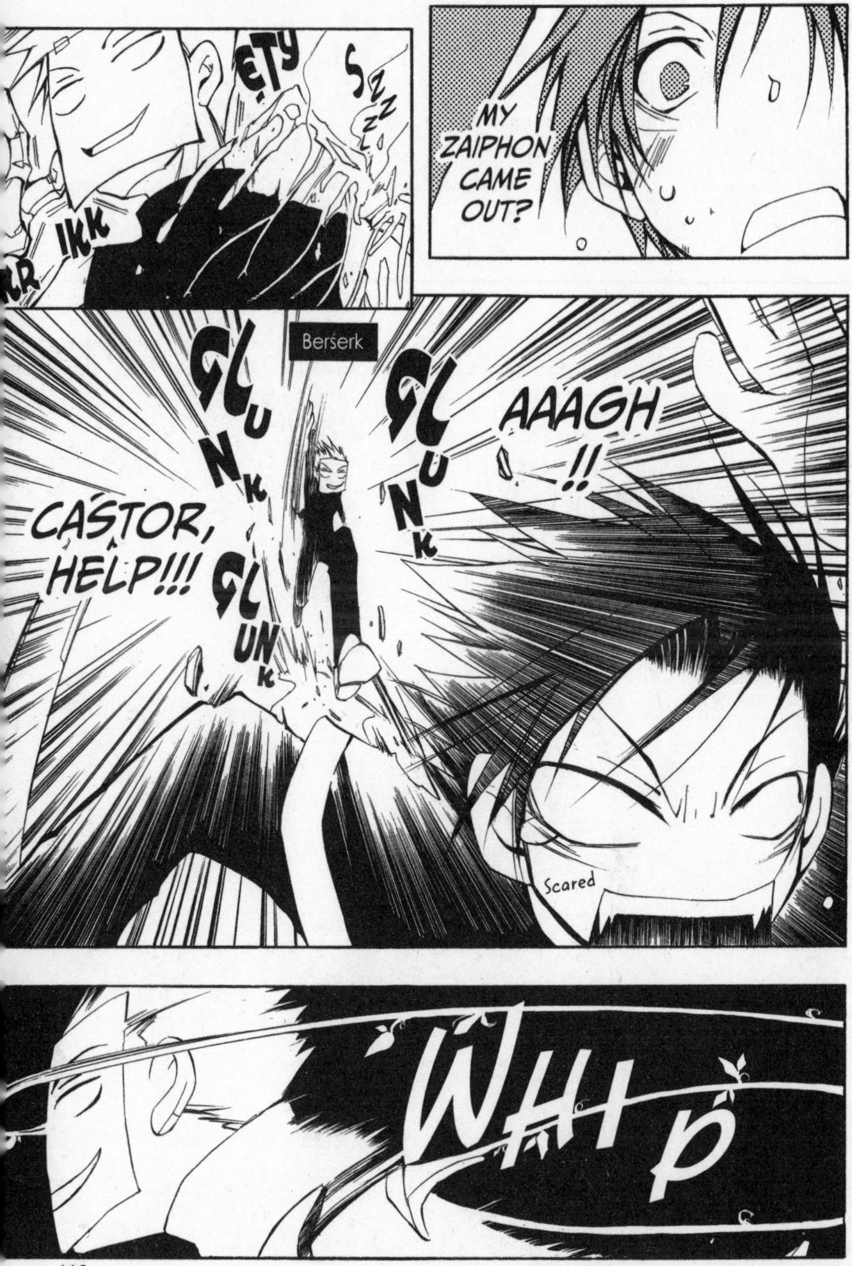
MY ZAIPHON CAME OUT?
ETY
SZZZL
IKK
AAAGH!!
GLUNK
Berserk
GLUNK
CASTOR, HELP!!!
GLUNK
Scared
WHIP

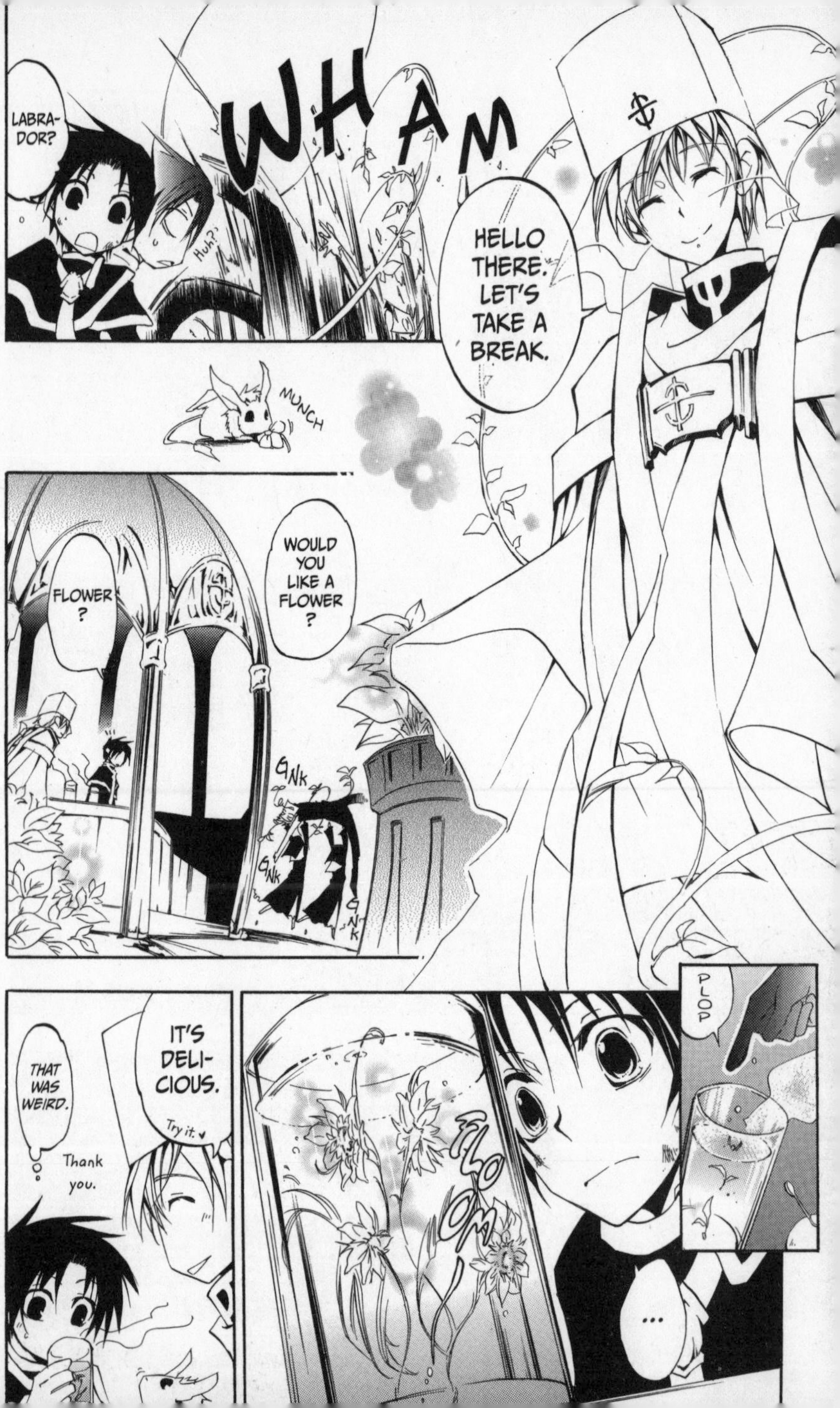

HELLO THERE. LET'S TAKE A BREAK.
WHAM
LABRA-DOR?
HUH?
MUNCH
WOULD YOU LIKE A FLOWER?
FLOWER?
GNK
GNK
GNK
PLOP
FLOOM
...
IT'S DELI-CIOUS.
Try it.
THAT WAS WEIRD.
Thank you.

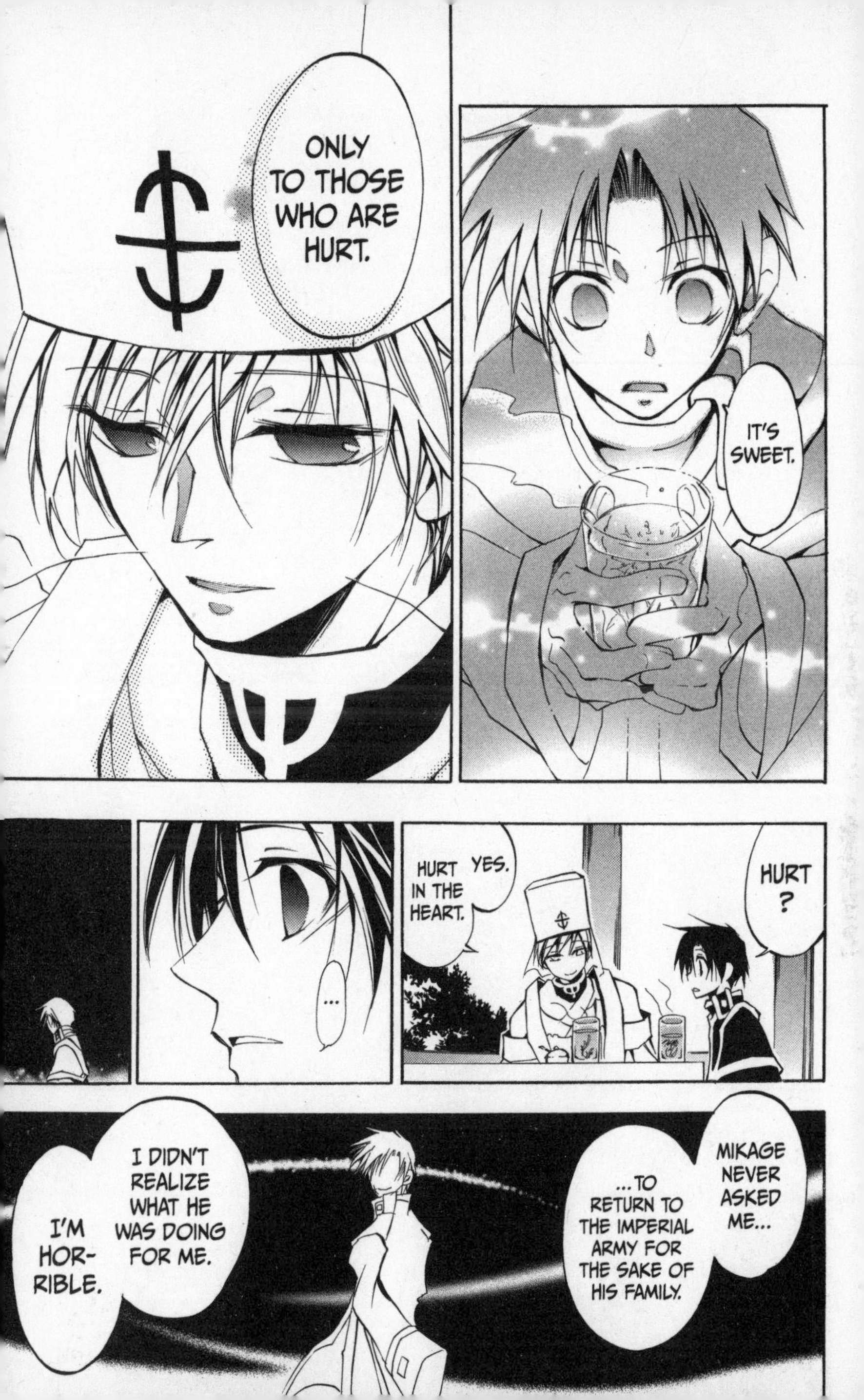
IT'S SWEET.
ONLY TO THOSE WHO ARE HURT.
HURT ?
YES.
HURT IN THE HEART.
...
MIKAGE NEVER ASKED ME...
...TO RETURN TO THE IMPERIAL ARMY FOR THE SAKE OF HIS FAMILY.
I DIDN'T REALIZE WHAT HE WAS DOING FOR ME.
I'M HOR-RIBLE.

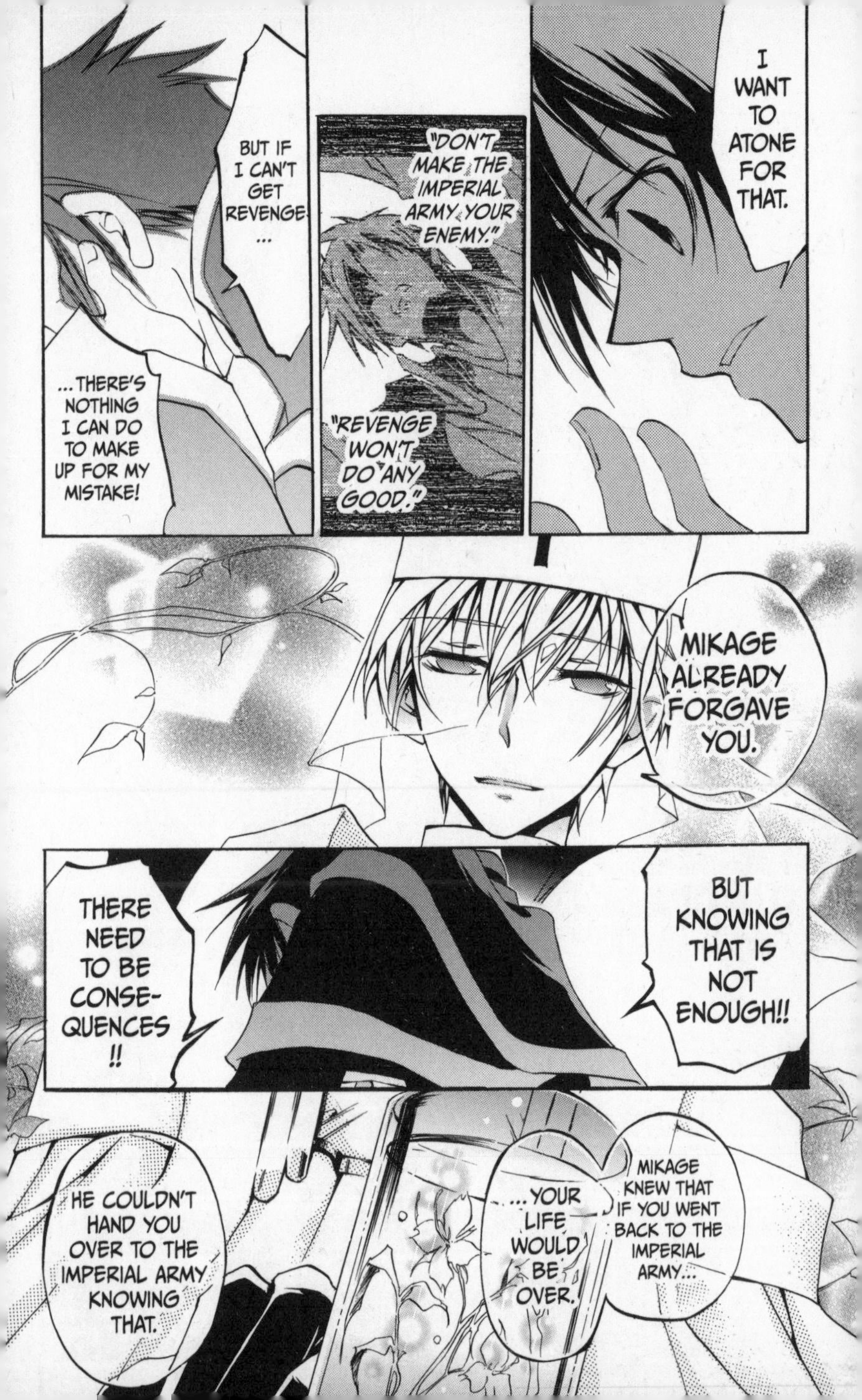
I WANT TO ATONE FOR THAT.
"DON'T MAKE THE IMPERIAL ARMY YOUR ENEMY."
"REVENGE WON'T DO ANY GOOD."
BUT IF I CAN'T GET REVENGE...
...THERE'S NOTHING I CAN DO TO MAKE UP FOR MY MISTAKE!
MIKAGE ALREADY FORGAVE YOU.
BUT KNOWING THAT IS NOT ENOUGH!!
THERE NEED TO BE CONSE-QUENCES!!
MIKAGE KNEW THAT IF YOU WENT BACK TO THE IMPERIAL ARMY...
...YOUR LIFE WOULD BE OVER.
HE COULDN'T HAND YOU OVER TO THE IMPERIAL ARMY KNOWING THAT.

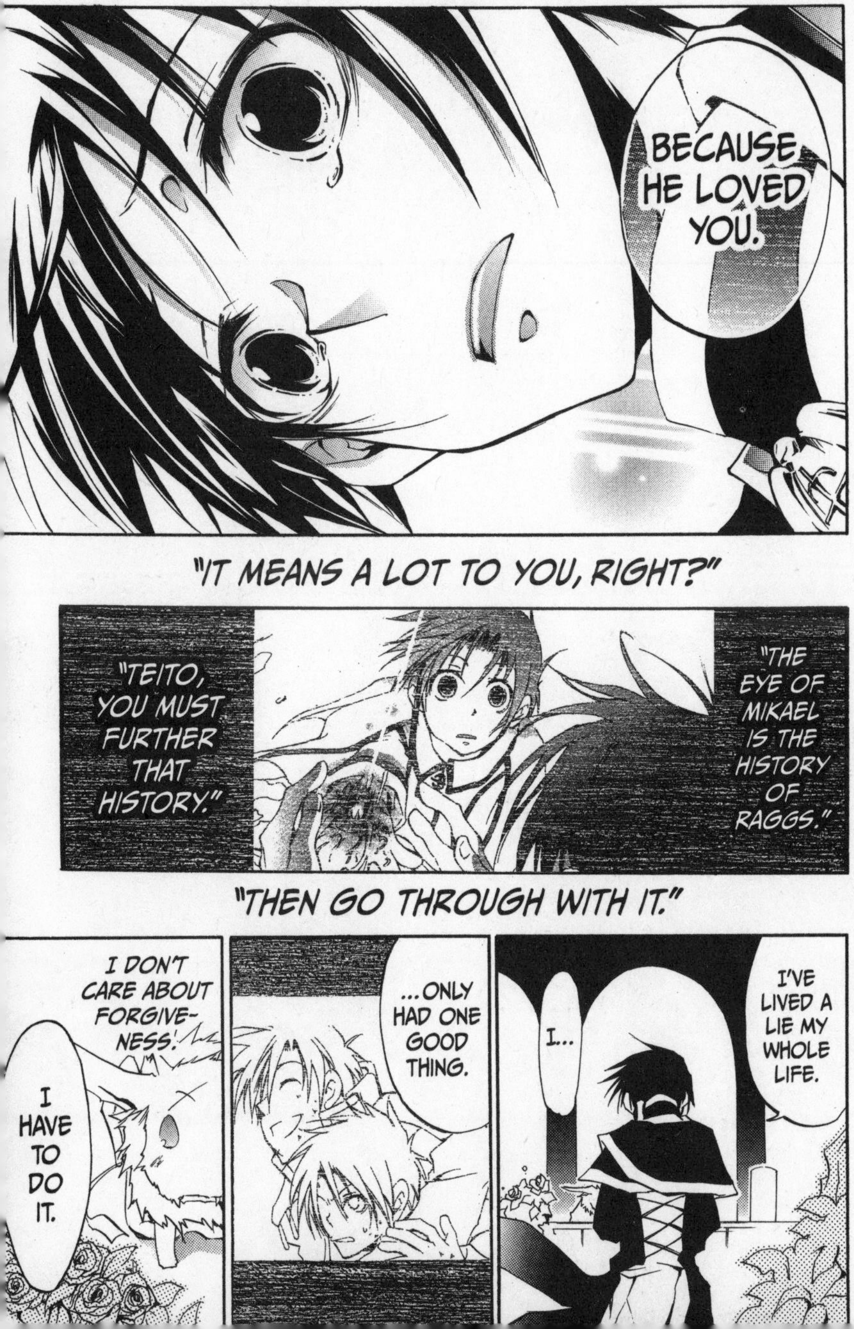
BECAUSE HE LOVED YOU.
"IT MEANS A LOT TO YOU, RIGHT?"
"THE EYE OF MIKAEL IS THE HISTORY OF RAGGS."
"TEITO, YOU MUST FURTHER THAT HISTORY."
"THEN GO THROUGH WITH IT."
I'VE LIVED A LIE MY WHOLE LIFE.
I...
...ONLY HAD ONE GOOD THING.
I DON'T CARE ABOUT FORGIVE-NESS!
I HAVE TO DO IT.

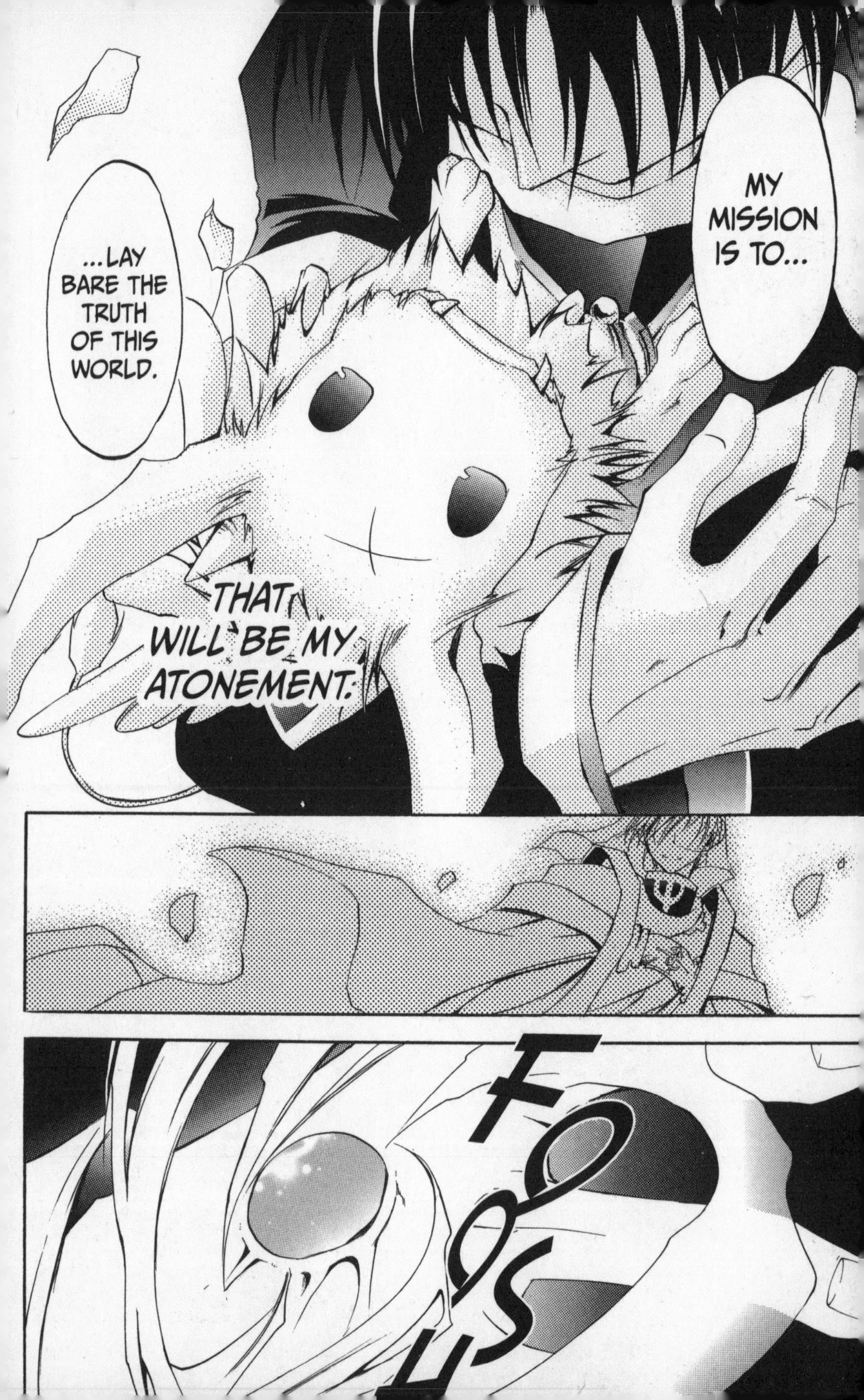
MY MISSION IS TO...
...LAY BARE THE TRUTH OF THIS WORLD.
THAT WILL BE MY ATONEMENT.
FOOSH

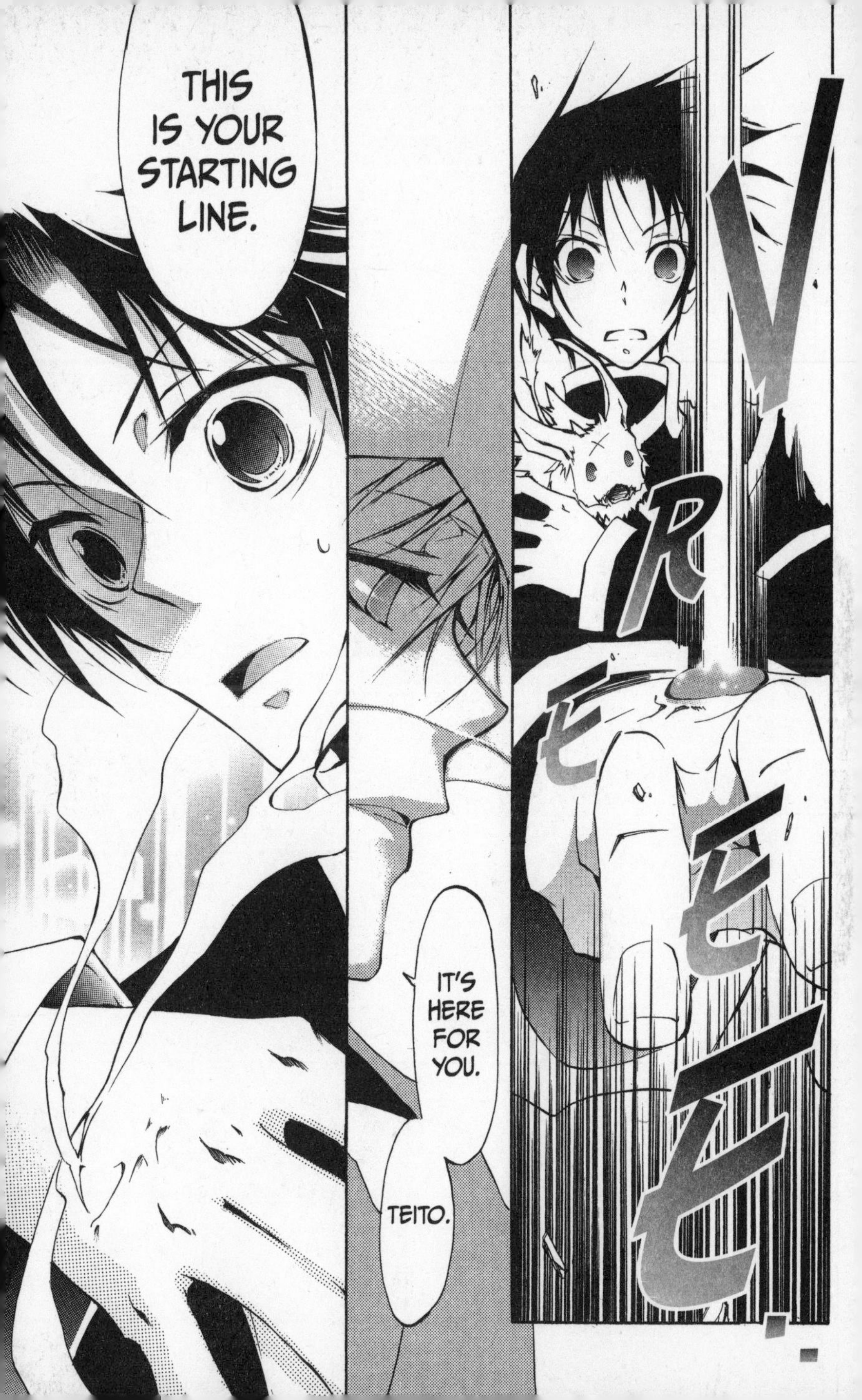
IT'S HERE FOR YOU.
TEITO.
THIS IS YOUR STARTING LINE.

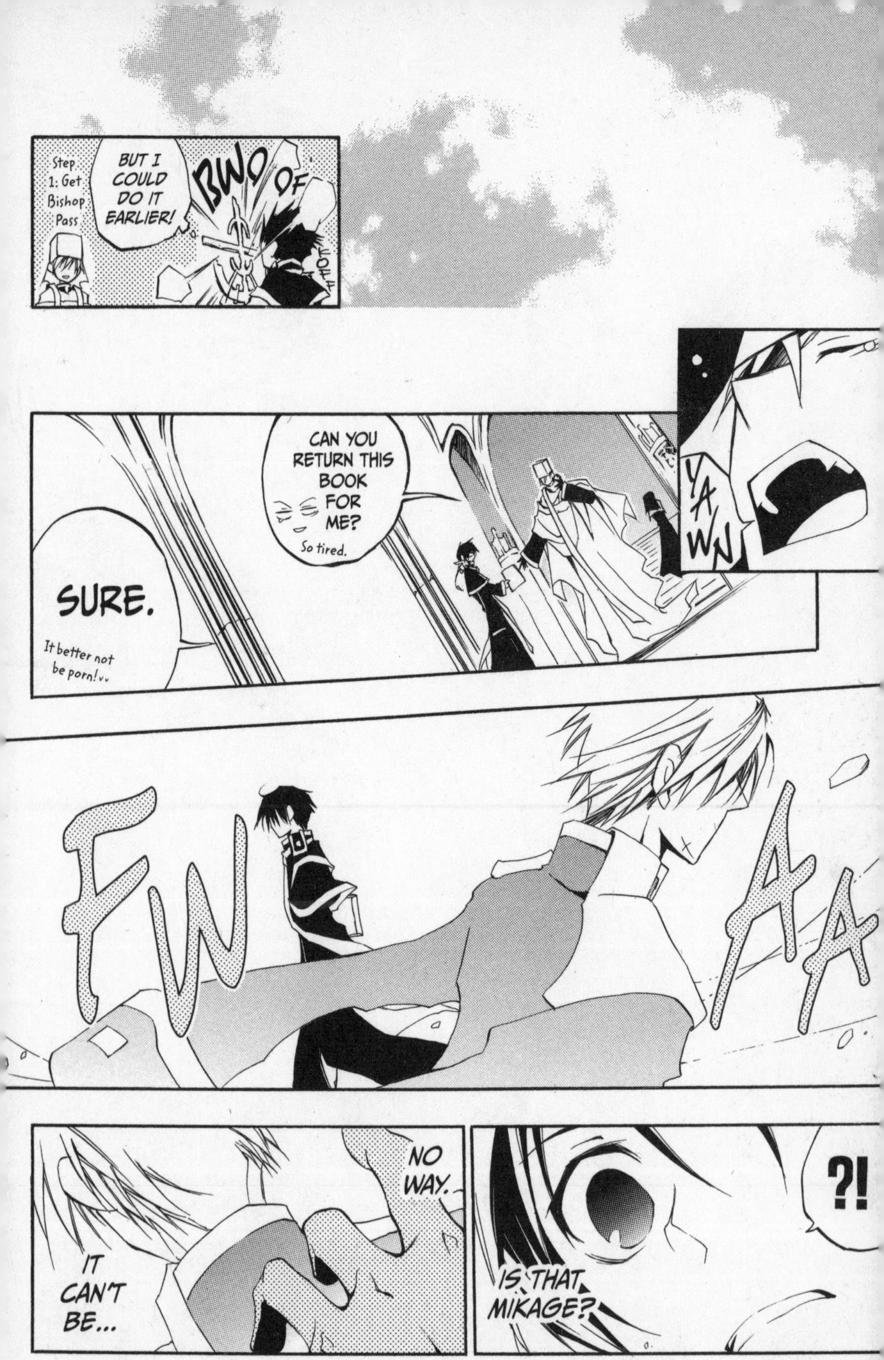
BWOOF
BUT I COULD DO IT EARLIER!
Step 1: Get Bishop Pass
YAWN
CAN YOU RETURN THIS BOOK FOR ME?
So tired.
SURE.
It better not be porn!
FWAA
?!
IS THAT MIKAGE?
NO WAY.
IT CAN'T BE...

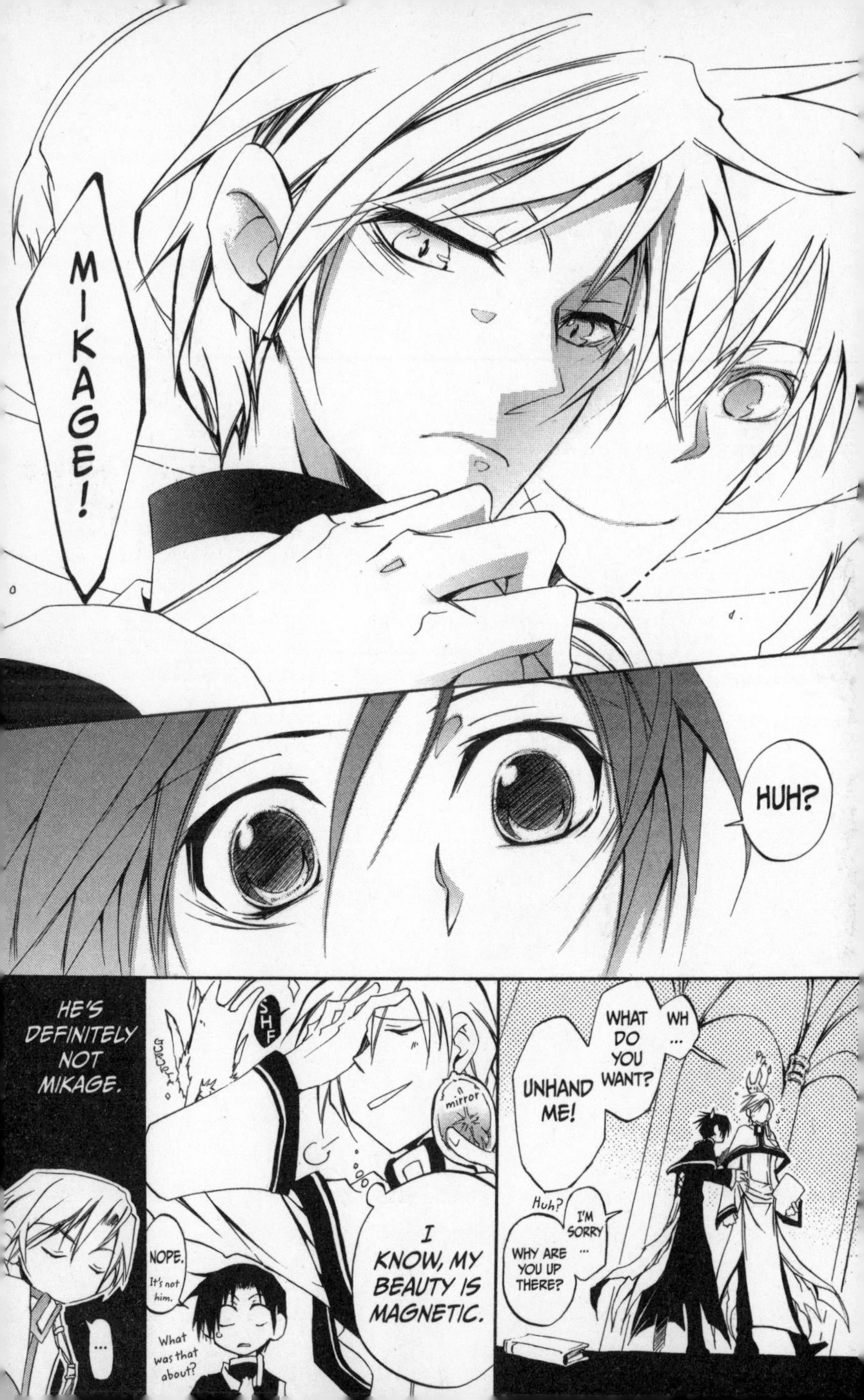
MIKAGE!
HUH?
WH ...
WHAT DO YOU WANT?
UNHAND ME!
I'M SORRY ...
Huh?
WHY ARE YOU UP THERE?
SHF
mirror
I KNOW, MY BEAUTY IS MAGNETIC.
HE'S DEFINITELY NOT MIKAGE.
NOPE.
It's not him.
...
What was that about?

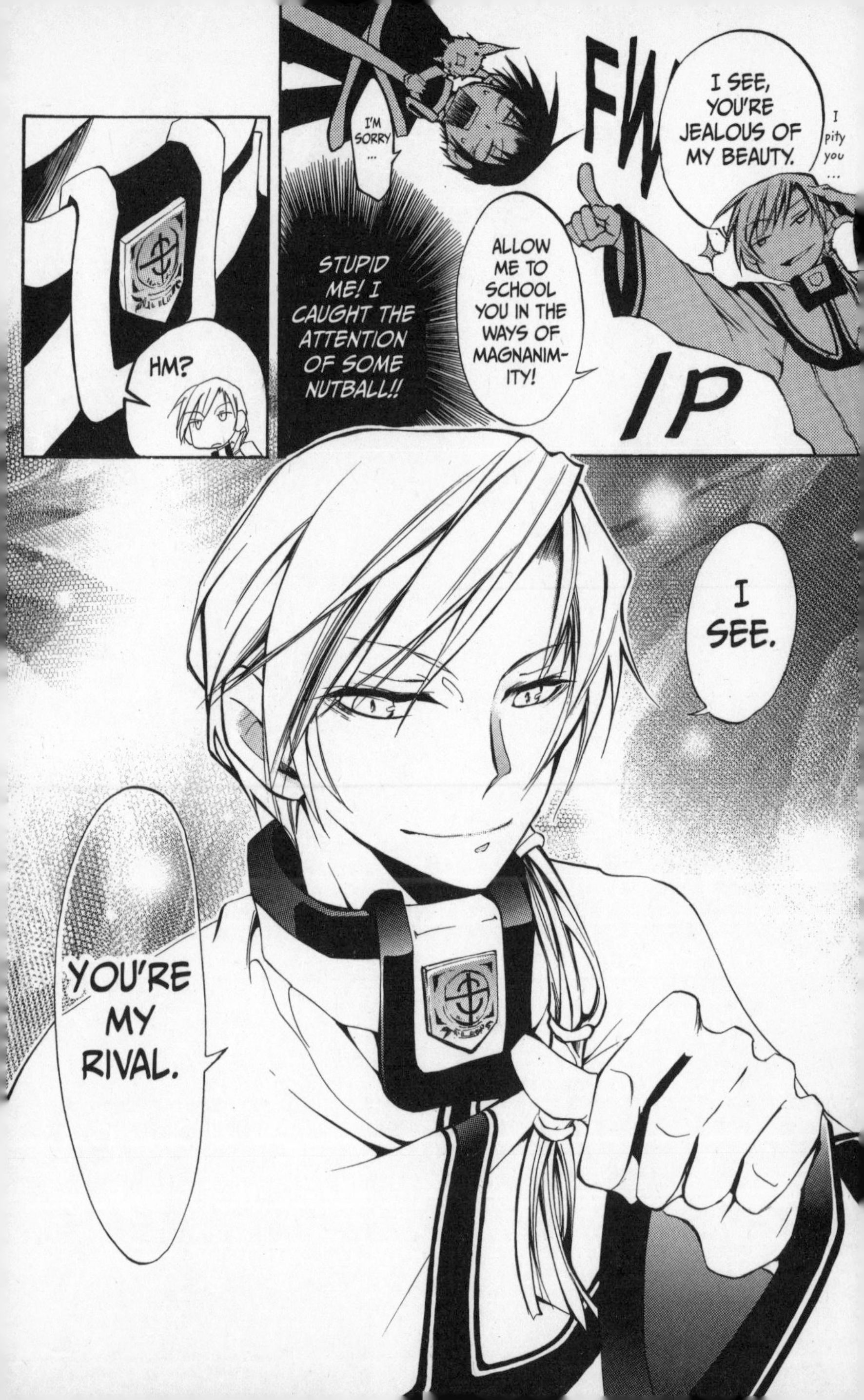
I SEE, YOU'RE JEALOUS OF MY BEAUTY.
I pity you...
FWIP
ALLOW ME TO SCHOOL YOU IN THE WAYS OF MAGNANIM-ITY!
I'M SORRY...
STUPID ME! I CAUGHT THE ATTENTION OF SOME NUTBALL!!
HM?
I SEE.
YOU'RE MY RIVAL.

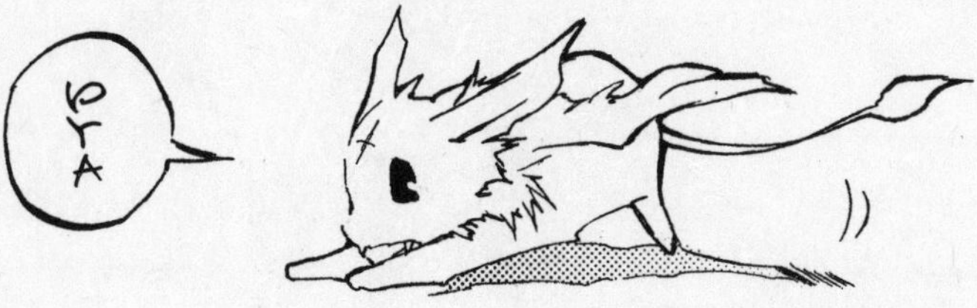
PYA

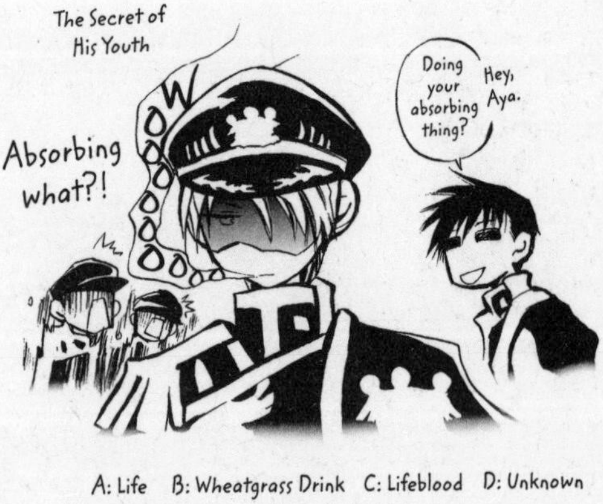
The Secret of His Youth
Hey, Aya.
Doing your absorbing thing?
Absorbing what?!
WOOOOOOOO

A: Life B: Wheatgrass Drink C: Lifeblood D: Unknown

Ayanami at age unknown

(always looks pale)

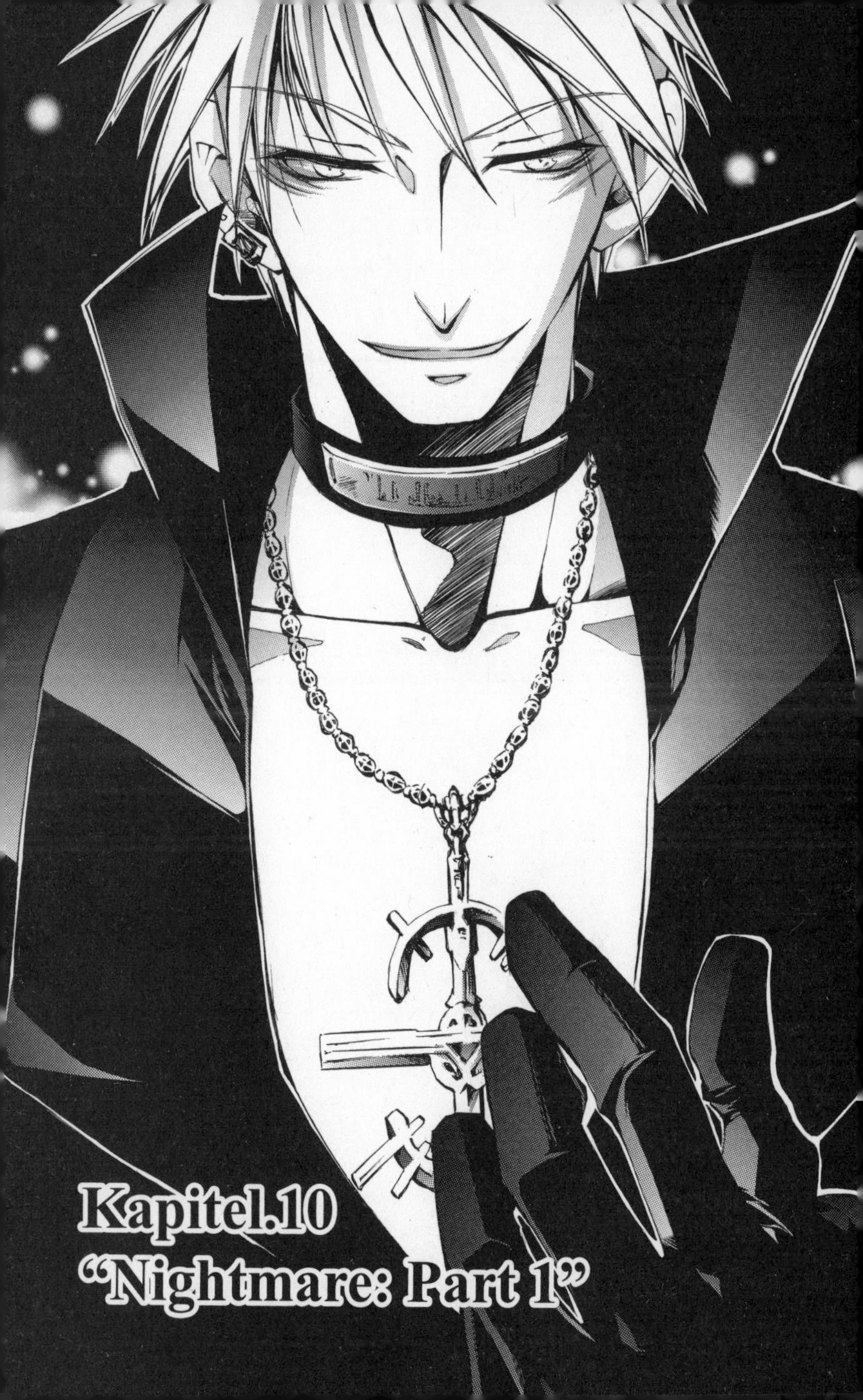
Kapitel.10
"Nightmare: Part 1"

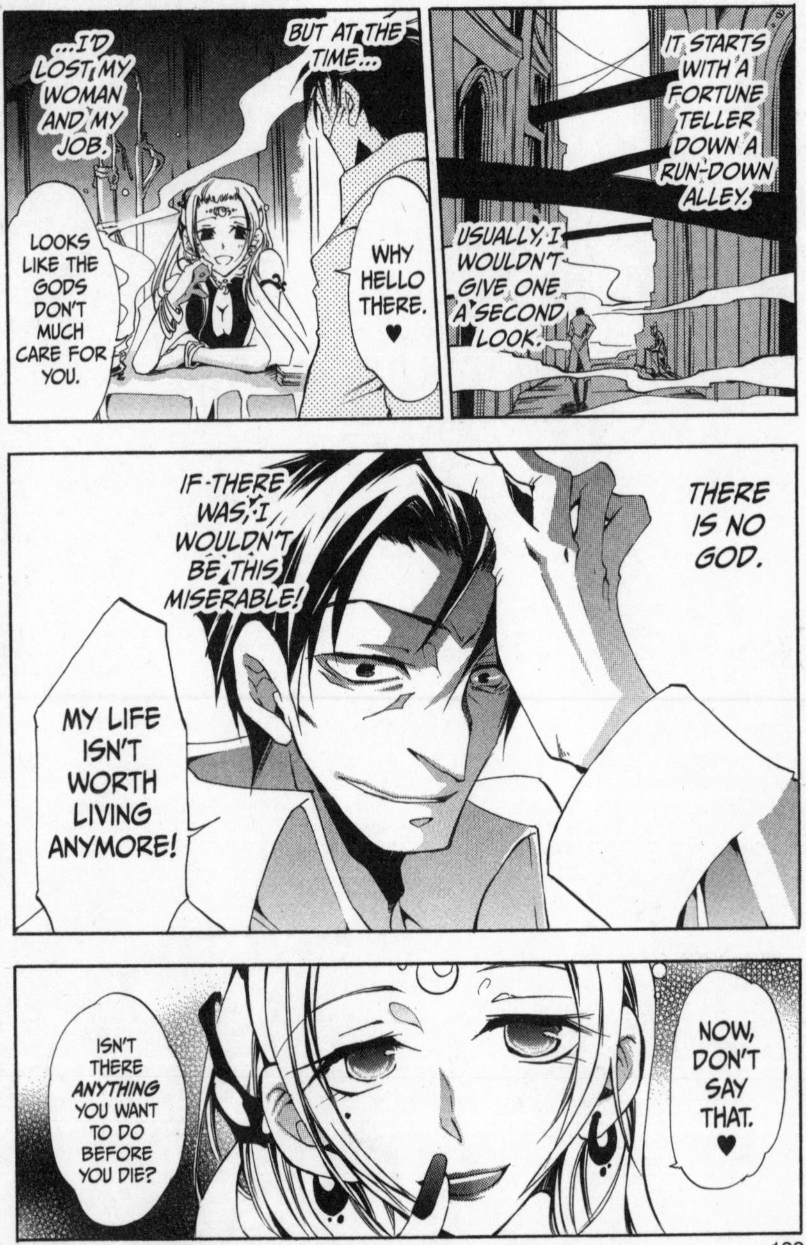
IT STARTS WITH A FORTUNE TELLER DOWN A RUN-DOWN ALLEY.
USUALLY, I WOULDN'T GIVE ONE A SECOND LOOK.
BUT AT THE TIME...
...I'D LOST MY WOMAN AND MY JOB.
WHY HELLO THERE. ♥
LOOKS LIKE THE GODS DON'T MUCH CARE FOR YOU.
THERE IS NO GOD.
IF THERE WAS, I WOULDN'T BE THIS MISERABLE!
MY LIFE ISN'T WORTH LIVING ANYMORE!
NOW, DON'T SAY THAT. ♥
ISN'T THERE *ANYTHING* YOU WANT TO DO BEFORE YOU DIE?

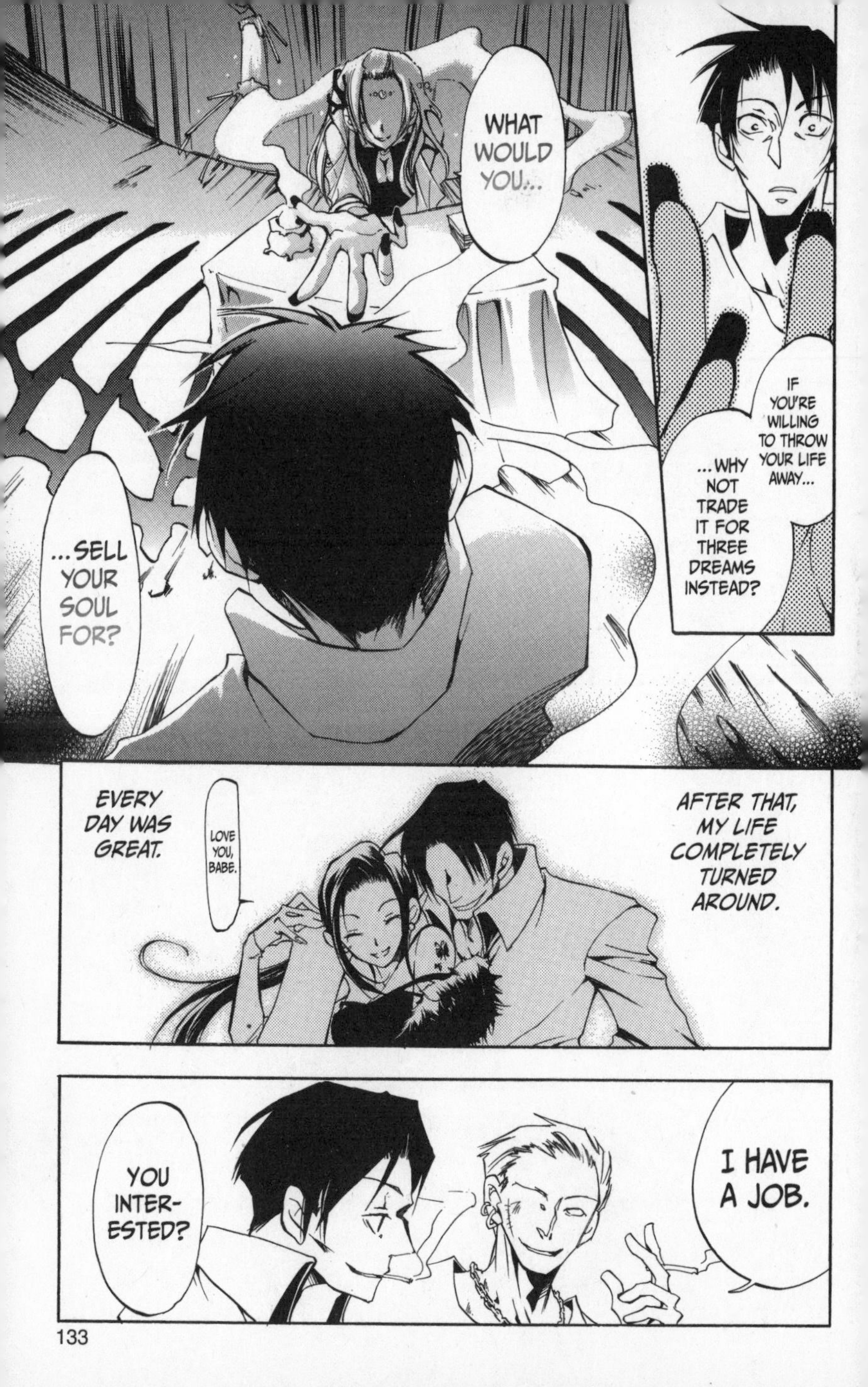
IF YOU'RE WILLING TO THROW YOUR LIFE AWAY...
...WHY NOT TRADE IT FOR THREE DREAMS INSTEAD?
WHAT WOULD YOU...
...SELL YOUR SOUL FOR?
AFTER THAT, MY LIFE COMPLETELY TURNED AROUND.
LOVE YOU, BABE.
EVERY DAY WAS GREAT.
I HAVE A JOB.
YOU INTER-ESTED?

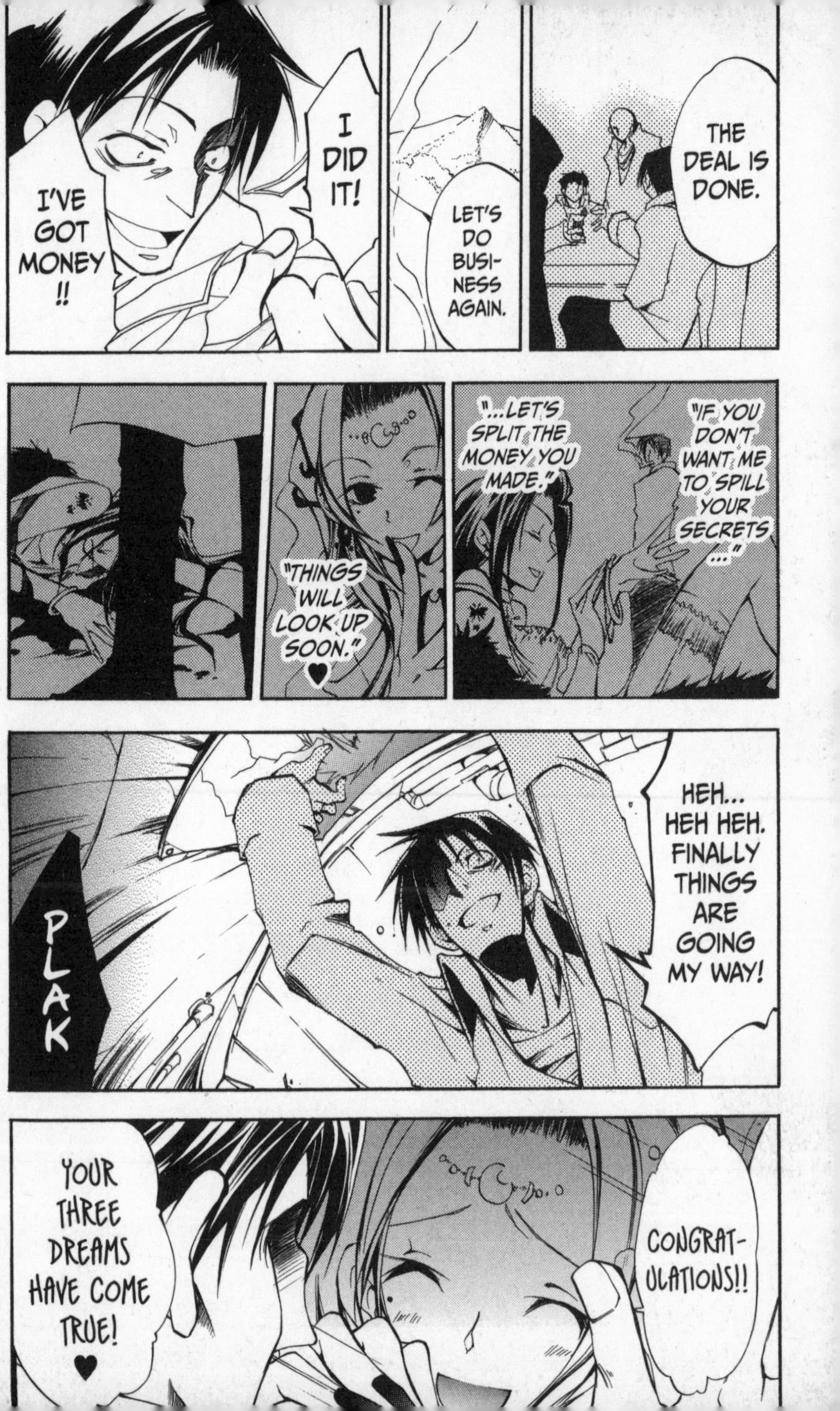
THE DEAL IS DONE.
LET'S DO BUSI-NESS AGAIN.
I DID IT!
I'VE GOT MONEY!!
"IF YOU DON'T WANT ME TO SPILL YOUR SECRETS..."
"...LET'S SPLIT THE MONEY YOU MADE."
"THINGS WILL LOOK UP SOON." ♥
HEH... HEH HEH. FINALLY THINGS ARE GOING MY WAY!
PLAK
CONGRAT-ULATIONS!!
YOUR THREE DREAMS HAVE COME TRUE! ♥

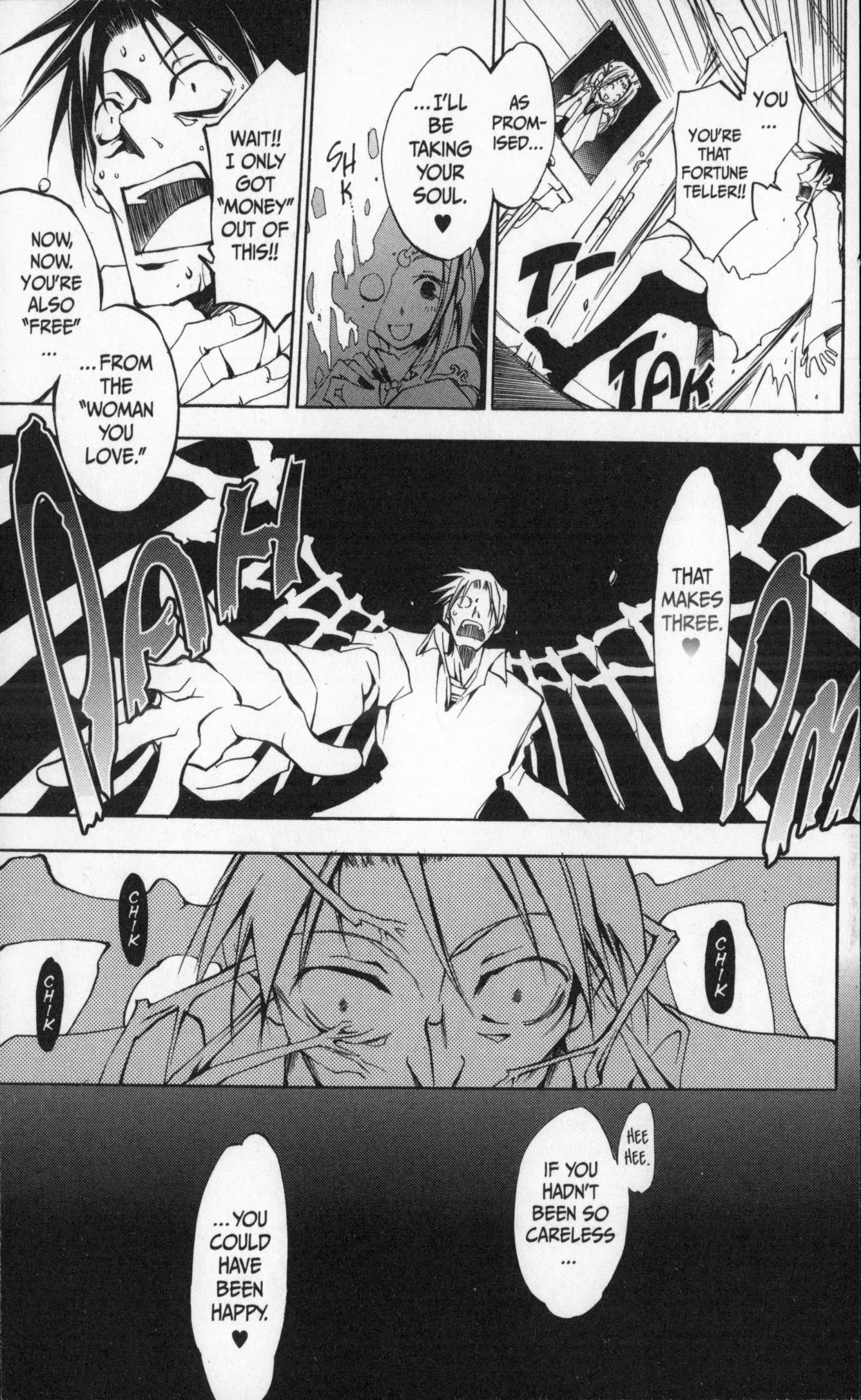
YOU ...
YOU'RE THAT FORTUNE TELLER!!
T-
TAK
AS PROMISED...
...I'LL BE TAKING YOUR SOUL. ♥
SHK
WAIT!! I ONLY GOT "MONEY" OUT OF THIS!!
NOW, NOW. YOU'RE ALSO "FREE" ...
...FROM THE "WOMAN YOU LOVE."
THAT MAKES THREE. ♥
CHIK
CHIK
CHIK
HEE HEE.
IF YOU HADN'T BEEN SO CARELESS ...
...YOU COULD HAVE BEEN HAPPY. ♥

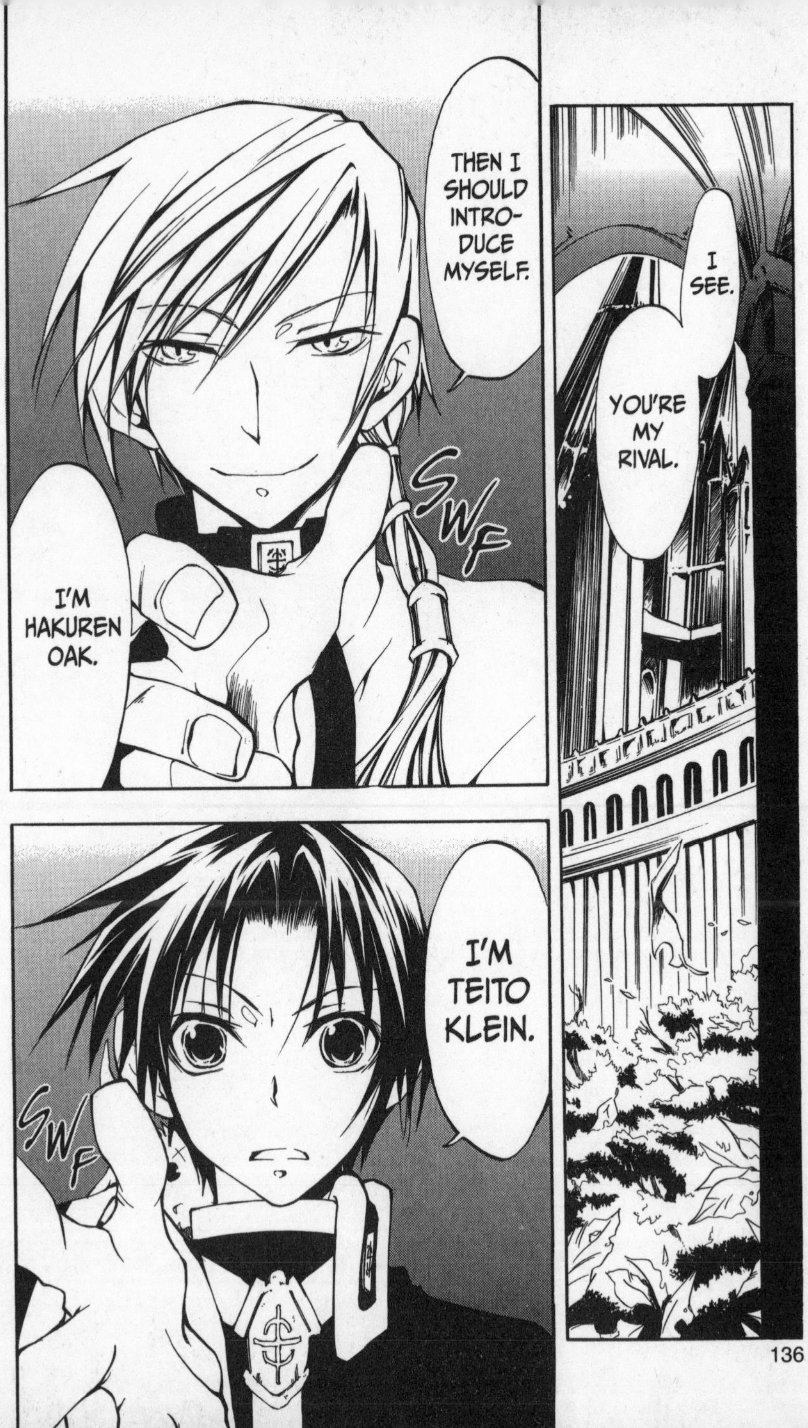
I SEE.
YOU'RE MY RIVAL.
THEN I SHOULD INTRO-DUCE MYSELF.
SWF
I'M HAKUREN OAK.
I'M TEITO KLEIN.
SWF

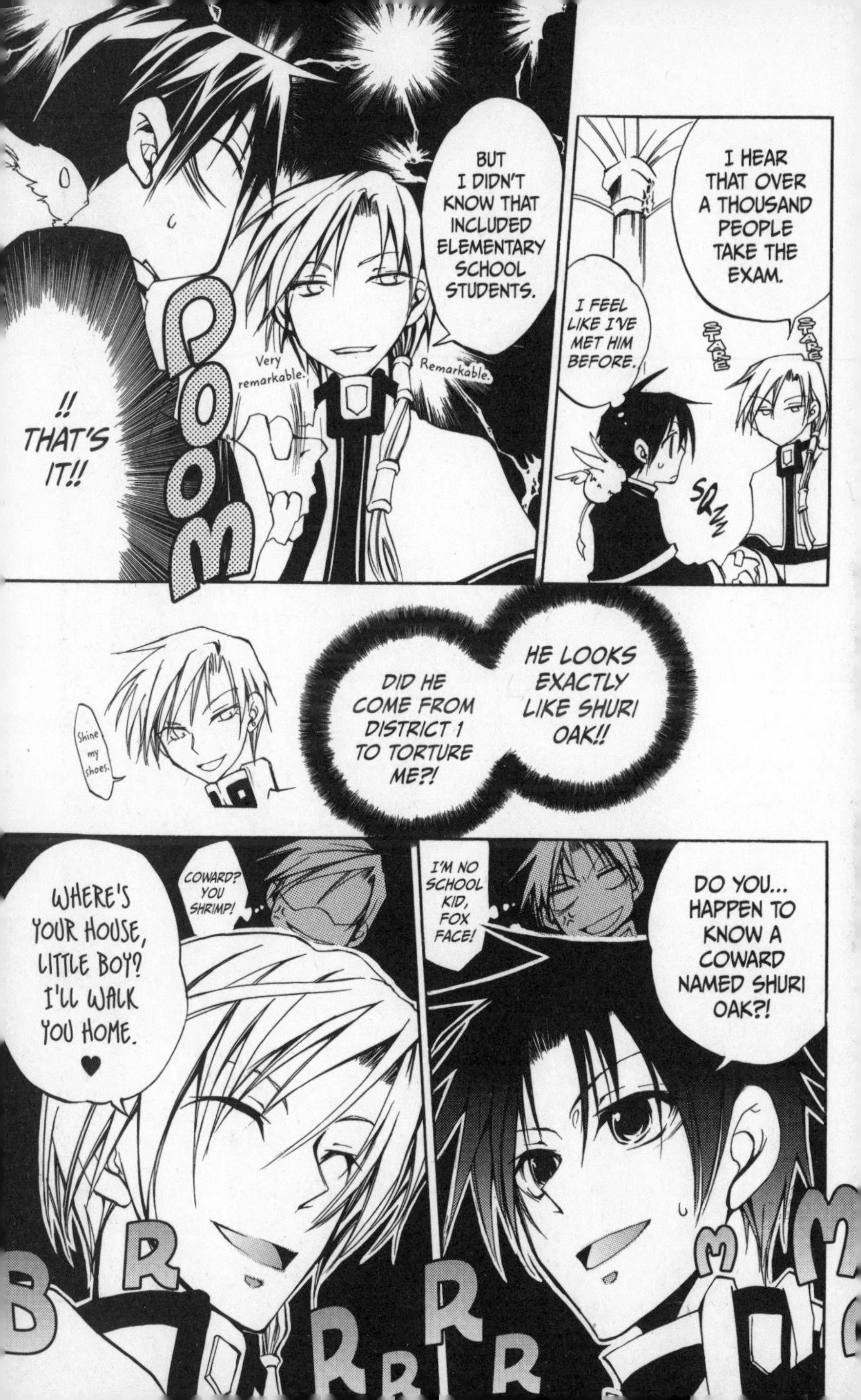
I HEAR THAT OVER A THOUSAND PEOPLE TAKE THE EXAM.
STARE
STARE
I FEEL LIKE I'VE MET HIM BEFORE.
SQZZ
BUT I DIDN'T KNOW THAT INCLUDED ELEMENTARY SCHOOL STUDENTS.
Remarkable.
Very remarkable.
!! THAT'S IT!!
HE LOOKS EXACTLY LIKE SHURI OAK!!
DID HE COME FROM DISTRICT 1 TO TORTURE ME?!
Shine my shoes.
DO YOU... HAPPEN TO KNOW A COWARD NAMED SHURI OAK?!
I'M NO SCHOOL KID, FOX FACE!
COWARD? YOU SHRIMP!
WHERE'S YOUR HOUSE, LITTLE BOY? I'LL WALK YOU HOME. ♥

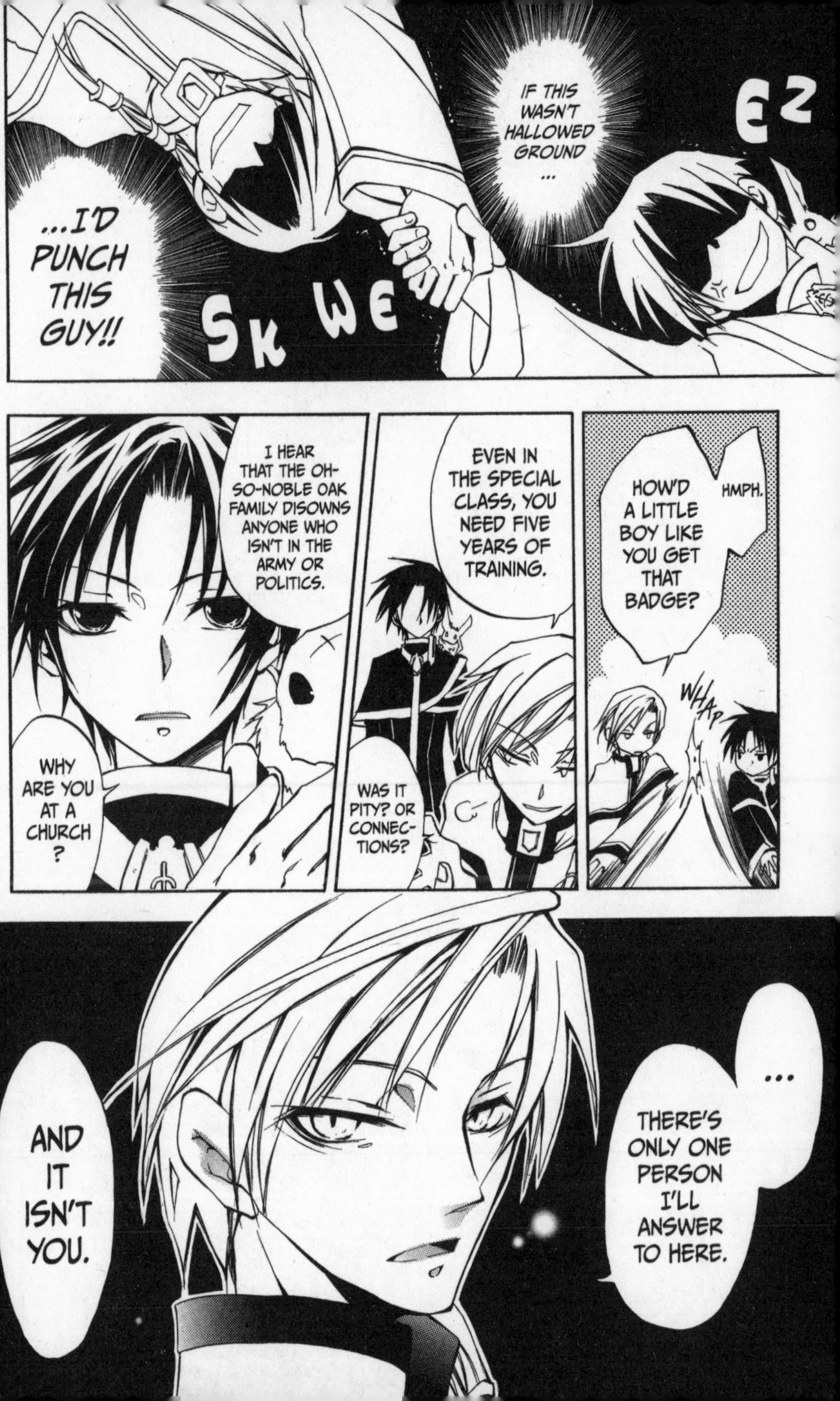
IF THIS WASN'T HALLOWED GROUND ...
...I'D PUNCH THIS GUY!!
HMPH.
HOW'D A LITTLE BOY LIKE YOU GET THAT BADGE?
WHAP
EVEN IN THE SPECIAL CLASS, YOU NEED FIVE YEARS OF TRAINING.
WAS IT PITY? OR CONNECTIONS?
I HEAR THAT THE OH-SO-NOBLE OAK FAMILY DISOWNS ANYONE WHO ISN'T IN THE ARMY OR POLITICS.
WHY ARE YOU AT A CHURCH?
...
THERE'S ONLY ONE PERSON I'LL ANSWER TO HERE.
AND IT ISN'T YOU.

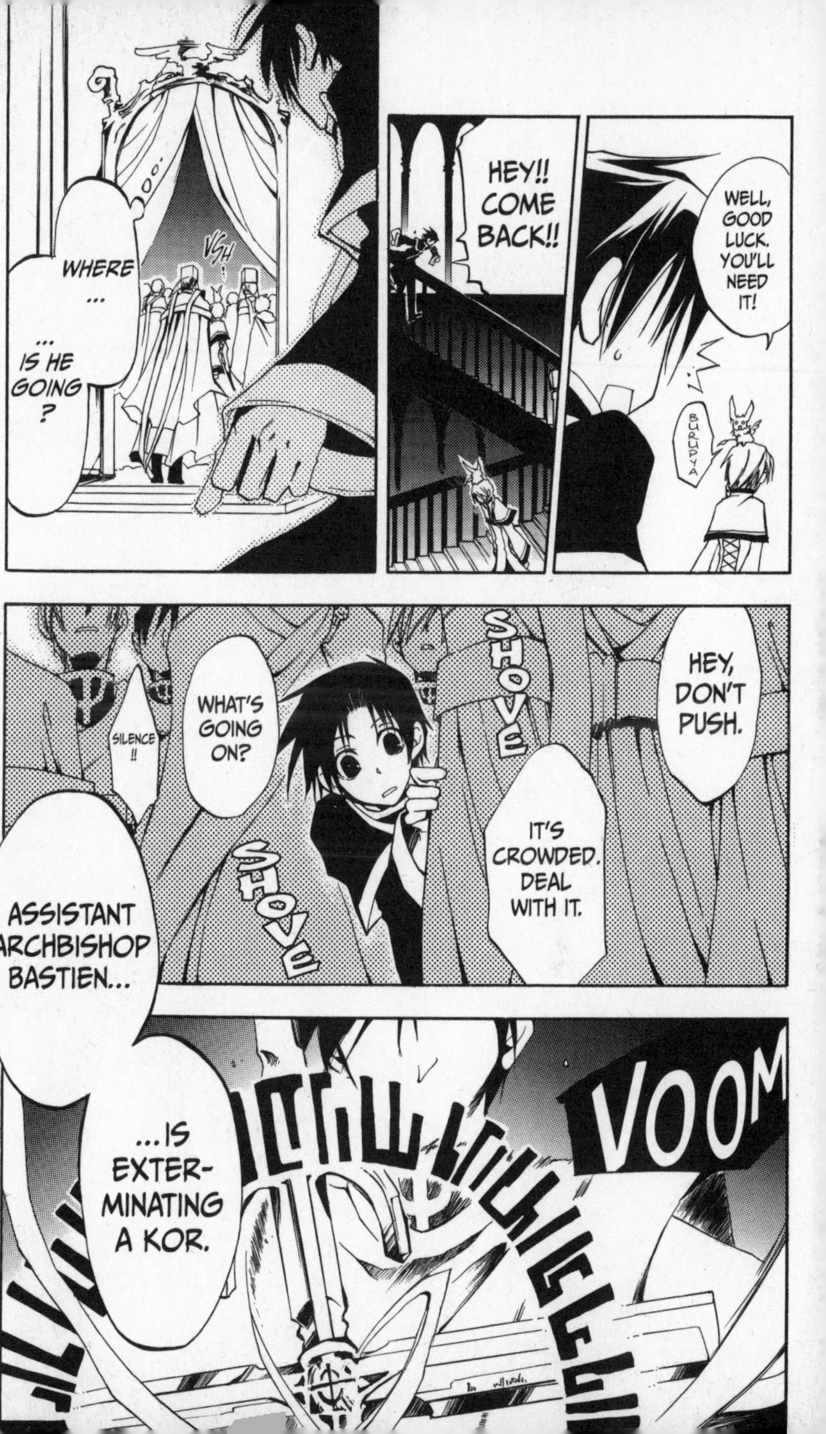
WELL, GOOD LUCK. YOU'LL NEED IT!
BURUPYA
HEY!! COME BACK!!
VSH
WHERE...
...IS HE GOING?
HEY, DON'T PUSH.
SHOVE
IT'S CROWDED. DEAL WITH IT.
WHAT'S GOING ON?
SILENCE!!
SHOVE
ASSISTANT ARCHBISHOP BASTIEN...
VOOM
...IS EXTERMINATING A KOR.

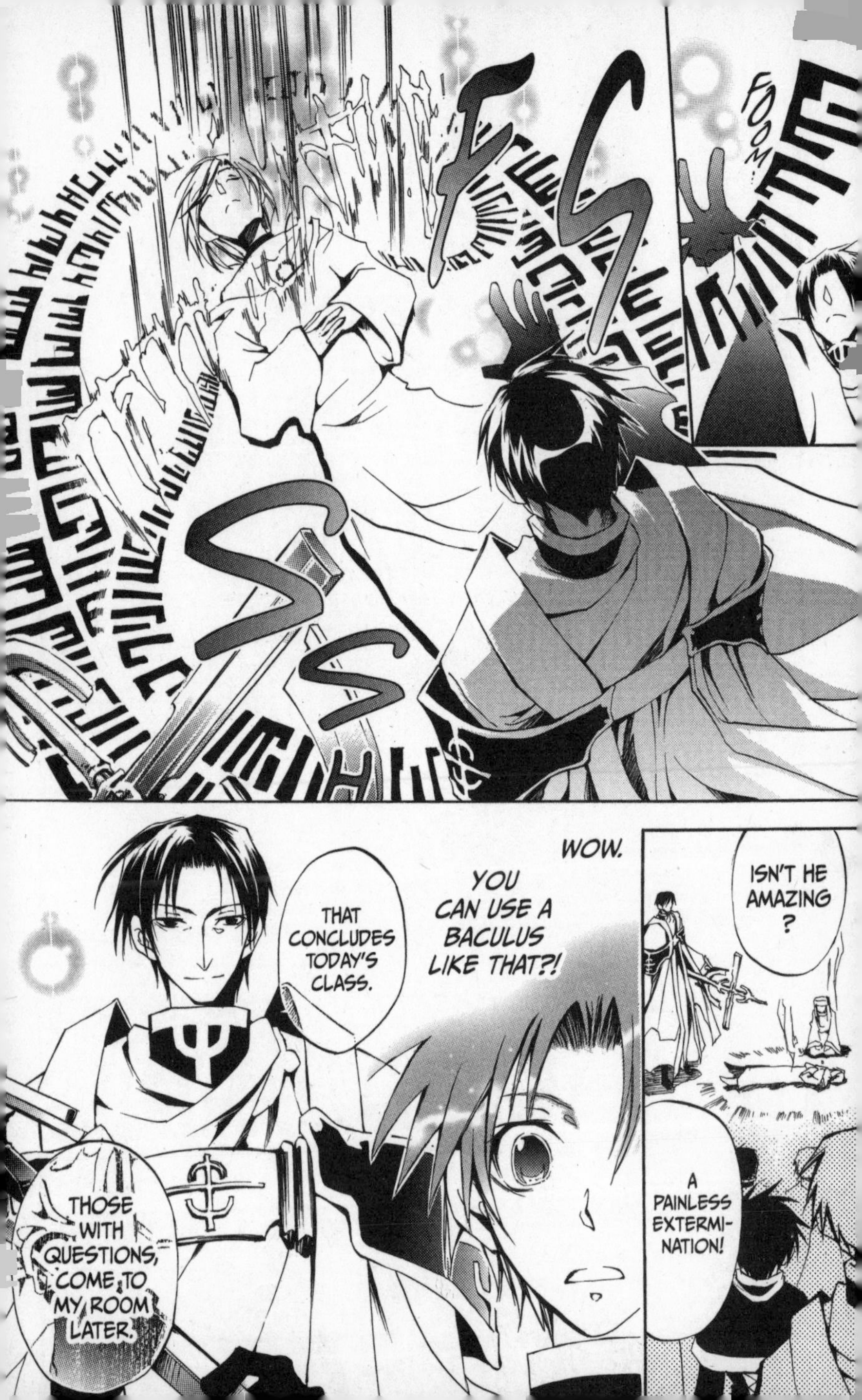
FOOM...
ISN'T HE AMAZING?
A PAINLESS EXTERMINATION!
WOW.
YOU CAN USE A BACULUS LIKE THAT?!
THAT CONCLUDES TODAY'S CLASS.
THOSE WITH QUESTIONS, COME TO MY ROOM LATER.

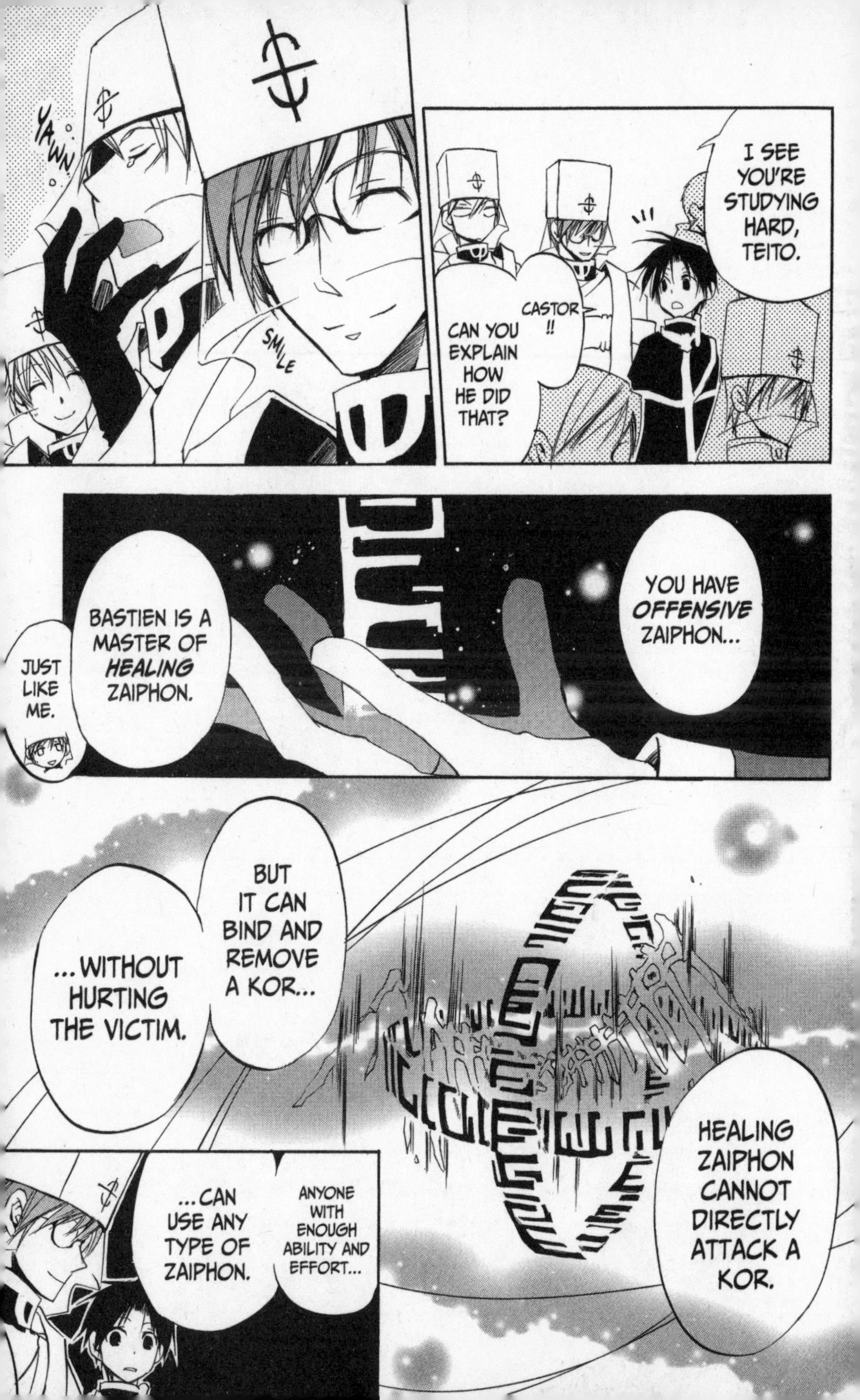
I SEE YOU'RE STUDYING HARD, TEITO.
CASTOR!!
CAN YOU EXPLAIN HOW HE DID THAT?
YAWN
SMILE
YOU HAVE *OFFENSIVE* ZAIPHON...
BASTIEN IS A MASTER OF *HEALING* ZAIPHON.
JUST LIKE ME.
HEALING ZAIPHON CANNOT DIRECTLY ATTACK A KOR.
BUT IT CAN BIND AND REMOVE A KOR...
...WITHOUT HURTING THE VICTIM.
ANYONE WITH ENOUGH ABILITY AND EFFORT...
...CAN USE ANY TYPE OF ZAIPHON.

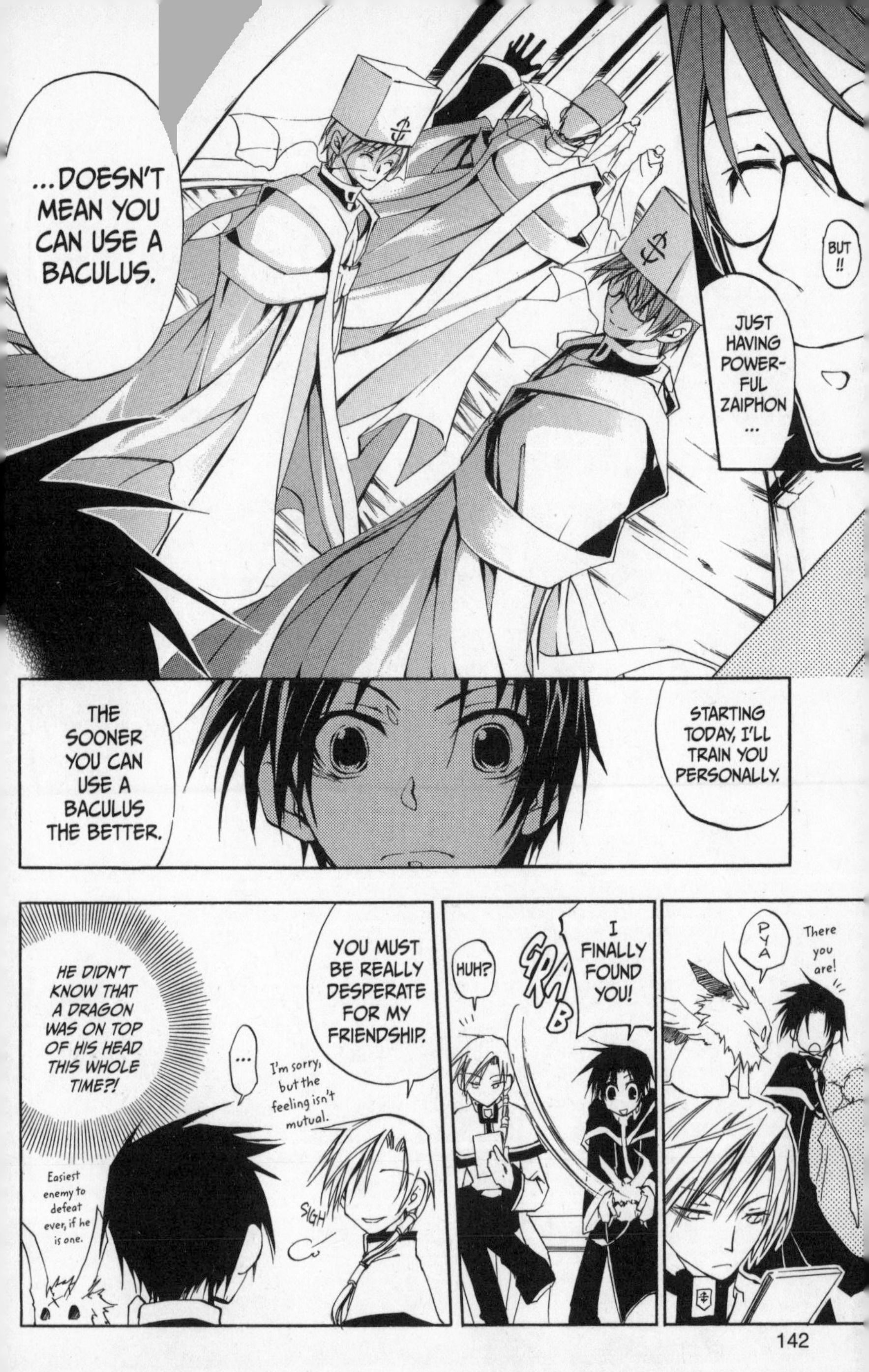
BUT !!
JUST HAVING POWER-FUL ZAIPHON ...
...DOESN'T MEAN YOU CAN USE A BACULUS.
STARTING TODAY, I'LL TRAIN YOU PERSONALLY.
THE SOONER YOU CAN USE A BACULUS THE BETTER.
PYA
There you are!
I FINALLY FOUND YOU!
GRAB
HUH?
YOU MUST BE REALLY DESPERATE FOR MY FRIENDSHIP.
I'm sorry, but the feeling isn't mutual.
SIGH
...
HE DIDN'T KNOW THAT A DRAGON WAS ON TOP OF HIS HEAD THIS WHOLE TIME?!
Easiest enemy to defeat ever, if he is one.

HUFF

HUFF

HUFF

GIVE...

I GAVE YOU YOUR MONEY.

NOW SCRAM.

You high or some-thing?

Ha ha ha.

OH, IT'S YOU.

KREE!

HM?

ZZHK

ZZHK

ZZHK

ZZHK

GIVE ME YOUR SOUL.

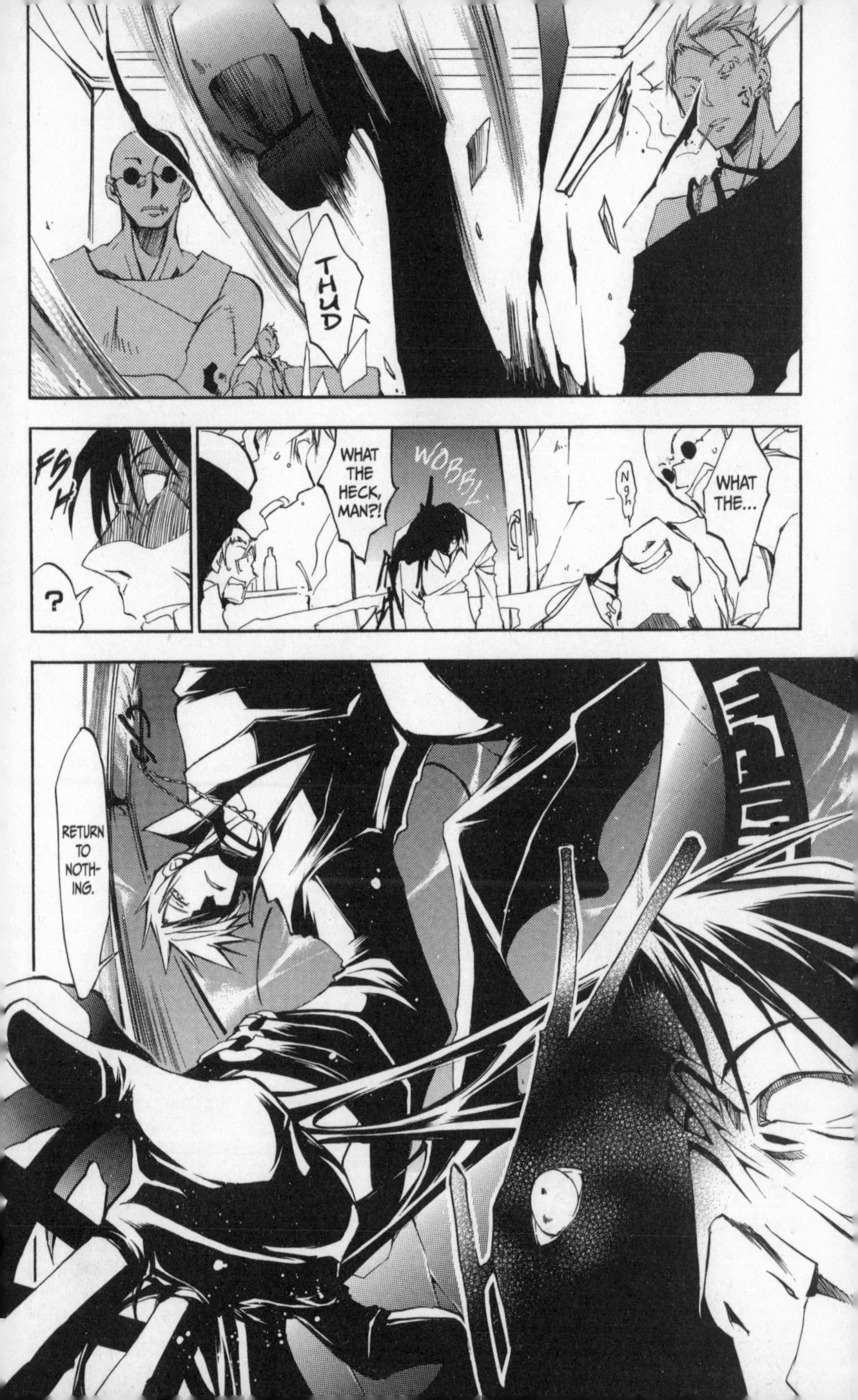
THUD
WHAT THE...
Ngh
WOBBLY
WHAT THE HECK, MAN?!
FSH
?
RETURN TO NOTHING.

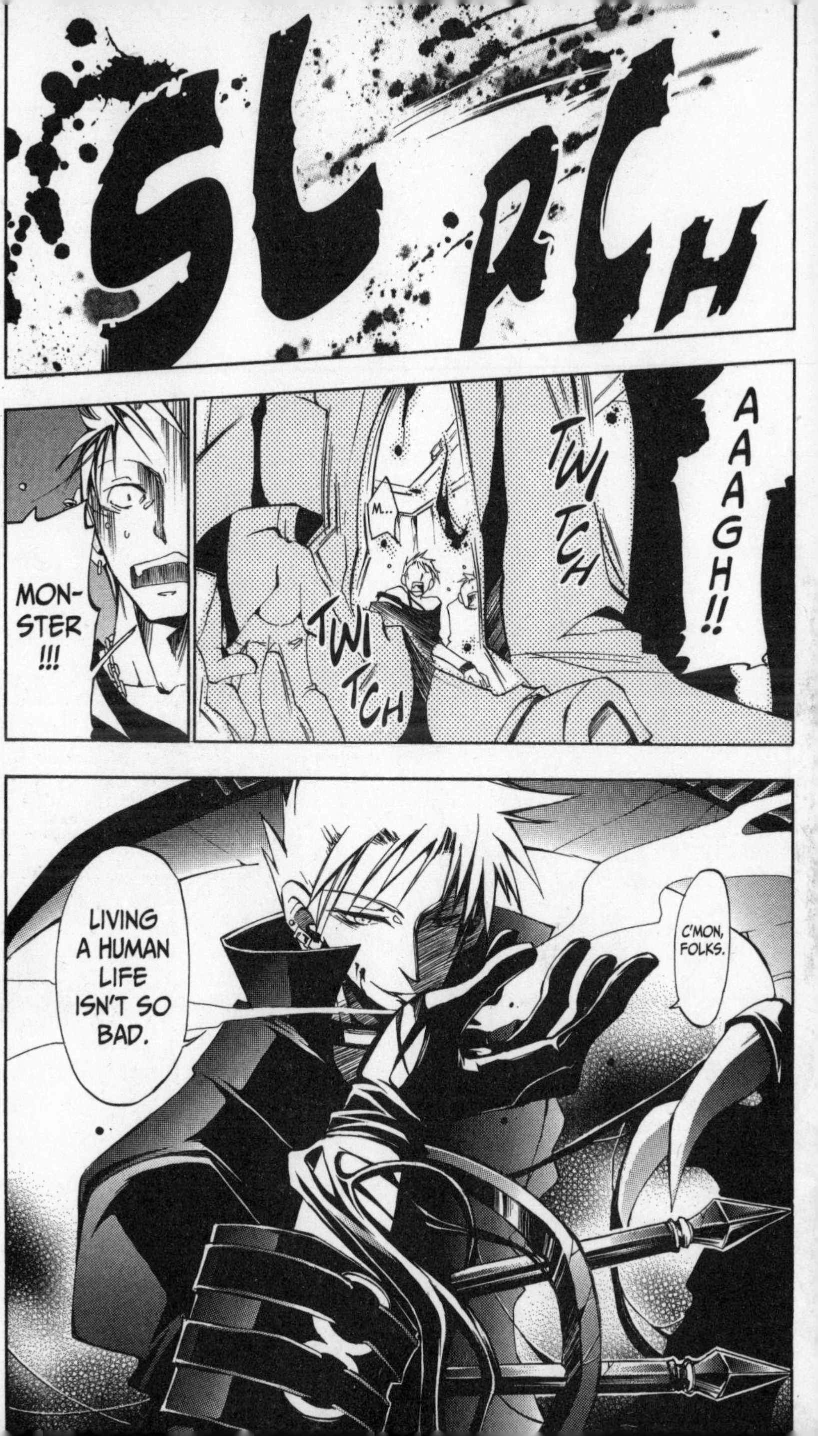
SLRCH
AAAAGH!!
TWITCH
M...
TWITCH
MON-STER!!!
C'MON, FOLKS.
LIVING A HUMAN LIFE ISN'T SO BAD.

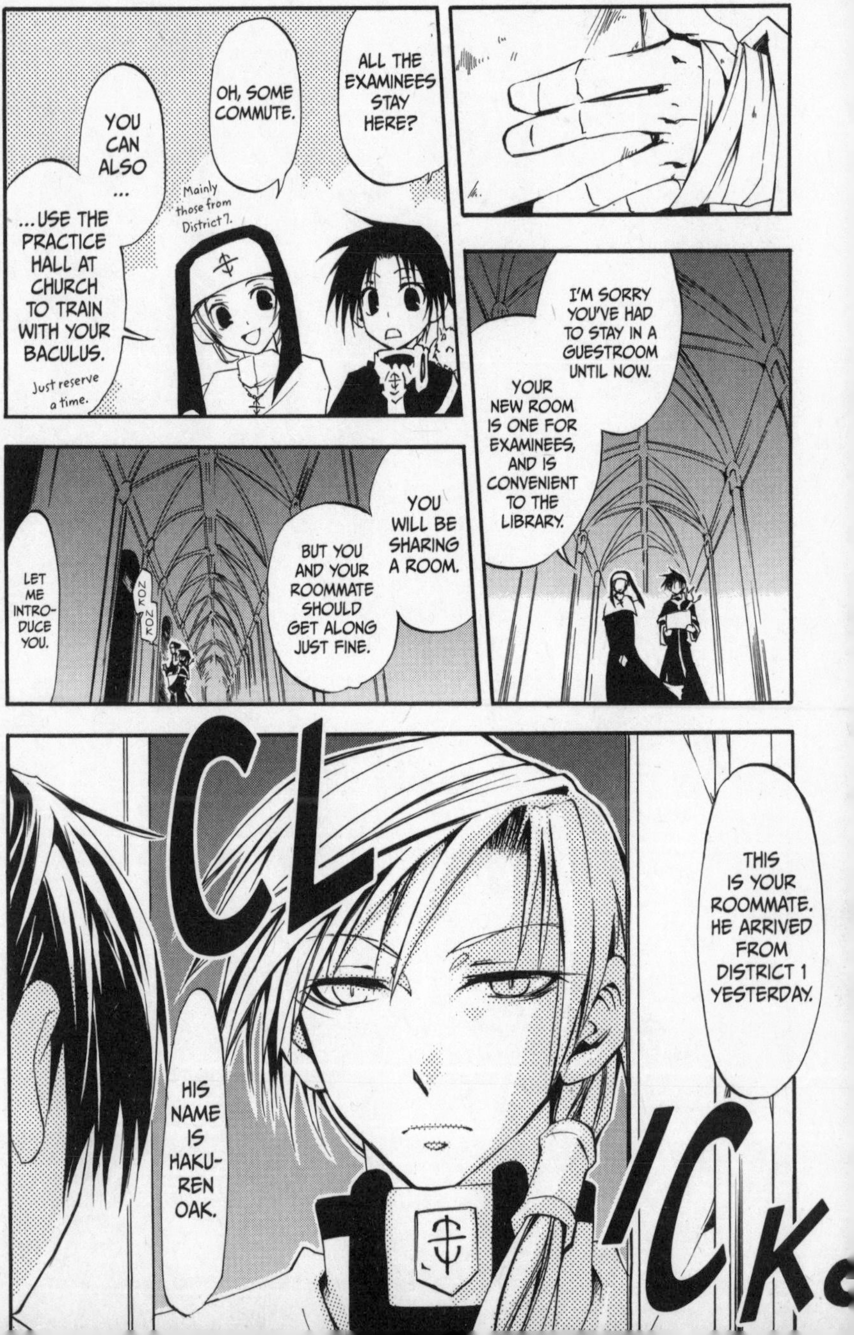
ALL THE EXAMINEES STAY HERE?
OH, SOME COMMUTE.
Mainly those from District 7.
YOU CAN ALSO ...
...USE THE PRACTICE HALL AT CHURCH TO TRAIN WITH YOUR BACULUS.
Just reserve a time.
I'M SORRY YOU'VE HAD TO STAY IN A GUESTROOM UNTIL NOW.
YOUR NEW ROOM IS ONE FOR EXAMINEES, AND IS CONVENIENT TO THE LIBRARY.
YOU WILL BE SHARING A ROOM.
BUT YOU AND YOUR ROOMMATE SHOULD GET ALONG JUST FINE.
NOK NOK
LET ME INTRO-DUCE YOU.
CLICK
THIS IS YOUR ROOMMATE. HE ARRIVED FROM DISTRICT 1 YESTERDAY.
HIS NAME IS HAKU-REN OAK.

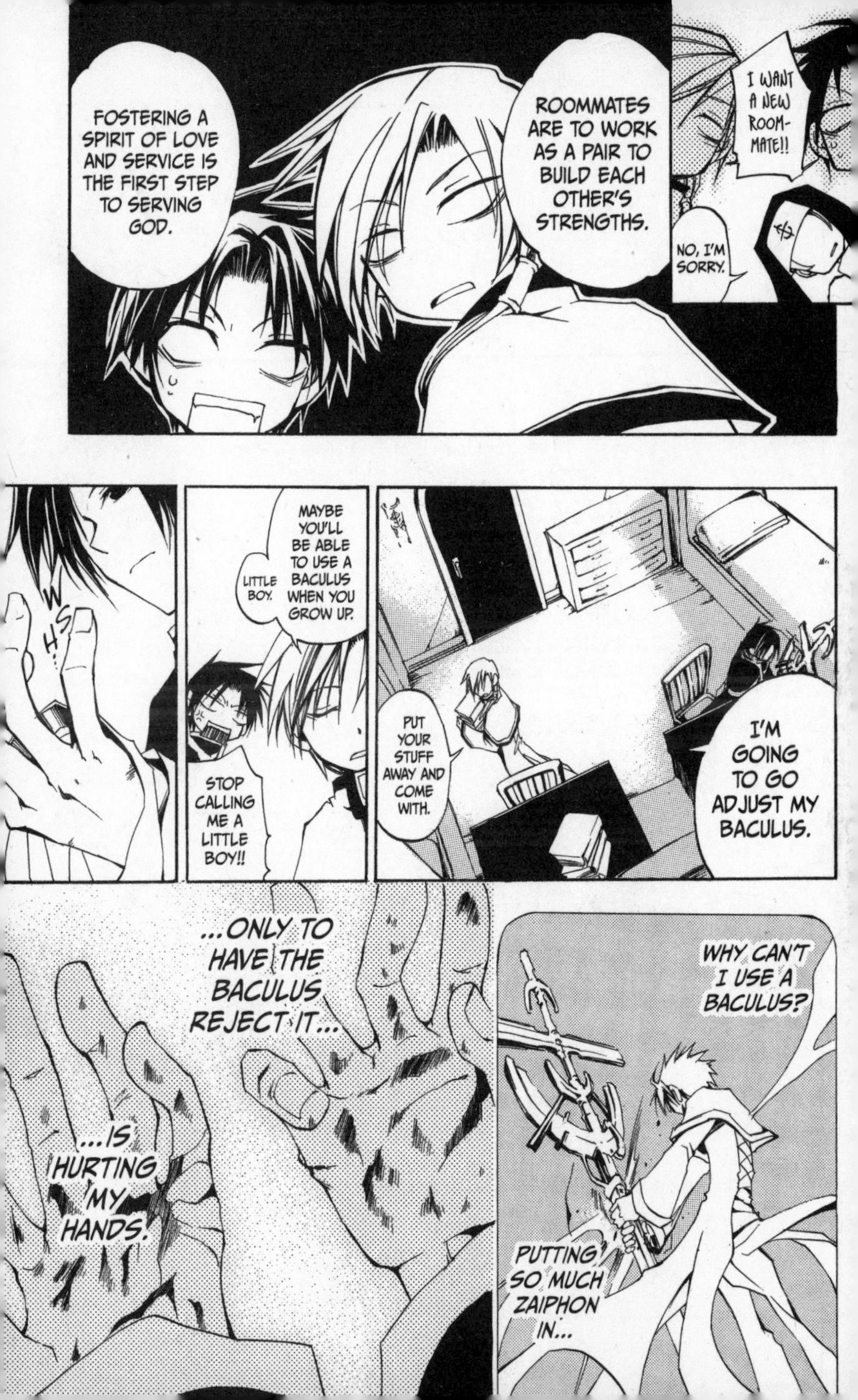
I WANT A NEW ROOMMATE!!
NO, I'M SORRY.
ROOMMATES ARE TO WORK AS A PAIR TO BUILD EACH OTHER'S STRENGTHS.
FOSTERING A SPIRIT OF LOVE AND SERVICE IS THE FIRST STEP TO SERVING GOD.
I'M GOING TO GO ADJUST MY BACULUS.
PUT YOUR STUFF AWAY AND COME WITH.
MAYBE YOU'LL BE ABLE TO USE A BACULUS WHEN YOU GROW UP.
LITTLE BOY.
STOP CALLING ME A LITTLE BOY!!
WHY CAN'T I USE A BACULUS?
PUTTING SO MUCH ZAIPHON IN...
...ONLY TO HAVE THE BACULUS REJECT IT...
...IS HURTING MY HANDS.

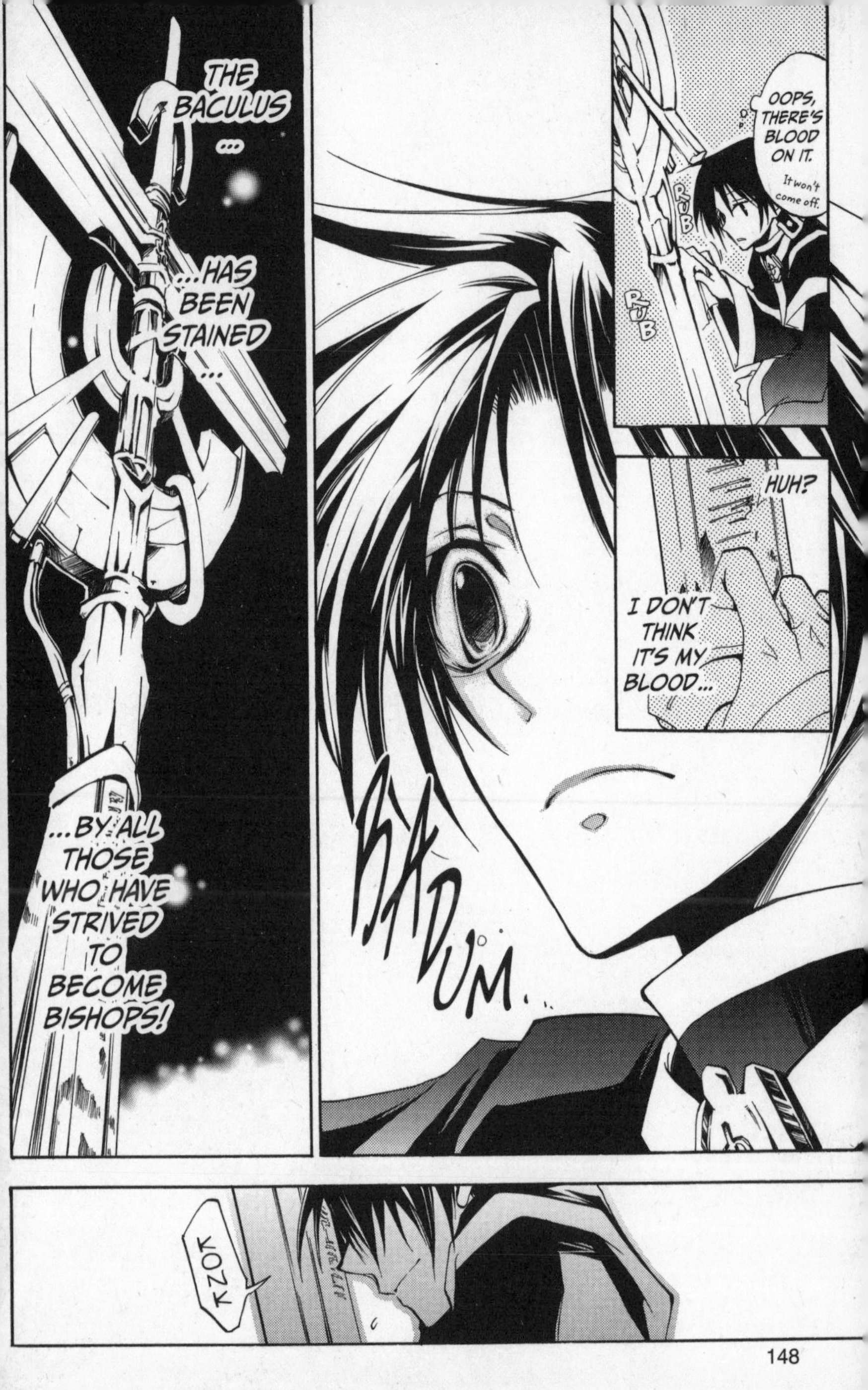
OOPS, THERE'S BLOOD ON IT.
It won't come off.
RUB
RUB
HUH?
I DON'T THINK IT'S MY BLOOD...
BADUM...
THE BACULUS...
...HAS BEEN STAINED...
...BY ALL THOSE WHO HAVE STRIVED TO BECOME BISHOPS!
KONK

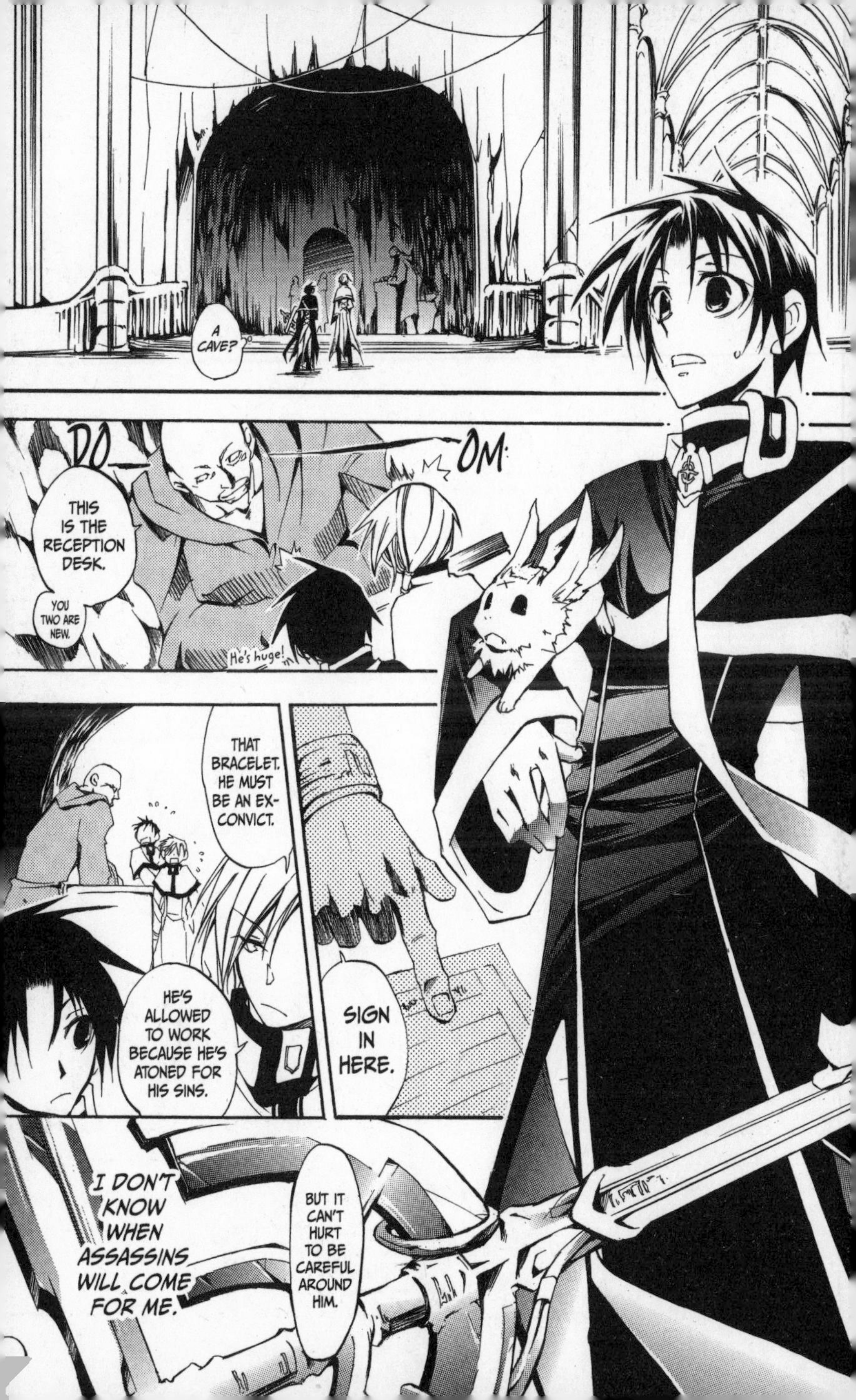
A CAVE?
DO-OM
THIS IS THE RECEPTION DESK.
YOU TWO ARE NEW.
He's huge!
SIGN IN HERE.
THAT BRACELET. HE MUST BE AN EX-CONVICT.
HE'S ALLOWED TO WORK BECAUSE HE'S ATONED FOR HIS SINS.
BUT IT CAN'T HURT TO BE CAREFUL AROUND HIM.
I DON'T KNOW WHEN ASSASSINS WILL COME FOR ME.

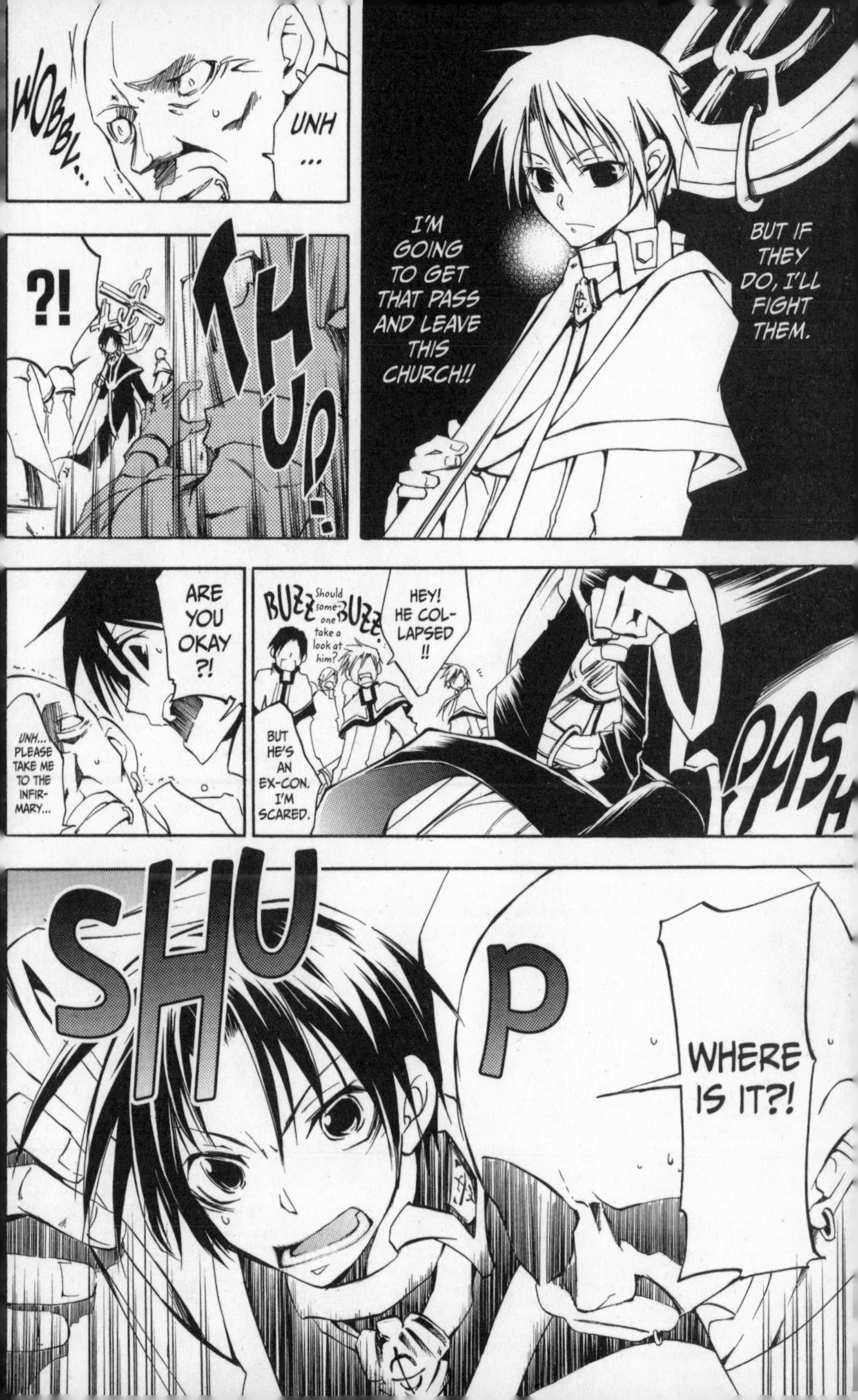
I'M GOING TO GET THAT PASS AND LEAVE THIS CHURCH!!
BUT IF THEY DO, I'LL FIGHT THEM.
UNH ...
WOBBLY...
THUD..
?!
PASH
HEY! HE COL-LAPSED!!
BUZZ
Should some-one take a look at him?
BUZZ
BUT HE'S AN EX-CON. I'M SCARED.
ARE YOU OKAY?!
UNH... PLEASE TAKE ME TO THE INFIRMARY...
WHERE IS IT?!
SHUP

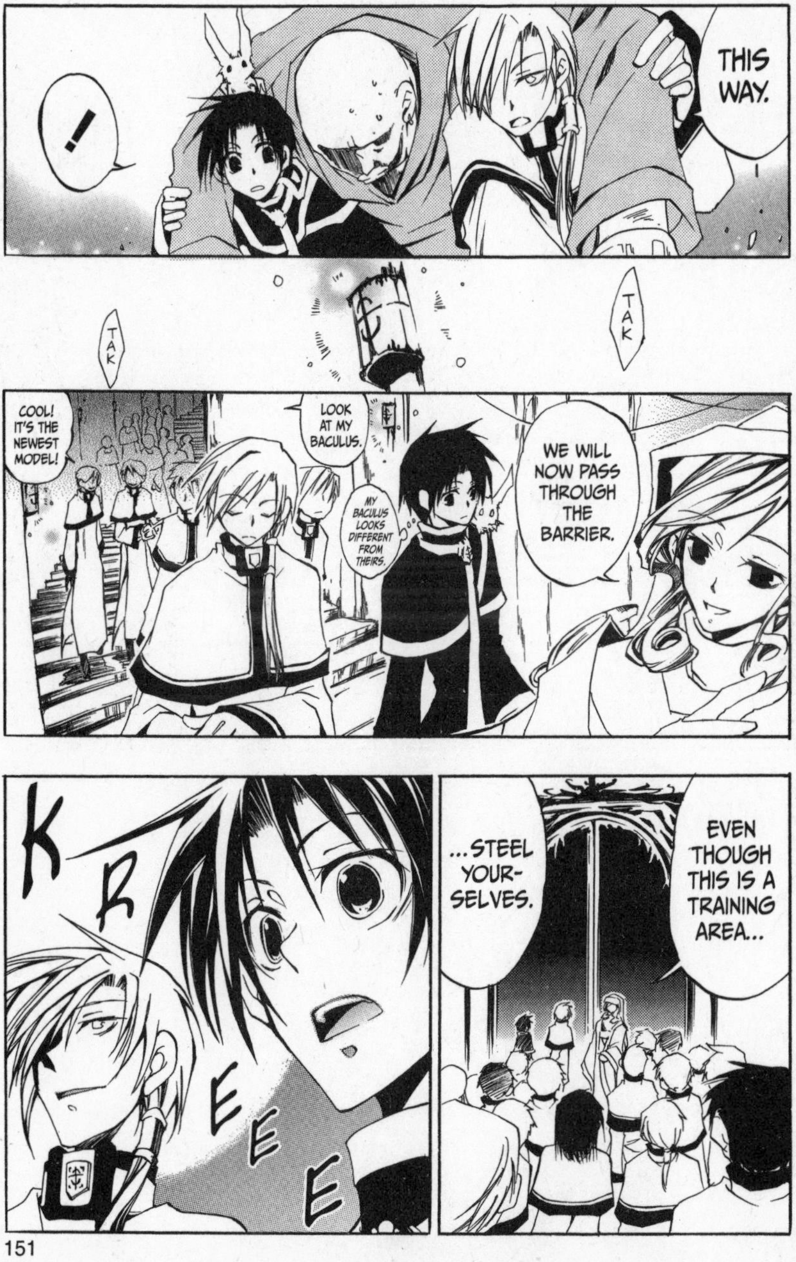
THIS WAY.
!
TAK
TAK
WE WILL NOW PASS THROUGH THE BARRIER.
MY BACULUS LOOKS DIFFERENT FROM THEIRS.
LOOK AT MY BACULUS.
COOL! IT'S THE NEWEST MODEL!
EVEN THOUGH THIS IS A TRAINING AREA...
...STEEL YOUR-SELVES.
KREEEE

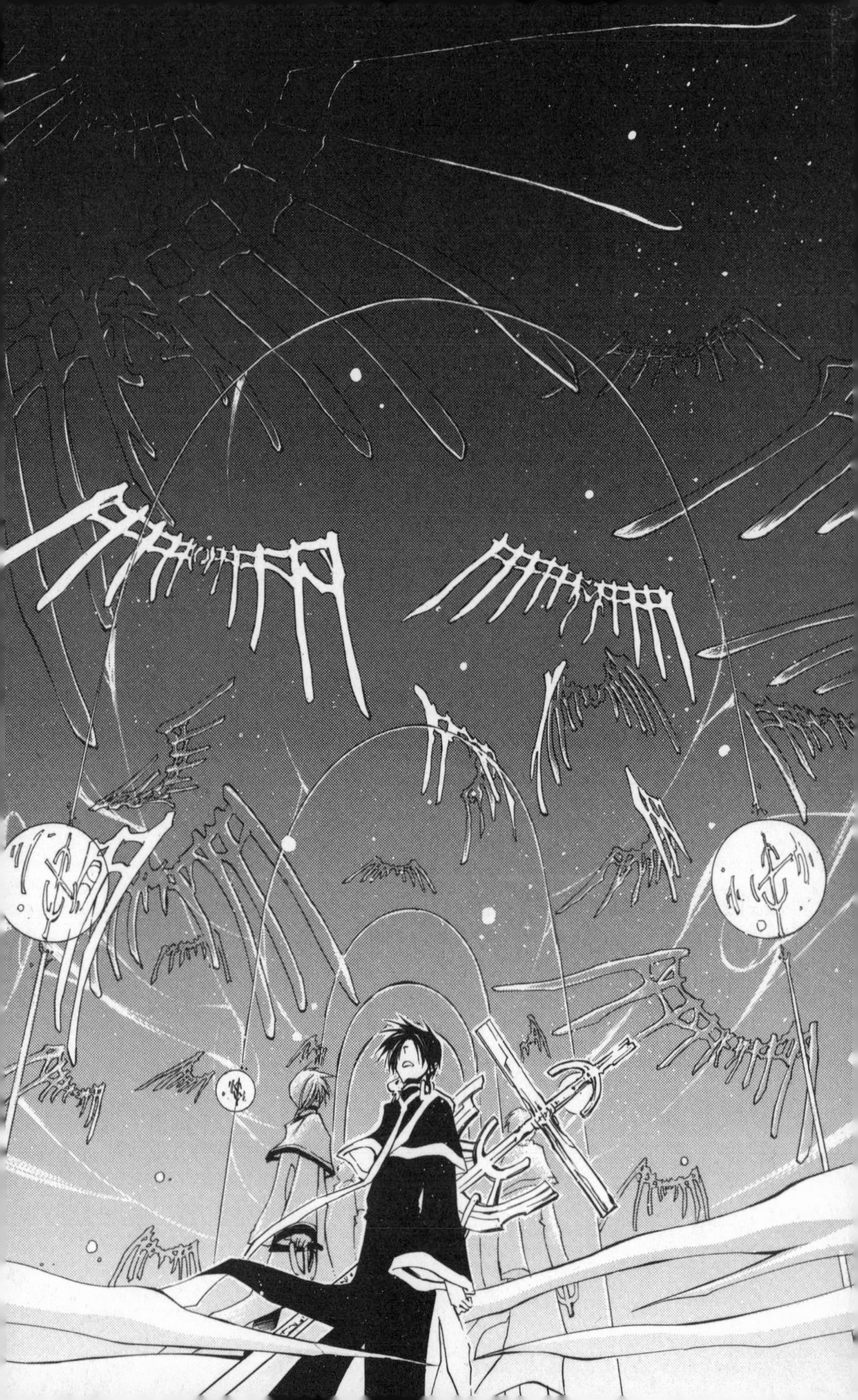

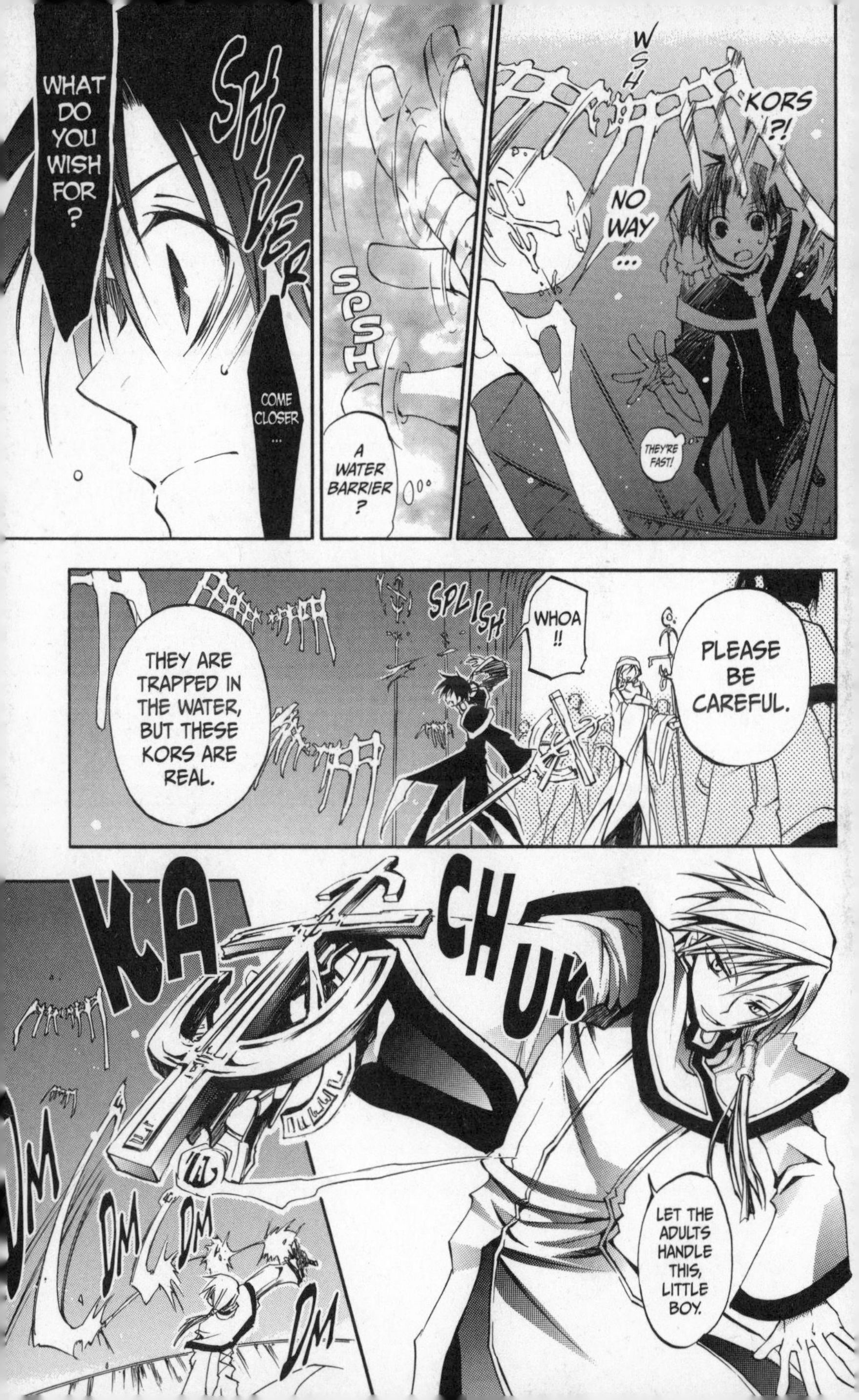
WSH
KORS ?!
NO WAY ...
THEY'RE FAST!
SPSH
A WATER BARRIER ?
WHAT DO YOU WISH FOR ?
SHIVER
COME CLOSER ...
PLEASE BE CAREFUL.
WHOA !!
SPLISH
THEY ARE TRAPPED IN THE WATER, BUT THESE KORS ARE REAL.
KA CHUK
LET THE ADULTS HANDLE THIS, LITTLE BOY.
DM DM DM DM

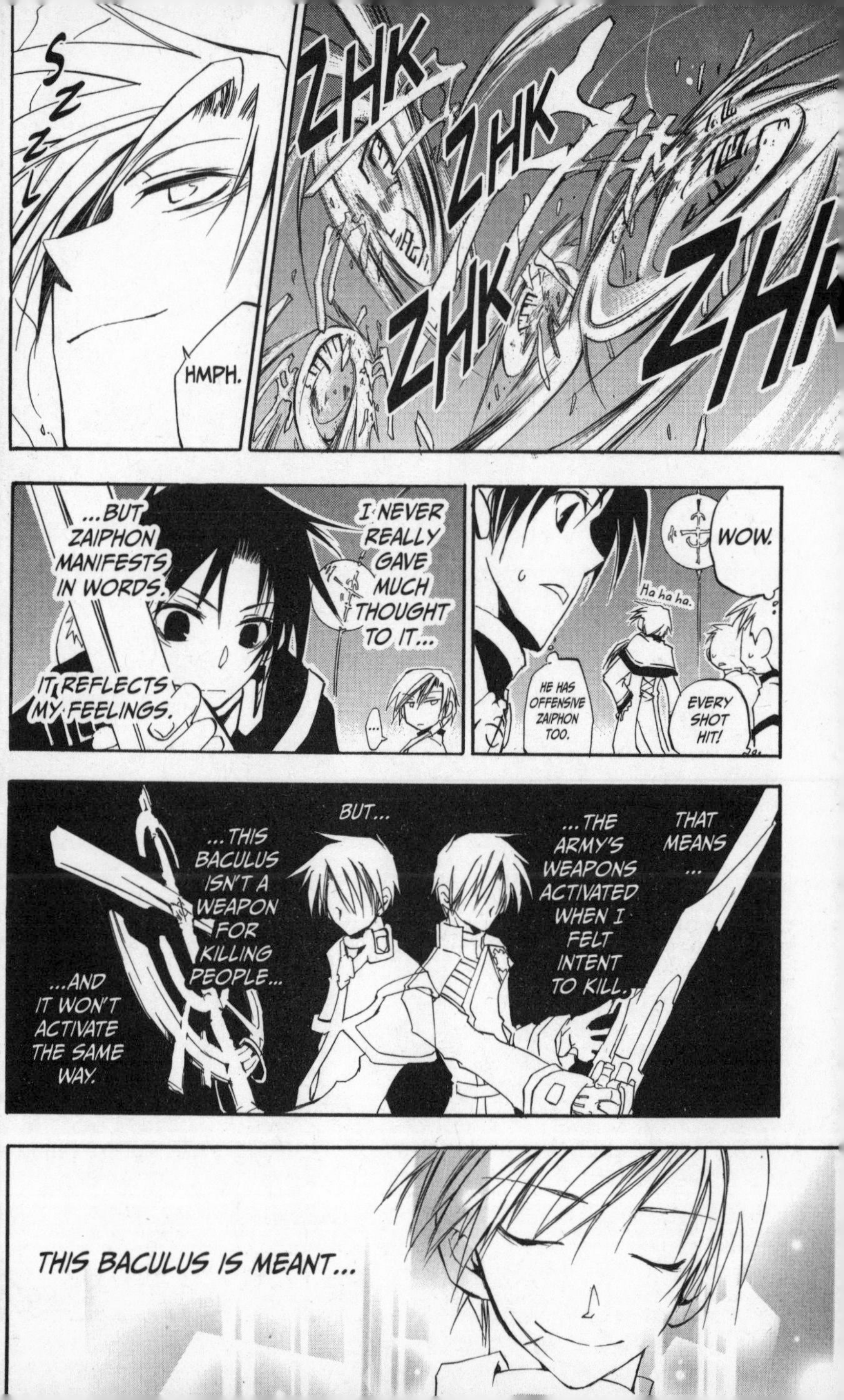
ZHK
ZHK
ZHK
ZHK
SZZZL
HMPH.
WOW.
Ha ha ha.
EVERY SHOT HIT!
HE HAS OFFENSIVE ZAIPHON TOO.
I NEVER REALLY GAVE MUCH THOUGHT TO IT...
...
...BUT ZAIPHON MANIFESTS IN WORDS.
IT REFLECTS MY FEELINGS.
THAT MEANS...
...THE ARMY'S WEAPONS ACTIVATED WHEN I FELT INTENT TO KILL.
BUT...
...THIS BACULUS ISN'T A WEAPON FOR KILLING PEOPLE...
...AND IT WON'T ACTIVATE THE SAME WAY.
THIS BACULUS IS MEANT...

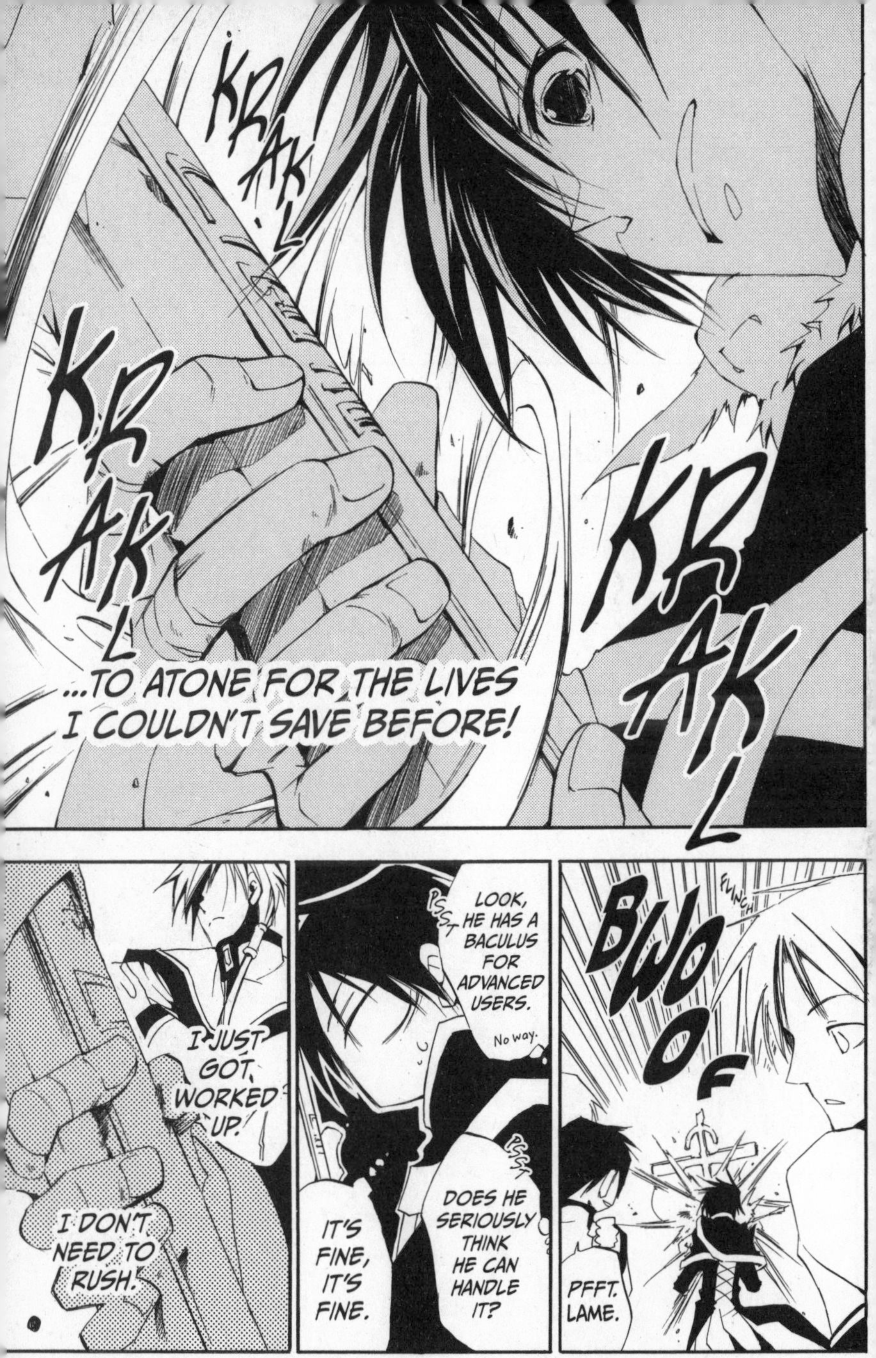
KRAKL
KRAKL
KRAKL
...TO ATONE FOR THE LIVES I COULDN'T SAVE BEFORE!
FLINCH
BWOOF
PFFT. LAME.
PSST
LOOK, HE HAS A BACULUS FOR ADVANCED USERS.
No way.
PSST
DOES HE SERIOUSLY THINK HE CAN HANDLE IT?
IT'S FINE, IT'S FINE.
I JUST GOT WORKED UP.
I DON'T NEED TO RUSH.

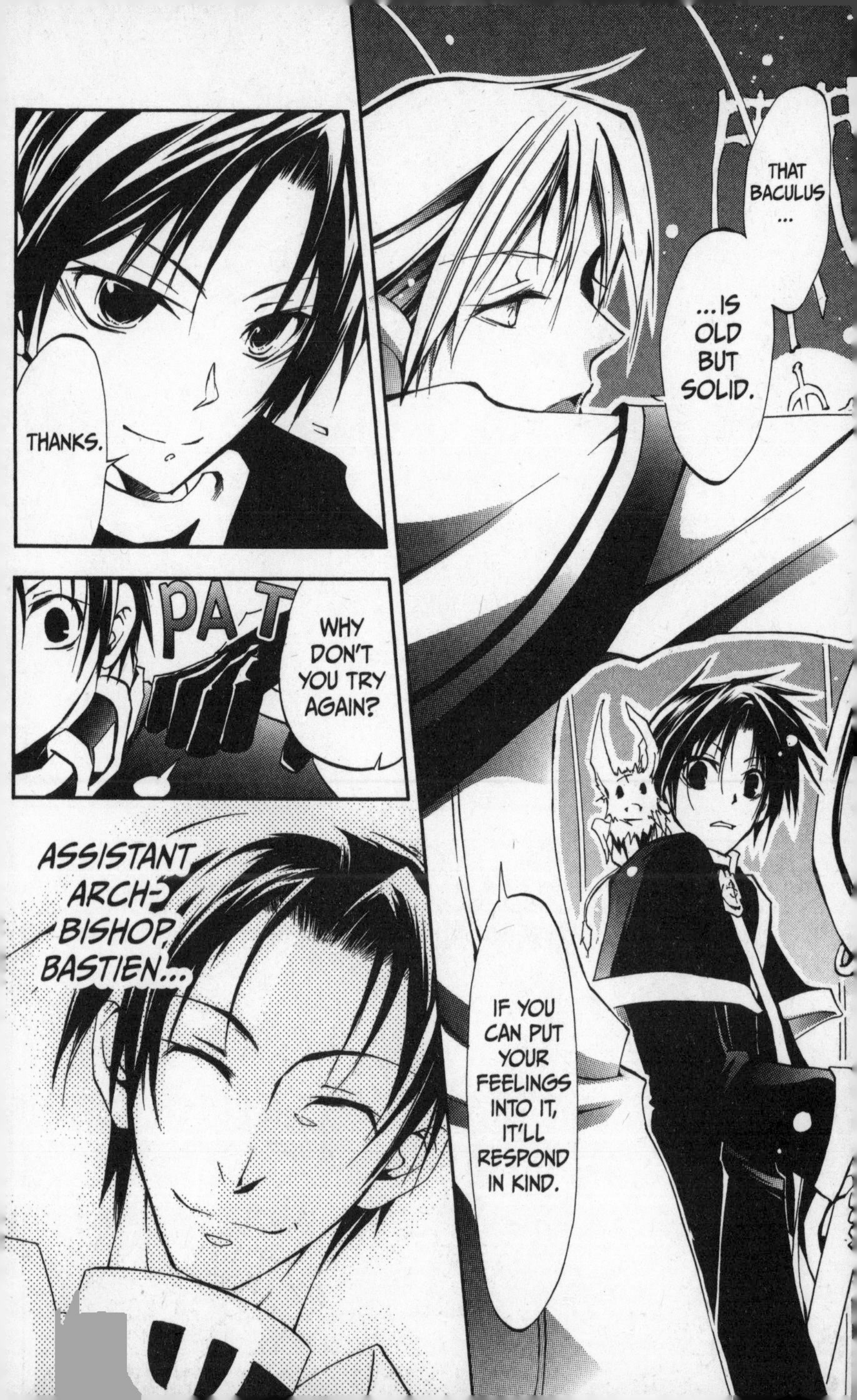
THAT BACULUS ...
...IS OLD BUT SOLID.
IF YOU CAN PUT YOUR FEELINGS INTO IT, IT'LL RESPOND IN KIND.
THANKS.
PAT
WHY DON'T YOU TRY AGAIN?
ASSISTANT ARCH-BISHOP BASTIEN...

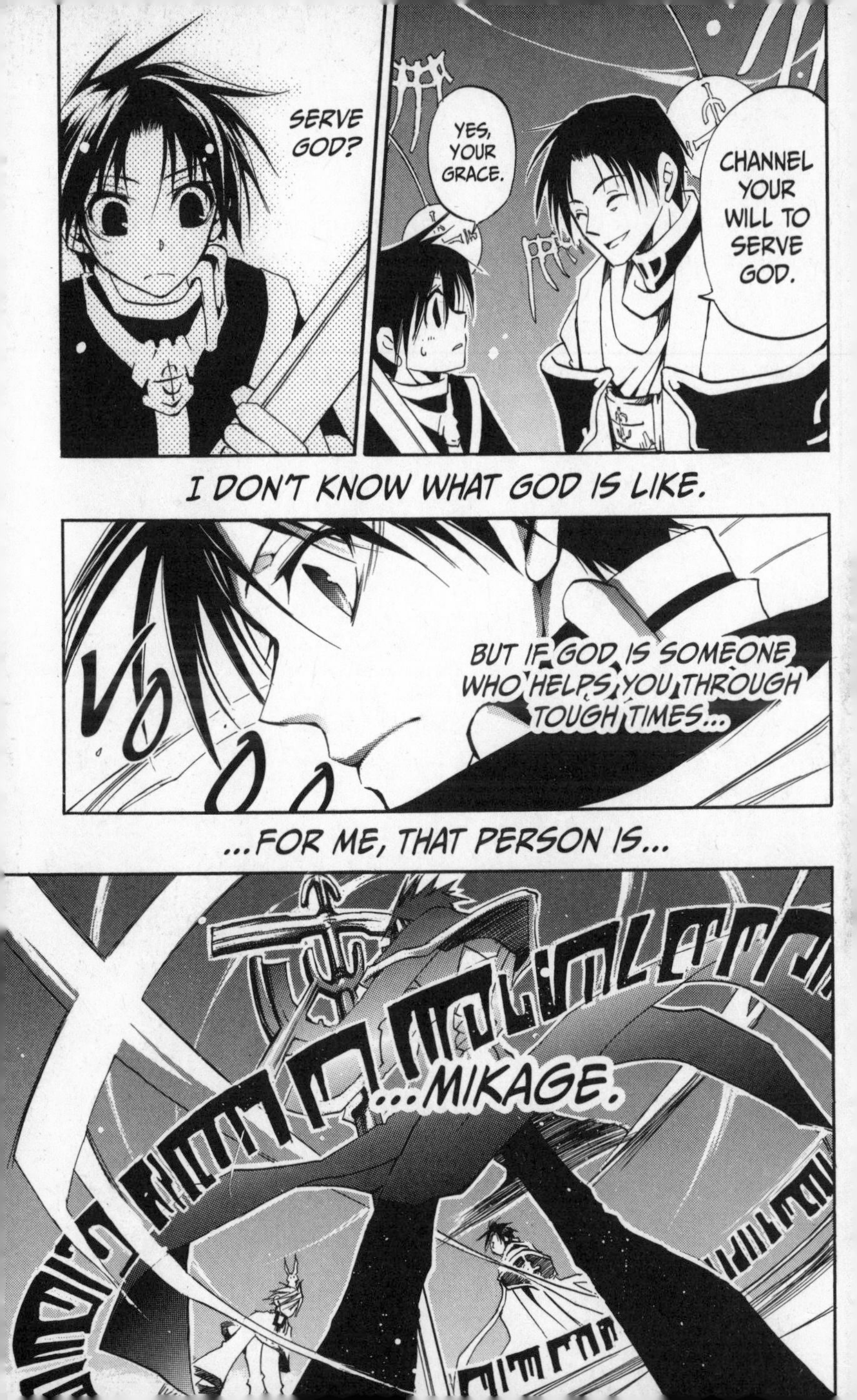
CHANNEL YOUR WILL TO SERVE GOD.
YES, YOUR GRACE.
SERVE GOD?
I DON'T KNOW WHAT GOD IS LIKE.
BUT IF GOD IS SOMEONE WHO HELPS YOU THROUGH TOUGH TIMES...
...FOR ME, THAT PERSON IS...
...MIKAGE.

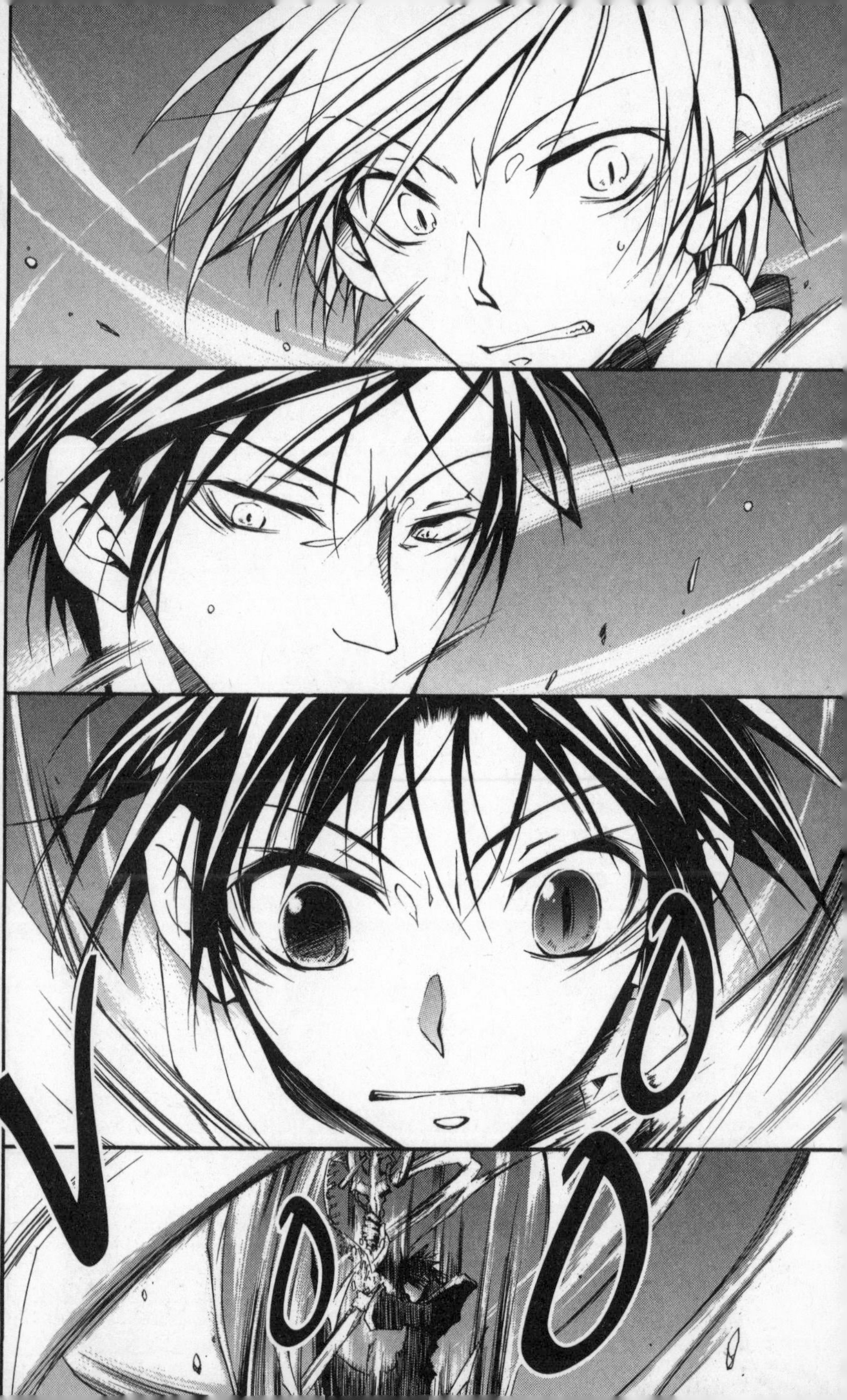

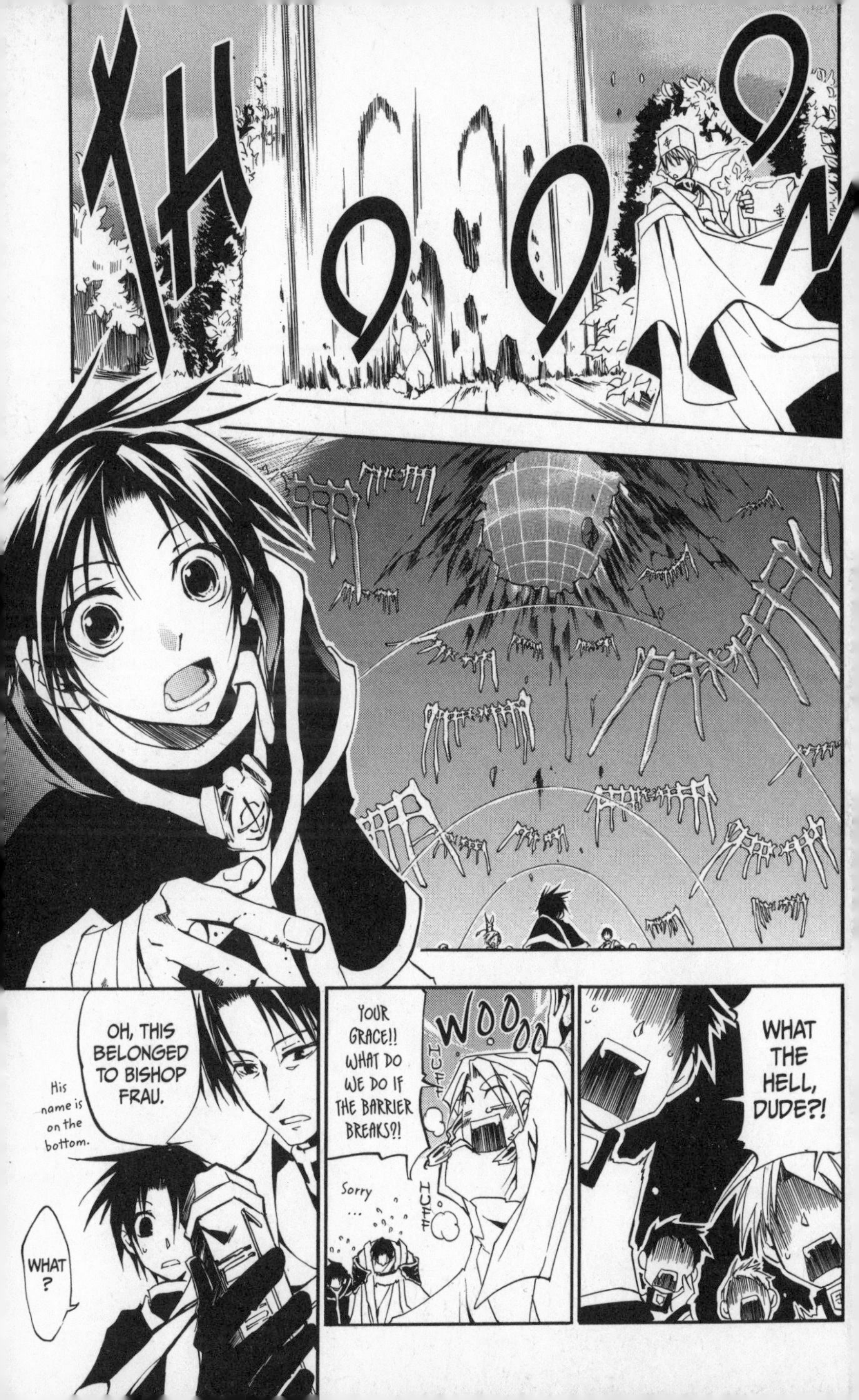
WHAT THE HELL, DUDE?!
YOUR GRACE!! WHAT DO WE DO IF THE BARRIER BREAKS?!
WOOOO
HUFF
HUFF
Sorry ...
OH, THIS BELONGED TO BISHOP FRAU.
His name is on the bottom.
WHAT?

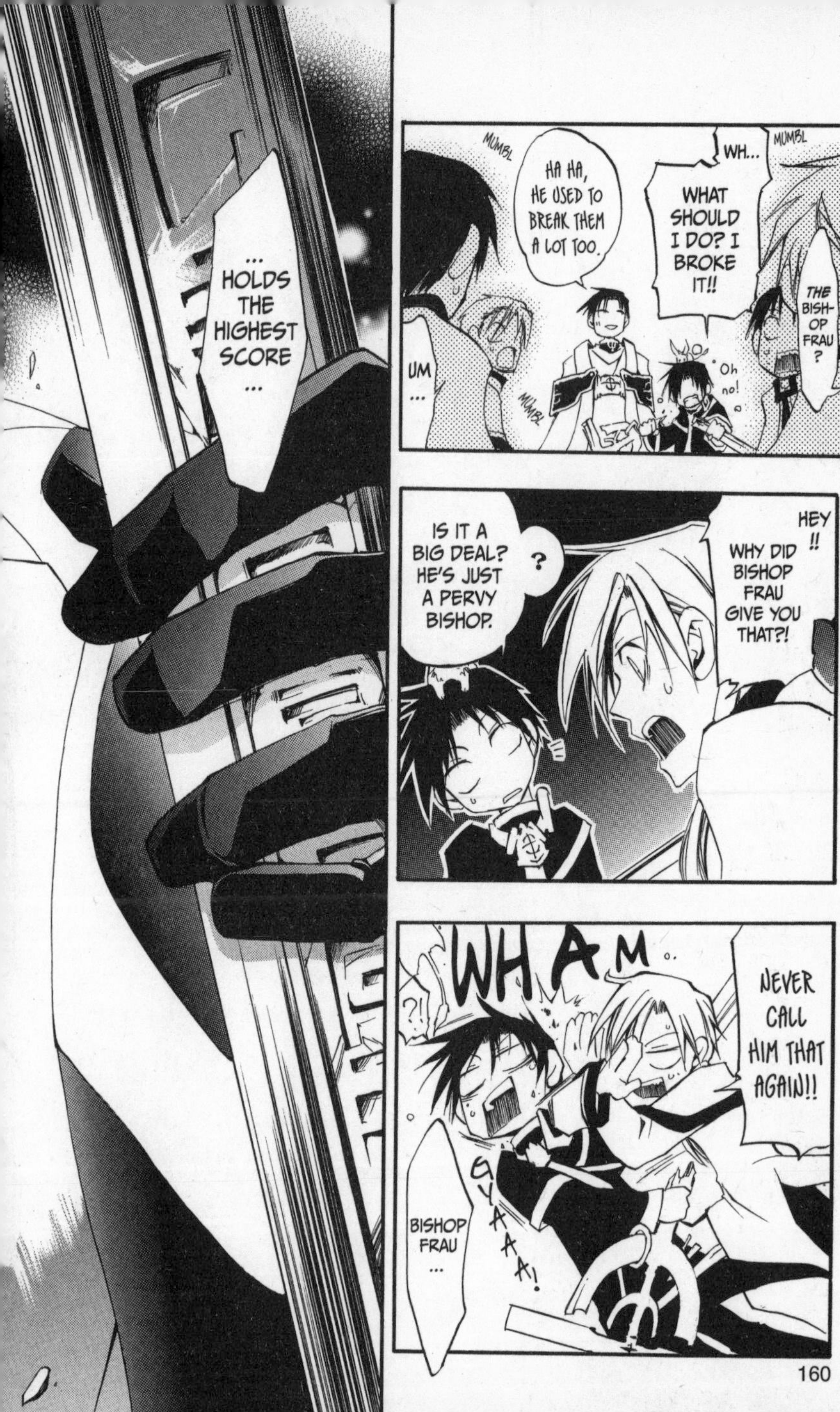
MUMBL
WH...
WHAT SHOULD I DO? I BROKE IT!!
THE BISH-OP FRAU?
HA HA, HE USED TO BREAK THEM A LOT TOO.
MUMBL
Oh no!
UM ...
MUMBL
HEY!!
WHY DID BISHOP FRAU GIVE YOU THAT?!
?
IS IT A BIG DEAL? HE'S JUST A PERVY BISHOP.
NEVER CALL HIM THAT AGAIN!!
WHAM
?!
GYAAAA!
BISHOP FRAU ...
... HOLDS THE HIGHEST SCORE ...

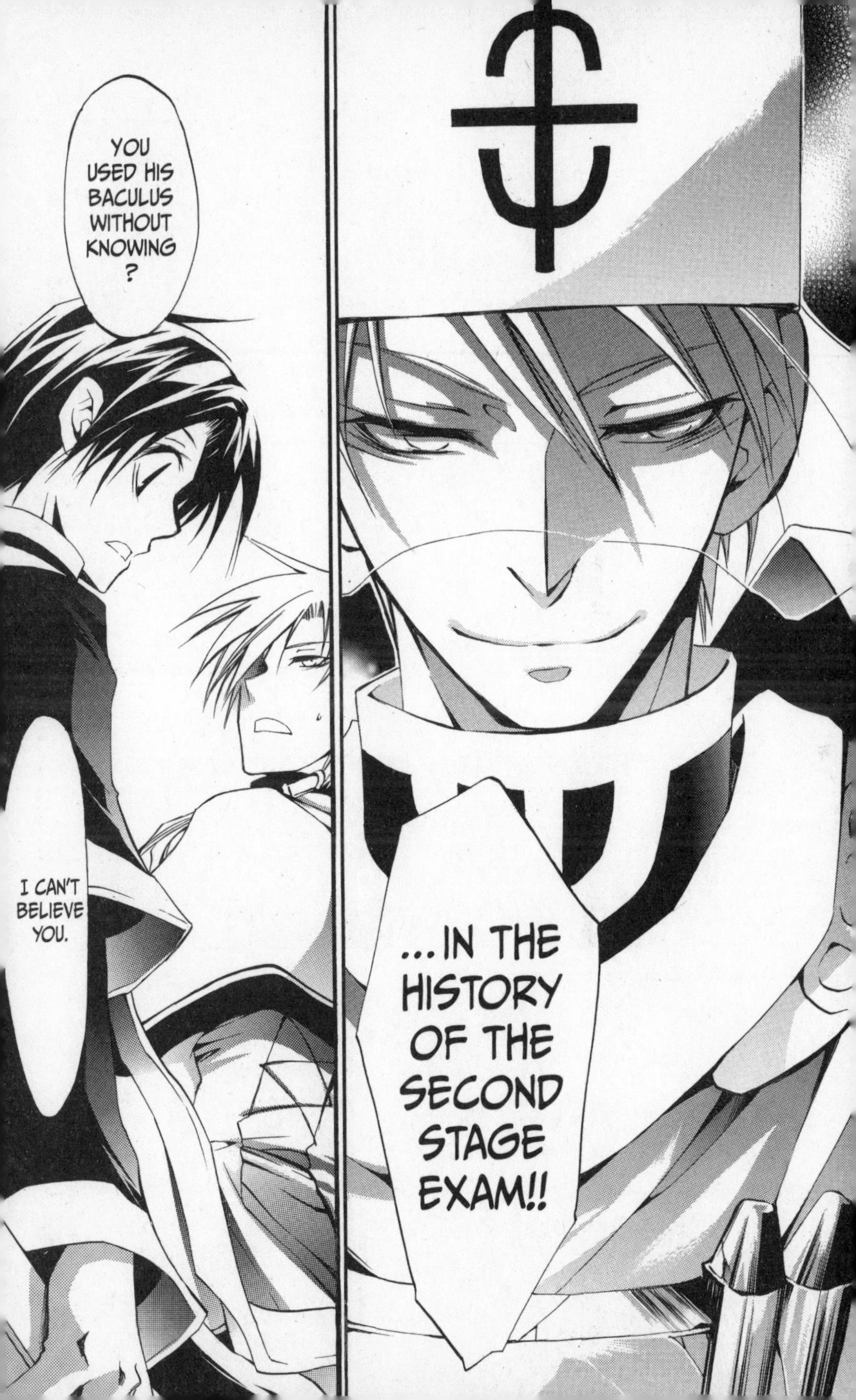
...IN THE HISTORY OF THE SECOND STAGE EXAM!!
YOU USED HIS BACULUS WITHOUT KNOWING?
I CAN'T BELIEVE YOU.

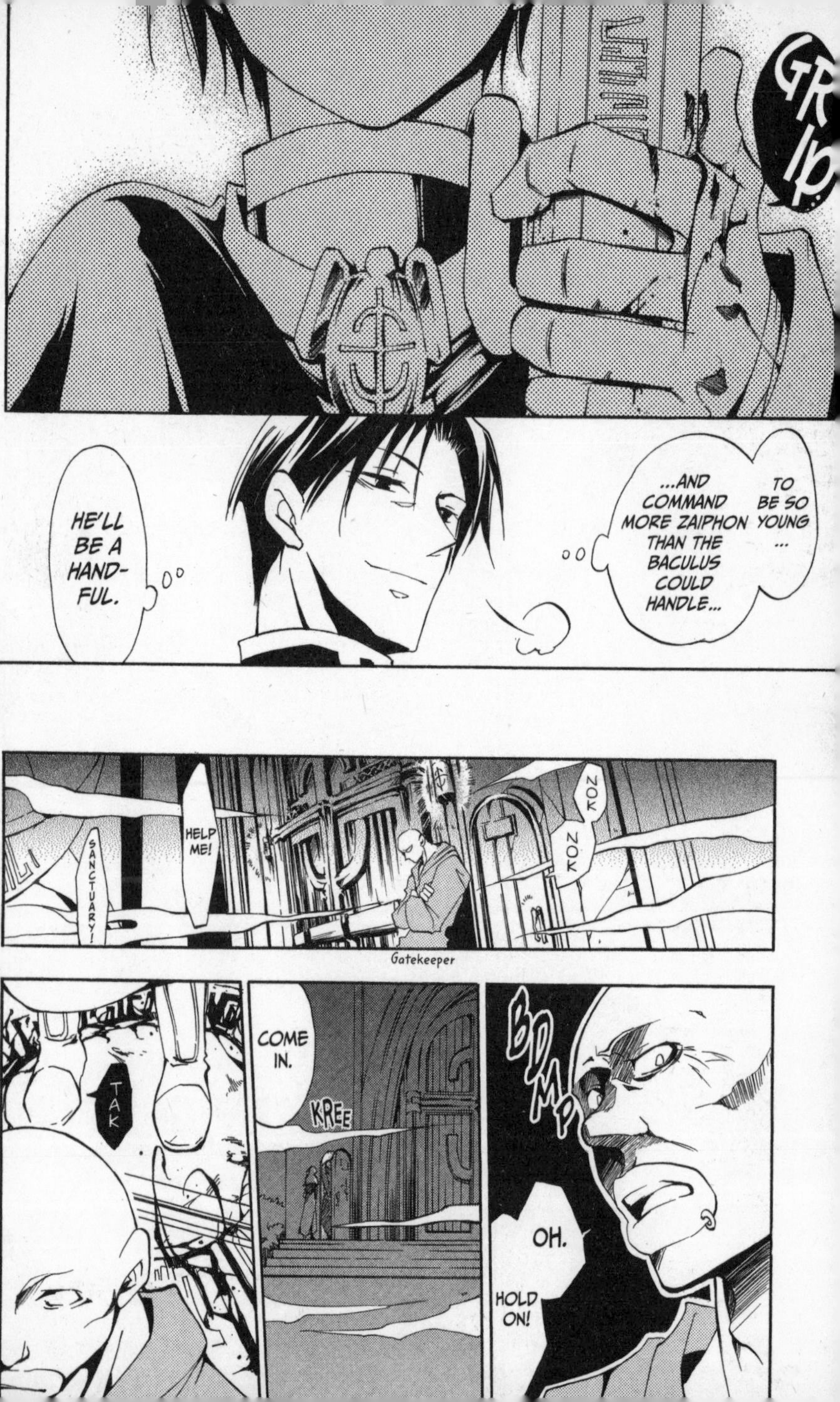
GRIP
TO BE SO YOUNG...
...AND COMMAND MORE ZAIPHON THAN THE BACULUS COULD HANDLE...
HE'LL BE A HANDFUL.
NOK NOK
HELP ME!
SANCTUARY!
Gatekeeper
BDMP
OH.
HOLD ON!
COME IN.
KREE
TAK

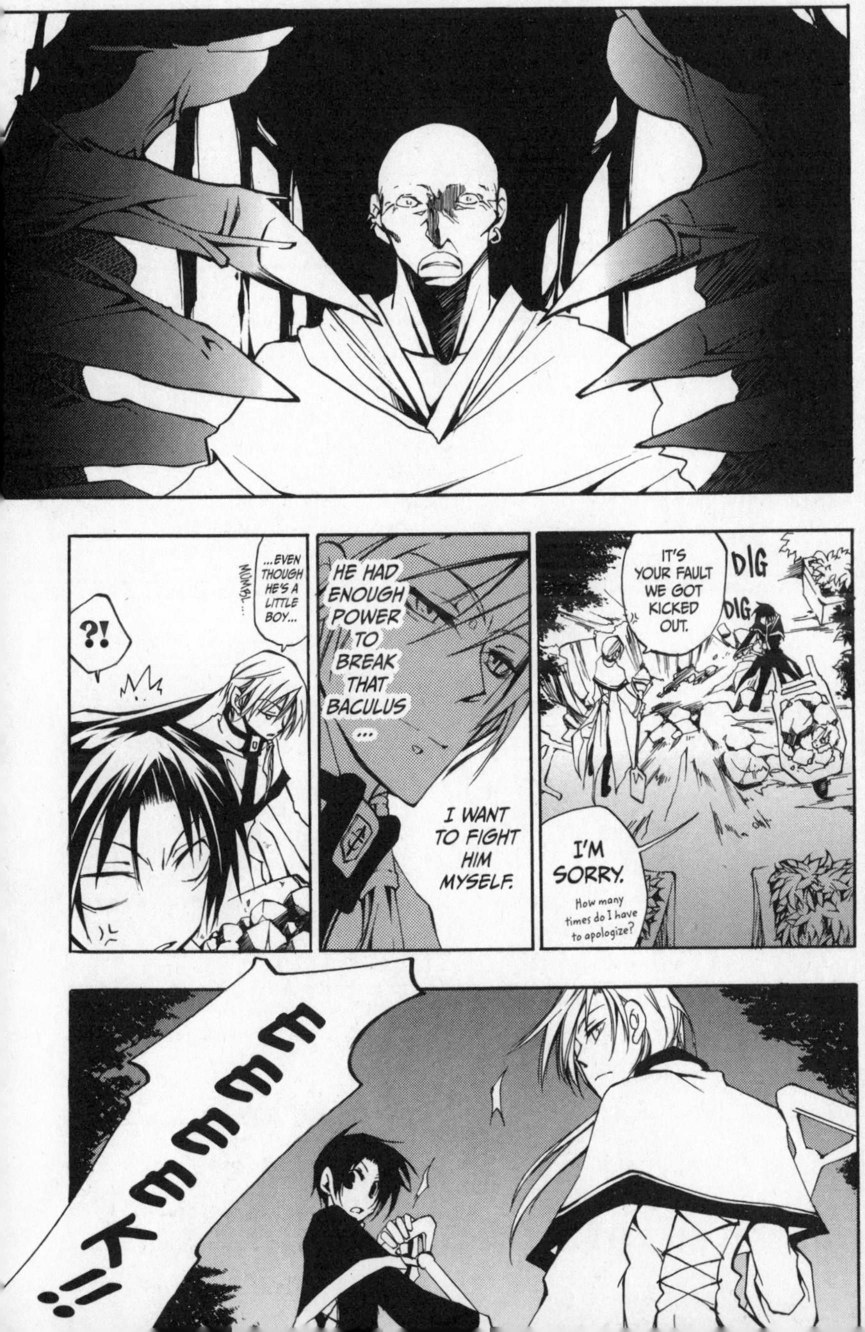
IT'S YOUR FAULT WE GOT KICKED OUT.
DIG
DIG
I'M SORRY.
How many times do I have to apologize?
HE HAD ENOUGH POWER TO BREAK THAT BACULUS...
I WANT TO FIGHT HIM MYSELF.
...EVEN THOUGH HE'S A LITTLE BOY...
MUMBL...
?!
EEEEEEK!!

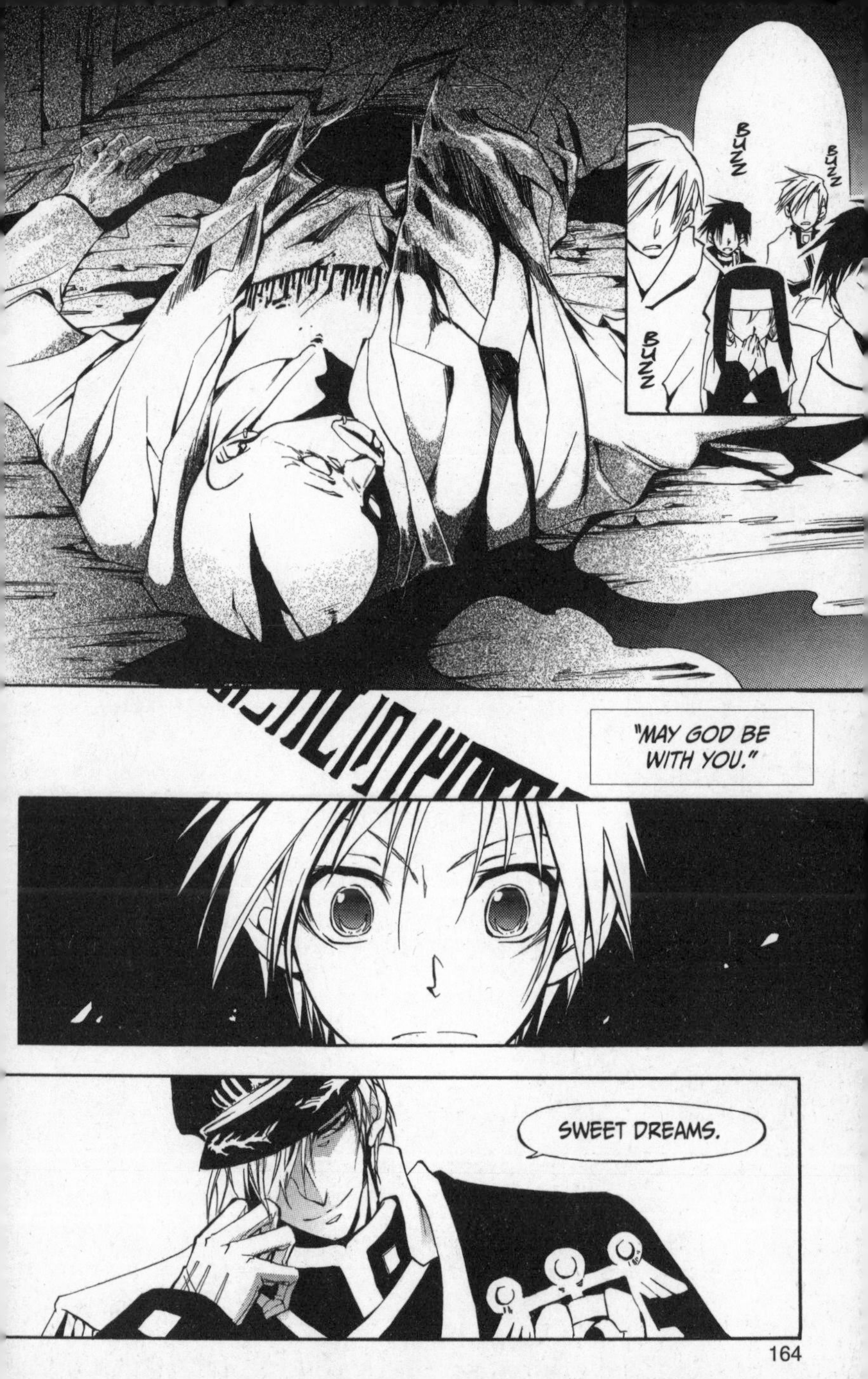
BUZZ
BUZZ
BUZZ
"MAY GOD BE WITH YOU."
SWEET DREAMS.

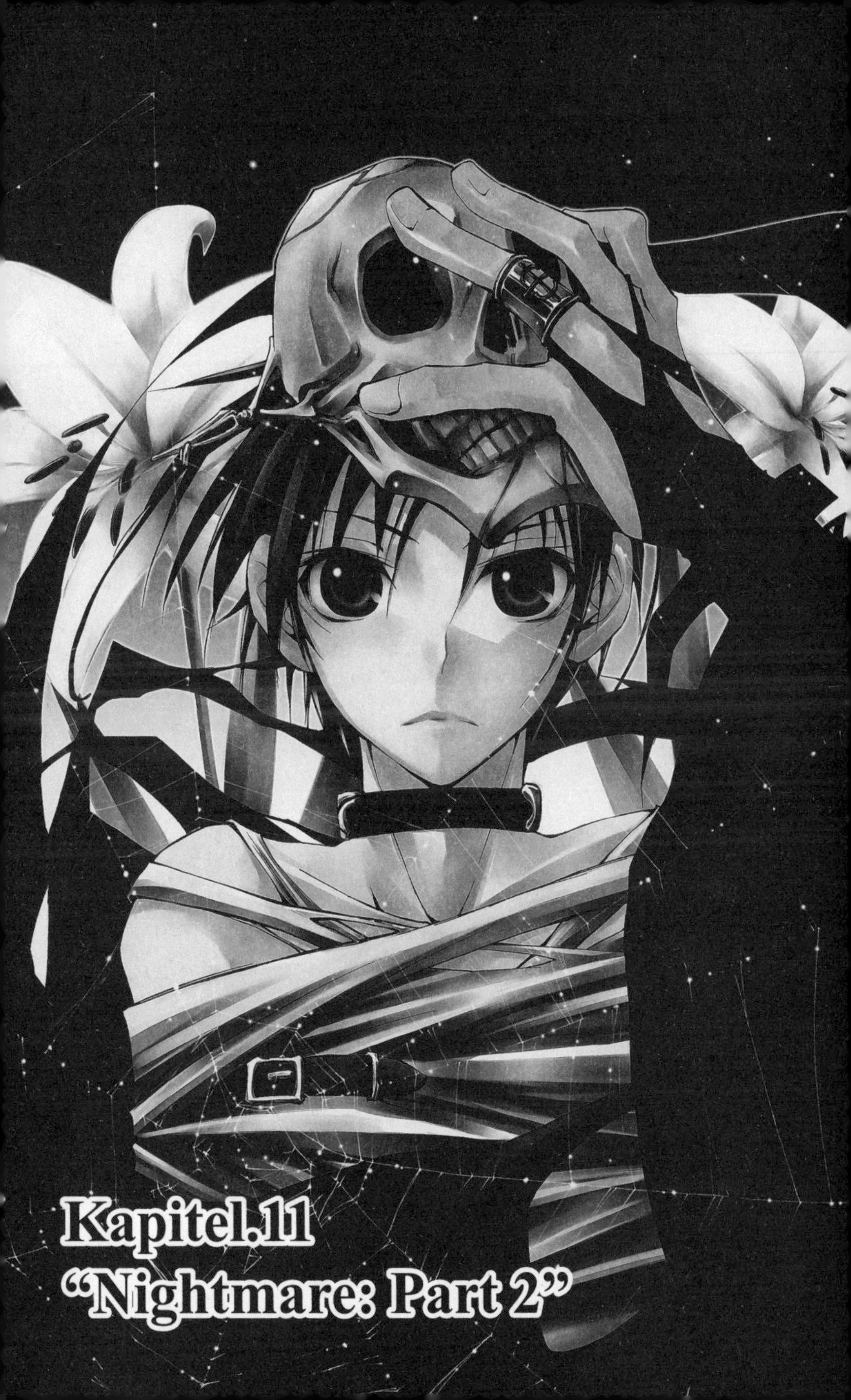
Kapitel.11
"Nightmare: Part 2"

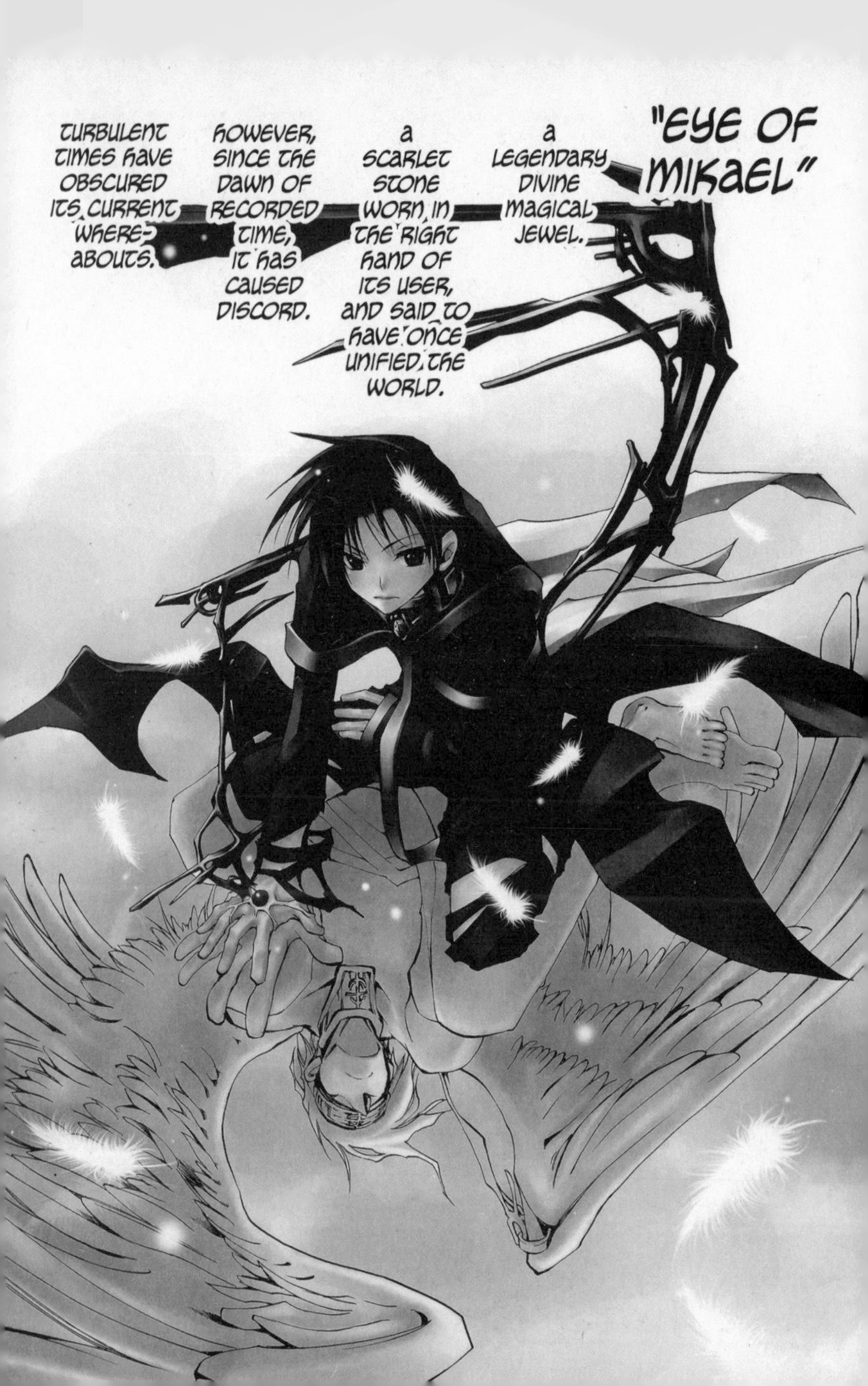
"EYE OF MIKAEL"
A LEGENDARY DIVINE MAGICAL JEWEL.
A SCARLET STONE WORN IN THE RIGHT HAND OF ITS USER, AND SAID TO HAVE ONCE UNIFIED THE WORLD.
HOWEVER, SINCE THE DAWN OF RECORDED TIME, IT HAS CAUSED DISCORD.
TURBULENT TIMES HAVE OBSCURED ITS CURRENT WHERE-ABOUTS.

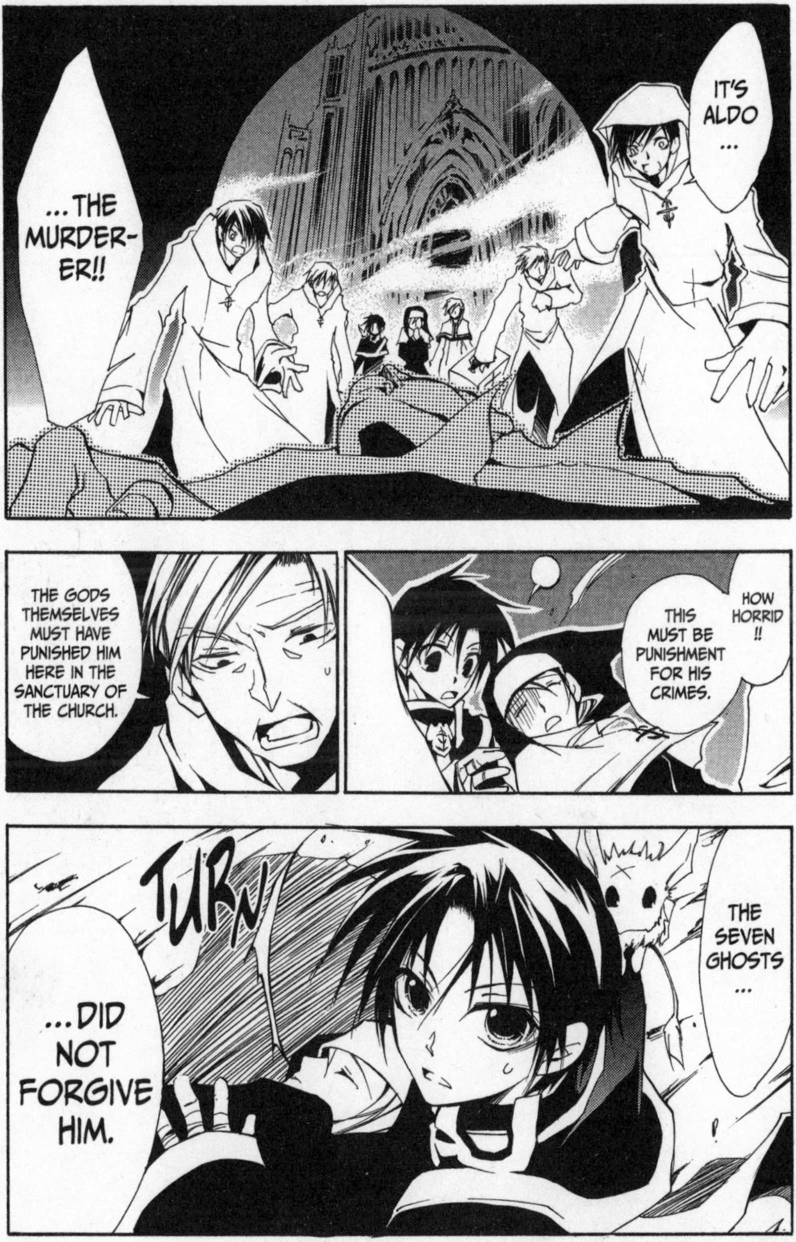
IT'S ALDO ...
...THE MURDERER!!
HOW HORRID!!
THIS MUST BE PUNISHMENT FOR HIS CRIMES.
THE GODS THEMSELVES MUST HAVE PUNISHED HIM HERE IN THE SANCTUARY OF THE CHURCH.
THE SEVEN GHOSTS ...
TURN
...DID NOT FORGIVE HIM.

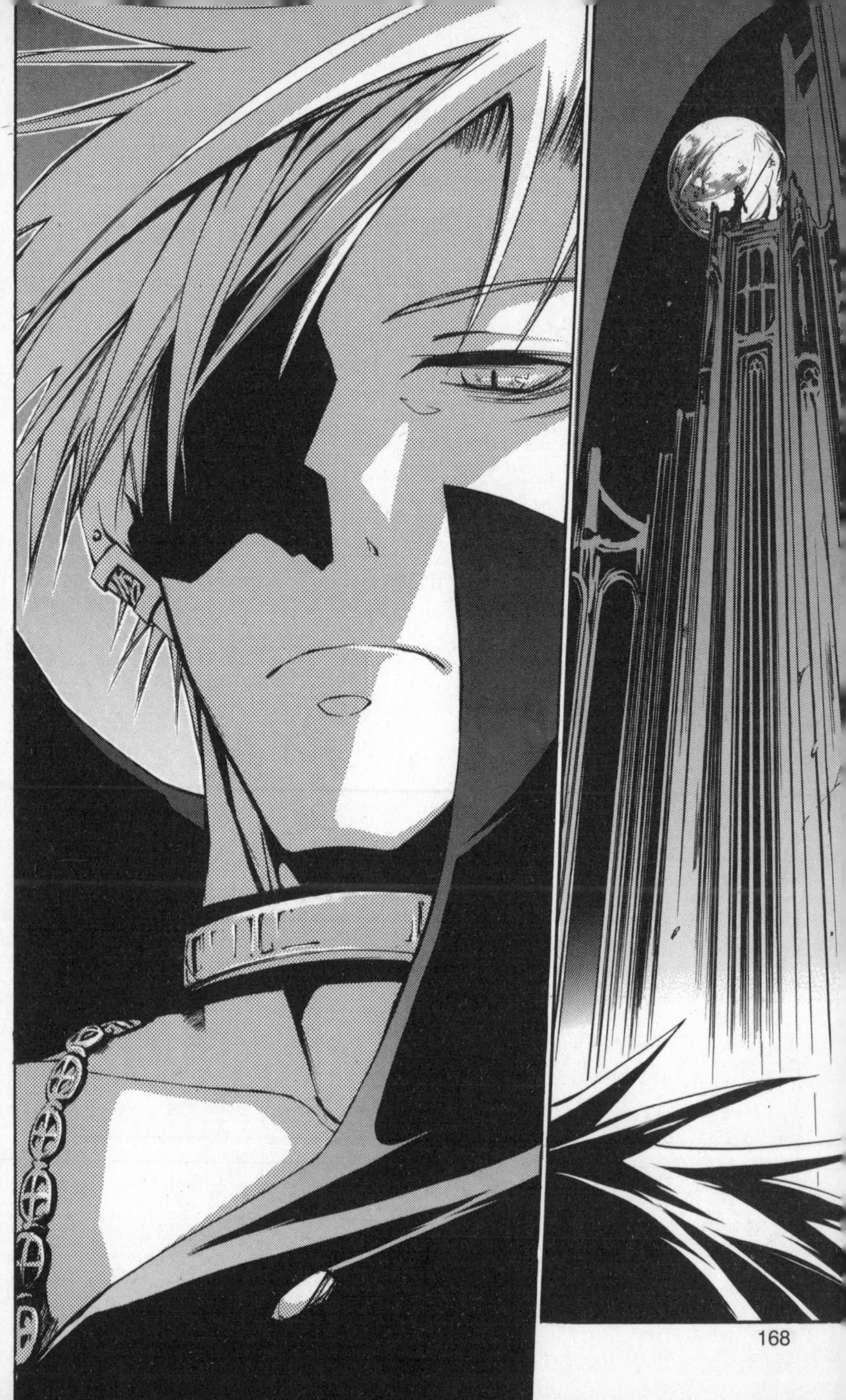

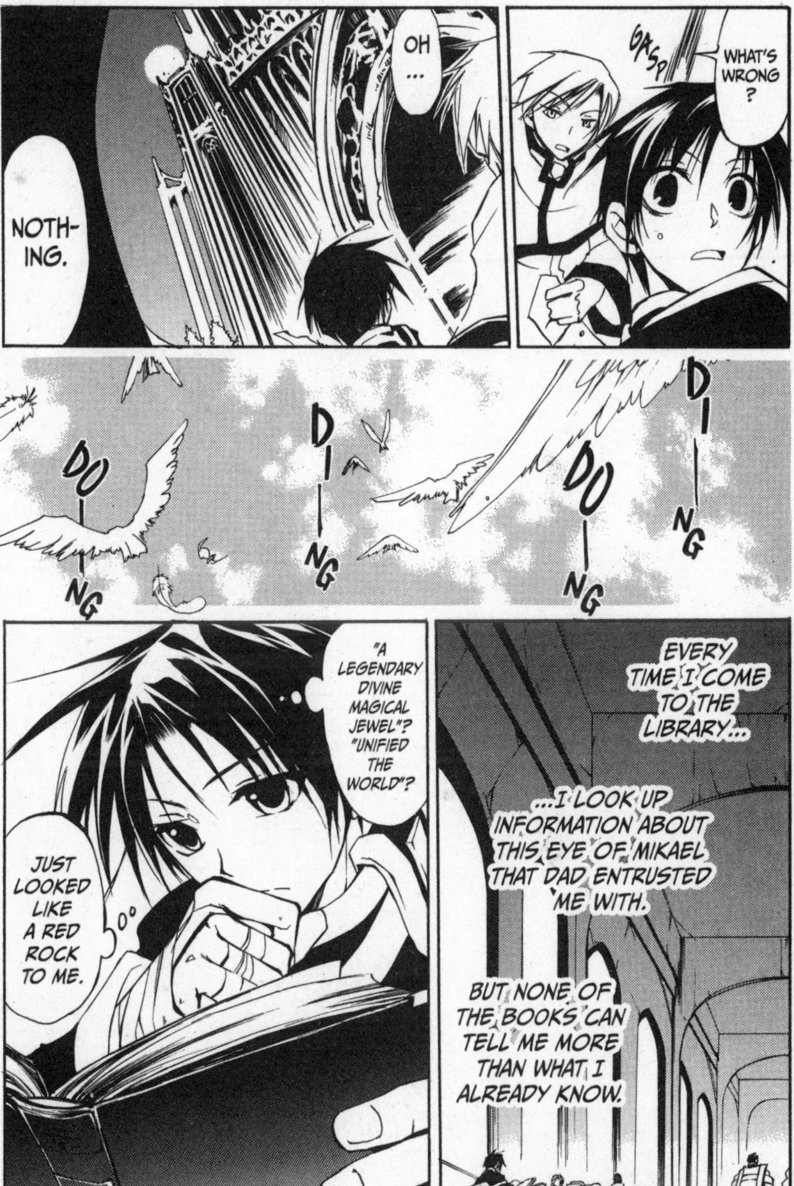
GASP
WHAT'S WRONG?
OH ...
NOTH-ING.
DI-I-NG
DO-NG
DI-I-NG
DO-NG
EVERY TIME I COME TO THE LIBRARY...
...I LOOK UP INFORMATION ABOUT THIS EYE OF MIKAEL THAT DAD ENTRUSTED ME WITH.
BUT NONE OF THE BOOKS CAN TELL ME MORE THAN WHAT I ALREADY KNOW.
"A LEGENDARY DIVINE MAGICAL JEWEL"? "UNIFIED THE WORLD"?
JUST LOOKED LIKE A RED ROCK TO ME.

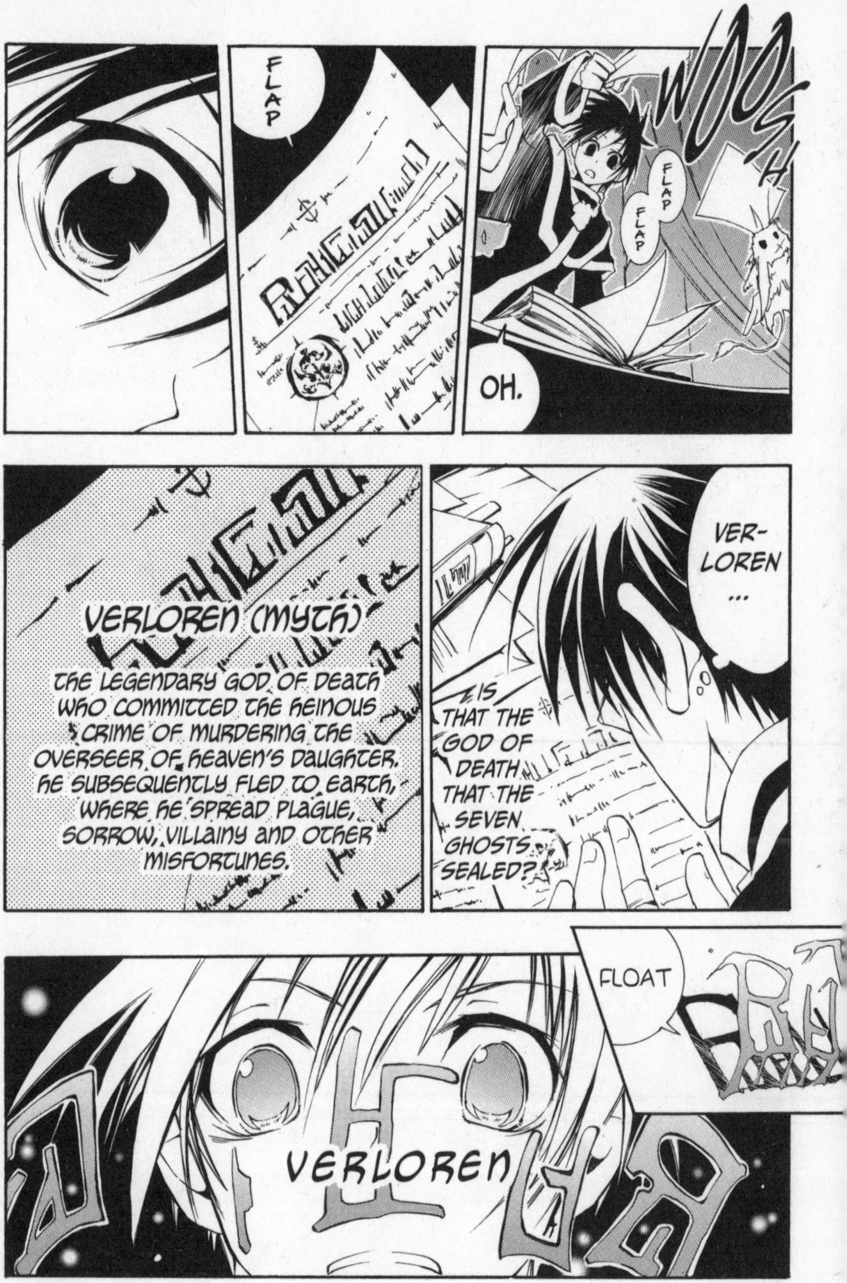
WOOSH
FLAP FLAP
OH.
FLAP
VER-LOREN...
IS THAT THE GOD OF DEATH THAT THE SEVEN GHOSTS SEALED?
VERLOREN (MYTH)
THE LEGENDARY GOD OF DEATH WHO COMMITTED THE HEINOUS CRIME OF MURDERING THE OVERSEER OF HEAVEN'S DAUGHTER. HE SUBSEQUENTLY FLED TO EARTH, WHERE HE SPREAD PLAGUE, SORROW, VILLAINY AND OTHER MISFORTUNES.
FLOAT
VERLOREN

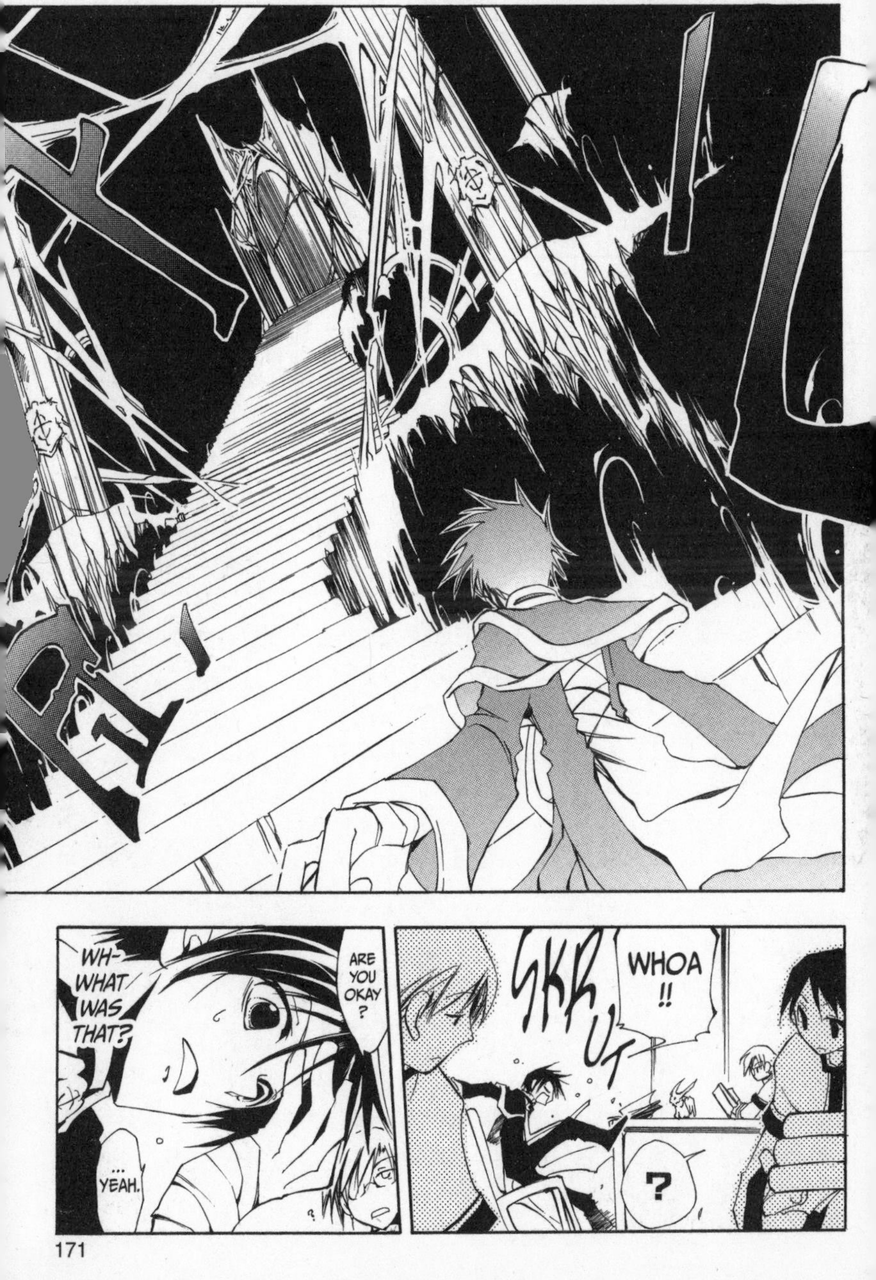
WHOA!!
SKRUT
?
ARE YOU OKAY?
WH-WHAT WAS THAT?
...YEAH.

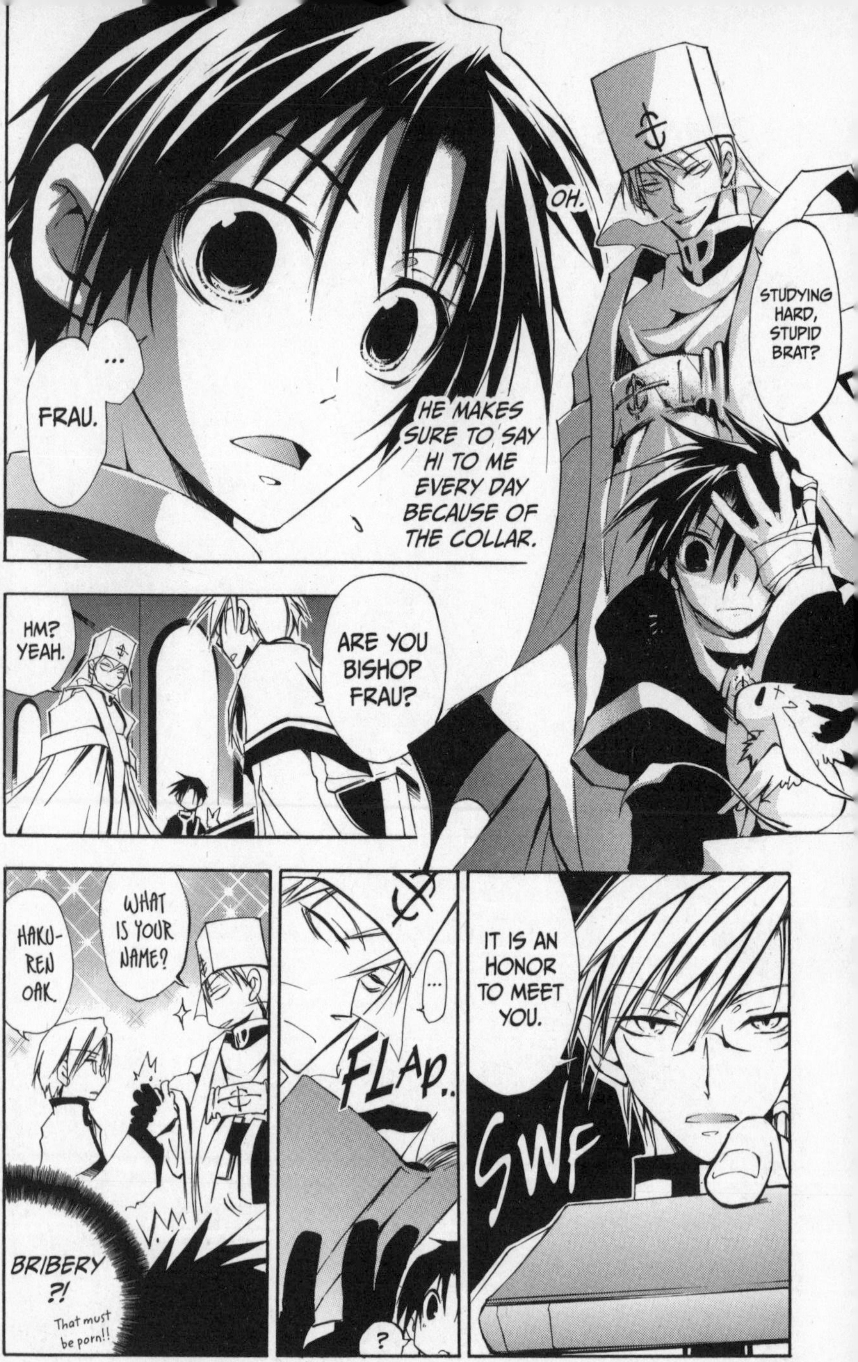
OH.
STUDYING HARD, STUPID BRAT?
...
FRAU.
HE MAKES SURE TO SAY HI TO ME EVERY DAY BECAUSE OF THE COLLAR.
ARE YOU BISHOP FRAU?
HM? YEAH.
IT IS AN HONOR TO MEET YOU.
SWF
...
FLAP..
?
WHAT IS YOUR NAME?
HAKU-REN OAK.
BRIBERY?!
That must be porn!!

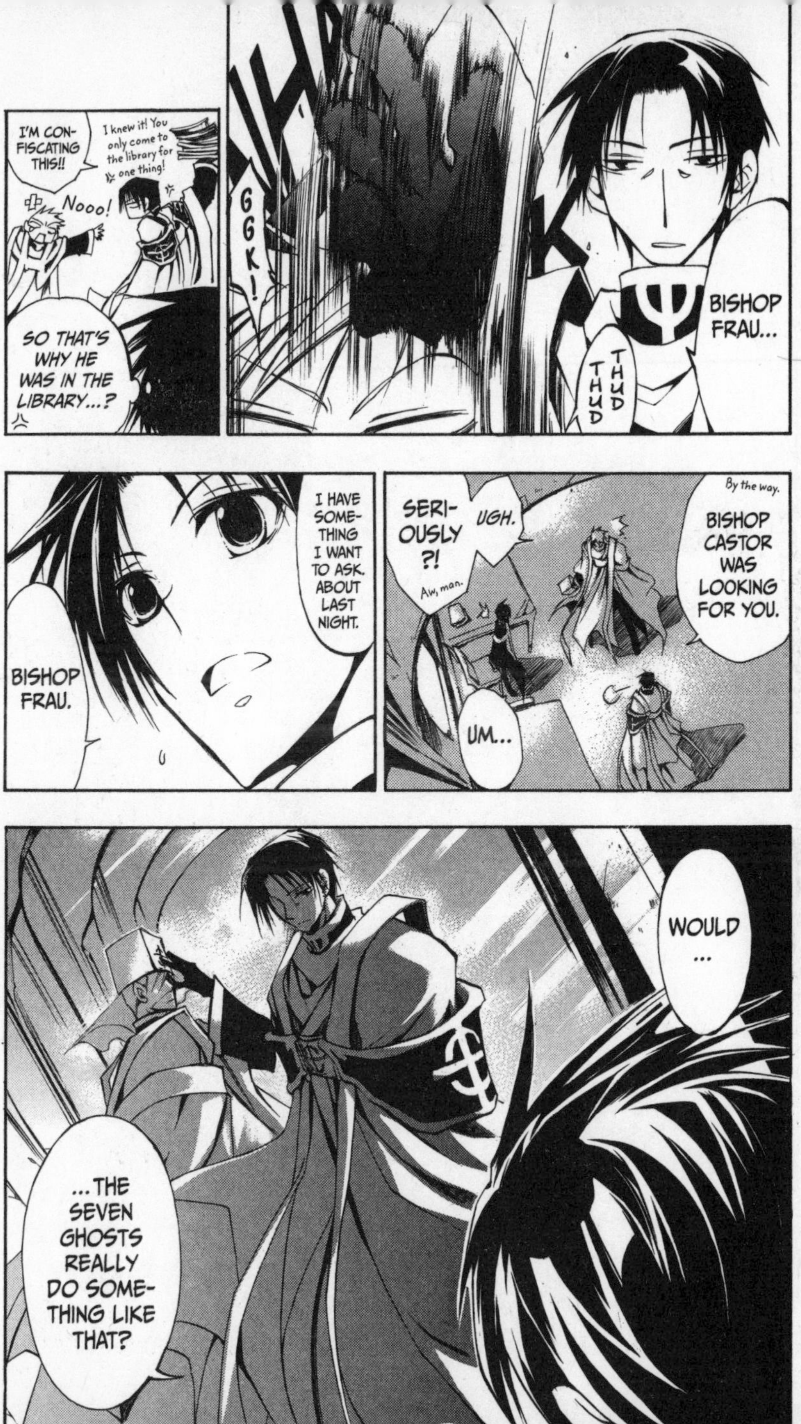
BISHOP FRAU...
THUD THUD
GGK!
I'M CONFISCATING THIS!!
I knew it! You only come to the library for one thing!
Nooo!
SO THAT'S WHY HE WAS IN THE LIBRARY...?
By the way.
BISHOP CASTOR WAS LOOKING FOR YOU.
UGH.
SERIOUSLY?!
Aw, man.
UM...
I HAVE SOMETHING I WANT TO ASK. ABOUT LAST NIGHT.
BISHOP FRAU.
WOULD...
...THE SEVEN GHOSTS REALLY DO SOMETHING LIKE THAT?

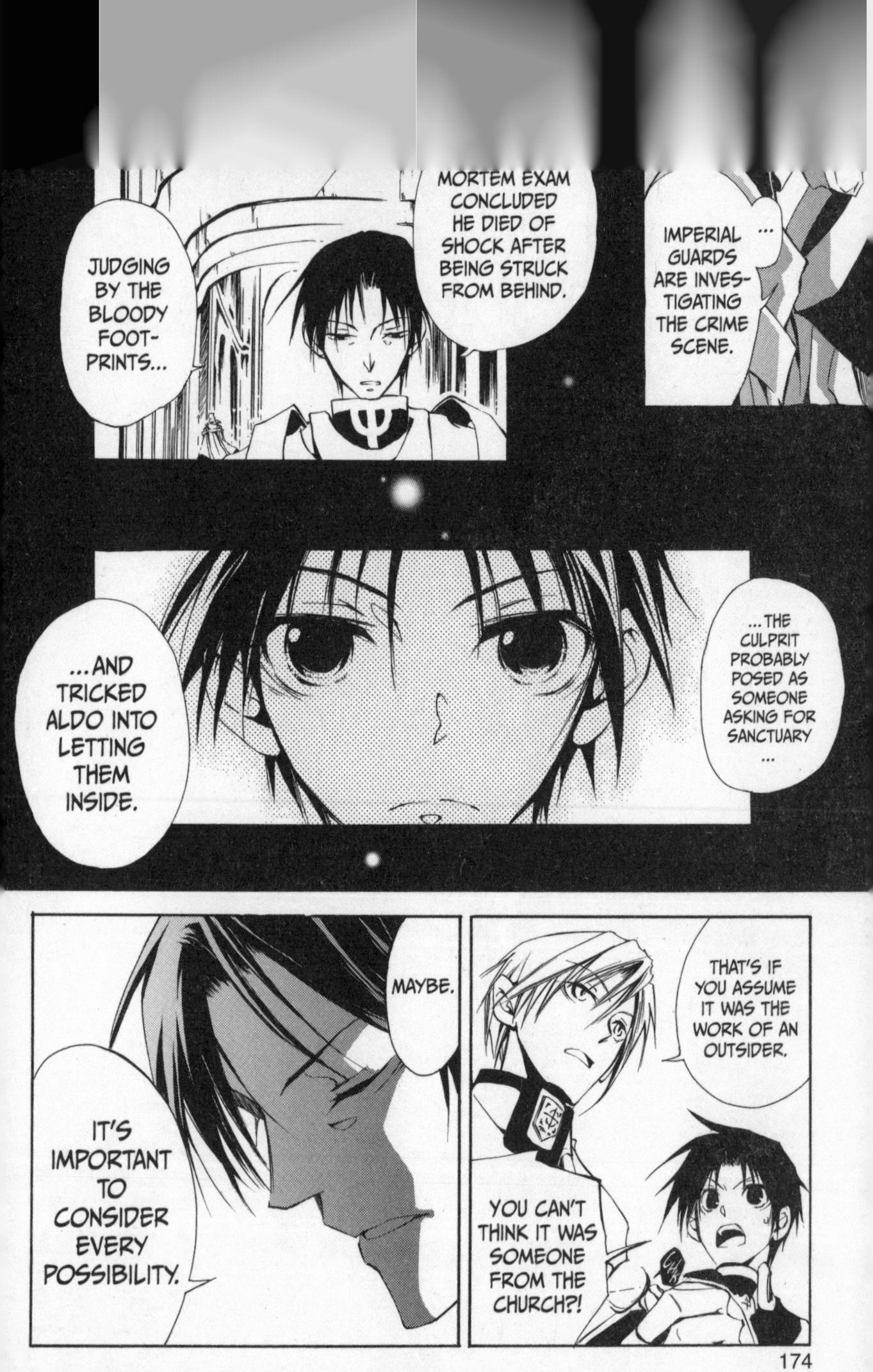
...
IMPERIAL GUARDS ARE INVES-TIGATING THE CRIME SCENE.
MORTEM EXAM CONCLUDED HE DIED OF SHOCK AFTER BEING STRUCK FROM BEHIND.
JUDGING BY THE BLOODY FOOT-PRINTS...
...THE CULPRIT PROBABLY POSED AS SOMEONE ASKING FOR SANCTUARY ...
...AND TRICKED ALDO INTO LETTING THEM INSIDE.
THAT'S IF YOU ASSUME IT WAS THE WORK OF AN OUTSIDER.
YOU CAN'T THINK IT WAS SOMEONE FROM THE CHURCH?!
MAYBE.
IT'S IMPORTANT TO CONSIDER EVERY POSSIBILITY.

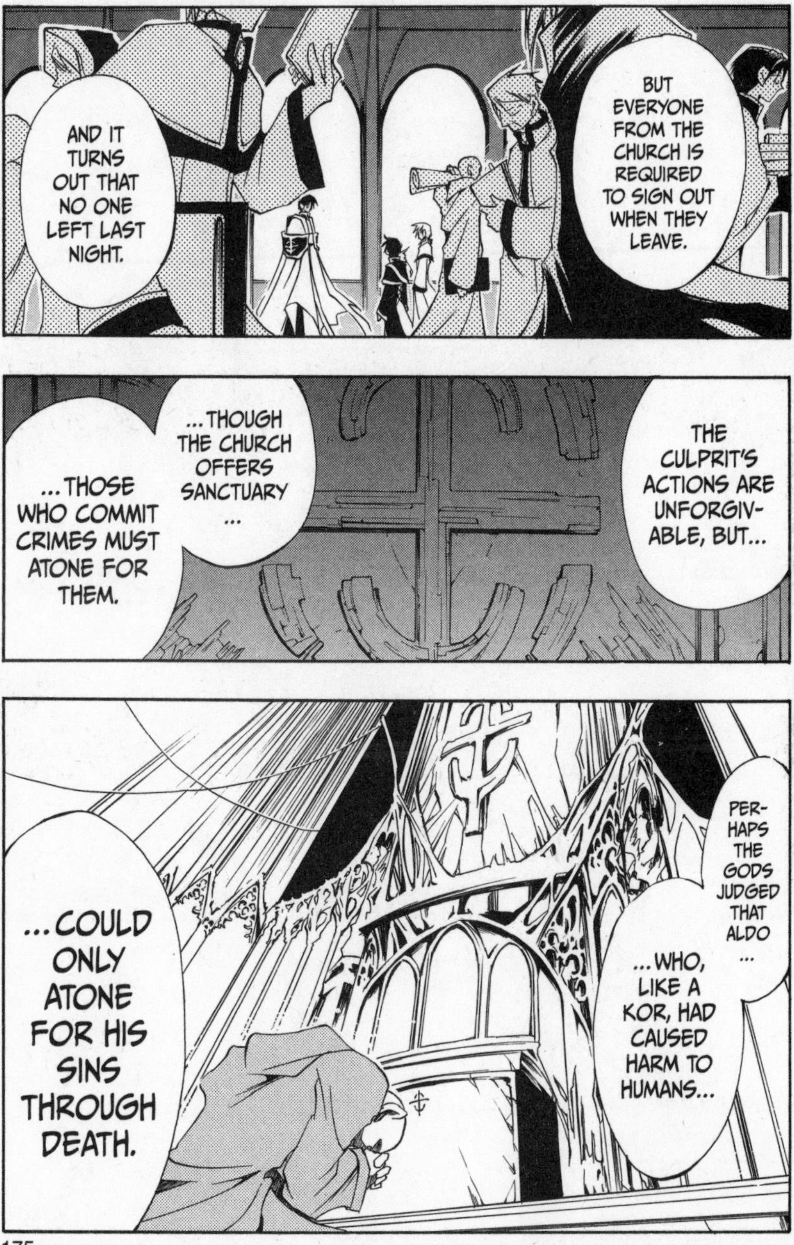
BUT EVERYONE FROM THE CHURCH IS REQUIRED TO SIGN OUT WHEN THEY LEAVE.
AND IT TURNS OUT THAT NO ONE LEFT LAST NIGHT.
THE CULPRIT'S ACTIONS ARE UNFORGIV-ABLE, BUT...
...THOUGH THE CHURCH OFFERS SANCTUARY ...
...THOSE WHO COMMIT CRIMES MUST ATONE FOR THEM.
PER-HAPS THE GODS JUDGED THAT ALDO ...
...WHO, LIKE A KOR, HAD CAUSED HARM TO HUMANS...
...COULD ONLY ATONE FOR HIS SINS THROUGH DEATH.

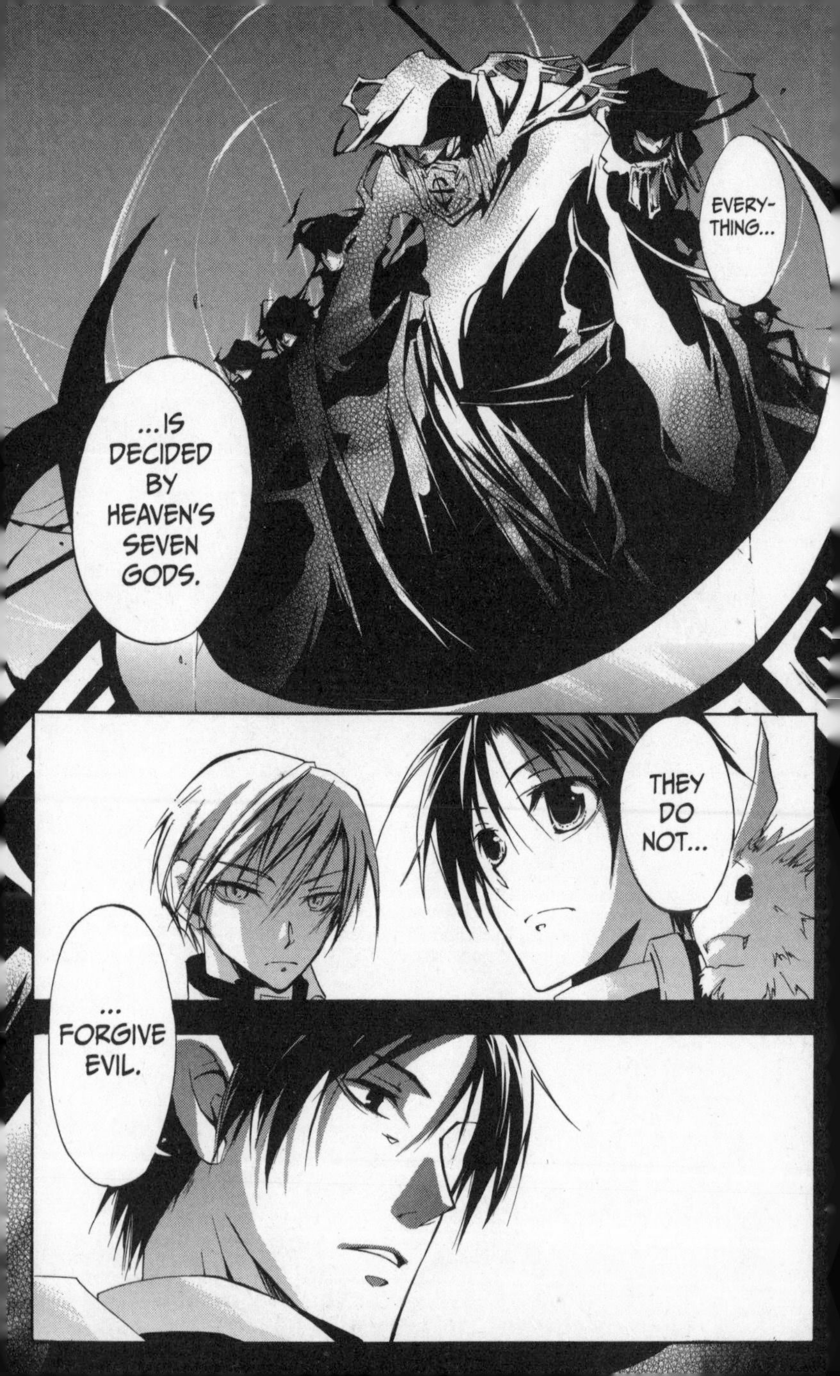
EVERY-THING...
...IS DECIDED BY HEAVEN'S SEVEN GODS.
THEY DO NOT...
... FORGIVE EVIL.

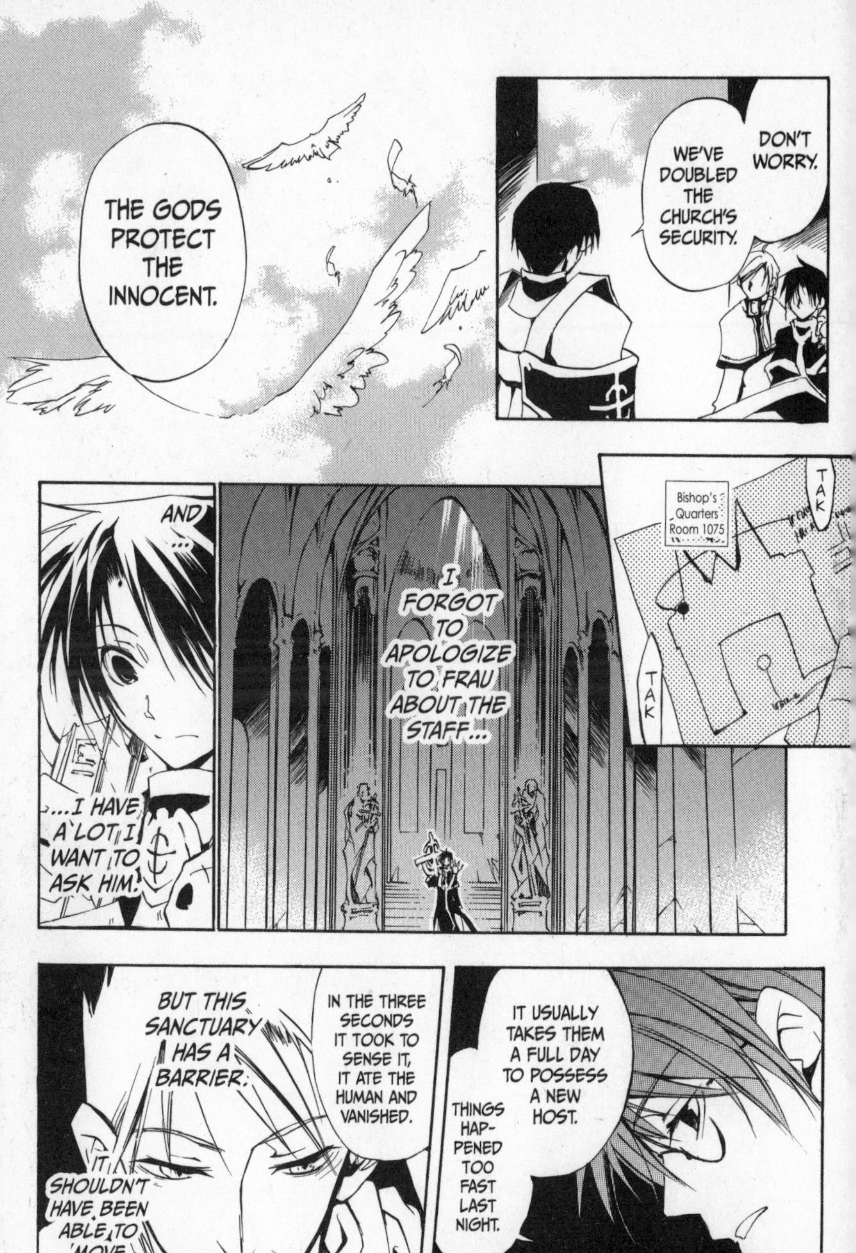
DON'T WORRY.
WE'VE DOUBLED THE CHURCH'S SECURITY.
THE GODS PROTECT THE INNOCENT.
TAK
Bishop's Quarters Room 1075
TAK
I FORGOT TO APOLOGIZE TO FRAU ABOUT THE STAFF...
AND ...
...I HAVE A LOT I WANT TO ASK HIM.
IT USUALLY TAKES THEM A FULL DAY TO POSSESS A NEW HOST.
THINGS HAP-PENED TOO FAST LAST NIGHT.
IN THE THREE SECONDS IT TOOK TO SENSE IT, IT ATE THE HUMAN AND VANISHED.
BUT THIS SANCTUARY HAS A BARRIER.
IT SHOULDN'T HAVE BEEN ABLE TO MOVE FREELY.

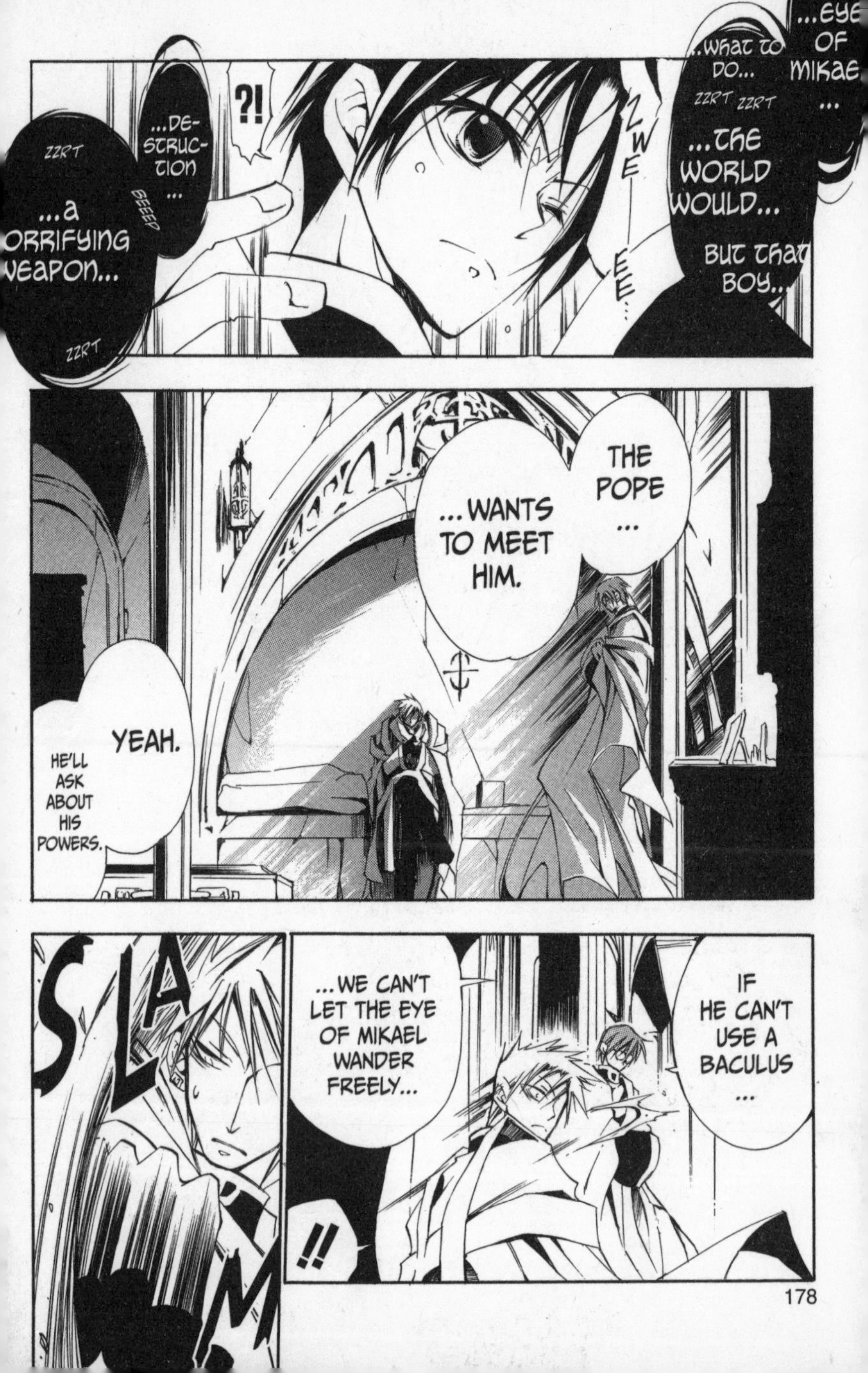
...EYE OF MIKAE ...
...WHAT TO DO...
ZZRT ZZRT
...THE WORLD WOULD...
BUT THAT BOY...
ZWEEE...
?!
...DE-STRUCTION ...
ZZRT
...a ORRIFYING VEAPON...
BEEEP
ZZRT
THE POPE ...
...WANTS TO MEET HIM.
YEAH.
HE'LL ASK ABOUT HIS POWERS.
IF HE CAN'T USE A BACULUS ...
...WE CAN'T LET THE EYE OF MIKAEL WANDER FREELY...
!!
SLAM

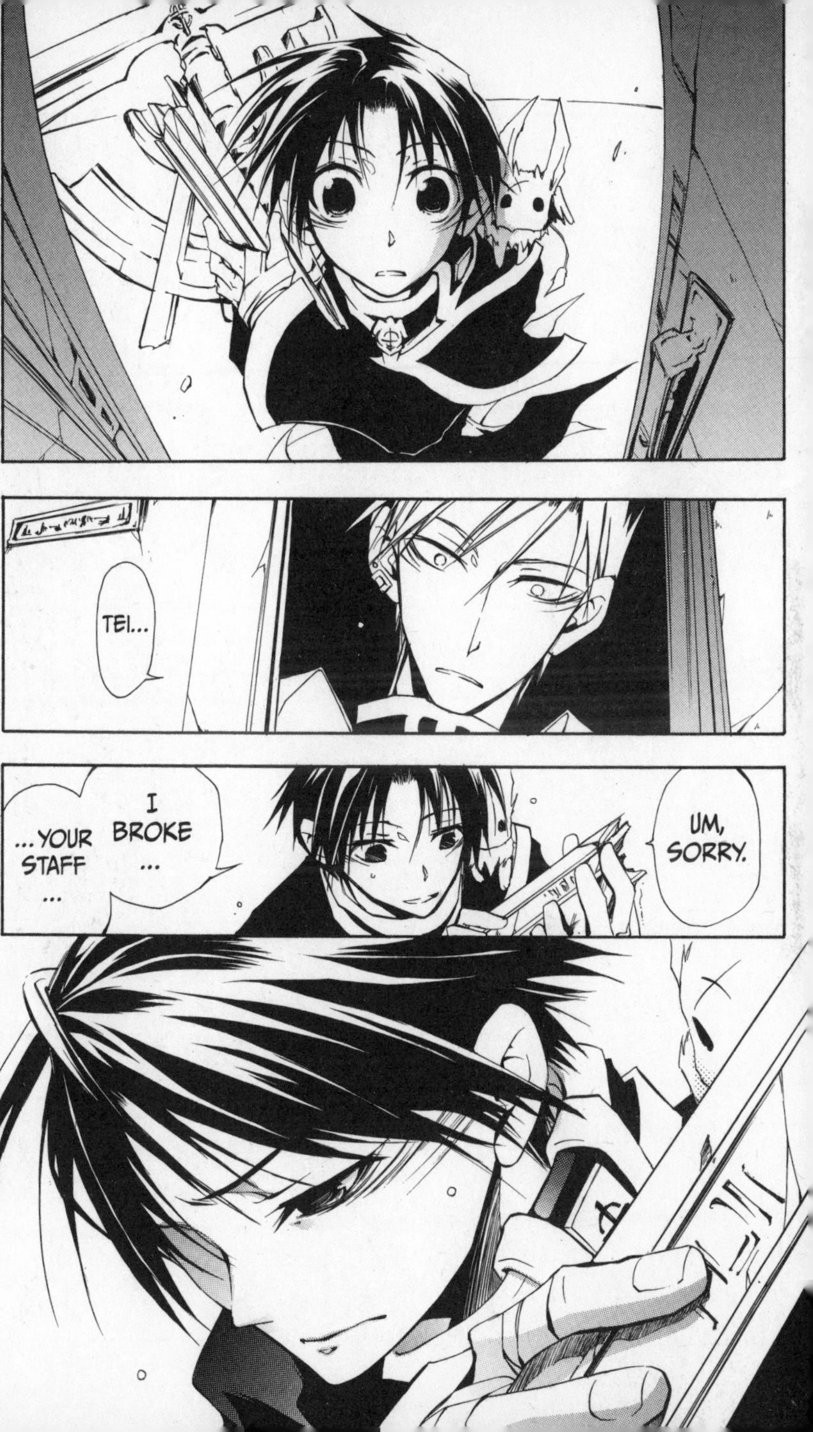
TEI...
UM, SORRY.
I BROKE ...
...YOUR STAFF ...

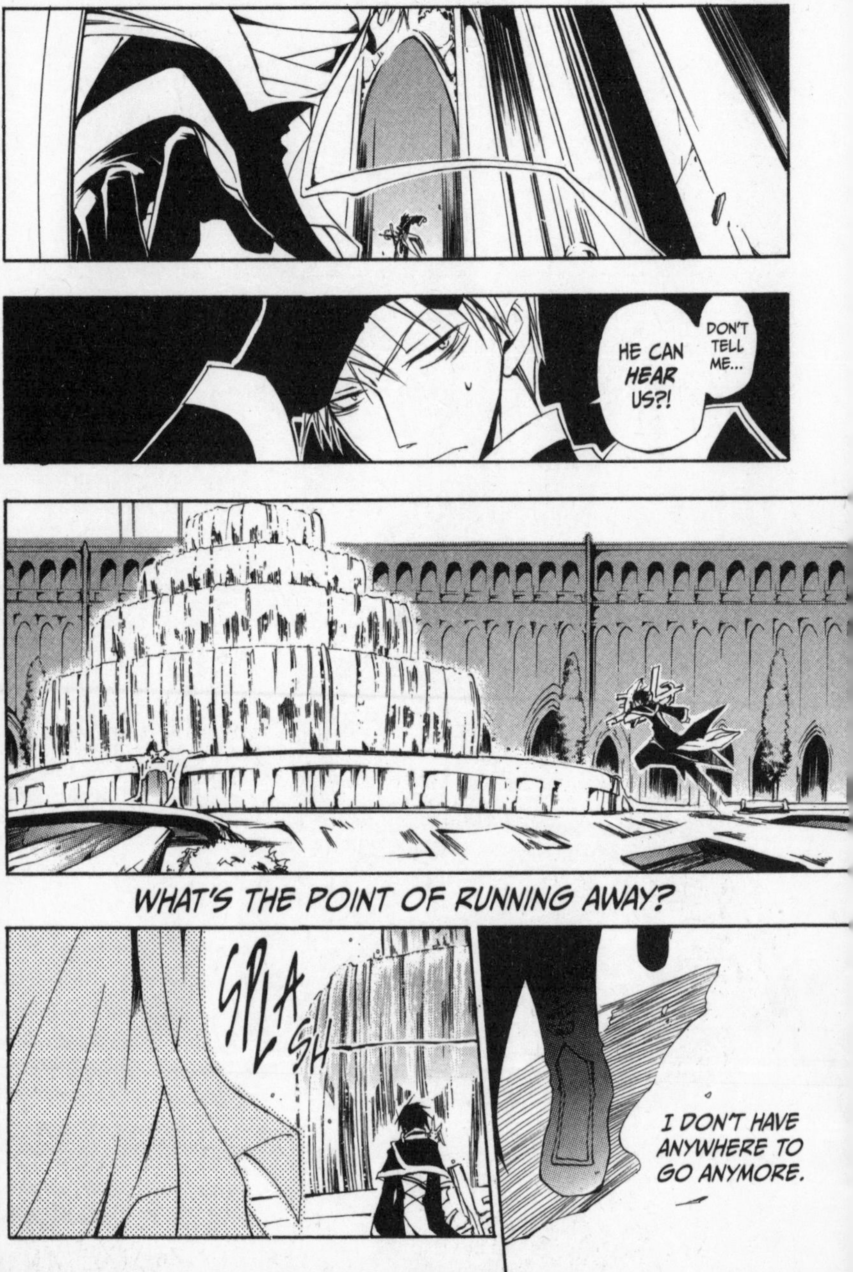
DON'T TELL ME...
HE CAN HEAR US?!
WHAT'S THE POINT OF RUNNING AWAY?
I DON'T HAVE ANYWHERE TO GO ANYMORE.
SPLASH

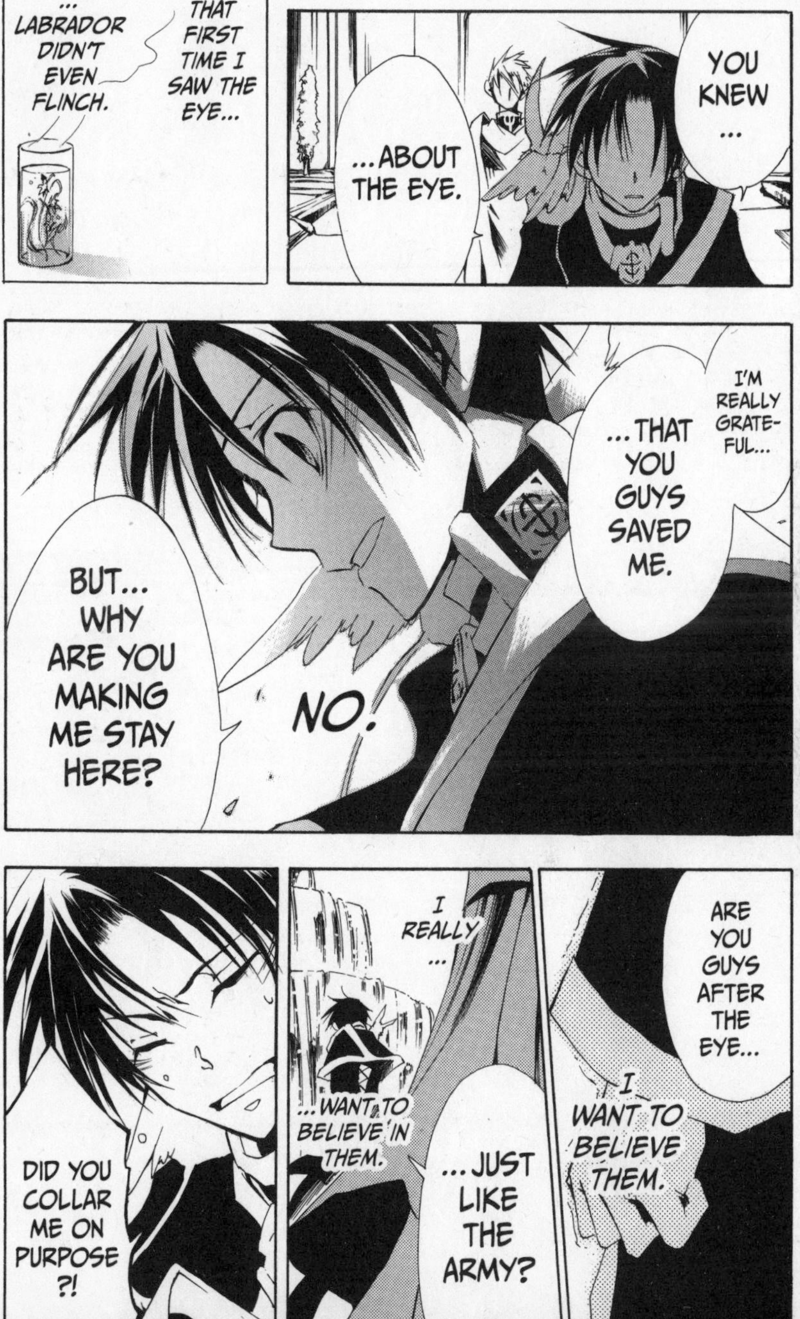
YOU KNEW...
...ABOUT THE EYE.
THAT FIRST TIME I SAW THE EYE...
...LABRADOR DIDN'T EVEN FLINCH.
I'M REALLY GRATE-FUL...
...THAT YOU GUYS SAVED ME.
NO.
BUT... WHY ARE YOU MAKING ME STAY HERE?
ARE YOU GUYS AFTER THE EYE...
...JUST LIKE THE ARMY?
I WANT TO BELIEVE THEM.
I REALLY...
...WANT TO BELIEVE IN THEM.
DID YOU COLLAR ME ON PURPOSE?!

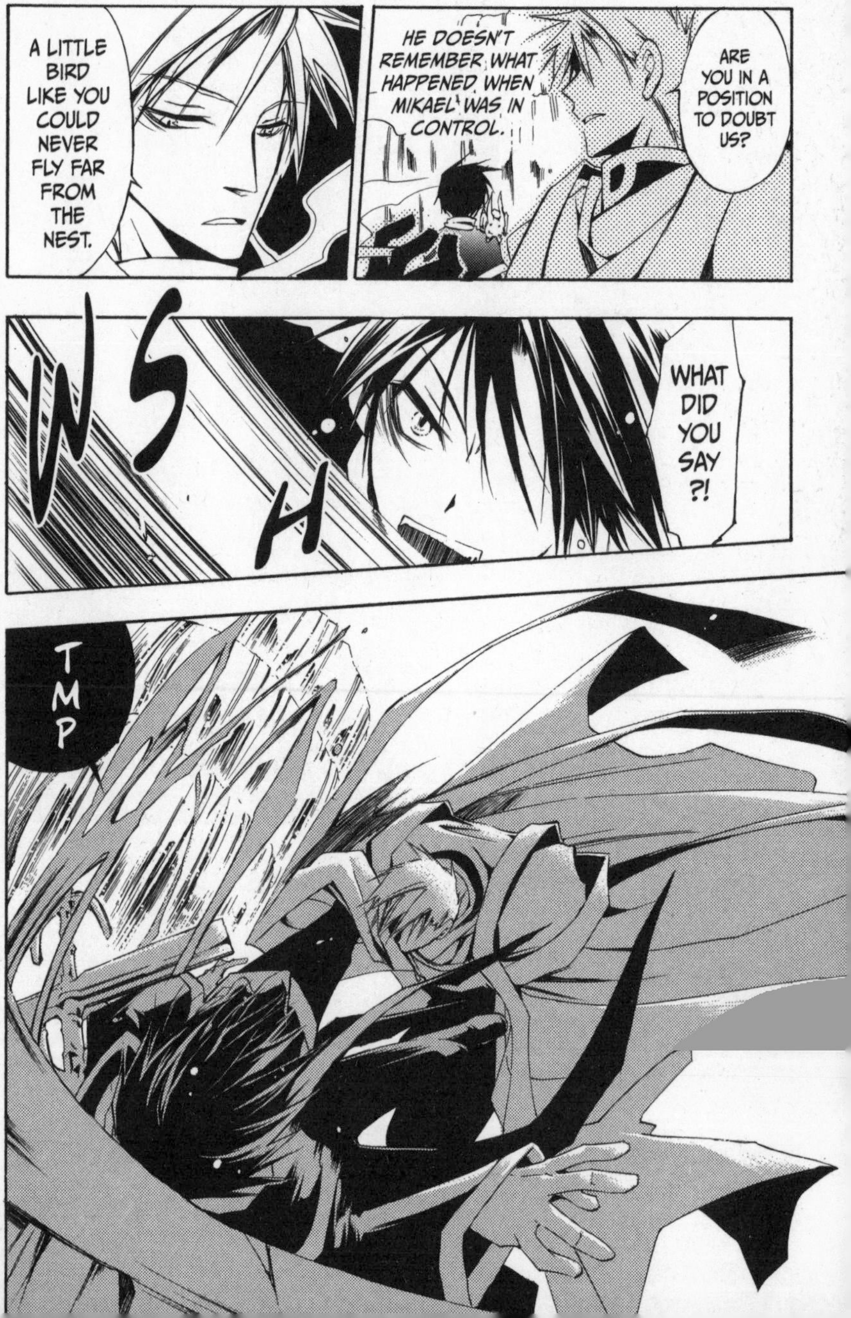
ARE YOU IN A POSITION TO DOUBT US?
HE DOESN'T REMEMBER WHAT HAPPENED WHEN MIKAEL WAS IN CONTROL.
A LITTLE BIRD LIKE YOU COULD NEVER FLY FAR FROM THE NEST.
WHAT DID YOU SAY ?!
WSH
TMP

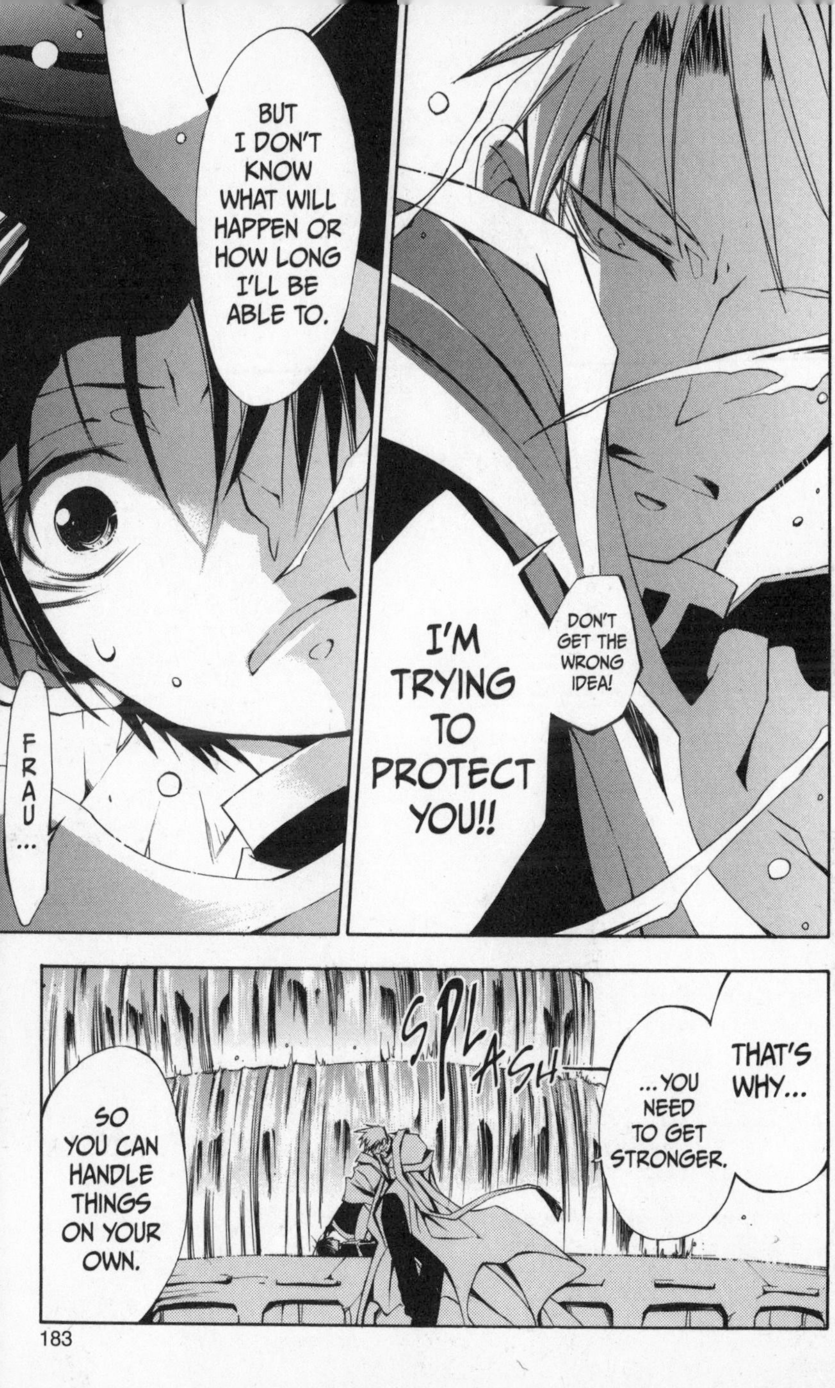
DON'T GET THE WRONG IDEA!
I'M TRYING TO PROTECT YOU!!
BUT I DON'T KNOW WHAT WILL HAPPEN OR HOW LONG I'LL BE ABLE TO.
FRAU...
THAT'S WHY...
...YOU NEED TO GET STRONGER.
SPLASH
SO YOU CAN HANDLE THINGS ON YOUR OWN.

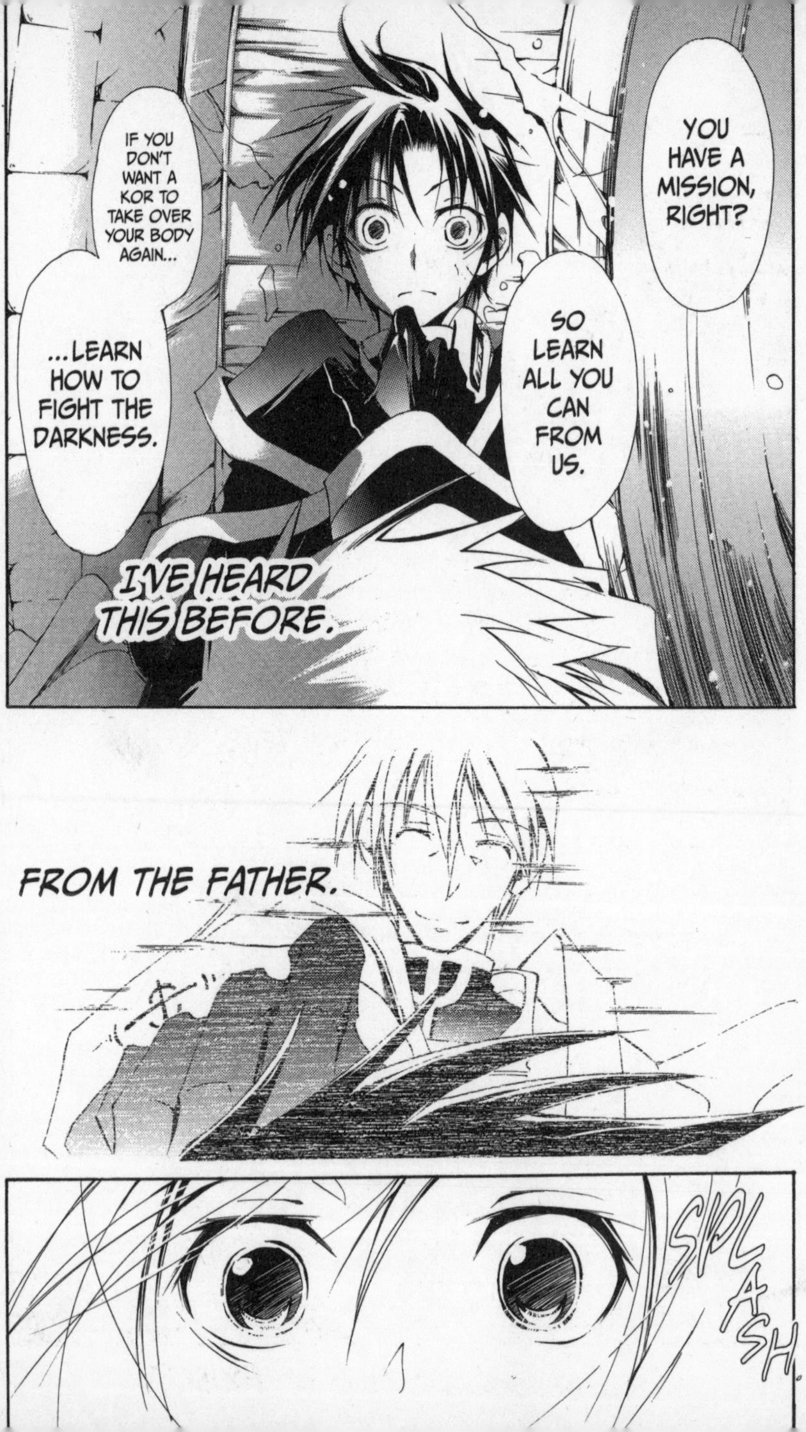
YOU HAVE A MISSION, RIGHT?
SO LEARN ALL YOU CAN FROM US.
IF YOU DON'T WANT A KOR TO TAKE OVER YOUR BODY AGAIN...
...LEARN HOW TO FIGHT THE DARKNESS.
I'VE HEARD THIS BEFORE.
FROM THE FATHER.
SPLASH

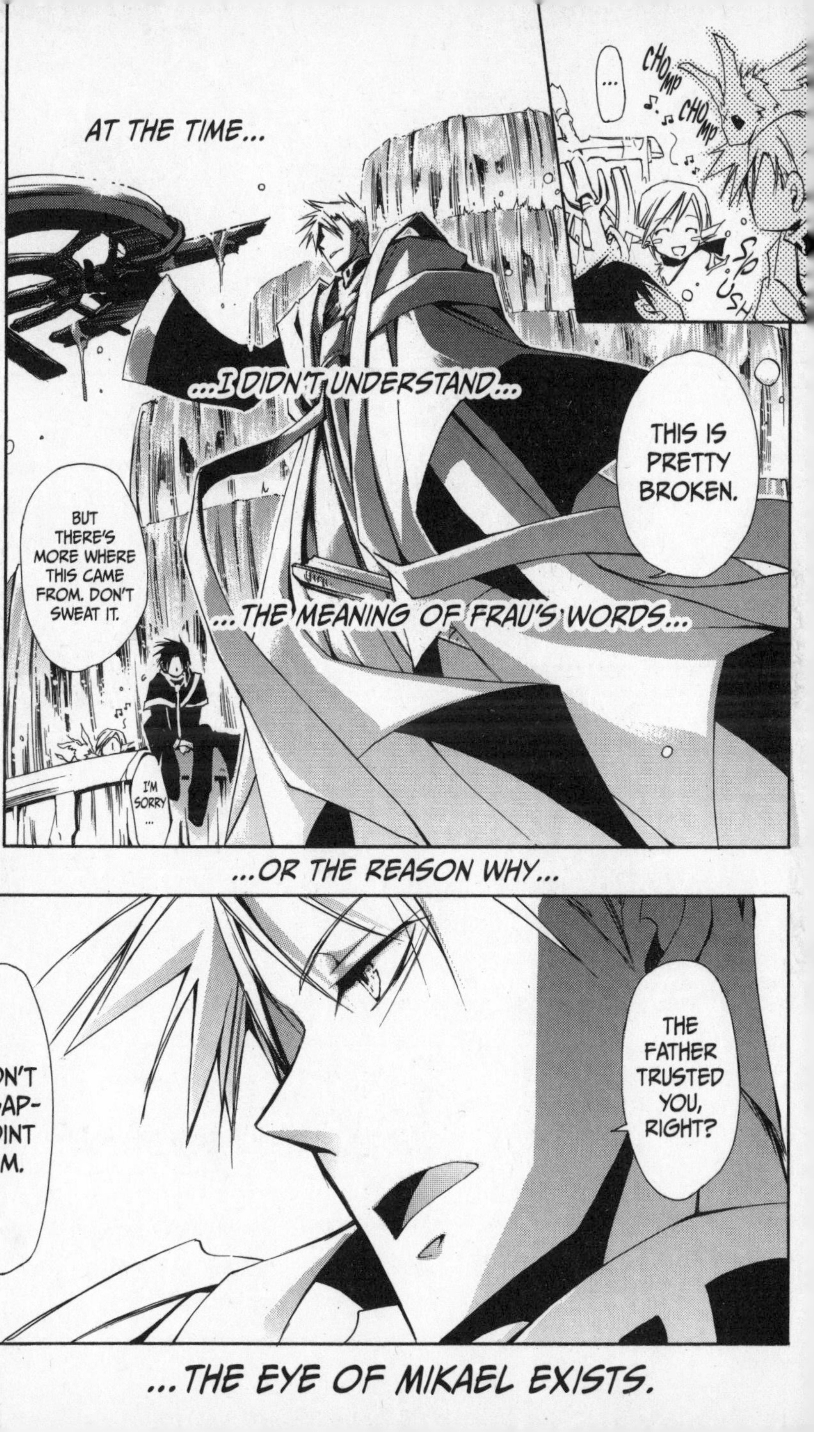
...
CHOMP CHOMP
SPLUSH
AT THE TIME...
...I DIDN'T UNDERSTAND...
THIS IS PRETTY BROKEN.
BUT THERE'S MORE WHERE THIS CAME FROM. DON'T SWEAT IT.
...THE MEANING OF FRAU'S WORDS...
I'M SORRY...
...OR THE REASON WHY...
THE FATHER TRUSTED YOU, RIGHT?
DON'T DISAPPOINT HIM.
...THE EYE OF MIKAEL EXISTS.

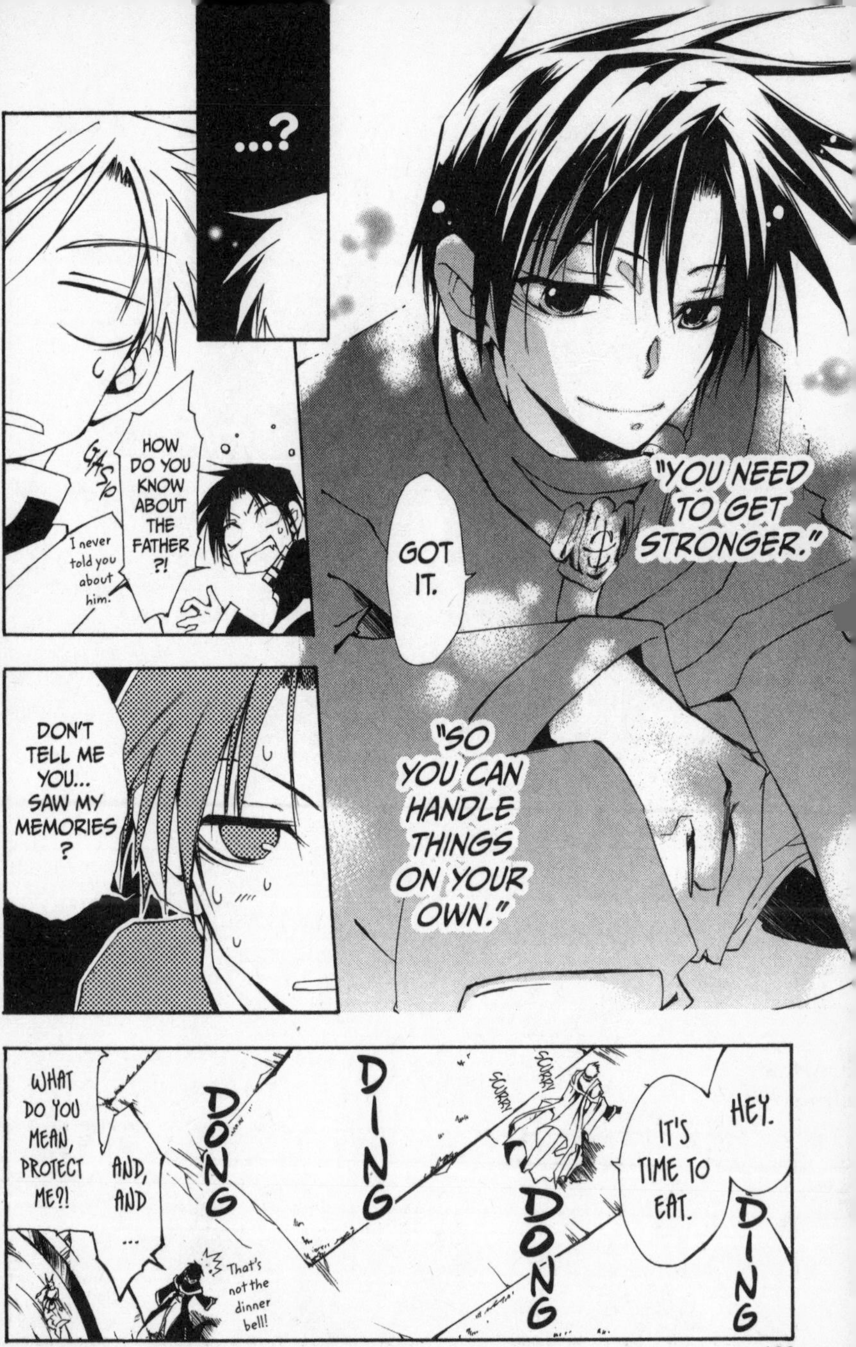
"YOU NEED TO GET STRONGER."
GOT IT.
"SO YOU CAN HANDLE THINGS ON YOUR OWN."
...?
HOW DO YOU KNOW ABOUT THE FATHER ?!
I never told you about him.
GASP
DON'T TELL ME YOU... SAW MY MEMORIES ?
HEY.
IT'S TIME TO EAT.
DING
DONG
SCURRY SCURRY
DING
DONG
AND, AND ...
WHAT DO YOU MEAN, PROTECT ME?!
That's not the dinner bell!

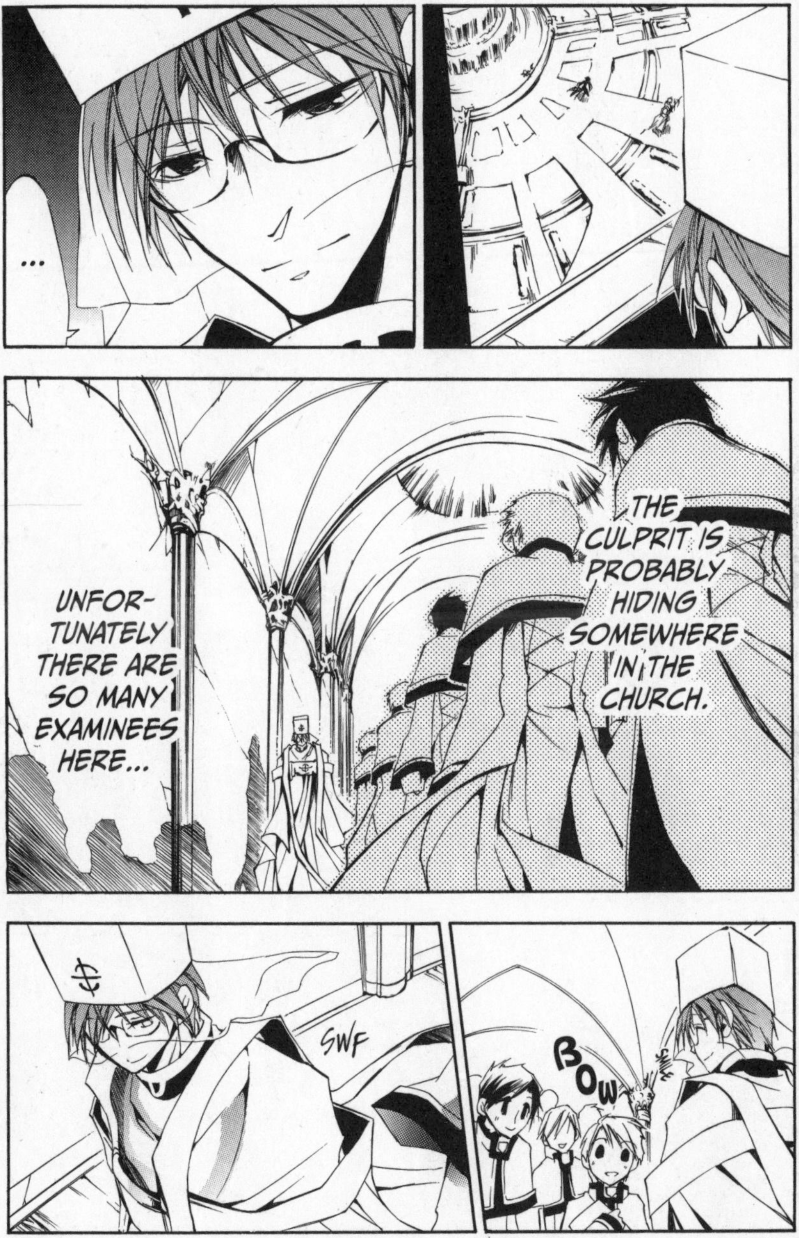
...
THE CULPRIT IS PROBABLY HIDING SOMEWHERE IN THE CHURCH.
UNFOR-TUNATELY THERE ARE SO MANY EXAMINEES HERE...
BOW
SWF

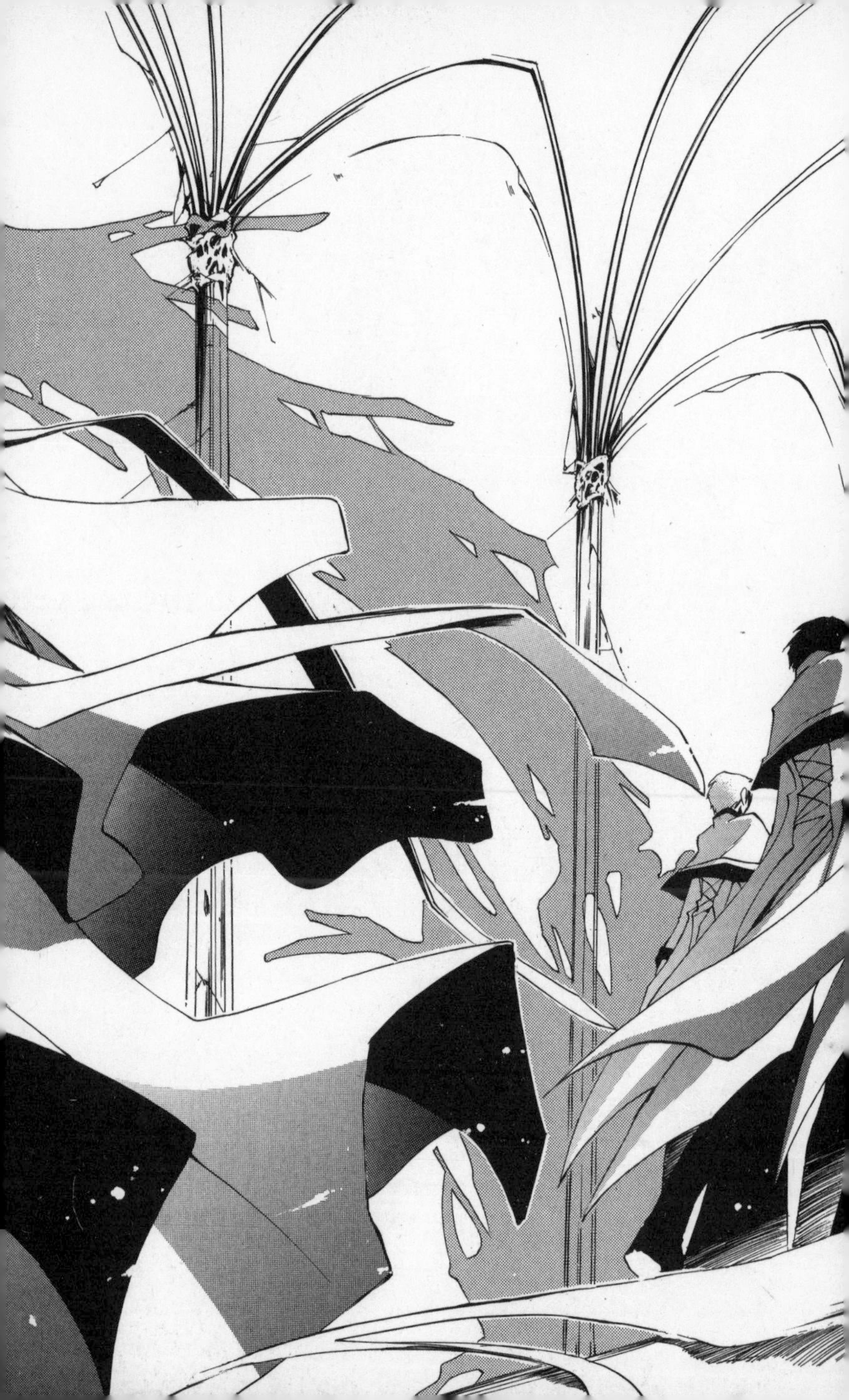

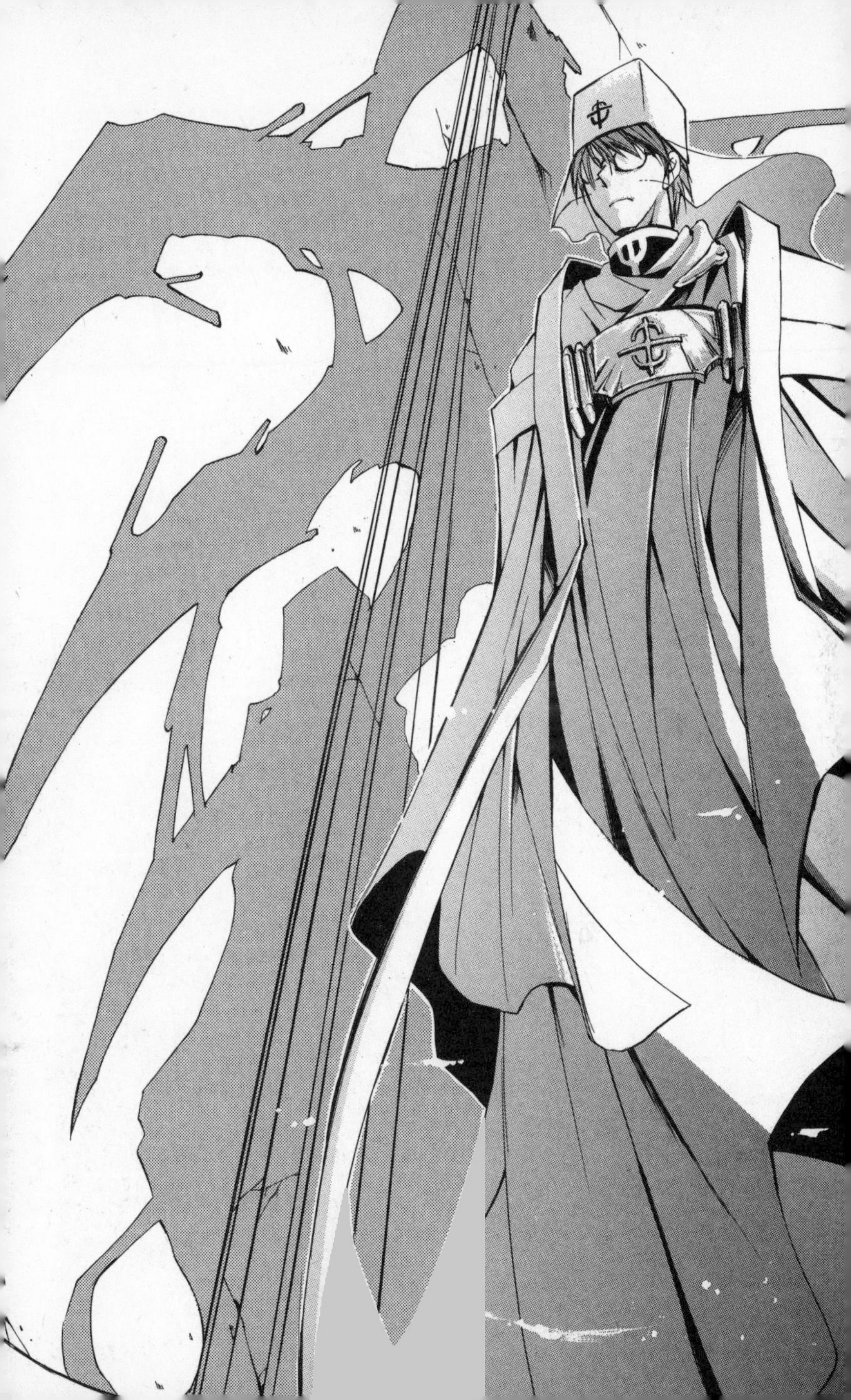

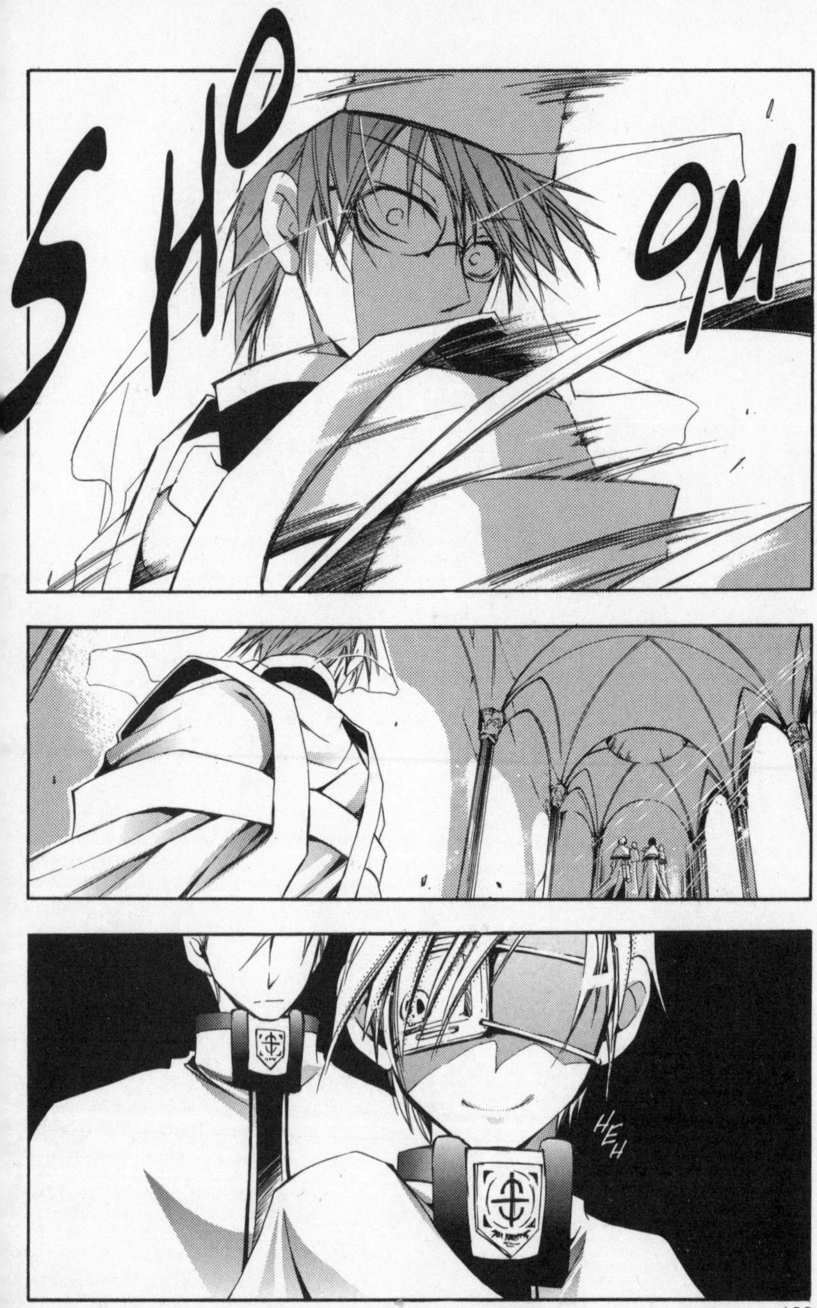
SHOOM
HEH

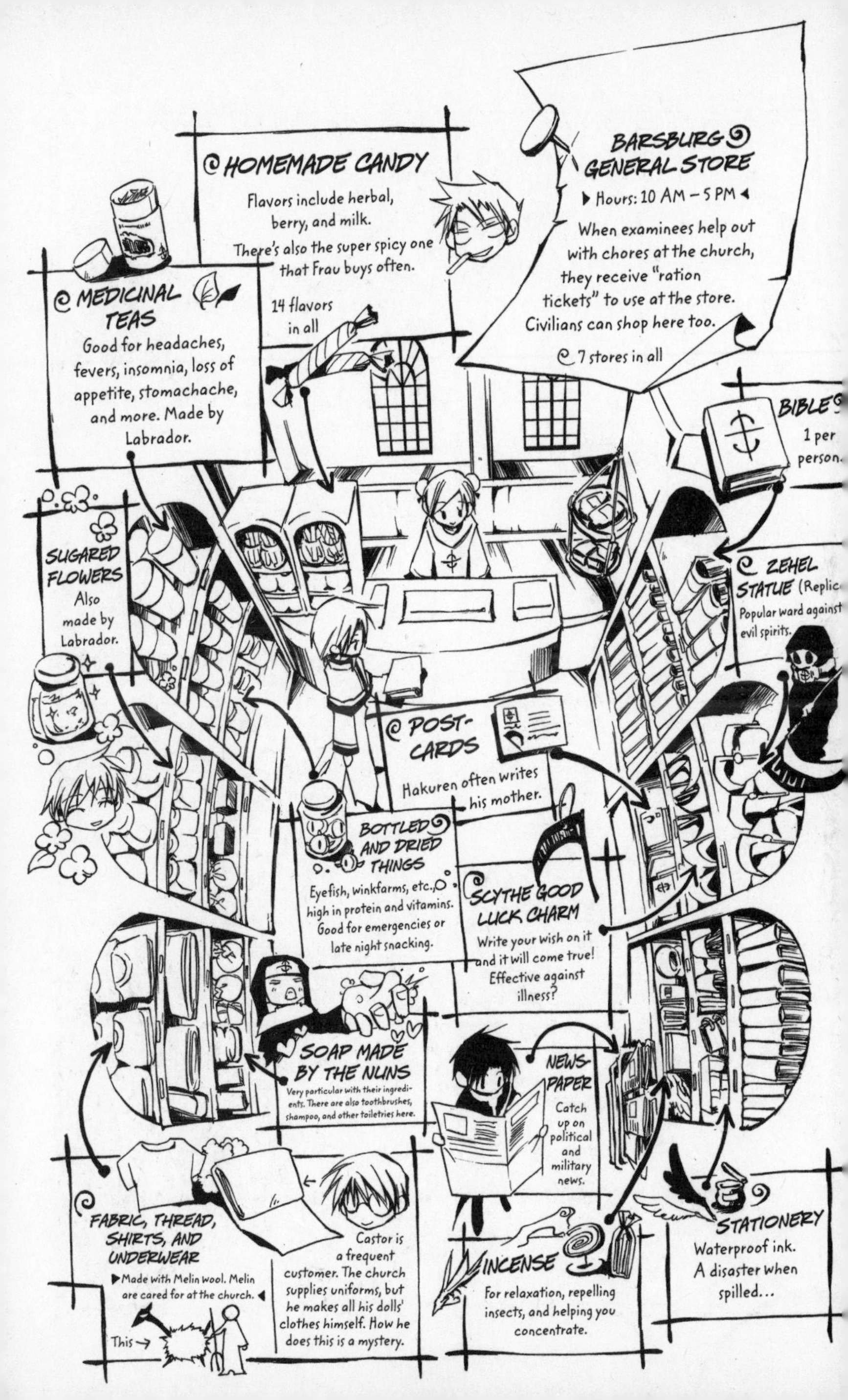
BARSBURG GENERAL STORE
Hours: 10 AM – 5 PM
When examinees help out with chores at the church, they receive "ration tickets" to use at the store. Civilians can shop here too.
7 stores in all
HOMEMADE CANDY
Flavors include herbal, berry, and milk.
There's also the super spicy one that Frau buys often.
14 flavors in all
MEDICINAL TEAS
Good for headaches, fevers, insomnia, loss of appetite, stomachache, and more. Made by Labrador.
BIBLES
1 per person.
ZEHEL STATUE (Replic
Popular ward against evil spirits.
SUGARED FLOWERS
Also made by Labrador.
POST-CARDS
Hakuren often writes his mother.
BOTTLED AND DRIED THINGS
Eyefish, winkfarms, etc., high in protein and vitamins. Good for emergencies or late night snacking.
SCYTHE GOOD LUCK CHARM
Write your wish on it and it will come true! Effective against illness?
SOAP MADE BY THE NUNS
Very particular with their ingredients. There are also toothbrushes, shampoo, and other toiletries here.
NEWS-PAPER
Catch up on political and military news.
FABRIC, THREAD, SHIRTS, AND UNDERWEAR
Made with Melin wool. Melin are cared for at the church.
This →
Castor is a frequent customer. The church supplies uniforms, but he makes all his dolls' clothes himself. How he does this is a mystery.
INCENSE
For relaxation, repelling insects, and helping you concentrate.
STATIONERY
Waterproof ink. A disaster when spilled...

Part 1

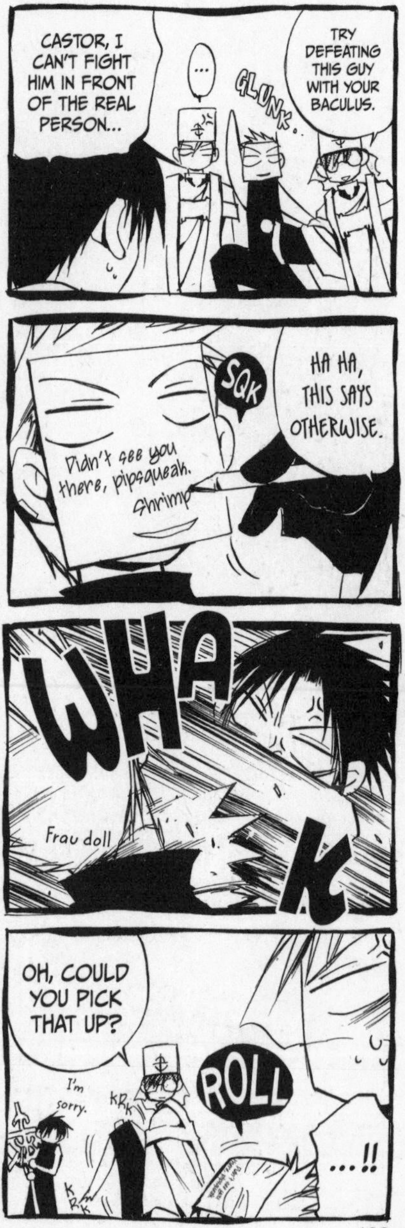
TRY DEFEATING THIS GUY WITH YOUR BACULUS.
GLUNK...
...
CASTOR, I CAN'T FIGHT HIM IN FRONT OF THE REAL PERSON...
HA HA, THIS SAYS OTHERWISE.
SQK
Didn't see you there, pipsqueak. Shrimp
WHAK
Frau doll
OH, COULD YOU PICK THAT UP?
ROLL
...!!
KRK
I'm sorry.
KRK

Part 2

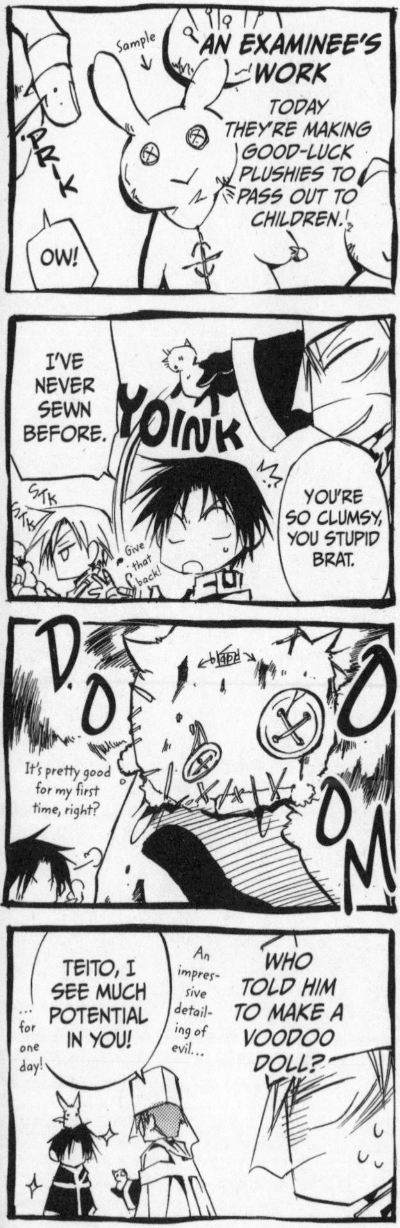
AN EXAMINEE'S WORK
TODAY THEY'RE MAKING GOOD-LUCK PLUSHIES TO PASS OUT TO CHILDREN.
Sample
PRIK
OW!
YOINK
YOU'RE SO CLUMSY, YOU STUPID BRAT.
I'VE NEVER SEWN BEFORE.
STK STK
Give that back!
DOOM
It's pretty good for my first time, right?
WHO TOLD HIM TO MAKE A VOODOO DOLL?
An impressive detailing of evil...
TEITO, I SEE MUCH POTENTIAL IN YOU!
...for one day!

Afterword

Thank you (very much) for picking up this book. It's thanks to our supporters that this volume exists.

For two volumes in a row now Teito has been losing things he holds dear, but we love people who triumph against the odds. We'd be delighted if you watched with us as Teito struggles to scramble up from rock bottom.

To the people who pick up this book, to the people who read our series in the magazine, to the people who send us letters and emails with suggestions and support, to the people who work hard alongside us to create this manga and give us advice, to our friends...
We love you all.

Thank you very much ♥♥ April 2006
Amemiya & Ichihara

Part 3

OOH, A PICNIC. ♡
Sweet!
K
YOU'RE WELCOME TO JOIN.
A PICNIC LUNCH MADE BY THE GREAT LIEUTENANT-COLONEL KUROYURI! I'M GLAD TO BE ALIVE! BUT WHAT'S THE RED THING, AND THE BROWN AND BLUE ONES?
Haruse
SASHIMI WITH STRAWBERRY JAM. BOILED EGG COVERED IN CHOCOLATE. THE BLUE ONE IS A SECRET. ♥
YUM! ♡
HUH?
Konatsu

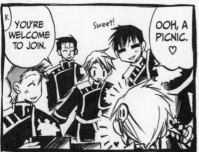

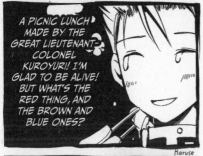

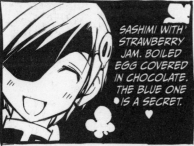

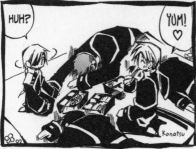

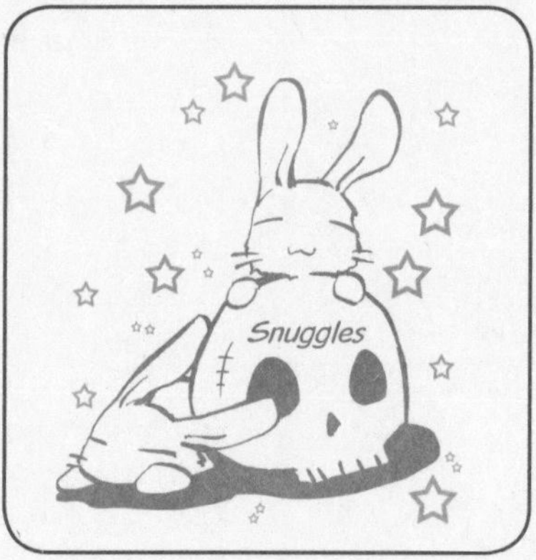
Snuggles

The path in front of our house is always packed with joggers. We joined the stampede in an effort to be more active, but all the fit old guys left us in the dust!

—Yuki Amemiya & Yukino Ichihara, 2006

Yuki Amemiya was born in Miyagi, Japan, on March 25. Yukino Ichihara was born in Fukushima, Japan, on November 24. Together they write and illustrate *07-Ghost*, the duo's first series. Since its debut in 2005, *07-Ghost* has been translated into a dozen languages, and in 2009 it was adapted into a TV anime series.

GON FREECSS

冨樫義博

My assistant made this—it's a double-layered sticker. The top layer is just the fishing rod, so if you peel it off, it's just Gon punching! That's so awesome!!

Yoshihiro Togashi

Yoshihiro Togashi's manga career began in 1986 at the age of 20, when he won the coveted Osamu Tezuka Award for new manga artists. He debuted in the Japanese **Weekly Shonen Jump** magazine in 1989 with the romantic comedy **Tende Shôwaru Cupid**. From 1990 to 1994 he wrote and drew the hit manga **YuYu Hakusho**, which was followed by the dark comedy science-fiction series **Level E**, and finally this adventure series, **Hunter x Hunter**, available from VIZ Media's SHONEN JUMP Advanced imprint. In 1999 he married the manga artist Naoko Takeuchi.

HUNTER X HUNTER Volume 24
SHONEN JUMP ADVANCED Manga Edition

STORY AND ART BY
YOSHIHIRO TOGASHI

English Adaptation & Translation/Lillian Olsen
Touch-up Art & Lettering/Mark McMurray
Design/Matt Hinrichs
Editor/Yuki Murashige

Printed in Canada

Published by VIZ Media, LLC
P.O. Box 77010
San Francisco, CA 94107

10 9 8 7 6 5 4 3 2
First printing, January 2009
Second printing, January 2016

www.viz.com

RATED T+ FOR OLDER TEEN

PARENTAL ADVISORY
HUNTER X HUNTER is rated T+ for Older Teen and is recommended for ages 16 and up. Contains realistic violence and mature language.

ratings.viz.com

www.shonenjump.com

SHONEN JUMP ADVANCED MANGA

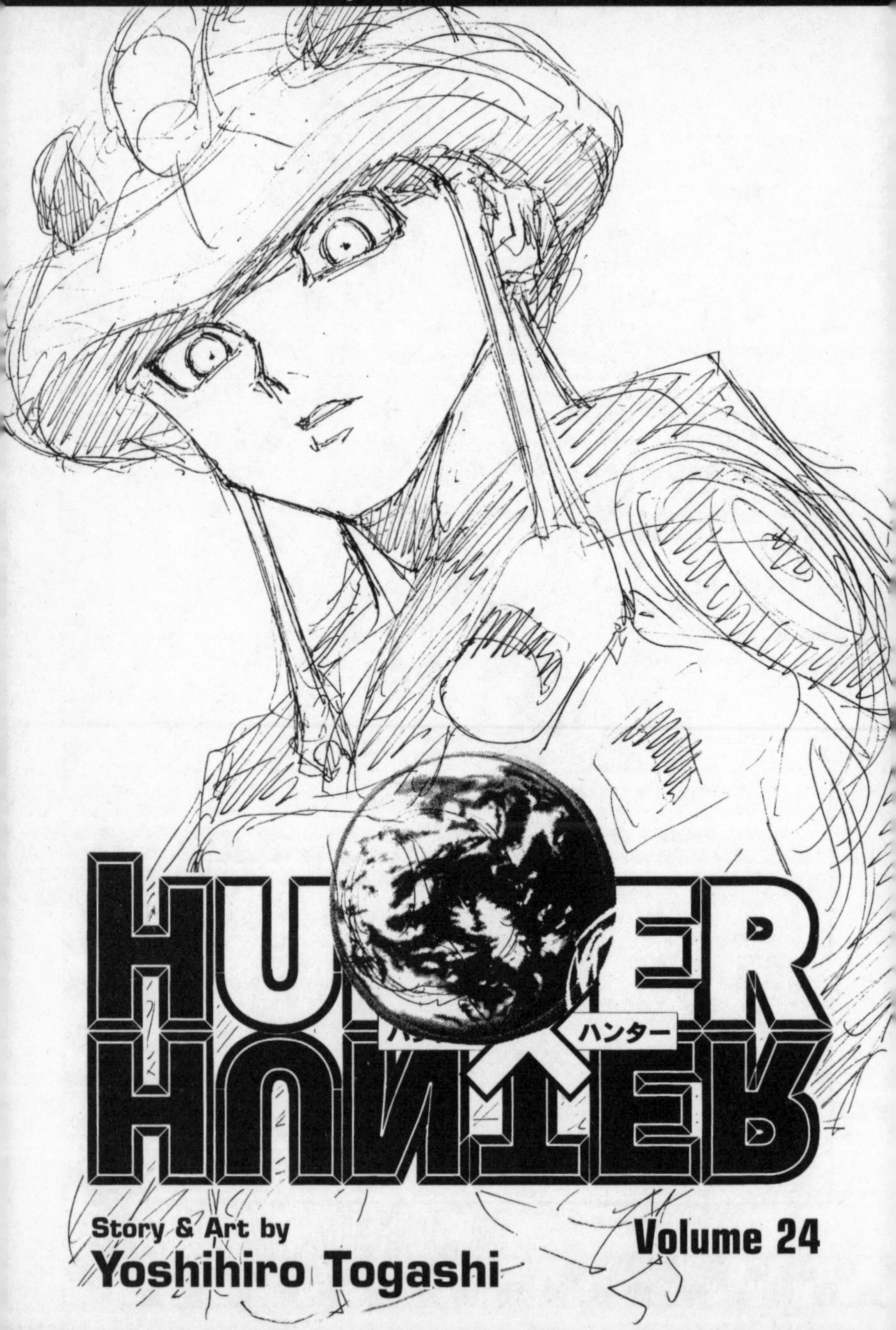

HUNTER × HUNTER

ハンター×ハンター

Story & Art by
Yoshihiro Togashi

Volume 24

Gon

OUR EAGER HERO. NOW A HUNTER, HE'S ON A SEARCH TO REUNITE WITH HIS FATHER!

The Story Thus Far

GON DREAMS OF BEING A HUNTER LIKE THE FATHER HE BARELY REMEMBERS, THE GREAT GING FREECSS. HE PASSES THE HIGHLY SELECTIVE LICENSING EXAM, BUT FINDING GING WILL BE EVEN HARDER.

GON REUNITES WITH GING'S OLD COMRADE KITE AND STARTS ON ANOTHER ADVENTURE IN NGL, WHERE THE VICIOUS CHIMERA ANTS HAVE BUILT THEIR NEST. GON AND KILLUA ESCAPE AN ENCOUNTER WITH THE FORMIDABLE NEFERPITOU, IN EXCHANGE FOR KITE'S CAPTURE. FINALLY, THE KING ANT IS BORN—A VICIOUS CREATURE WHO WOULD EVEN EAT HIS OWN KIND. THE KING LEAVES THE NEST BEHIND AND TAKES OVER THE REPUBLIC OF EAST GORTEAU. KITE IS RECOVERED BY THE HUNTERS, BUT HE IS NO LONGER THE MAN HE USED TO BE... AND GON VOWS TO TURN HIM BACK!

OUR HEROES SNEAK INTO EAST GORTEAU TO DEFEAT THE KING, SPLITTING UP TO EXECUTE THEIR PLANS. THEIR GUERILLA BATTLE AGAINST THE ANTS BEGINS!!

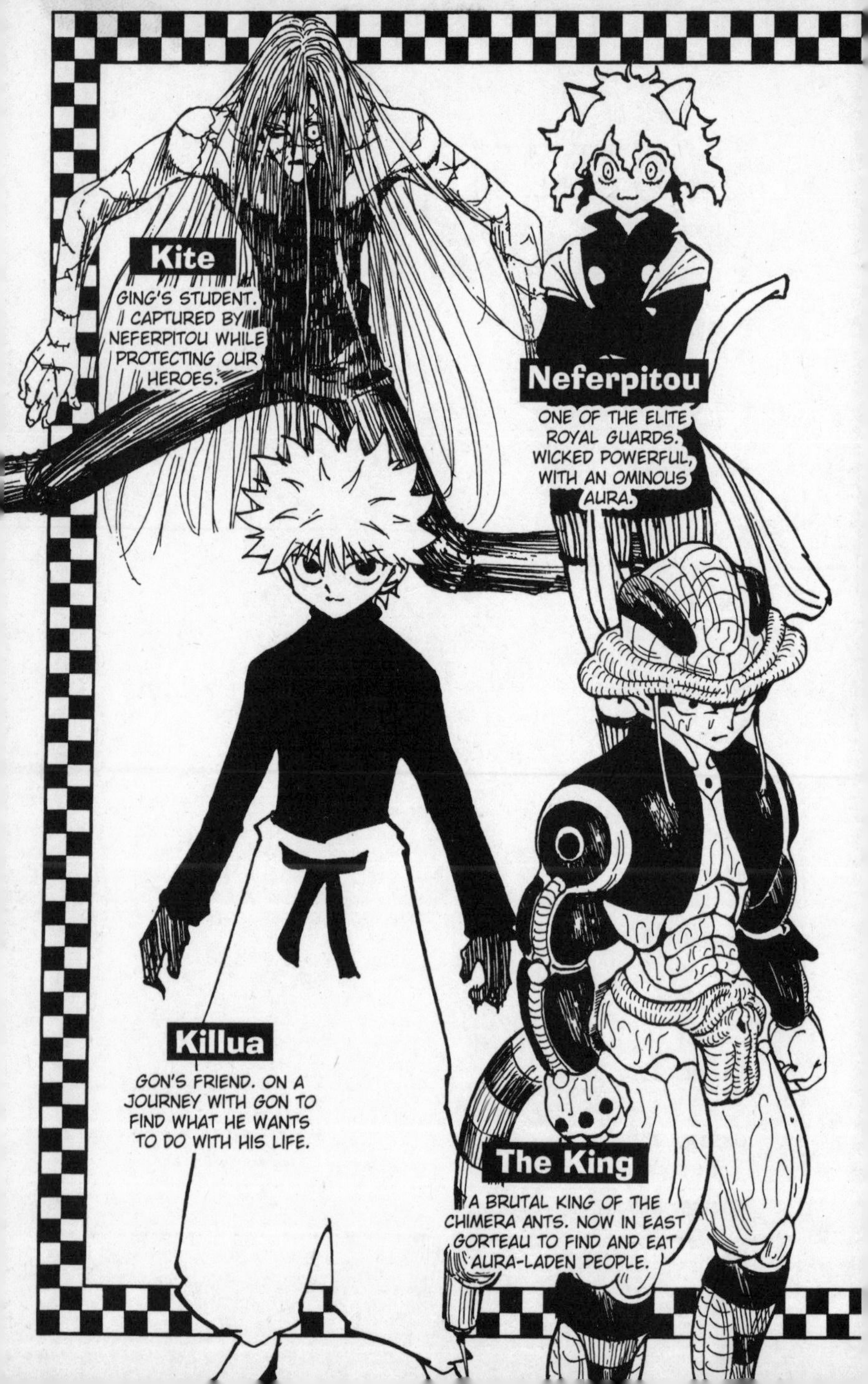
Kite
GING'S STUDENT. CAPTURED BY NEFERPITOU WHILE PROTECTING OUR HEROES.
Neferpitou
ONE OF THE ELITE ROYAL GUARDS. WICKED POWERFUL, WITH AN OMINOUS AURA.
Killua
GON'S FRIEND. ON A JOURNEY WITH GON TO FIND WHAT HE WANTS TO DO WITH HIS LIFE.
The King
A BRUTAL KING OF THE CHIMERA ANTS. NOW IN EAST GORTEAU TO FIND AND EAT AURA-LADEN PEOPLE.

HUNTER×HUNTER

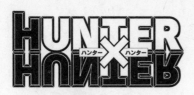

Volume 24

CONTENTS

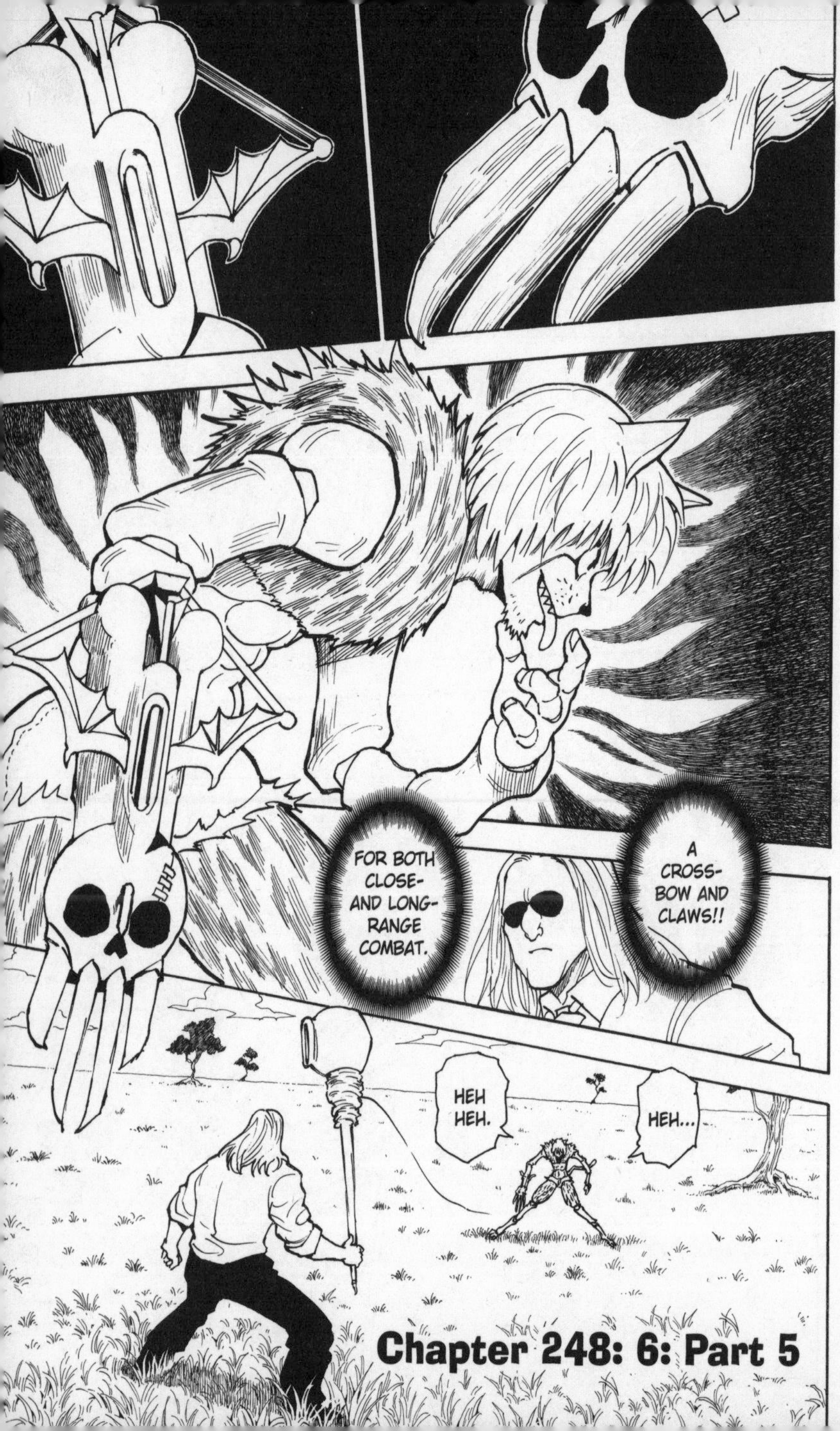
A CROSS-BOW AND CLAWS!!
FOR BOTH CLOSE- AND LONG-RANGE COMBAT.
HEH...
HEH HEH.
Chapter 248: 6: Part 5

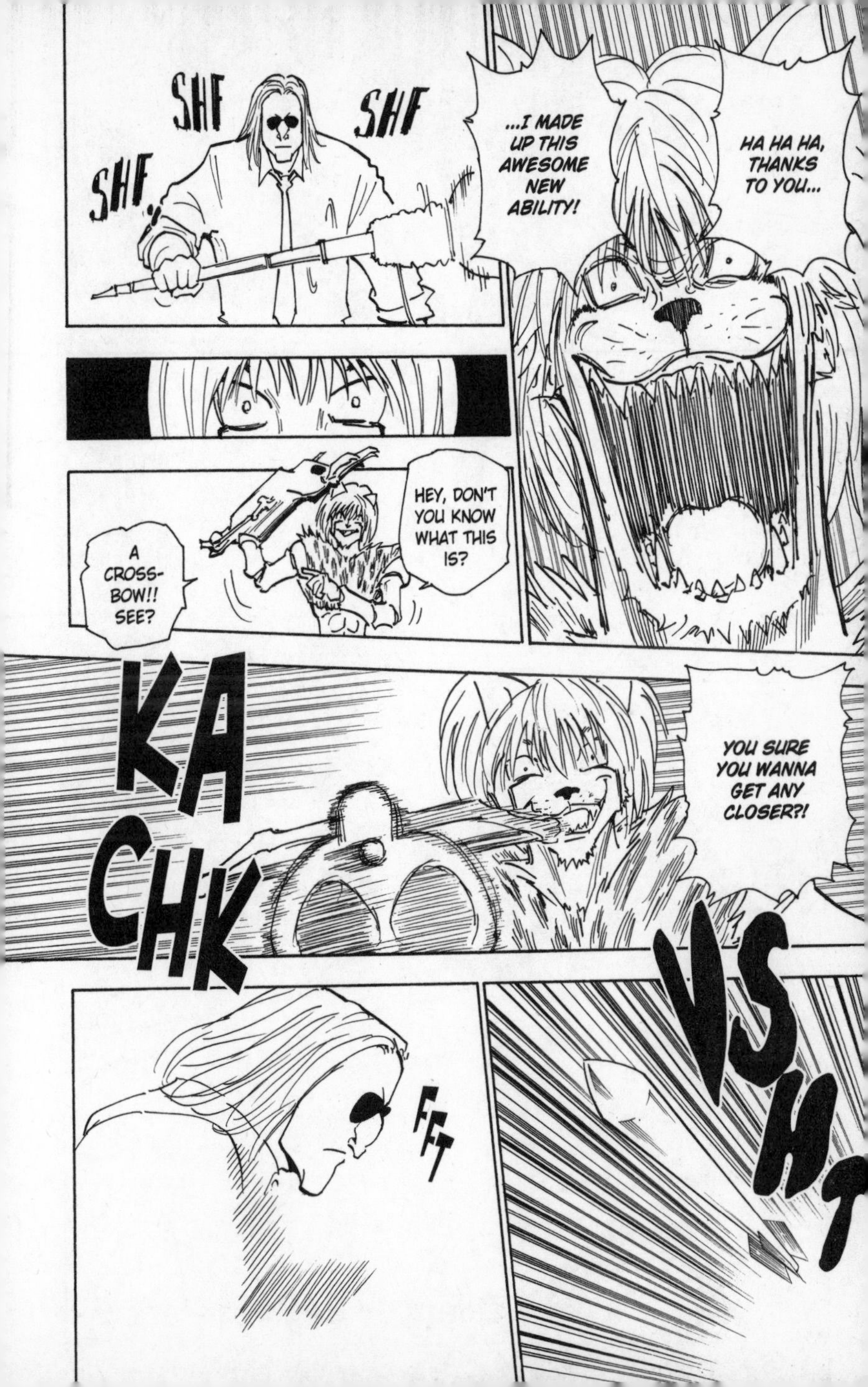
HA HA HA, THANKS TO YOU...
...I MADE UP THIS AWESOME NEW ABILITY!
SHF
SHF
SHF
HEY, DON'T YOU KNOW WHAT THIS IS?
A CROSS-BOW!! SEE?
YOU SURE YOU WANNA GET ANY CLOSER?!
KA CHK
VSHT
FFT

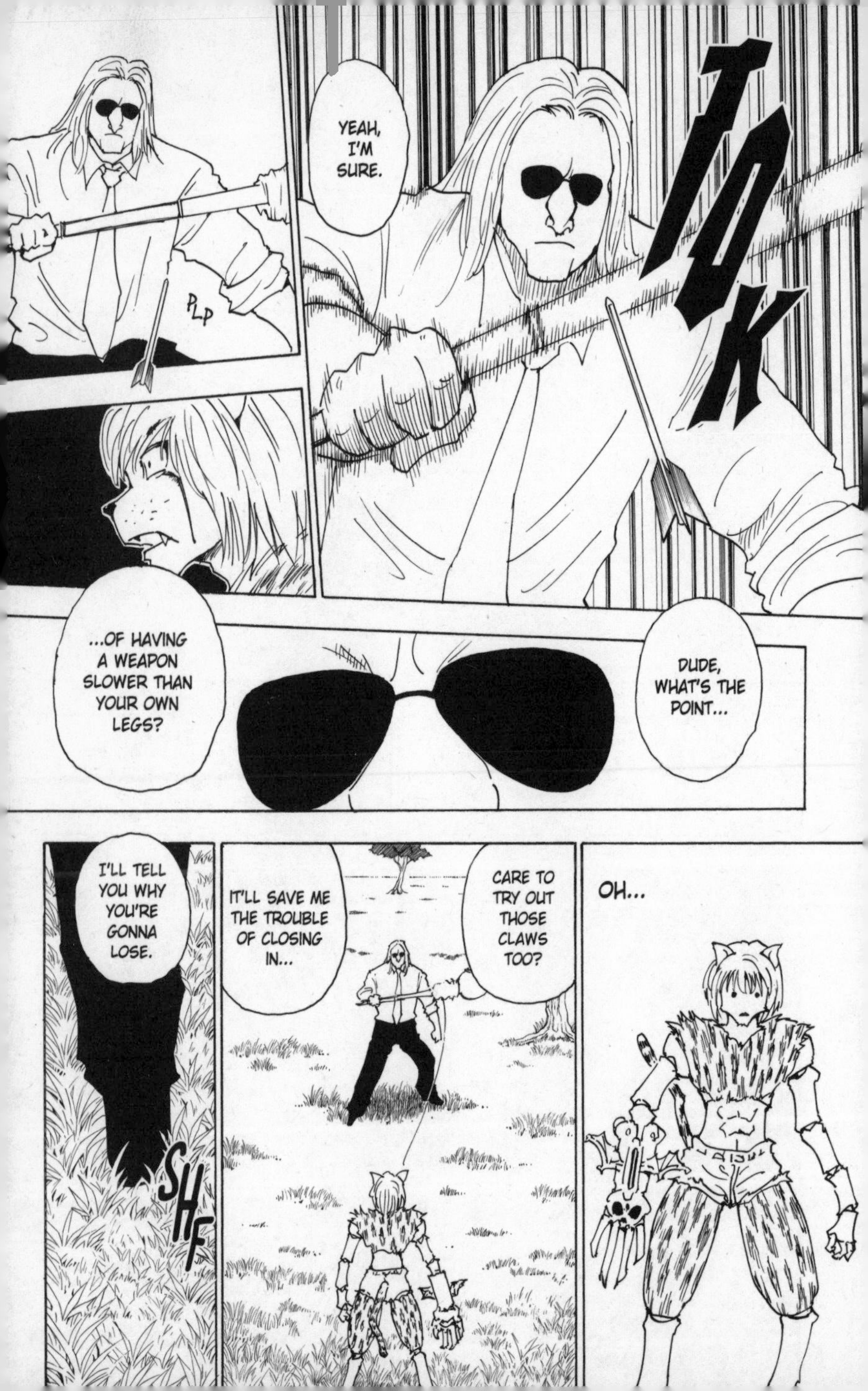
YEAH, I'M SURE.
TOK
PLP
DUDE, WHAT'S THE POINT...
...OF HAVING A WEAPON SLOWER THAN YOUR OWN LEGS?
OH...
CARE TO TRY OUT THOSE CLAWS TOO?
IT'LL SAVE ME THE TROUBLE OF CLOSING IN...
I'LL TELL YOU WHY YOU'RE GONNA LOSE.
SHF

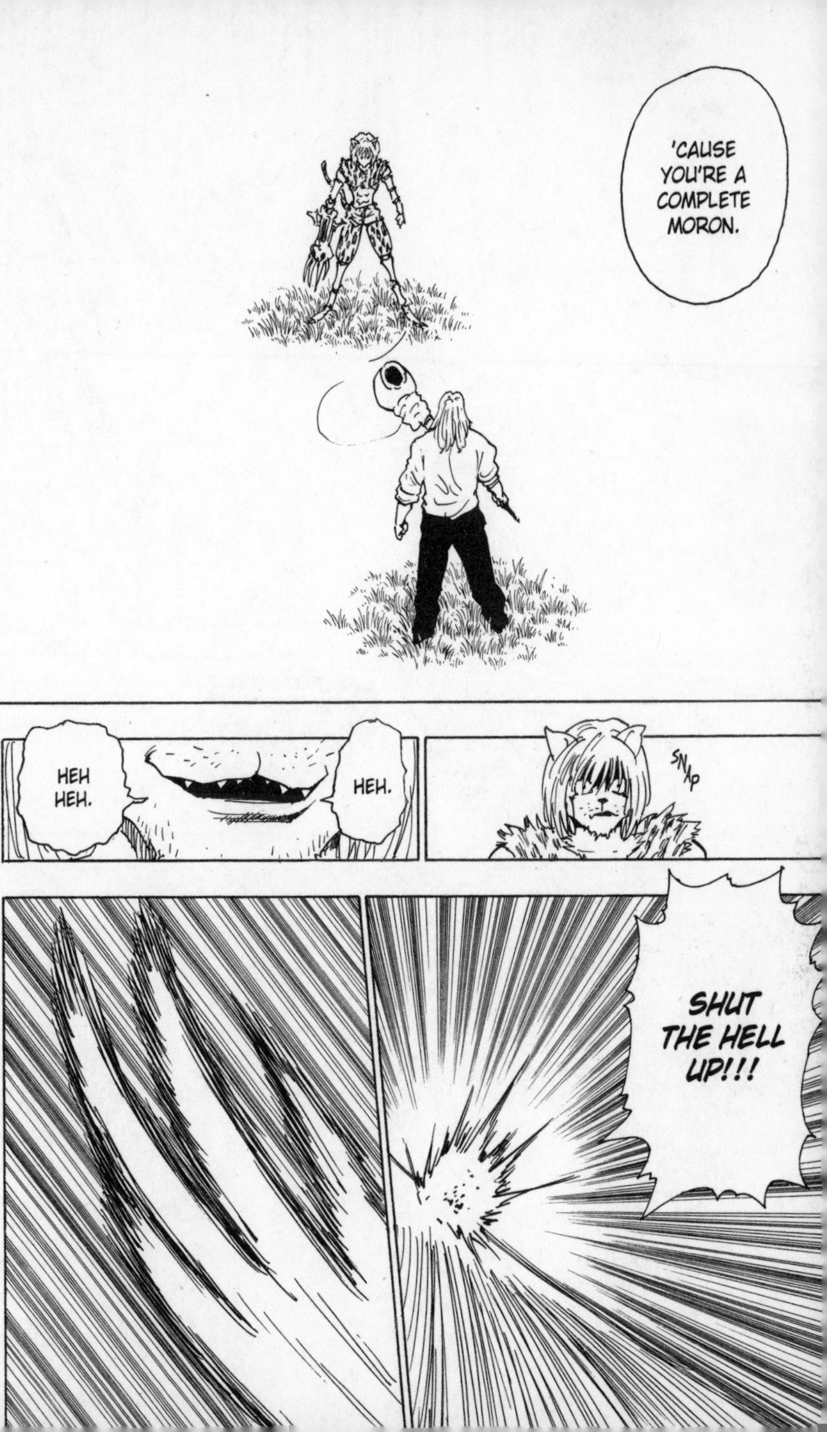
'CAUSE YOU'RE A COMPLETE MORON.
SNAP
HEH.
HEH HEH.
SHUT THE HELL UP!!!

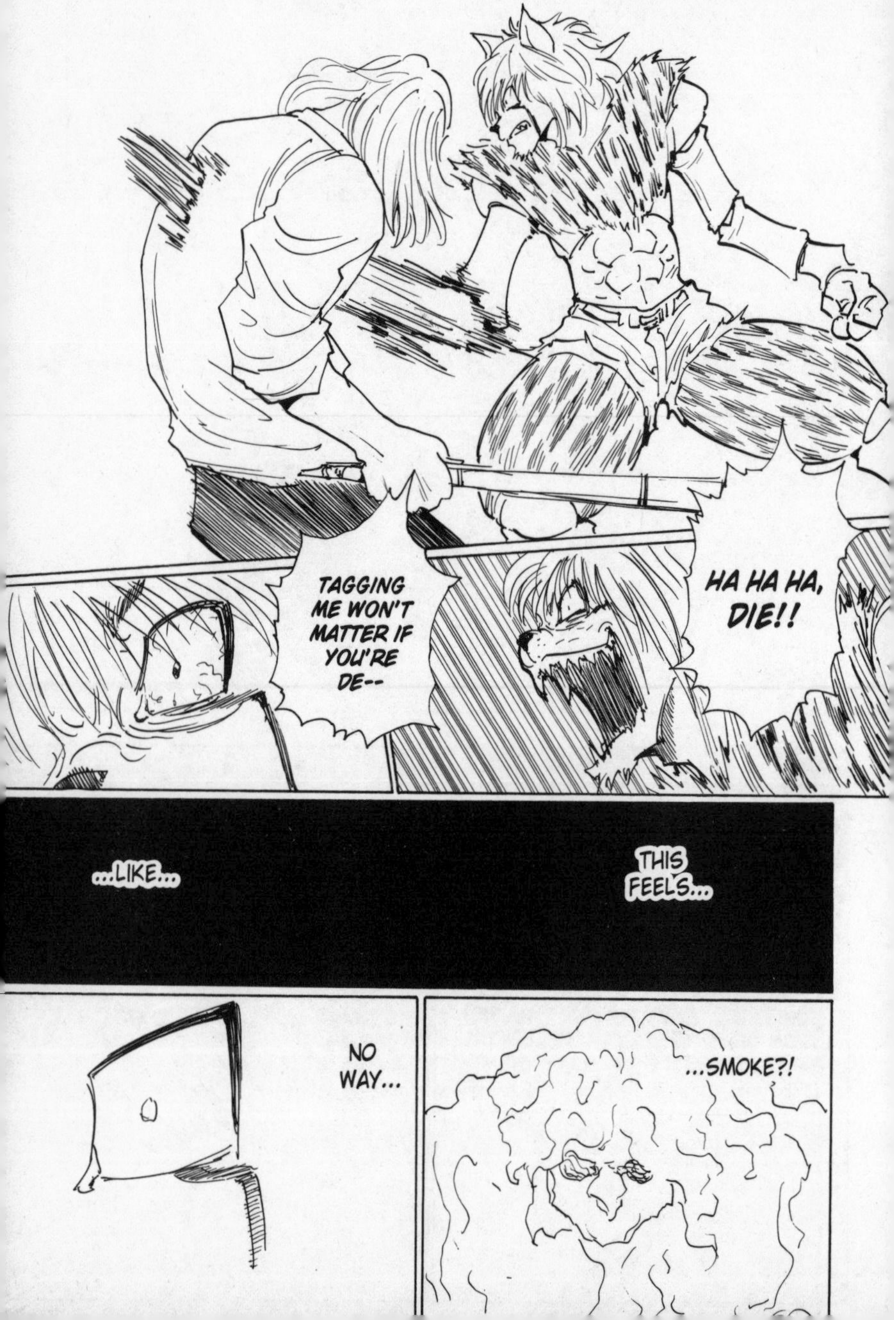
HA HA HA, DIE!!
TAGGING ME WON'T MATTER IF YOU'RE DE--
THIS FEELS...
...LIKE...
...SMOKE?!
NO WAY...

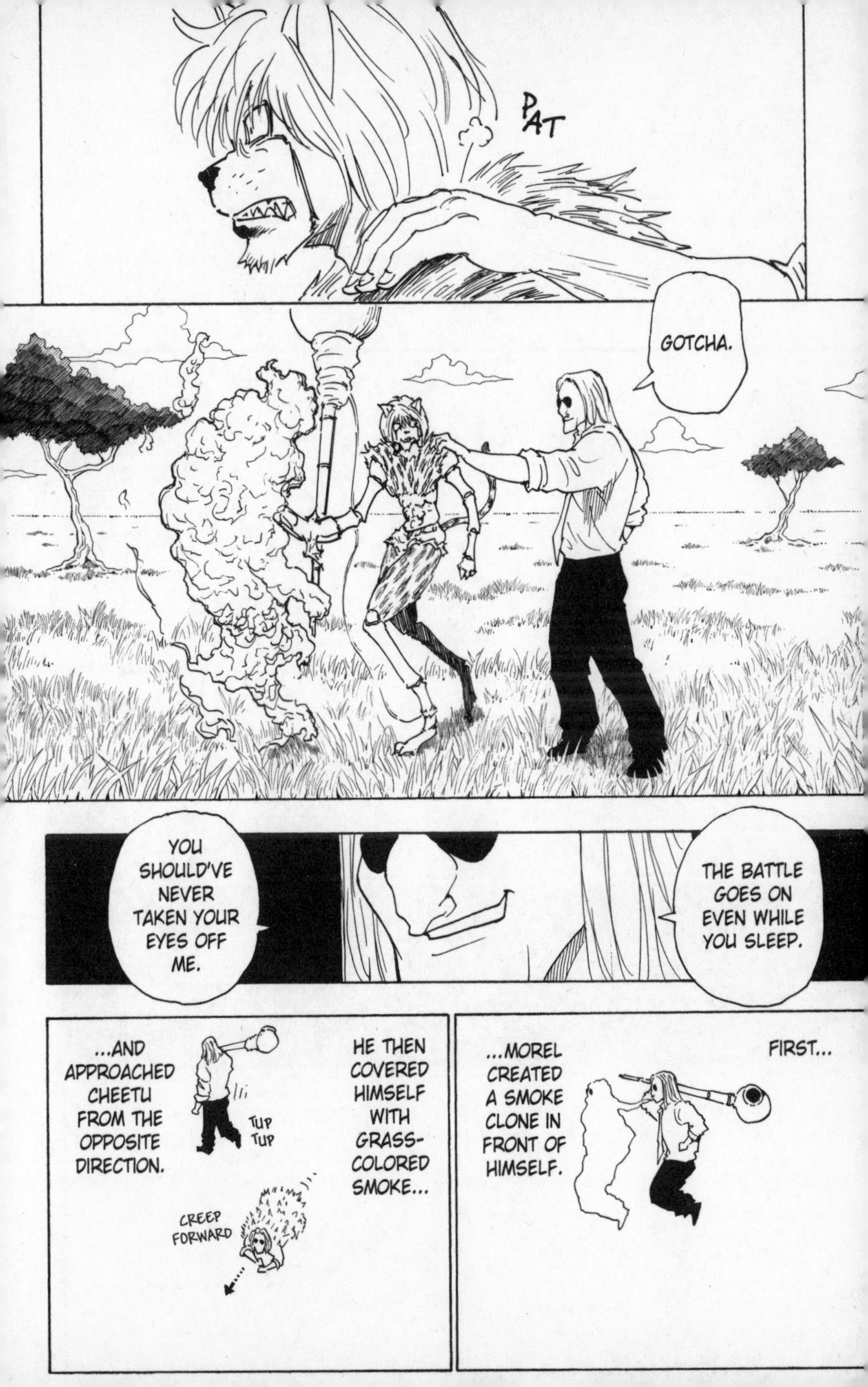
PAT
GOTCHA.
THE BATTLE GOES ON EVEN WHILE YOU SLEEP.
YOU SHOULD'VE NEVER TAKEN YOUR EYES OFF ME.
FIRST...
...MOREL CREATED A SMOKE CLONE IN FRONT OF HIMSELF.
HE THEN COVERED HIMSELF WITH GRASS-COLORED SMOKE...
...AND APPROACHED CHEETU FROM THE OPPOSITE DIRECTION.
TUP TUP
CREEP FORWARD

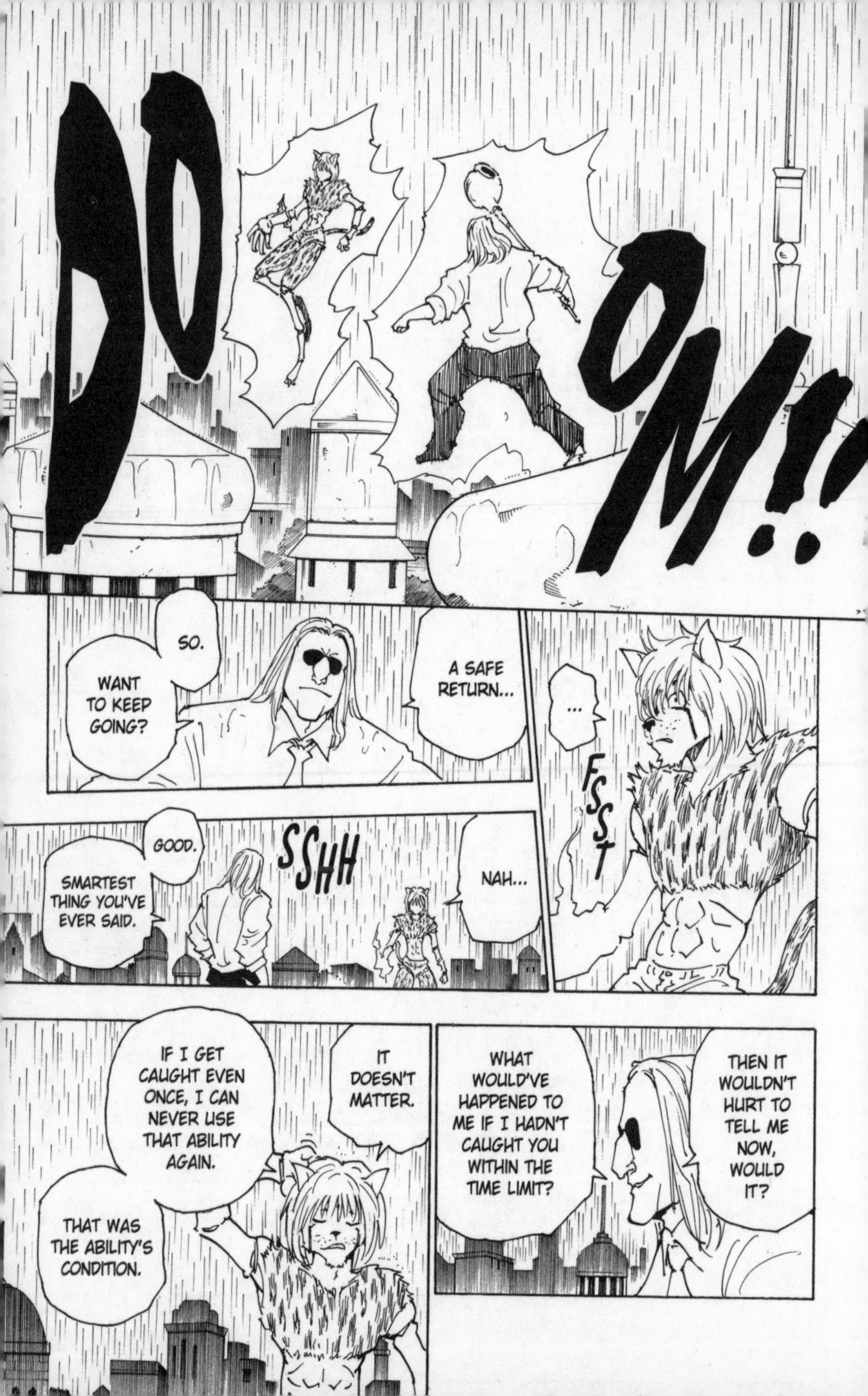
DO
OM!!
...
FSST
A SAFE RETURN...
SO.
WANT TO KEEP GOING?
NAH...
SSHH
GOOD.
SMARTEST THING YOU'VE EVER SAID.
THEN IT WOULDN'T HURT TO TELL ME NOW, WOULD IT?
WHAT WOULD'VE HAPPENED TO ME IF I HADN'T CAUGHT YOU WITHIN THE TIME LIMIT?
IT DOESN'T MATTER.
IF I GET CAUGHT EVEN ONCE, I CAN NEVER USE THAT ABILITY AGAIN.
THAT WAS THE ABILITY'S CONDITION.

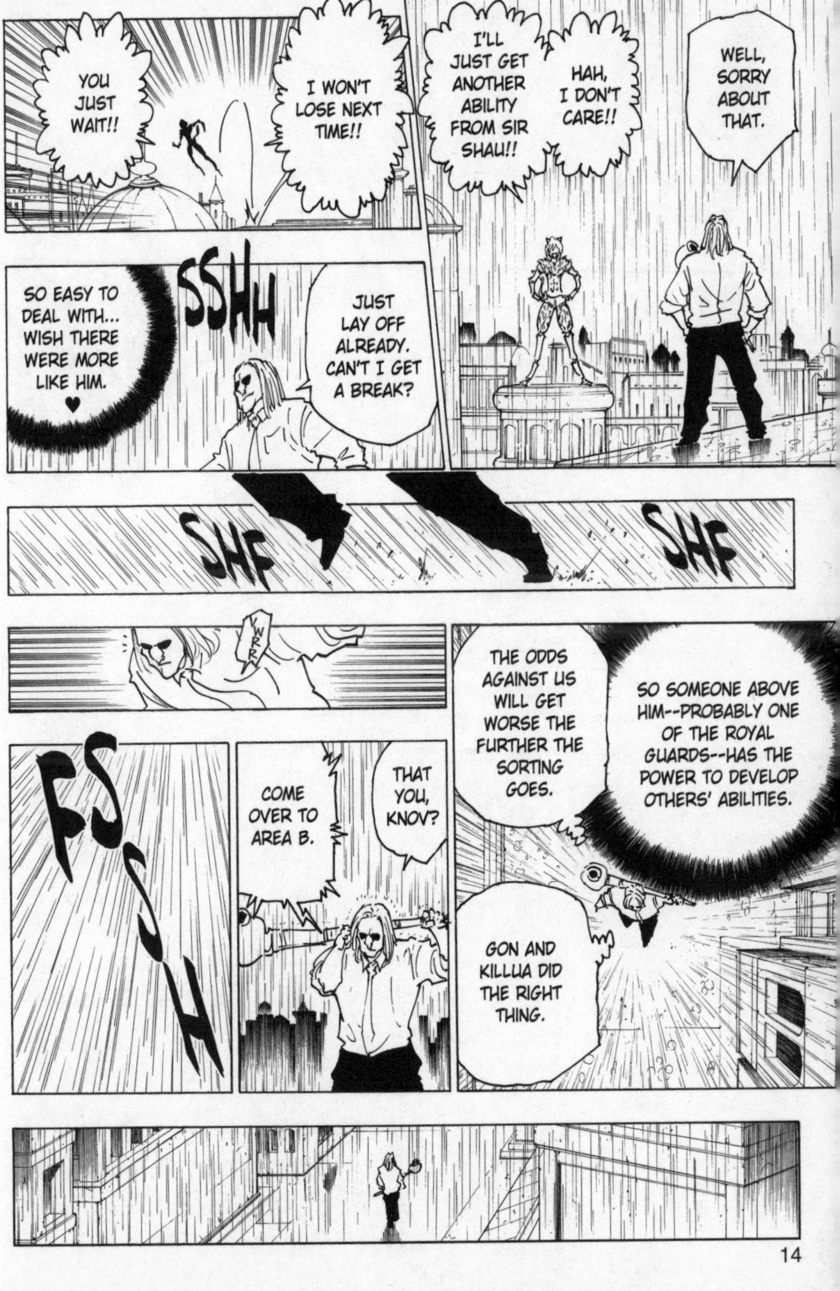
WELL, SORRY ABOUT THAT.
HAH, I DON'T CARE!!
I'LL JUST GET ANOTHER ABILITY FROM SIR SHAU!!
I WON'T LOSE NEXT TIME!!
YOU JUST WAIT!!
JUST LAY OFF ALREADY. CAN'T I GET A BREAK?
SSHH
SO EASY TO DEAL WITH... WISH THERE WERE MORE LIKE HIM. ♥
SHF
SHF
SO SOMEONE ABOVE HIM--PROBABLY ONE OF THE ROYAL GUARDS--HAS THE POWER TO DEVELOP OTHERS' ABILITIES.
THE ODDS AGAINST US WILL GET WORSE THE FURTHER THE SORTING GOES.
GON AND KILLUA DID THE RIGHT THING.
WRR
THAT YOU, KNOV?
COME OVER TO AREA B.
FSSH

READ THIS WAY

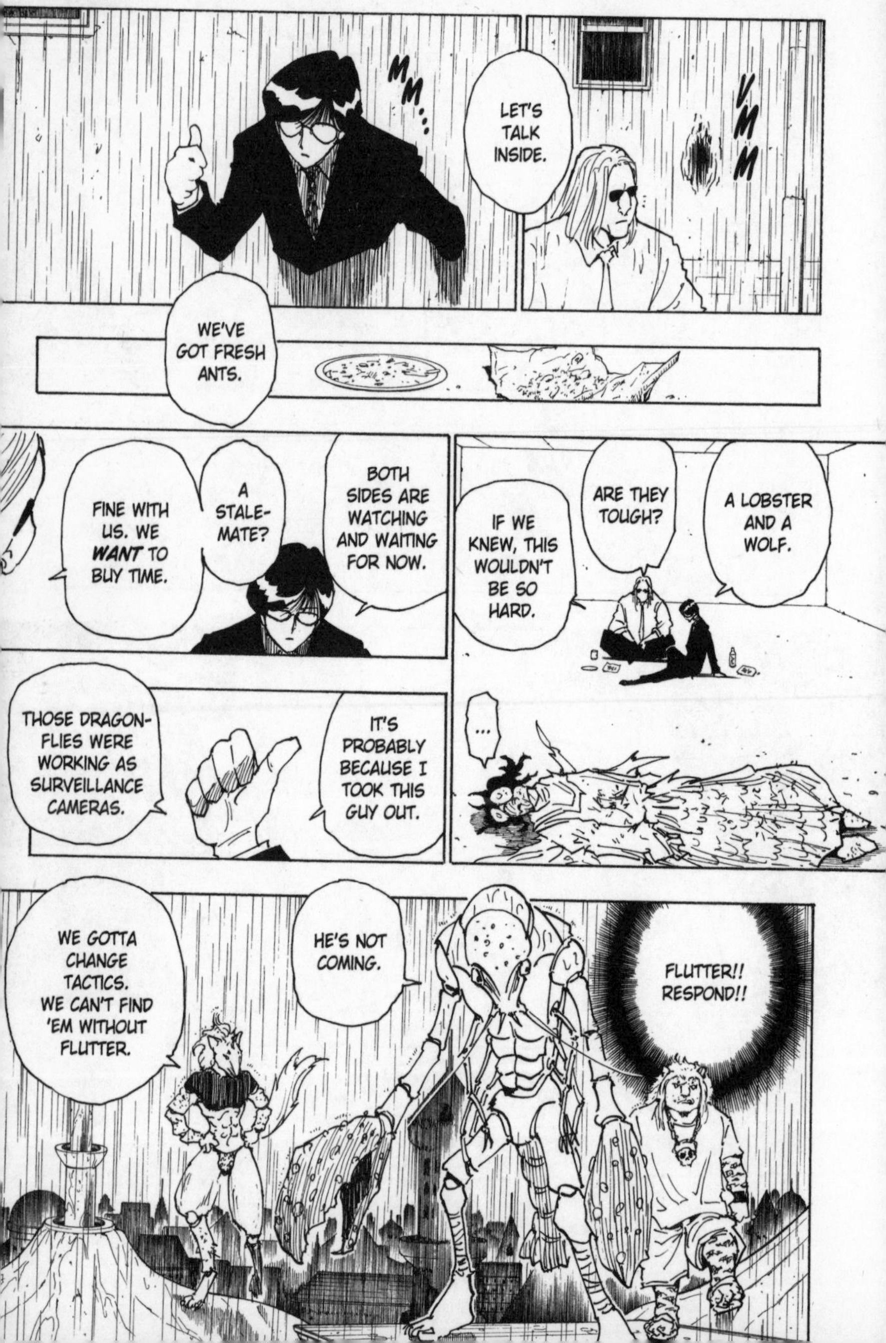
LET'S TALK INSIDE.
VMM
MM...
WE'VE GOT FRESH ANTS.
A LOBSTER AND A WOLF.
ARE THEY TOUGH?
IF WE KNEW, THIS WOULDN'T BE SO HARD.
BOTH SIDES ARE WATCHING AND WAITING FOR NOW.
A STALEMATE?
FINE WITH US. WE *WANT* TO BUY TIME.
...
IT'S PROBABLY BECAUSE I TOOK THIS GUY OUT.
THOSE DRAGONFLIES WERE WORKING AS SURVEILLANCE CAMERAS.
FLUTTER!! RESPOND!!
HE'S NOT COMING.
WE GOTTA CHANGE TACTICS. WE CAN'T FIND 'EM WITHOUT FLUTTER.

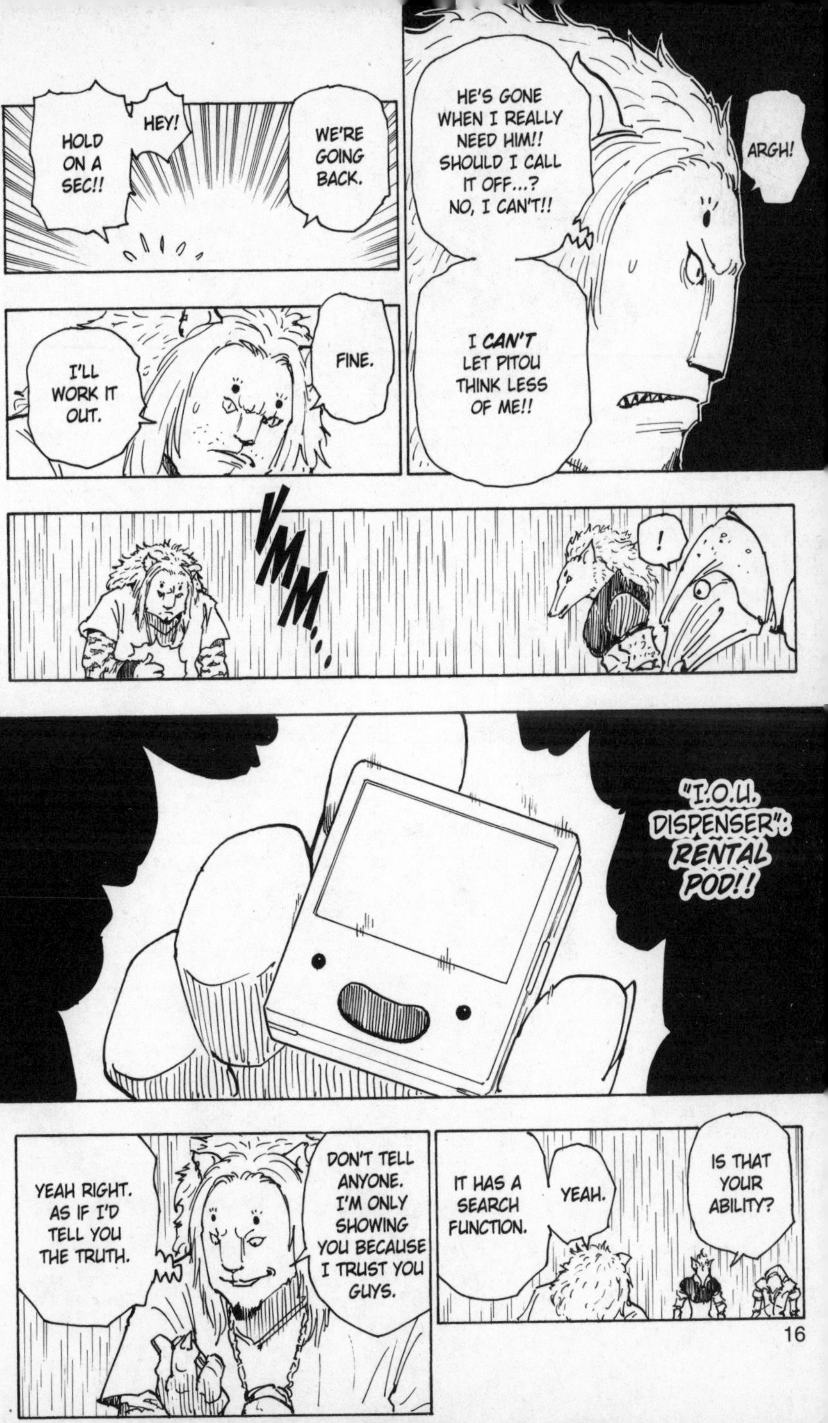
ARGH!
HE'S GONE WHEN I REALLY NEED HIM!! SHOULD I CALL IT OFF...? NO, I CAN'T!!
I CAN'T LET PITOU THINK LESS OF ME!!
WE'RE GOING BACK.
HEY!
HOLD ON A SEC!!
FINE.
I'LL WORK IT OUT.
!
VMM..
"I.O.U. DISPENSER": RENTAL POD!!
IS THAT YOUR ABILITY?
YEAH.
IT HAS A SEARCH FUNCTION.
DON'T TELL ANYONE. I'M ONLY SHOWING YOU BECAUSE I TRUST YOU GUYS.
YEAH RIGHT. AS IF I'D TELL YOU THE TRUTH.

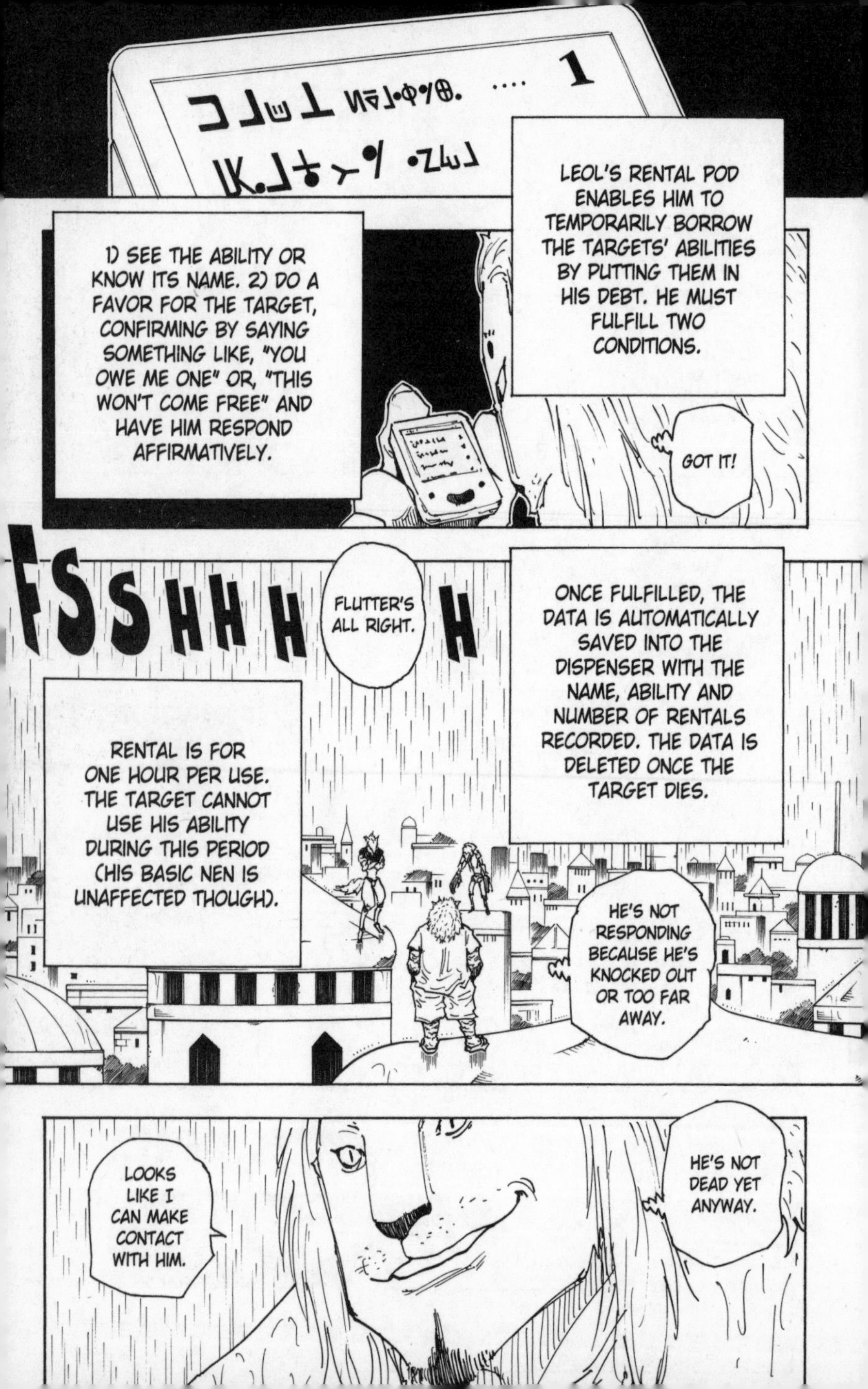
LEOL'S RENTAL POD ENABLES HIM TO TEMPORARILY BORROW THE TARGETS' ABILITIES BY PUTTING THEM IN HIS DEBT. HE MUST FULFILL TWO CONDITIONS.
1) SEE THE ABILITY OR KNOW ITS NAME. 2) DO A FAVOR FOR THE TARGET, CONFIRMING BY SAYING SOMETHING LIKE, "YOU OWE ME ONE" OR, "THIS WON'T COME FREE" AND HAVE HIM RESPOND AFFIRMATIVELY.
GOT IT!
ONCE FULFILLED, THE DATA IS AUTOMATICALLY SAVED INTO THE DISPENSER WITH THE NAME, ABILITY AND NUMBER OF RENTALS RECORDED. THE DATA IS DELETED ONCE THE TARGET DIES.
FLUTTER'S ALL RIGHT.
FSSHHHH
RENTAL IS FOR ONE HOUR PER USE. THE TARGET CANNOT USE HIS ABILITY DURING THIS PERIOD (HIS BASIC NEN IS UNAFFECTED THOUGH).
HE'S NOT RESPONDING BECAUSE HE'S KNOCKED OUT OR TOO FAR AWAY.
HE'S NOT DEAD YET ANYWAY.
LOOKS LIKE I CAN MAKE CONTACT WITH HIM.

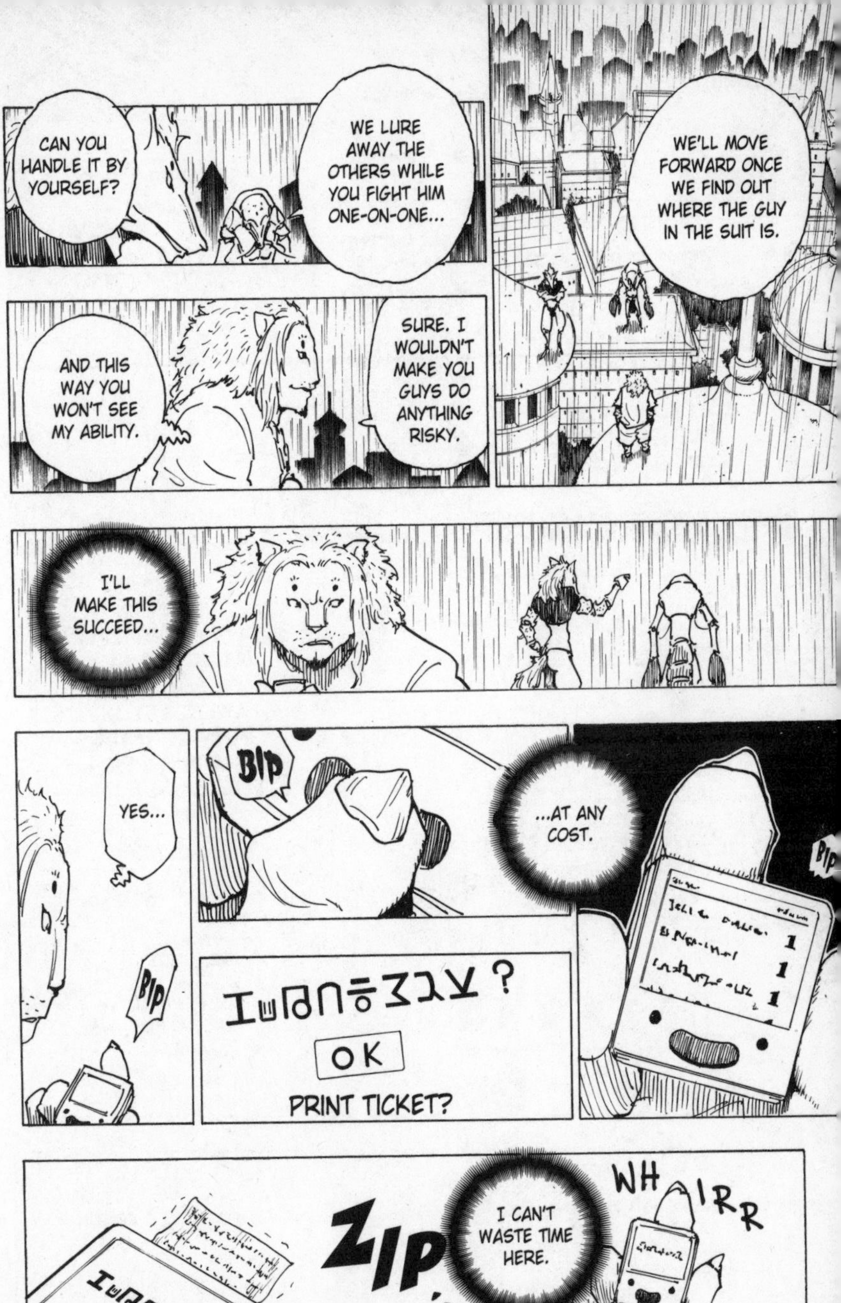

WE'LL MOVE FORWARD ONCE WE FIND OUT WHERE THE GUY IN THE SUIT IS.
WE LURE AWAY THE OTHERS WHILE YOU FIGHT HIM ONE-ON-ONE...
CAN YOU HANDLE IT BY YOURSELF?
SURE. I WOULDN'T MAKE YOU GUYS DO ANYTHING RISKY.
AND THIS WAY YOU WON'T SEE MY ABILITY.
I'LL MAKE THIS SUCCEED...
BIP
...AT ANY COST.
BIP
OK
PRINT TICKET?
YES...
BIP
WHIRR
I CAN'T WASTE TIME HERE.
ZIP

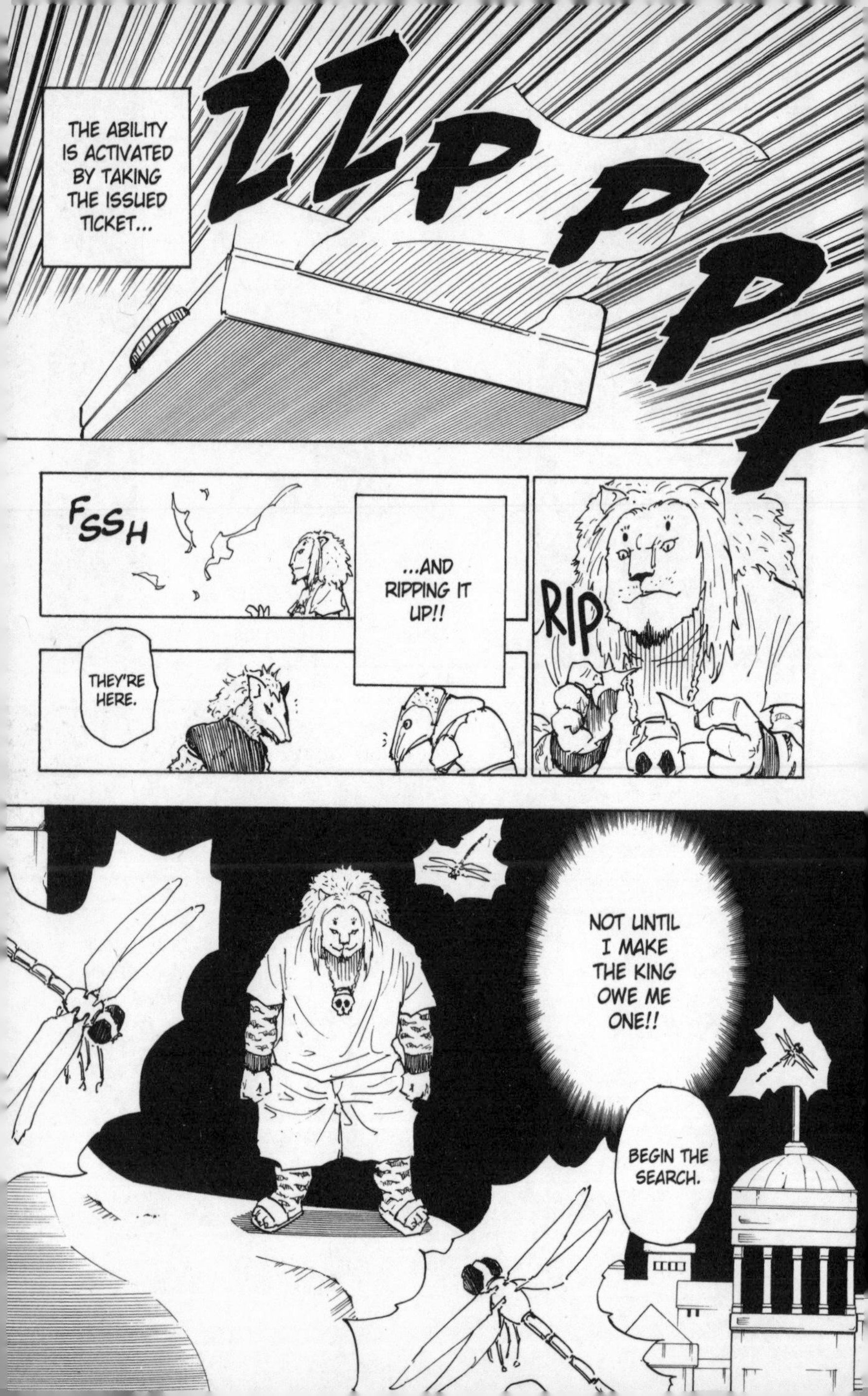
ZZPPPF
THE ABILITY IS ACTIVATED BY TAKING THE ISSUED TICKET...
...AND RIPPING IT UP!!
RIP
FSSH
THEY'RE HERE.
NOT UNTIL I MAKE THE KING OWE ME ONE!!
BEGIN THE SEARCH.

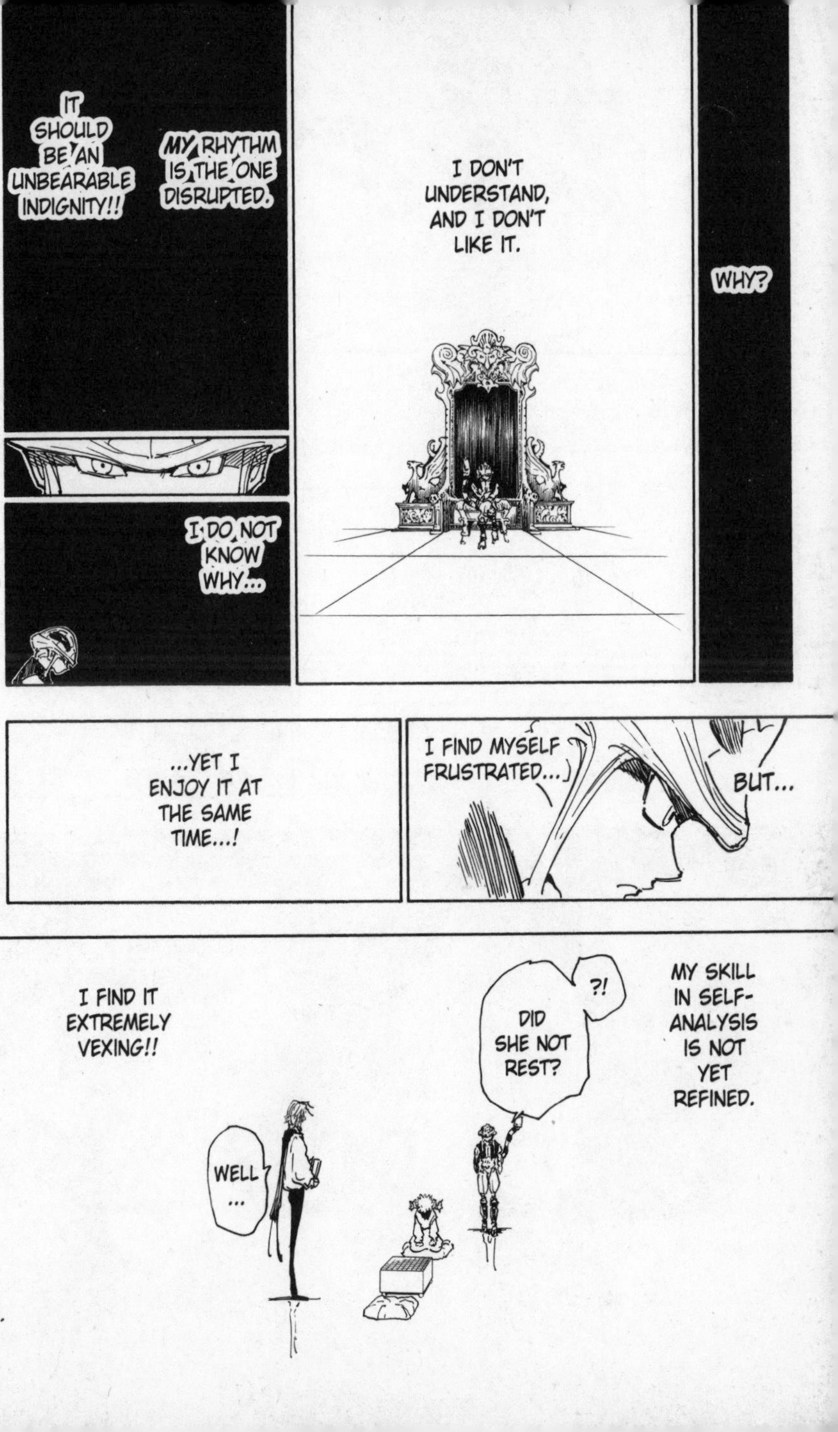
WHY?
I DON'T UNDERSTAND, AND I DON'T LIKE IT.
MY RHYTHM IS THE ONE DISRUPTED.
IT SHOULD BE AN UNBEARABLE INDIGNITY!!
I DO NOT KNOW WHY...
I FIND MYSELF FRUSTRATED...
BUT...
...YET I ENJOY IT AT THE SAME TIME...!
MY SKILL IN SELF-ANALYSIS IS NOT YET REFINED.
?!
DID SHE NOT REST?
I FIND IT EXTREMELY VEXING!!
WELL ...

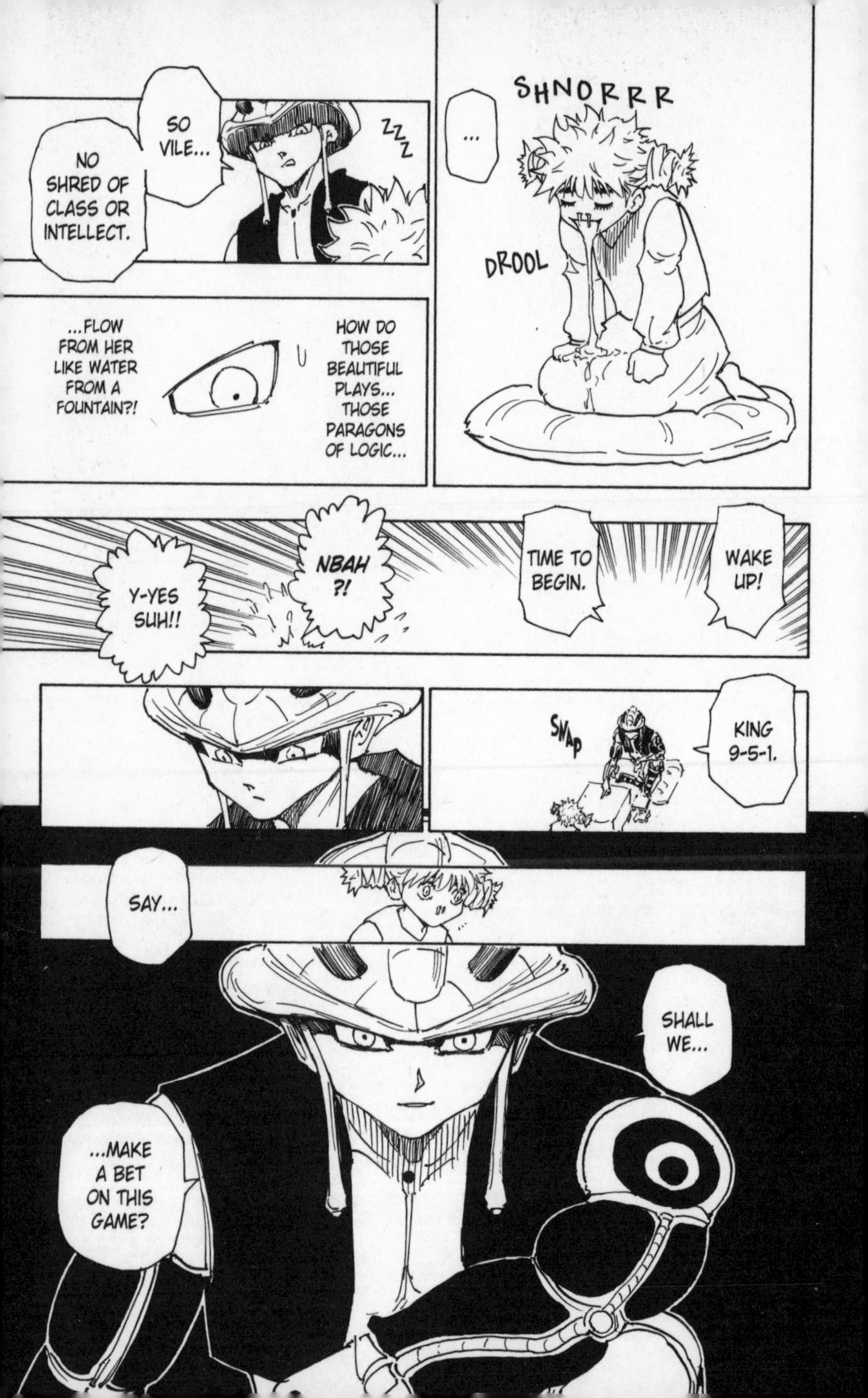
SHNORRR
...
DROOL
ZZZ
SO VILE...
NO SHRED OF CLASS OR INTELLECT.
HOW DO THOSE BEAUTIFUL PLAYS... THOSE PARAGONS OF LOGIC...
...FLOW FROM HER LIKE WATER FROM A FOUNTAIN?!
WAKE UP!
TIME TO BEGIN.
NBAH ?!
Y-YES SUH!!
KING 9-5-1.
SNAP
SAY...
SHALL WE...
...MAKE A BET ON THIS GAME?

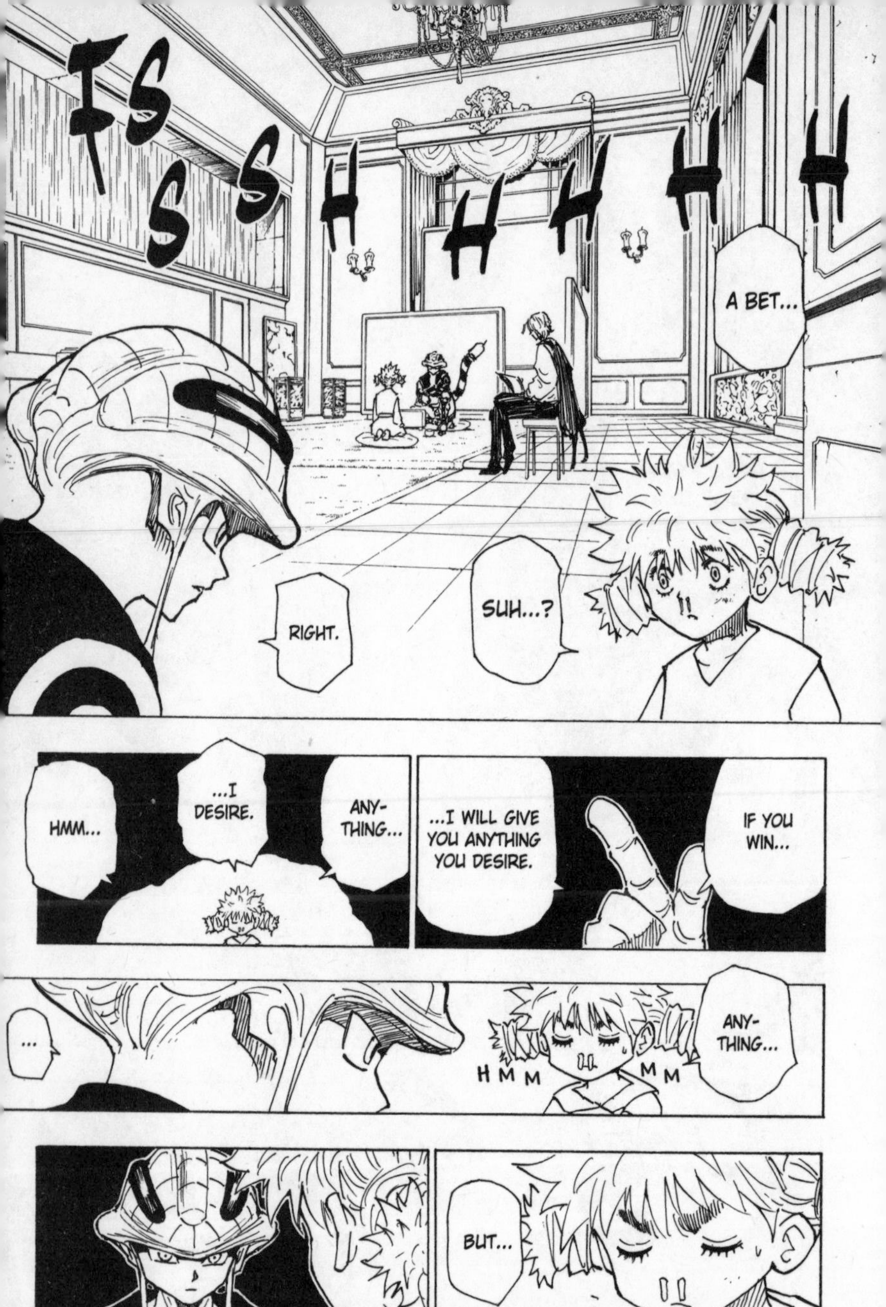
FSSSHHHHH
A BET...
SUH...?
RIGHT.
IF YOU WIN...
...I WILL GIVE YOU ANYTHING YOU DESIRE.
ANY-THING...
...I DESIRE.
HMM...
ANY-THING...
HMMMM
...
BUT...

Chapter 249: 6: Part 6

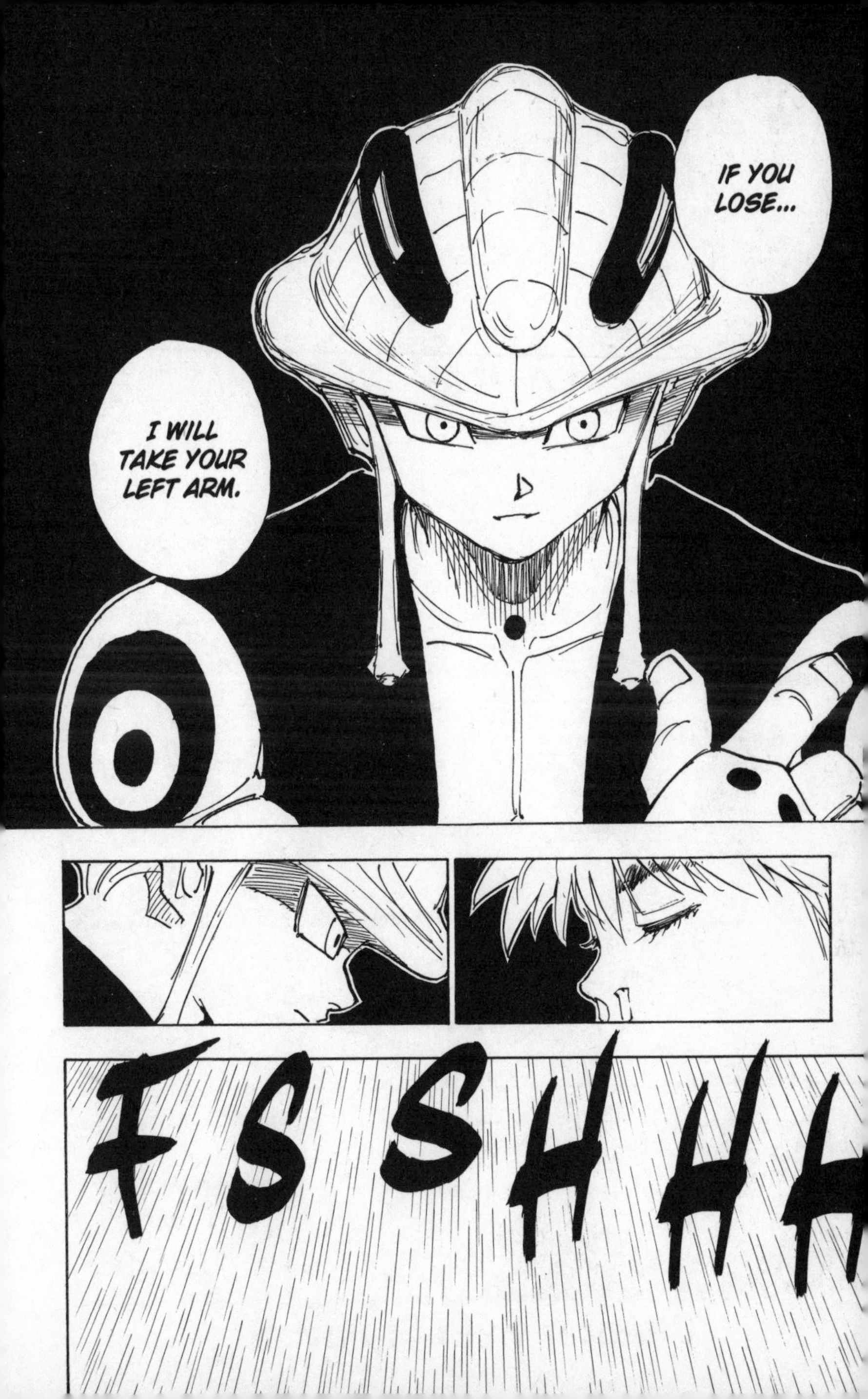
IF YOU LOSE...
I WILL TAKE YOUR LEFT ARM.
FSHHH

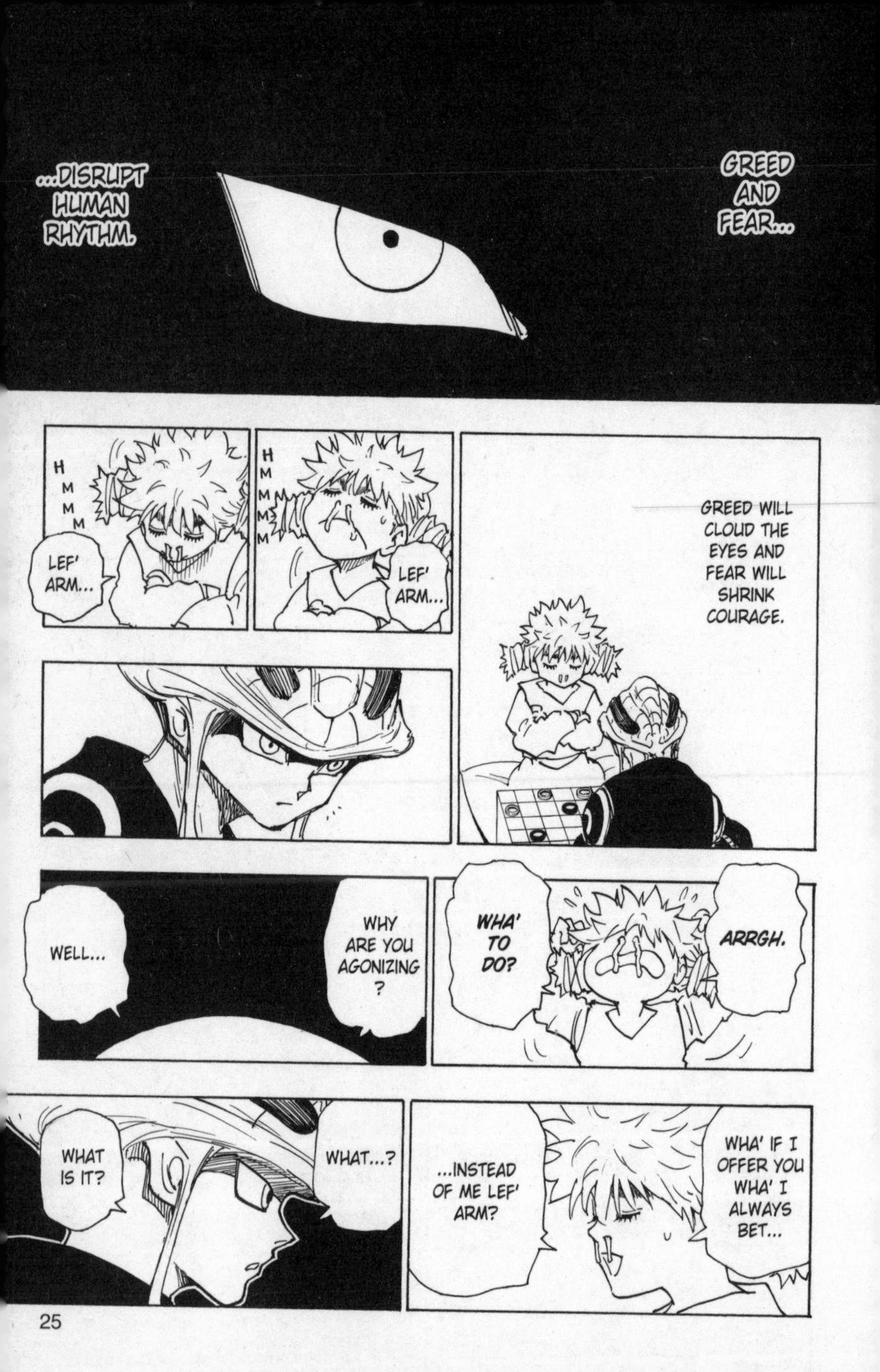
GREED AND FEAR...
...DISRUPT HUMAN RHYTHM.
GREED WILL CLOUD THE EYES AND FEAR WILL SHRINK COURAGE.
HMMMMM
LEF' ARM...
HMMM
LEF' ARM...
ARRGH.
WHA' TO DO?
WHY ARE YOU AGONIZING?
WELL...
WHA' IF I OFFER YOU WHA' I ALWAYS BET...
...INSTEAD OF ME LEF' ARM?
WHAT...?
WHAT IS IT?

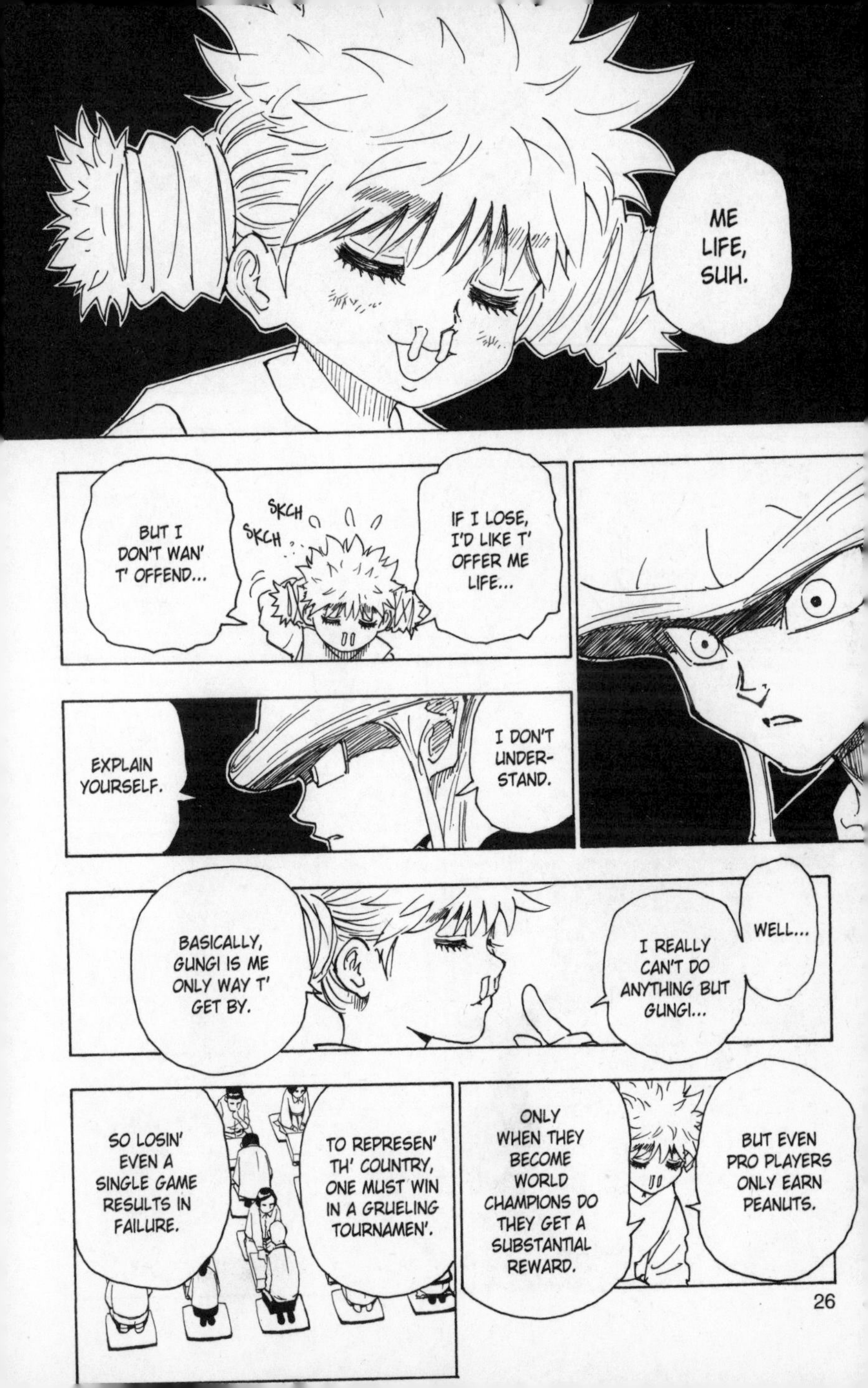
ME LIFE, SUH.
IF I LOSE, I'D LIKE T' OFFER ME LIFE...
SKCH
SKCH
BUT I DON'T WAN' T' OFFEND...
I DON'T UNDERSTAND.
EXPLAIN YOURSELF.
WELL...
I REALLY CAN'T DO ANYTHING BUT GUNGI...
BASICALLY, GUNGI IS ME ONLY WAY T' GET BY.
BUT EVEN PRO PLAYERS ONLY EARN PEANUTS.
ONLY WHEN THEY BECOME WORLD CHAMPIONS DO THEY GET A SUBSTANTIAL REWARD.
TO REPRESEN' TH' COUNTRY, ONE MUST WIN IN A GRUELING TOURNAMEN'.
SO LOSIN' EVEN A SINGLE GAME RESULTS IN FAILURE.

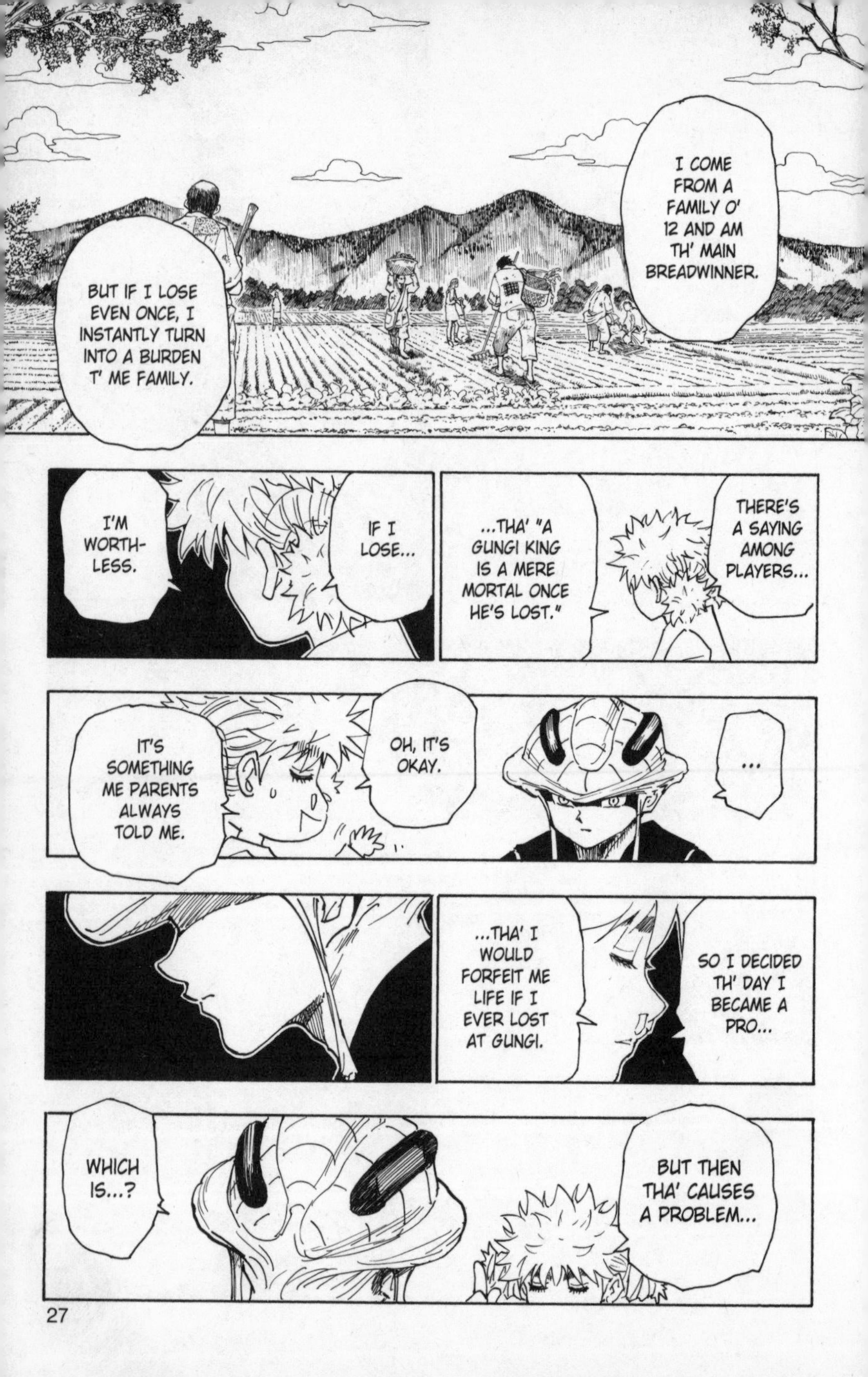
I COME FROM A FAMILY O' 12 AND AM TH' MAIN BREADWINNER.
BUT IF I LOSE EVEN ONCE, I INSTANTLY TURN INTO A BURDEN T' ME FAMILY.
THERE'S A SAYING AMONG PLAYERS...
...THA' "A GUNGI KING IS A MERE MORTAL ONCE HE'S LOST."
IF I LOSE...
I'M WORTHLESS.
...
OH, IT'S OKAY.
IT'S SOMETHING ME PARENTS ALWAYS TOLD ME.
SO I DECIDED TH' DAY I BECAME A PRO...
...THA' I WOULD FORFEIT ME LIFE IF I EVER LOST AT GUNGI.
BUT THEN THA' CAUSES A PROBLEM...
WHICH IS...?

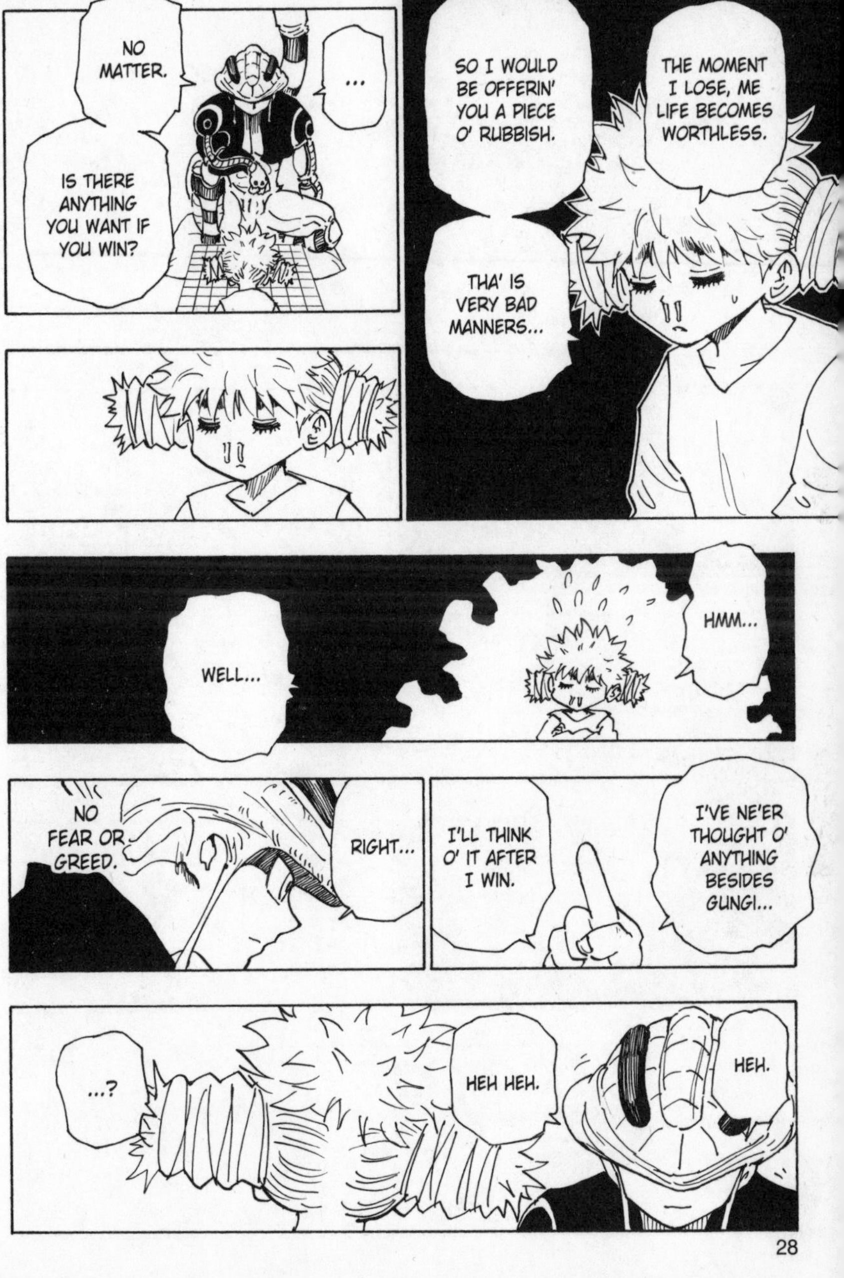
THE MOMENT I LOSE, ME LIFE BECOMES WORTHLESS.
SO I WOULD BE OFFERIN' YOU A PIECE O' RUBBISH.
THA' IS VERY BAD MANNERS...
...
NO MATTER.
IS THERE ANYTHING YOU WANT IF YOU WIN?
HMM...
WELL...
I'VE NE'ER THOUGHT O' ANYTHING BESIDES GUNGI...
I'LL THINK O' IT AFTER I WIN.
RIGHT...
NO FEAR OR GREED.
HEH.
HEH HEH.
...?

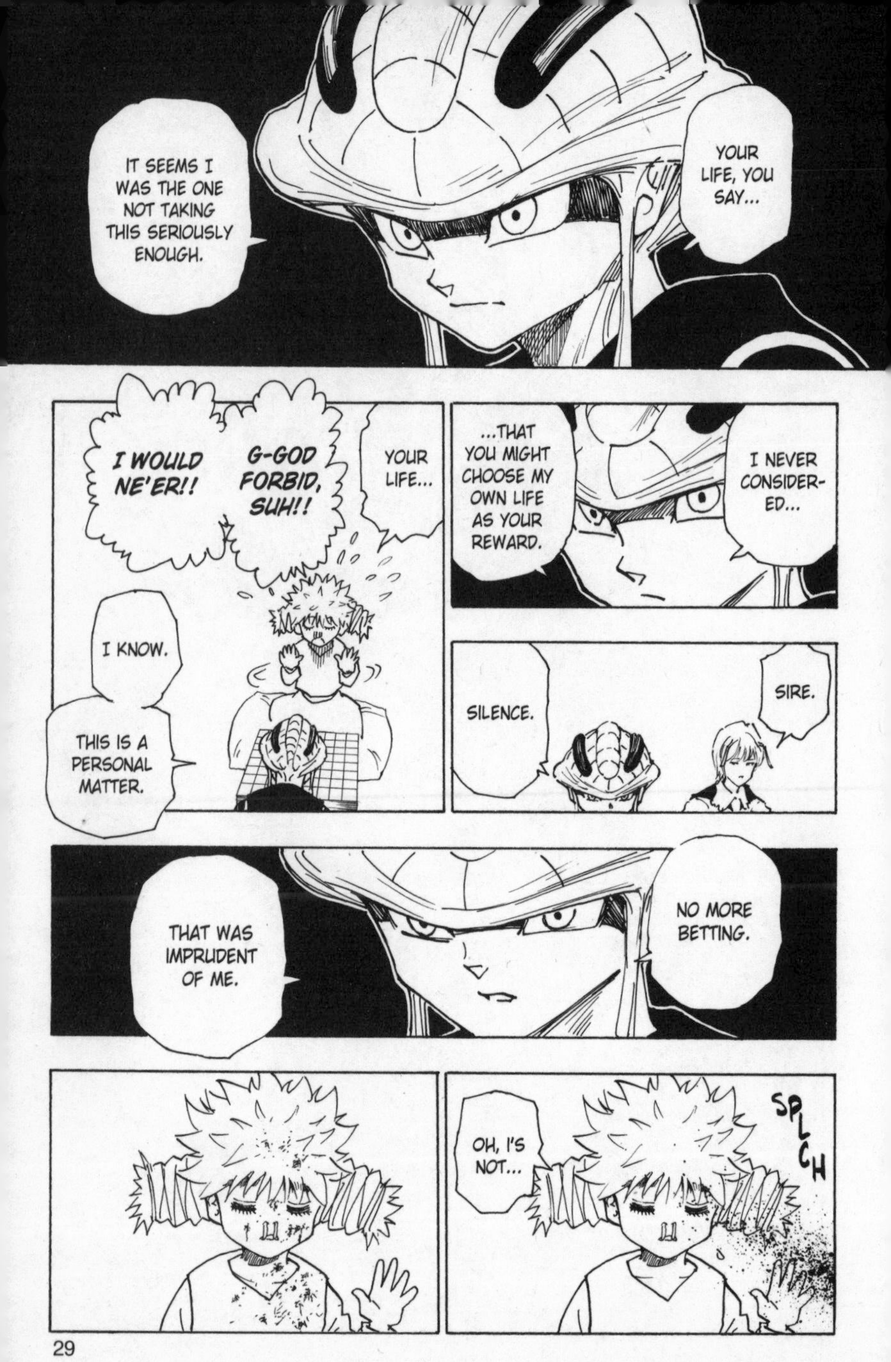
YOUR LIFE, YOU SAY...
IT SEEMS I WAS THE ONE NOT TAKING THIS SERIOUSLY ENOUGH.
I NEVER CONSIDERED...
...THAT YOU MIGHT CHOOSE MY OWN LIFE AS YOUR REWARD.
SIRE.
SILENCE.
YOUR LIFE...
G-GOD FORBID, SUH!!
I WOULD NE'ER!!
I KNOW.
THIS IS A PERSONAL MATTER.
NO MORE BETTING.
THAT WAS IMPRUDENT OF ME.
SPLCH
OH, I'S NOT...

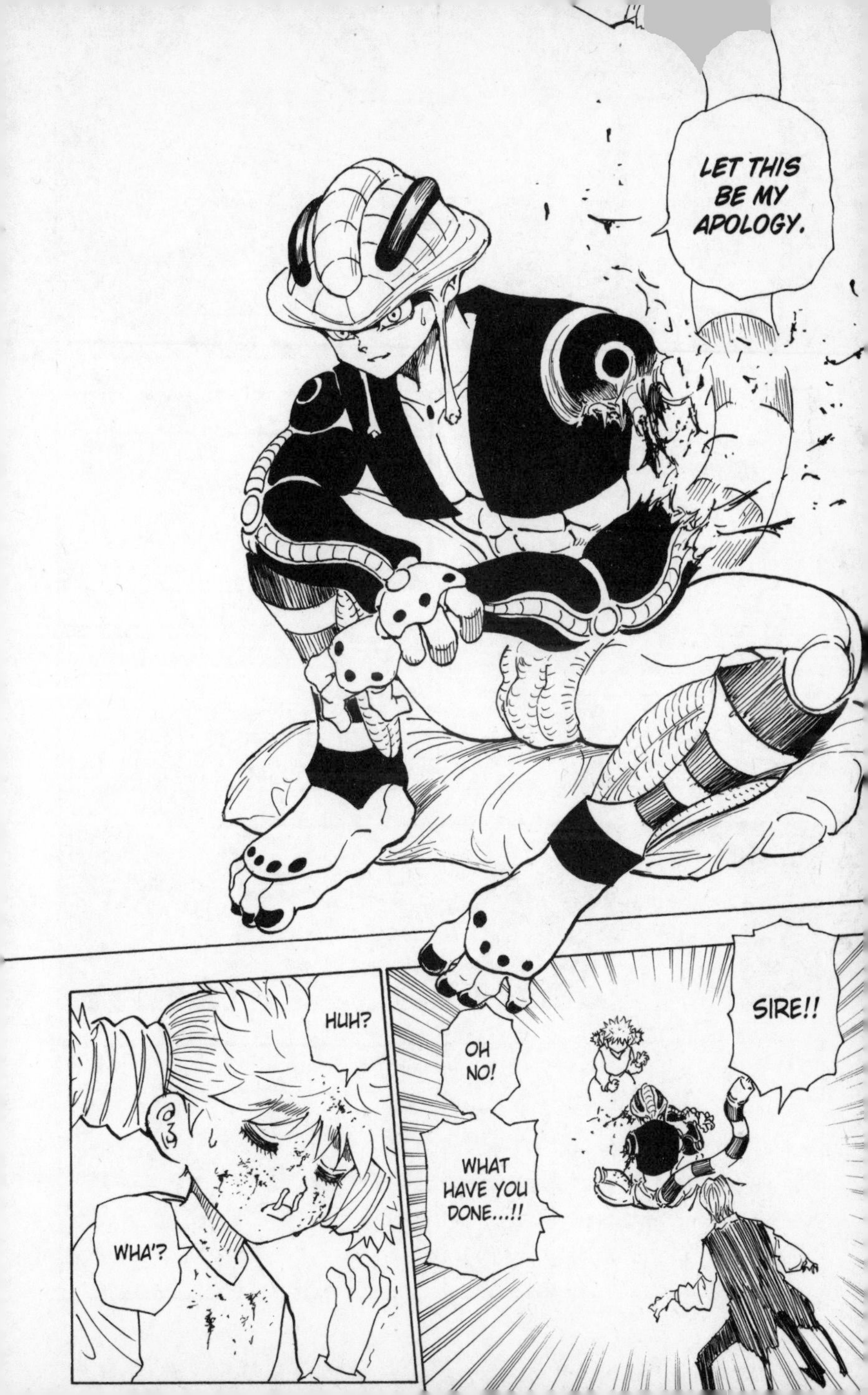
LET THIS BE MY APOLOGY.
SIRE!!
OH NO!
WHAT HAVE YOU DONE...!!
HUH?
WHA'?

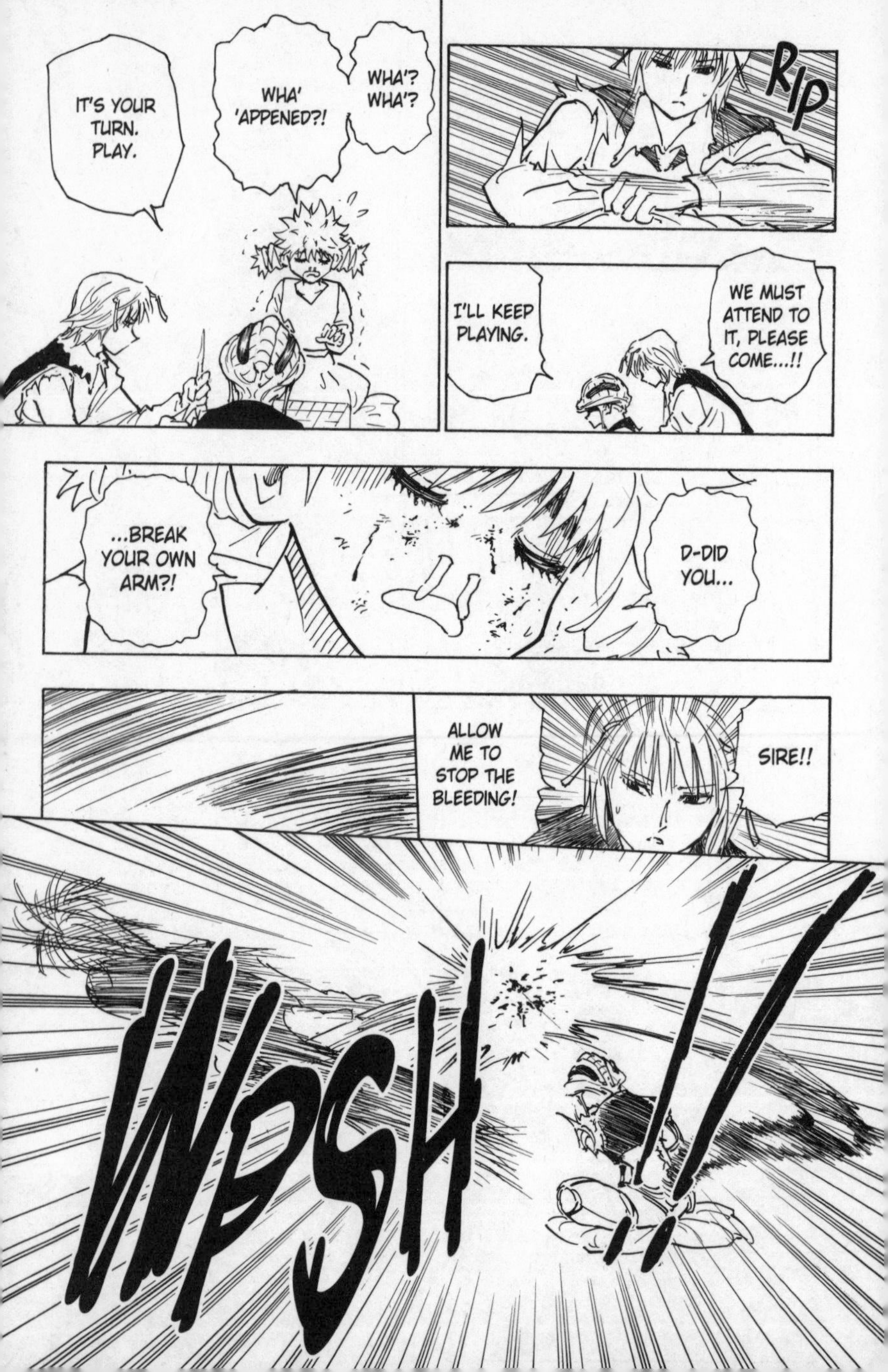
RIP
WE MUST ATTEND TO IT, PLEASE COME...!!
I'LL KEEP PLAYING.
WHA'? WHA'?
WHA' 'APPENED?!
IT'S YOUR TURN. PLAY.
D-DID YOU...
...BREAK YOUR OWN ARM?!
SIRE!!
ALLOW ME TO STOP THE BLEEDING!
WPSH!!

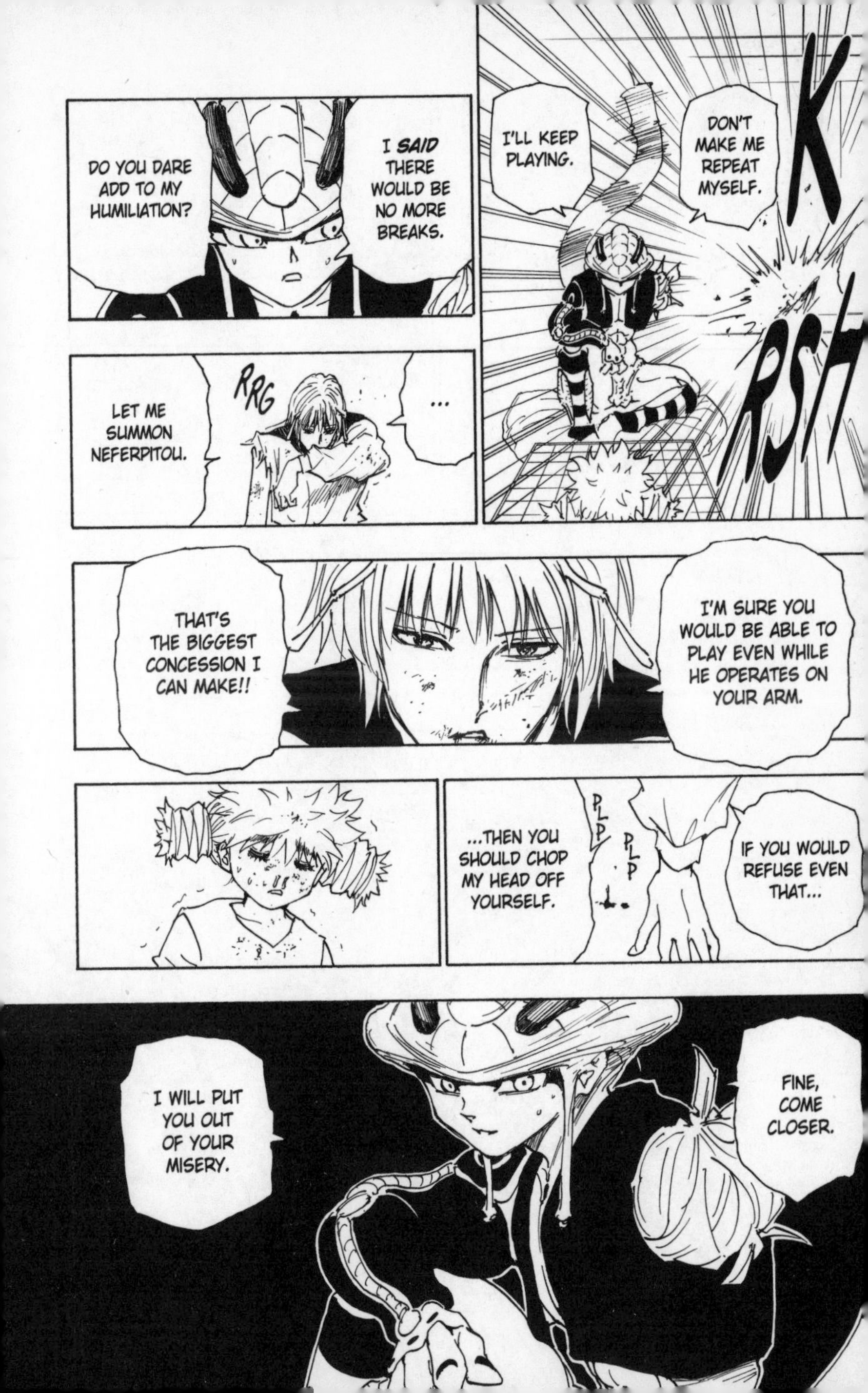
KRSH
DON'T MAKE ME REPEAT MYSELF.
I'LL KEEP PLAYING.
I *SAID* THERE WOULD BE NO MORE BREAKS.
DO YOU DARE ADD TO MY HUMILIATION?
...
RRG
LET ME SUMMON NEFERPITOU.
I'M SURE YOU WOULD BE ABLE TO PLAY EVEN WHILE HE OPERATES ON YOUR ARM.
THAT'S THE BIGGEST CONCESSION I CAN MAKE!!
IF YOU WOULD REFUSE EVEN THAT...
PLP
PLP
...THEN YOU SHOULD CHOP MY HEAD OFF YOURSELF.
FINE, COME CLOSER.
I WILL PUT YOU OUT OF YOUR MISERY.

READ THIS WAY

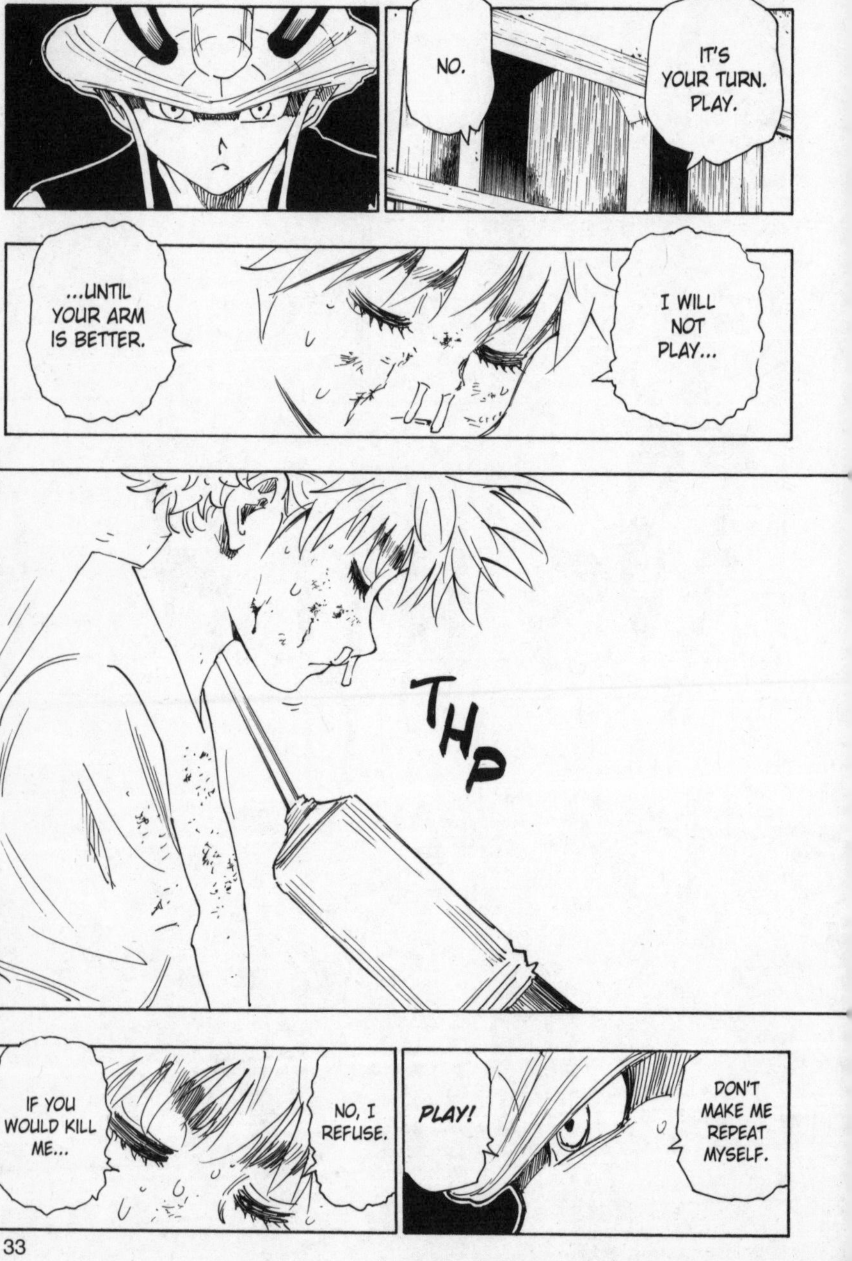
IT'S YOUR TURN. PLAY.
NO.
I WILL NOT PLAY...
...UNTIL YOUR ARM IS BETTER.
THP
DON'T MAKE ME REPEAT MYSELF.
PLAY!
NO, I REFUSE.
IF YOU WOULD KILL ME...

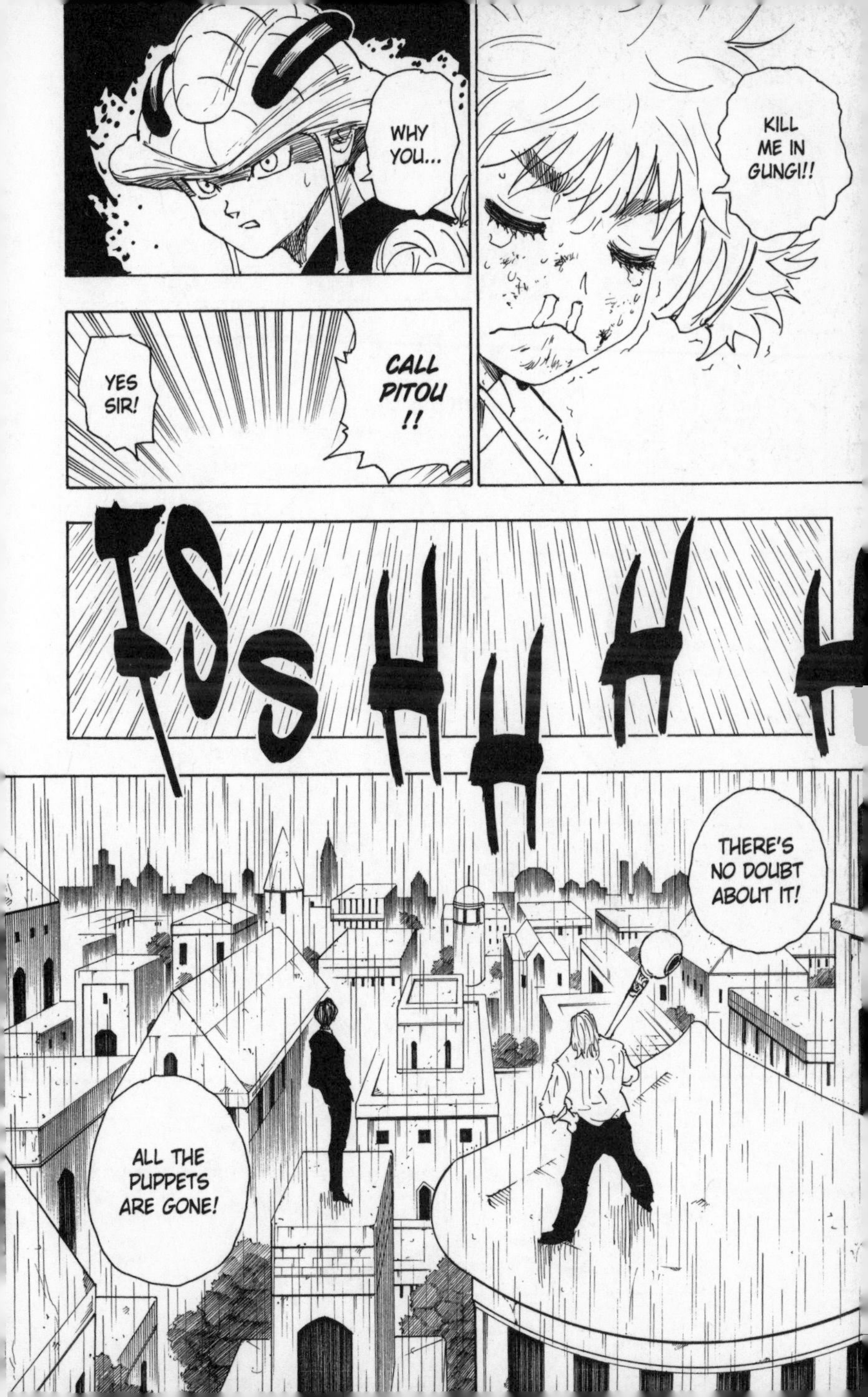
KILL ME IN GUNGI!!
WHY YOU...
CALL PITOU!!
YES SIR!
TSHHHH
THERE'S NO DOUBT ABOUT IT!
ALL THE PUPPETS ARE GONE!

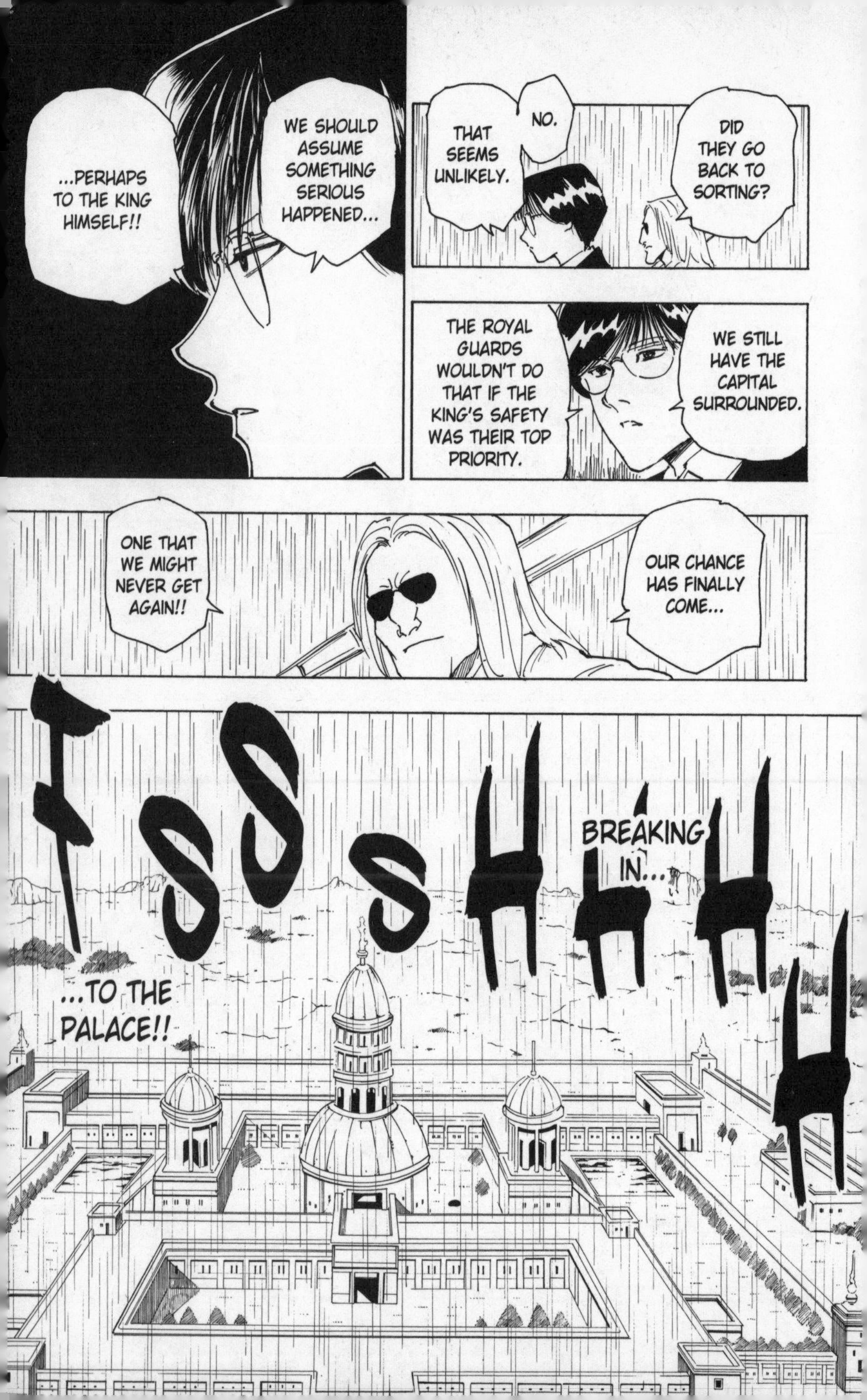
DID THEY GO BACK TO SORTING?
NO.
THAT SEEMS UNLIKELY.
WE STILL HAVE THE CAPITAL SURROUNDED.
THE ROYAL GUARDS WOULDN'T DO THAT IF THE KING'S SAFETY WAS THEIR TOP PRIORITY.
WE SHOULD ASSUME SOMETHING SERIOUS HAPPENED...
...PERHAPS TO THE KING HIMSELF!!
OUR CHANCE HAS FINALLY COME...
ONE THAT WE MIGHT NEVER GET AGAIN!!
FSSSHHHH
BREAKING IN...
...TO THE PALACE!!

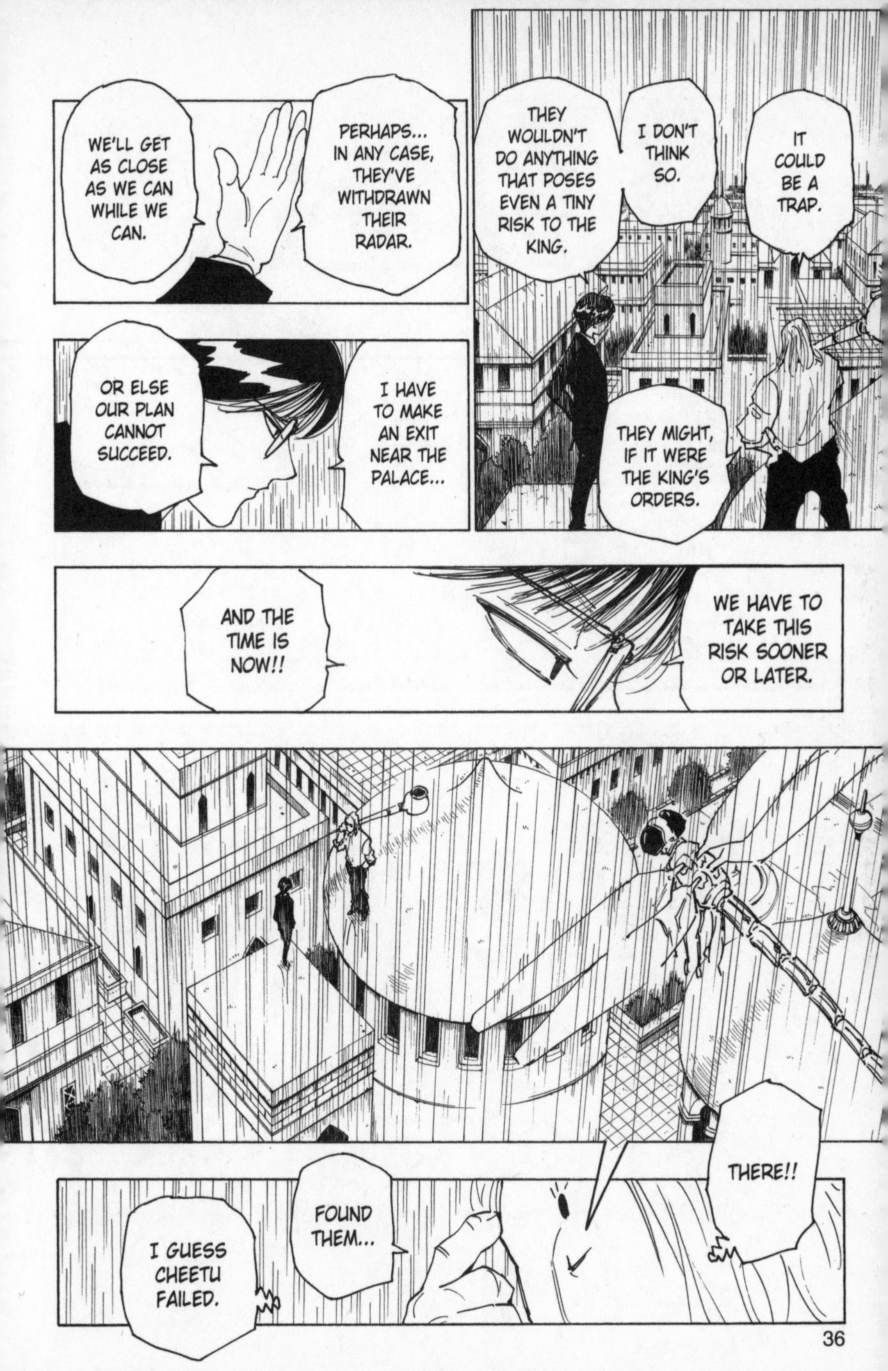
IT COULD BE A TRAP.
I DON'T THINK SO.
THEY WOULDN'T DO ANYTHING THAT POSES EVEN A TINY RISK TO THE KING.
THEY MIGHT, IF IT WERE THE KING'S ORDERS.
PERHAPS... IN ANY CASE, THEY'VE WITHDRAWN THEIR RADAR.
WE'LL GET AS CLOSE AS WE CAN WHILE WE CAN.
I HAVE TO MAKE AN EXIT NEAR THE PALACE...
OR ELSE OUR PLAN CANNOT SUCCEED.
WE HAVE TO TAKE THIS RISK SOONER OR LATER.
AND THE TIME IS NOW!!
THERE!!
FOUND THEM...
I GUESS CHEETU FAILED.

READ THIS WAY

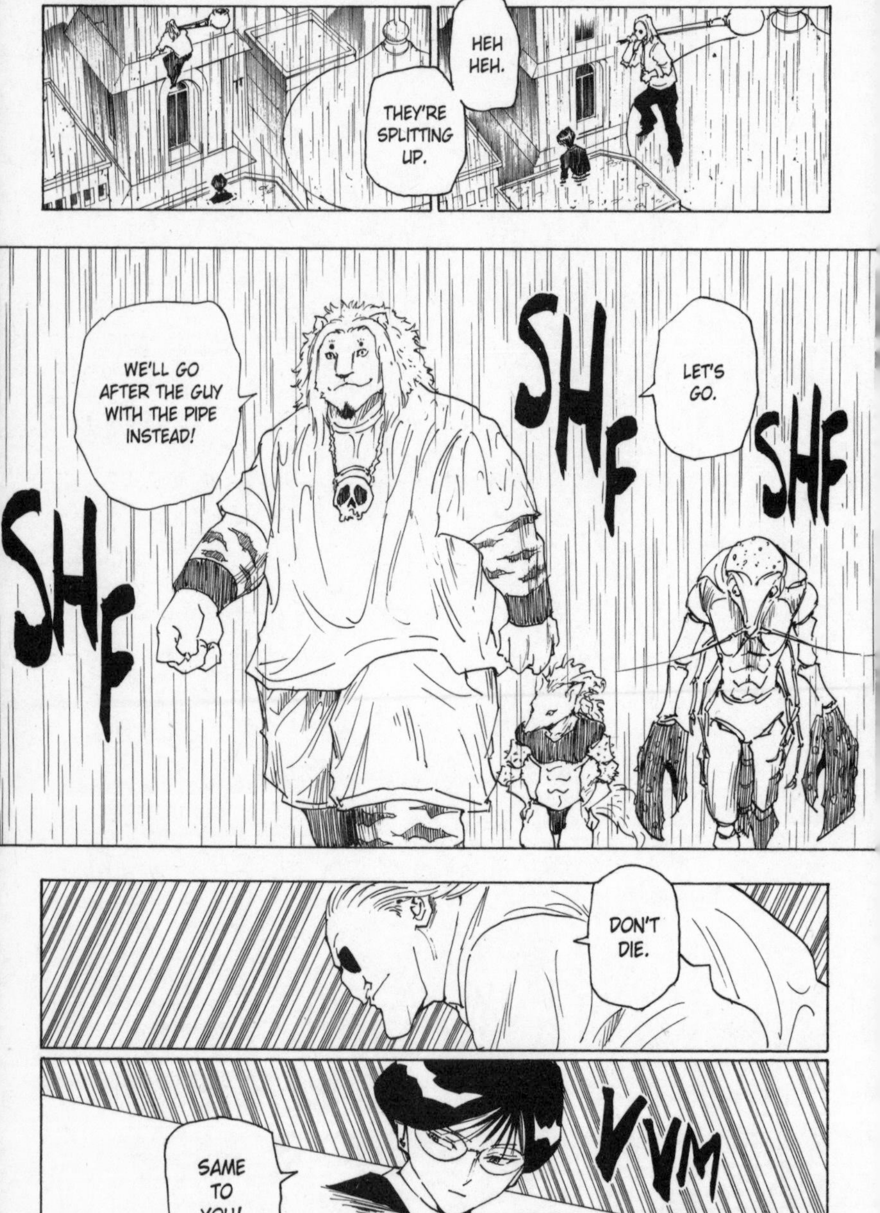
HEH HEH.
THEY'RE SPLITTING UP.
SHF
LET'S GO.
SHF
SHF
WE'LL GO AFTER THE GUY WITH THE PIPE INSTEAD!
SHF
DON'T DIE.
VVM
SAME TO YOU!

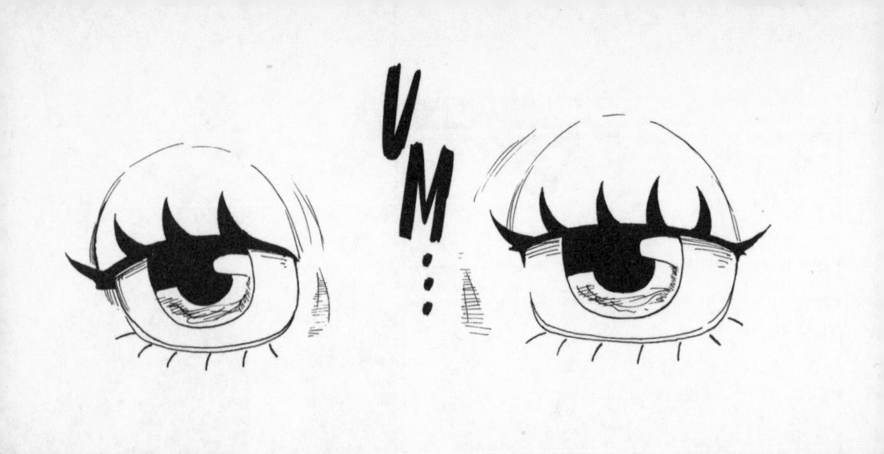
UM...

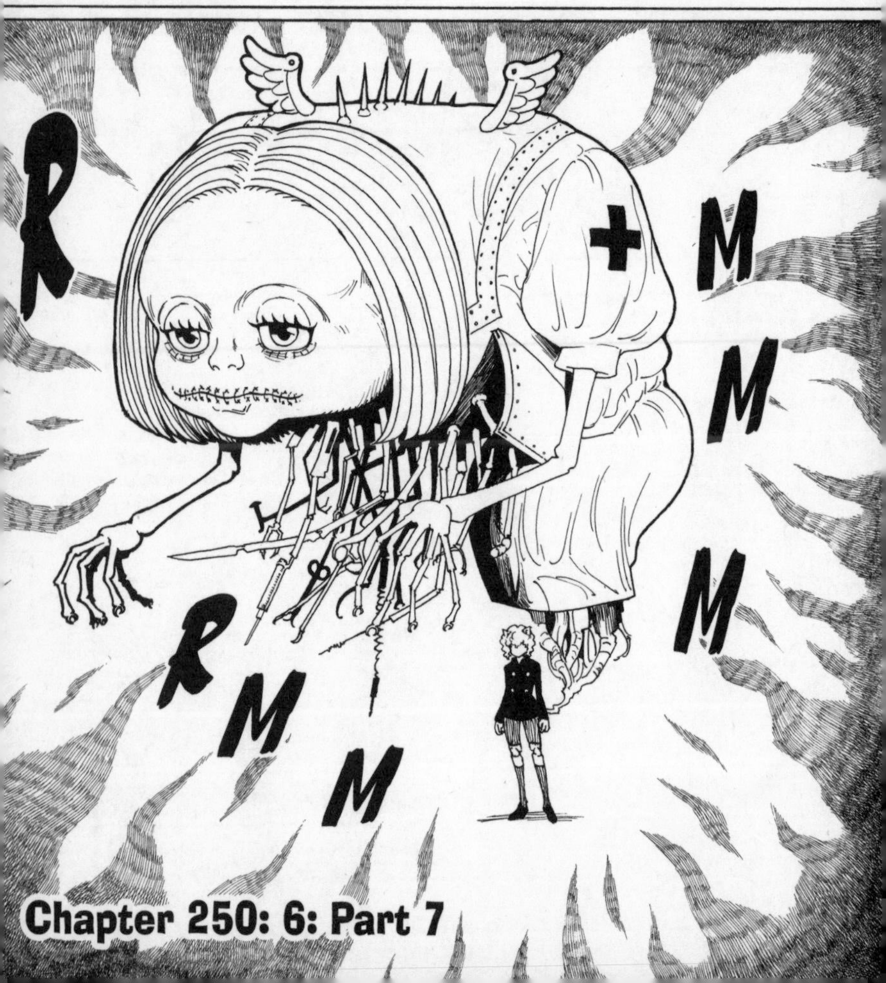
MMMM
R
RMM

Chapter 250: 6: Part 7

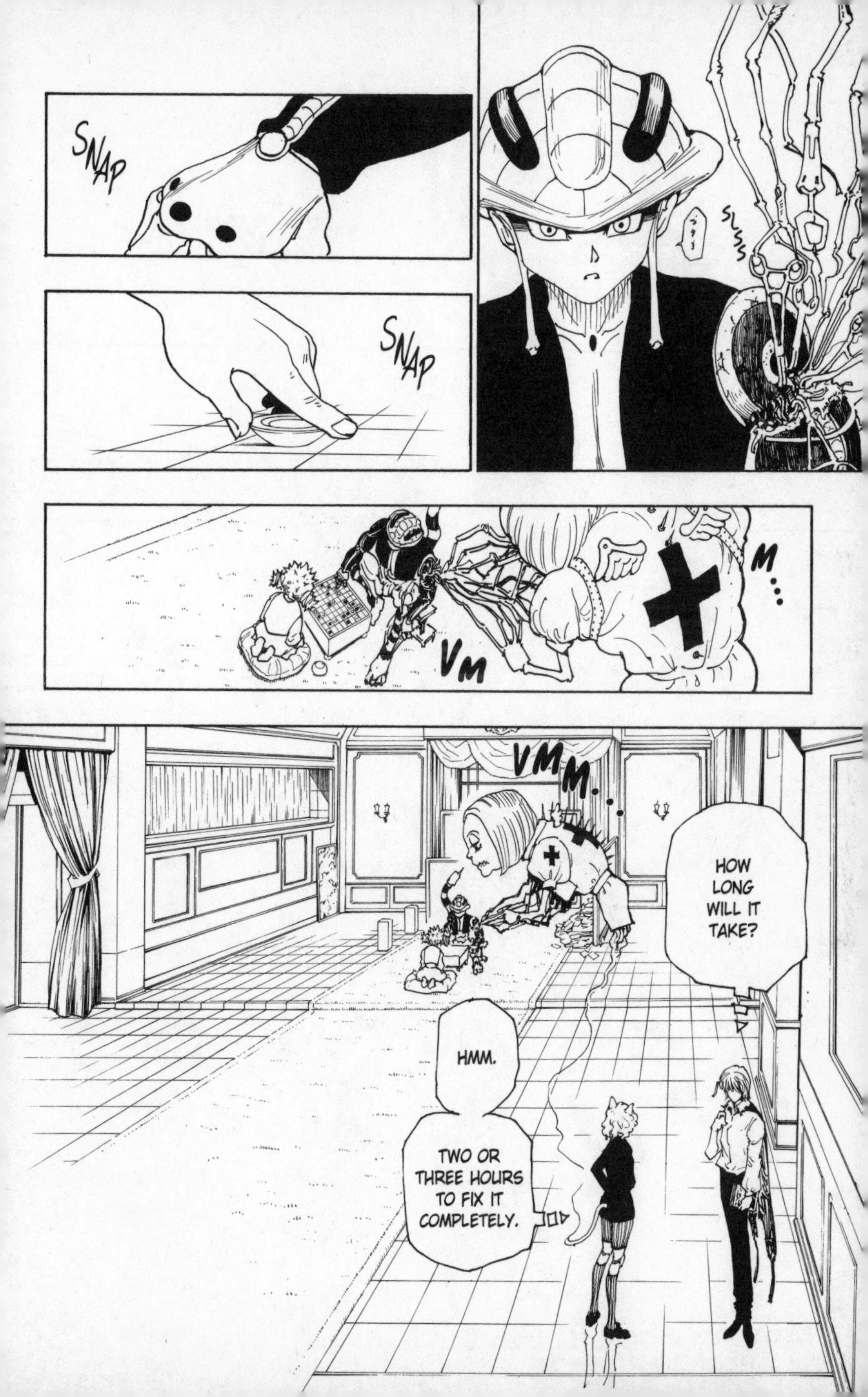
SLSS
SNAP
SNAP
M...
VM
VMM...
HOW LONG WILL IT TAKE?
HMM.
TWO OR THREE HOURS TO FIX IT COMPLETELY.

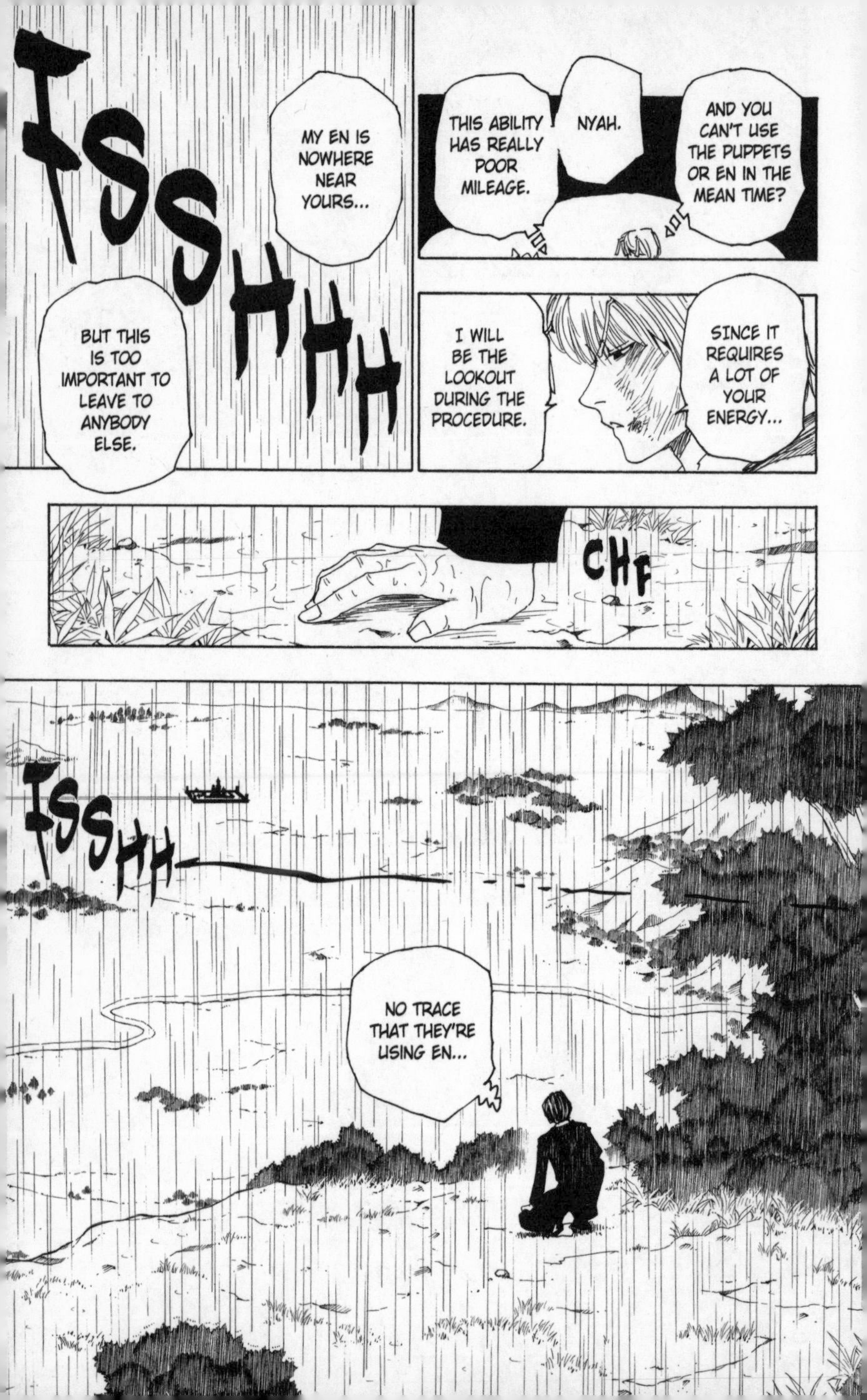
AND YOU CAN'T USE THE PUPPETS OR EN IN THE MEAN TIME?
NYAH.
THIS ABILITY HAS REALLY POOR MILEAGE.
SINCE IT REQUIRES A LOT OF YOUR ENERGY...
I WILL BE THE LOOKOUT DURING THE PROCEDURE.
TSSHHH
MY EN IS NOWHERE NEAR YOURS...
BUT THIS IS TOO IMPORTANT TO LEAVE TO ANYBODY ELSE.
CHF
TSSHH
NO TRACE THAT THEY'RE USING EN...

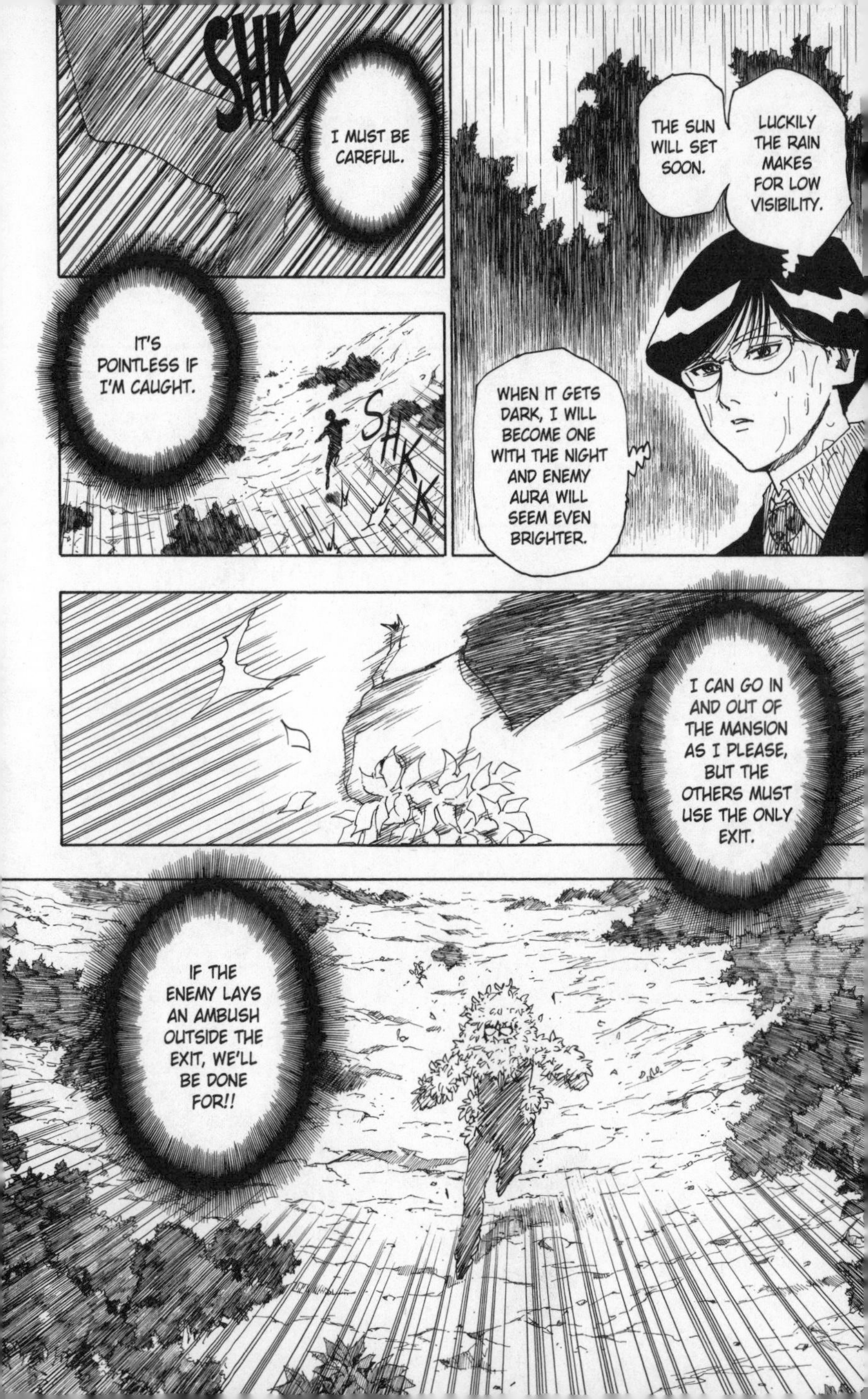
LUCKILY THE RAIN MAKES FOR LOW VISIBILITY.
THE SUN WILL SET SOON.
WHEN IT GETS DARK, I WILL BECOME ONE WITH THE NIGHT AND ENEMY AURA WILL SEEM EVEN BRIGHTER.
SHK
I MUST BE CAREFUL.
IT'S POINTLESS IF I'M CAUGHT.
SHKK
I CAN GO IN AND OUT OF THE MANSION AS I PLEASE, BUT THE OTHERS MUST USE THE ONLY EXIT.
IF THE ENEMY LAYS AN AMBUSH OUTSIDE THE EXIT, WE'LL BE DONE FOR!!

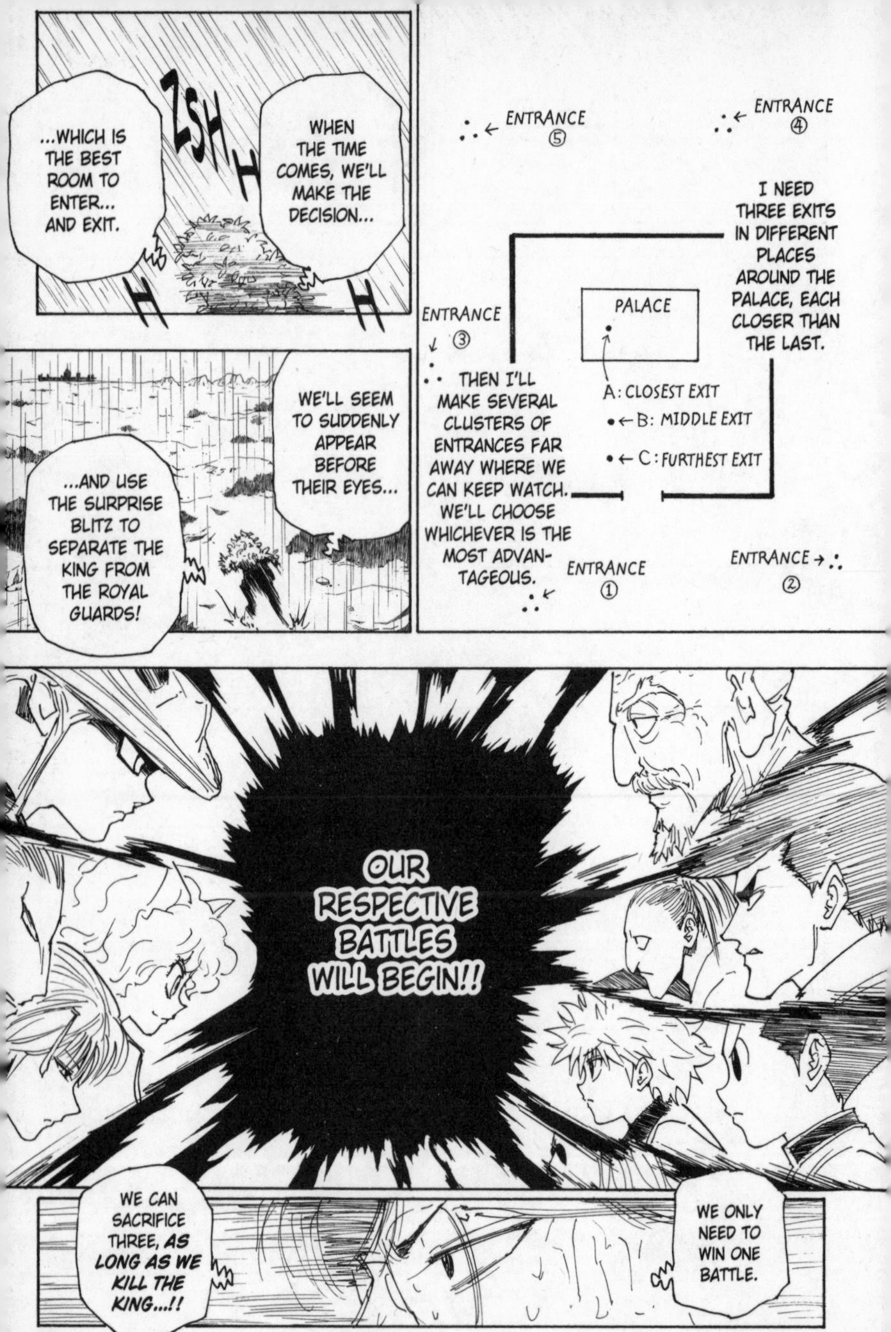
ENTRANCE ④
ENTRANCE ⑤
I NEED THREE EXITS IN DIFFERENT PLACES AROUND THE PALACE, EACH CLOSER THAN THE LAST.
PALACE
ENTRANCE ③
A: CLOSEST EXIT
B: MIDDLE EXIT
C: FURTHEST EXIT
THEN I'LL MAKE SEVERAL CLUSTERS OF ENTRANCES FAR AWAY WHERE WE CAN KEEP WATCH. WE'LL CHOOSE WHICHEVER IS THE MOST ADVANTAGEOUS.
ENTRANCE ②
ENTRANCE ①
WHEN THE TIME COMES, WE'LL MAKE THE DECISION...
ZSHHHH
...WHICH IS THE BEST ROOM TO ENTER... AND EXIT.
WE'LL SEEM TO SUDDENLY APPEAR BEFORE THEIR EYES...
...AND USE THE SURPRISE BLITZ TO SEPARATE THE KING FROM THE ROYAL GUARDS!
OUR RESPECTIVE BATTLES WILL BEGIN!!
WE ONLY NEED TO WIN ONE BATTLE.
WE CAN SACRIFICE THREE, AS LONG AS WE KILL THE KING...!!

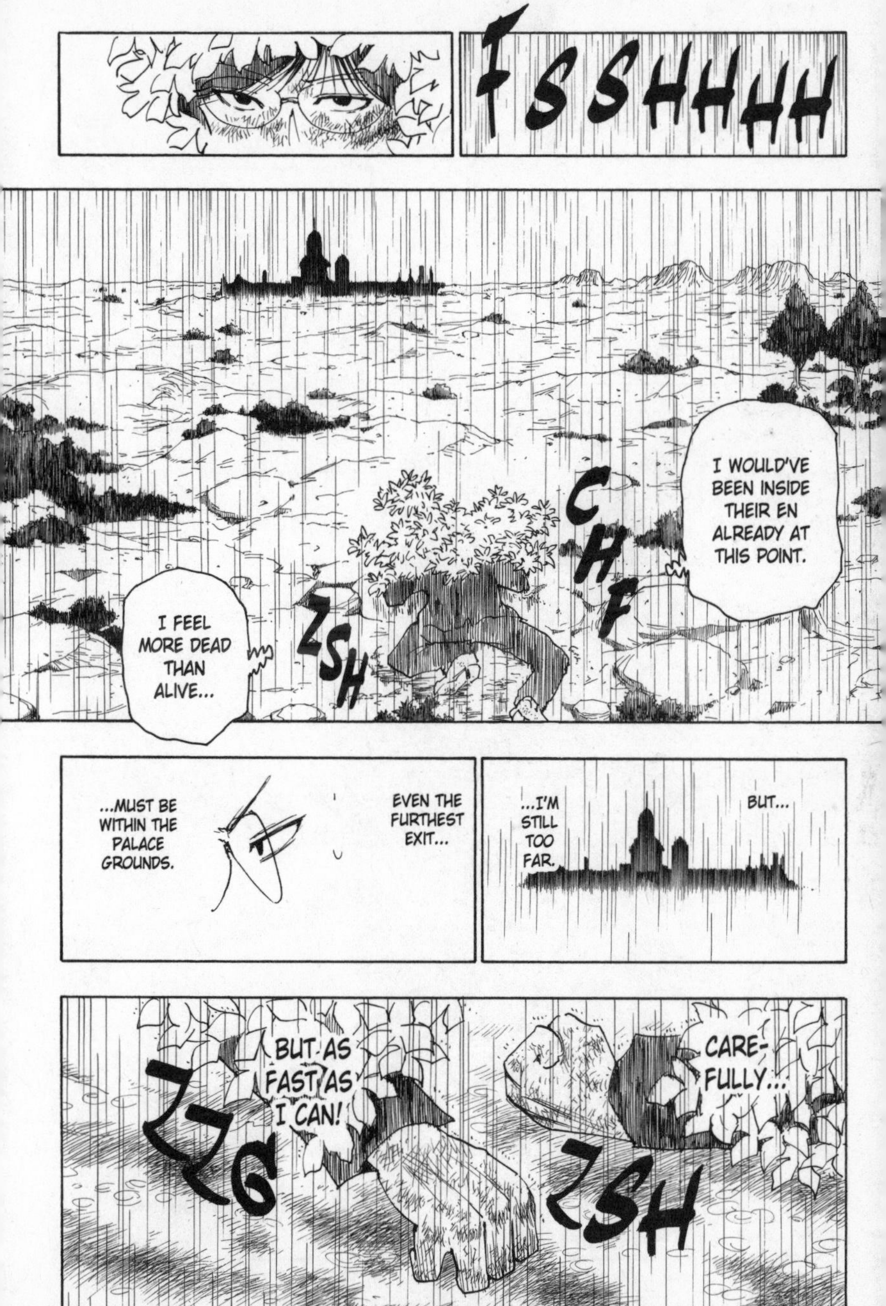
FSSHHHH
I WOULD'VE BEEN INSIDE THEIR EN ALREADY AT THIS POINT.
CHF
ZSH
I FEEL MORE DEAD THAN ALIVE...
BUT...
...I'M STILL TOO FAR.
EVEN THE FURTHEST EXIT...
...MUST BE WITHIN THE PALACE GROUNDS.
CARE-FULLY...
ZSH
BUT AS FAST AS I CAN!
ZZG

READ THIS WAY

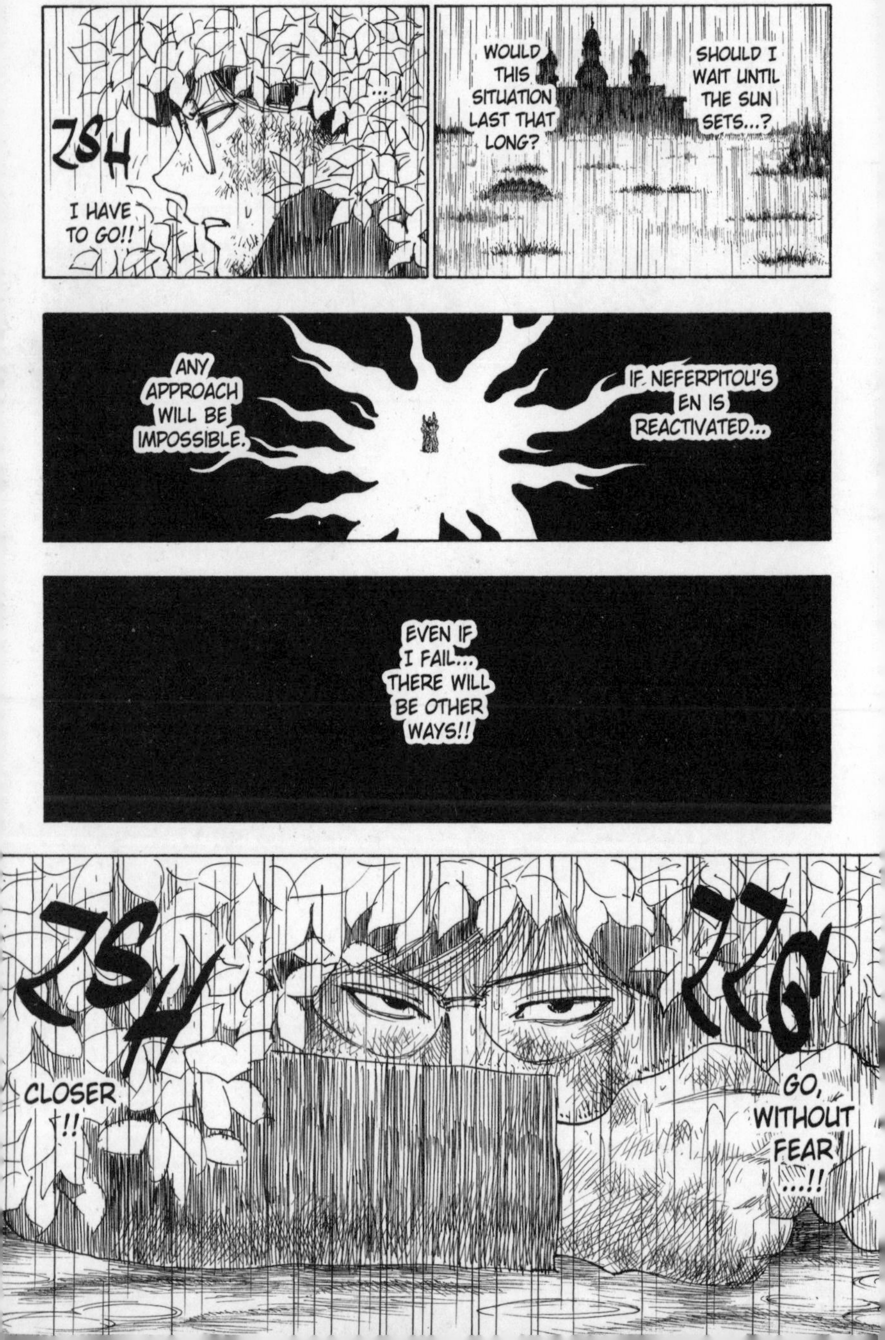
SHOULD I WAIT UNTIL THE SUN SETS...?
WOULD THIS SITUATION LAST THAT LONG?
...
ZSH
I HAVE TO GO!!
IF NEFERPITOU'S EN IS REACTIVATED...
ANY APPROACH WILL BE IMPOSSIBLE.
EVEN IF I FAIL... THERE WILL BE OTHER WAYS!!
ZZG
GO, WITHOUT FEAR ...!!
ZSH
CLOSER !!

THERE ARE CURRENTLY THREE HUMANS IN THE PALACE WHO ARE NOT KEPT FOR FOOD.

...

ONE IS THE YOUNG GUNGI PLAYER, ANOTHER IS MING...

AND THE THIRD IS...

TK

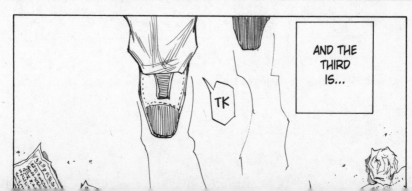

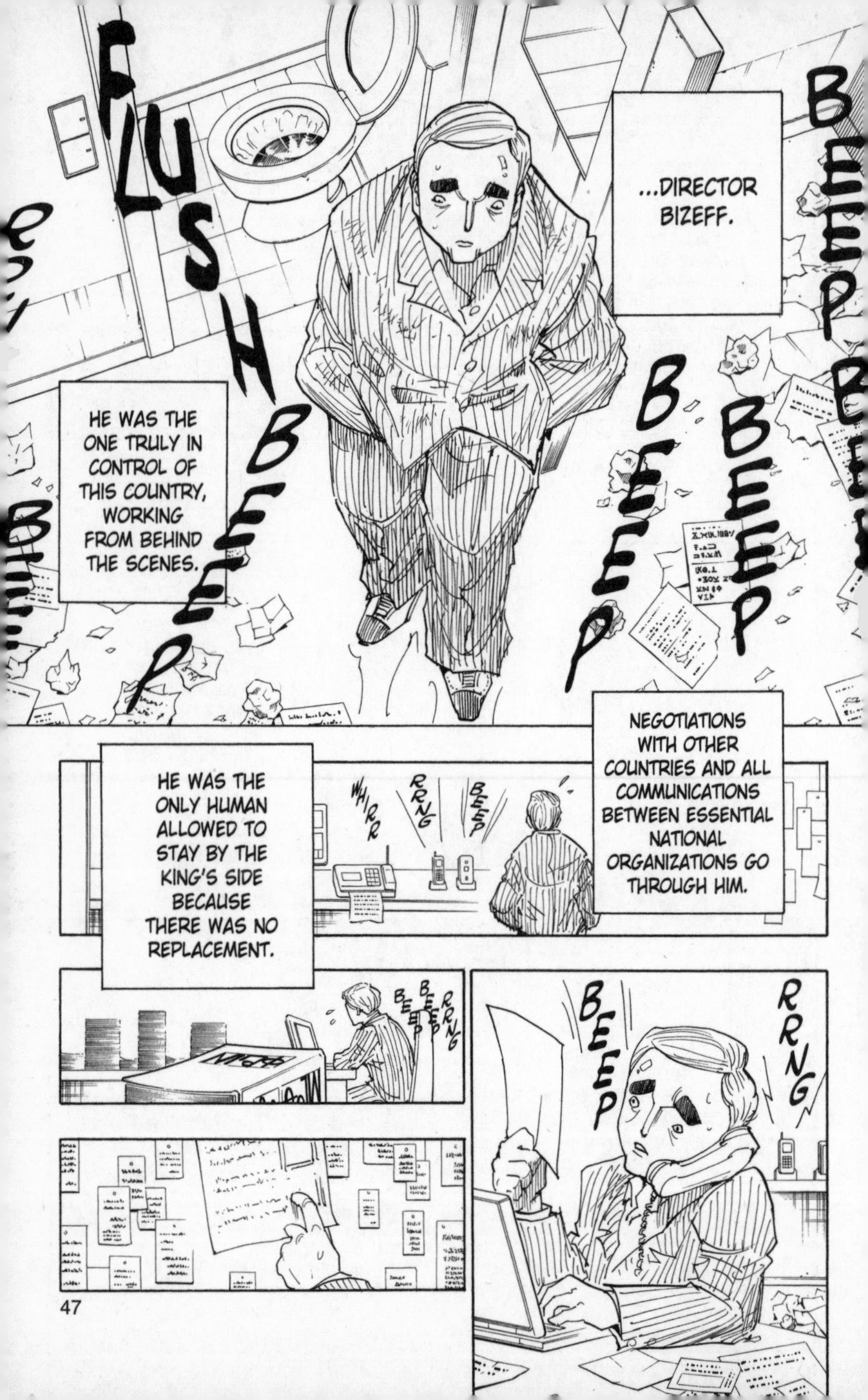

BEEP BEEP
...DIRECTOR BIZEFF.
BEEP
BEEP
FLUSH
HE WAS THE ONE TRULY IN CONTROL OF THIS COUNTRY, WORKING FROM BEHIND THE SCENES.
BEEP
NEGOTIATIONS WITH OTHER COUNTRIES AND ALL COMMUNICATIONS BETWEEN ESSENTIAL NATIONAL ORGANIZATIONS GO THROUGH HIM.
BEEP
RRNG
WHIRR
HE WAS THE ONLY HUMAN ALLOWED TO STAY BY THE KING'S SIDE BECAUSE THERE WAS NO REPLACEMENT.
RRNG
BEEP
RRNG
BEEP
BEEP

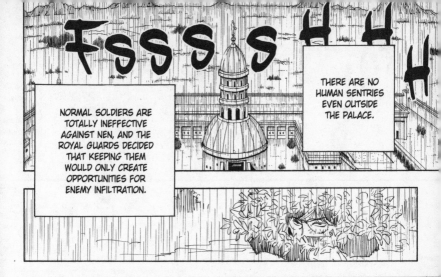

FSSSSHHHH
THERE ARE NO HUMAN SENTRIES EVEN OUTSIDE THE PALACE.
NORMAL SOLDIERS ARE TOTALLY INEFFECTIVE AGAINST NEN, AND THE ROYAL GUARDS DECIDED THAT KEEPING THEM WOULD ONLY CREATE OPPORTUNITIES FOR ENEMY INFILTRATION.
CHEETU, WHO JUST RETURNED, IS THE ONLY SQUADRON LEADER CURRENTLY HERE, ALONG WITH SIX LESSER ANTS.
ZZH
ZZH
ZISH
THEREFORE, THERE ARE CURRENTLY ONLY THREE HUMANS (BESIDES THOSE KEPT FOR FOOD) AND ELEVEN ANTS WITHIN THE PALACE.
ZISH

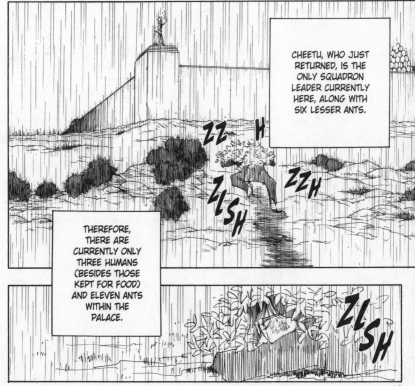

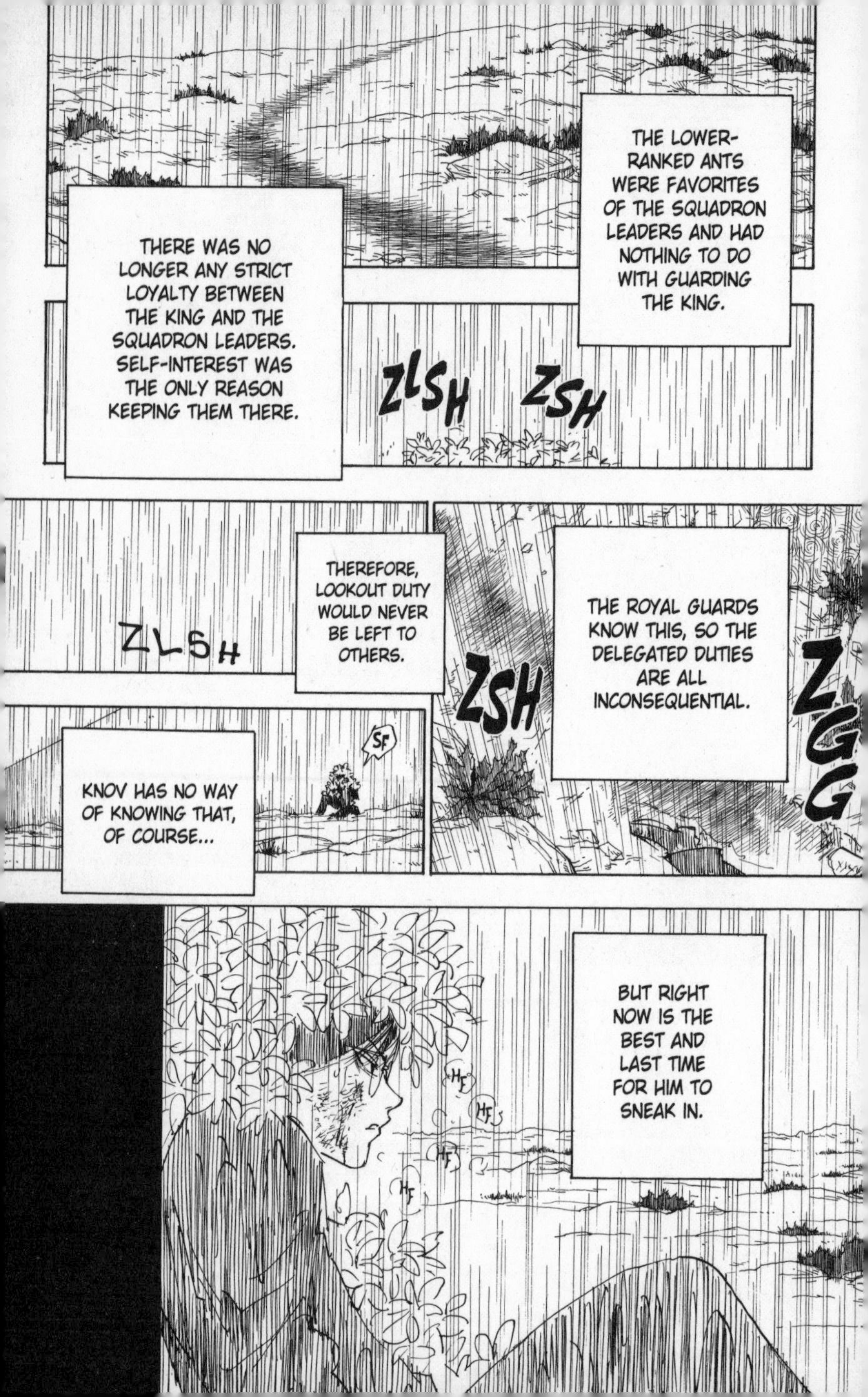
THE LOWER-RANKED ANTS WERE FAVORITES OF THE SQUADRON LEADERS AND HAD NOTHING TO DO WITH GUARDING THE KING.
THERE WAS NO LONGER ANY STRICT LOYALTY BETWEEN THE KING AND THE SQUADRON LEADERS. SELF-INTEREST WAS THE ONLY REASON KEEPING THEM THERE.
ZSH
ZLSH
ZGG
THE ROYAL GUARDS KNOW THIS, SO THE DELEGATED DUTIES ARE ALL INCONSEQUENTIAL.
ZSH
THEREFORE, LOOKOUT DUTY WOULD NEVER BE LEFT TO OTHERS.
ZLSH
SF
KNOV HAS NO WAY OF KNOWING THAT, OF COURSE...
BUT RIGHT NOW IS THE BEST AND LAST TIME FOR HIM TO SNEAK IN.
HF
HF
HF
HF

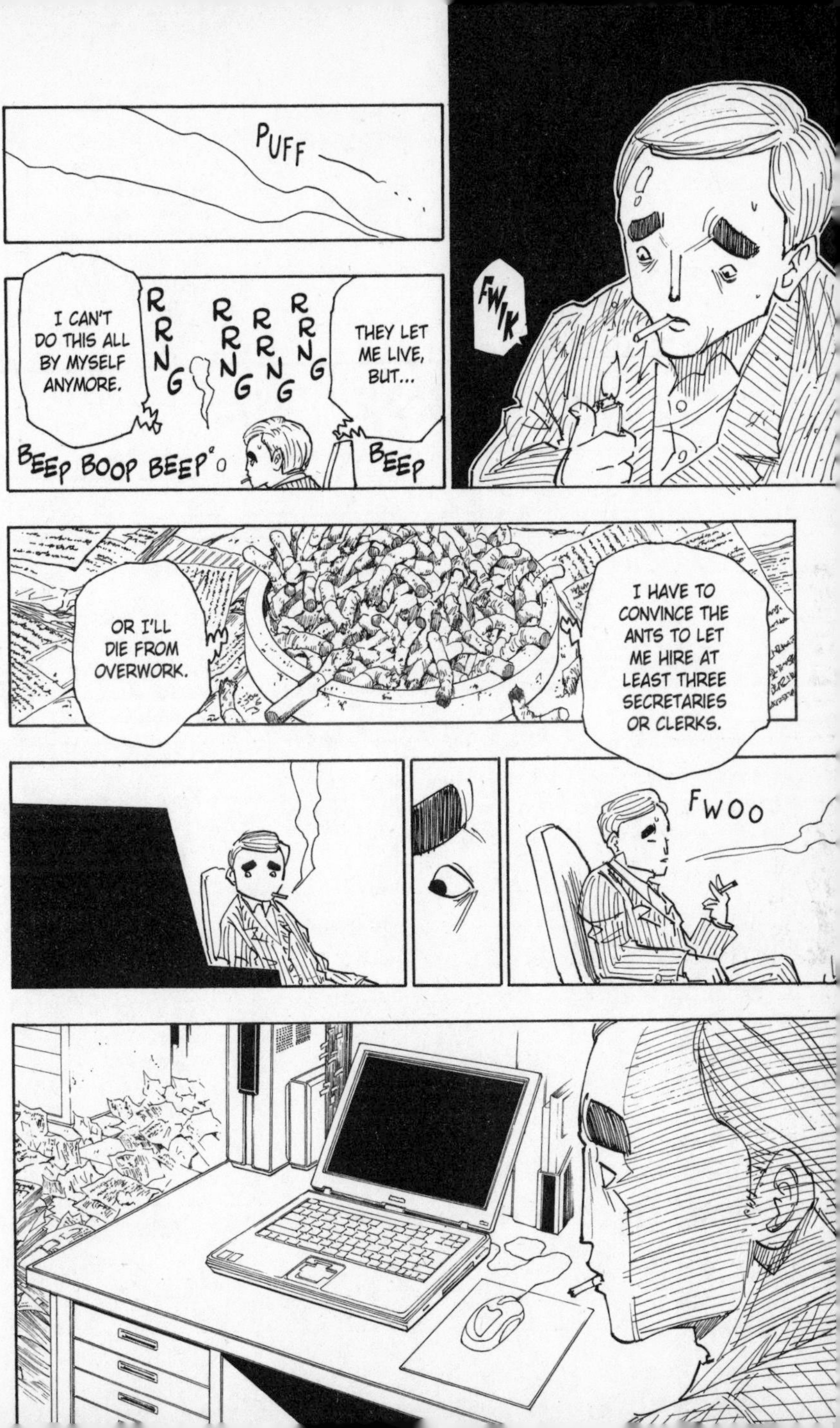
FWIK
PUFF
THEY LET ME LIVE, BUT...
BEEP
RRNG RRNG RRNG RRNG
I CAN'T DO THIS ALL BY MYSELF ANYMORE.
BEEP BOOP BEEP
I HAVE TO CONVINCE THE ANTS TO LET ME HIRE AT LEAST THREE SECRETARIES OR CLERKS.
OR I'LL DIE FROM OVERWORK.
FWOO

READ THIS WAY

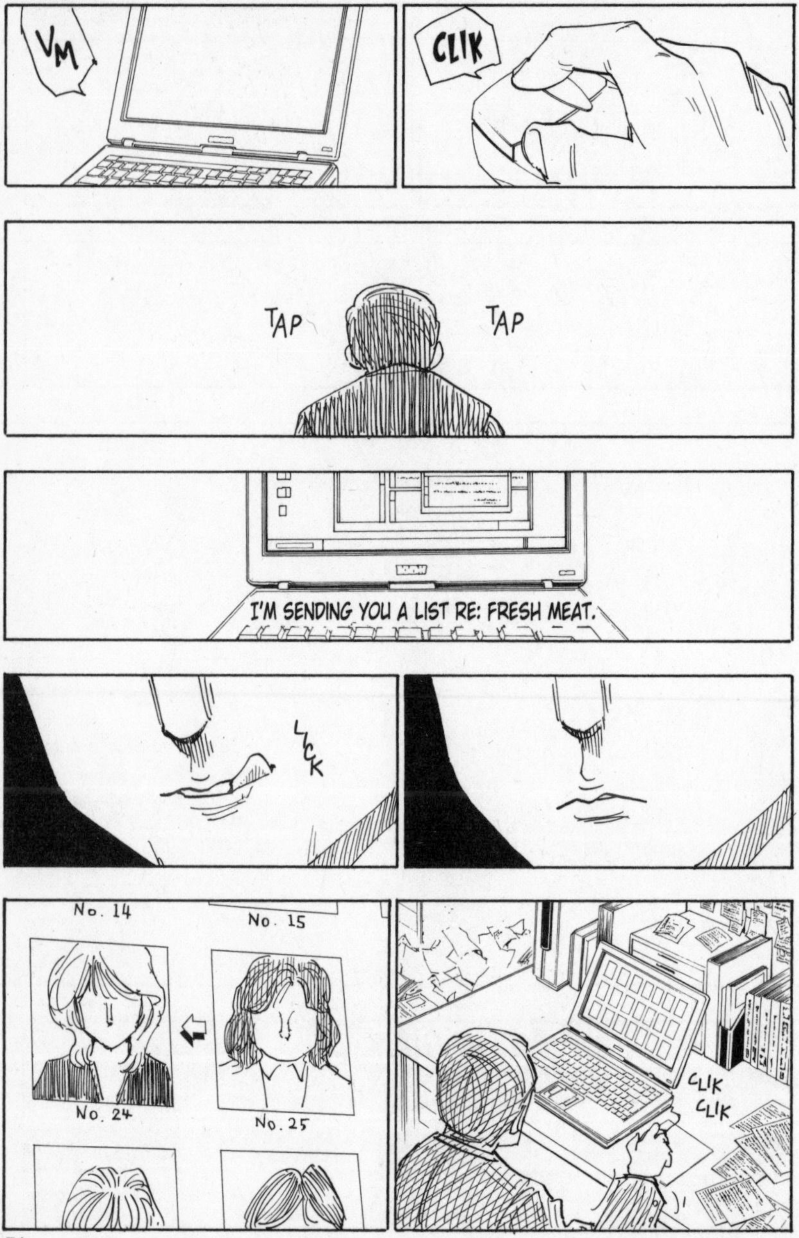
CLIK
VM
TAP
TAP
I'M SENDING YOU A LIST RE: FRESH MEAT.
LICK
CLIK
CLIK
No. 15
No. 14
No. 25
No. 24

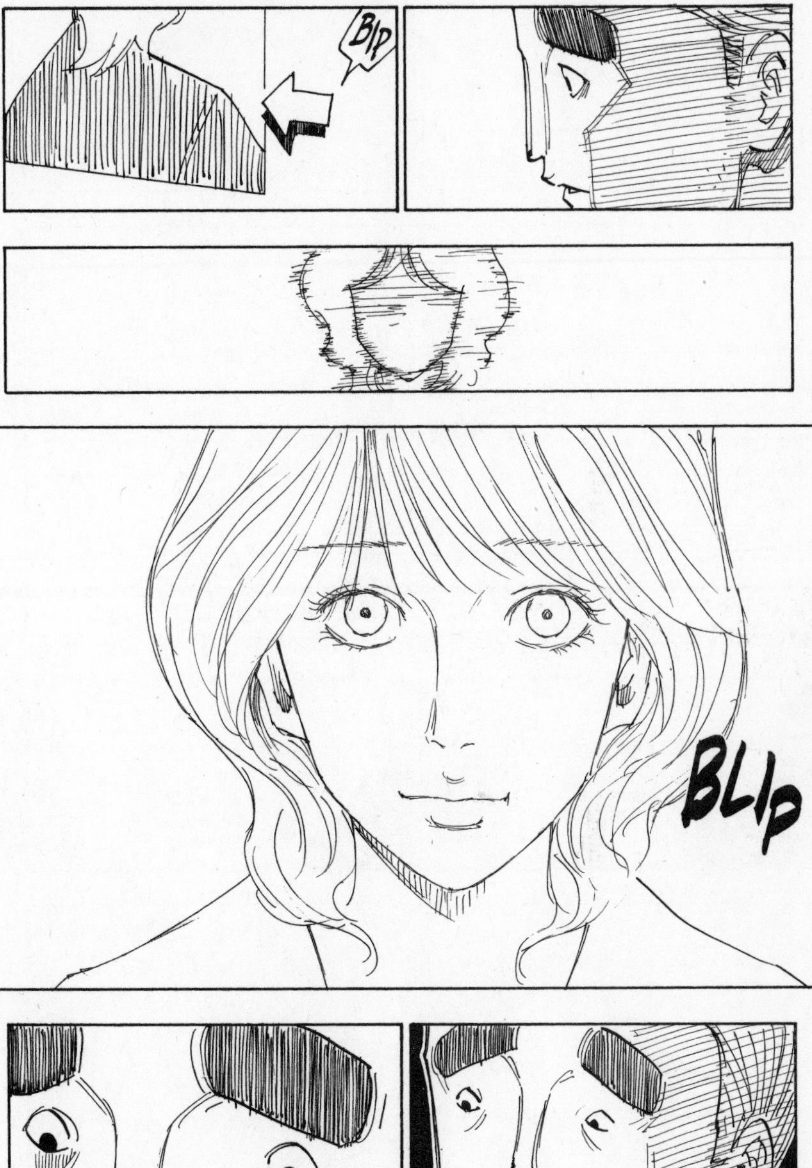
BLIP
BLIP

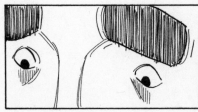

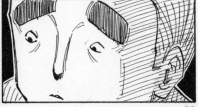

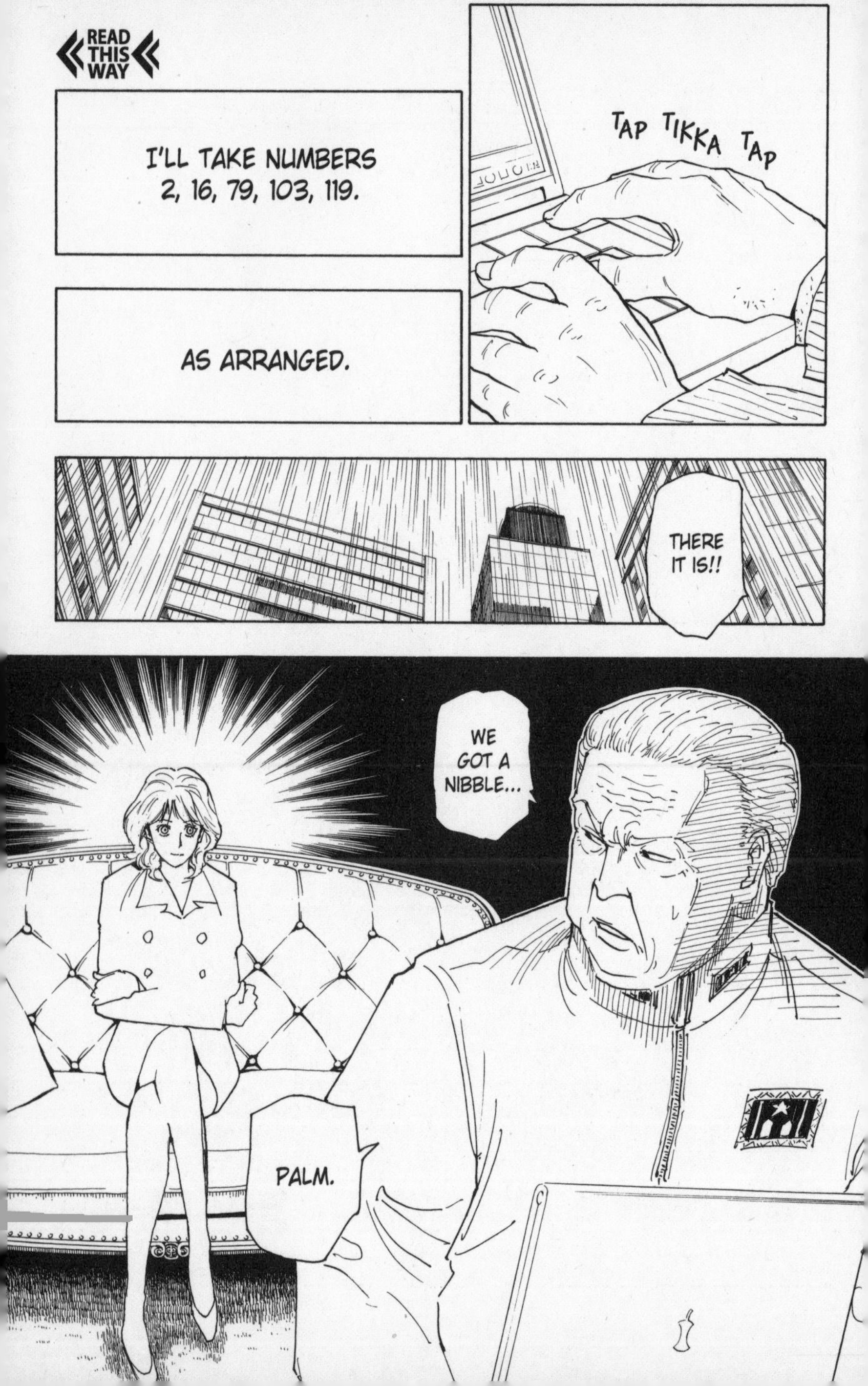
READ THIS WAY
TAP TIKKA TAP
I'LL TAKE NUMBERS 2, 16, 79, 103, 119.
AS ARRANGED.
THERE IT IS!!
WE GOT A NIBBLE...
PALM.

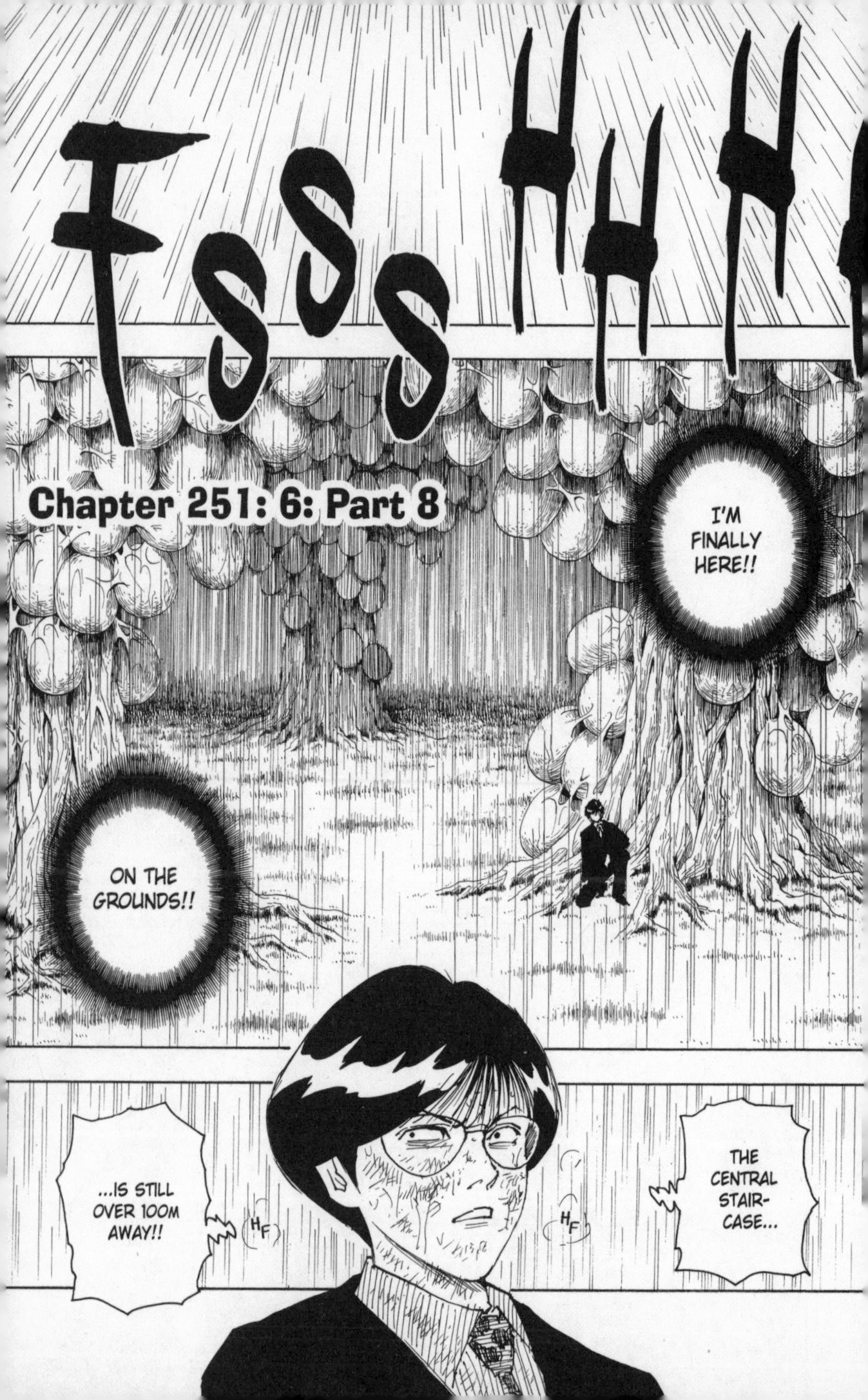
FSSSHHH
Chapter 251: 6: Part 8
I'M FINALLY HERE!!
ON THE GROUNDS!!
THE CENTRAL STAIR-CASE...
HF
HF
...IS STILL OVER 100M AWAY!!

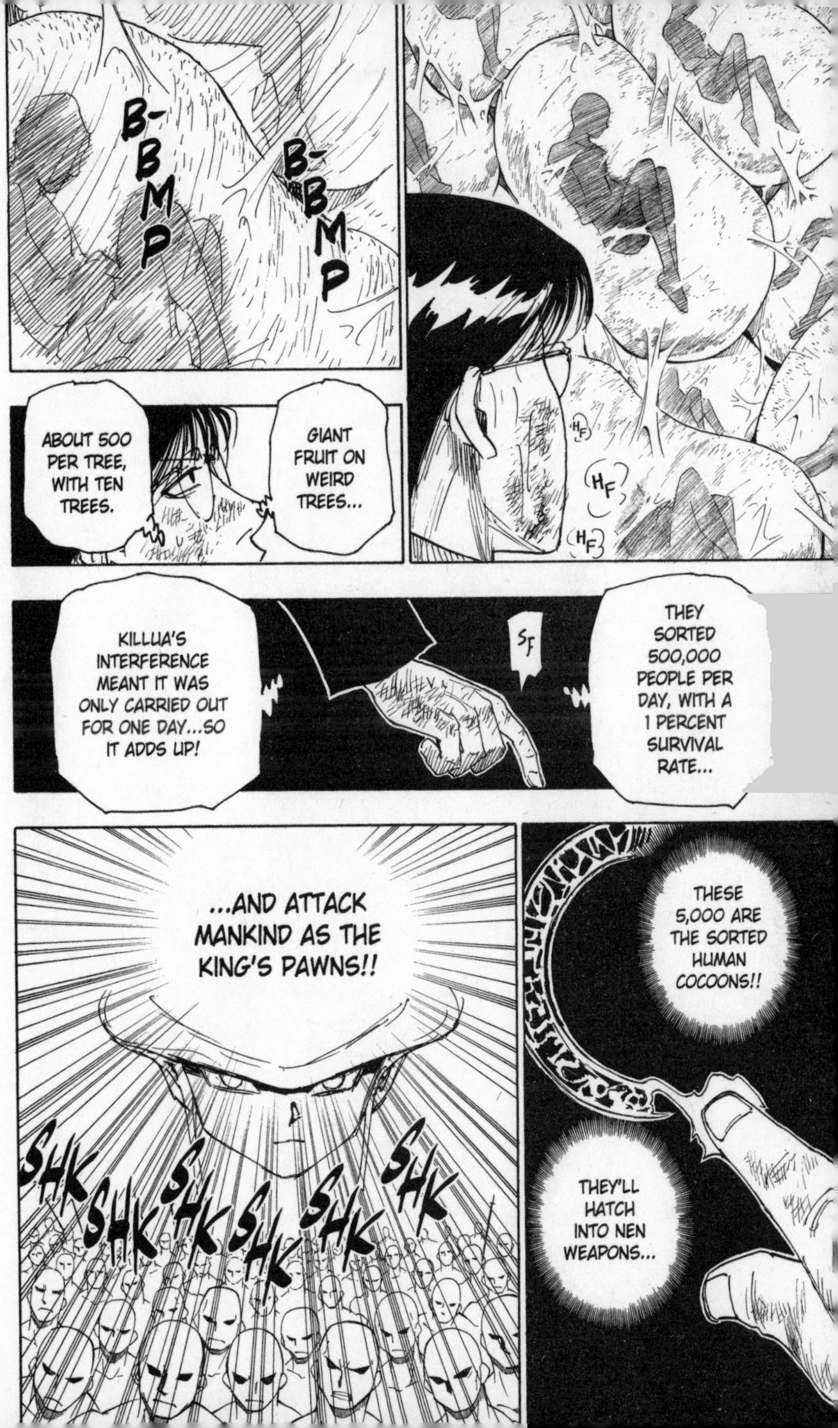
HF
HF
HF
B-BMP
B-BMP
GIANT FRUIT ON WEIRD TREES...
ABOUT 500 PER TREE, WITH TEN TREES.
THEY SORTED 500,000 PEOPLE PER DAY, WITH A 1 PERCENT SURVIVAL RATE...
SF
KILLUA'S INTERFERENCE MEANT IT WAS ONLY CARRIED OUT FOR ONE DAY...SO IT ADDS UP!
THESE 5,000 ARE THE SORTED HUMAN COCOONS!!
THEY'LL HATCH INTO NEN WEAPONS...
...AND ATTACK MANKIND AS THE KING'S PAWNS!!
SHK SHK SHK SHK SHK SHK SHK SHK

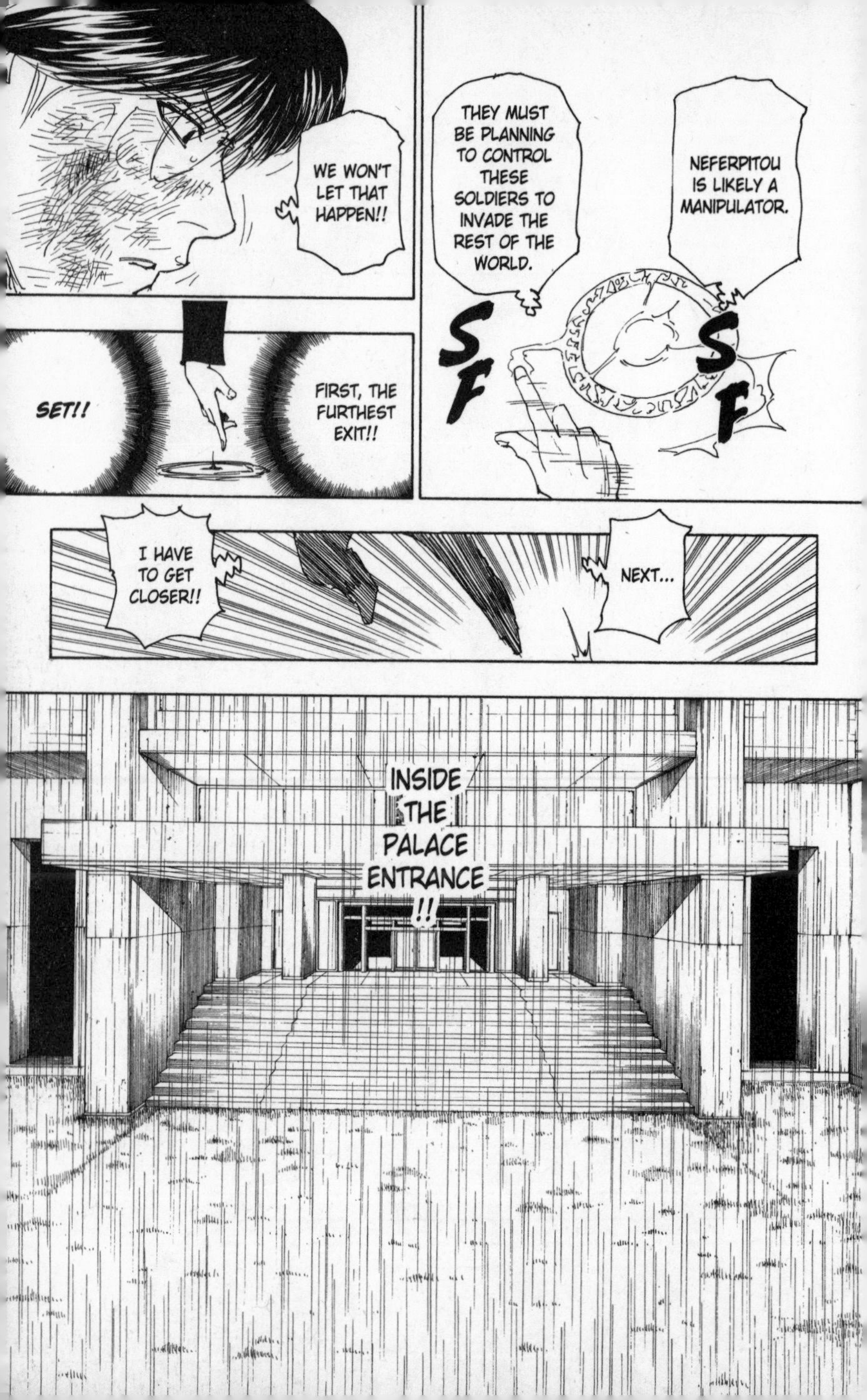
NEFERPITOU IS LIKELY A MANIPULATOR.
THEY MUST BE PLANNING TO CONTROL THESE SOLDIERS TO INVADE THE REST OF THE WORLD.
SF
SF
WE WON'T LET THAT HAPPEN!!
FIRST, THE FURTHEST EXIT!!
SET!!
NEXT...
I HAVE TO GET CLOSER!!
INSIDE THE PALACE ENTRANCE!!

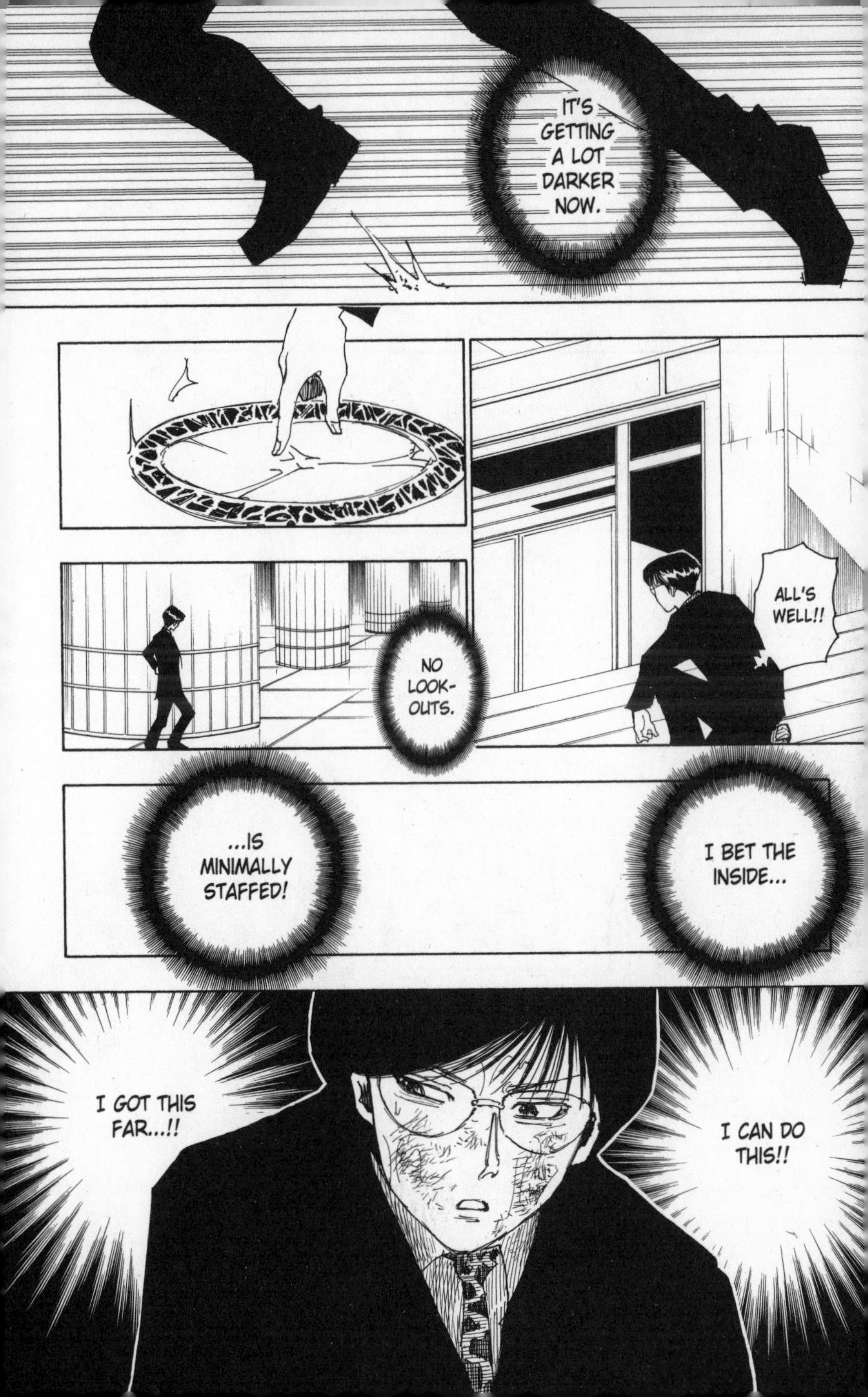
IT'S GETTING A LOT DARKER NOW.
ALL'S WELL!!
NO LOOK-OUTS.
I BET THE INSIDE...
...IS MINIMALLY STAFFED!
I CAN DO THIS!!
I GOT THIS FAR...!!

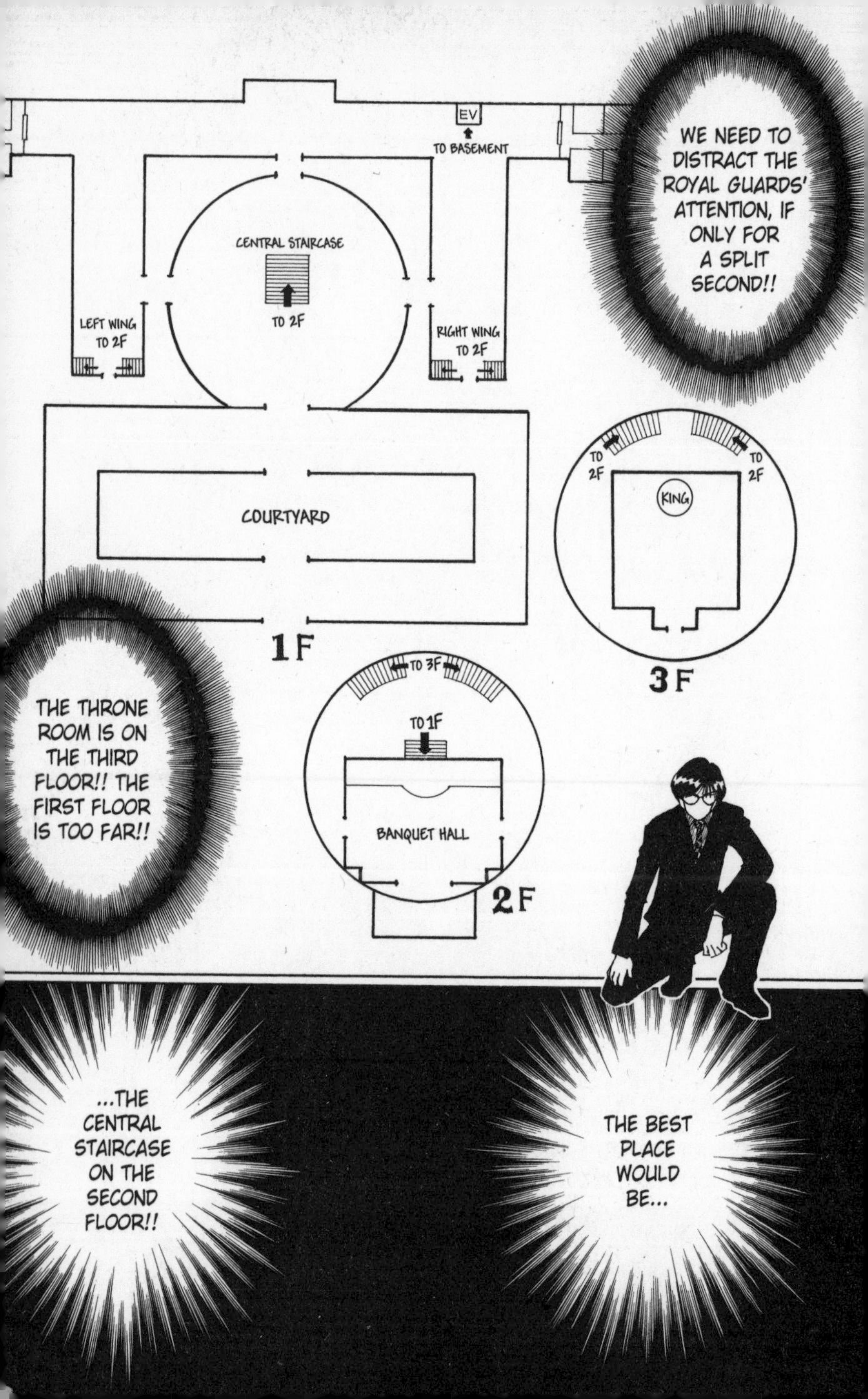
WE NEED TO DISTRACT THE ROYAL GUARDS' ATTENTION, IF ONLY FOR A SPLIT SECOND!!
EV
TO BASEMENT
CENTRAL STAIRCASE
TO 2F
LEFT WING TO 2F
RIGHT WING TO 2F
COURTYARD
1F
TO 2F
TO 2F
KING
3F
THE THRONE ROOM IS ON THE THIRD FLOOR!! THE FIRST FLOOR IS TOO FAR!!
TO 3F
TO 1F
BANQUET HALL
2F
THE BEST PLACE WOULD BE...
...THE CENTRAL STAIRCASE ON THE SECOND FLOOR!!

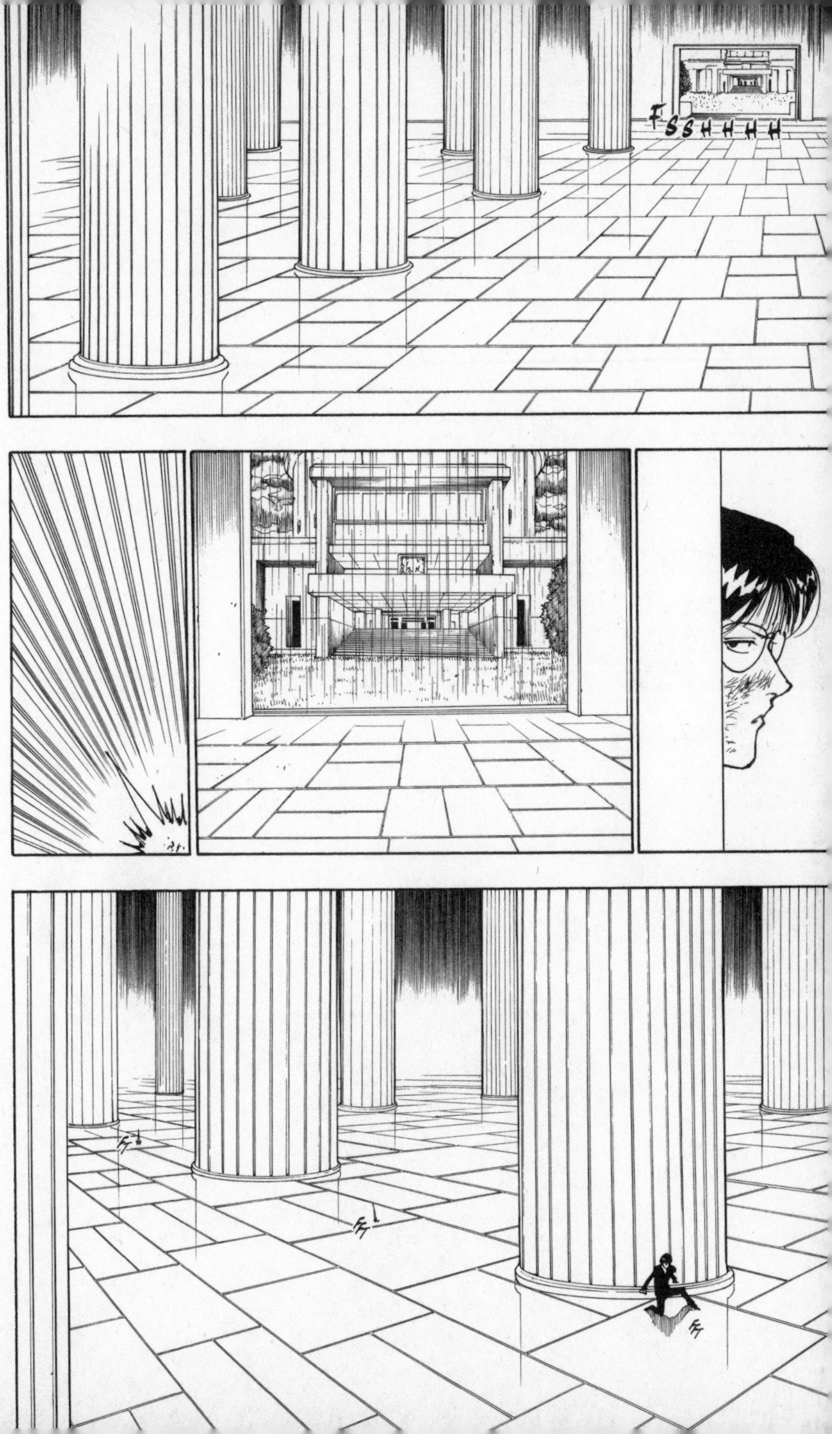
FSSHHHHH

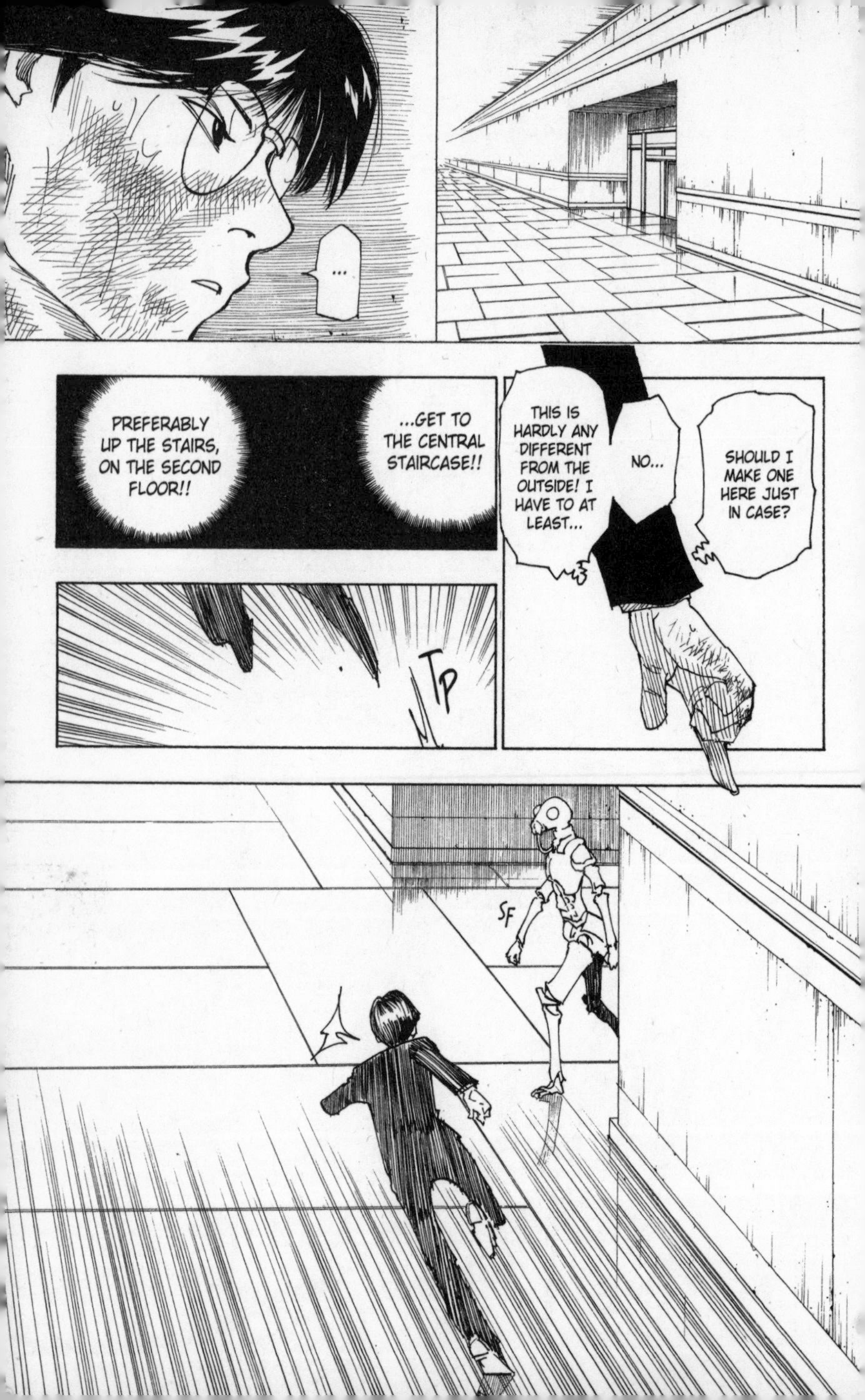
...
SHOULD I MAKE ONE HERE JUST IN CASE?
NO...
THIS IS HARDLY ANY DIFFERENT FROM THE OUTSIDE! I HAVE TO AT LEAST...
...GET TO THE CENTRAL STAIRCASE!!
PREFERABLY UP THE STAIRS, ON THE SECOND FLOOR!!
TP
SF

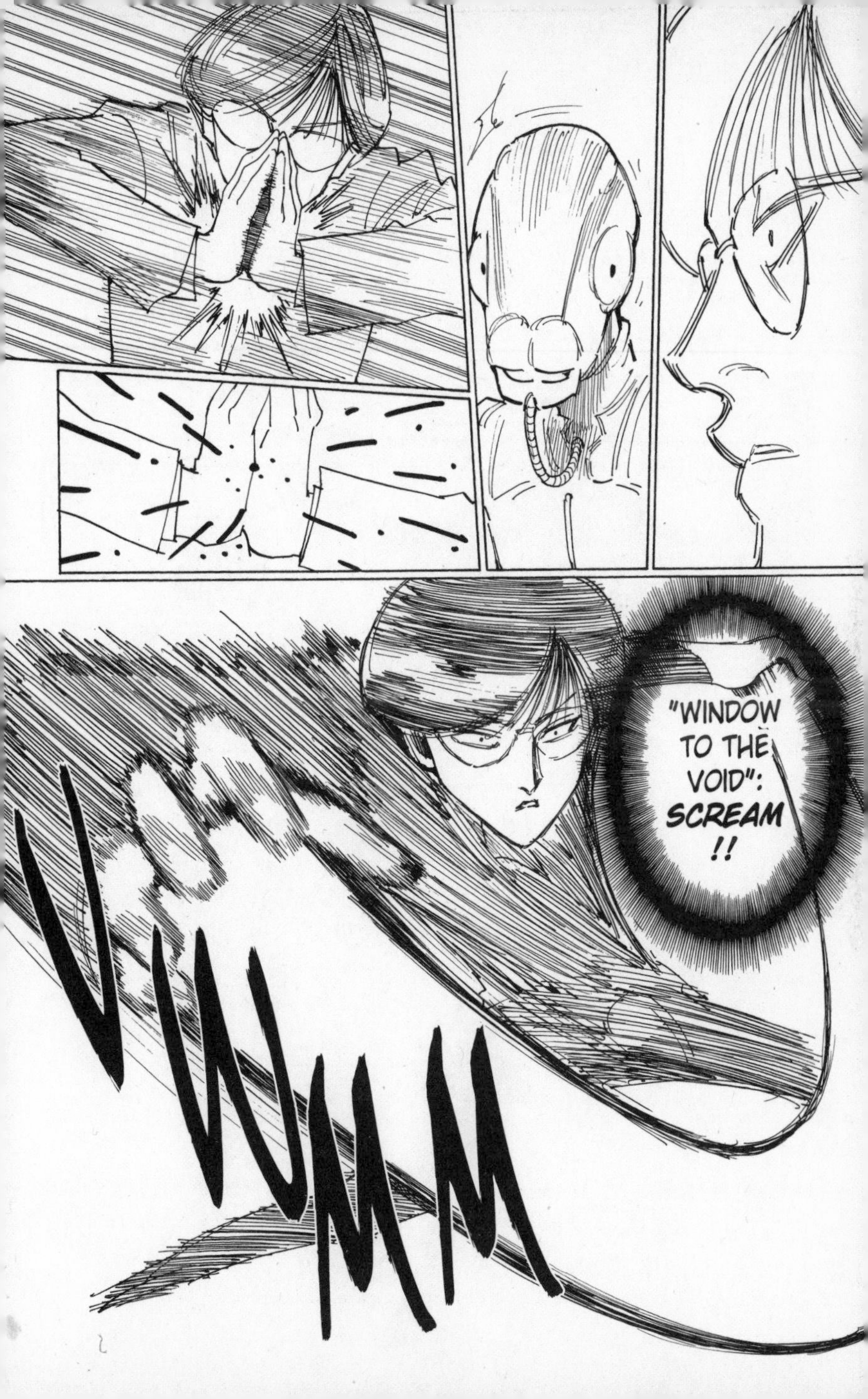
"WINDOW TO THE VOID": SCREAM !!
VWMM

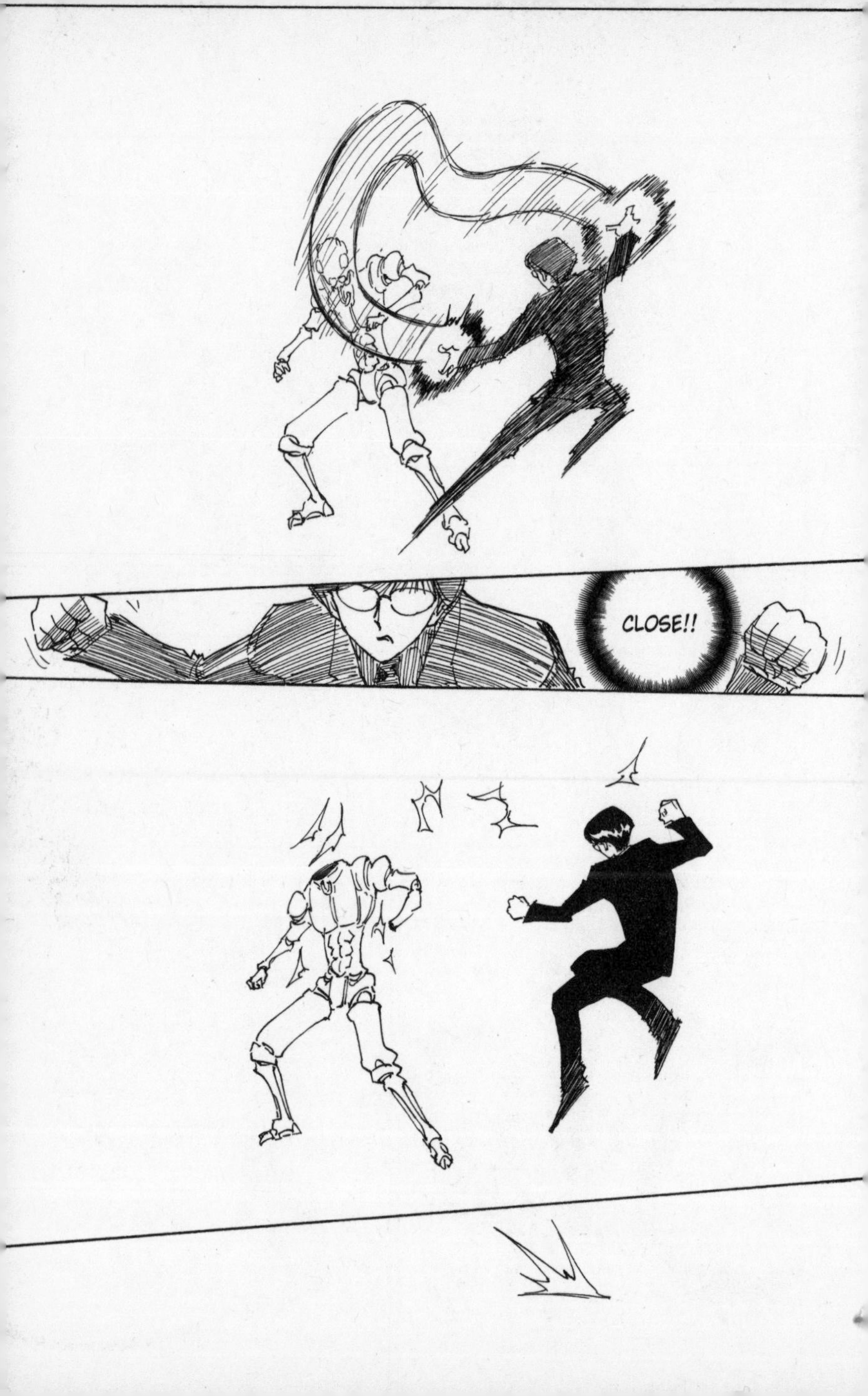
CLOSE!!

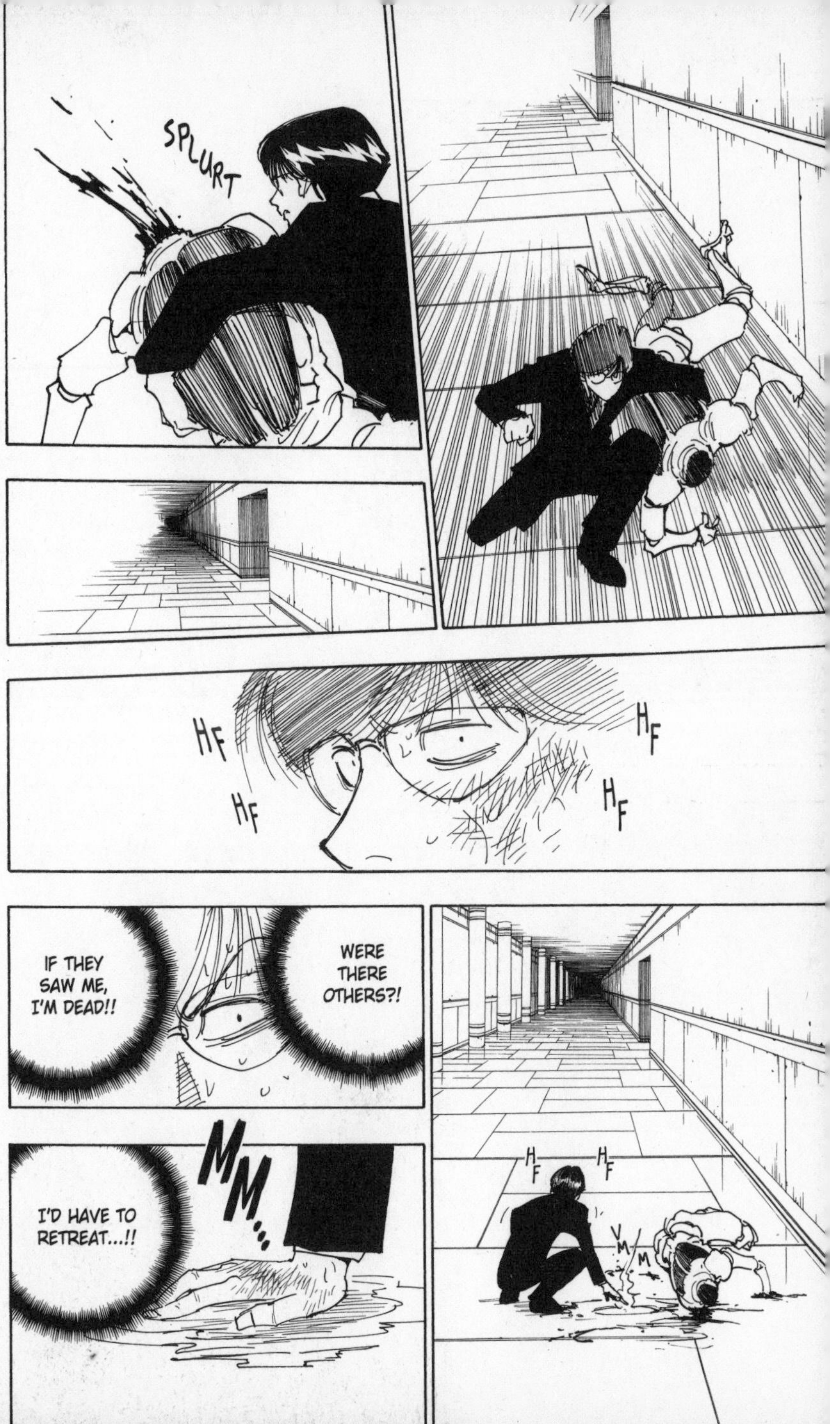
SPLURT
HF
HF
HF
HF
HF
HF
VM
M
WERE THERE OTHERS?!
IF THEY SAW ME, I'M DEAD!!
MM...
I'D HAVE TO RETREAT...!!

READ THIS WAY

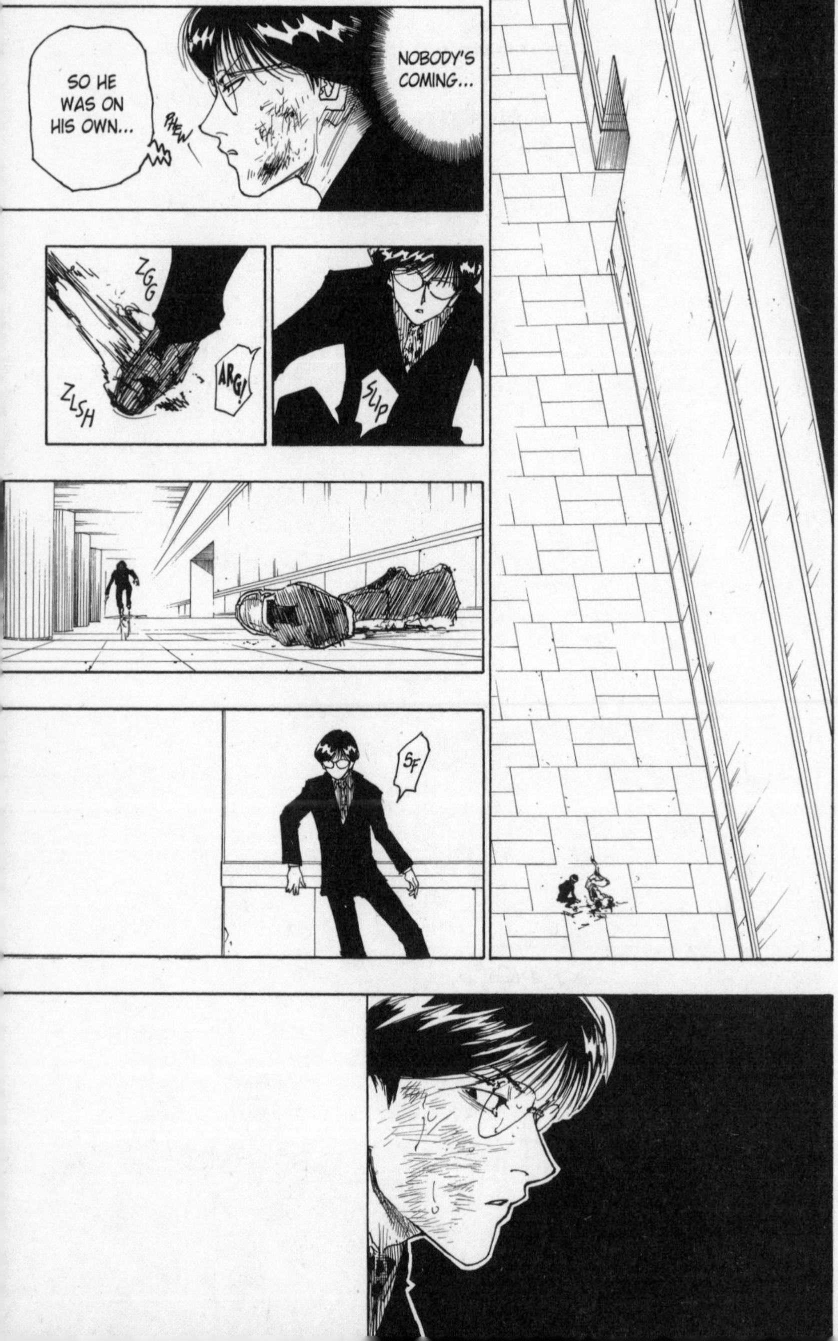
NOBODY'S COMING...
PHEW
SO HE WAS ON HIS OWN...
SLIP
ARG!
ZGG
ZLSH
SF

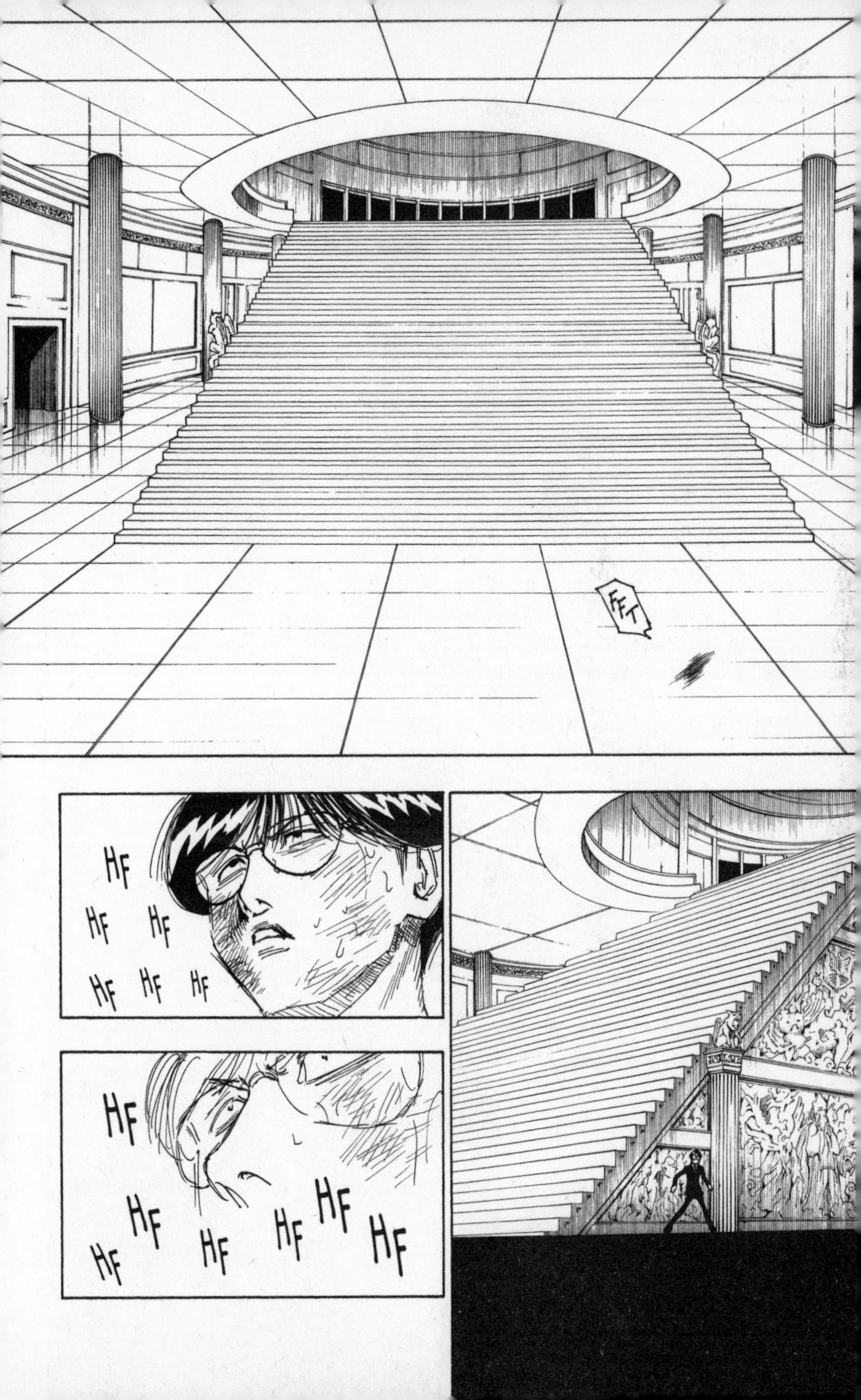
FFT
HF
HF
HF
HF
HF
HF
HF
HF
HF
HF
HF
HF
HF

READ THIS WAY

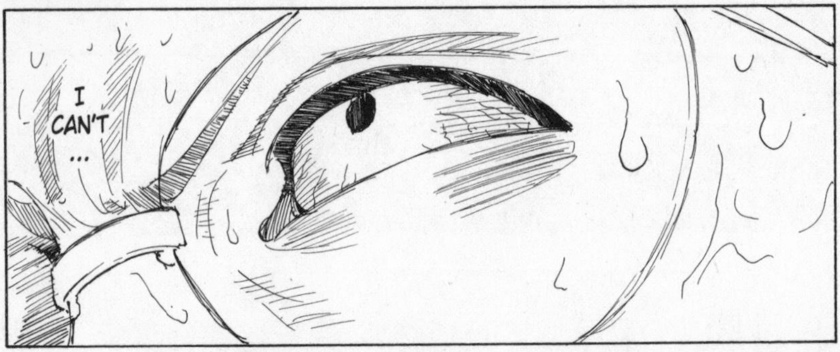
I CAN'T ...

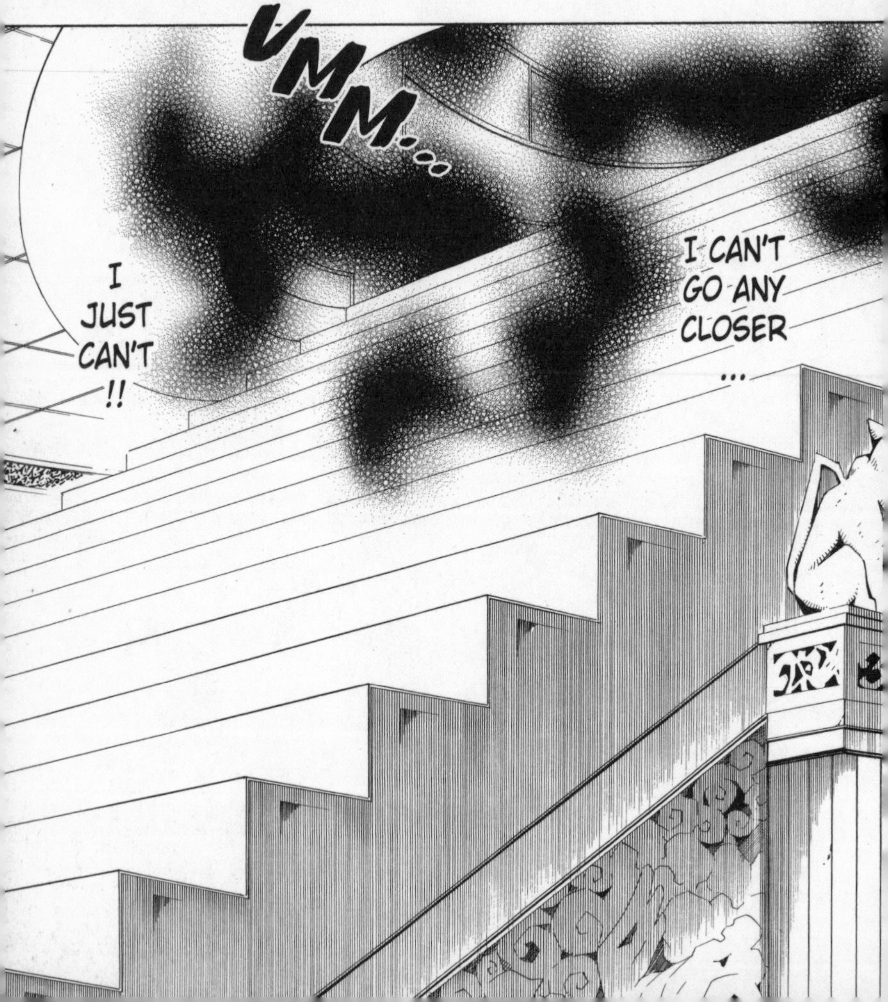
UMM...
I CAN'T GO ANY CLOSER ...
I JUST CAN'T !!

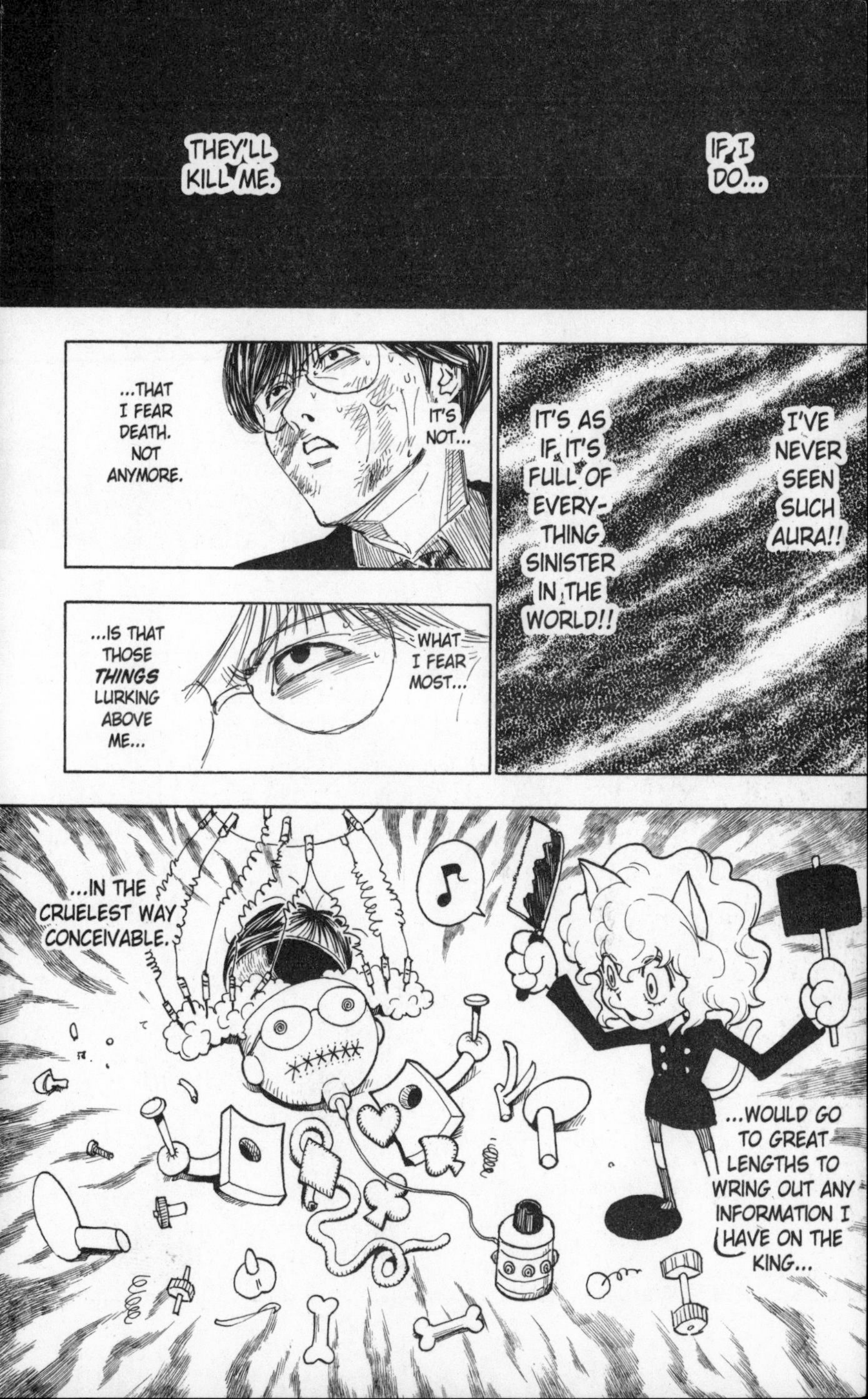
IF I DO...
THEY'LL KILL ME.
I'VE NEVER SEEN SUCH AURA!!
IT'S AS IF IT'S FULL OF EVERYTHING SINISTER IN THE WORLD!!
IT'S NOT...
...THAT I FEAR DEATH. NOT ANYMORE.
WHAT I FEAR MOST...
...IS THAT THOSE *THINGS* LURKING ABOVE ME...
...WOULD GO TO GREAT LENGTHS TO WRING OUT ANY INFORMATION I HAVE ON THE KING...
...IN THE CRUELEST WAY CONCEIVABLE.

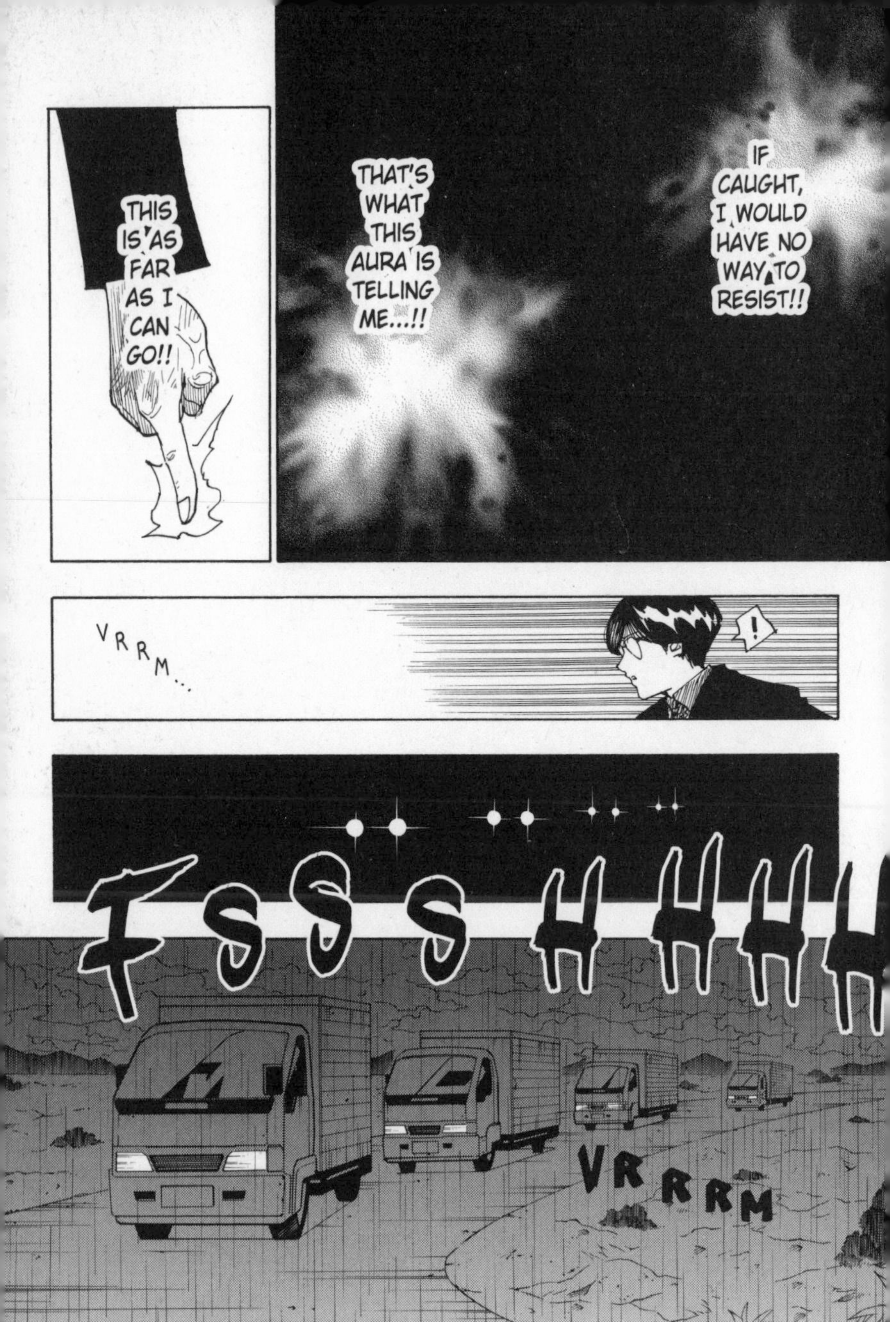
IF CAUGHT, I WOULD HAVE NO WAY TO RESIST!!
THAT'S WHAT THIS AURA IS TELLING ME...!!
THIS IS AS FAR AS I CAN GO!!
!
VRRM...
FSSSHHHH
VRRRM

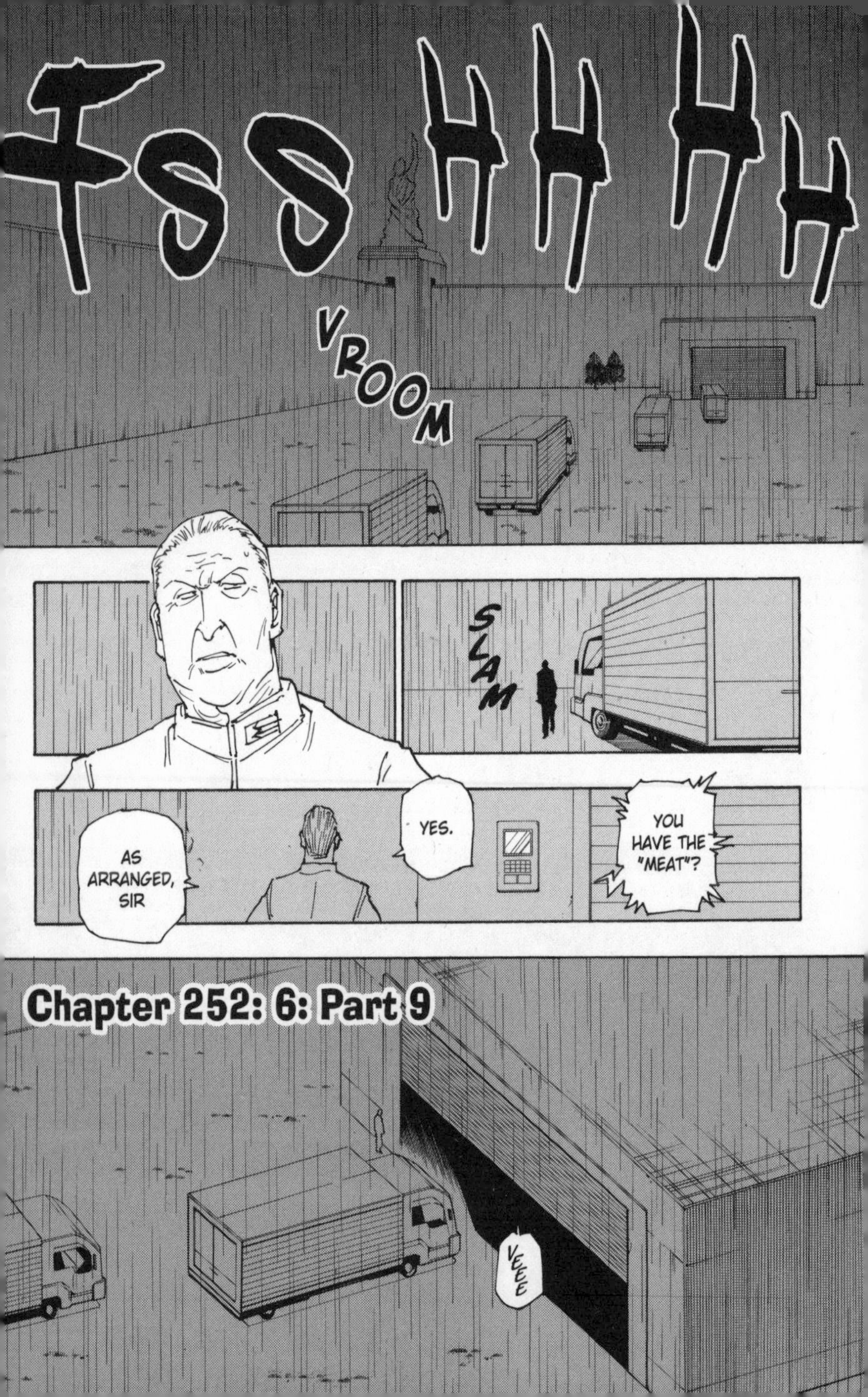
FSSHHHHH
VROOM
SLAM
YOU HAVE THE "MEAT"?
YES.
AS ARRANGED, SIR
Chapter 252: 6: Part 9
VEEE

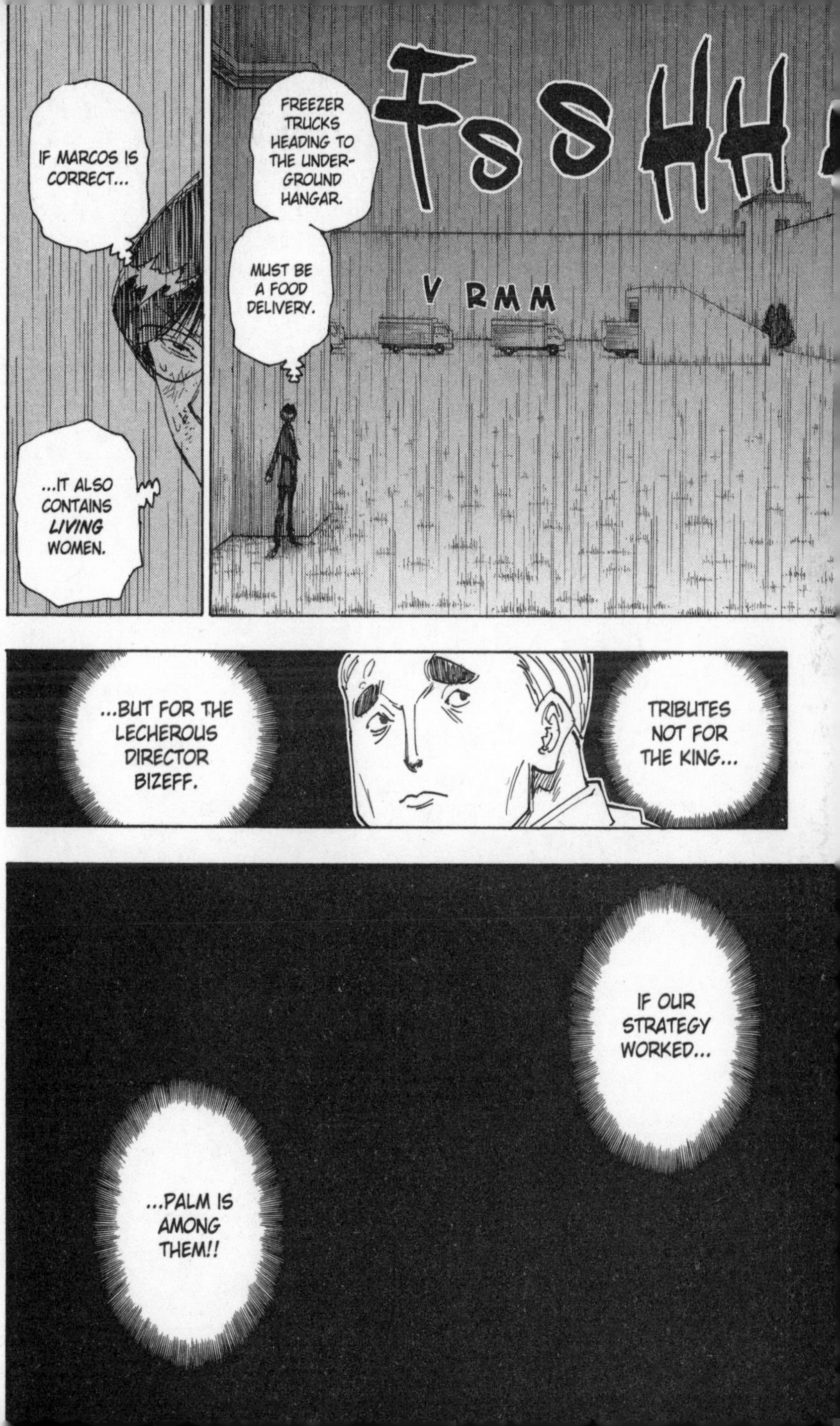
FSSHH
FREEZER TRUCKS HEADING TO THE UNDER-GROUND HANGAR.
MUST BE A FOOD DELIVERY.
VRMM
IF MARCOS IS CORRECT...
...IT ALSO CONTAINS *LIVING* WOMEN.
TRIBUTES NOT FOR THE KING...
...BUT FOR THE LECHEROUS DIRECTOR BIZEFF.
IF OUR STRATEGY WORKED...
...PALM IS AMONG THEM!!

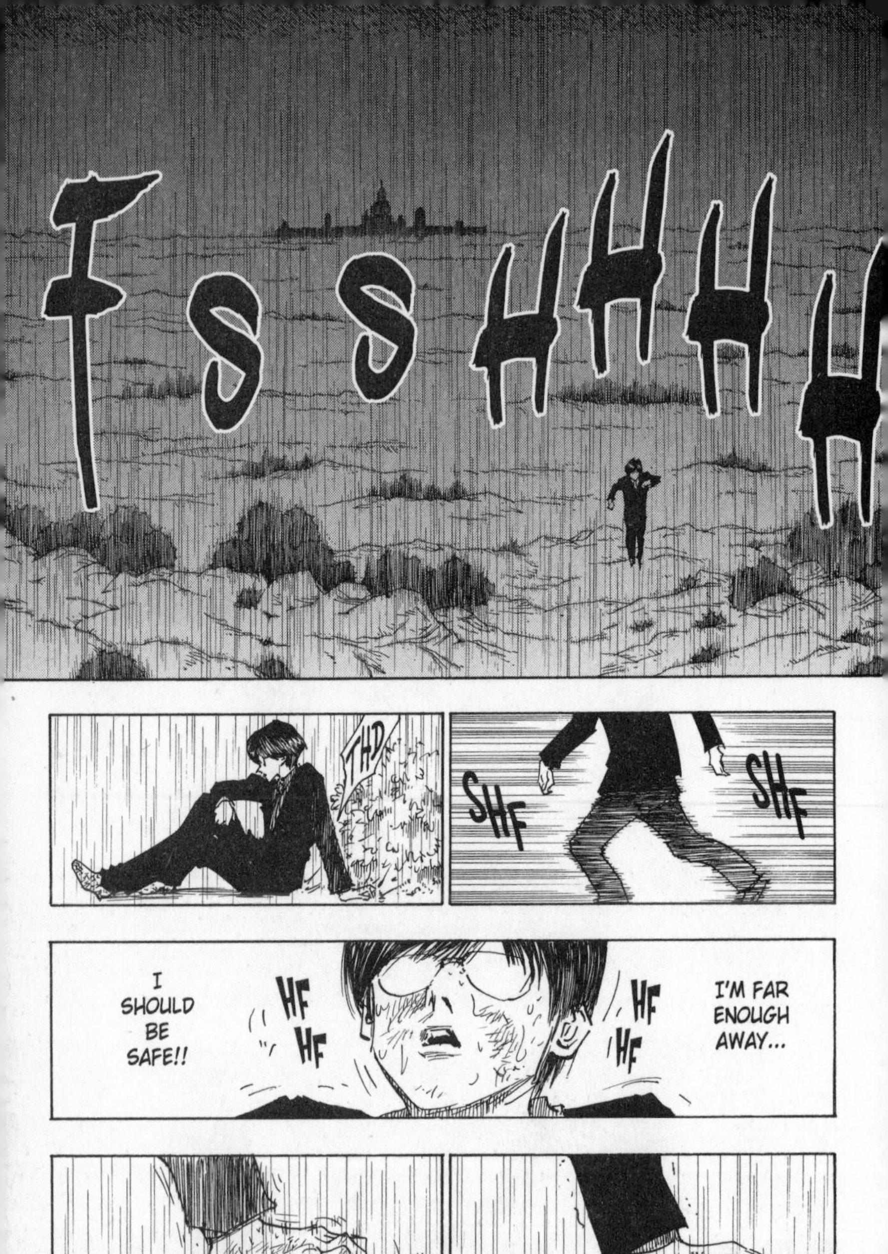
FSSHHHH
SHF
SHF
THD
I'M FAR ENOUGH AWAY...
HF
HF
HF
HF
I SHOULD BE SAFE!!

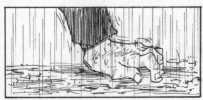

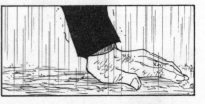

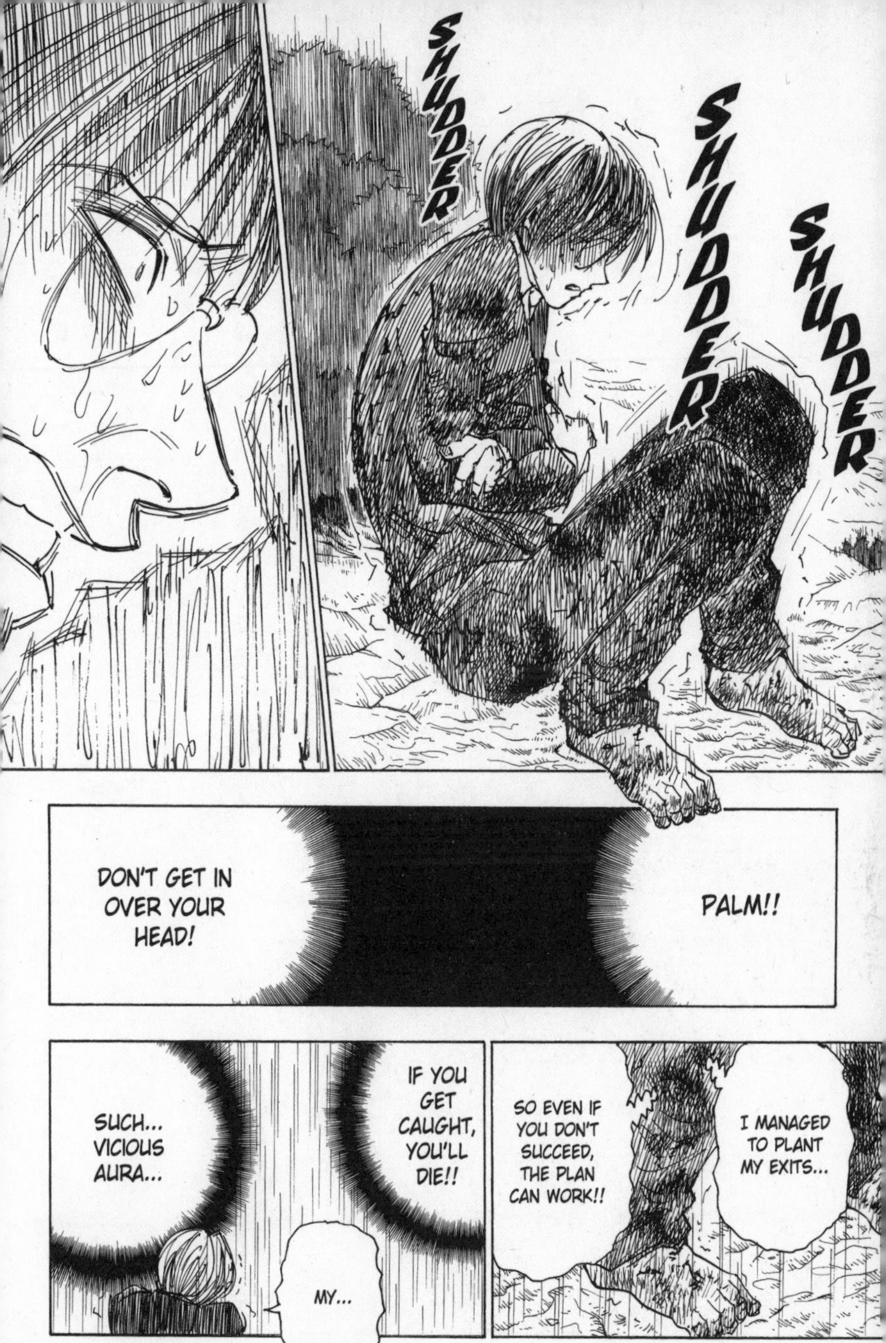
SHUDDER
SHUDDER
SHUDDER
PALM!!
DON'T GET IN OVER YOUR HEAD!
I MANAGED TO PLANT MY EXITS...
SO EVEN IF YOU DON'T SUCCEED, THE PLAN CAN WORK!!
IF YOU GET CAUGHT, YOU'LL DIE!!
SUCH... VICIOUS AURA...
MY...

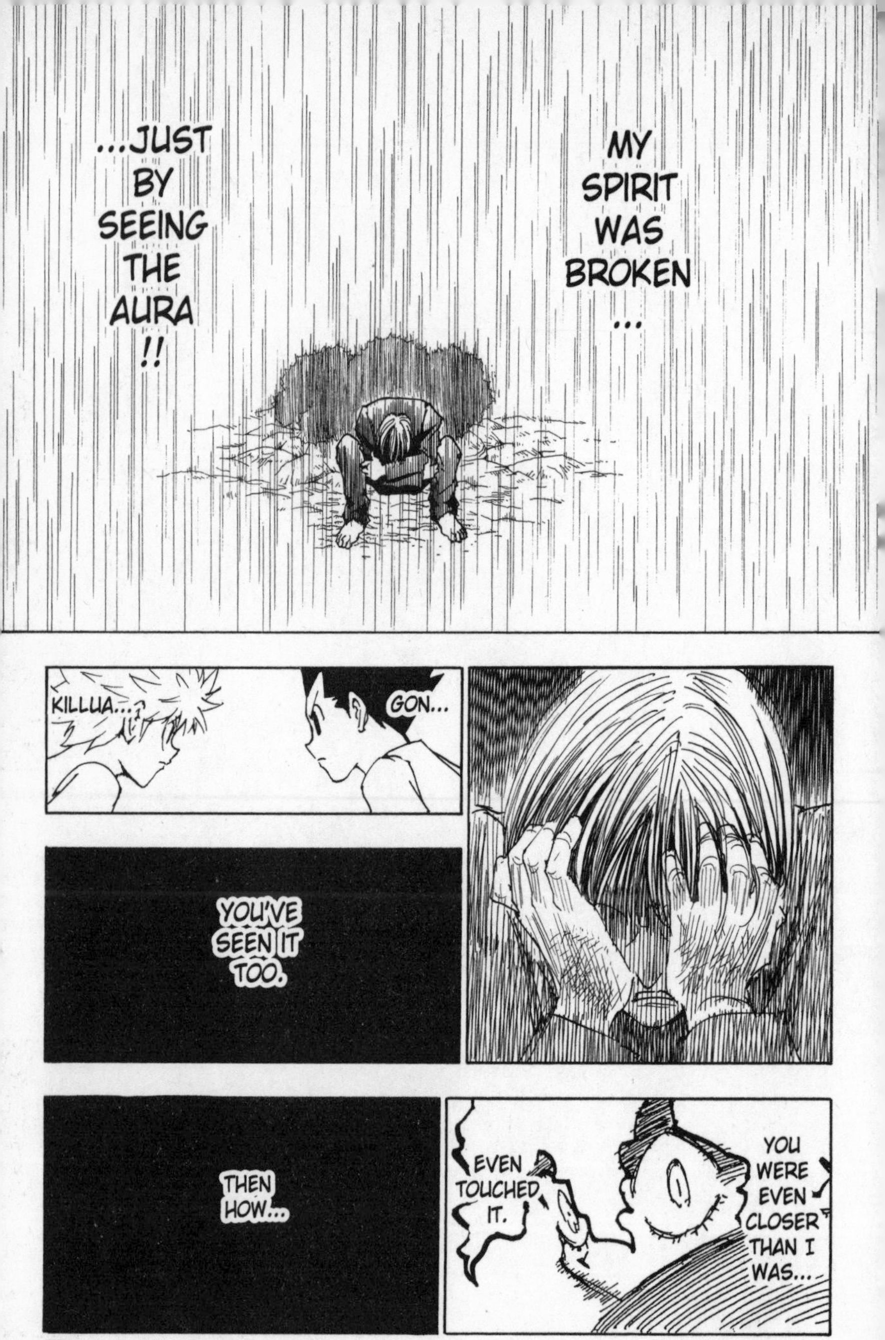
MY SPIRIT WAS BROKEN ...
...JUST BY SEEING THE AURA !!
GON...
KILLUA...
YOU'VE SEEN IT TOO.
YOU WERE EVEN CLOSER THAN I WAS...
EVEN TOUCHED IT.
THEN HOW...

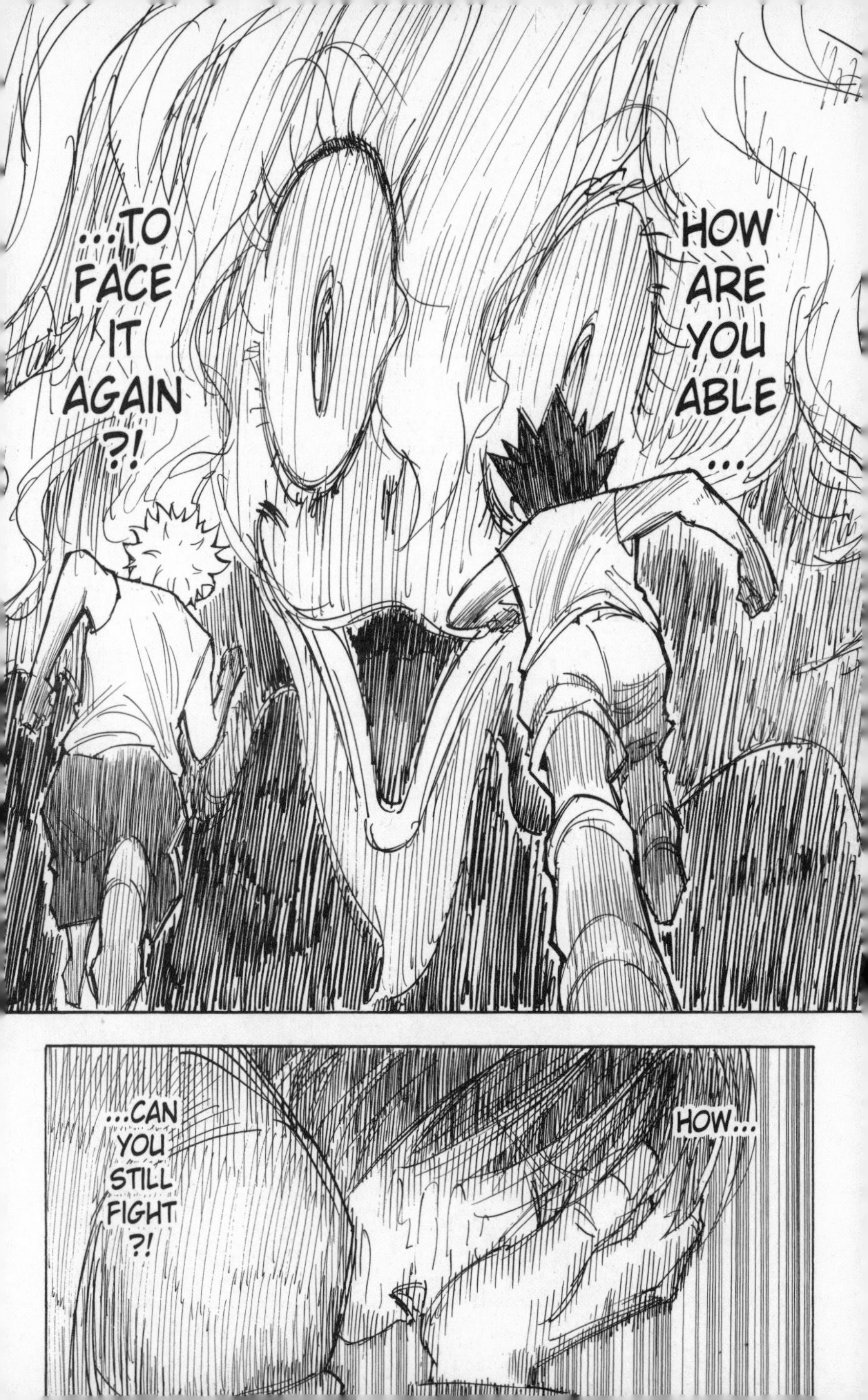
HOW ARE YOU ABLE...
...TO FACE IT AGAIN?!
HOW...
...CAN YOU STILL FIGHT?!

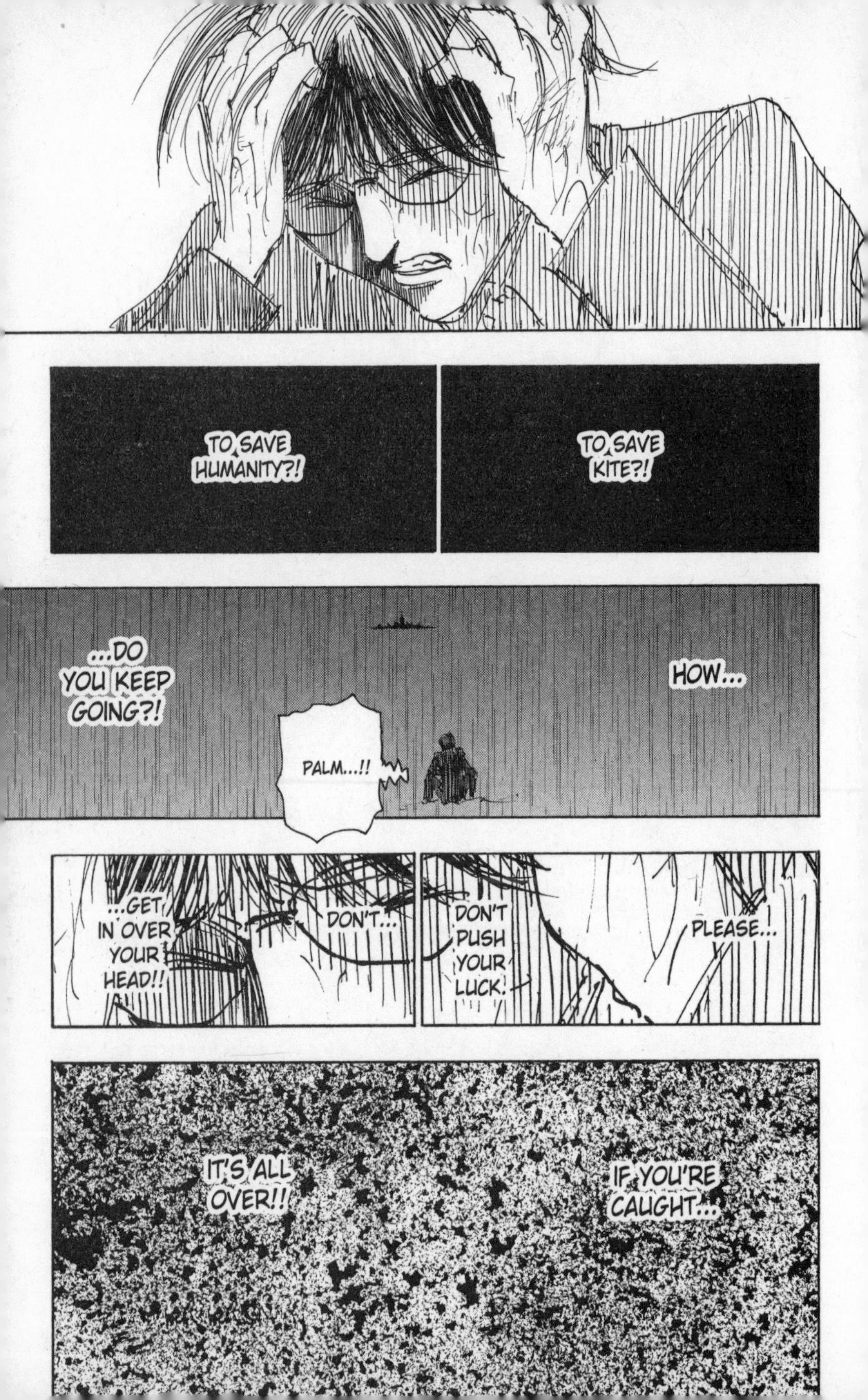
TO SAVE KITE?!
TO SAVE HUMANITY?!
HOW...
...DO YOU KEEP GOING?!
PALM...!!
PLEASE...
DON'T PUSH YOUR LUCK.
DON'T...
...GET IN OVER YOUR HEAD!!
IF YOU'RE CAUGHT...
IT'S ALL OVER!!

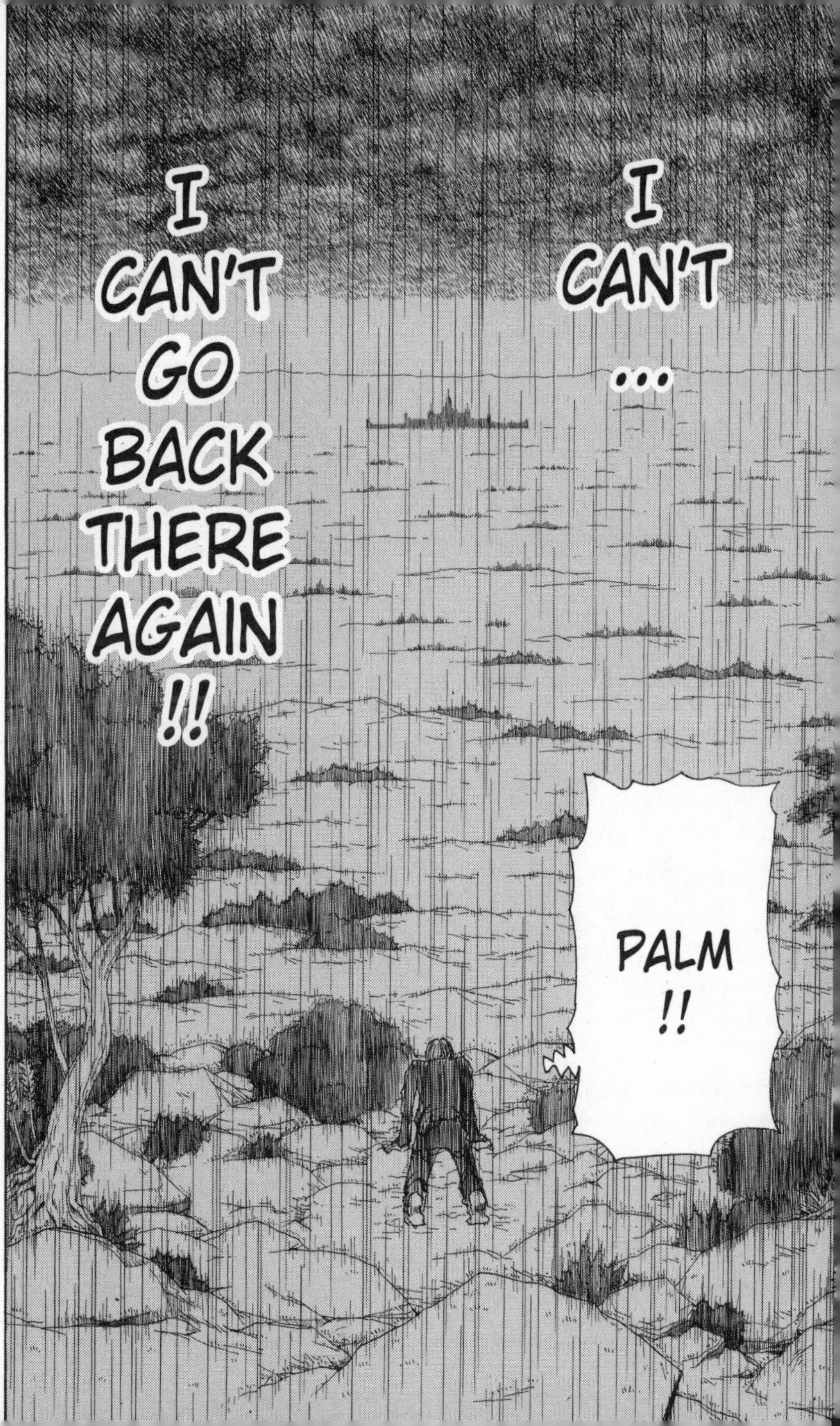
I CAN'T ...
I CAN'T GO BACK THERE AGAIN!!
PALM!!

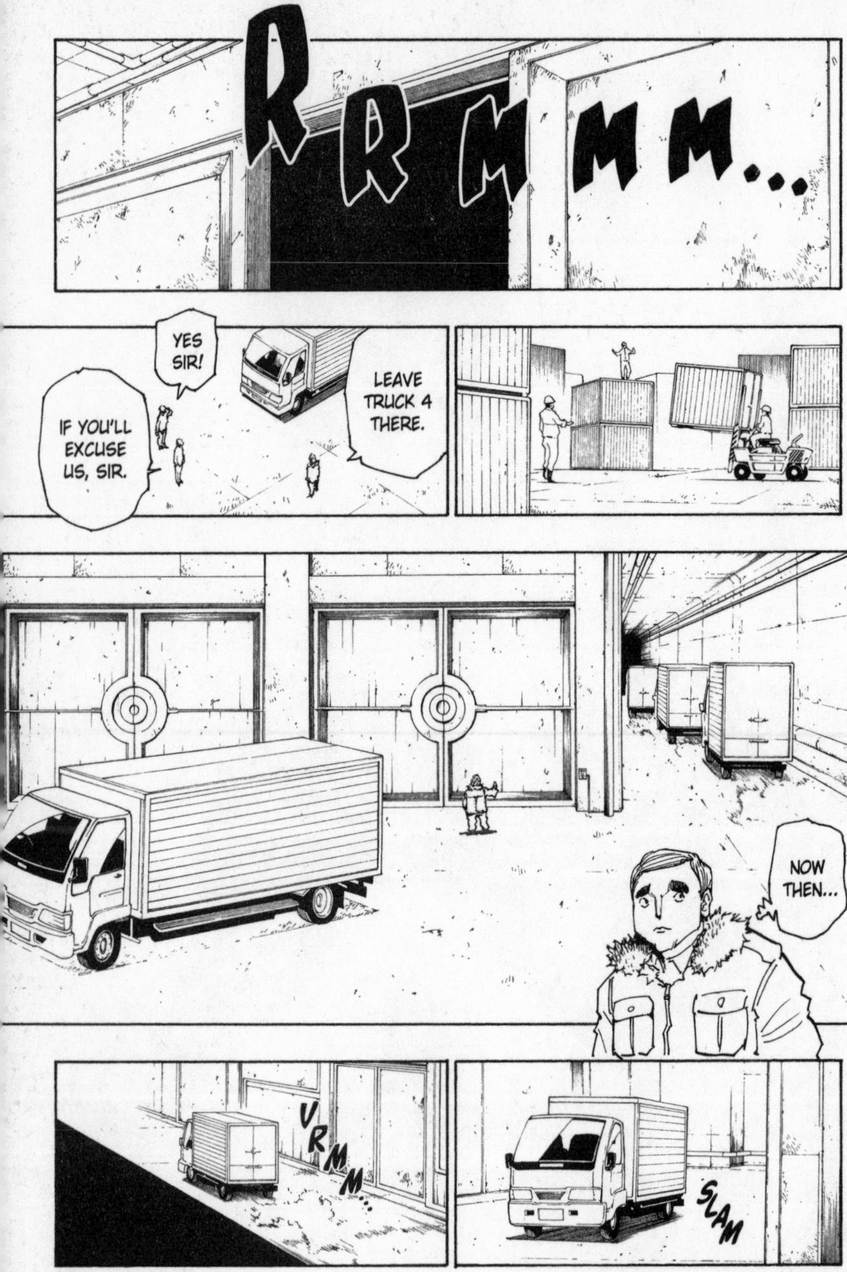
RRMMM...
LEAVE TRUCK 4 THERE.
YES SIR!
IF YOU'LL EXCUSE US, SIR.
NOW THEN...
SLAM
VRMM...

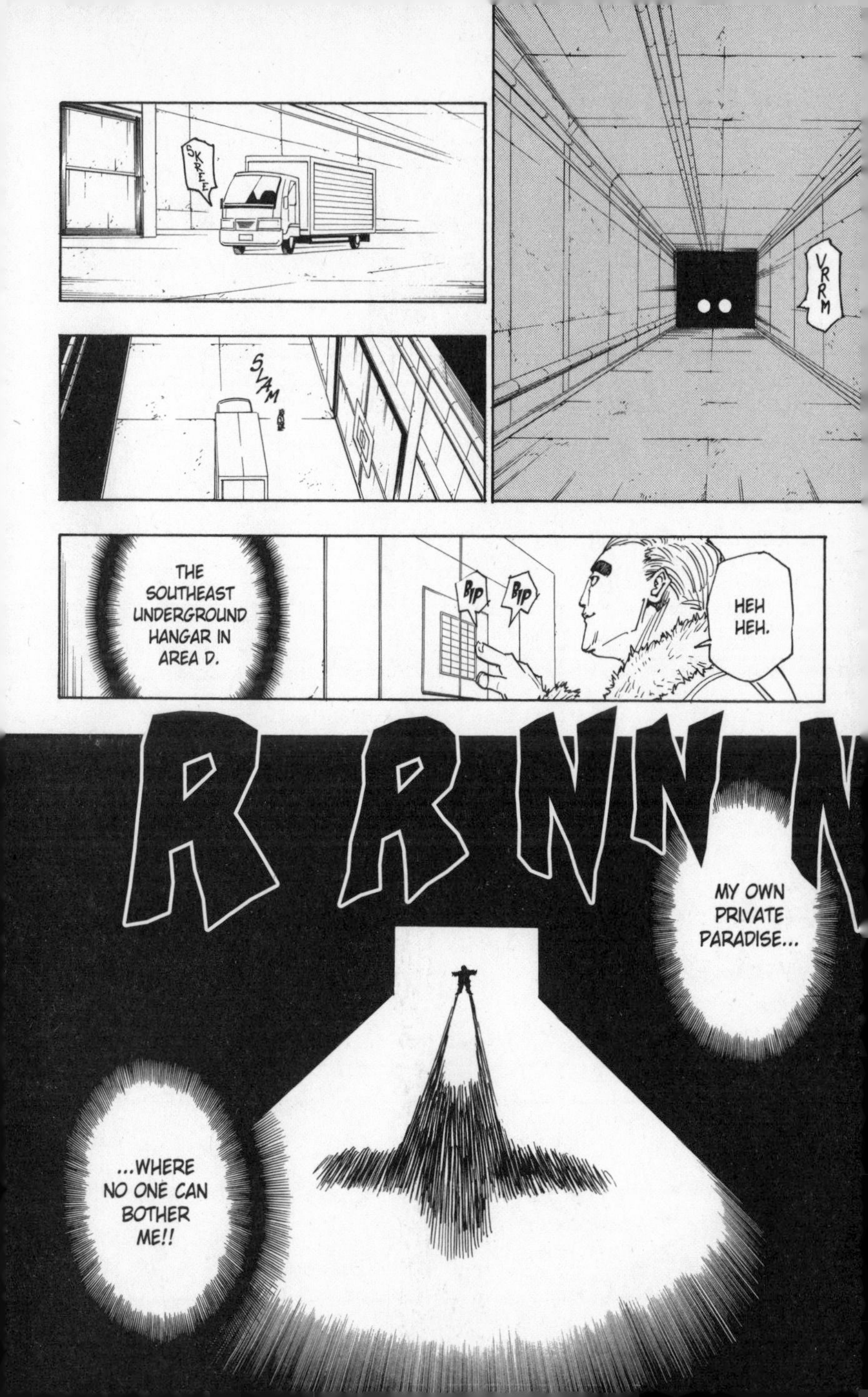
VRRM
SKREE
SLAM
HEH HEH.
BIP
BIP
THE SOUTHEAST UNDERGROUND HANGAR IN AREA D.
RRNNN
MY OWN PRIVATE PARADISE...
...WHERE NO ONE CAN BOTHER ME!!

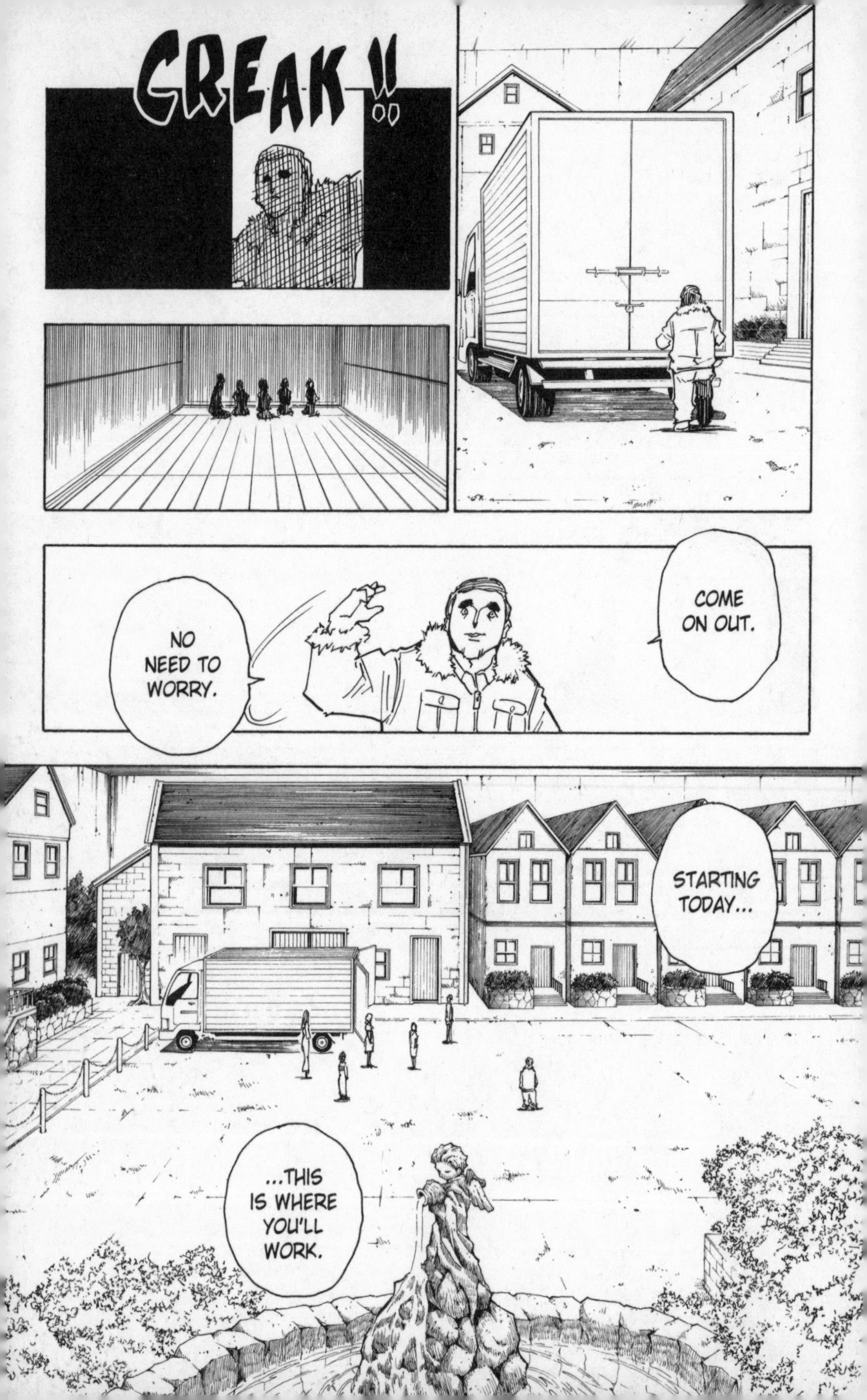
GREAK!!
COME ON OUT.
NO NEED TO WORRY.
STARTING TODAY...
...THIS IS WHERE YOU'LL WORK.

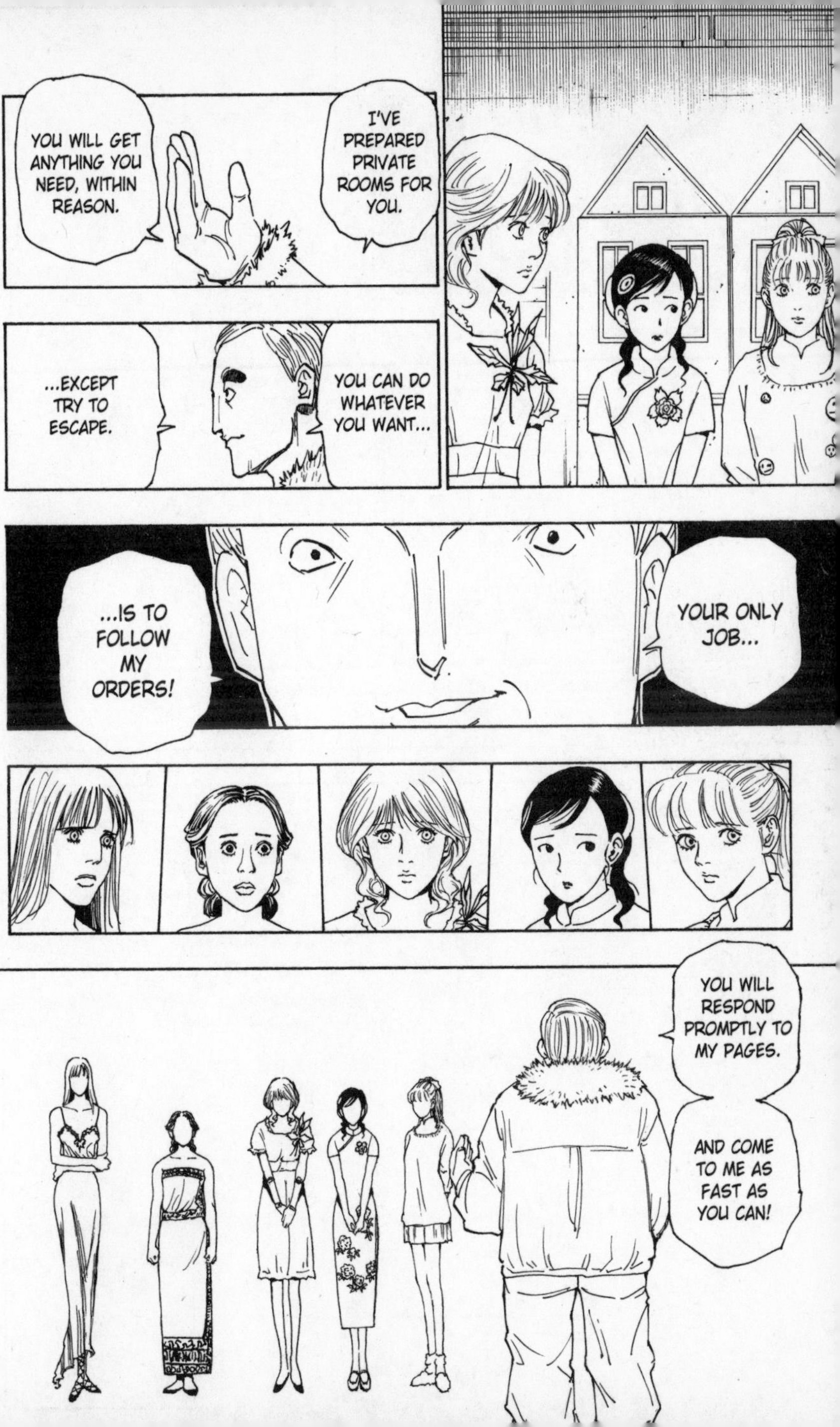
I'VE PREPARED PRIVATE ROOMS FOR YOU.
YOU WILL GET ANYTHING YOU NEED, WITHIN REASON.
YOU CAN DO WHATEVER YOU WANT...
...EXCEPT TRY TO ESCAPE.
YOUR ONLY JOB...
...IS TO FOLLOW MY ORDERS!
YOU WILL RESPOND PROMPTLY TO MY PAGES.
AND COME TO ME AS FAST AS YOU CAN!

READ THIS WAY

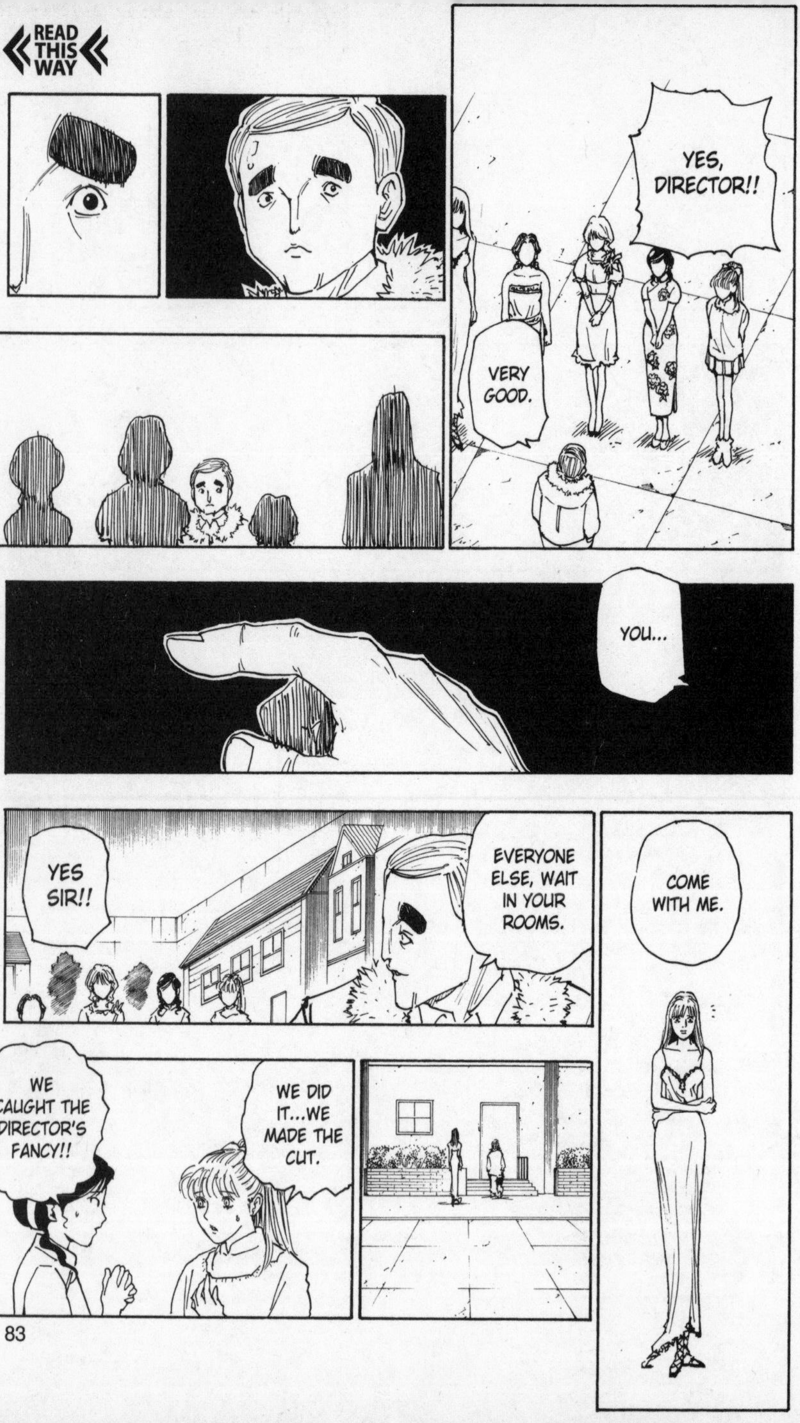
YES, DIRECTOR!!
VERY GOOD.
YOU...
COME WITH ME.
EVERYONE ELSE, WAIT IN YOUR ROOMS.
YES SIR!!
WE DID IT...WE MADE THE CUT.
WE CAUGHT THE DIRECTOR'S FANCY!!

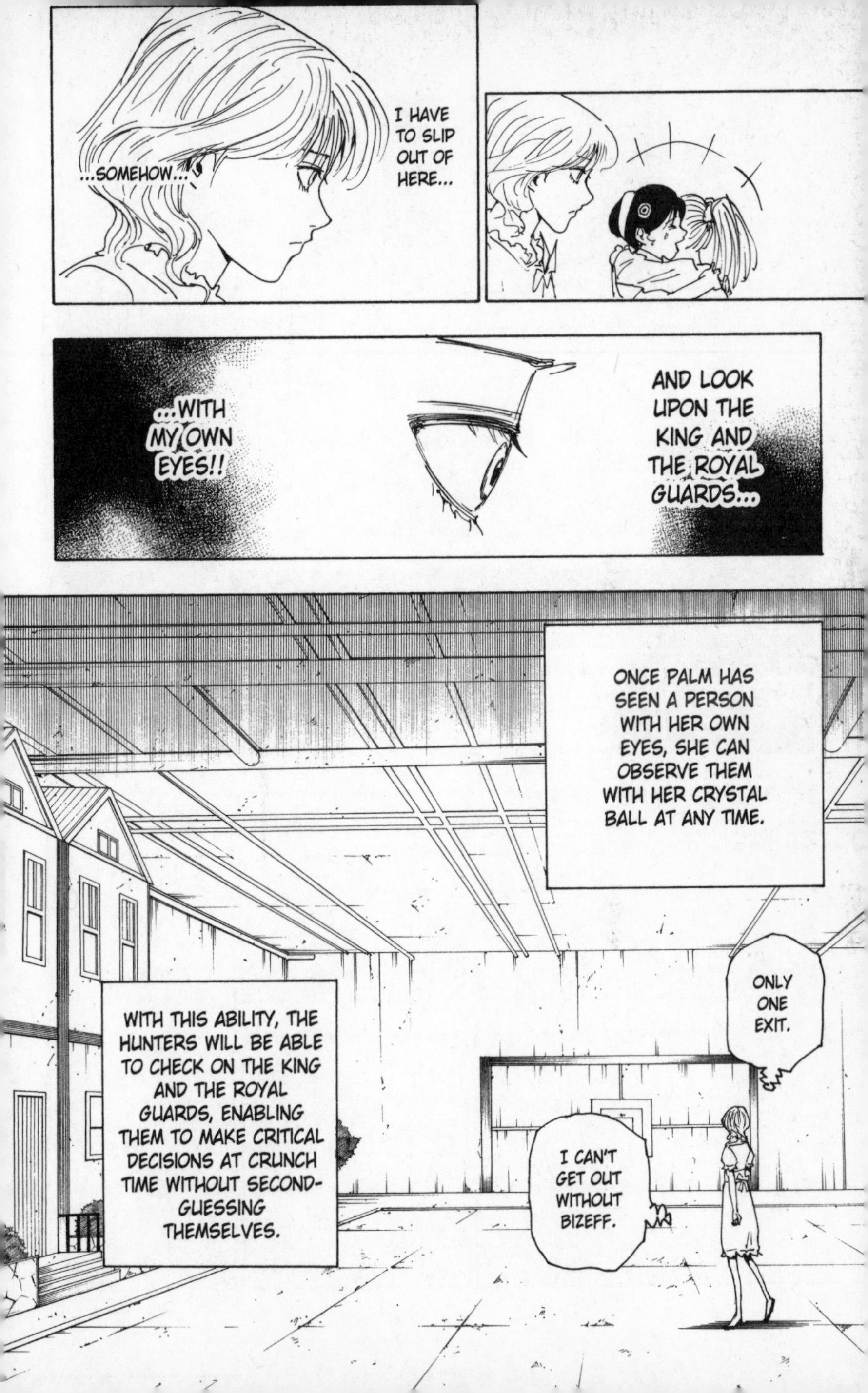
I HAVE TO SLIP OUT OF HERE...
...SOMEHOW...
AND LOOK UPON THE KING AND THE ROYAL GUARDS...
...WITH MY OWN EYES!!
ONCE PALM HAS SEEN A PERSON WITH HER OWN EYES, SHE CAN OBSERVE THEM WITH HER CRYSTAL BALL AT ANY TIME.
ONLY ONE EXIT.
WITH THIS ABILITY, THE HUNTERS WILL BE ABLE TO CHECK ON THE KING AND THE ROYAL GUARDS, ENABLING THEM TO MAKE CRITICAL DECISIONS AT CRUNCH TIME WITHOUT SECOND-GUESSING THEMSELVES.
I CAN'T GET OUT WITHOUT BIZEFF.

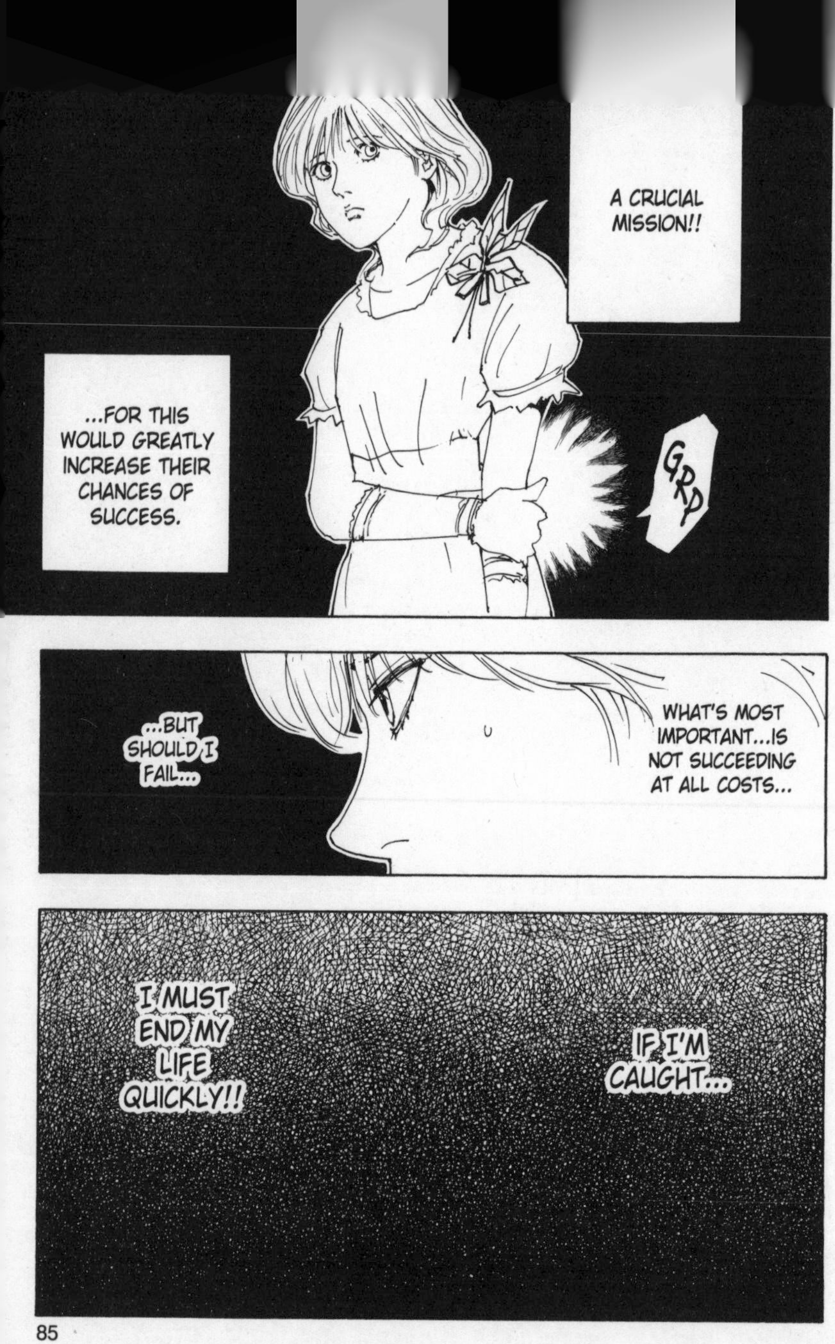
A CRUCIAL MISSION!!
...FOR THIS WOULD GREATLY INCREASE THEIR CHANCES OF SUCCESS.
GRP
WHAT'S MOST IMPORTANT...IS NOT SUCCEEDING AT ALL COSTS...
...BUT SHOULD I FAIL...
IF I'M CAUGHT...
I MUST END MY LIFE QUICKLY!!

Chapter 253: 6: Part 10

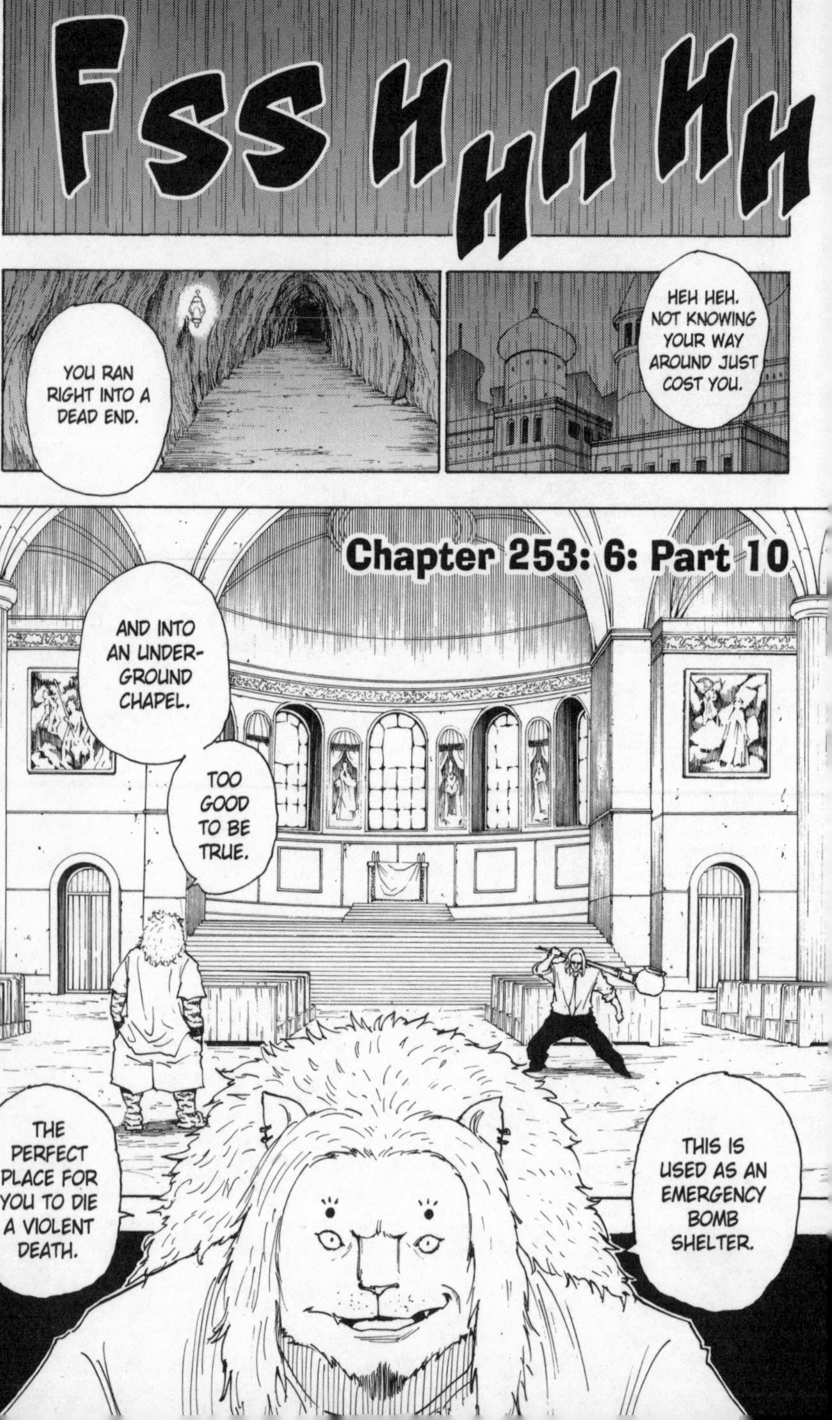
FSSHHHHHH
HEH HEH. NOT KNOWING YOUR WAY AROUND JUST COST YOU.
YOU RAN RIGHT INTO A DEAD END.
AND INTO AN UNDER-GROUND CHAPEL.
TOO GOOD TO BE TRUE.
THIS IS USED AS AN EMERGENCY BOMB SHELTER.
THE PERFECT PLACE FOR YOU TO DIE A VIOLENT DEATH.

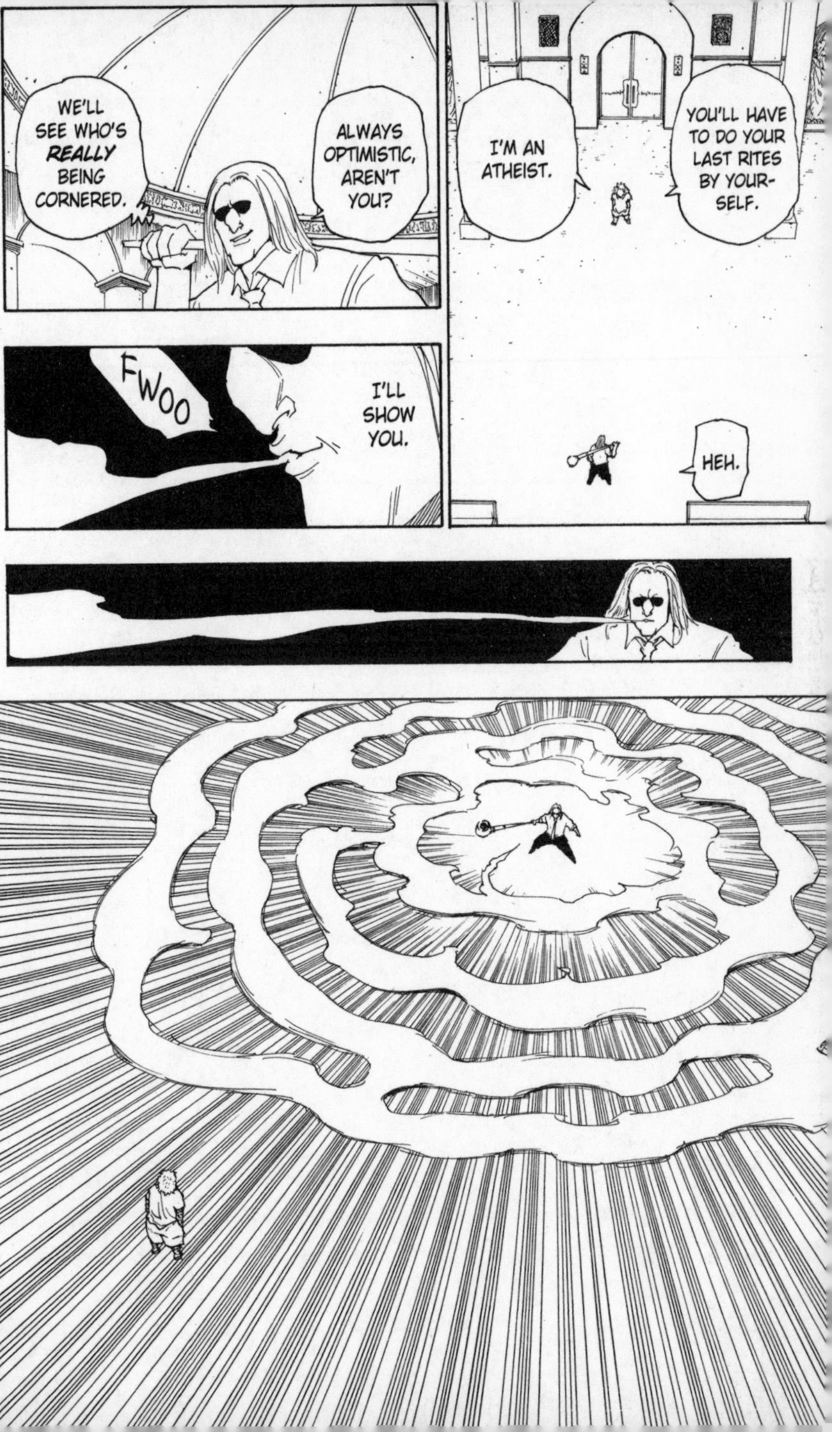
YOU'LL HAVE TO DO YOUR LAST RITES BY YOUR-SELF.
I'M AN ATHEIST.
HEH.
ALWAYS OPTIMISTIC, AREN'T YOU?
WE'LL SEE WHO'S *REALLY* BEING CORNERED.
I'LL SHOW YOU.
FWOO

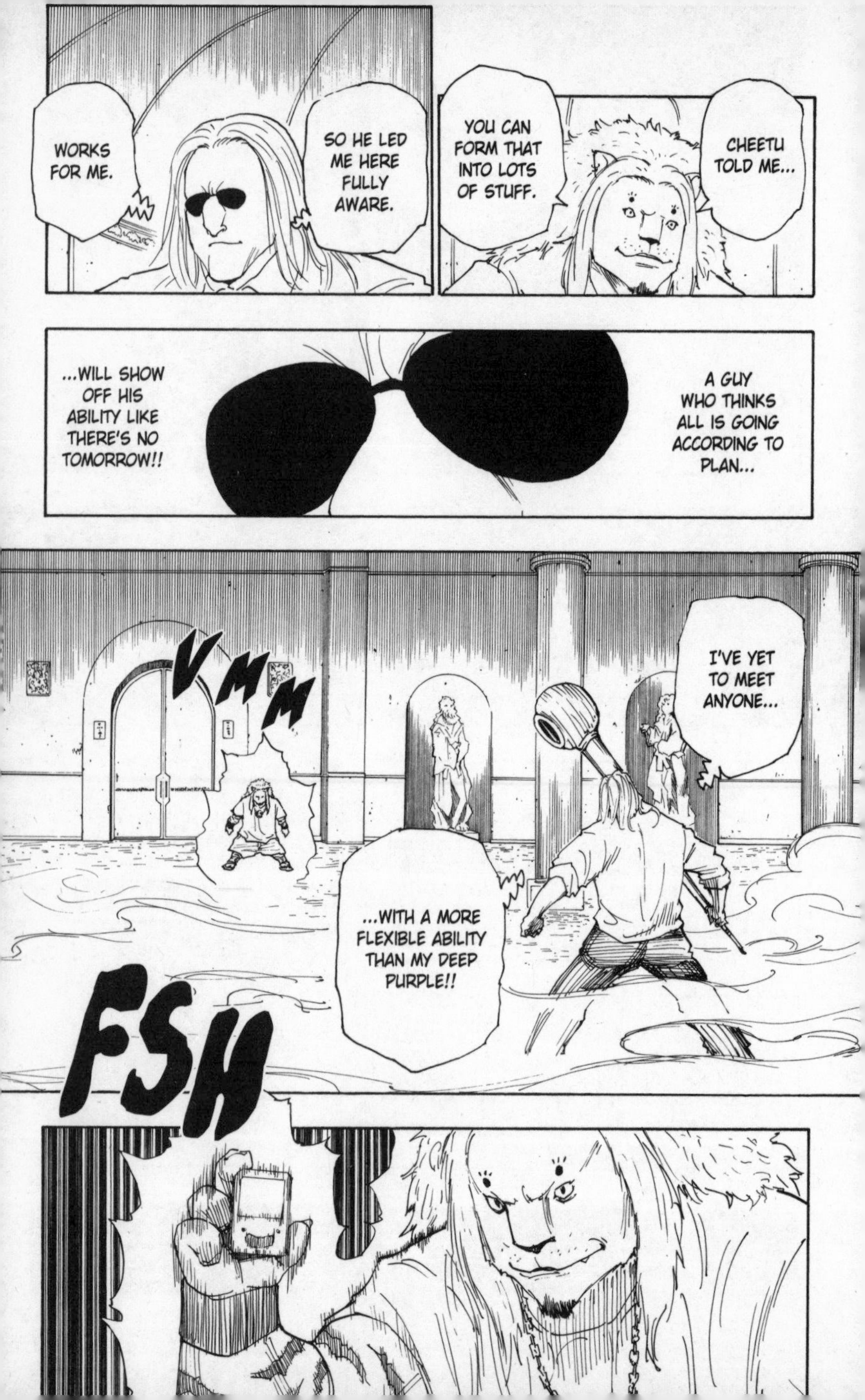
CHEETU TOLD ME...
YOU CAN FORM THAT INTO LOTS OF STUFF.
SO HE LED ME HERE FULLY AWARE.
WORKS FOR ME.
A GUY WHO THINKS ALL IS GOING ACCORDING TO PLAN...
...WILL SHOW OFF HIS ABILITY LIKE THERE'S NO TOMORROW!!
I'VE YET TO MEET ANYONE...
VMMM
...WITH A MORE FLEXIBLE ABILITY THAN MY DEEP PURPLE!!
FSH

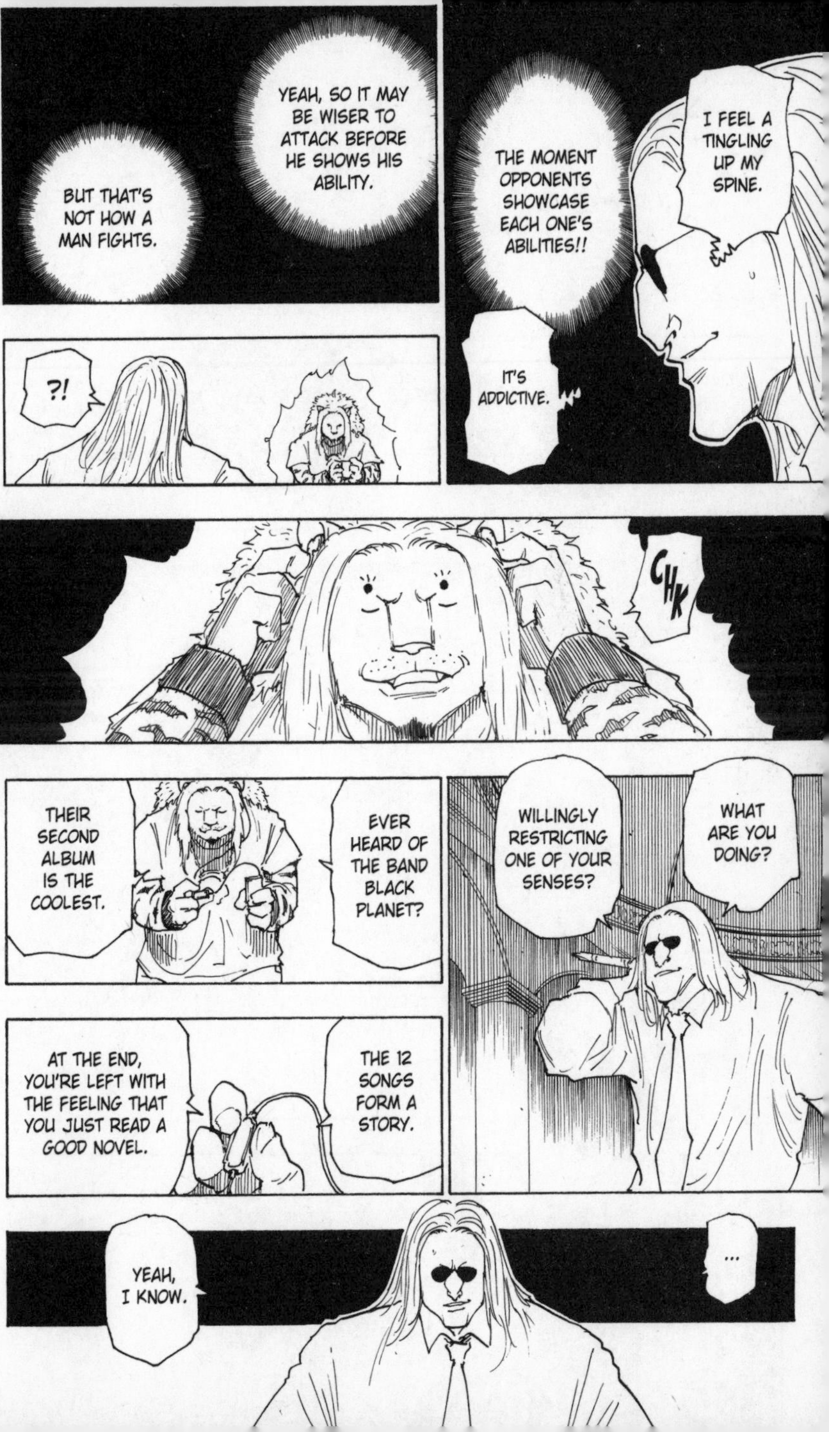
I FEEL A TINGLING UP MY SPINE.
THE MOMENT OPPONENTS SHOWCASE EACH ONE'S ABILITIES!!
IT'S ADDICTIVE.
YEAH, SO IT MAY BE WISER TO ATTACK BEFORE HE SHOWS HIS ABILITY.
BUT THAT'S NOT HOW A MAN FIGHTS.
?!
CHK
WHAT ARE YOU DOING?
WILLINGLY RESTRICTING ONE OF YOUR SENSES?
EVER HEARD OF THE BAND BLACK PLANET?
THEIR SECOND ALBUM IS THE COOLEST.
THE 12 SONGS FORM A STORY.
AT THE END, YOU'RE LEFT WITH THE FEELING THAT YOU JUST READ A GOOD NOVEL.
...
YEAH, I KNOW.

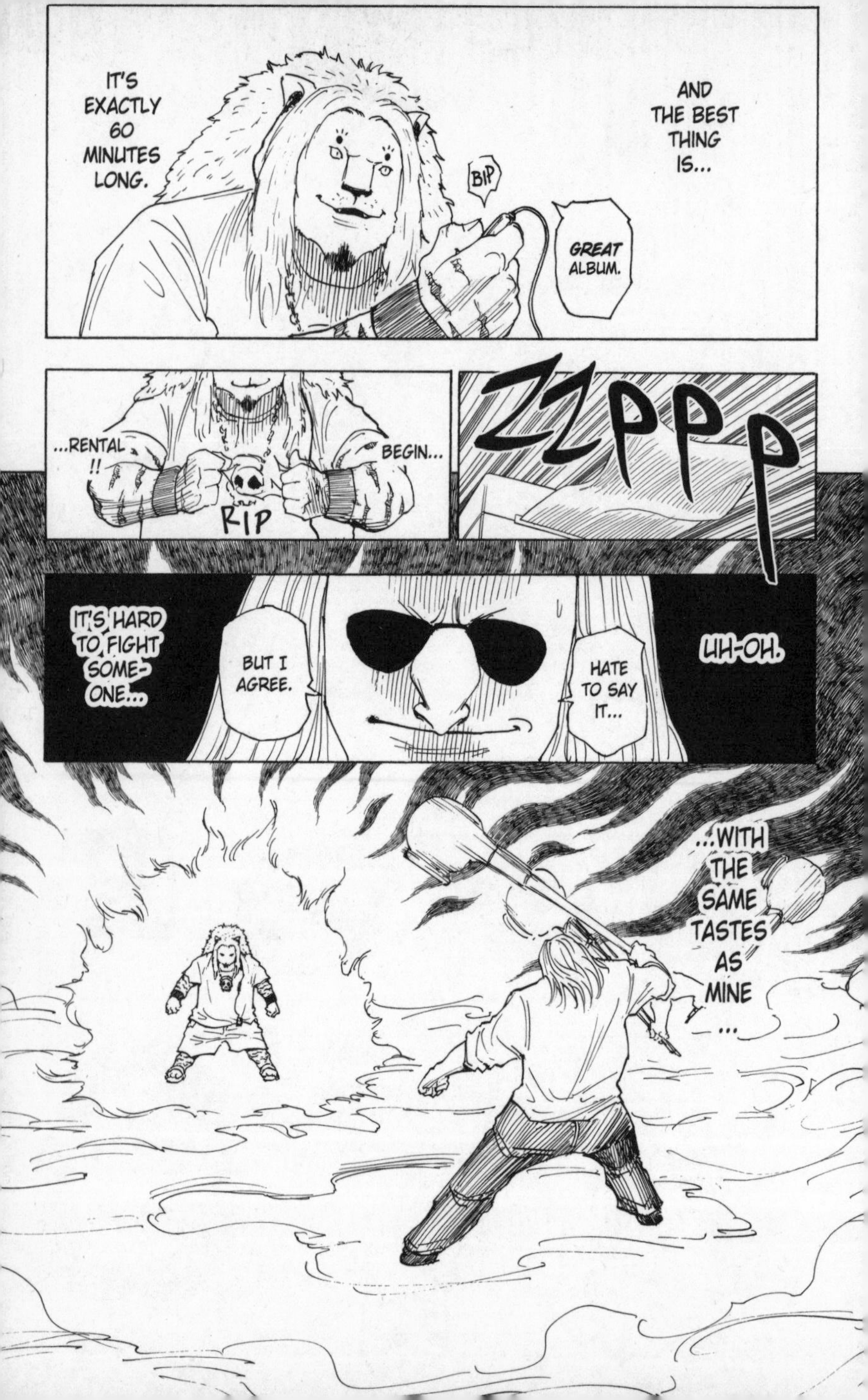
AND THE BEST THING IS...
BIP
GREAT ALBUM.
IT'S EXACTLY 60 MINUTES LONG.
ZZPPPP
BEGIN...
RIP
...RENTAL !!
UH-OH.
HATE TO SAY IT...
BUT I AGREE.
IT'S HARD TO FIGHT SOME-ONE...
...WITH THE SAME TASTES AS MINE...

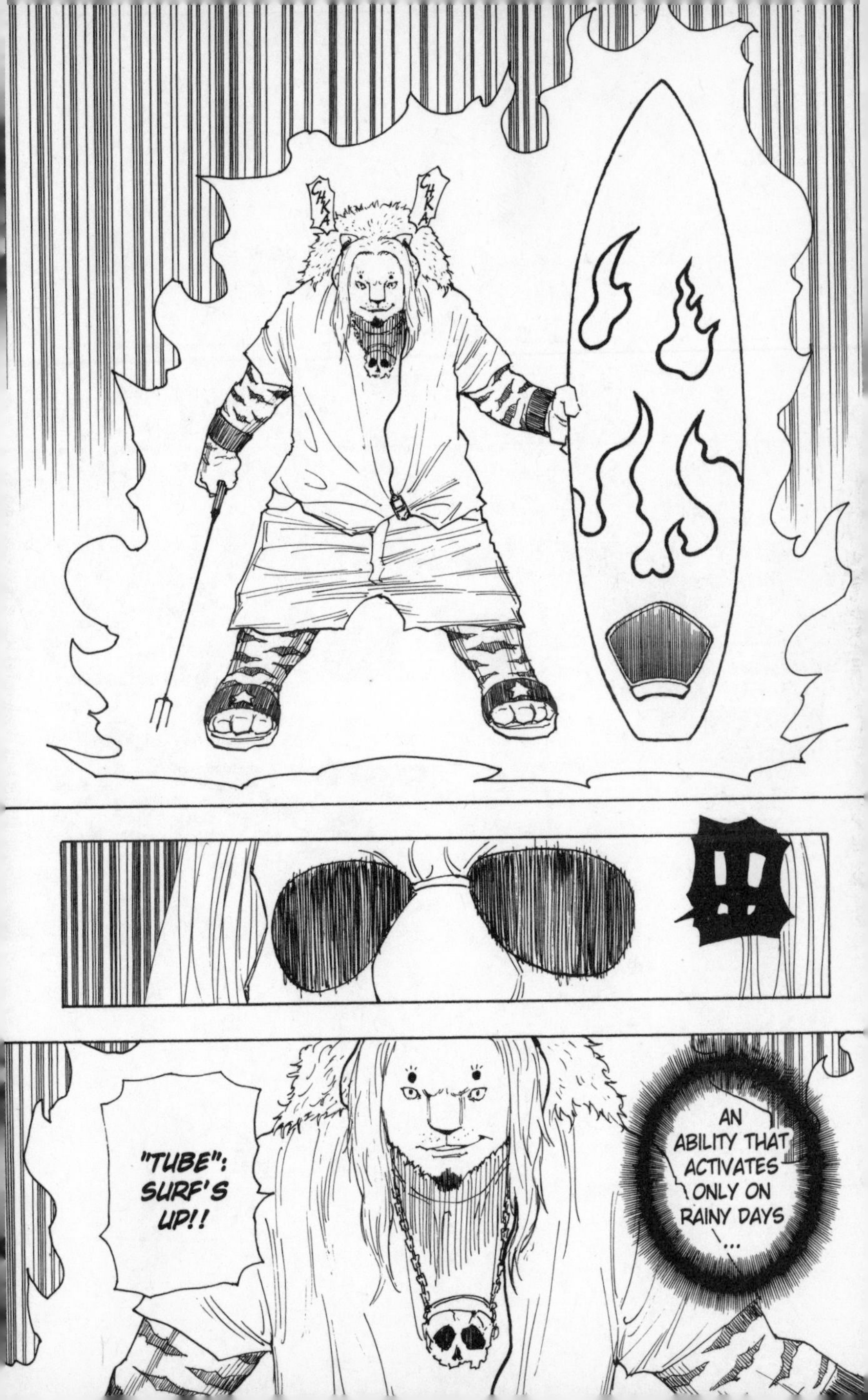
CHKA
CHKA
!!
AN ABILITY THAT ACTIVATES ONLY ON RAINY DAYS...
"TUBE": SURF'S UP!!

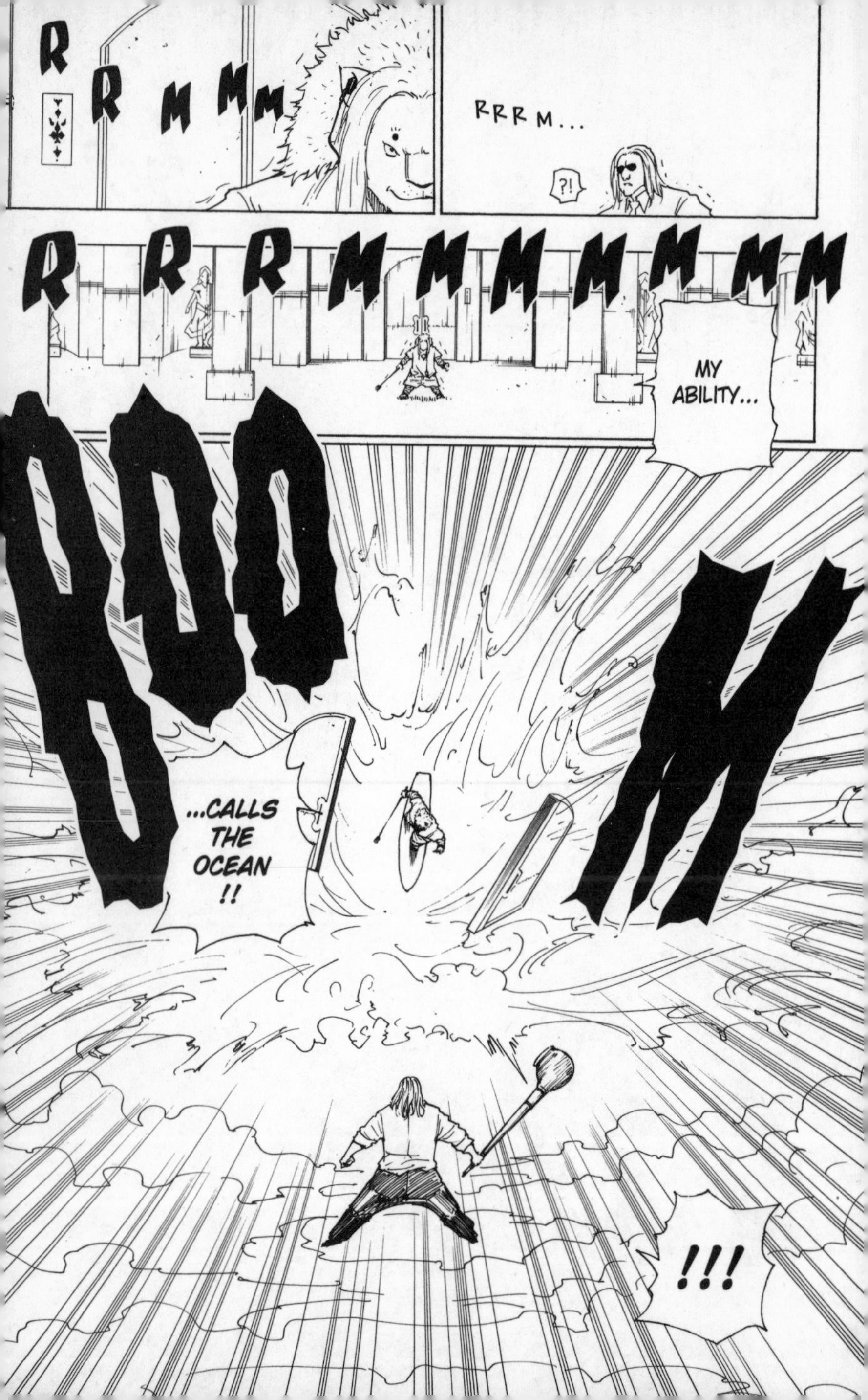
RRRM...
?!
RRMMM
RRRMMMMMMM
MY ABILITY...
ROOM
...CALLS THE OCEAN !!
!!!

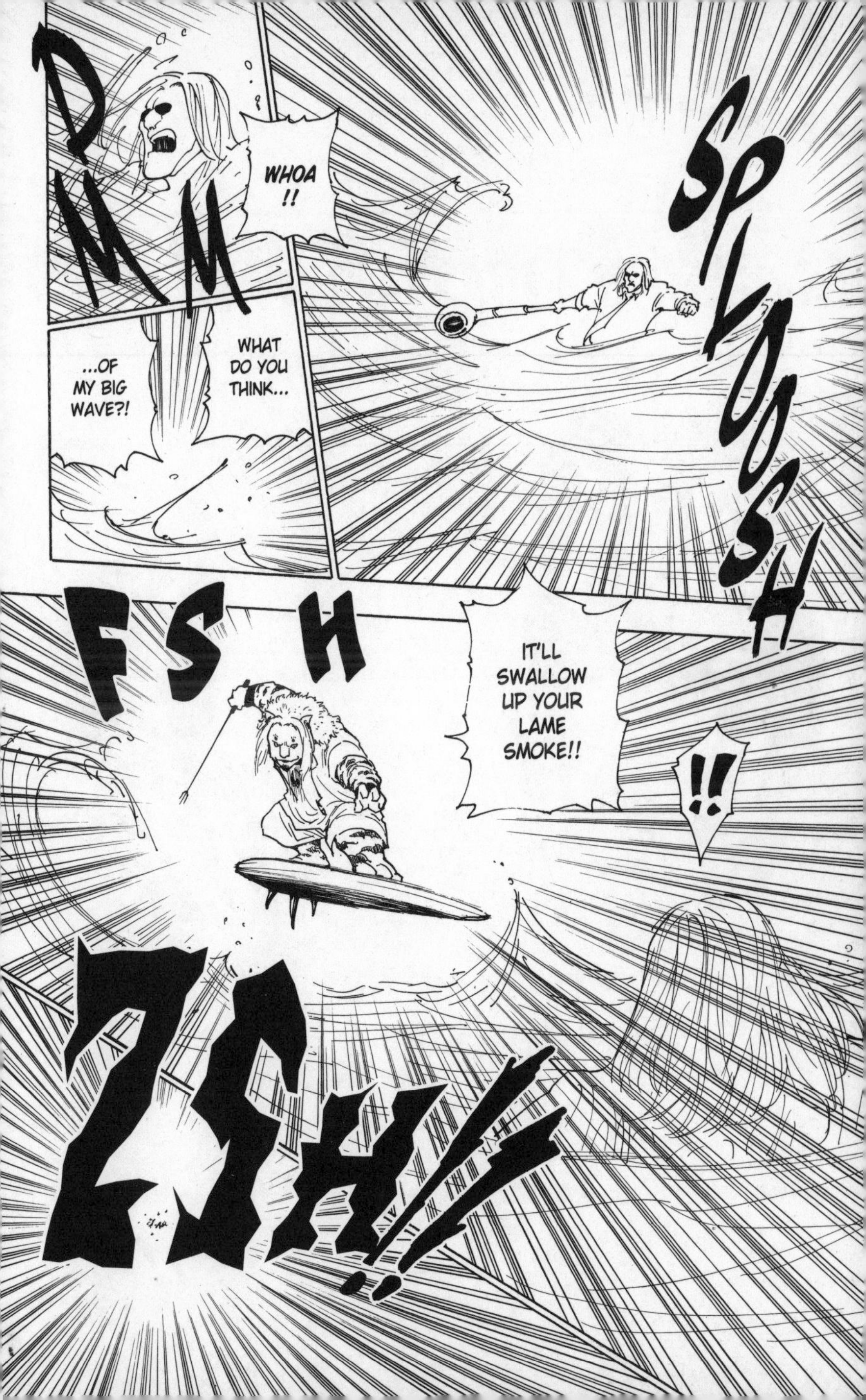
SPLOOSH
DMM
WHOA !!
WHAT DO YOU THINK...
...OF MY BIG WAVE?!
FSH
IT'LL SWALLOW UP YOUR LAME SMOKE!!
!!

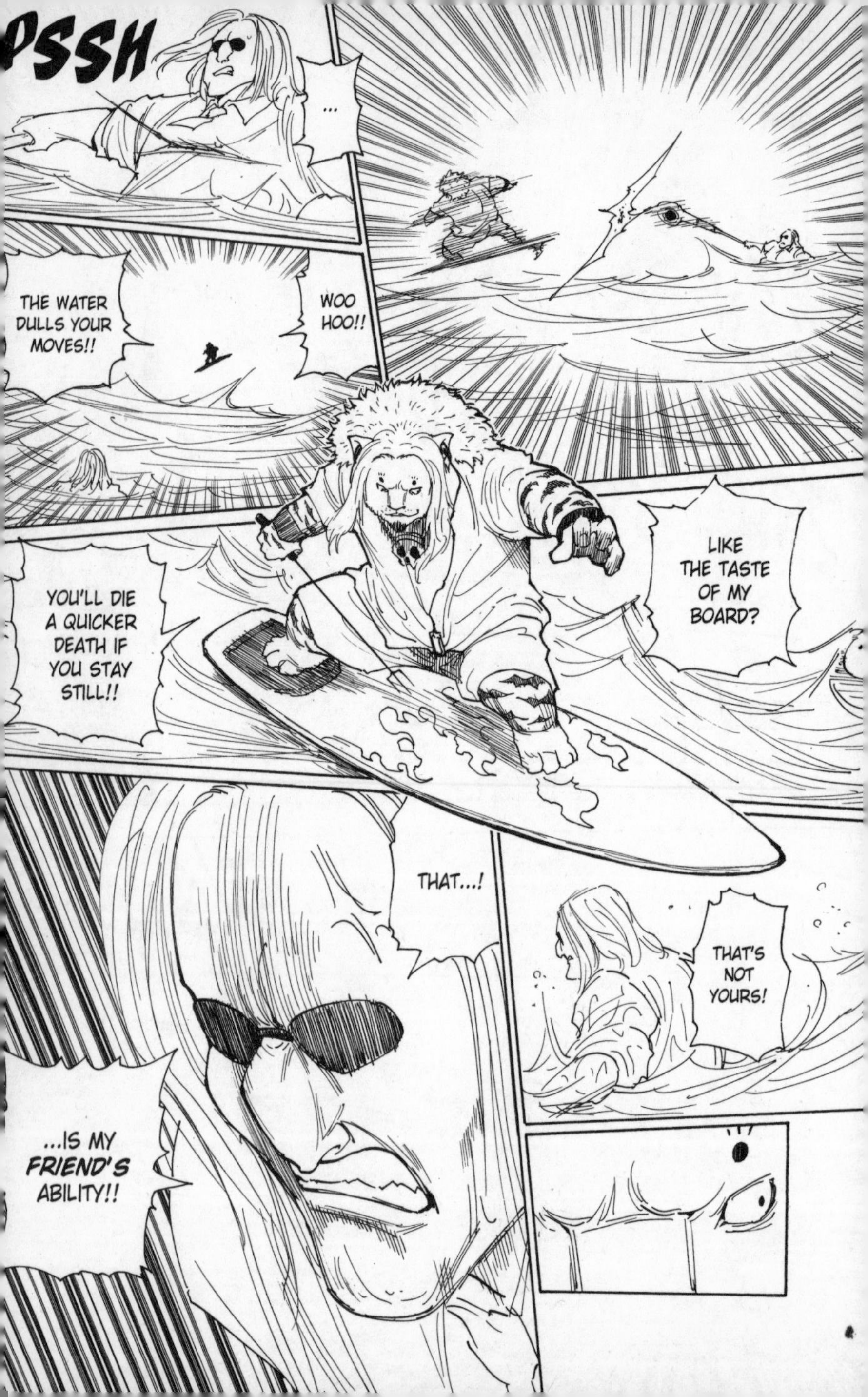
PSSH
...
WOO HOO!!
THE WATER DULLS YOUR MOVES!!
LIKE THE TASTE OF MY BOARD?
YOU'LL DIE A QUICKER DEATH IF YOU STAY STILL!!
THAT'S NOT YOURS!
THAT...!
...IS MY *FRIEND'S* ABILITY!!

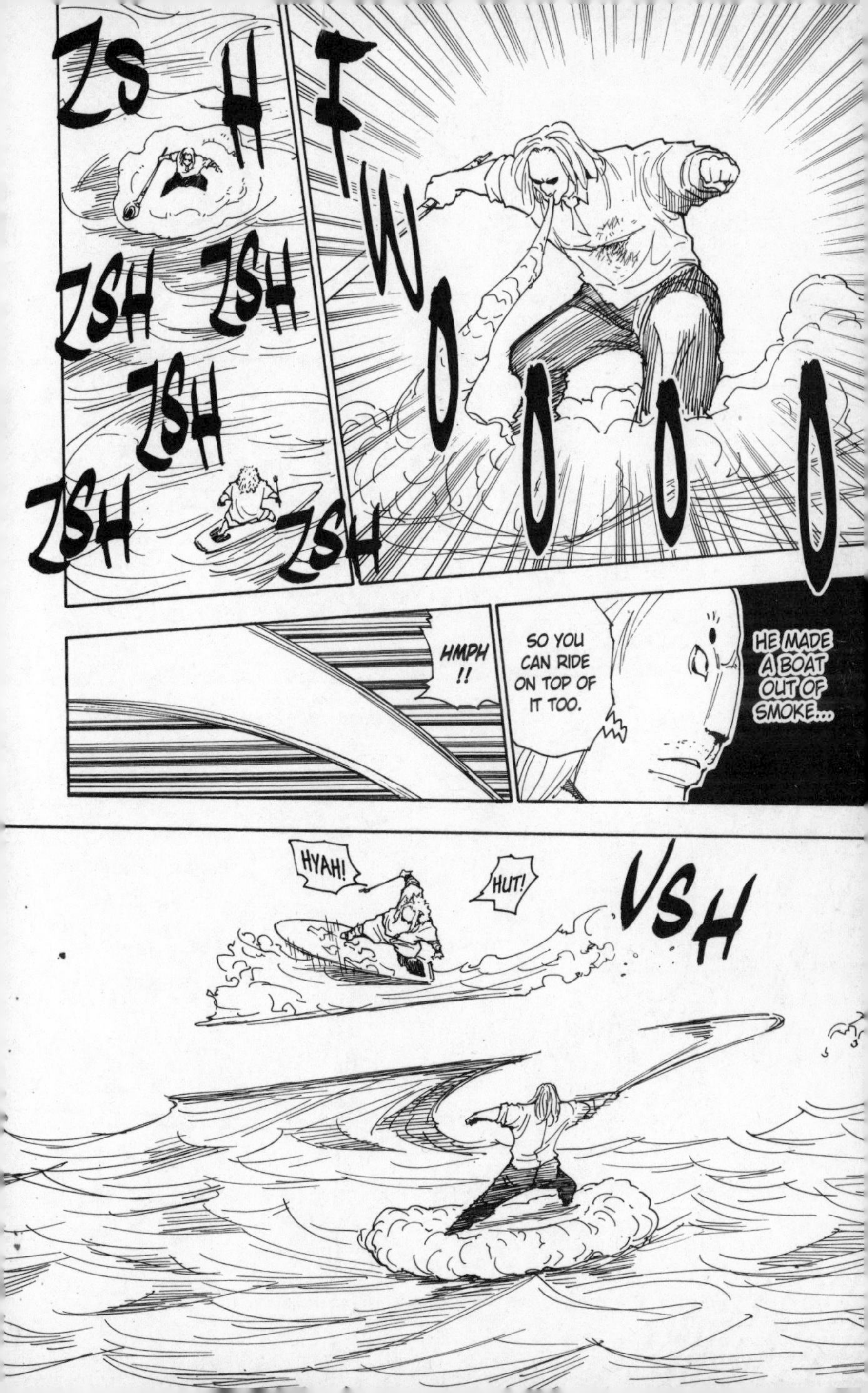
FWOOOO
ZSH
ZSH
ZSH
ZSH
ZSH
ZSH
HE MADE A BOAT OUT OF SMOKE...
SO YOU CAN RIDE ON TOP OF IT TOO.
HMPH !!
VSH
HUT!
HYAH!

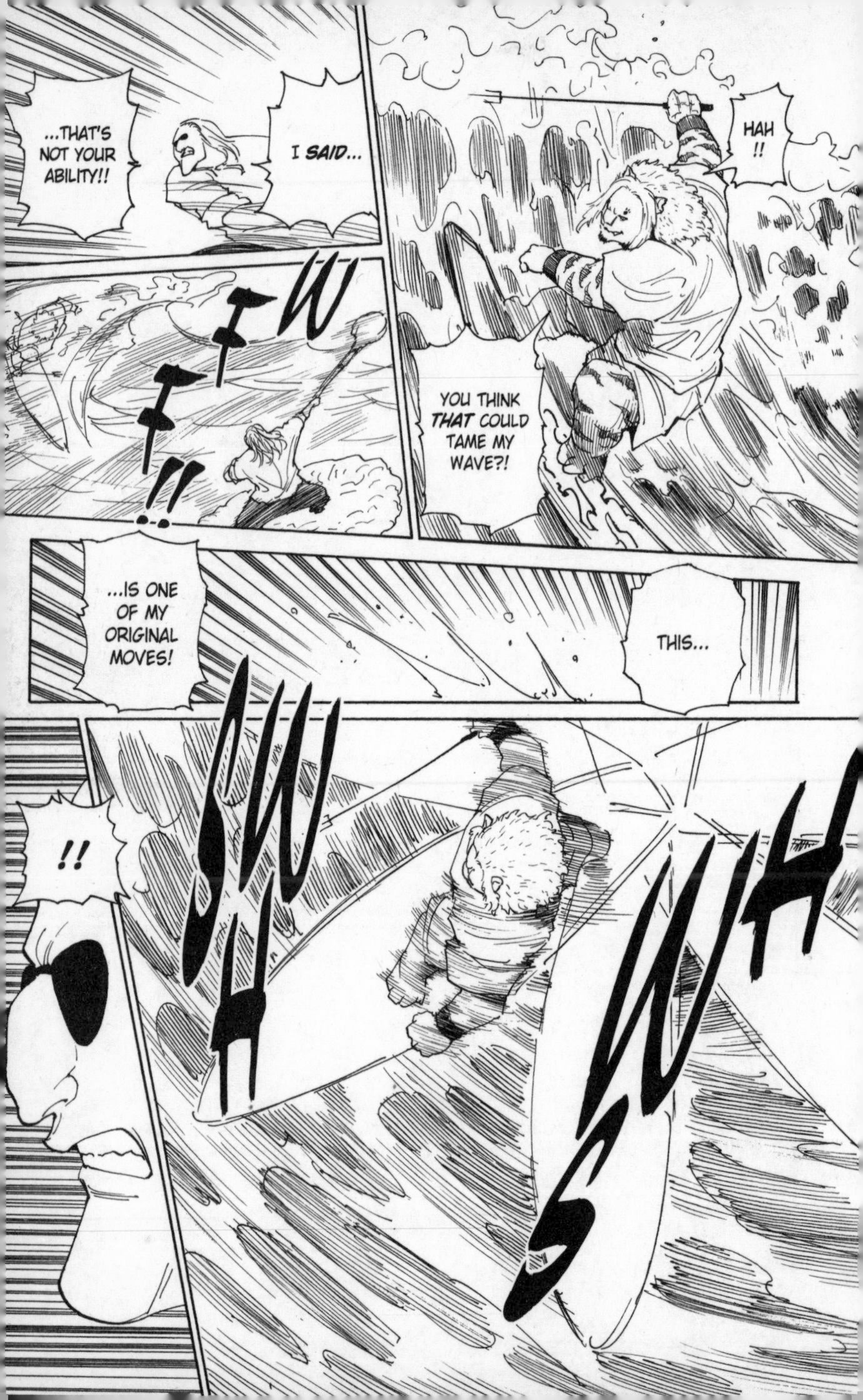
HAH !!
YOU THINK THAT COULD TAME MY WAVE?!
I SAID...
...THAT'S NOT YOUR ABILITY!!
THIS...
...IS ONE OF MY ORIGINAL MOVES!
!!

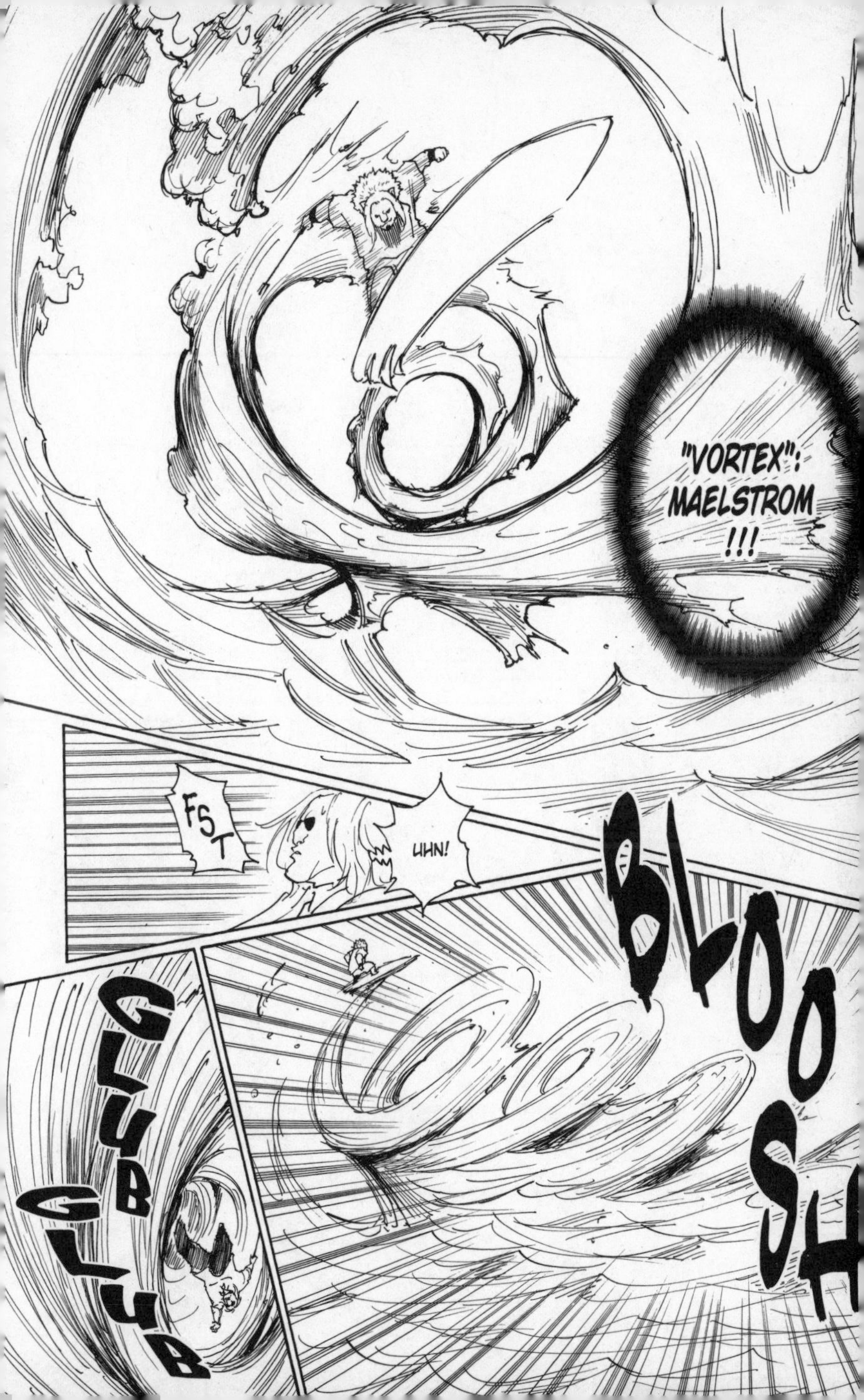

"VORTEX":
MAELSTROM
!!!
BLOOOSH
UHN!
FST
GLUB GLUB

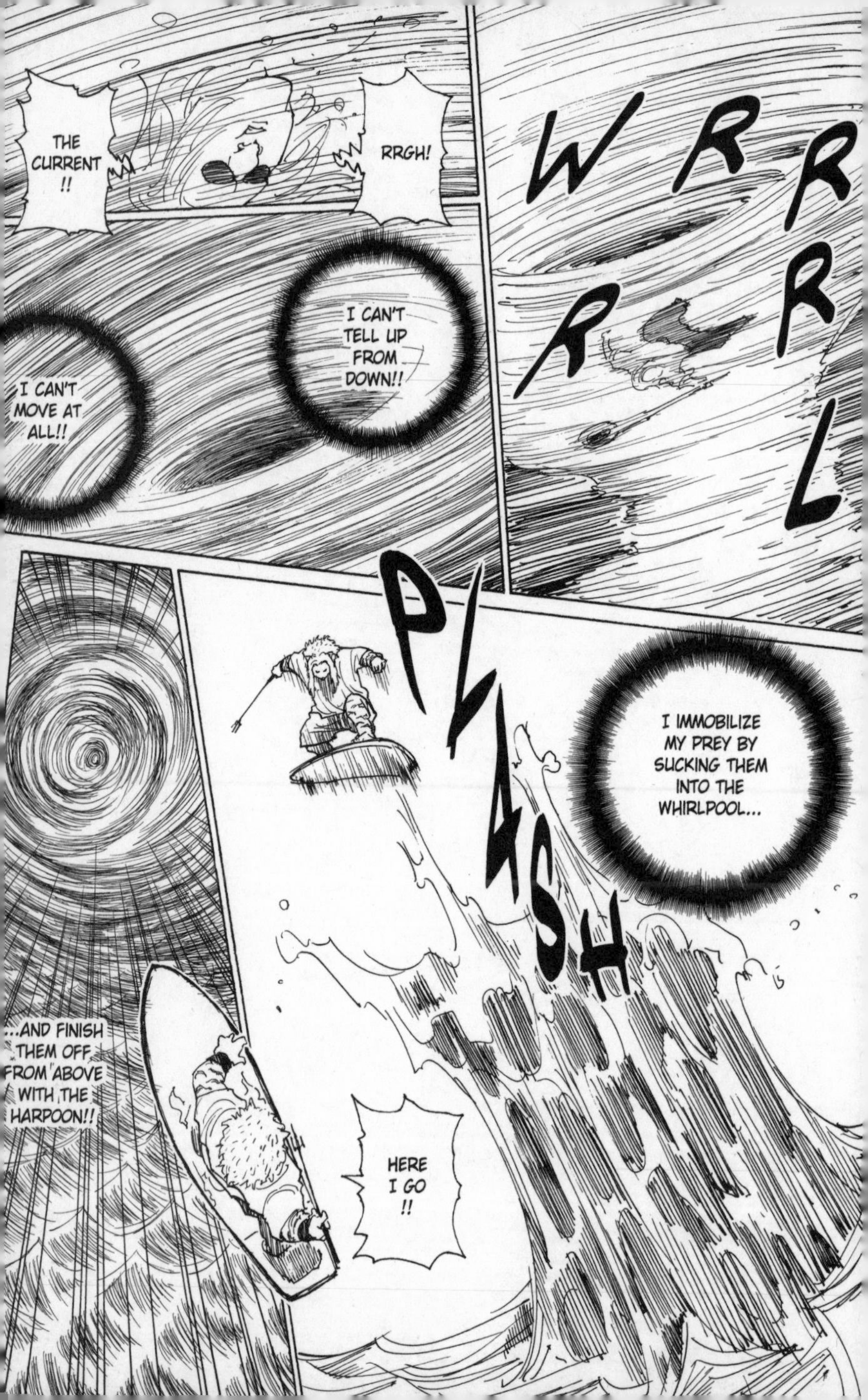
WRRRRL
RRGH!
THE CURRENT!!
I CAN'T TELL UP FROM DOWN!!
I CAN'T MOVE AT ALL!!
I IMMOBILIZE MY PREY BY SUCKING THEM INTO THE WHIRLPOOL...
PLASH
HERE I GO!!
...AND FINISH THEM OFF FROM ABOVE WITH THE HARPOON!!

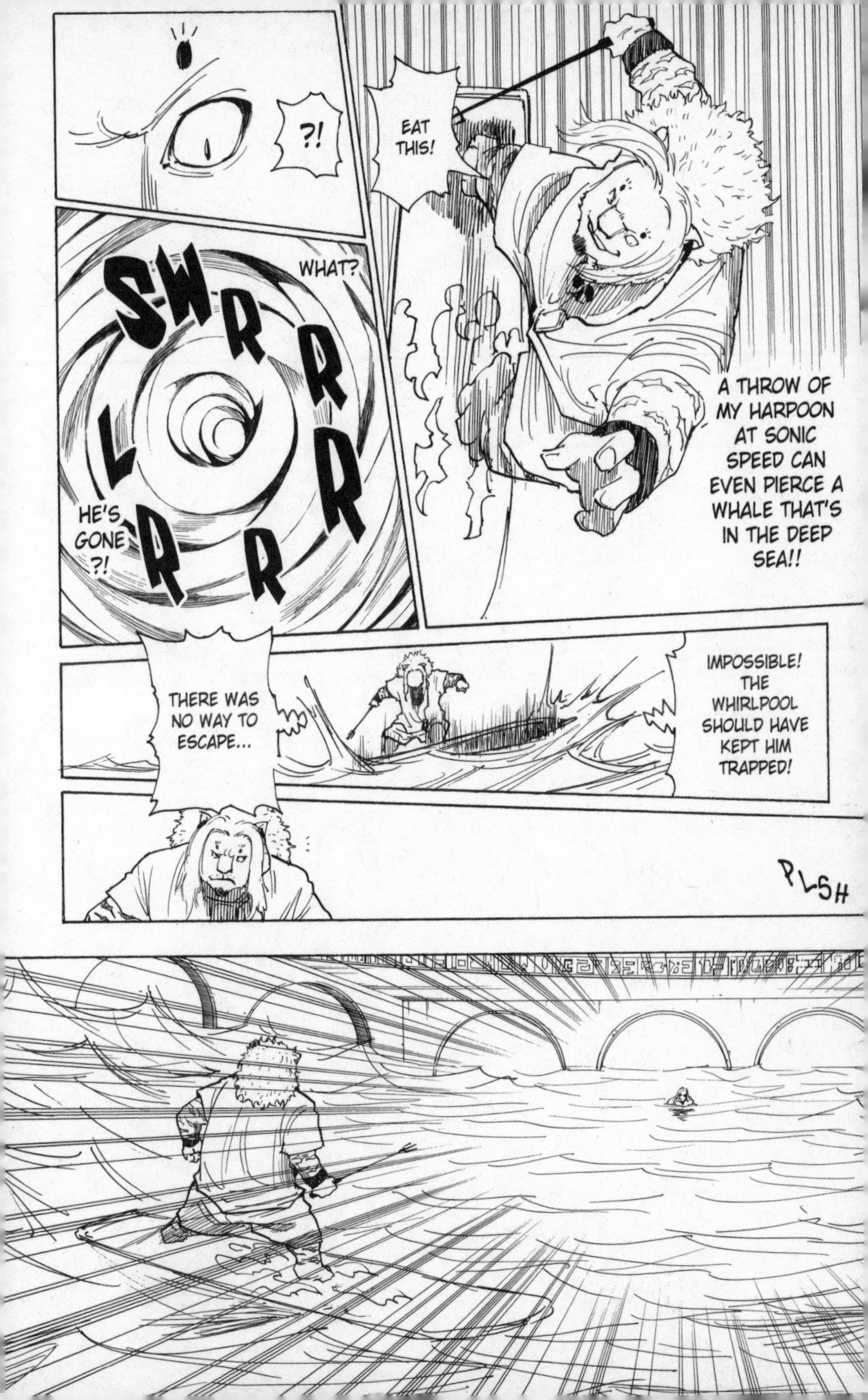
EAT THIS!
A THROW OF MY HARPOON AT SONIC SPEED CAN EVEN PIERCE A WHALE THAT'S IN THE DEEP SEA!!
?!
WHAT?
SWRRRRRRL
HE'S GONE ?!
IMPOSSIBLE! THE WHIRLPOOL SHOULD HAVE KEPT HIM TRAPPED!
THERE WAS NO WAY TO ESCAPE...
PLSH

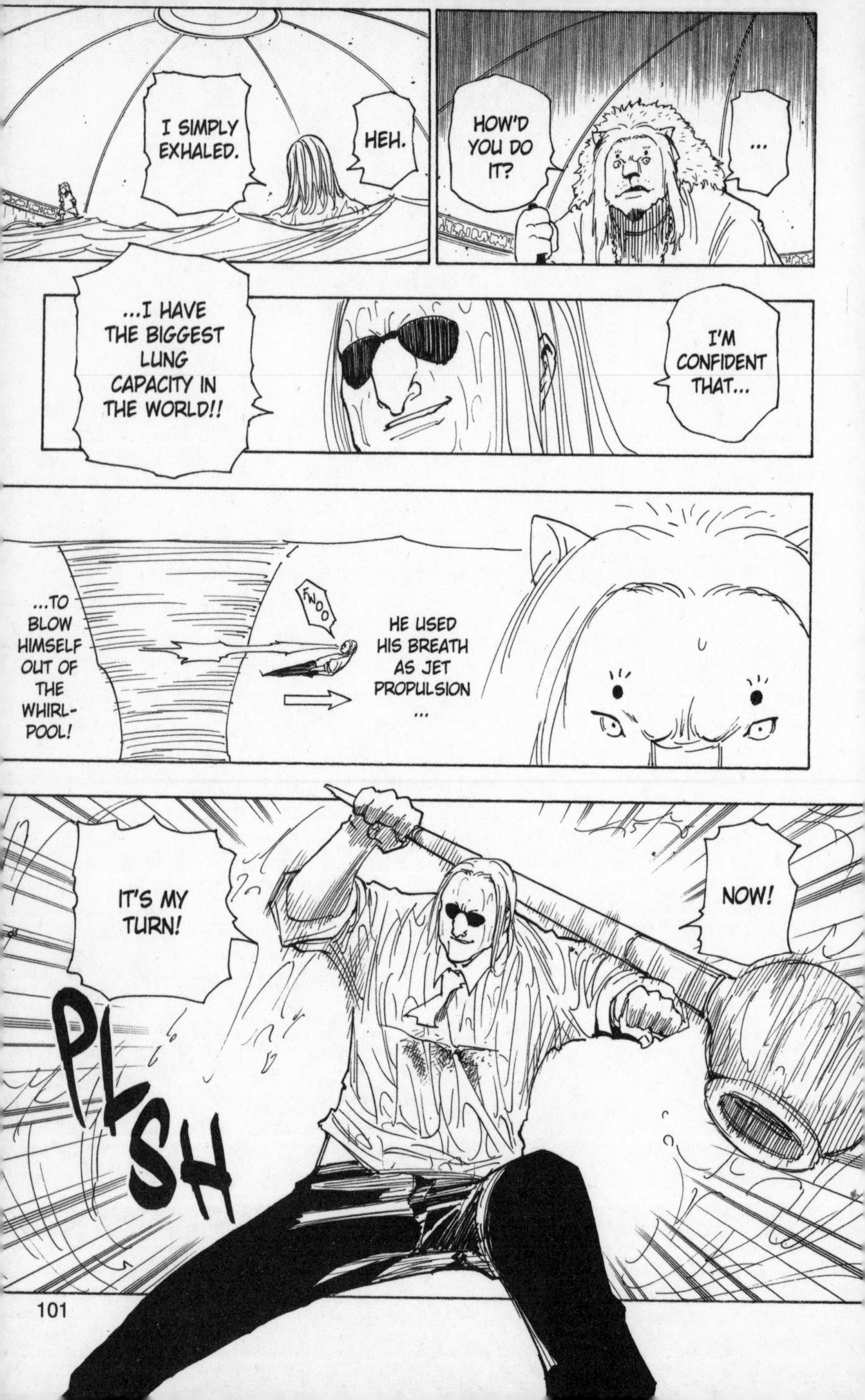
...
HOW'D YOU DO IT?
HEH.
I SIMPLY EXHALED.
I'M CONFIDENT THAT...
...I HAVE THE BIGGEST LUNG CAPACITY IN THE WORLD!!
HE USED HIS BREATH AS JET PROPULSION ...
FWOO
...TO BLOW HIMSELF OUT OF THE WHIRL-POOL!
NOW!
IT'S MY TURN!
PLSH

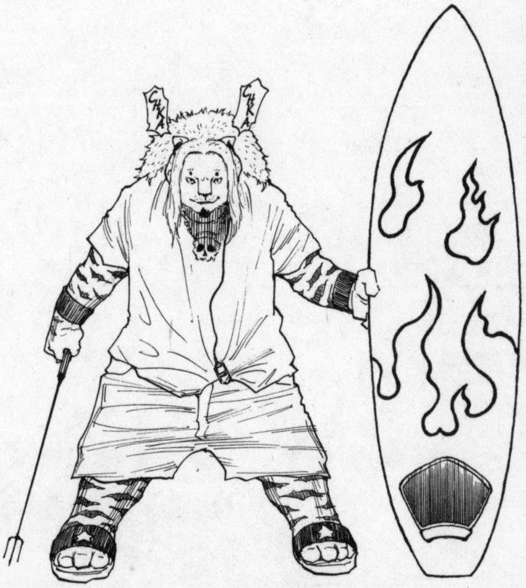

CHKA
CHKA

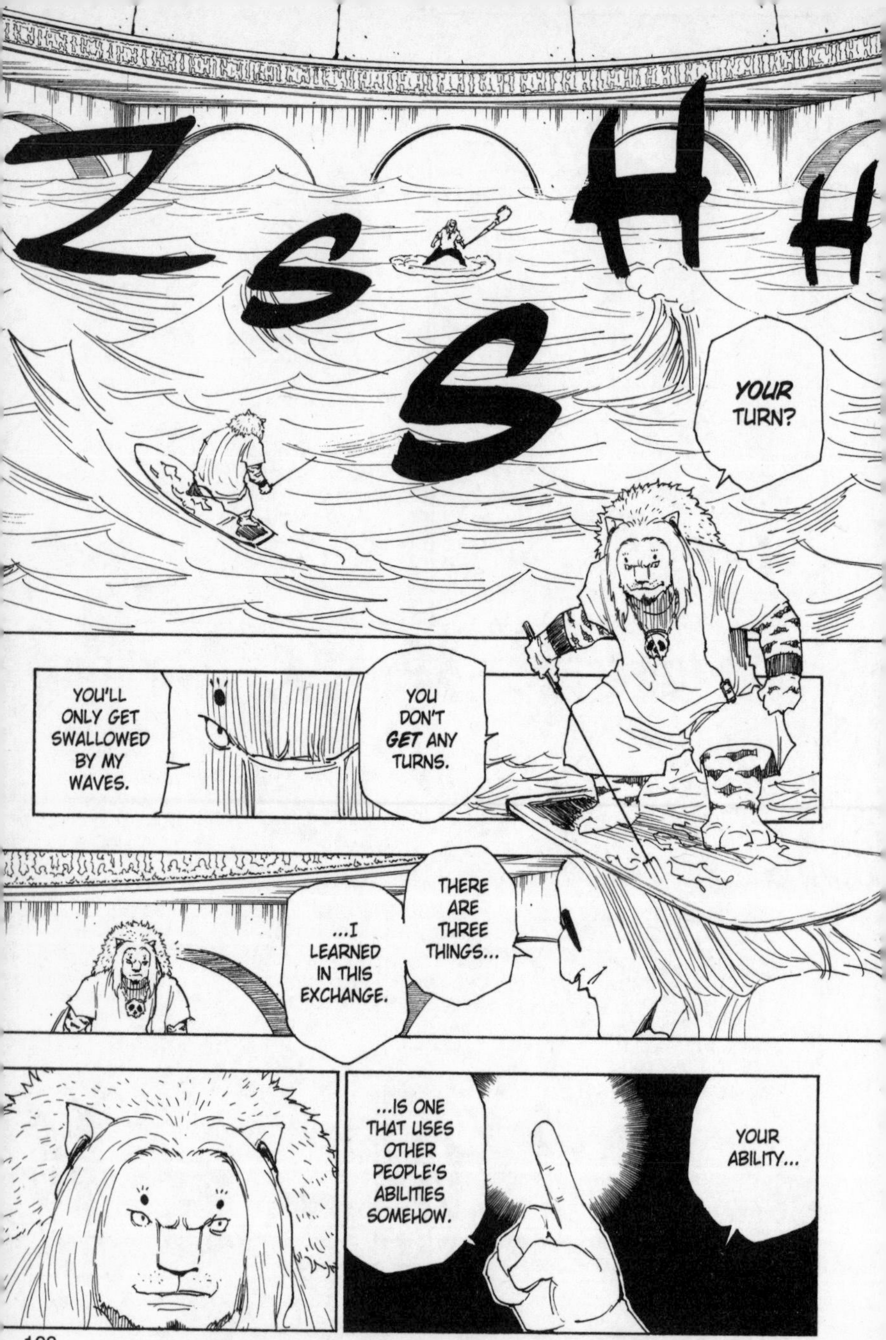
ZSSHH
YOUR TURN?
YOU DON'T GET ANY TURNS.
YOU'LL ONLY GET SWALLOWED BY MY WAVES.
THERE ARE THREE THINGS...
...I LEARNED IN THIS EXCHANGE.
YOUR ABILITY...
...IS ONE THAT USES OTHER PEOPLE'S ABILITIES SOMEHOW.

Chapter 254: 6: Part 11

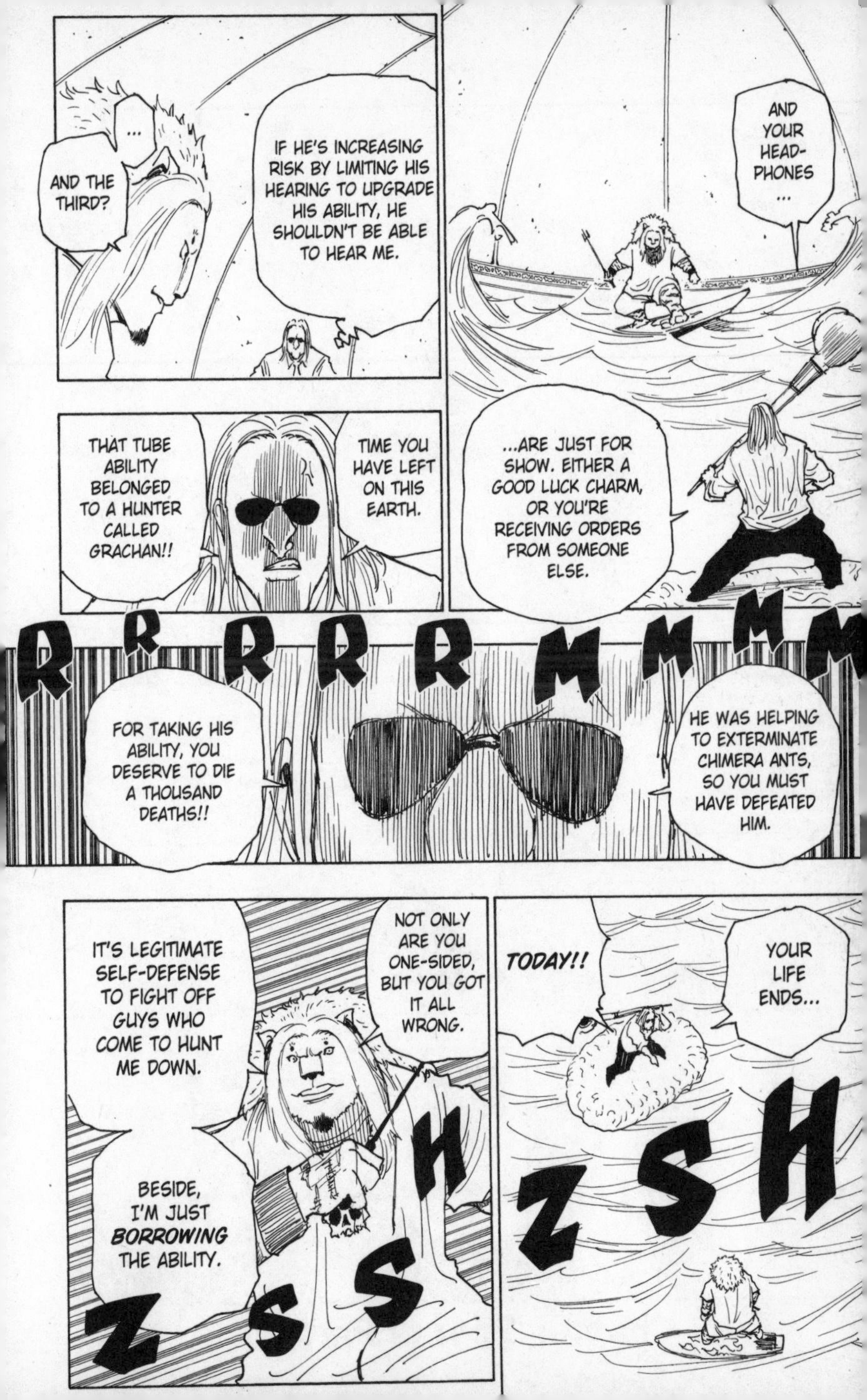
AND YOUR HEADPHONES ...
...ARE JUST FOR SHOW. EITHER A GOOD LUCK CHARM, OR YOU'RE RECEIVING ORDERS FROM SOMEONE ELSE.
IF HE'S INCREASING RISK BY LIMITING HIS HEARING TO UPGRADE HIS ABILITY, HE SHOULDN'T BE ABLE TO HEAR ME.
...
AND THE THIRD?
TIME YOU HAVE LEFT ON THIS EARTH.
THAT TUBE ABILITY BELONGED TO A HUNTER CALLED GRACHAN!!
RRRRRMMMMM
HE WAS HELPING TO EXTERMINATE CHIMERA ANTS, SO YOU MUST HAVE DEFEATED HIM.
FOR TAKING HIS ABILITY, YOU DESERVE TO DIE A THOUSAND DEATHS!!
YOUR LIFE ENDS...
TODAY!!
ZSSH
NOT ONLY ARE YOU ONE-SIDED, BUT YOU GOT IT ALL WRONG.
IT'S LEGITIMATE SELF-DEFENSE TO FIGHT OFF GUYS WHO COME TO HUNT ME DOWN.
BESIDE, I'M JUST BORROWING THE ABILITY.
ZSSH

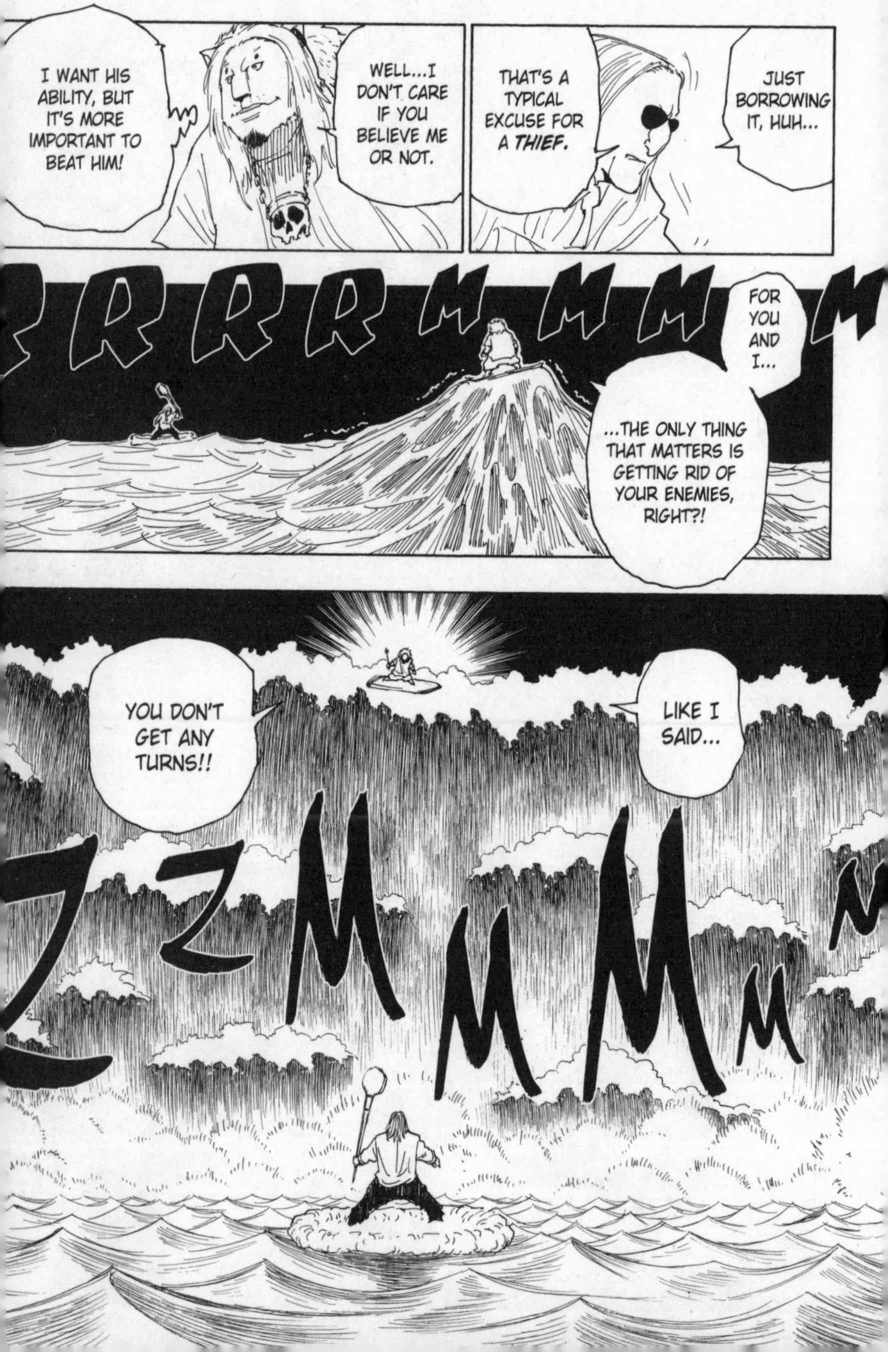
JUST BORROWING IT, HUH...
THAT'S A TYPICAL EXCUSE FOR A *THIEF*.
WELL...I DON'T CARE IF YOU BELIEVE ME OR NOT.
I WANT HIS ABILITY, BUT IT'S MORE IMPORTANT TO BEAT HIM!
RRRRMMMM
FOR YOU AND I...
...THE ONLY THING THAT MATTERS IS GETTING RID OF YOUR ENEMIES, RIGHT?!
LIKE I SAID...
YOU DON'T GET ANY TURNS!!
ZZMMMMM

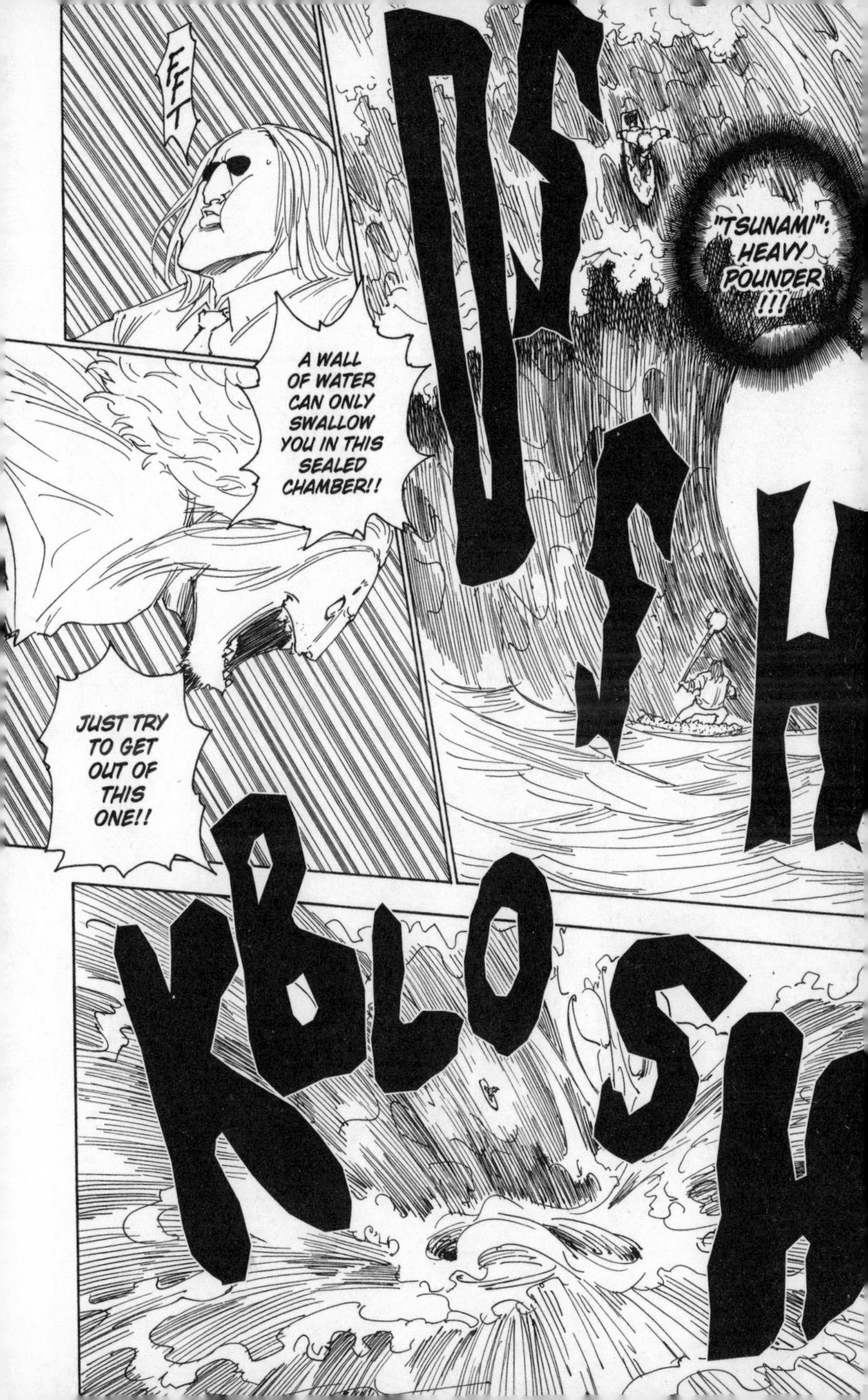
"TSUNAMI": HEAVY POUNDER!!!
FFT
A WALL OF WATER CAN ONLY SWALLOW YOU IN THIS SEALED CHAMBER!!
JUST TRY TO GET OUT OF THIS ONE!!
KBLOSH

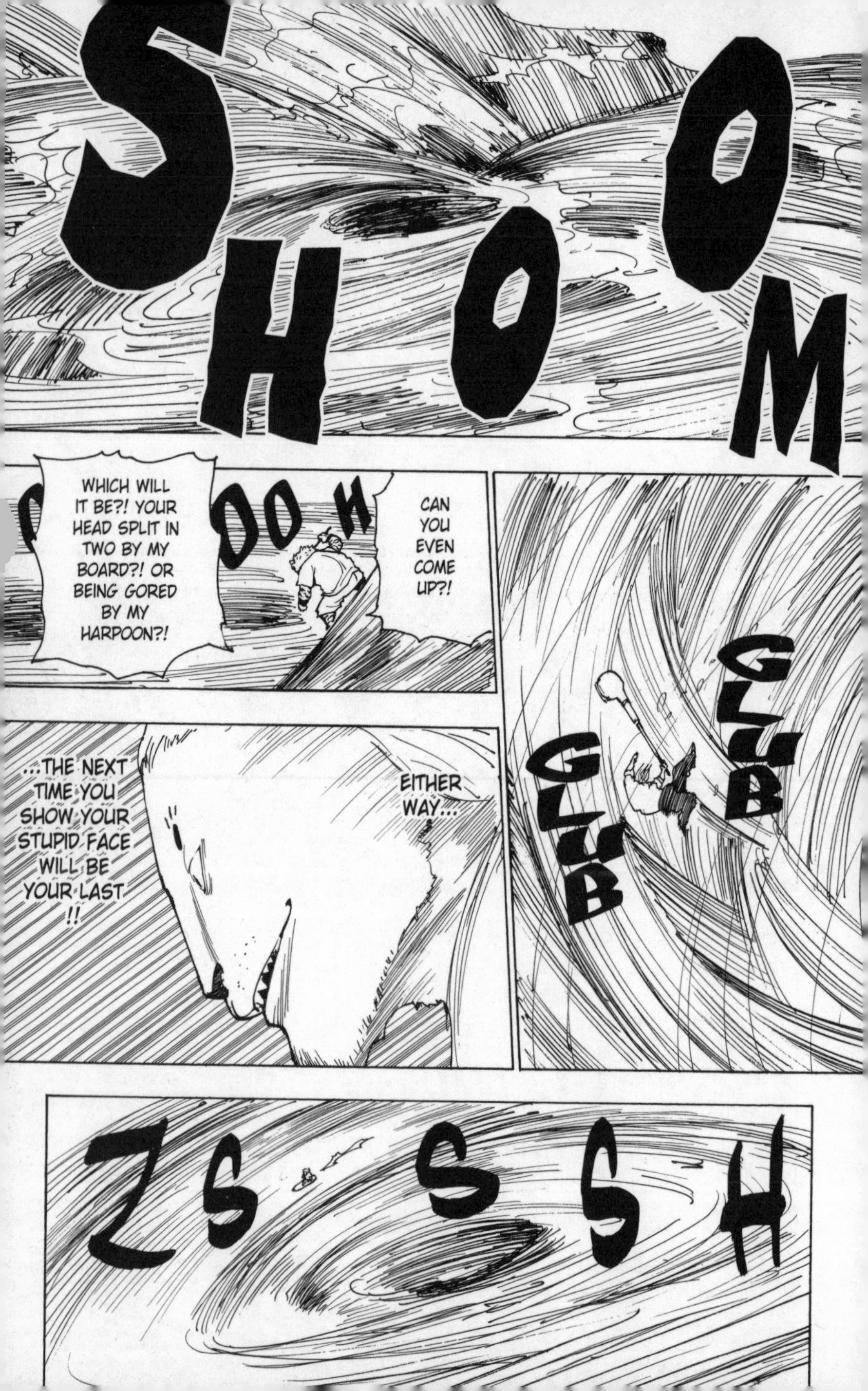
SHOOOM
GLUB GLUB
CAN YOU EVEN COME UP?!
WHICH WILL IT BE?! YOUR HEAD SPLIT IN TWO BY MY BOARD?! OR BEING GORED BY MY HARPOON?!
EITHER WAY...
...THE NEXT TIME YOU SHOW YOUR STUPID FACE WILL BE YOUR LAST!!
ZSSSH

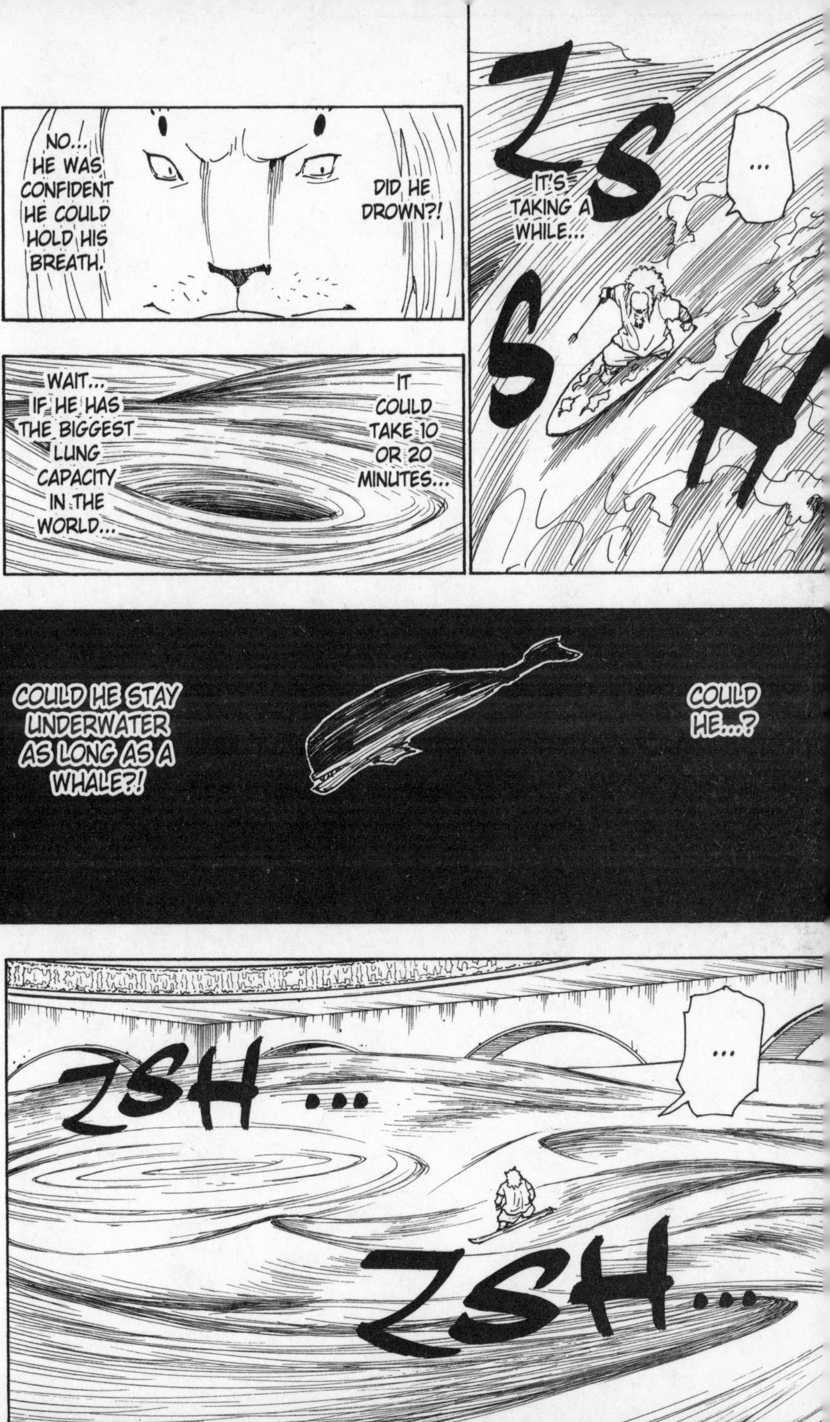
...
IT'S TAKING A WHILE...
ZSSH
DID HE DROWN?!
NO... HE WAS CONFIDENT HE COULD HOLD HIS BREATH.
IT COULD TAKE 10 OR 20 MINUTES...
WAIT... IF HE HAS THE BIGGEST LUNG CAPACITY IN THE WORLD...
COULD HE...?
COULD HE STAY UNDERWATER AS LONG AS A WHALE?!
...
ZSH...
ZSH...

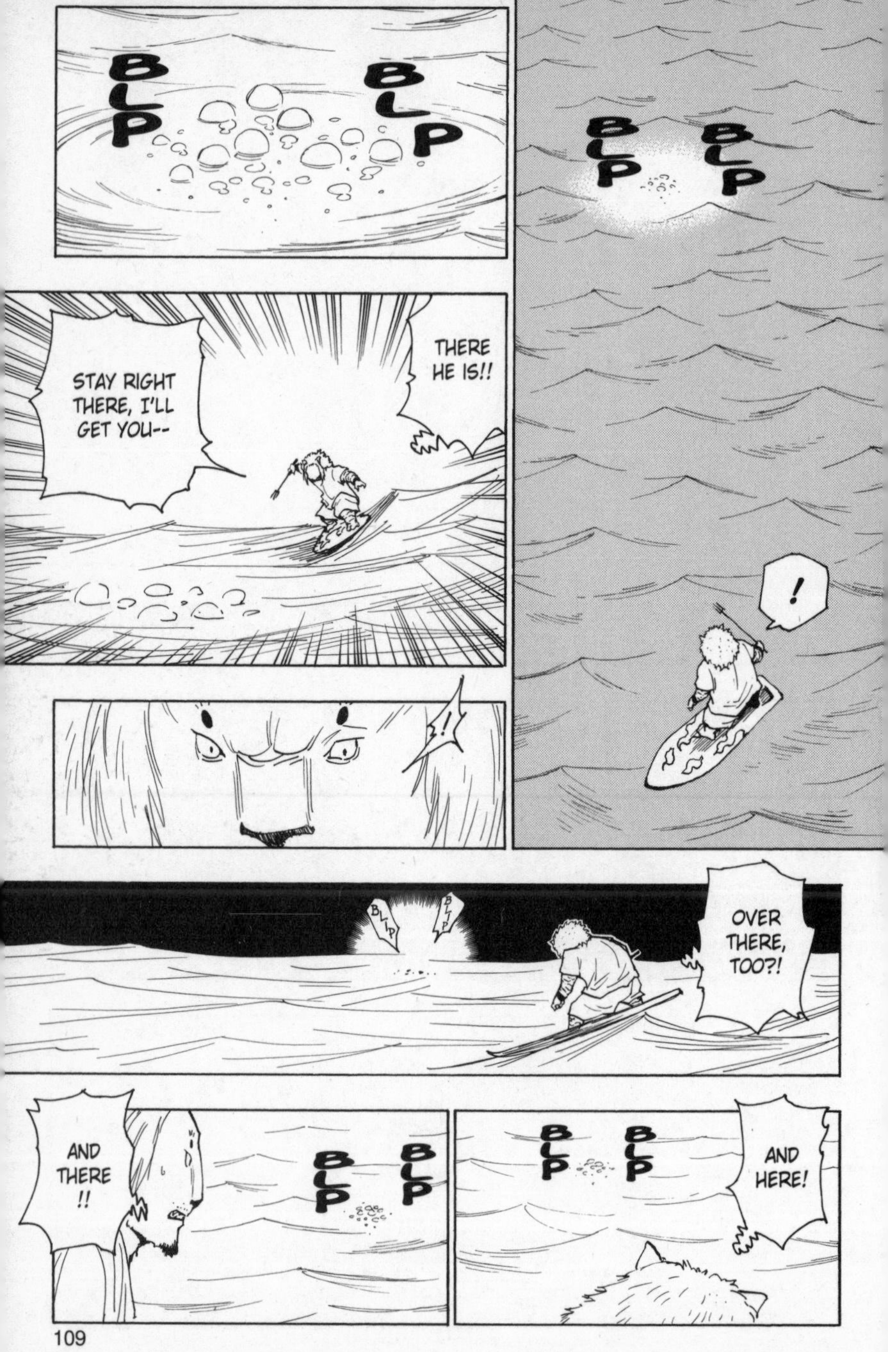
BLP
BLP
!
BLP
BLP
THERE HE IS!!
STAY RIGHT THERE, I'LL GET YOU--
!
OVER THERE, TOO?!
BLIP
BLIP
AND HERE!
BLP
BLP
BLP
BLP
AND THERE !!

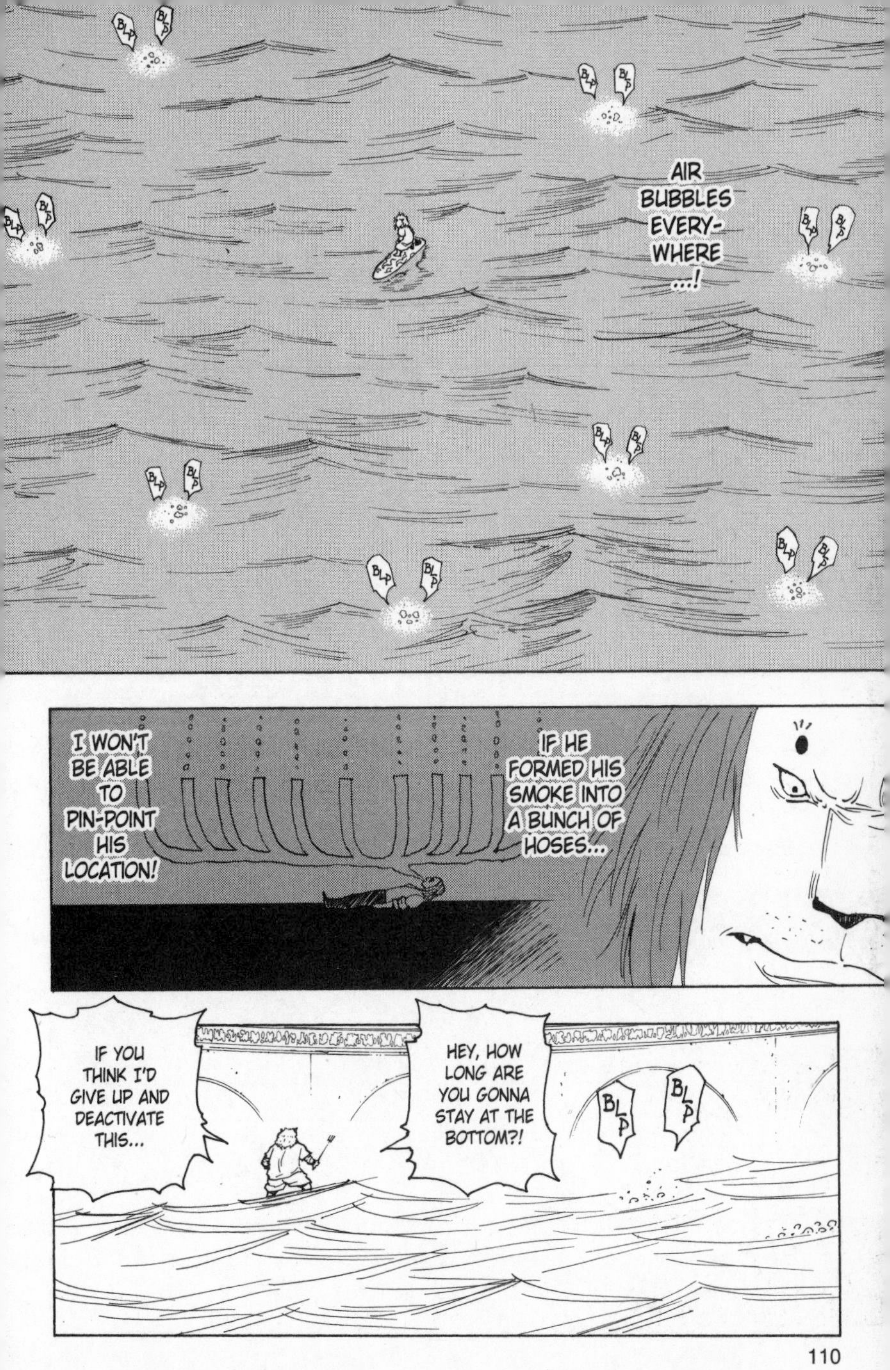
BLP BLP
AIR BUBBLES EVERY-WHERE ...!
BLP BLP
IF HE FORMED HIS SMOKE INTO A BUNCH OF HOSES...
I WON'T BE ABLE TO PIN-POINT HIS LOCATION!
BLP BLP
HEY, HOW LONG ARE YOU GONNA STAY AT THE BOTTOM?!
IF YOU THINK I'D GIVE UP AND DEACTIVATE THIS...

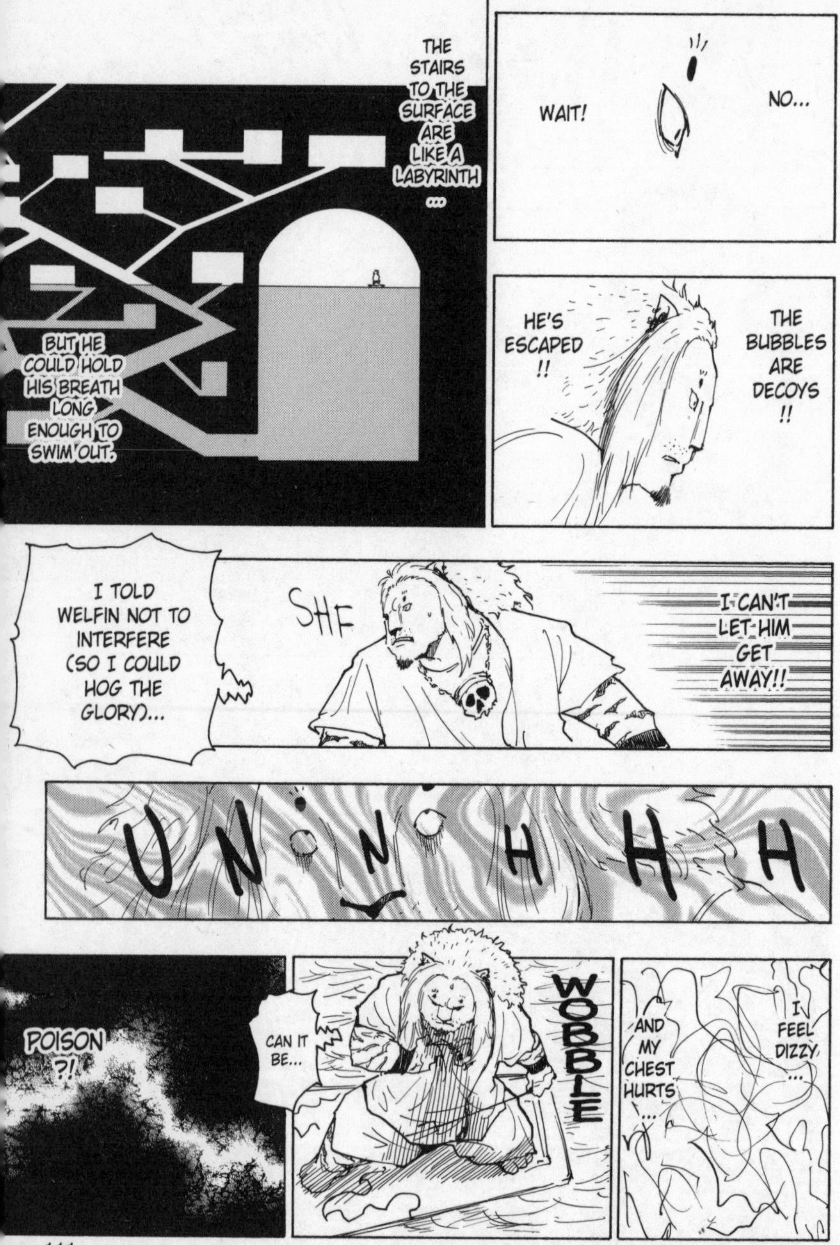
NO...
WAIT!
THE BUBBLES ARE DECOYS!!
HE'S ESCAPED!!
THE STAIRS TO THE SURFACE ARE LIKE A LABYRINTH...
BUT HE COULD HOLD HIS BREATH LONG ENOUGH TO SWIM OUT.
I CAN'T LET HIM GET AWAY!!
SHF
I TOLD WELFIN NOT TO INTERFERE (SO I COULD HOG THE GLORY)...
UNNHHH
I FEEL DIZZY...
AND MY CHEST HURTS...
WOBBLE
CAN IT BE...
POISON?!

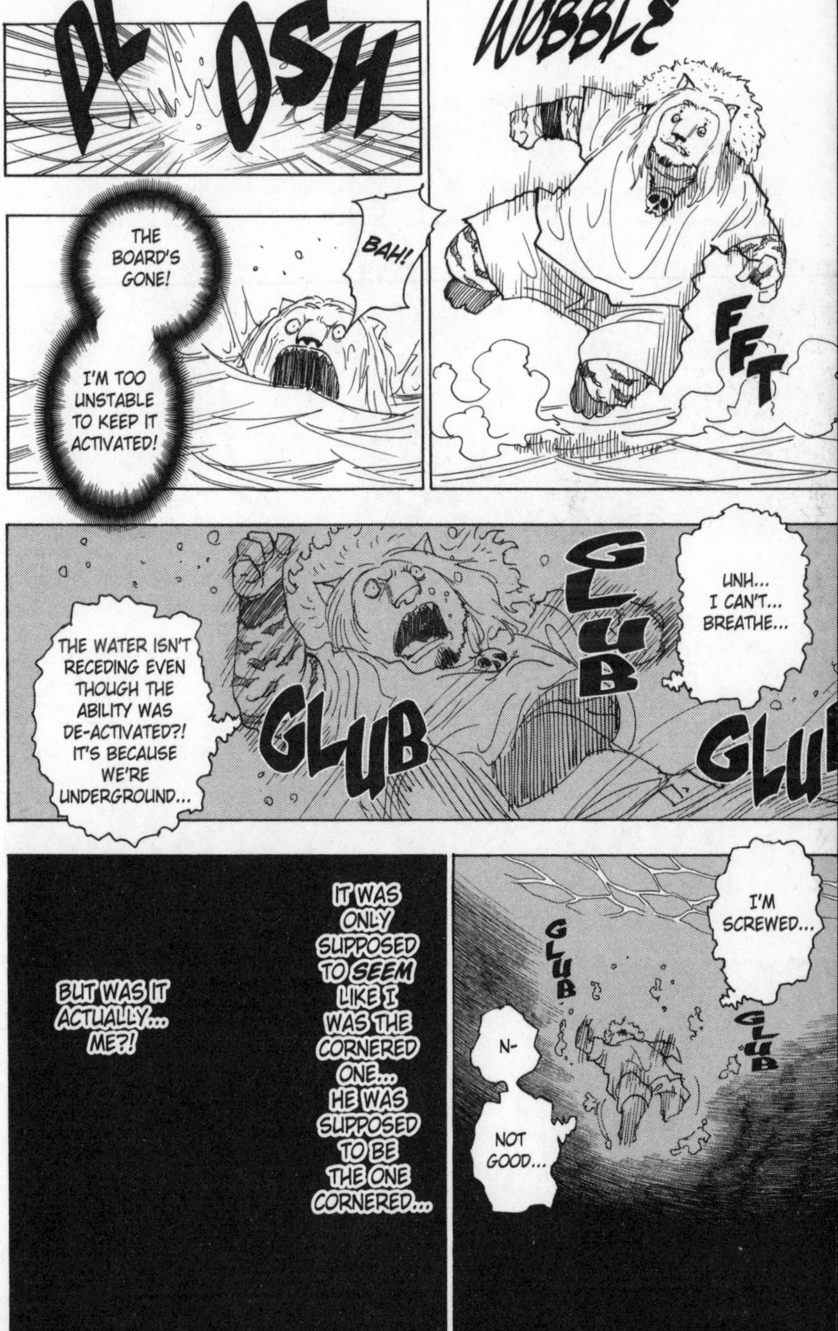
WOBBLE
PLOSH
FFT
BAH!
THE BOARD'S GONE!
I'M TOO UNSTABLE TO KEEP IT ACTIVATED!
UNH... I CAN'T... BREATHE...
GLUB
GLUB
GLUB
THE WATER ISN'T RECEDING EVEN THOUGH THE ABILITY WAS DE-ACTIVATED?! IT'S BECAUSE WE'RE UNDERGROUND...
I'M SCREWED...
GLUB
GLUB
N-
NOT GOOD...
IT WAS ONLY SUPPOSED TO SEEM LIKE I WAS THE CORNERED ONE... HE WAS SUPPOSED TO BE THE ONE CORNERED...
BUT WAS IT ACTUALLY... ME?!

READ THIS WAY

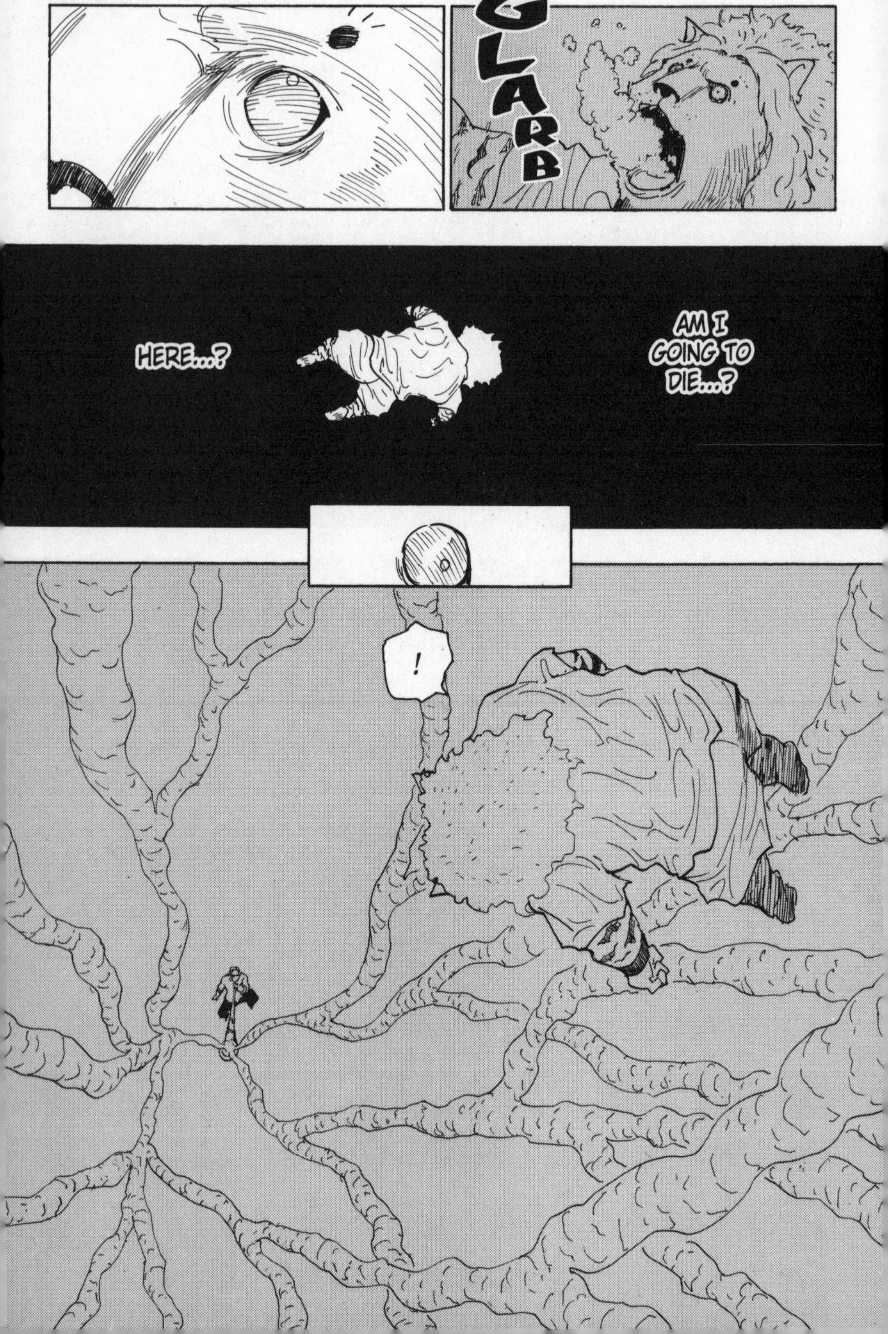
GLARB
AM I GOING TO DIE...?
HERE...?
!

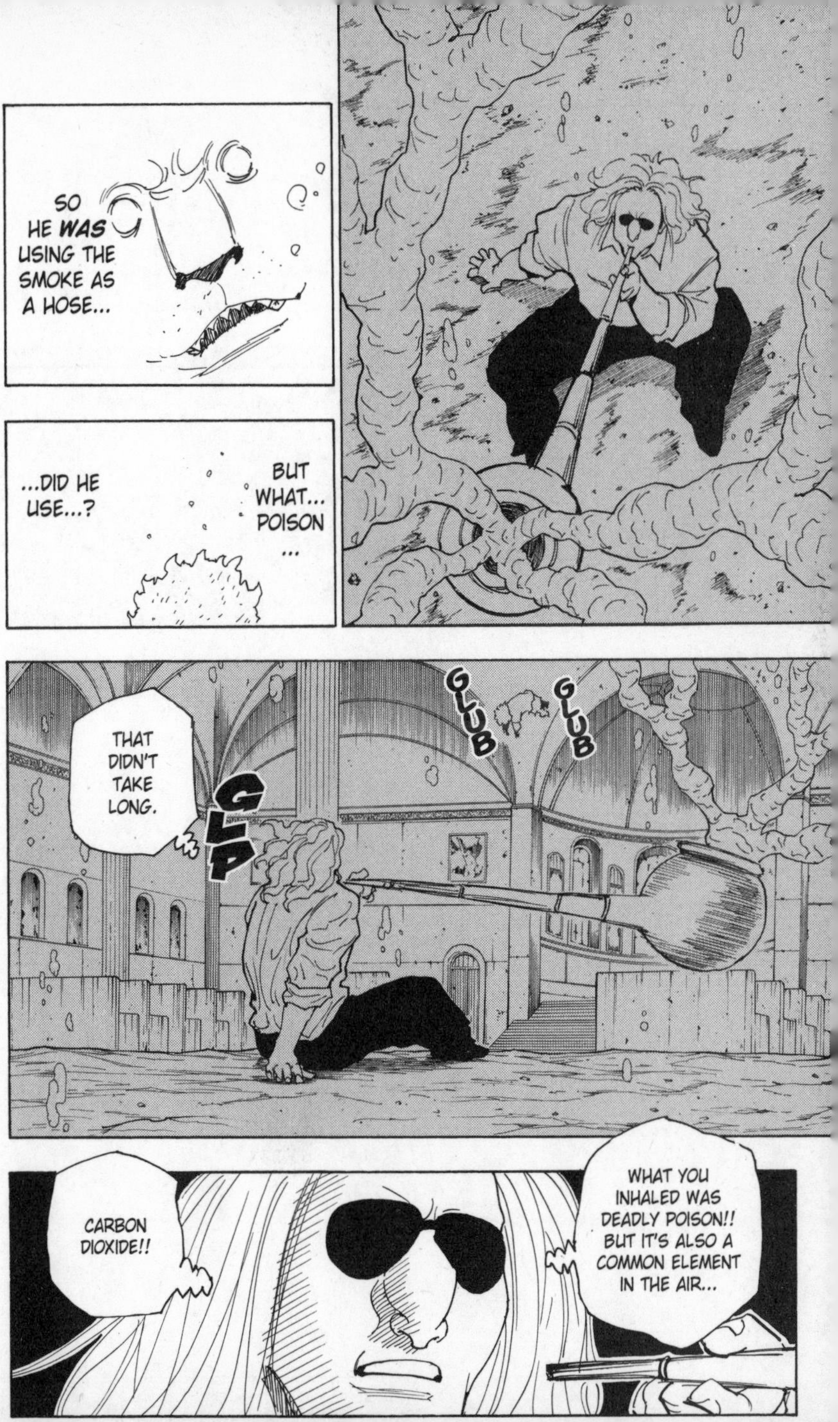
SO HE WAS USING THE SMOKE AS A HOSE...
BUT WHAT... POISON ...
...DID HE USE...?
GLUB
GLUB
THAT DIDN'T TAKE LONG.
GLP
WHAT YOU INHALED WAS DEADLY POISON!! BUT IT'S ALSO A COMMON ELEMENT IN THE AIR...
CARBON DIOXIDE!!

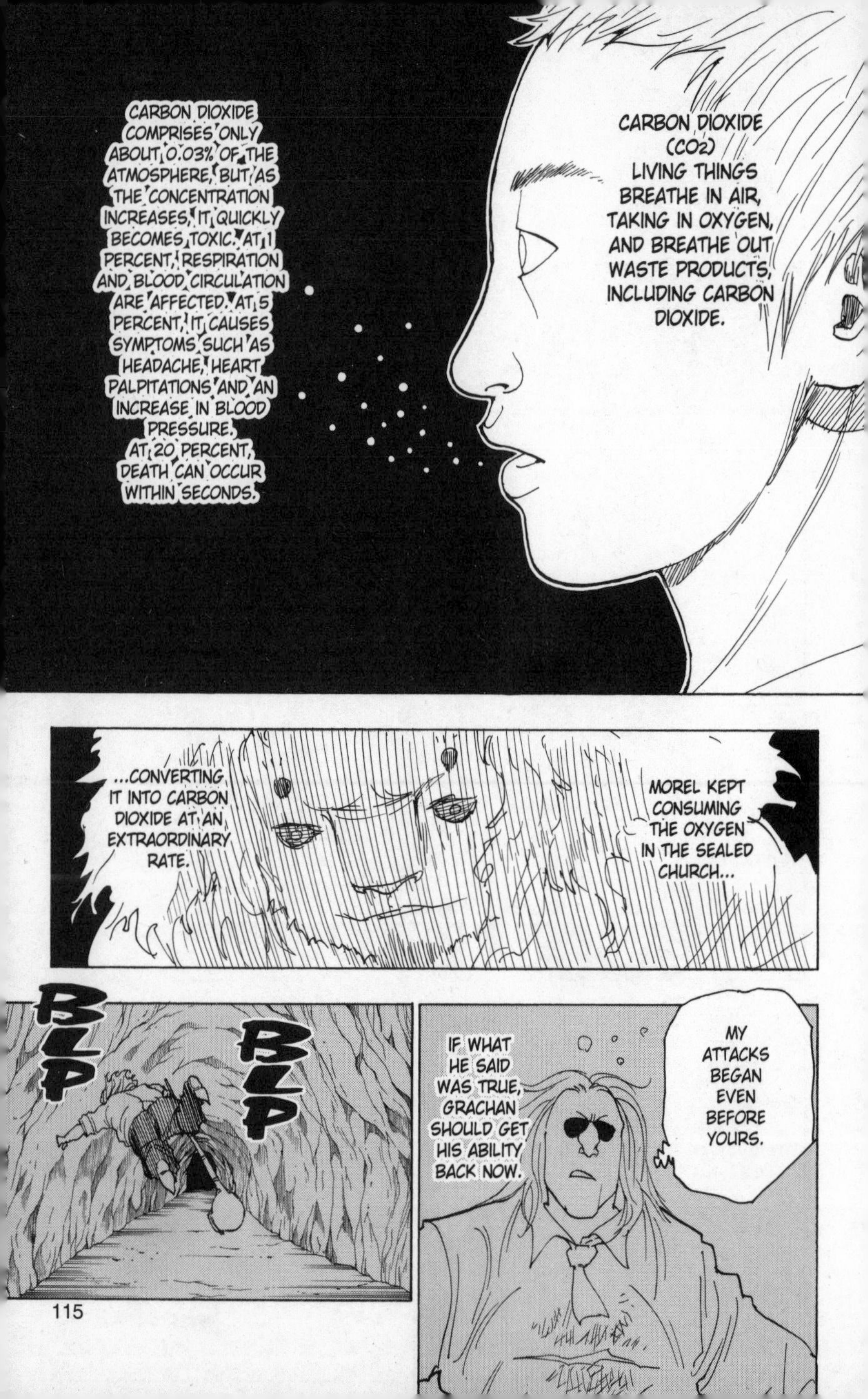
CARBON DIOXIDE (CO2) LIVING THINGS BREATHE IN AIR, TAKING IN OXYGEN, AND BREATHE OUT WASTE PRODUCTS, INCLUDING CARBON DIOXIDE.
CARBON DIOXIDE COMPRISES ONLY ABOUT 0.03% OF THE ATMOSPHERE, BUT AS THE CONCENTRATION INCREASES, IT QUICKLY BECOMES TOXIC. AT 1 PERCENT, RESPIRATION AND BLOOD CIRCULATION ARE AFFECTED. AT 5 PERCENT, IT CAUSES SYMPTOMS SUCH AS HEADACHE, HEART PALPITATIONS AND AN INCREASE IN BLOOD PRESSURE. AT 20 PERCENT, DEATH CAN OCCUR WITHIN SECONDS.
MOREL KEPT CONSUMING THE OXYGEN IN THE SEALED CHURCH...
...CONVERTING IT INTO CARBON DIOXIDE AT AN EXTRAORDINARY RATE.
MY ATTACKS BEGAN EVEN BEFORE YOURS.
IF WHAT HE SAID WAS TRUE, GRACHAN SHOULD GET HIS ABILITY BACK NOW.
BLP
BLP

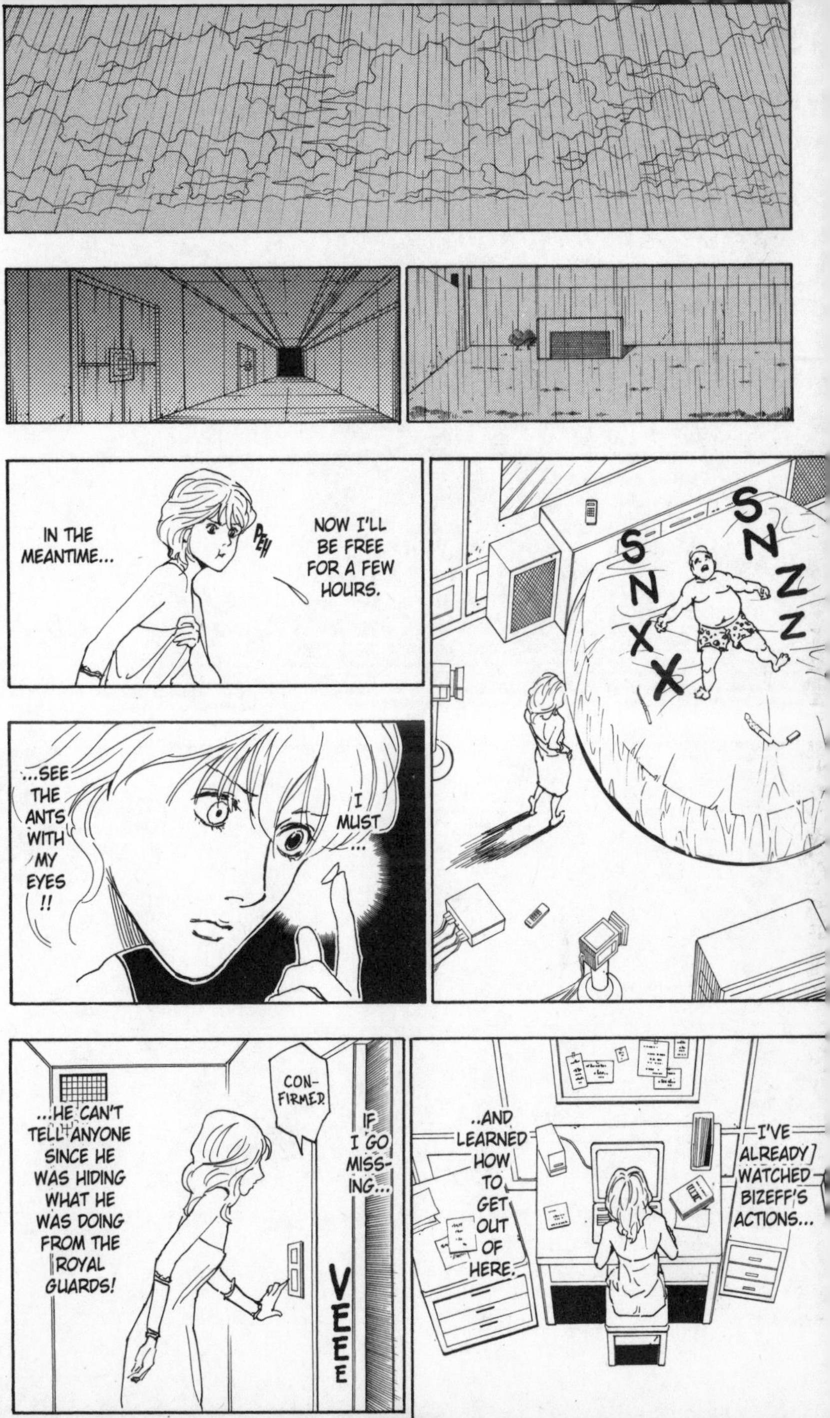
SNZZ
SNXX
NOW I'LL BE FREE FOR A FEW HOURS.
PEH
IN THE MEANTIME...
I MUST...
...SEE THE ANTS WITH MY EYES!!
I'VE ALREADY WATCHED BIZEFF'S ACTIONS...
..AND LEARNED HOW TO GET OUT OF HERE.
CON-FIRMED.
IF I GO MISS-ING...
VEEE
...HE CAN'T TELL ANYONE SINCE HE WAS HIDING WHAT HE WAS DOING FROM THE ROYAL GUARDS!

READ THIS WAY

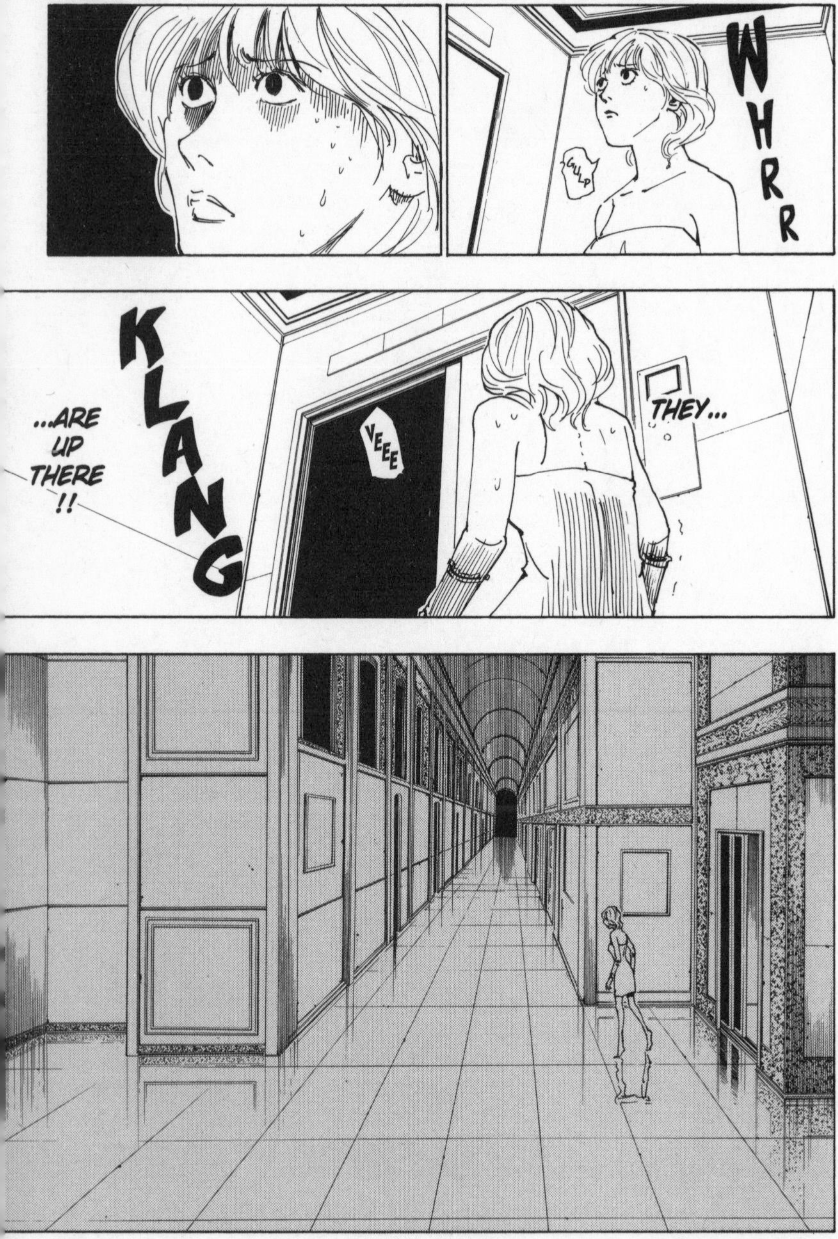
WHRR
GULP
THEY...
VEEE
KLANG
...ARE UP THERE!!

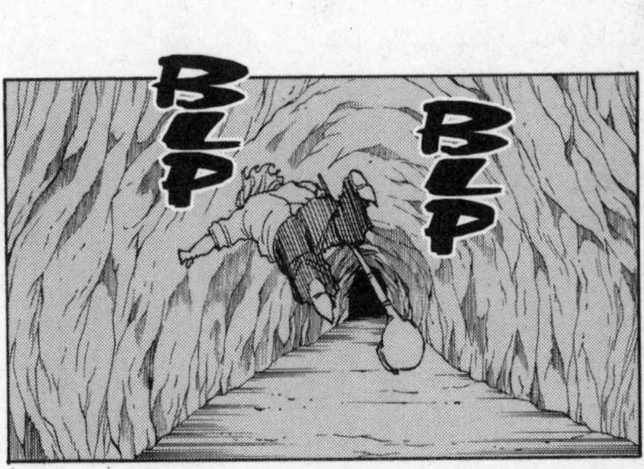
BLP
BLP

Chapter 255: 5: Part 1 to 2: Part 1

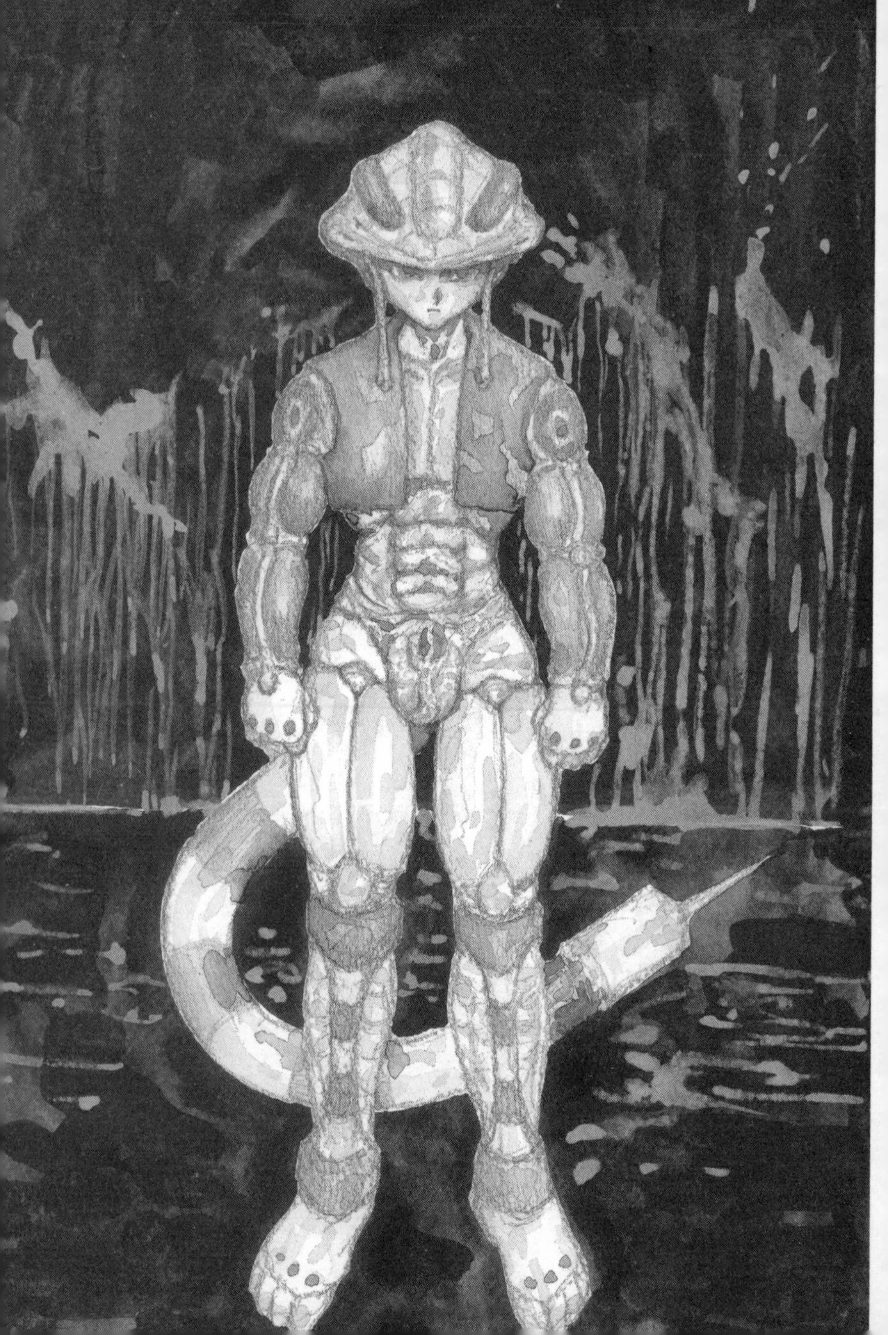

Chapter 255: 5: Part 1 to 2: Part 1

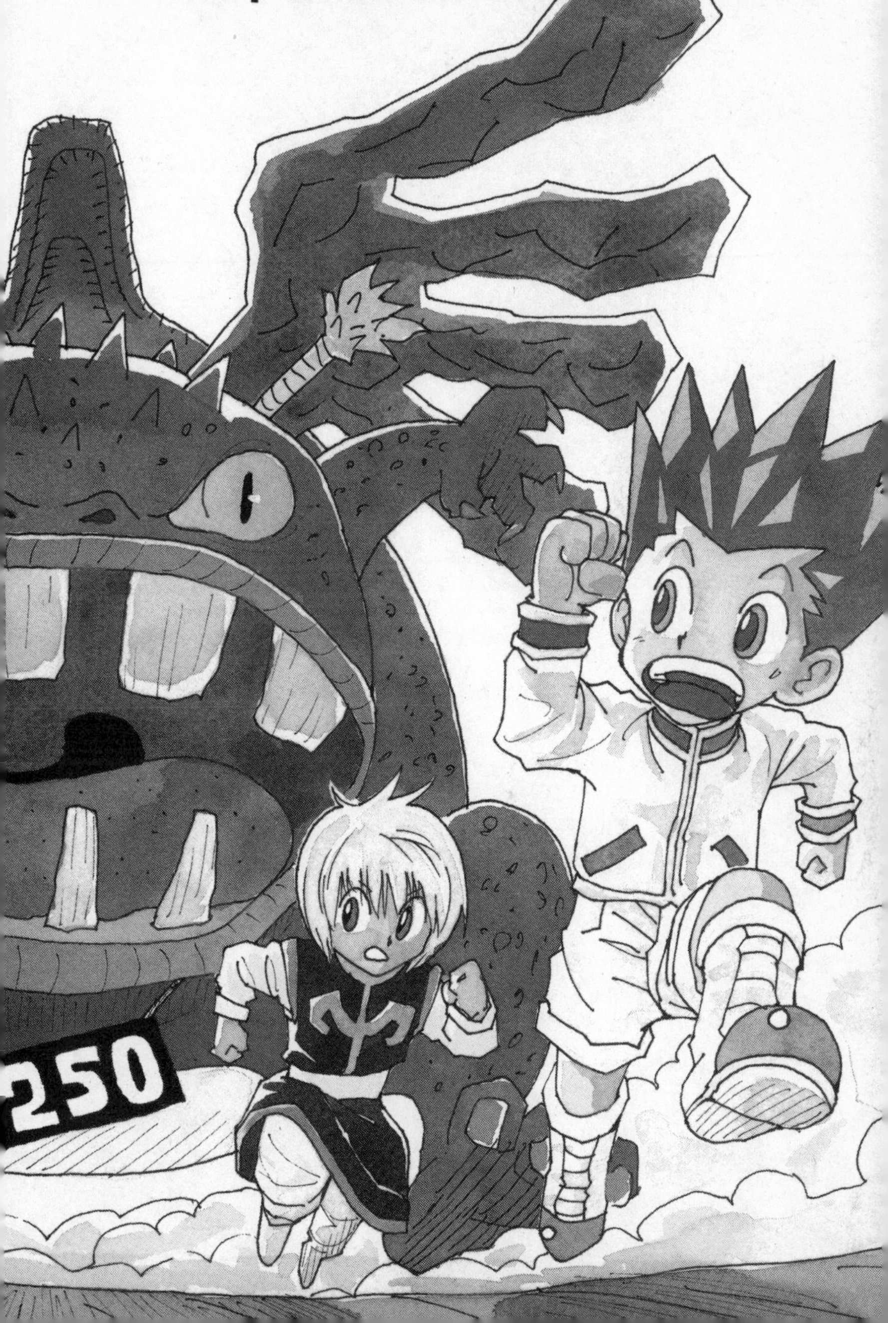
250

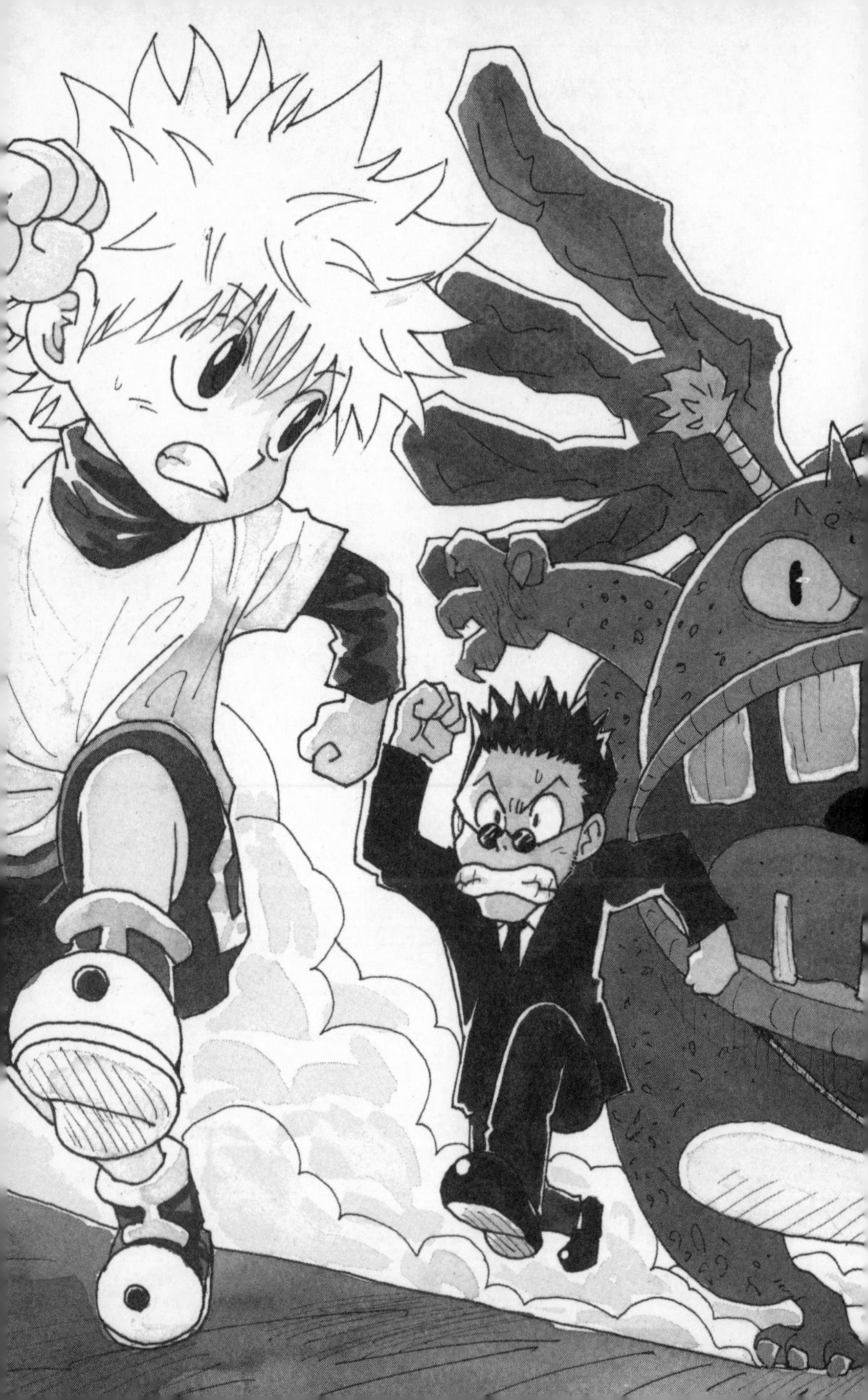

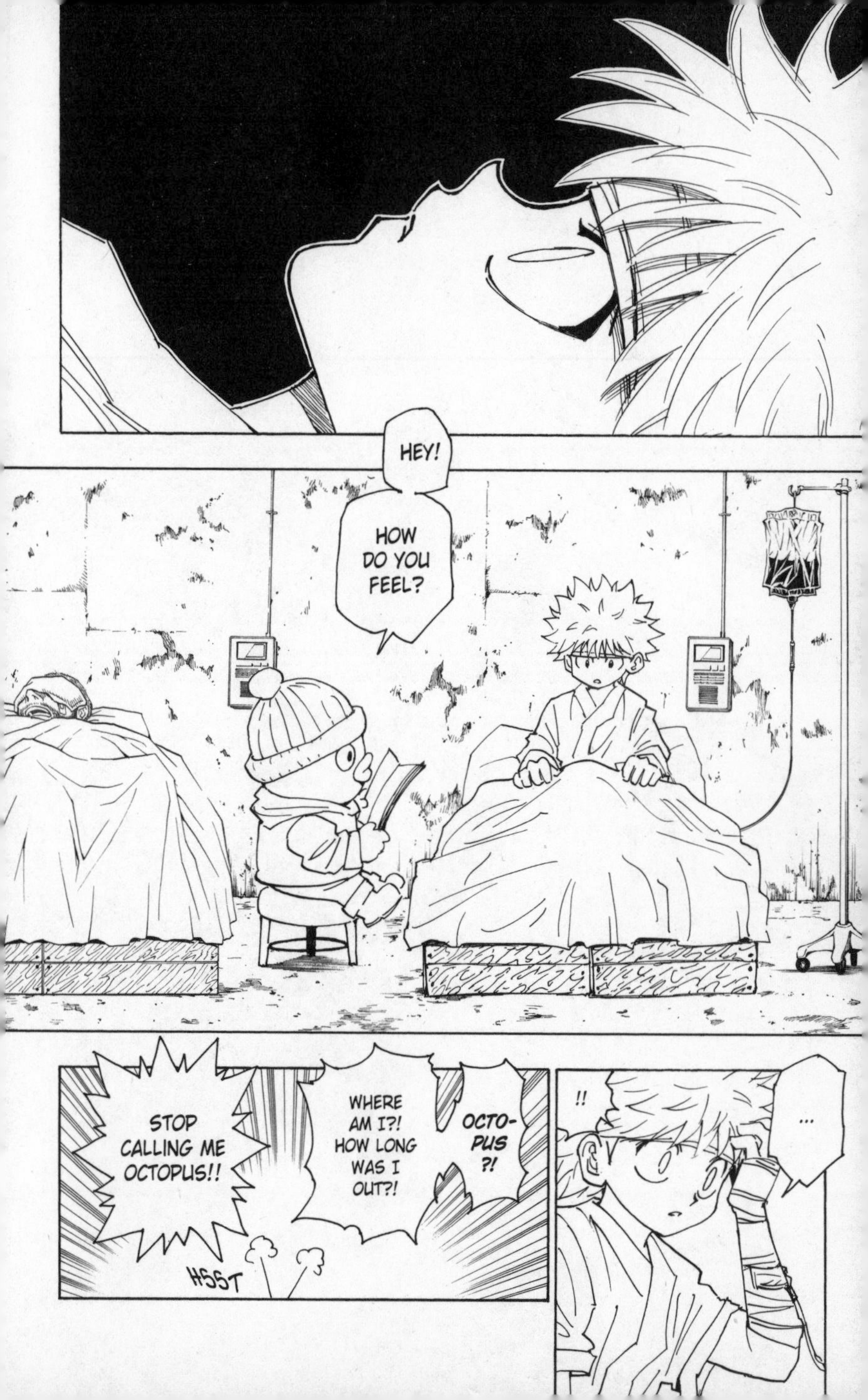
HEY!
HOW DO YOU FEEL?
...
!!
OCTO-PUS?!
WHERE AM I?! HOW LONG WAS I OUT?!
STOP CALLING ME OCTOPUS!!
HSST

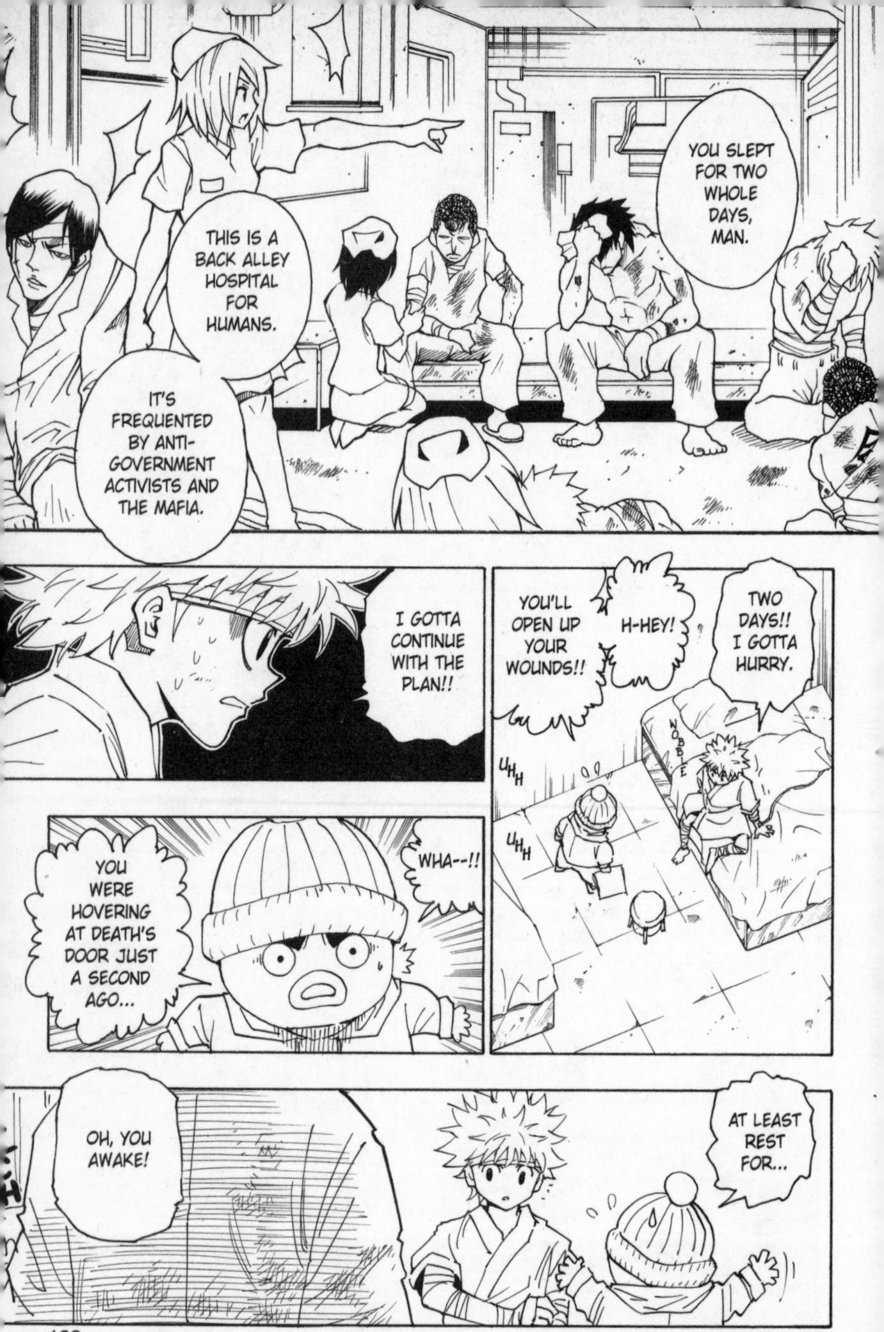
YOU SLEPT FOR TWO WHOLE DAYS, MAN.
THIS IS A BACK ALLEY HOSPITAL FOR HUMANS.
IT'S FREQUENTED BY ANTI-GOVERNMENT ACTIVISTS AND THE MAFIA.
TWO DAYS!! I GOTTA HURRY.
H-HEY!
YOU'LL OPEN UP YOUR WOUNDS!!
WOBBLE
UHH
UHH
I GOTTA CONTINUE WITH THE PLAN!!
WHA--!!
YOU WERE HOVERING AT DEATH'S DOOR JUST A SECOND AGO...
AT LEAST REST FOR...
OH, YOU AWAKE!

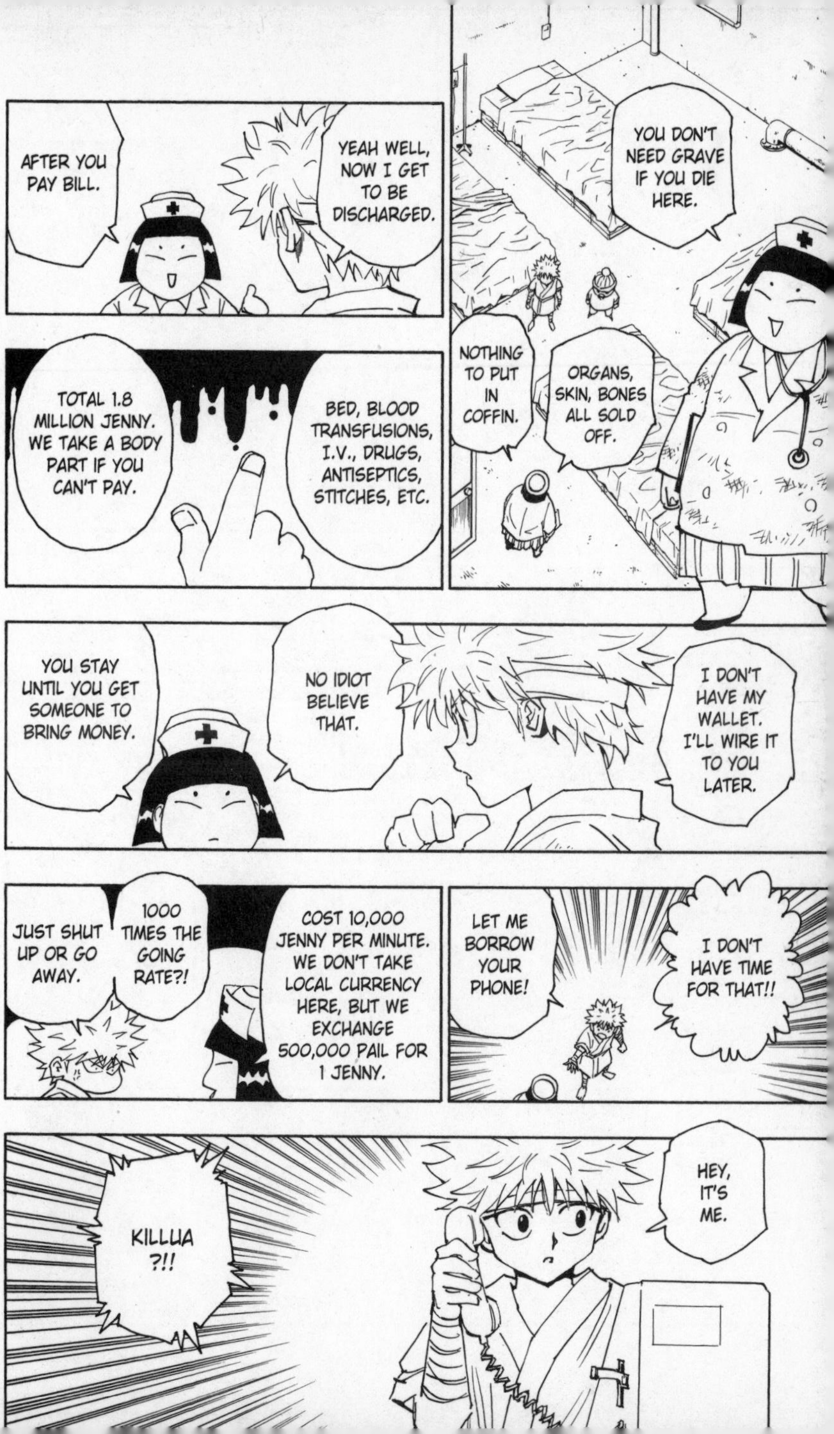
YOU DON'T NEED GRAVE IF YOU DIE HERE.
ORGANS, SKIN, BONES ALL SOLD OFF.
NOTHING TO PUT IN COFFIN.
YEAH WELL, NOW I GET TO BE DISCHARGED.
AFTER YOU PAY BILL.
BED, BLOOD TRANSFUSIONS, I.V., DRUGS, ANTISEPTICS, STITCHES, ETC.
TOTAL 1.8 MILLION JENNY. WE TAKE A BODY PART IF YOU CAN'T PAY.
I DON'T HAVE MY WALLET. I'LL WIRE IT TO YOU LATER.
NO IDIOT BELIEVE THAT.
YOU STAY UNTIL YOU GET SOMEONE TO BRING MONEY.
I DON'T HAVE TIME FOR THAT!!
LET ME BORROW YOUR PHONE!
COST 10,000 JENNY PER MINUTE. WE DON'T TAKE LOCAL CURRENCY HERE, BUT WE EXCHANGE 500,000 PAIL FOR 1 JENNY.
1000 TIMES THE GOING RATE?!
JUST SHUT UP OR GO AWAY.
HEY, IT'S ME.
KILLUA ?!!

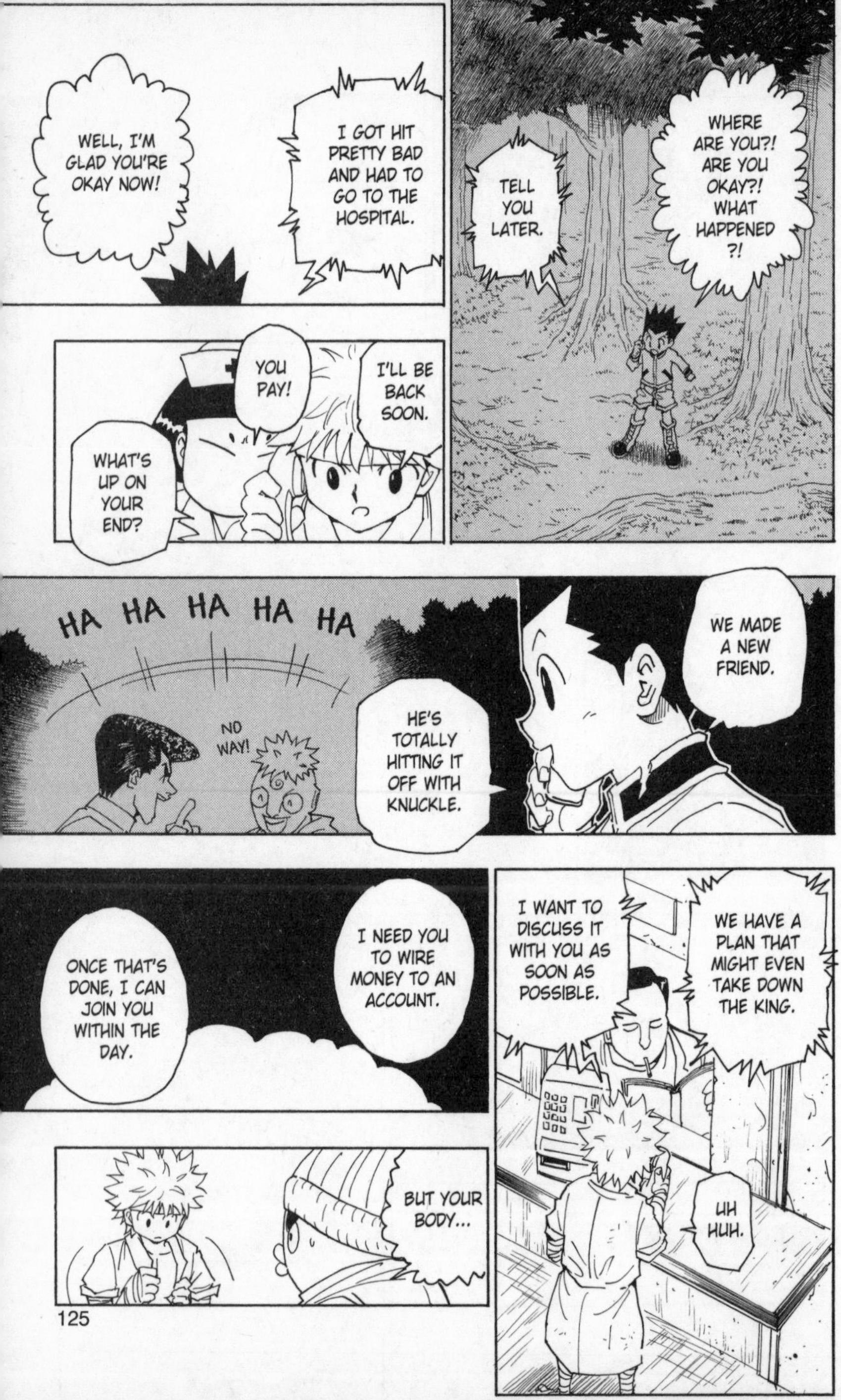
WHERE ARE YOU?! ARE YOU OKAY?! WHAT HAPPENED?!
TELL YOU LATER.
I GOT HIT PRETTY BAD AND HAD TO GO TO THE HOSPITAL.
WELL, I'M GLAD YOU'RE OKAY NOW!
I'LL BE BACK SOON.
YOU PAY!
WHAT'S UP ON YOUR END?
WE MADE A NEW FRIEND.
HE'S TOTALLY HITTING IT OFF WITH KNUCKLE.
HA HA HA HA HA
NO WAY!
WE HAVE A PLAN THAT MIGHT EVEN TAKE DOWN THE KING.
I WANT TO DISCUSS IT WITH YOU AS SOON AS POSSIBLE.
UH HUH.
I NEED YOU TO WIRE MONEY TO AN ACCOUNT.
ONCE THAT'S DONE, I CAN JOIN YOU WITHIN THE DAY.
BUT YOUR BODY...

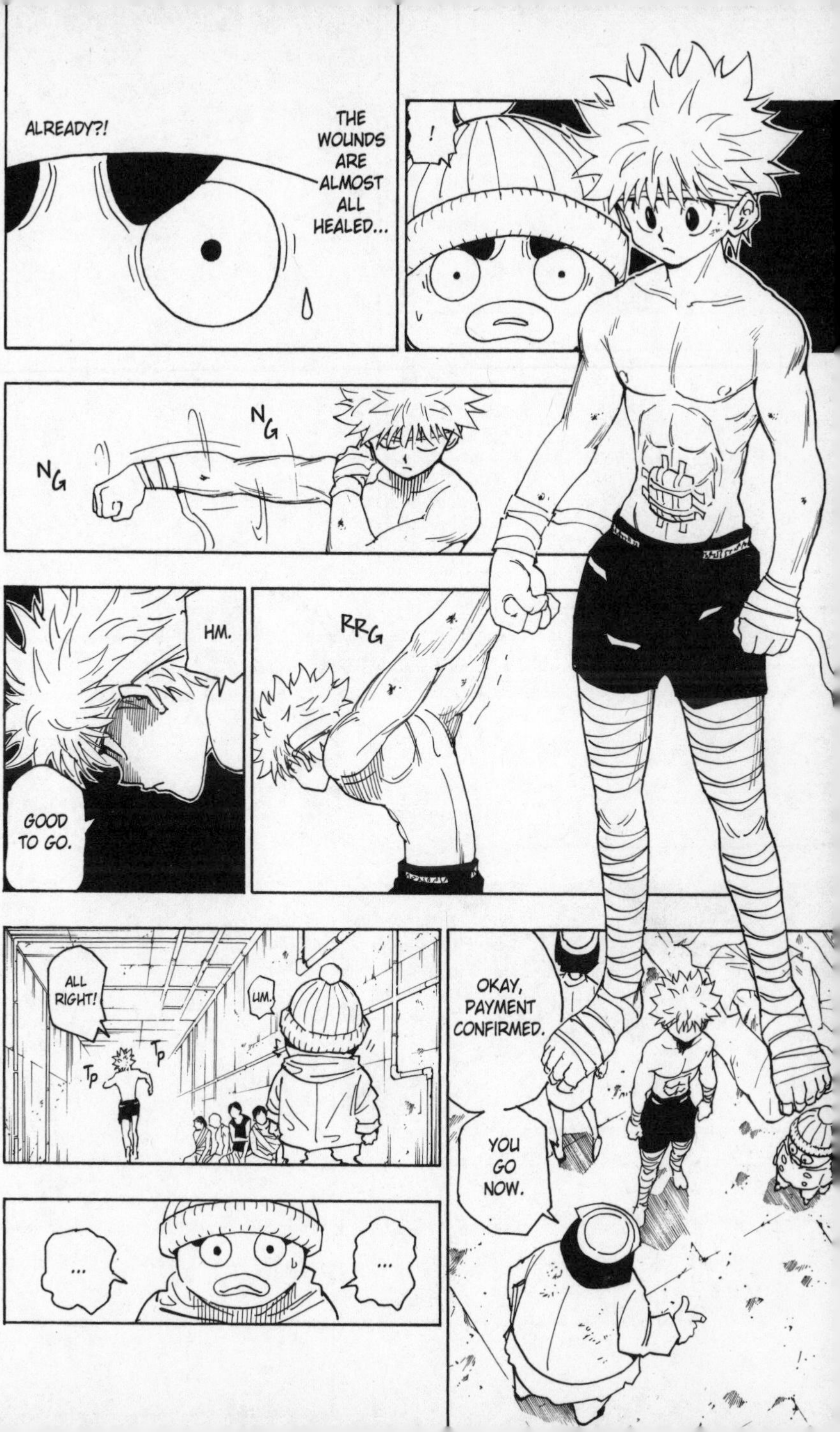
!
THE WOUNDS ARE ALMOST ALL HEALED...
ALREADY?!
NG
NG
RRG
HM.
GOOD TO GO.
OKAY, PAYMENT CONFIRMED.
YOU GO NOW.
ALL RIGHT!
UM.
TP
TP
...
...

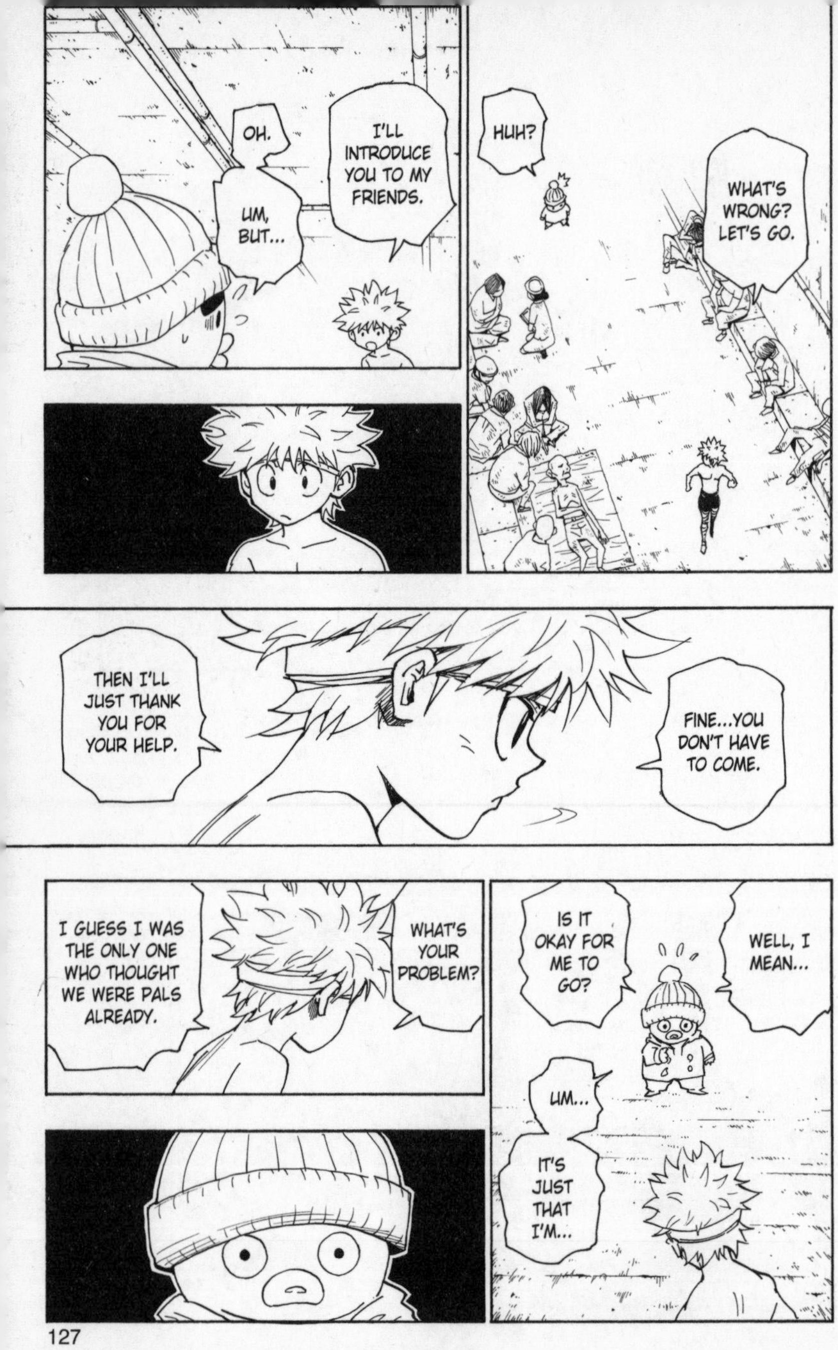
HUH?
WHAT'S WRONG? LET'S GO.
I'LL INTRODUCE YOU TO MY FRIENDS.
OH.
UM, BUT...
FINE...YOU DON'T HAVE TO COME.
THEN I'LL JUST THANK YOU FOR YOUR HELP.
WELL, I MEAN...
IS IT OKAY FOR ME TO GO?
UM...
IT'S JUST THAT I'M...
WHAT'S YOUR PROBLEM?
I GUESS I WAS THE ONLY ONE WHO THOUGHT WE WERE PALS ALREADY.

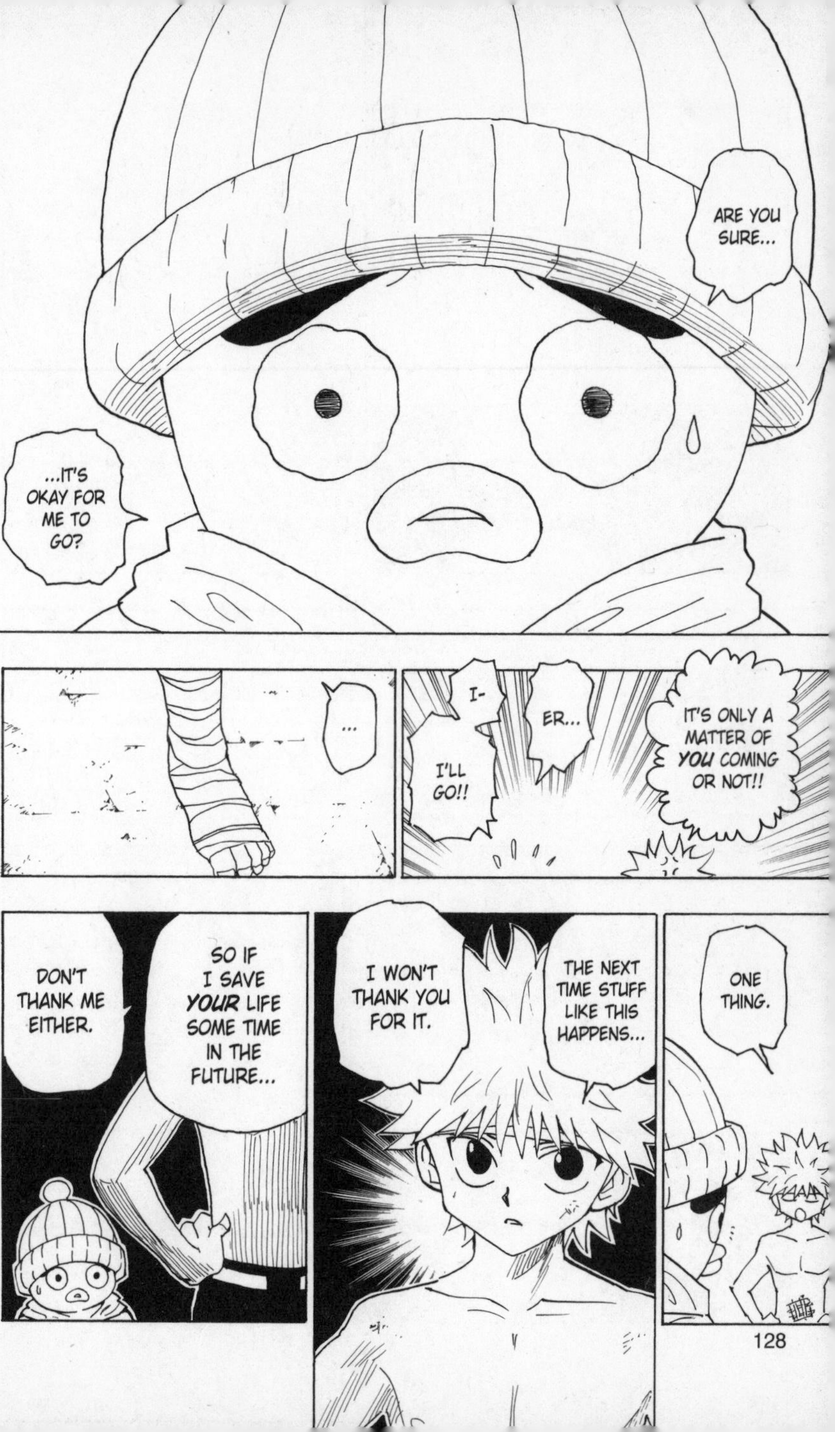
ARE YOU SURE...
...IT'S OKAY FOR ME TO GO?
IT'S ONLY A MATTER OF **YOU** COMING OR NOT!!
ER...
I-
I'LL GO!!
...
ONE THING.
THE NEXT TIME STUFF LIKE THIS HAPPENS...
I WON'T THANK YOU FOR IT.
SO IF I SAVE **YOUR** LIFE SOME TIME IN THE FUTURE...
DON'T THANK ME EITHER.

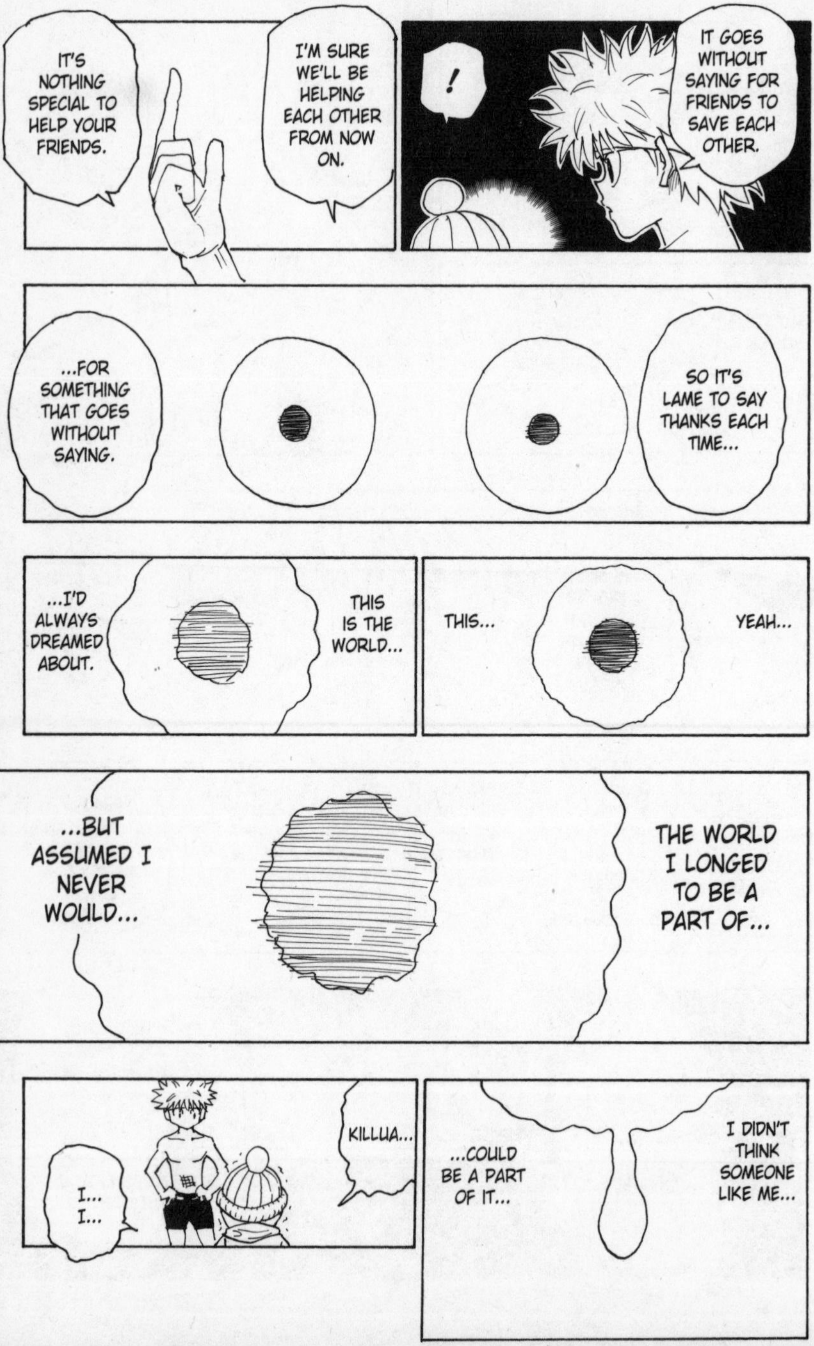
IT GOES WITHOUT SAYING FOR FRIENDS TO SAVE EACH OTHER.
!
I'M SURE WE'LL BE HELPING EACH OTHER FROM NOW ON.
IT'S NOTHING SPECIAL TO HELP YOUR FRIENDS.
SO IT'S LAME TO SAY THANKS EACH TIME...
...FOR SOMETHING THAT GOES WITHOUT SAYING.
YEAH...
THIS...
THIS IS THE WORLD...
...I'D ALWAYS DREAMED ABOUT.
THE WORLD I LONGED TO BE A PART OF...
...BUT ASSUMED I NEVER WOULD...
I DIDN'T THINK SOMEONE LIKE ME...
...COULD BE A PART OF IT...
KILLUA...
I... I...

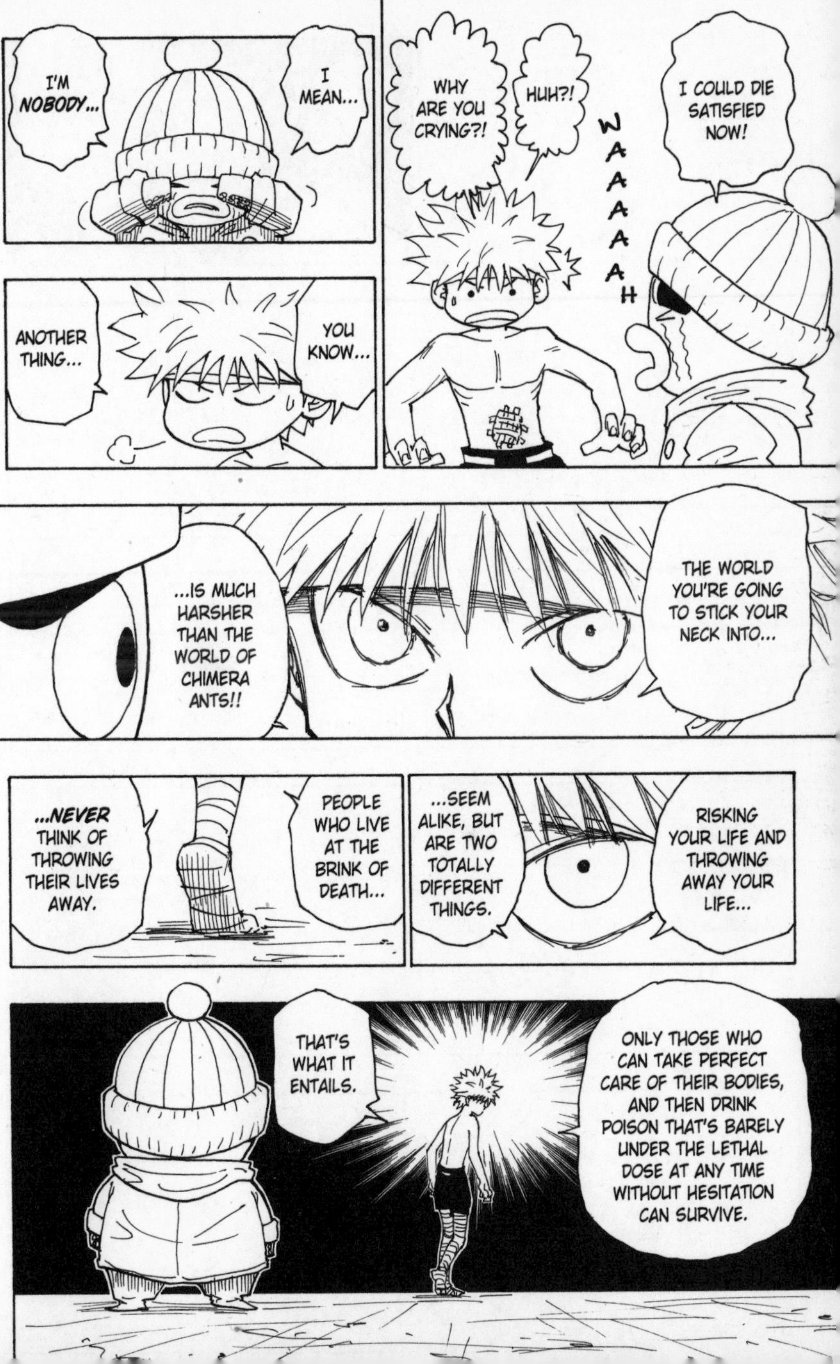
I COULD DIE SATISFIED NOW!
WAAAAAH
HUH?!
WHY ARE YOU CRYING?!
I MEAN...
I'M *NOBODY*...
YOU KNOW...
ANOTHER THING...
THE WORLD YOU'RE GOING TO STICK YOUR NECK INTO...
...IS MUCH HARSHER THAN THE WORLD OF CHIMERA ANTS!!
RISKING YOUR LIFE AND THROWING AWAY YOUR LIFE...
...SEEM ALIKE, BUT ARE TWO TOTALLY DIFFERENT THINGS.
PEOPLE WHO LIVE AT THE BRINK OF DEATH...
...NEVER THINK OF THROWING THEIR LIVES AWAY.
ONLY THOSE WHO CAN TAKE PERFECT CARE OF THEIR BODIES, AND THEN DRINK POISON THAT'S BARELY UNDER THE LETHAL DOSE AT ANY TIME WITHOUT HESITATION CAN SURVIVE.
THAT'S WHAT IT ENTAILS.

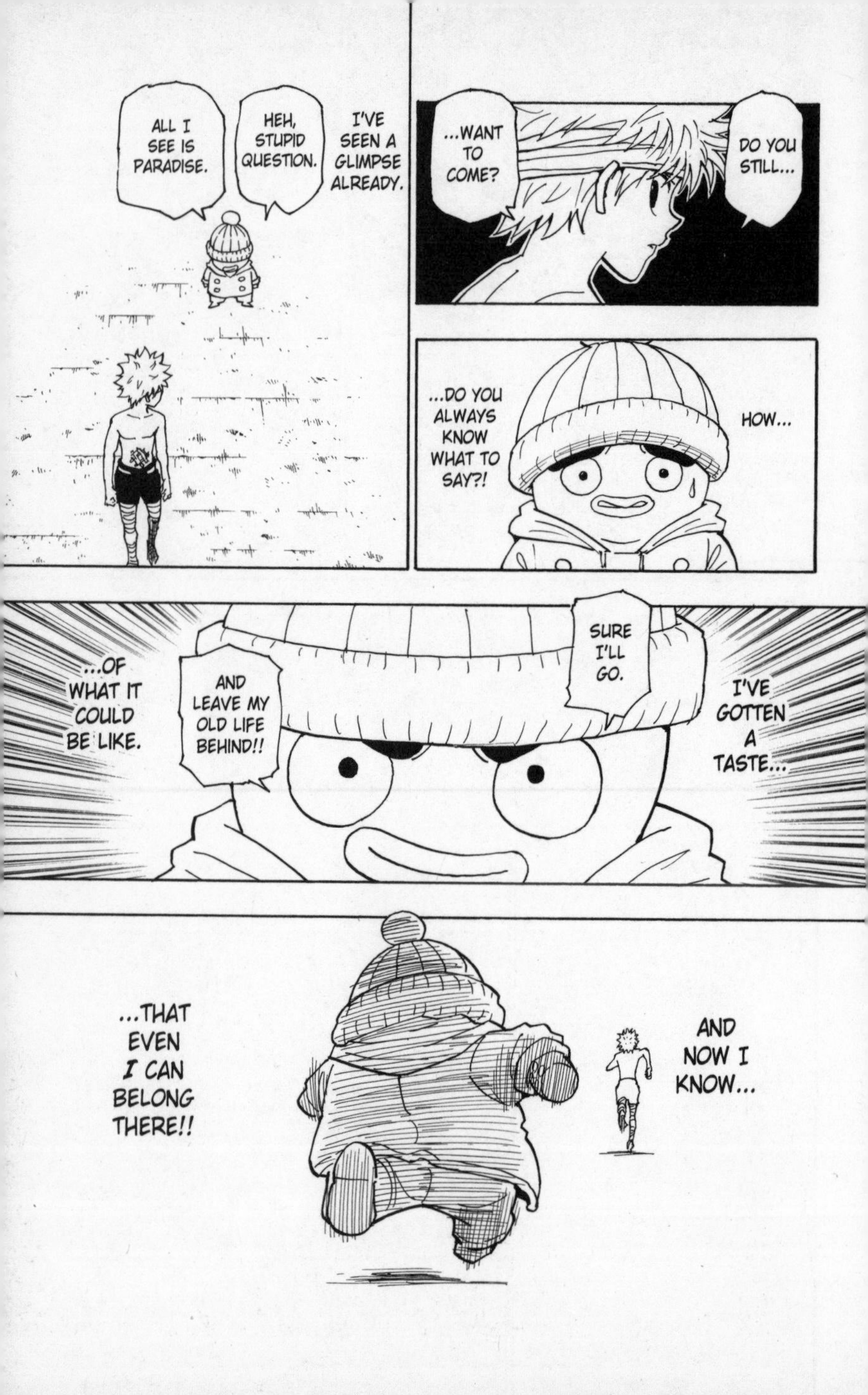
DO YOU STILL...
...WANT TO COME?
HOW...
...DO YOU ALWAYS KNOW WHAT TO SAY?!
I'VE SEEN A GLIMPSE ALREADY.
HEH, STUPID QUESTION.
ALL I SEE IS PARADISE.
I'VE GOTTEN A TASTE...
SURE I'LL GO.
AND LEAVE MY OLD LIFE BEHIND!!
...OF WHAT IT COULD BE LIKE.
AND NOW I KNOW...
...THAT EVEN *I* CAN BELONG THERE!!

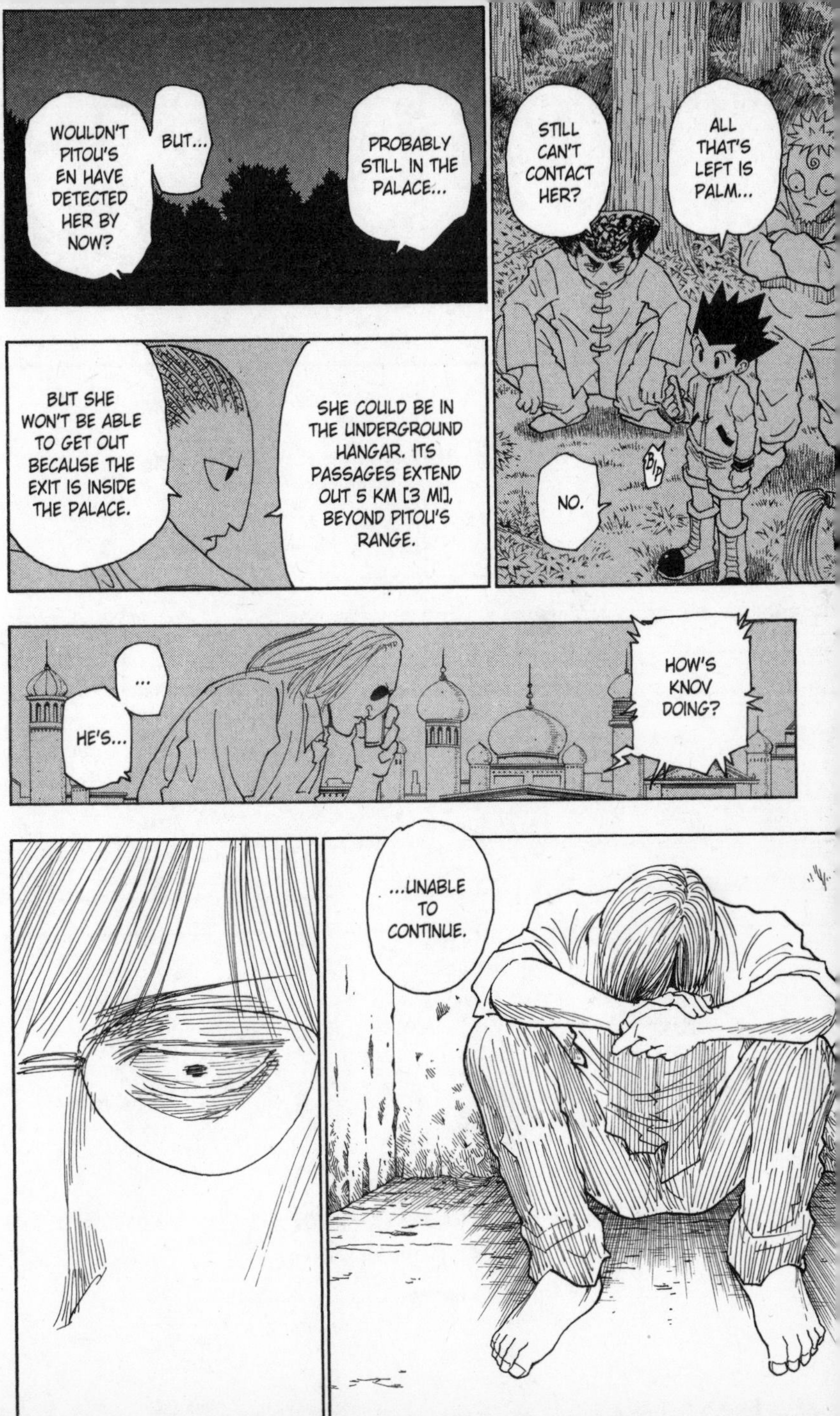
ALL THAT'S LEFT IS PALM...
STILL CAN'T CONTACT HER?
BIP
NO.
PROBABLY STILL IN THE PALACE...
BUT...
WOULDN'T PITOU'S EN HAVE DETECTED HER BY NOW?
SHE COULD BE IN THE UNDERGROUND HANGAR. ITS PASSAGES EXTEND OUT 5 KM [3 MI], BEYOND PITOU'S RANGE.
BUT SHE WON'T BE ABLE TO GET OUT BECAUSE THE EXIT IS INSIDE THE PALACE.
HOW'S KNOV DOING?
...
HE'S...
...UNABLE TO CONTINUE.

READ THIS WAY

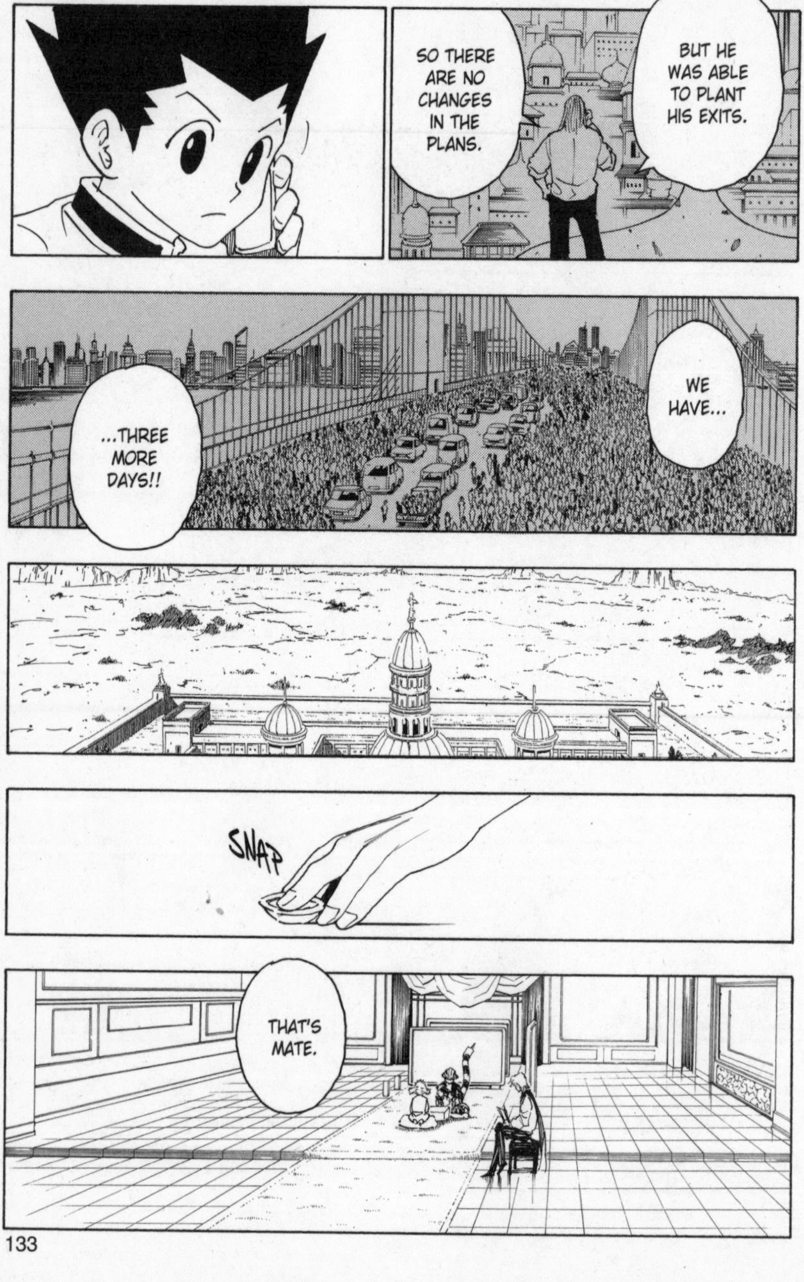

BUT HE WAS ABLE TO PLANT HIS EXITS.
SO THERE ARE NO CHANGES IN THE PLANS.
WE HAVE...
...THREE MORE DAYS!!
SNAP
THAT'S MATE.

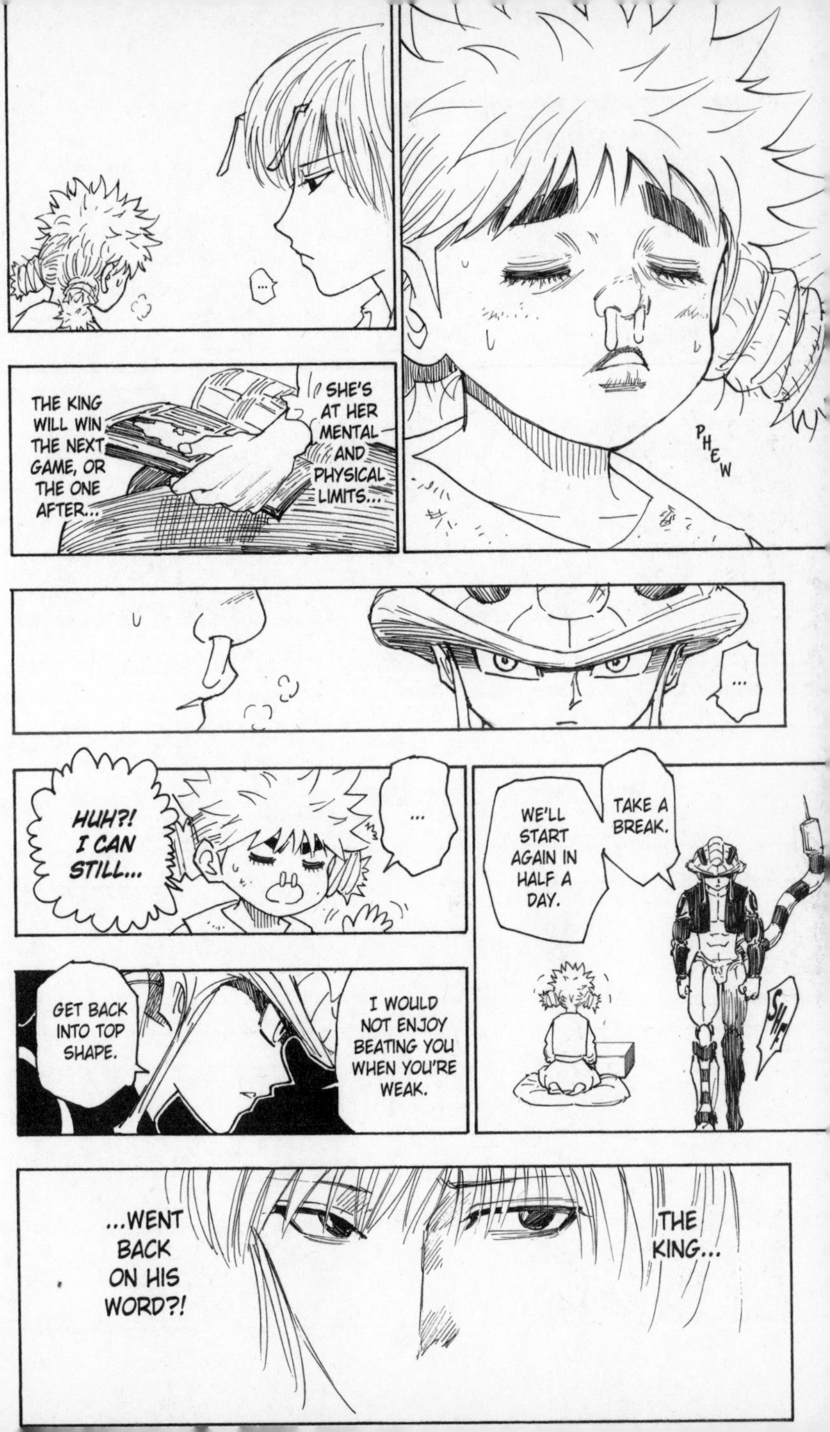
PHEW
...
SHE'S AT HER MENTAL AND PHYSICAL LIMITS...
THE KING WILL WIN THE NEXT GAME, OR THE ONE AFTER...
...
TAKE A BREAK.
WE'LL START AGAIN IN HALF A DAY.
SHF
...
HUH?! I CAN STILL...
I WOULD NOT ENJOY BEATING YOU WHEN YOU'RE WEAK.
GET BACK INTO TOP SHAPE.
THE KING...
...WENT BACK ON HIS WORD?!

READ THIS WAY

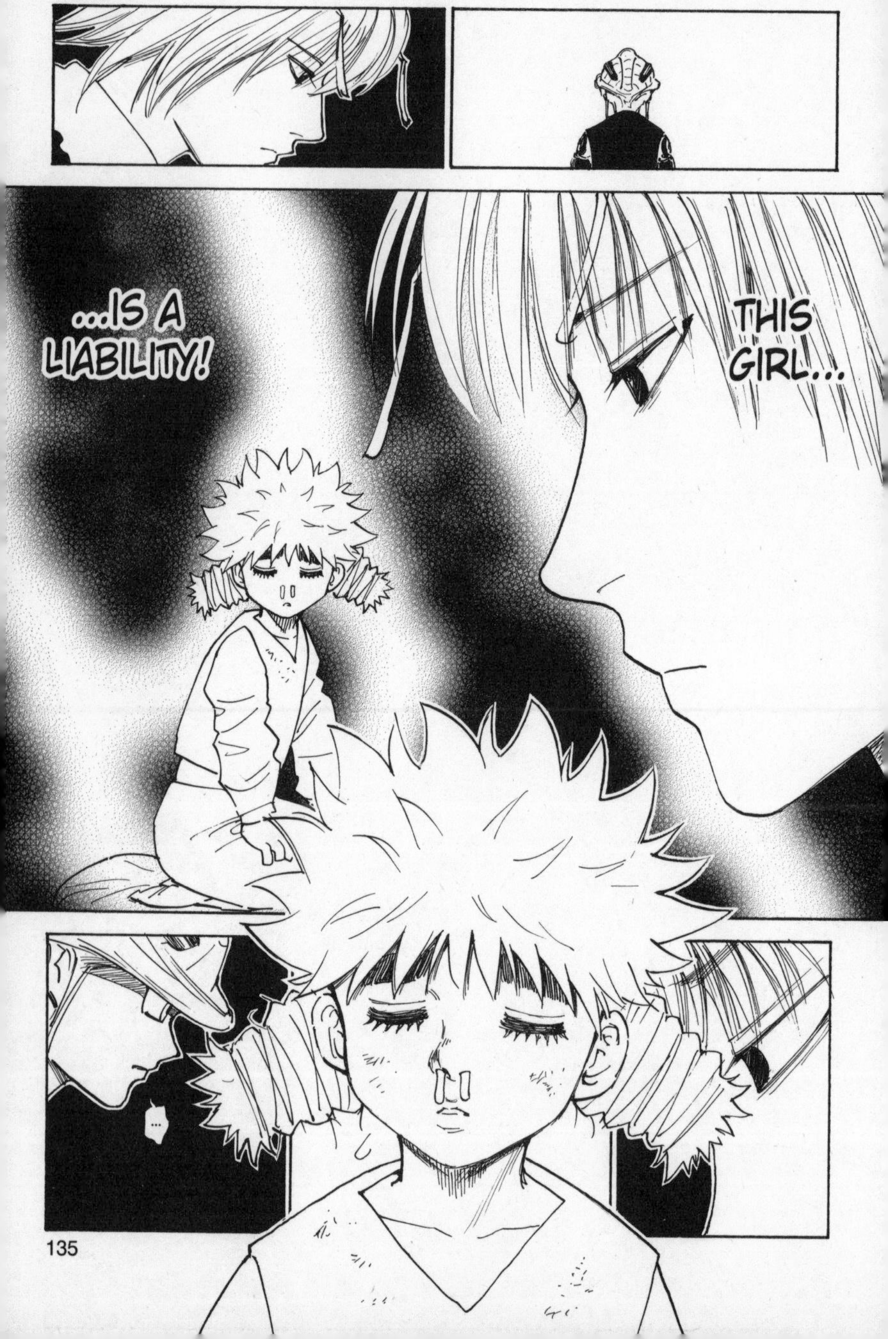
THIS GIRL...
...IS A LIABILITY!
...

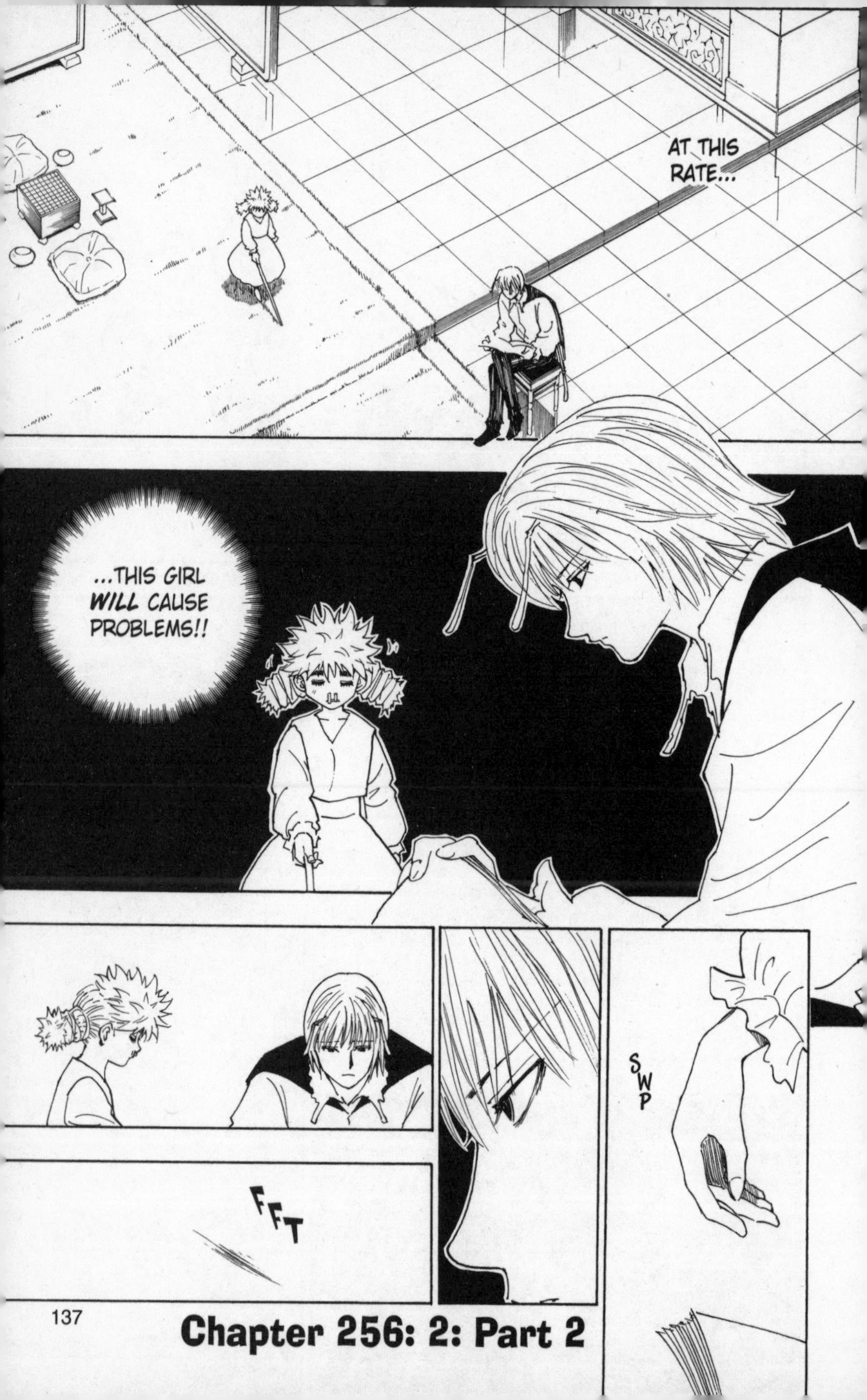
AT THIS RATE...
...THIS GIRL *WILL* CAUSE PROBLEMS!!
SWP
FFT

Chapter 256: 2: Part 2

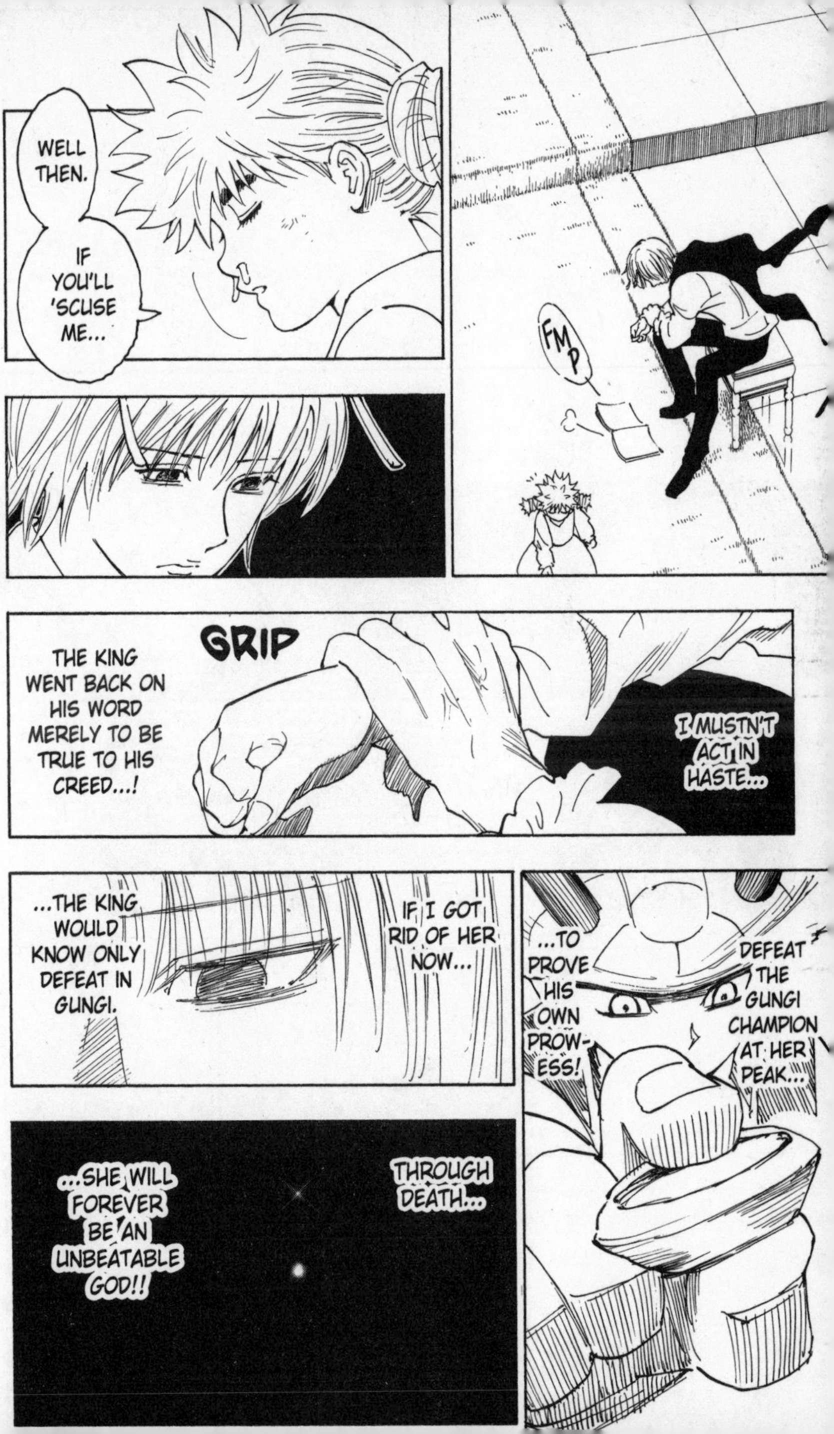
FMP
WELL THEN.
IF YOU'LL 'SCUSE ME...
GRIP
I MUSTN'T ACT IN HASTE...
THE KING WENT BACK ON HIS WORD MERELY TO BE TRUE TO HIS CREED...!
DEFEAT THE GUNGI CHAMPION AT HER PEAK...
...TO PROVE HIS OWN PROW-ESS!
IF I GOT RID OF HER NOW...
...THE KING WOULD KNOW ONLY DEFEAT IN GUNGI.
THROUGH DEATH...
...SHE WILL FOREVER BE AN UNBEATABLE GOD!!

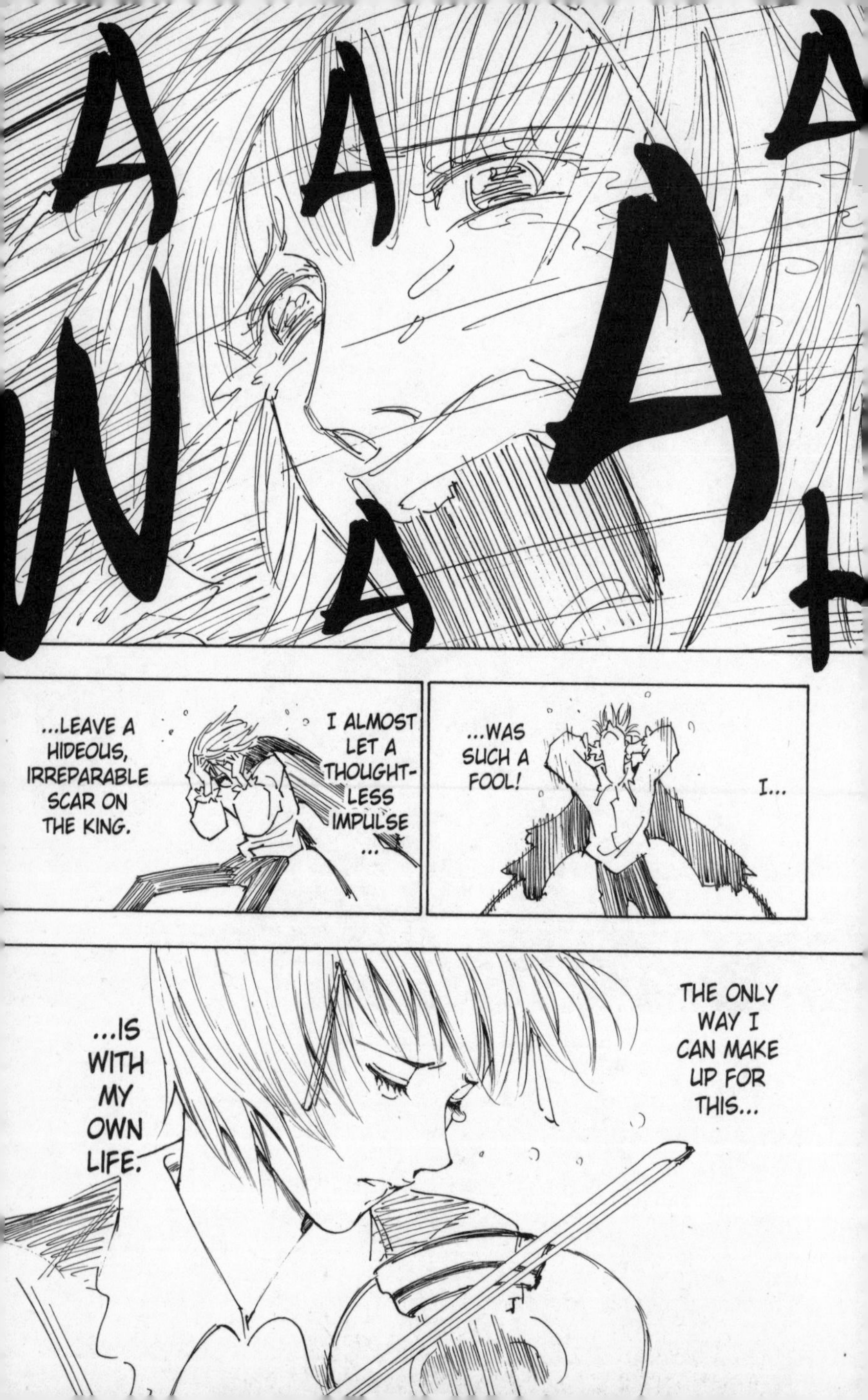
I...
...WAS SUCH A FOOL!
I ALMOST LET A THOUGHTLESS IMPULSE...
...LEAVE A HIDEOUS, IRREPARABLE SCAR ON THE KING.
THE ONLY WAY I CAN MAKE UP FOR THIS...
...IS WITH MY OWN LIFE.

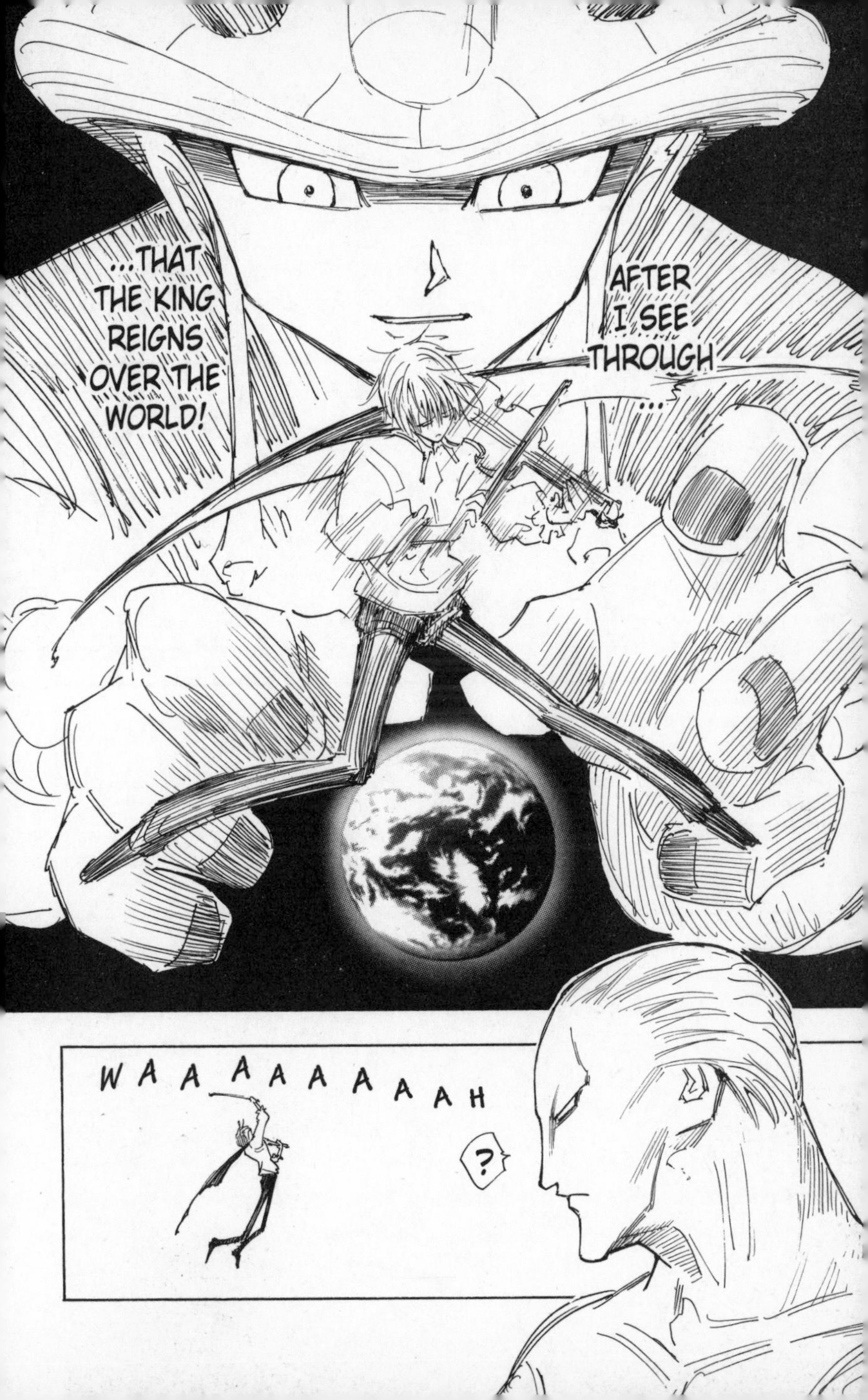
AFTER I SEE THROUGH...
...THAT THE KING REIGNS OVER THE WORLD!
WAAAAAAAAAH
?

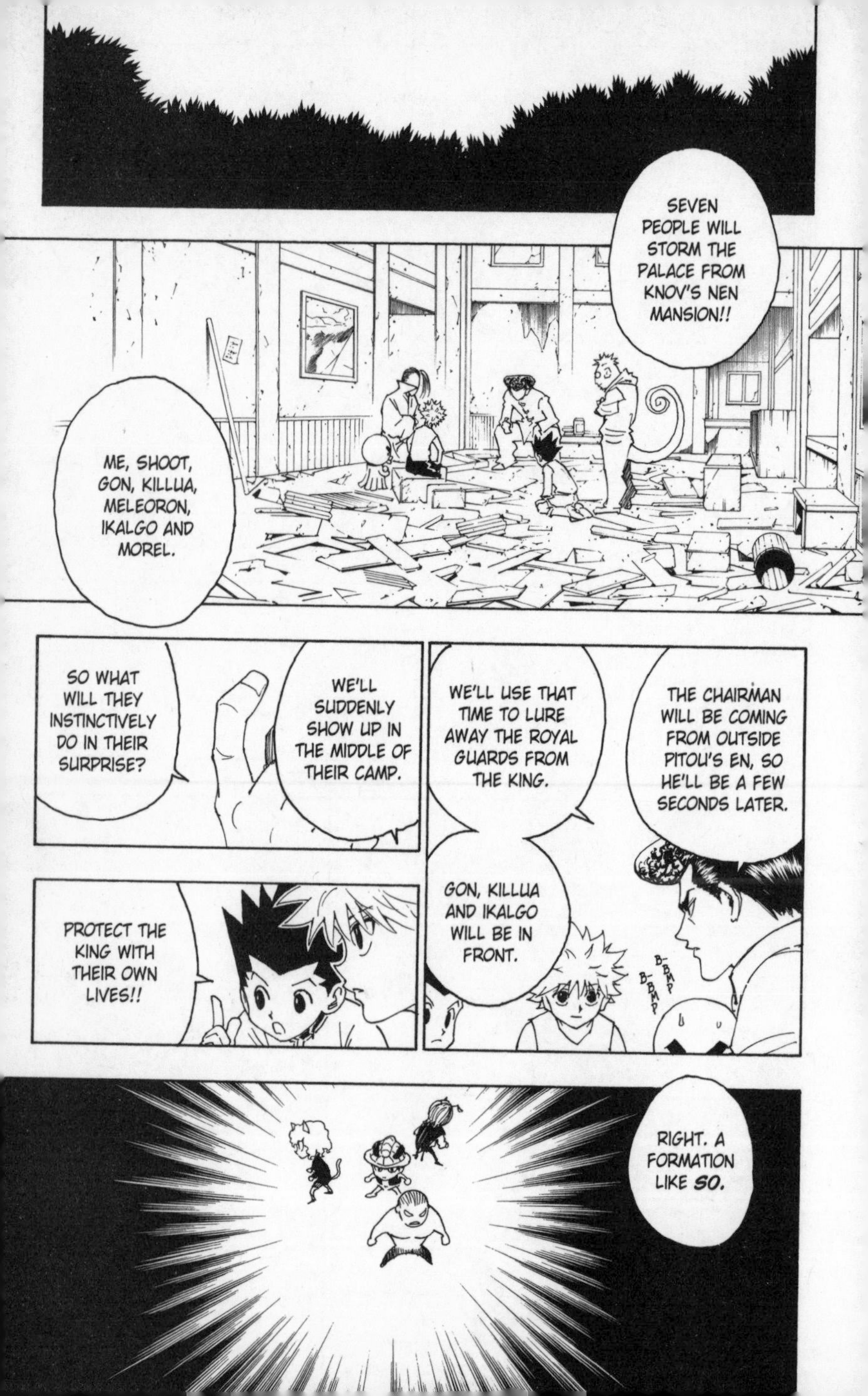
SEVEN PEOPLE WILL STORM THE PALACE FROM KNOV'S NEN MANSION!!
ME, SHOOT, GON, KILLUA, MELEORON, IKALGO AND MOREL.
THE CHAIRMAN WILL BE COMING FROM OUTSIDE PITOU'S EN, SO HE'LL BE A FEW SECONDS LATER.
WE'LL USE THAT TIME TO LURE AWAY THE ROYAL GUARDS FROM THE KING.
GON, KILLUA AND IKALGO WILL BE IN FRONT.
B-BMP
B-BMP
WE'LL SUDDENLY SHOW UP IN THE MIDDLE OF THEIR CAMP.
SO WHAT WILL THEY INSTINCTIVELY DO IN THEIR SURPRISE?
PROTECT THE KING WITH THEIR OWN LIVES!!
RIGHT. A FORMATION LIKE *SO.*

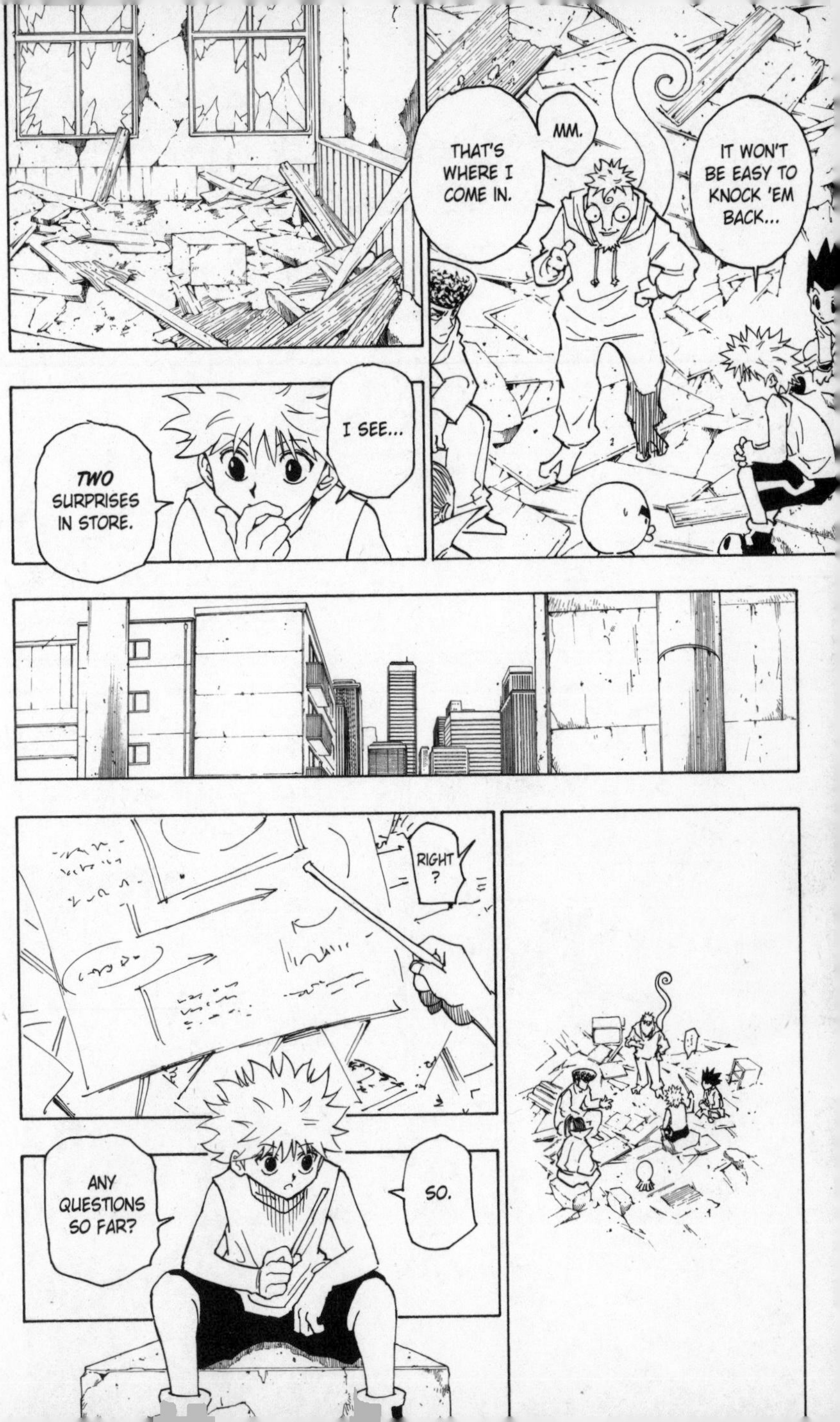
IT WON'T BE EASY TO KNOCK 'EM BACK...
MM.
THAT'S WHERE I COME IN.
I SEE...
TWO SURPRISES IN STORE.
RIGHT?
SO.
ANY QUESTIONS SO FAR?

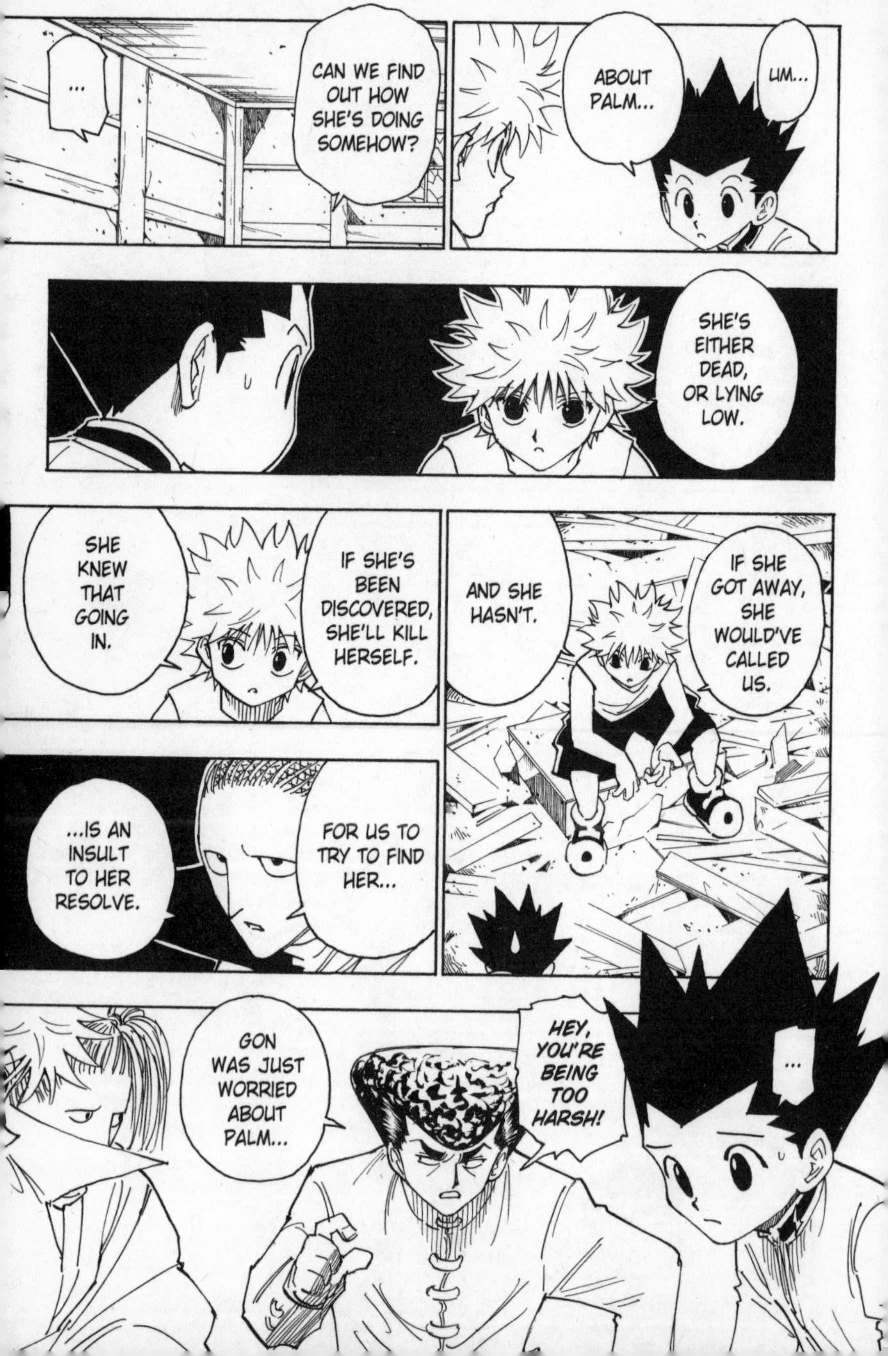
UM...
ABOUT PALM...
CAN WE FIND OUT HOW SHE'S DOING SOMEHOW?
...
SHE'S EITHER DEAD, OR LYING LOW.
IF SHE GOT AWAY, SHE WOULD'VE CALLED US.
AND SHE HASN'T.
IF SHE'S BEEN DISCOVERED, SHE'LL KILL HERSELF.
SHE KNEW THAT GOING IN.
FOR US TO TRY TO FIND HER...
...IS AN INSULT TO HER RESOLVE.
...
HEY, YOU'RE BEING TOO HARSH!
GON WAS JUST WORRIED ABOUT PALM...

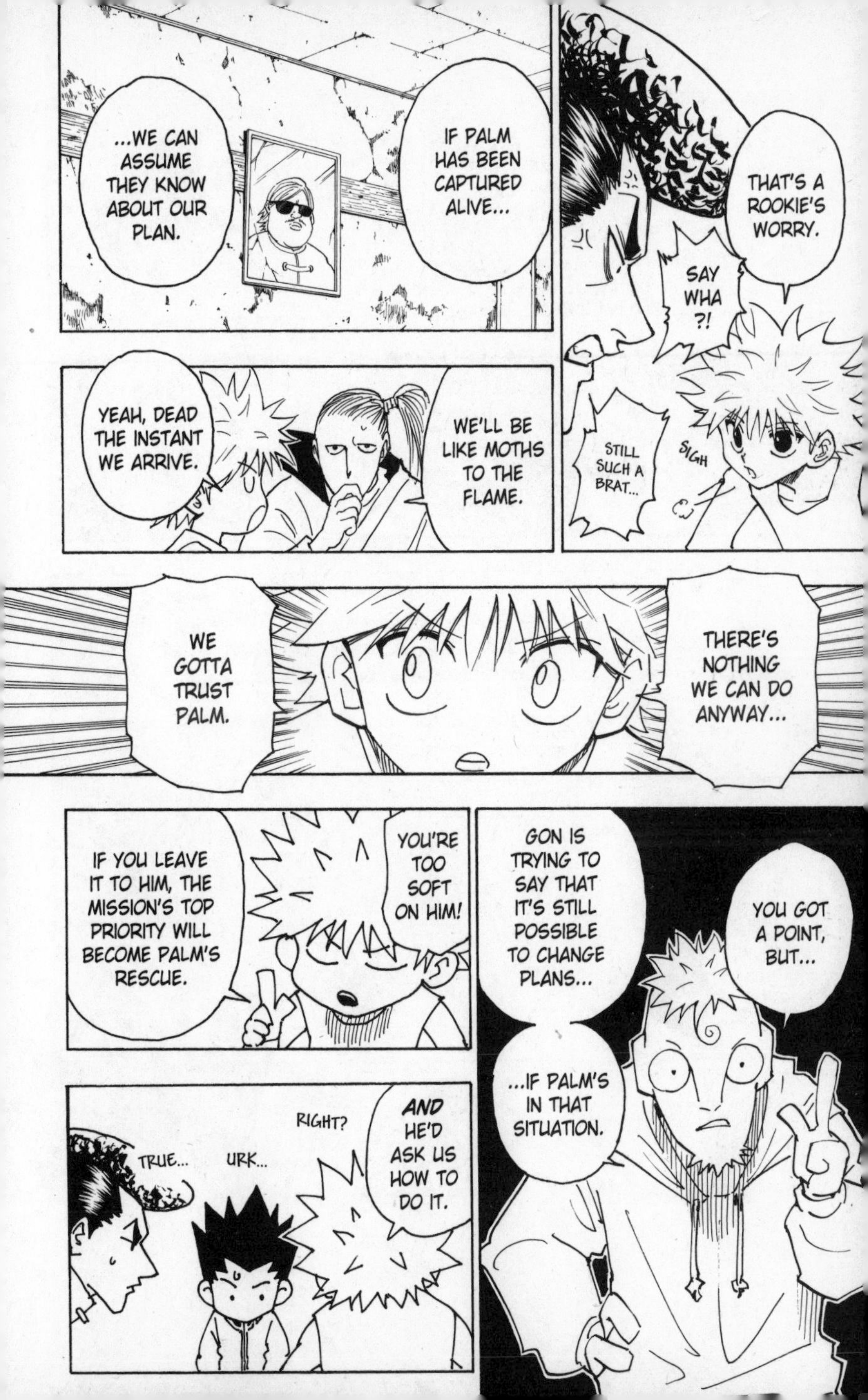

THAT'S A ROOKIE'S WORRY.
SAY WHA ?!
STILL SUCH A BRAT...
SIGH
IF PALM HAS BEEN CAPTURED ALIVE...
...WE CAN ASSUME THEY KNOW ABOUT OUR PLAN.
WE'LL BE LIKE MOTHS TO THE FLAME.
YEAH, DEAD THE INSTANT WE ARRIVE.
THERE'S NOTHING WE CAN DO ANYWAY...
WE GOTTA TRUST PALM.
YOU GOT A POINT, BUT...
GON IS TRYING TO SAY THAT IT'S STILL POSSIBLE TO CHANGE PLANS...
...IF PALM'S IN THAT SITUATION.
YOU'RE TOO SOFT ON HIM!
IF YOU LEAVE IT TO HIM, THE MISSION'S TOP PRIORITY WILL BECOME PALM'S RESCUE.
AND HE'D ASK US HOW TO DO IT.
RIGHT?
URK...
TRUE...

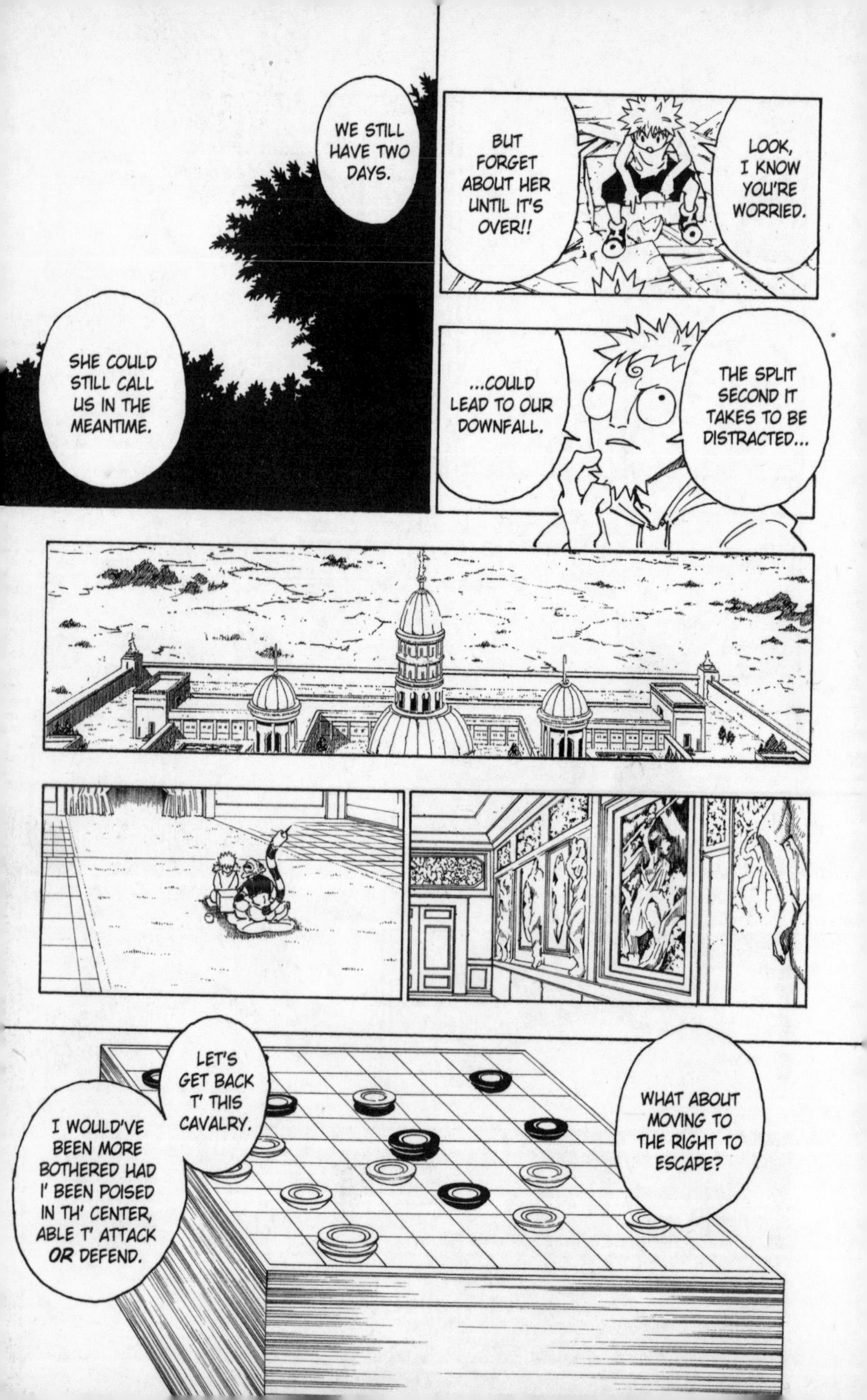
LOOK, I KNOW YOU'RE WORRIED.
BUT FORGET ABOUT HER UNTIL IT'S OVER!!
THE SPLIT SECOND IT TAKES TO BE DISTRACTED...
...COULD LEAD TO OUR DOWNFALL.
WE STILL HAVE TWO DAYS.
SHE COULD STILL CALL US IN THE MEANTIME.
WHAT ABOUT MOVING TO THE RIGHT TO ESCAPE?
LET'S GET BACK T' THIS CAVALRY.
I WOULD'VE BEEN MORE BOTHERED HAD I' BEEN POISED IN TH' CENTER, ABLE T' ATTACK **OR** DEFEND.

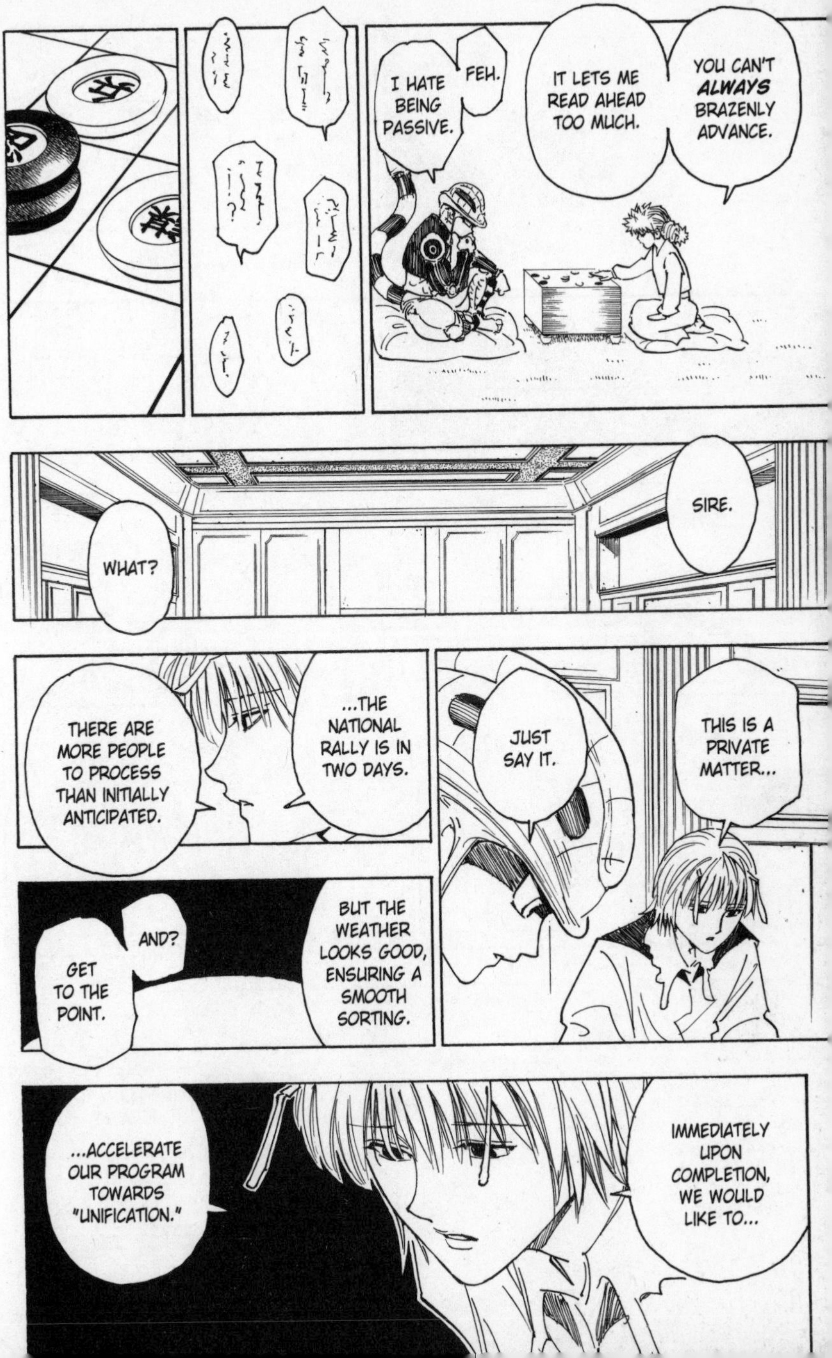
YOU CAN'T ***ALWAYS*** BRAZENLY ADVANCE.
IT LETS ME READ AHEAD TOO MUCH.
FEH.
I HATE BEING PASSIVE.
SIRE.
WHAT?
THIS IS A PRIVATE MATTER...
JUST SAY IT.
...THE NATIONAL RALLY IS IN TWO DAYS.
THERE ARE MORE PEOPLE TO PROCESS THAN INITIALLY ANTICIPATED.
BUT THE WEATHER LOOKS GOOD, ENSURING A SMOOTH SORTING.
AND?
GET TO THE POINT.
IMMEDIATELY UPON COMPLETION, WE WOULD LIKE TO...
...ACCELERATE OUR PROGRAM TOWARDS "UNIFICATION."

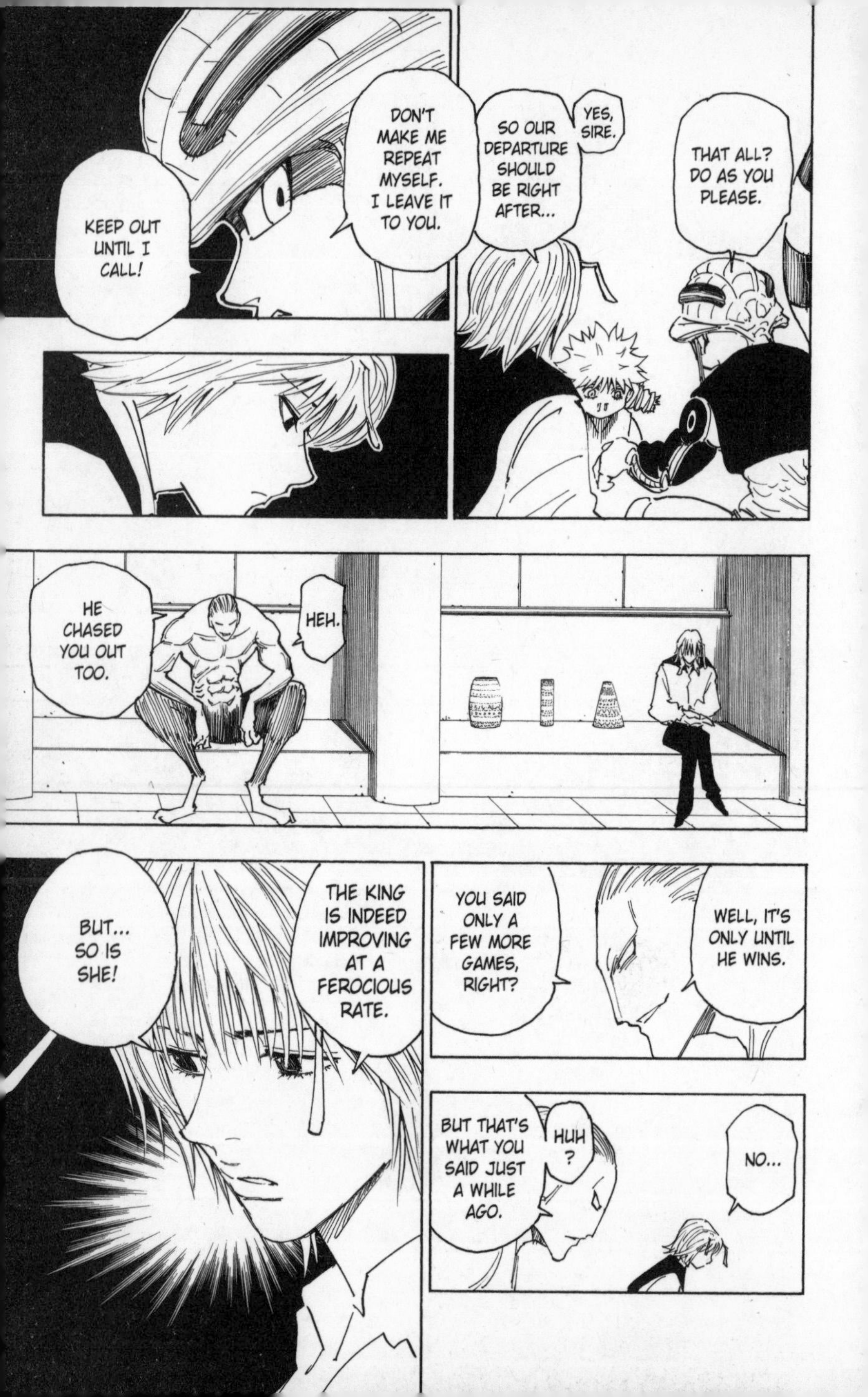
THAT ALL? DO AS YOU PLEASE.
YES, SIRE.
SO OUR DEPARTURE SHOULD BE RIGHT AFTER...
DON'T MAKE ME REPEAT MYSELF. I LEAVE IT TO YOU.
KEEP OUT UNTIL I CALL!
HEH.
HE CHASED YOU OUT TOO.
WELL, IT'S ONLY UNTIL HE WINS.
YOU SAID ONLY A FEW MORE GAMES, RIGHT?
NO...
HUH?
BUT THAT'S WHAT YOU SAID JUST A WHILE AGO.
THE KING IS INDEED IMPROVING AT A FEROCIOUS RATE.
BUT... SO IS SHE!

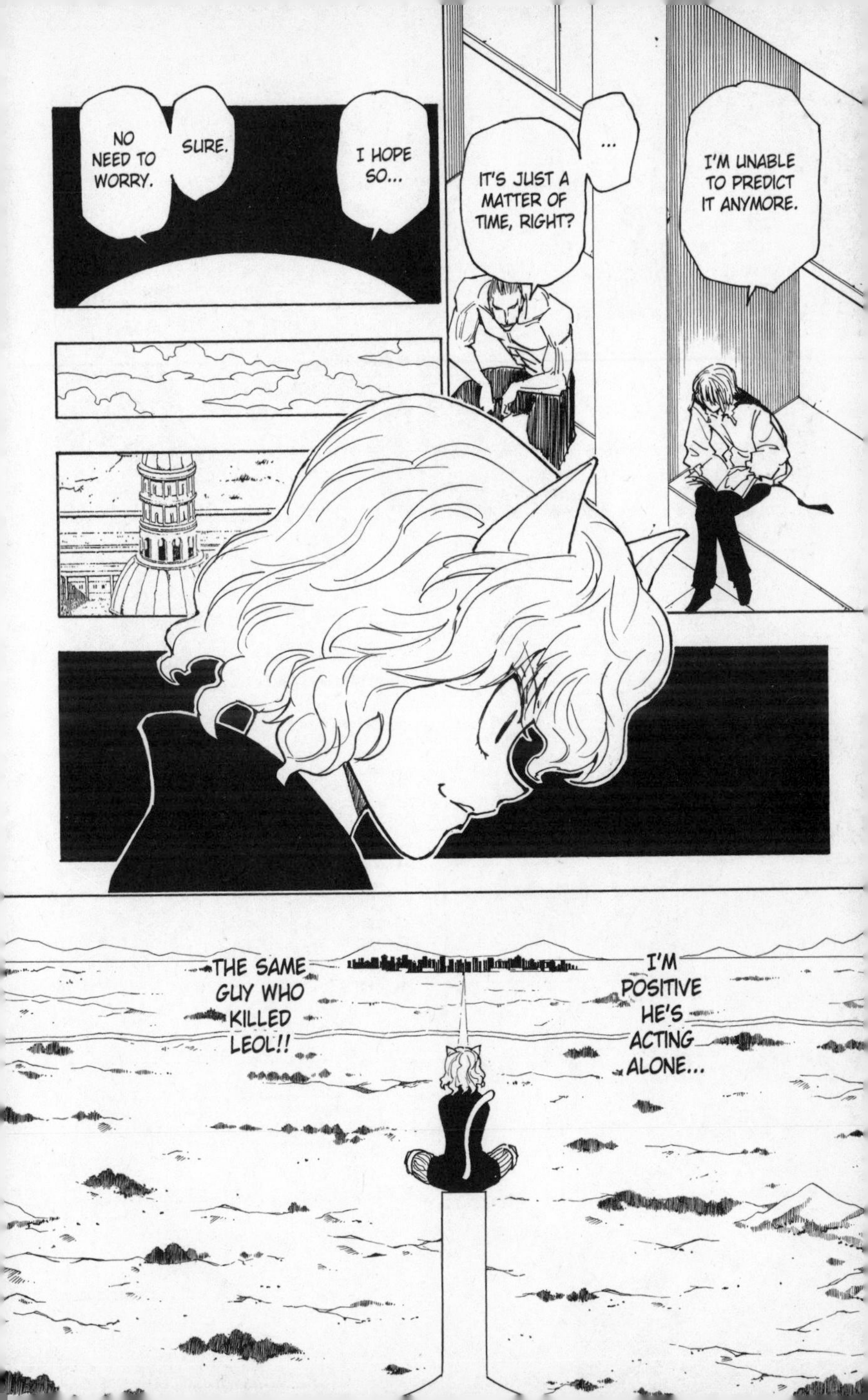
I'M UNABLE TO PREDICT IT ANYMORE.
...
IT'S JUST A MATTER OF TIME, RIGHT?
I HOPE SO...
SURE.
NO NEED TO WORRY.
I'M POSITIVE HE'S ACTING ALONE...
THE SAME GUY WHO KILLED LEOL!!

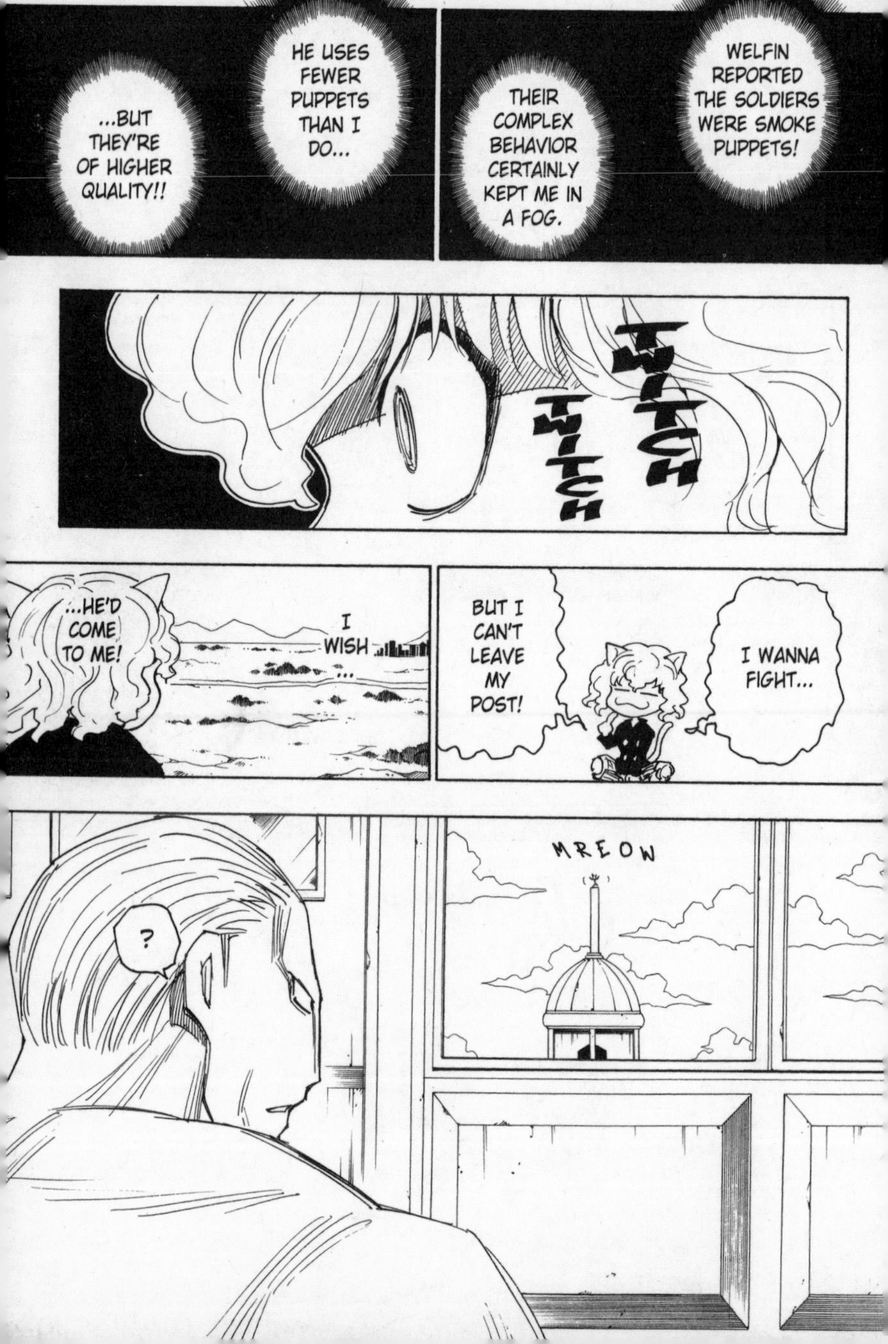
WELFIN REPORTED THE SOLDIERS WERE SMOKE PUPPETS!
THEIR COMPLEX BEHAVIOR CERTAINLY KEPT ME IN A FOG.
HE USES FEWER PUPPETS THAN I DO...
...BUT THEY'RE OF HIGHER QUALITY!!
TWITCH
TWITCH
I WANNA FIGHT...
BUT I CAN'T LEAVE MY POST!
I WISH ...
...HE'D COME TO ME!
MREOW
?

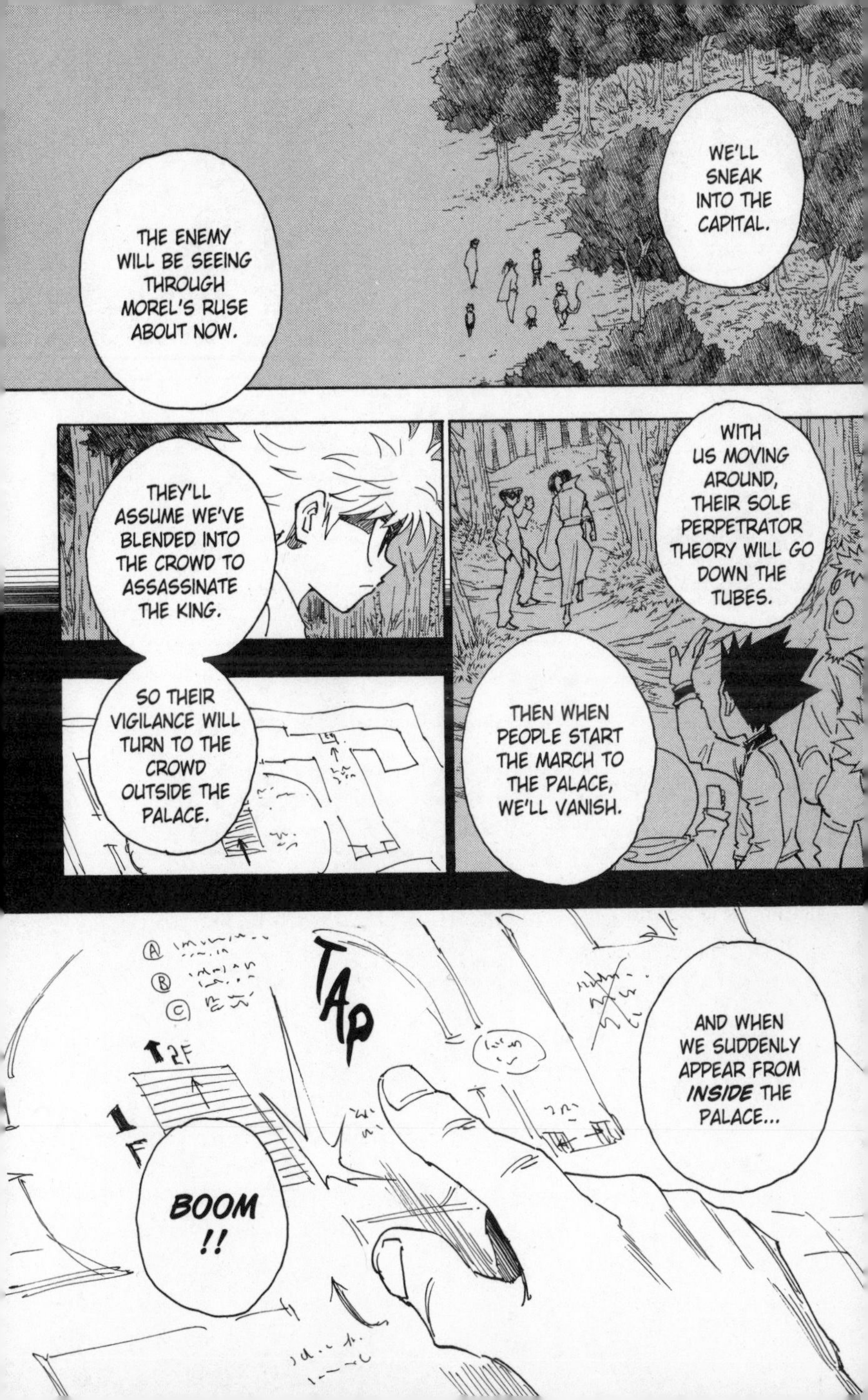

WE'LL SNEAK INTO THE CAPITAL.
THE ENEMY WILL BE SEEING THROUGH MOREL'S RUSE ABOUT NOW.
WITH US MOVING AROUND, THEIR SOLE PERPETRATOR THEORY WILL GO DOWN THE TUBES.
THEN WHEN PEOPLE START THE MARCH TO THE PALACE, WE'LL VANISH.
THEY'LL ASSUME WE'VE BLENDED INTO THE CROWD TO ASSASSINATE THE KING.
SO THEIR VIGILANCE WILL TURN TO THE CROWD OUTSIDE THE PALACE.
AND WHEN WE SUDDENLY APPEAR FROM *INSIDE* THE PALACE...
TAP
2F
1F
BOOM !!

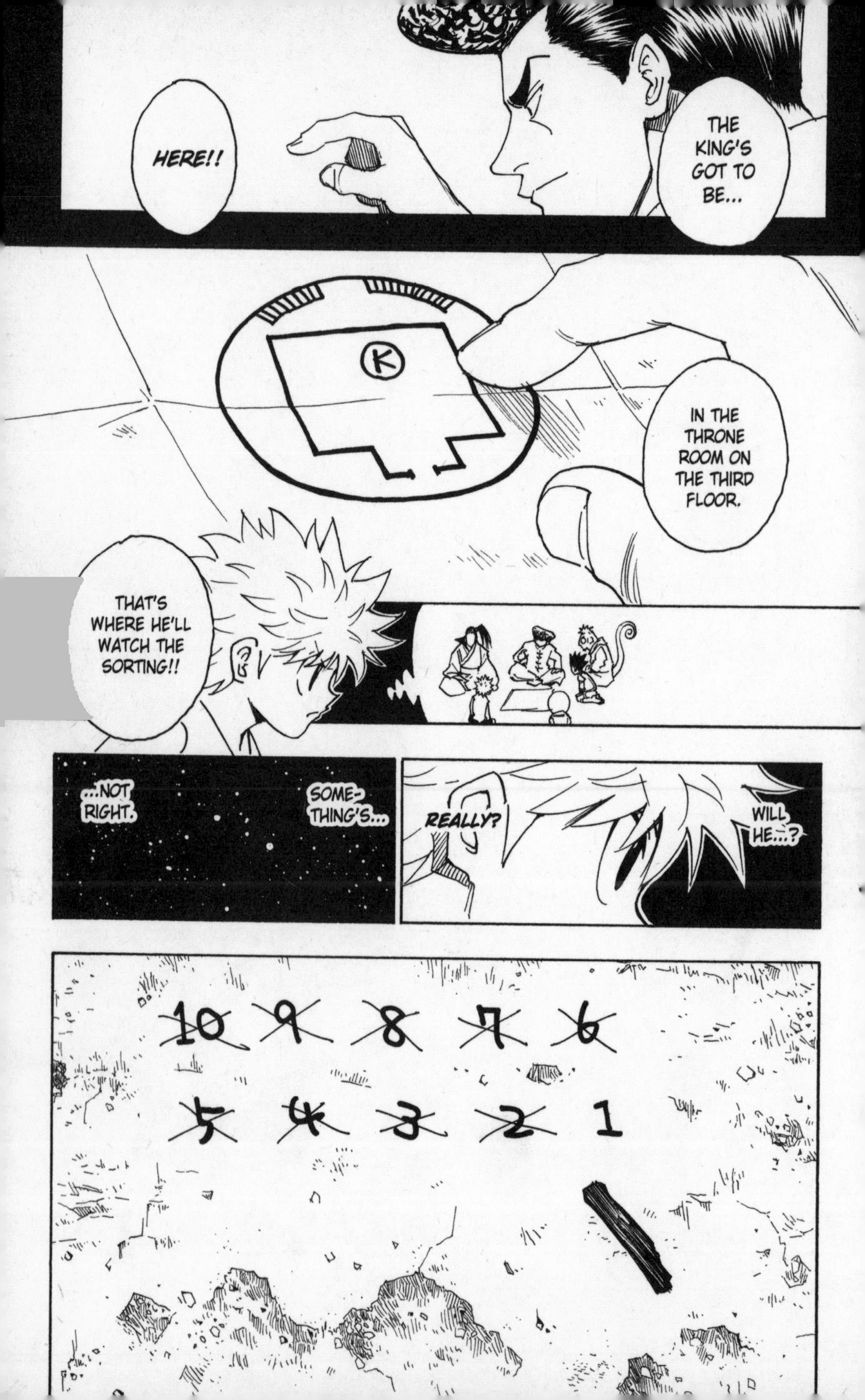
THE KING'S GOT TO BE...
HERE!!
K
IN THE THRONE ROOM ON THE THIRD FLOOR.
THAT'S WHERE HE'LL WATCH THE SORTING!!
WILL HE...?
REALLY?
SOME-THING'S...
...NOT RIGHT.
10 9 8 7 6
5 4 3 2 1

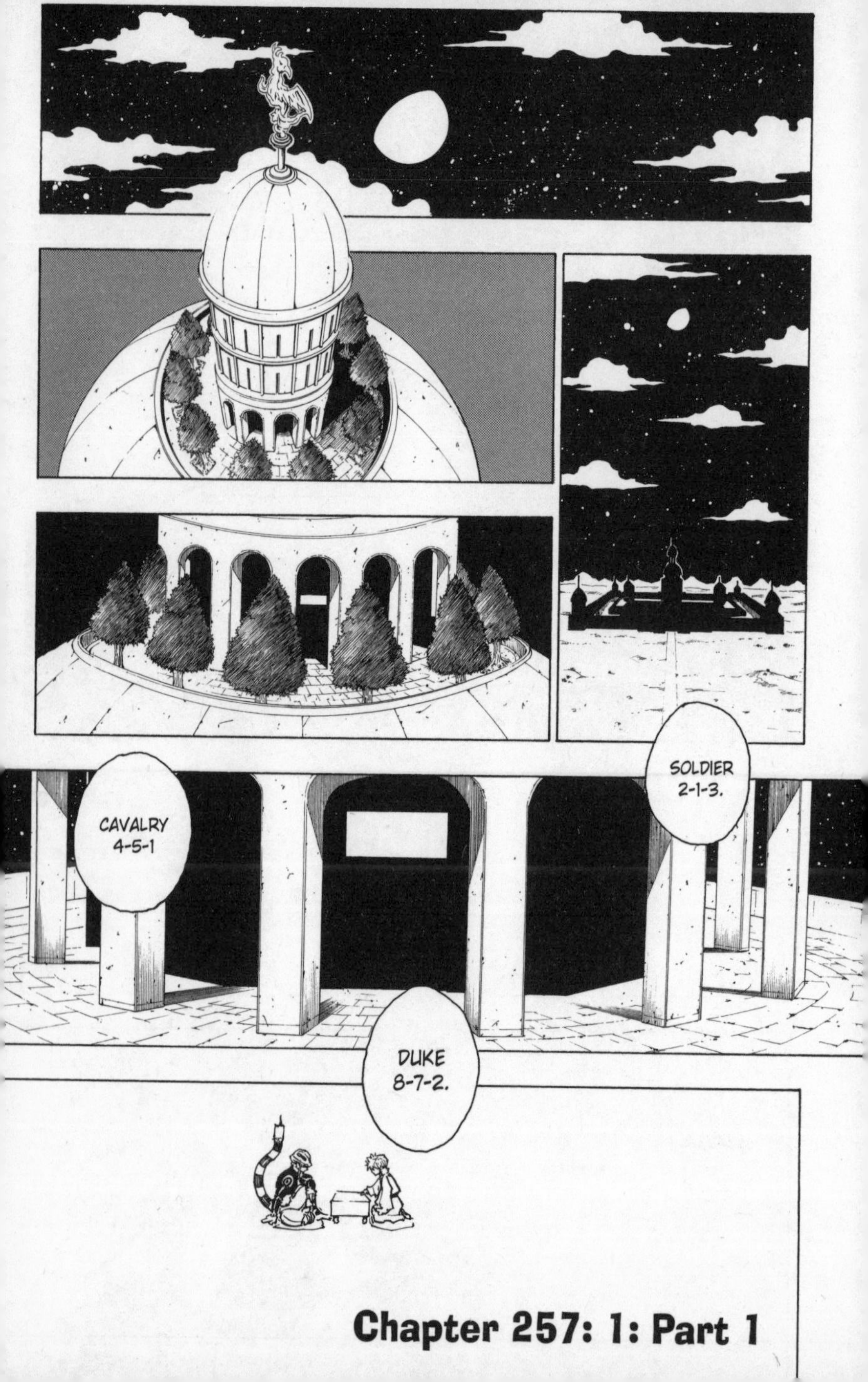
SOLDIER 2-1-3.
CAVALRY 4-5-1
DUKE 8-7-2.

Chapter 257: 1: Part 1

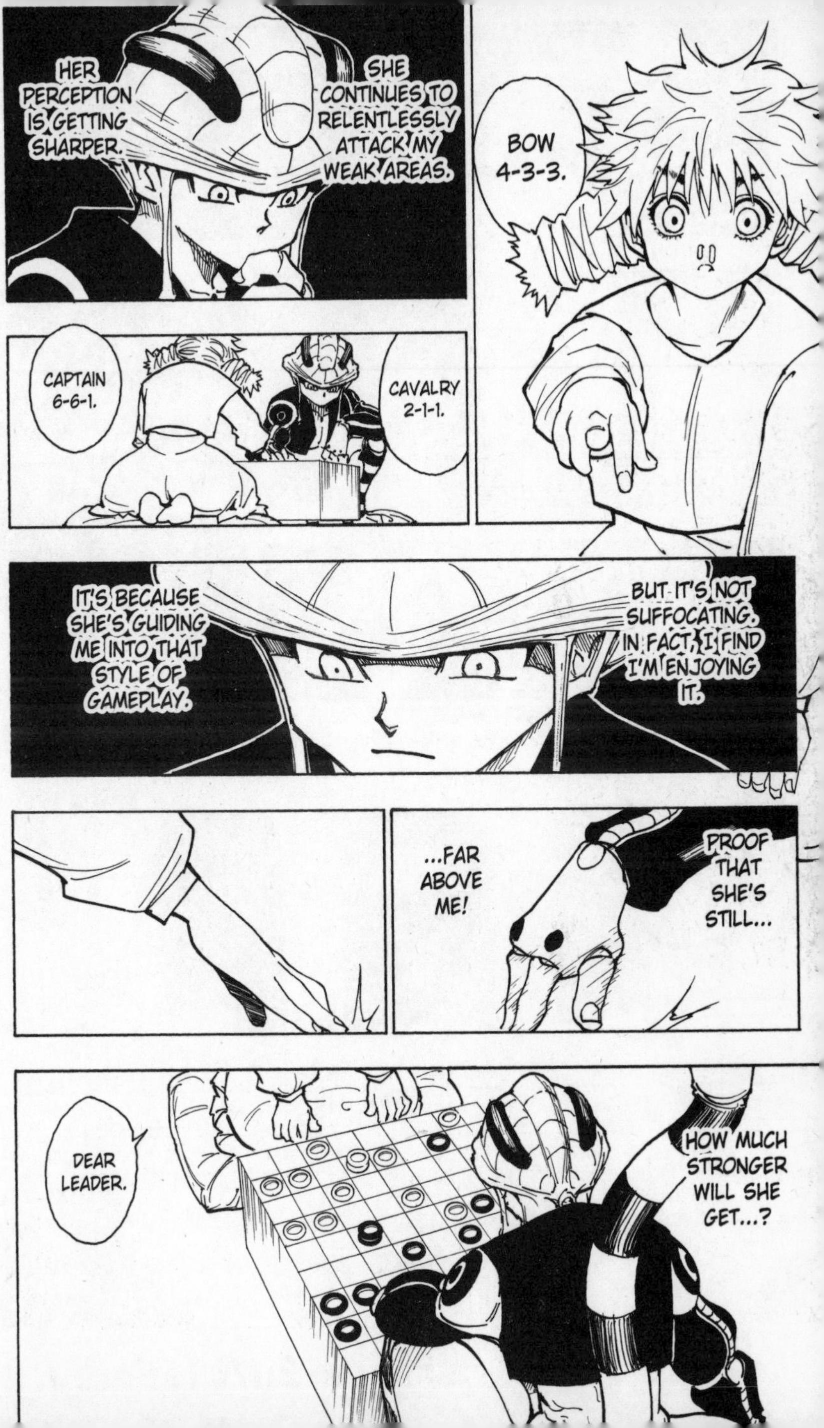
BOW 4-3-3.
SHE CONTINUES TO RELENTLESSLY ATTACK MY WEAK AREAS.
HER PERCEPTION IS GETTING SHARPER.
CAVALRY 2-1-1.
CAPTAIN 6-6-1.
BUT IT'S NOT SUFFOCATING. IN FACT, I FIND I'M ENJOYING IT.
IT'S BECAUSE SHE'S GUIDING ME INTO THAT STYLE OF GAMEPLAY.
PROOF THAT SHE'S STILL...
...FAR ABOVE ME!
HOW MUCH STRONGER WILL SHE GET...?
DEAR LEADER.

READ THIS WAY

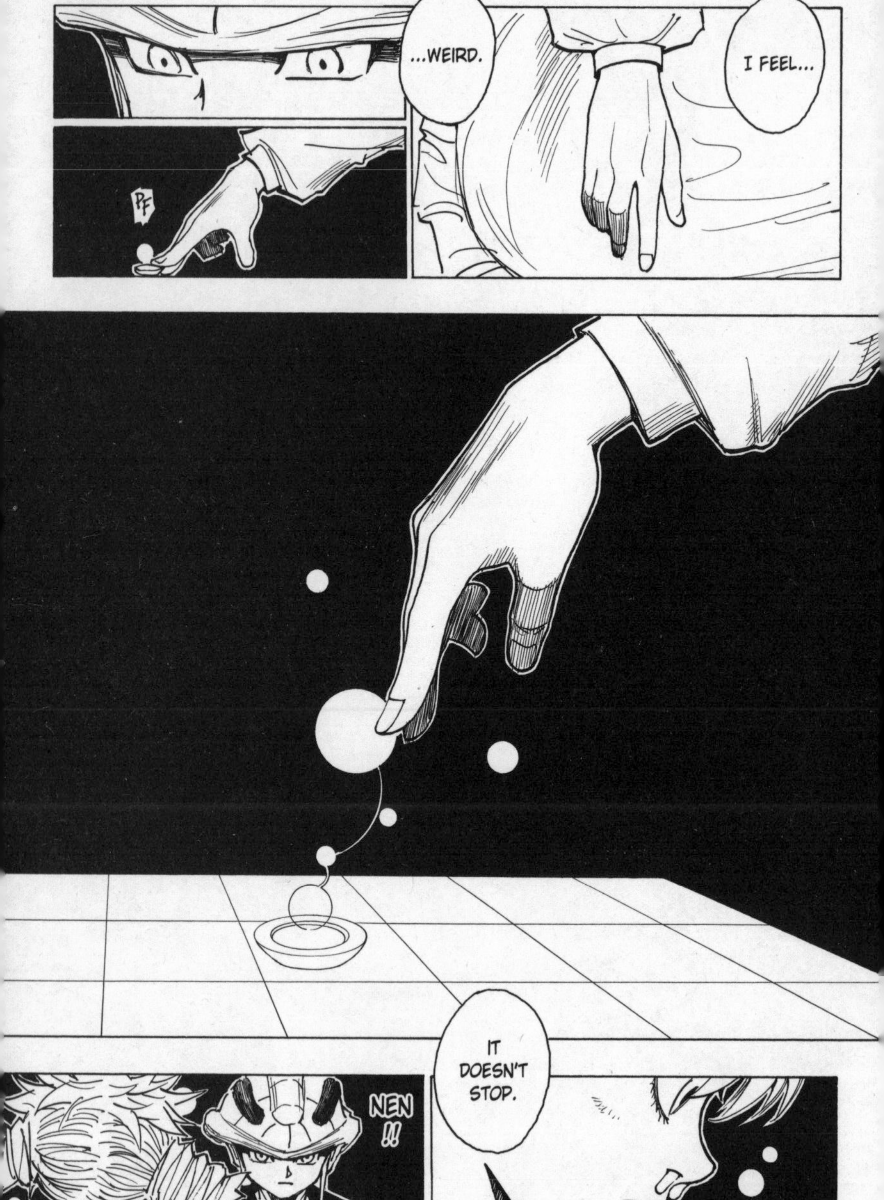

I FEEL...
...WEIRD.
PF
IT DOESN'T STOP.
NEN !!

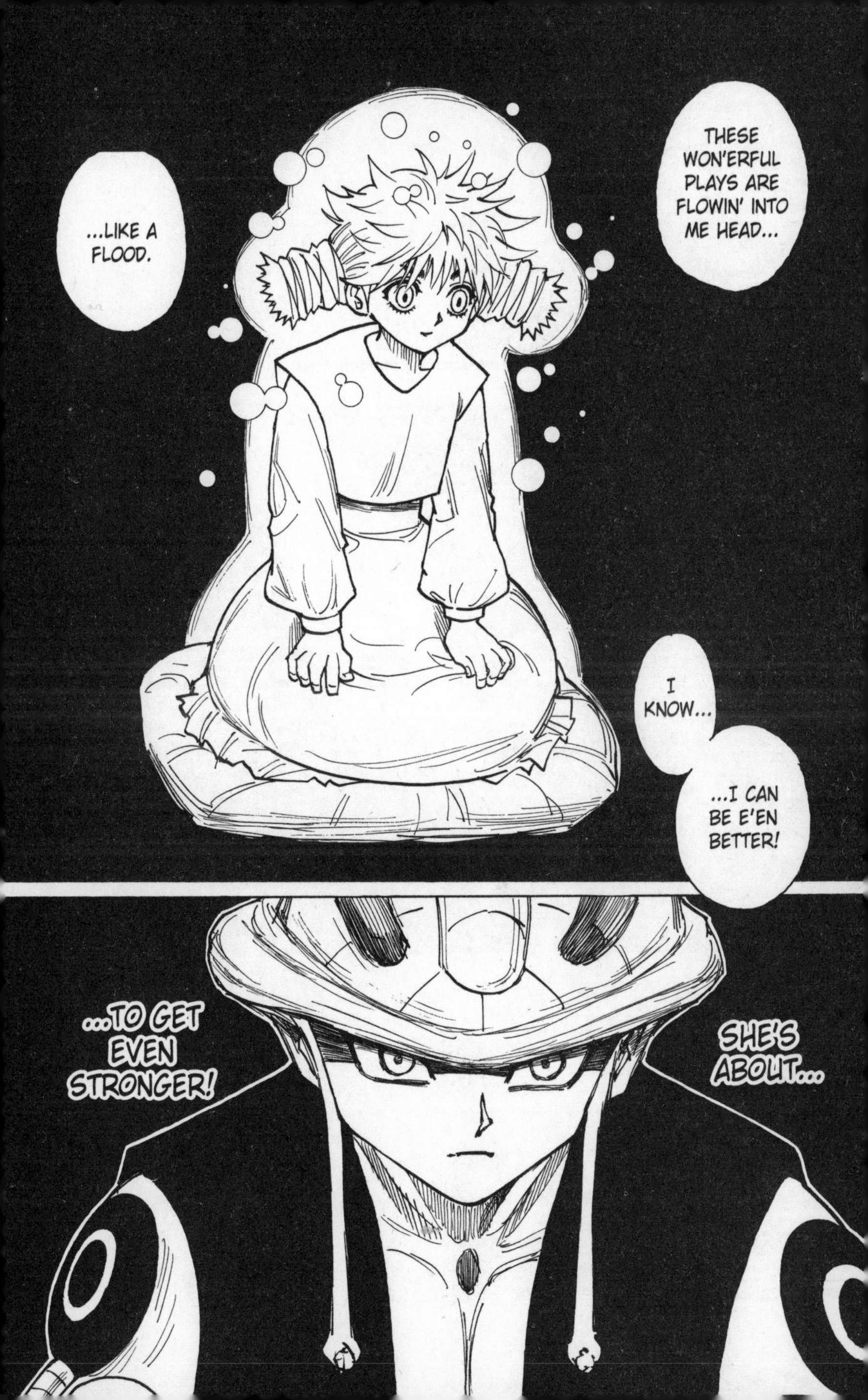
THESE WON'ERFUL PLAYS ARE FLOWIN' INTO ME HEAD...
...LIKE A FLOOD.
I KNOW...
...I CAN BE E'EN BETTER!
SHE'S ABOUT...
...TO GET EVEN STRONGER!

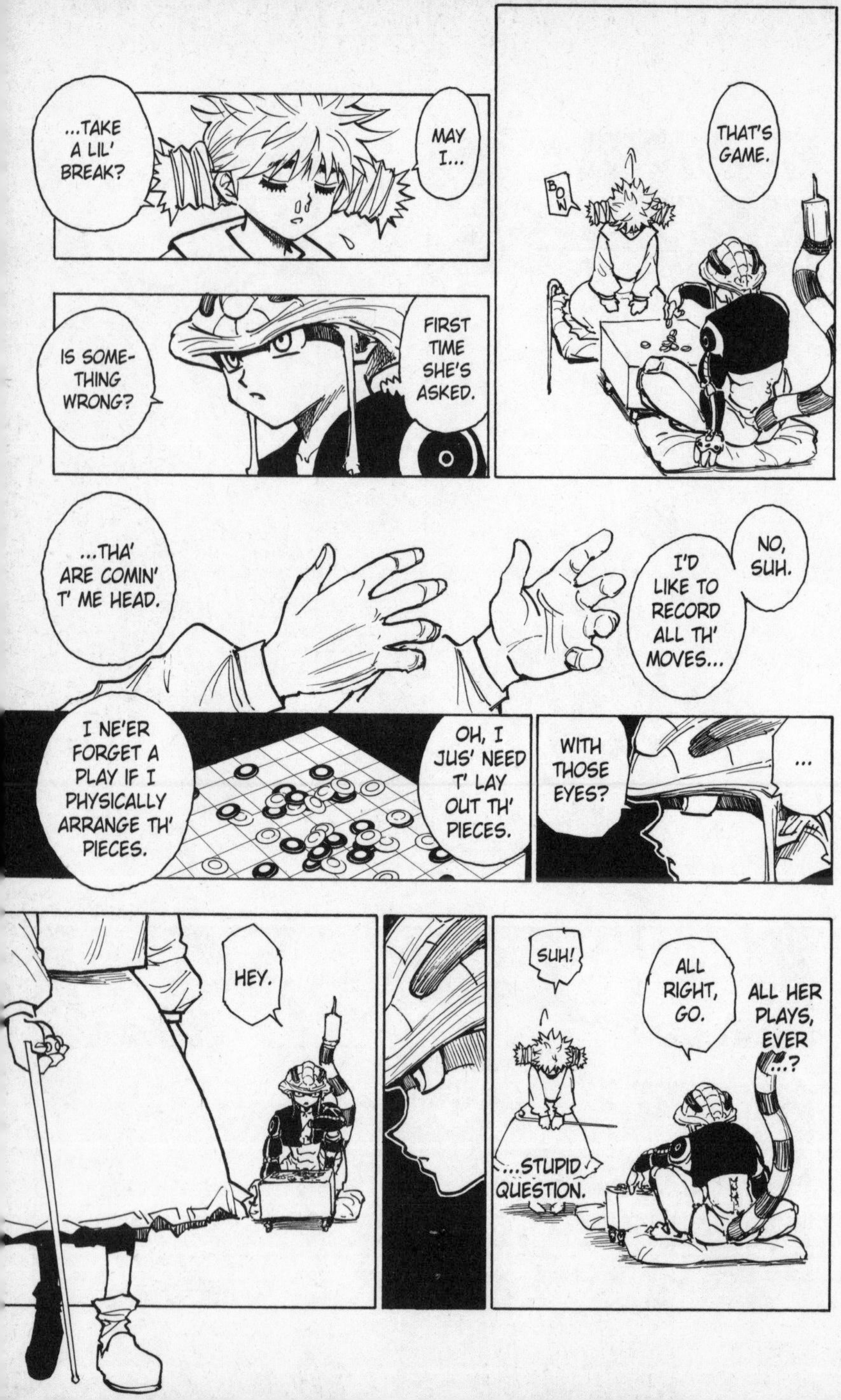
THAT'S GAME.
BOW
MAY I...
...TAKE A LIL' BREAK?
FIRST TIME SHE'S ASKED.
IS SOME-THING WRONG?
NO, SUH.
I'D LIKE TO RECORD ALL TH' MOVES...
...THA' ARE COMIN' T' ME HEAD.
...
WITH THOSE EYES?
OH, I JUS' NEED T' LAY OUT TH' PIECES.
I NE'ER FORGET A PLAY IF I PHYSICALLY ARRANGE TH' PIECES.
ALL HER PLAYS, EVER ...?
ALL RIGHT, GO.
SUH!
...STUPID QUESTION.
HEY.

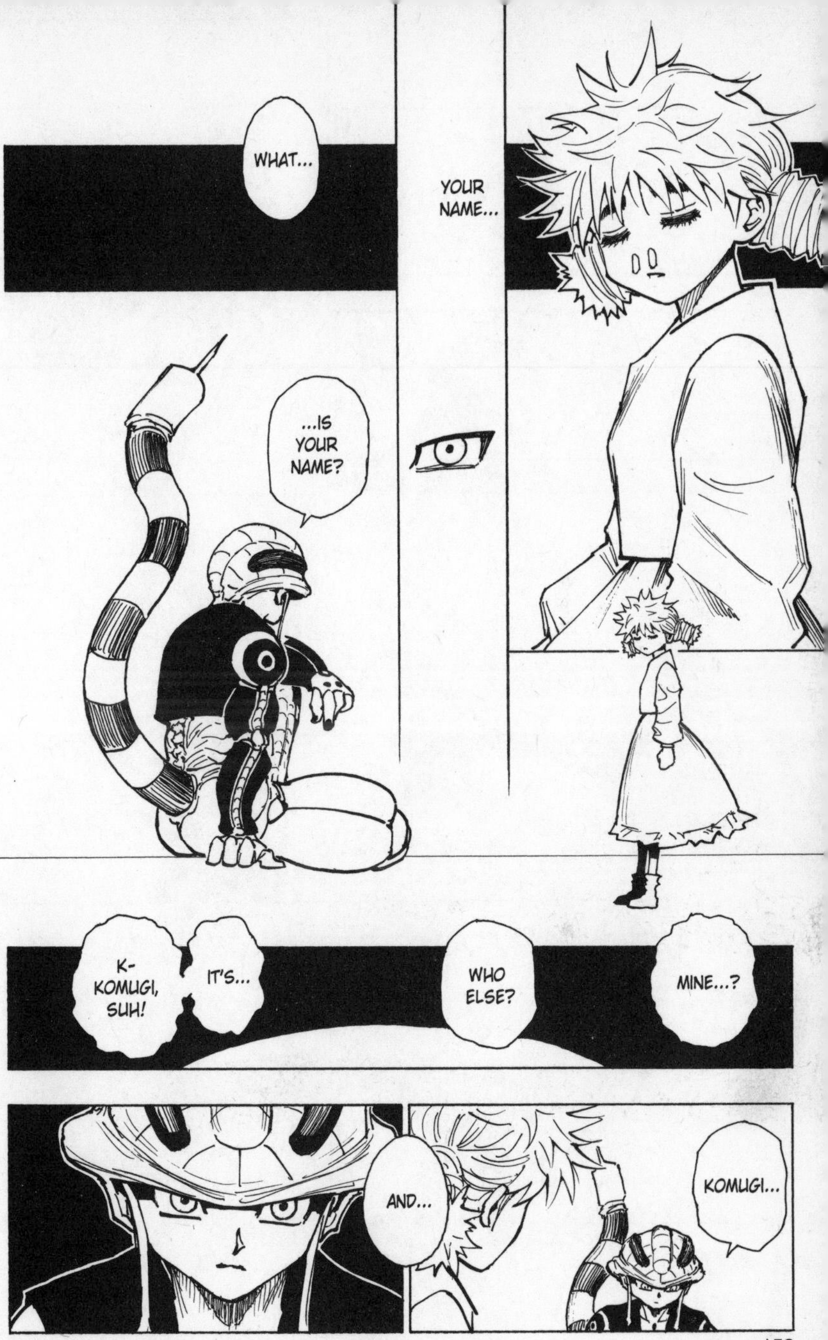

YOUR NAME...
WHAT...
...IS YOUR NAME?
MINE...?
WHO ELSE?
IT'S...
K-KOMUGI, SUH!
KOMUGI...
AND...

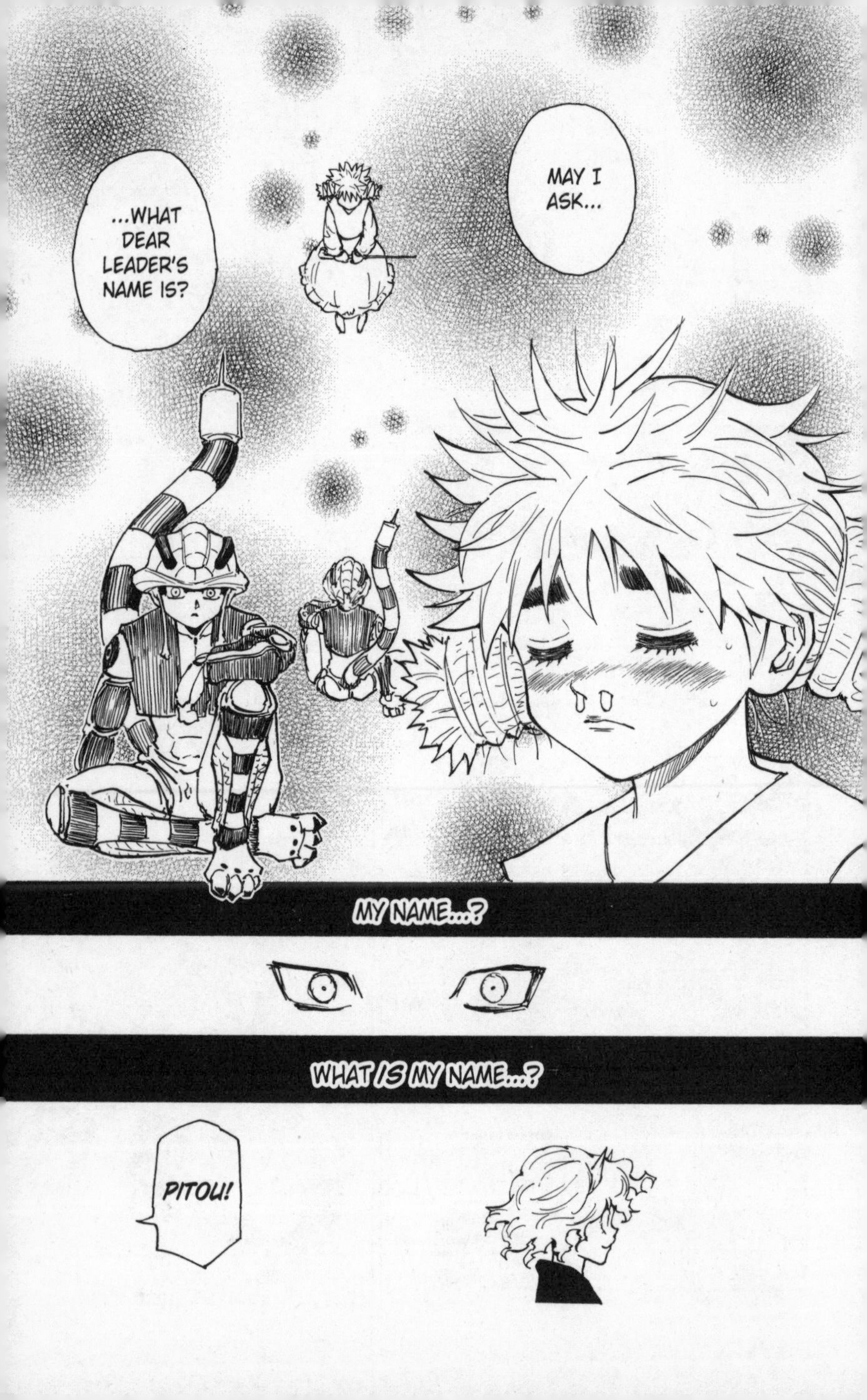
MAY I ASK...
...WHAT DEAR LEADER'S NAME IS?
MY NAME...?
WHAT IS MY NAME...?
PITOU!

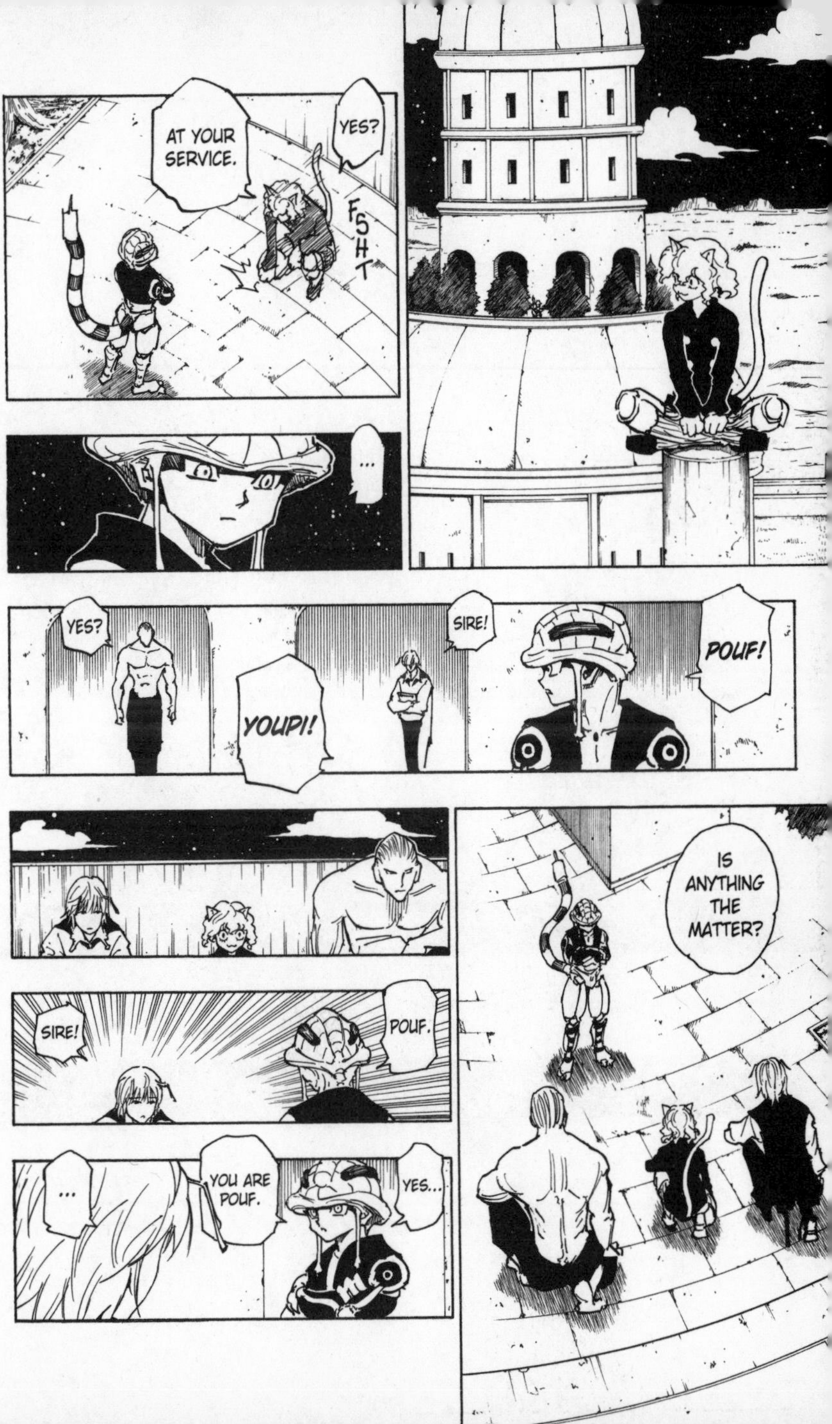
YES?
AT YOUR SERVICE.
FSHT
...
POUF!
SIRE!
YOUPI!
YES?
IS ANYTHING THE MATTER?
POUF.
SIRE!
YES...
YOU ARE POUF.
...

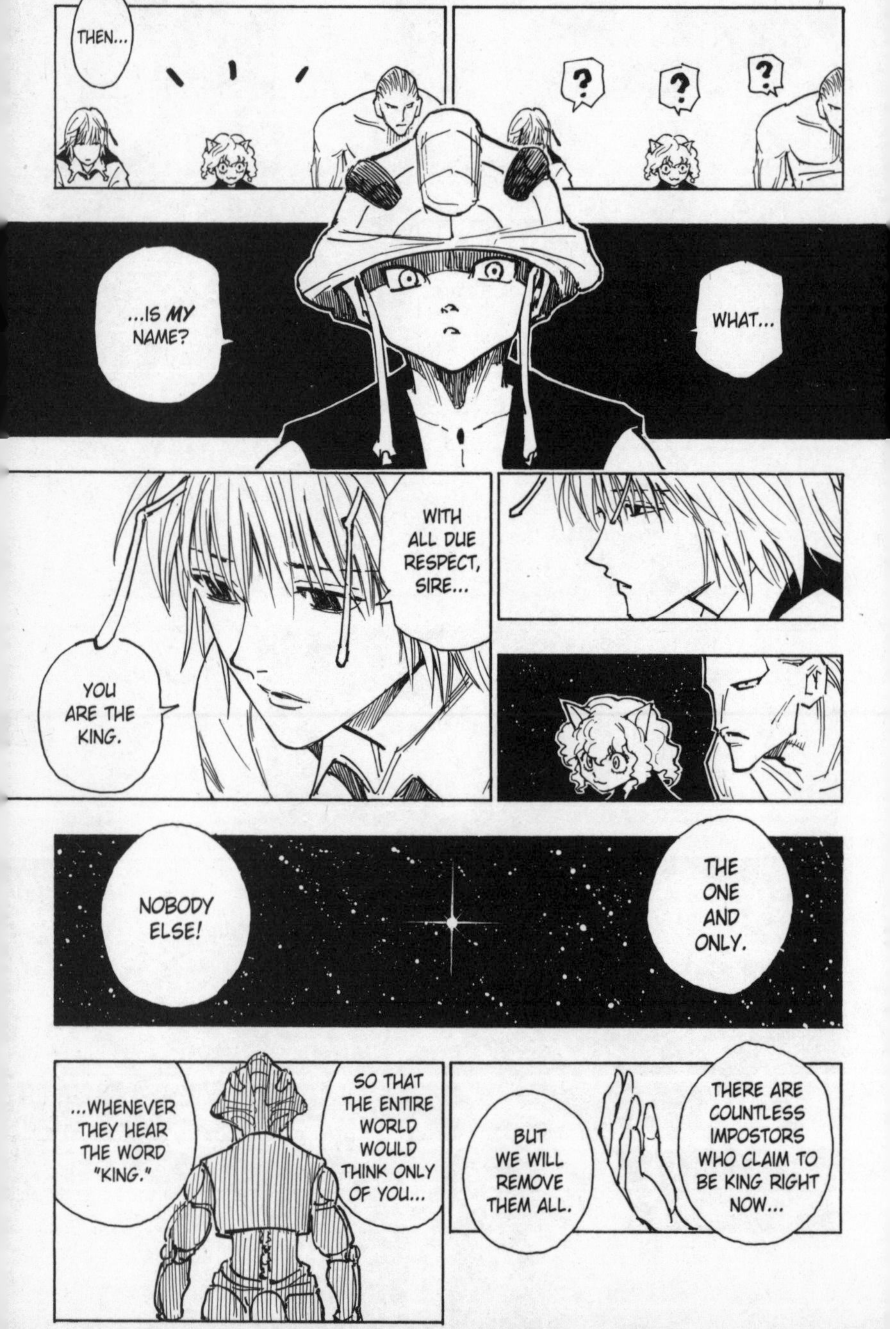
?
?
?
THEN...
WHAT...
...IS MY NAME?
WITH ALL DUE RESPECT, SIRE...
YOU ARE THE KING.
THE ONE AND ONLY.
NOBODY ELSE!
THERE ARE COUNTLESS IMPOSTORS WHO CLAIM TO BE KING RIGHT NOW...
BUT WE WILL REMOVE THEM ALL.
SO THAT THE ENTIRE WORLD WOULD THINK ONLY OF YOU...
...WHENEVER THEY HEAR THE WORD "KING."

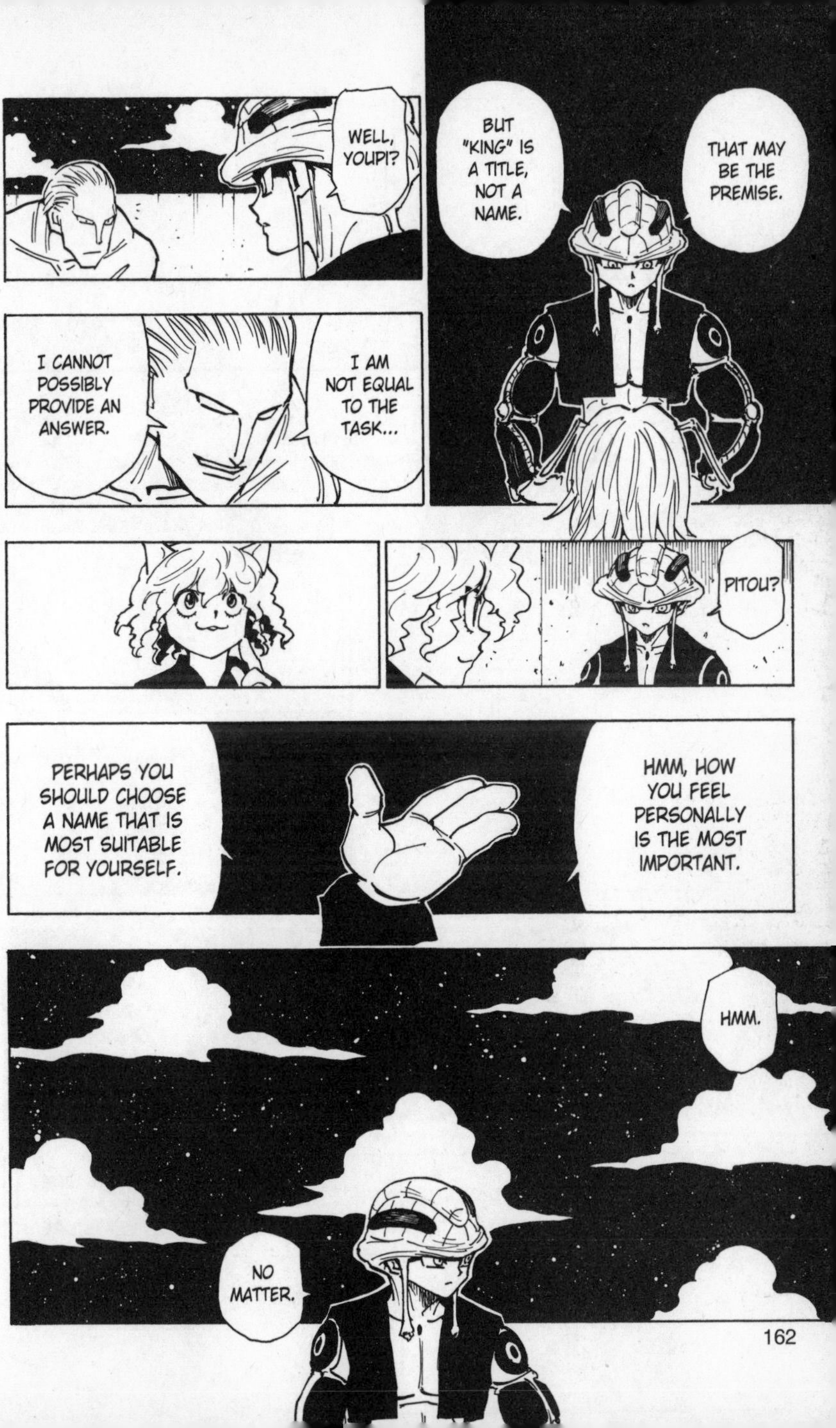
THAT MAY BE THE PREMISE.
BUT "KING" IS A TITLE, NOT A NAME.
WELL, YOUPI?
I AM NOT EQUAL TO THE TASK...
I CANNOT POSSIBLY PROVIDE AN ANSWER.
PITOU?
HMM, HOW YOU FEEL PERSONALLY IS THE MOST IMPORTANT.
PERHAPS YOU SHOULD CHOOSE A NAME THAT IS MOST SUITABLE FOR YOURSELF.
HMM.
NO MATTER.

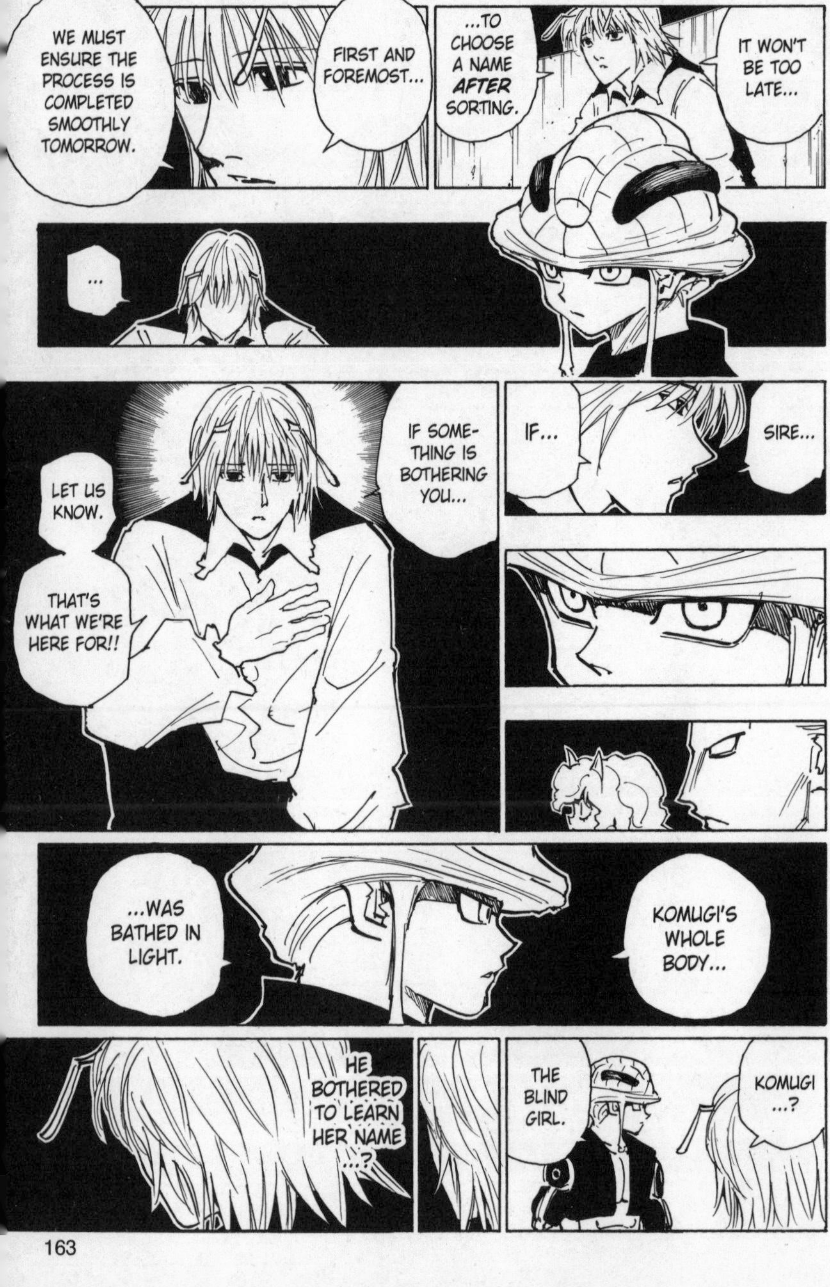
IT WON'T BE TOO LATE...
...TO CHOOSE A NAME **AFTER** SORTING.
FIRST AND FOREMOST...
WE MUST ENSURE THE PROCESS IS COMPLETED SMOOTHLY TOMORROW.
...
SIRE...
IF...
IF SOME-THING IS BOTHERING YOU...
LET US KNOW.
THAT'S WHAT WE'RE HERE FOR!!
KOMUGI'S WHOLE BODY...
...WAS BATHED IN LIGHT.
KOMUGI ...?
THE BLIND GIRL.
HE BOTHERED TO LEARN HER NAME ...?

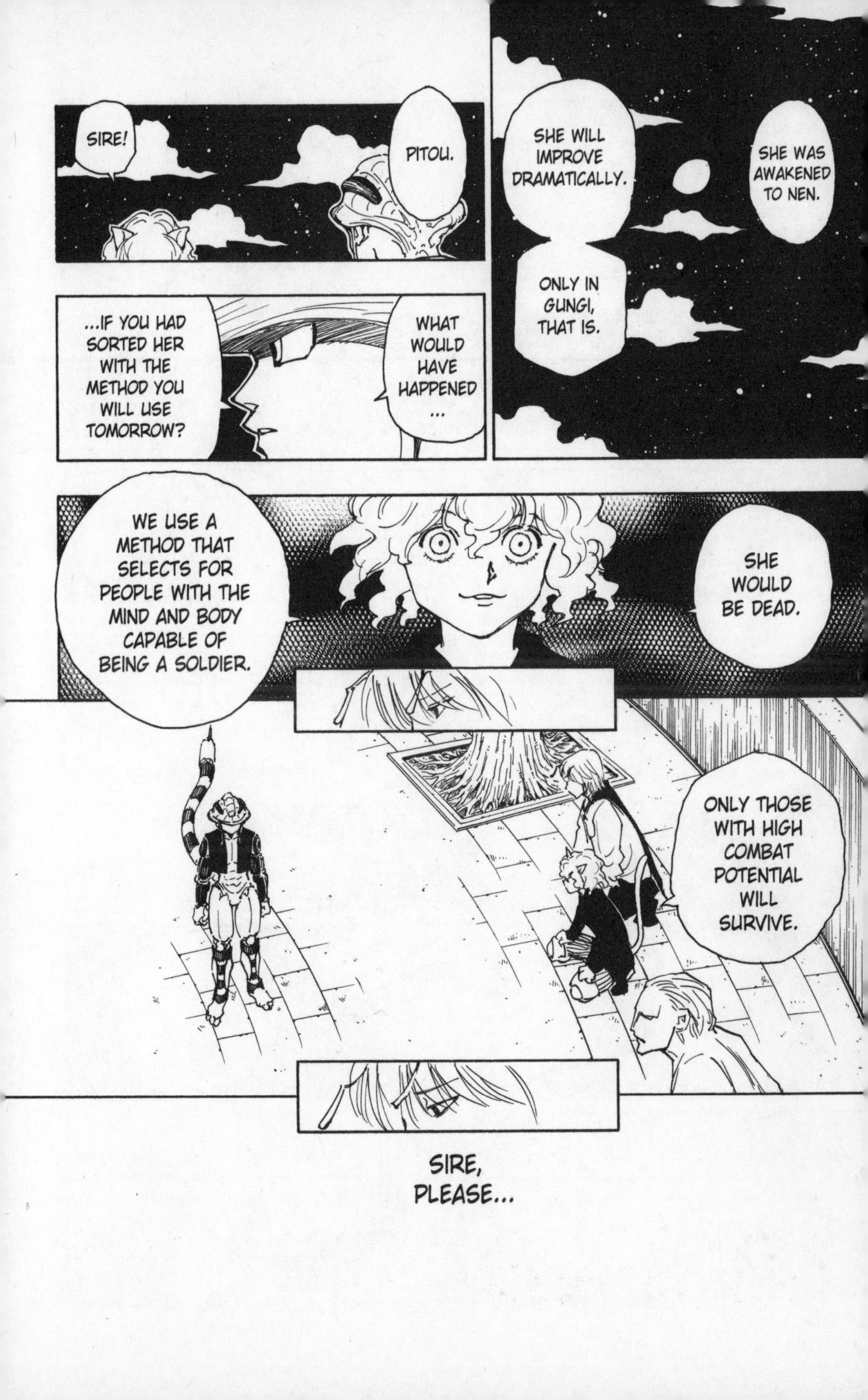
SHE WAS AWAKENED TO NEN.
SHE WILL IMPROVE DRAMATICALLY.
ONLY IN GUNGI, THAT IS.
PITOU.
SIRE!
WHAT WOULD HAVE HAPPENED ...
...IF YOU HAD SORTED HER WITH THE METHOD YOU WILL USE TOMORROW?
SHE WOULD BE DEAD.
WE USE A METHOD THAT SELECTS FOR PEOPLE WITH THE MIND AND BODY CAPABLE OF BEING A SOLDIER.
ONLY THOSE WITH HIGH COMBAT POTENTIAL WILL SURVIVE.
SIRE, PLEASE...

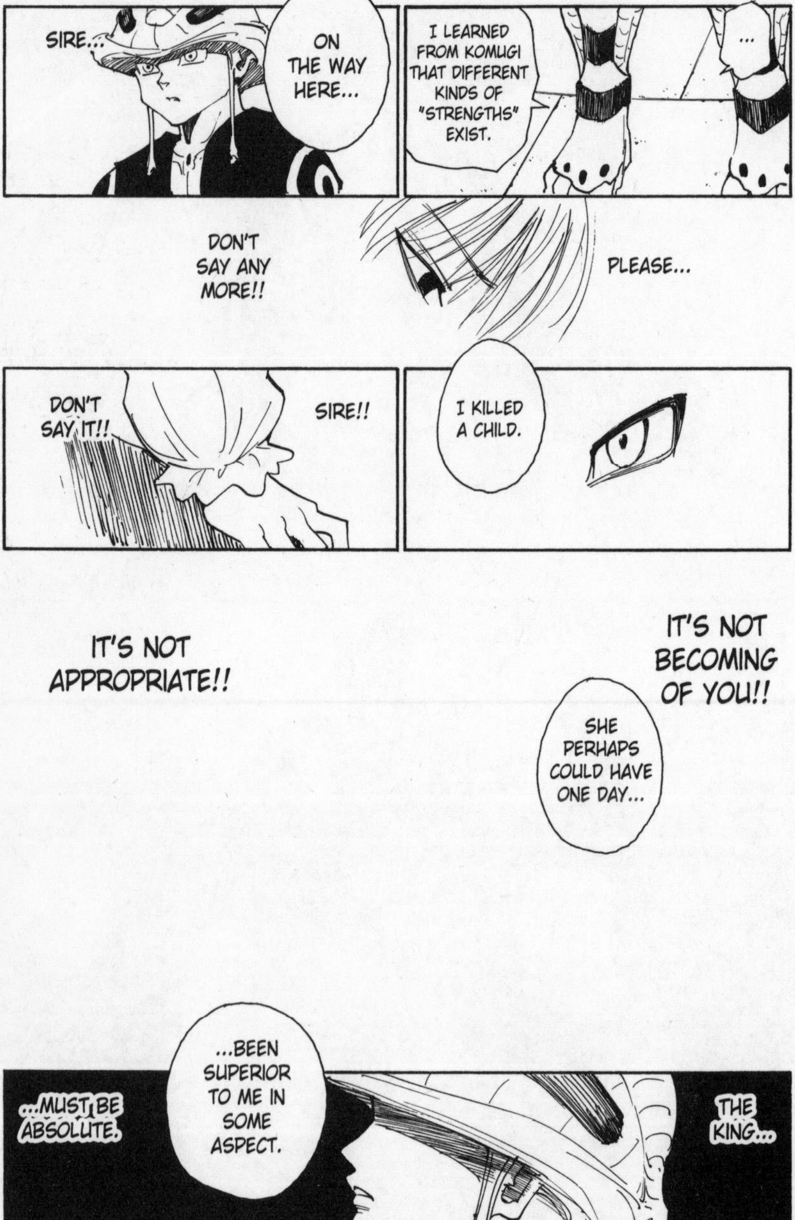
...
I LEARNED FROM KOMUGI THAT DIFFERENT KINDS OF "STRENGTHS" EXIST.
ON THE WAY HERE...
SIRE...
PLEASE...
DON'T SAY ANY MORE!!
I KILLED A CHILD.
SIRE!!
DON'T SAY IT!!
IT'S NOT BECOMING OF YOU!!
SHE PERHAPS COULD HAVE ONE DAY...
IT'S NOT APPROPRIATE!!
THE KING...
...BEEN SUPERIOR TO ME IN SOME ASPECT.
...MUST BE ABSOLUTE.

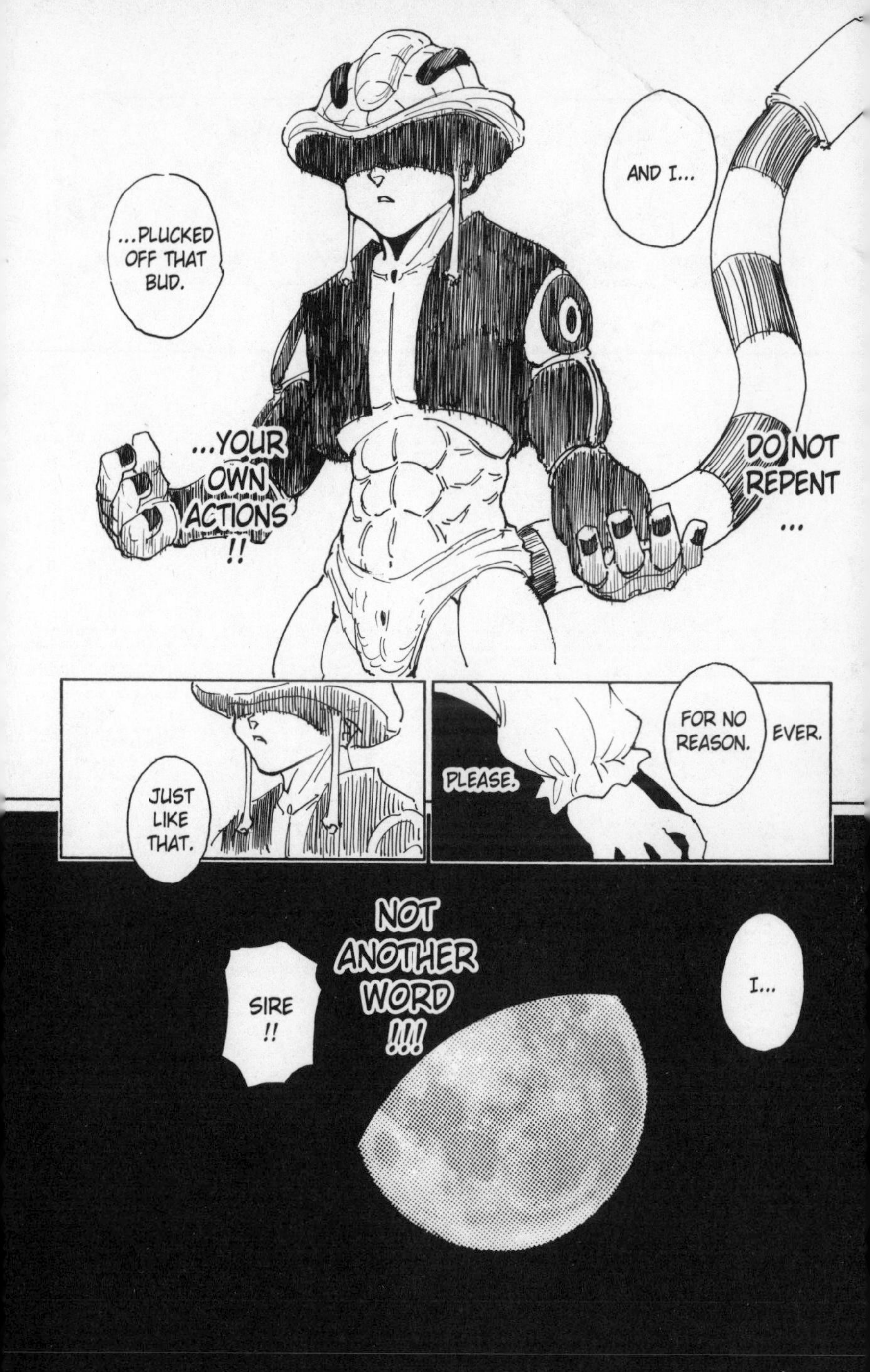
AND I...
...PLUCKED OFF THAT BUD.
DO NOT REPENT ...
...YOUR OWN ACTIONS !!
EVER.
FOR NO REASON.
PLEASE.
JUST LIKE THAT.
I...
NOT ANOTHER WORD !!!
SIRE !!

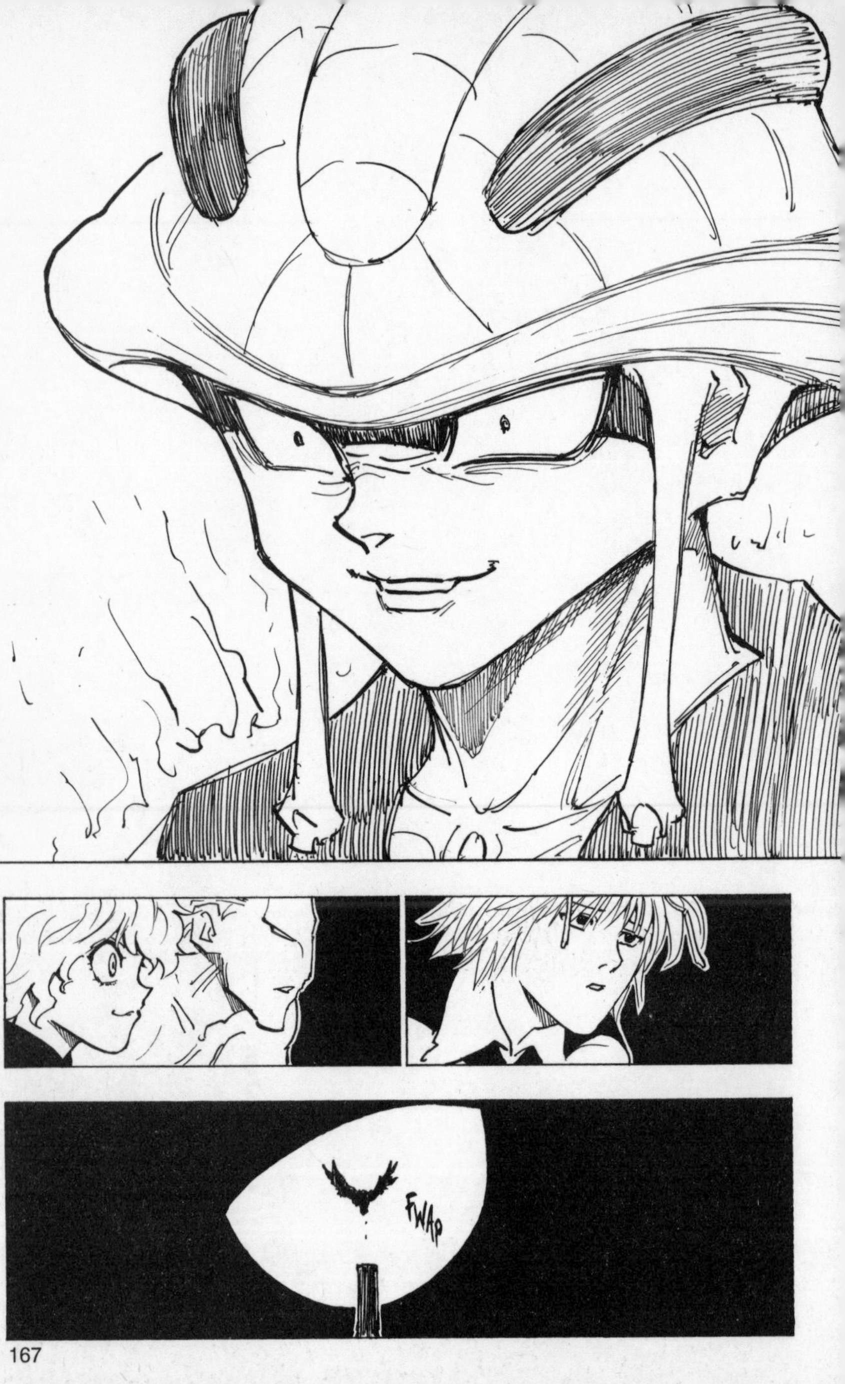
FWAP

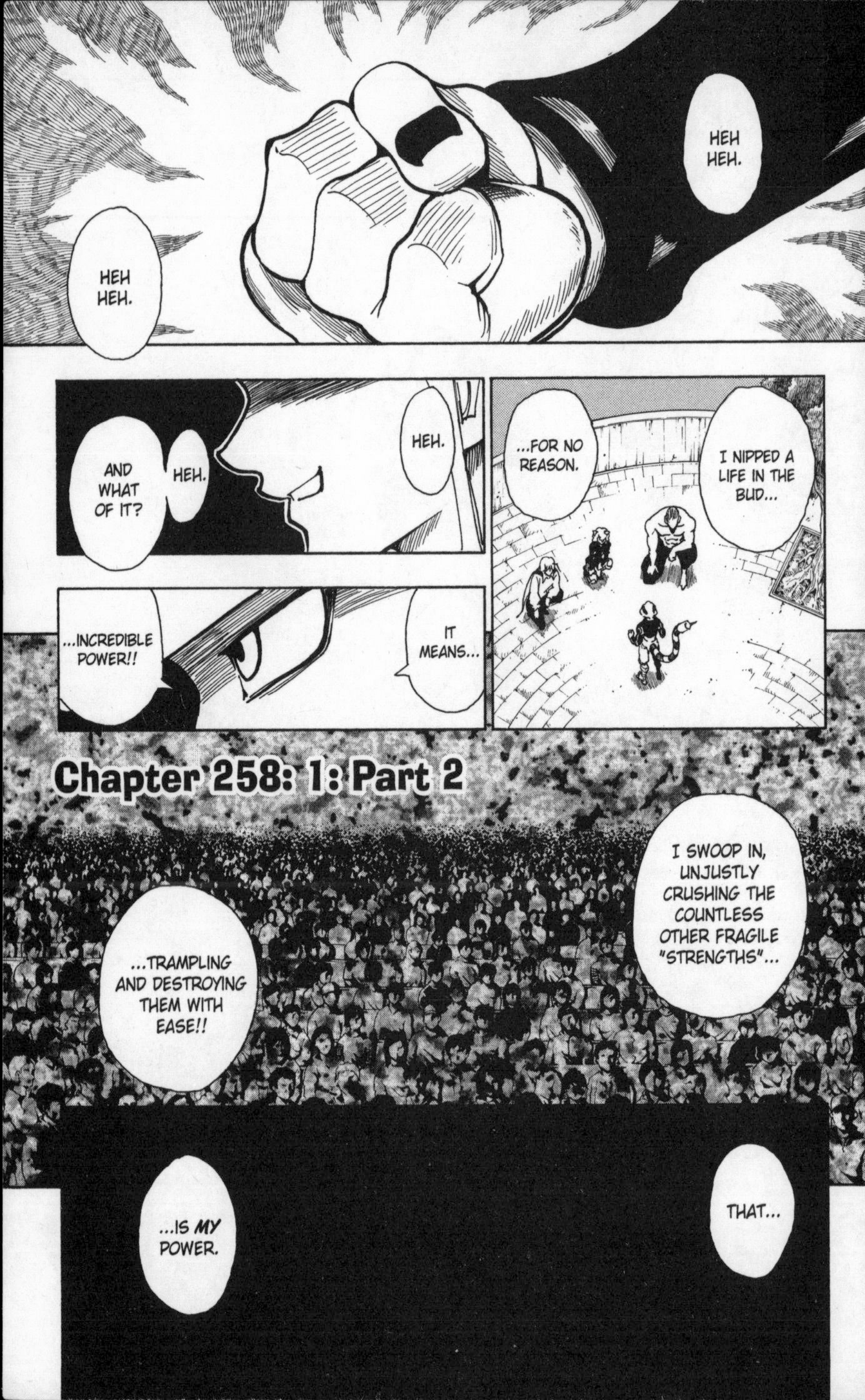
HEH HEH.
HEH HEH.
I NIPPED A LIFE IN THE BUD...
...FOR NO REASON.
HEH.
HEH.
AND WHAT OF IT?
IT MEANS...
...INCREDIBLE POWER!!
Chapter 258: 1: Part 2
I SWOOP IN, UNJUSTLY CRUSHING THE COUNTLESS OTHER FRAGILE "STRENGTHS"...
...TRAMPLING AND DESTROYING THEM WITH EASE!!
THAT...
...IS *MY* POWER.

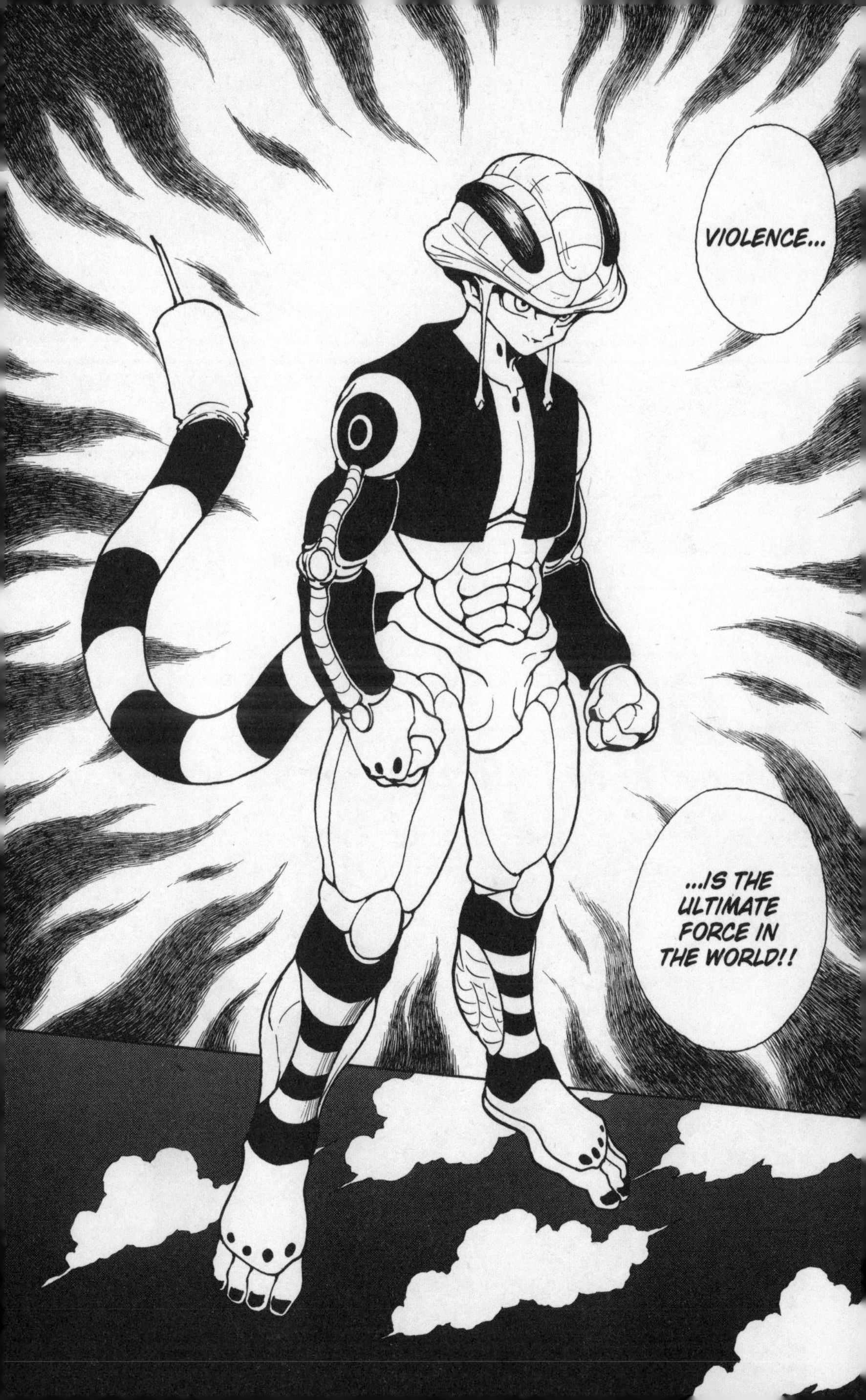
VIOLENCE...
...IS THE ULTIMATE FORCE IN THE WORLD!!

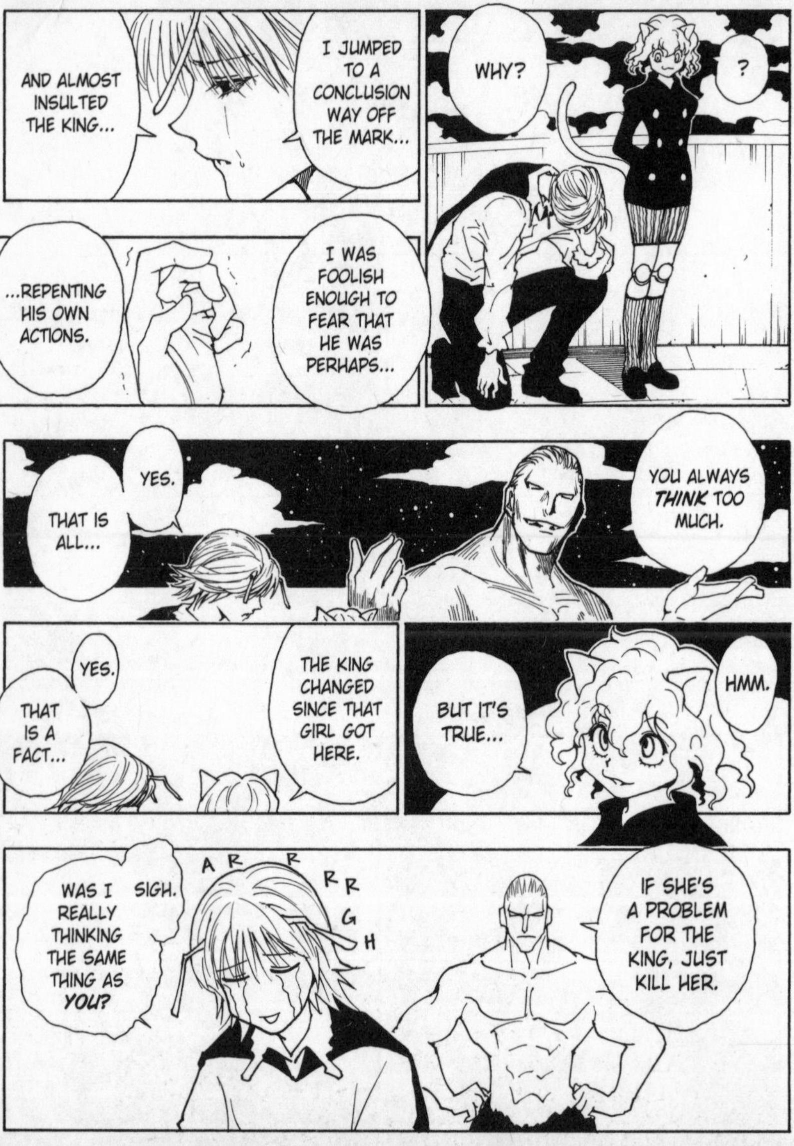
?
WHY?
I JUMPED TO A CONCLUSION WAY OFF THE MARK...
AND ALMOST INSULTED THE KING...
I WAS FOOLISH ENOUGH TO FEAR THAT HE WAS PERHAPS...
...REPENTING HIS OWN ACTIONS.
YOU ALWAYS *THINK* TOO MUCH.
YES.
THAT IS ALL...
HMM.
BUT IT'S TRUE...
THE KING CHANGED SINCE THAT GIRL GOT HERE.
YES.
THAT IS A FACT...
IF SHE'S A PROBLEM FOR THE KING, JUST KILL HER.
ARRRRGH
SIGH.
WAS I REALLY THINKING THE SAME THING AS *YOU?*

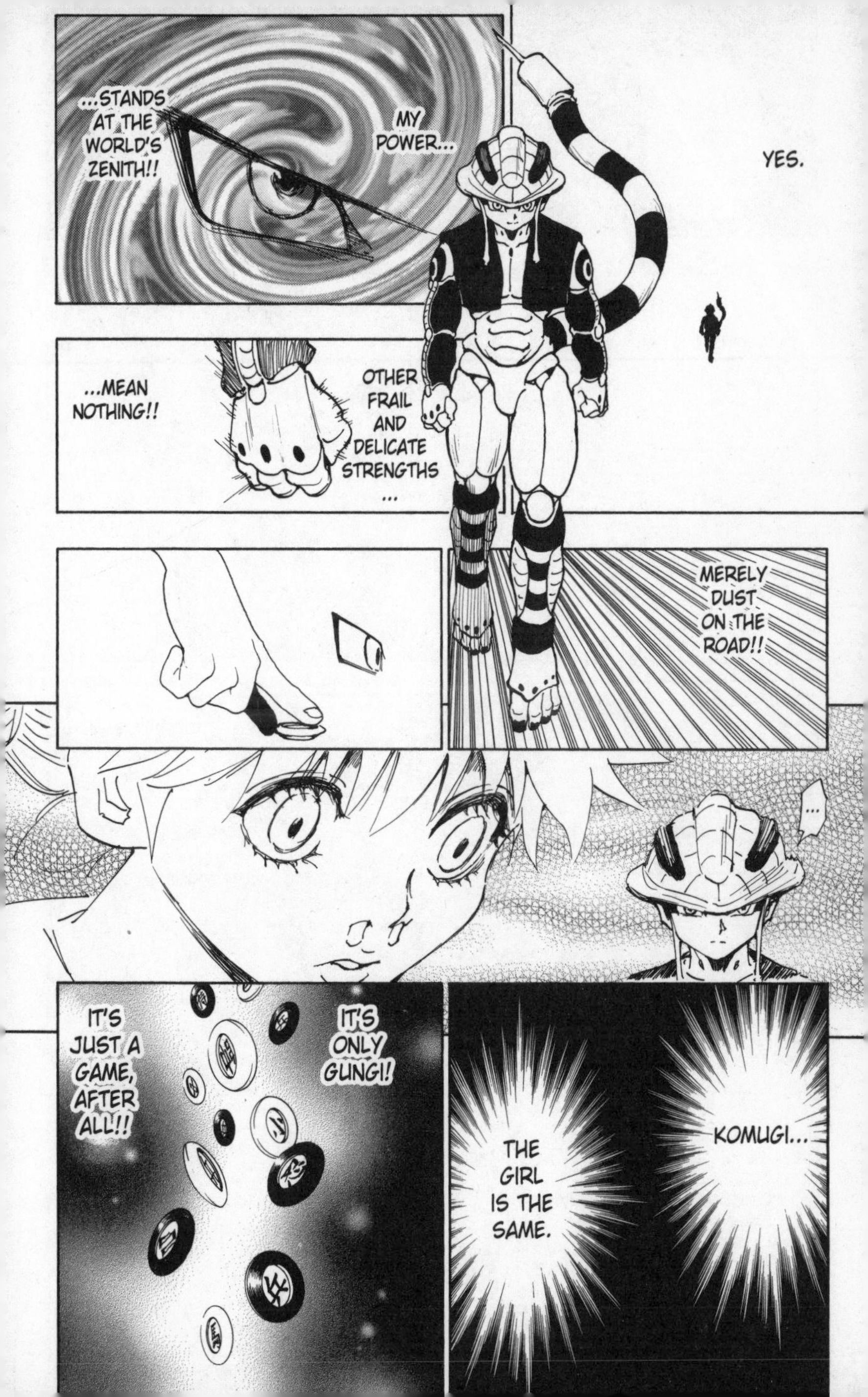
YES.
MY POWER...
...STANDS AT THE WORLD'S ZENITH!!
OTHER FRAIL AND DELICATE STRENGTHS...
...MEAN NOTHING!!
MERELY DUST ON THE ROAD!!
...
KOMUGI...
THE GIRL IS THE SAME.
IT'S ONLY GUNGI!
IT'S JUST A GAME, AFTER ALL!!

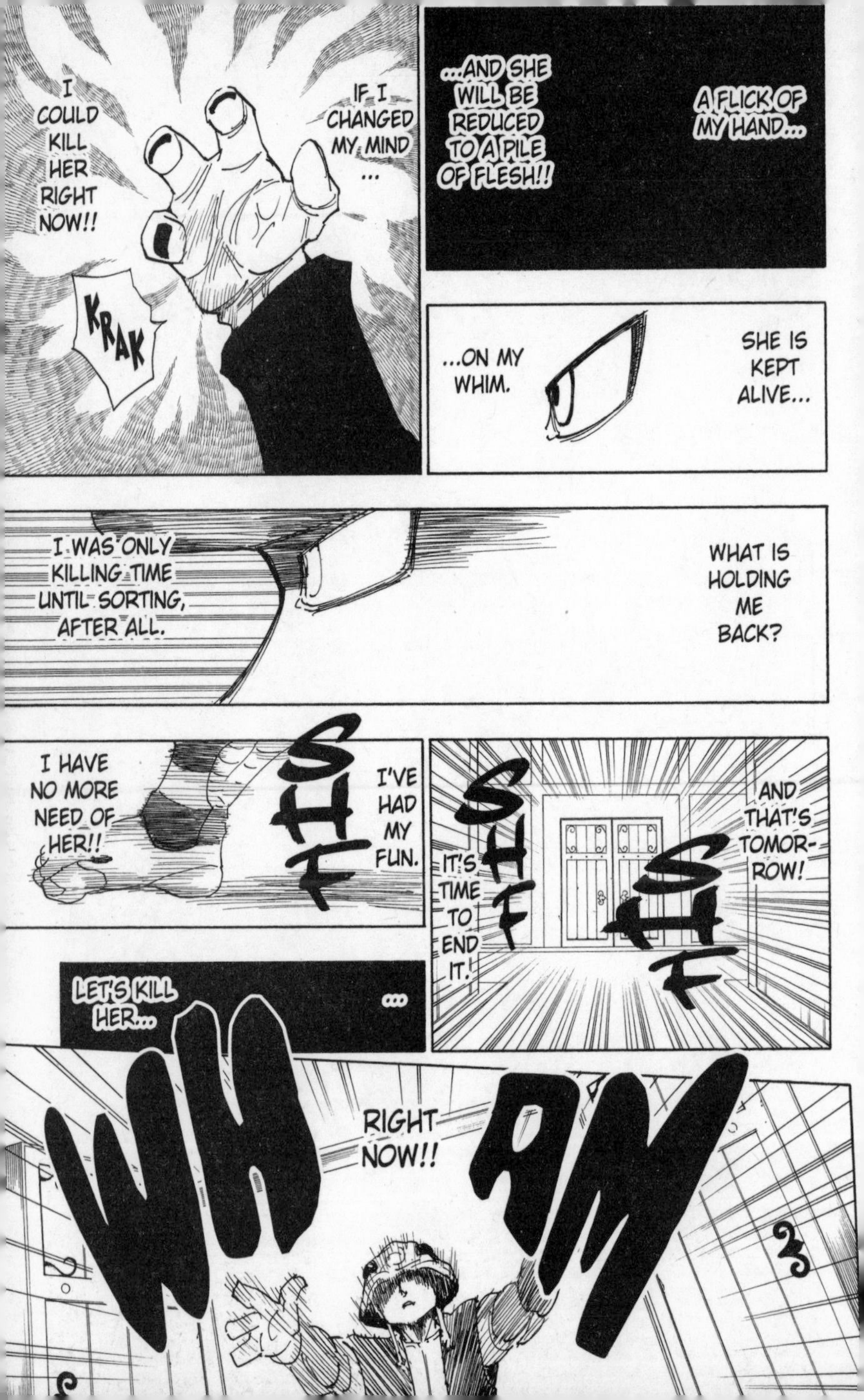
A FLICK OF MY HAND...
...AND SHE WILL BE REDUCED TO A PILE OF FLESH!!
SHE IS KEPT ALIVE...
...ON MY WHIM.
IF I CHANGED MY MIND ...
I COULD KILL HER RIGHT NOW!!
KRAK
WHAT IS HOLDING ME BACK?
I WAS ONLY KILLING TIME UNTIL SORTING, AFTER ALL.
AND THAT'S TOMORROW!
SHF
SHF
IT'S TIME TO END IT.
I'VE HAD MY FUN.
SHF
I HAVE NO MORE NEED OF HER!!
...
LET'S KILL HER...
WHAM
RIGHT NOW!!

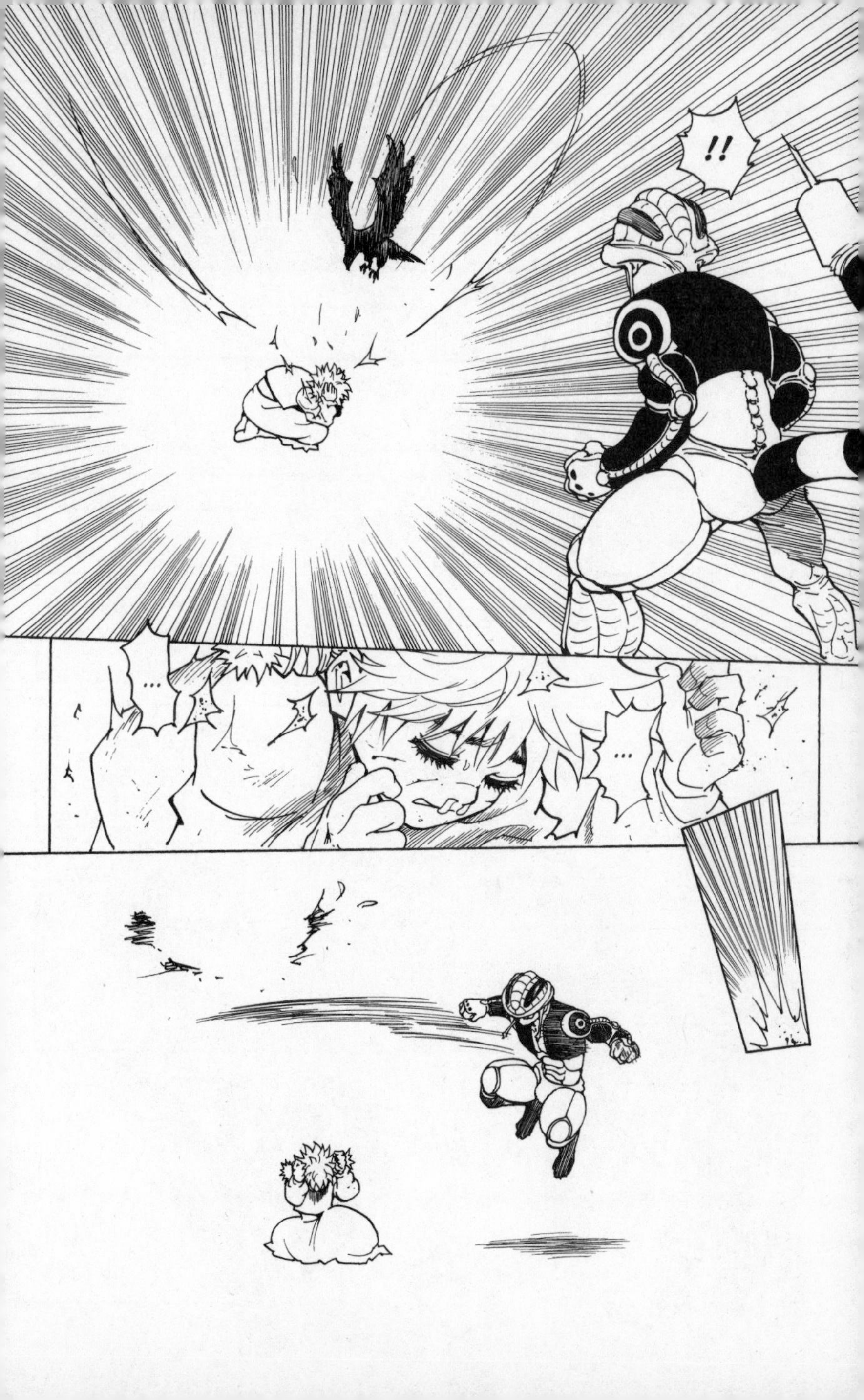
!!
...
...

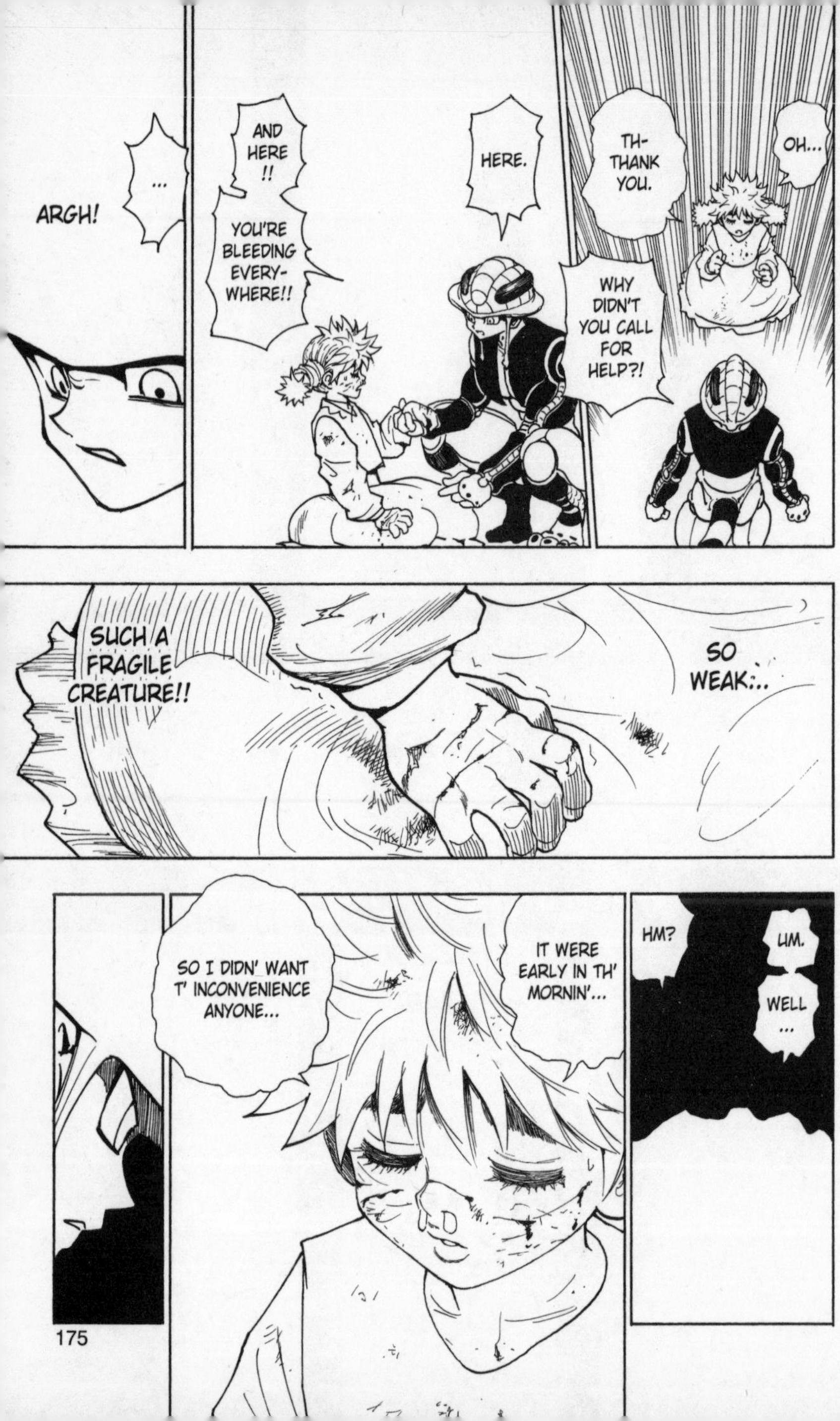
OH...
TH- THANK YOU.
WHY DIDN'T YOU CALL FOR HELP?!
HERE.
AND HERE !!
YOU'RE BLEEDING EVERY-WHERE!!
...
ARGH!
SO WEAK...
SUCH A FRAGILE CREATURE!!
UM.
WELL ...
HM?
IT WERE EARLY IN TH' MORNIN'...
SO I DIDN' WANT T' INCONVENIENCE ANYONE...

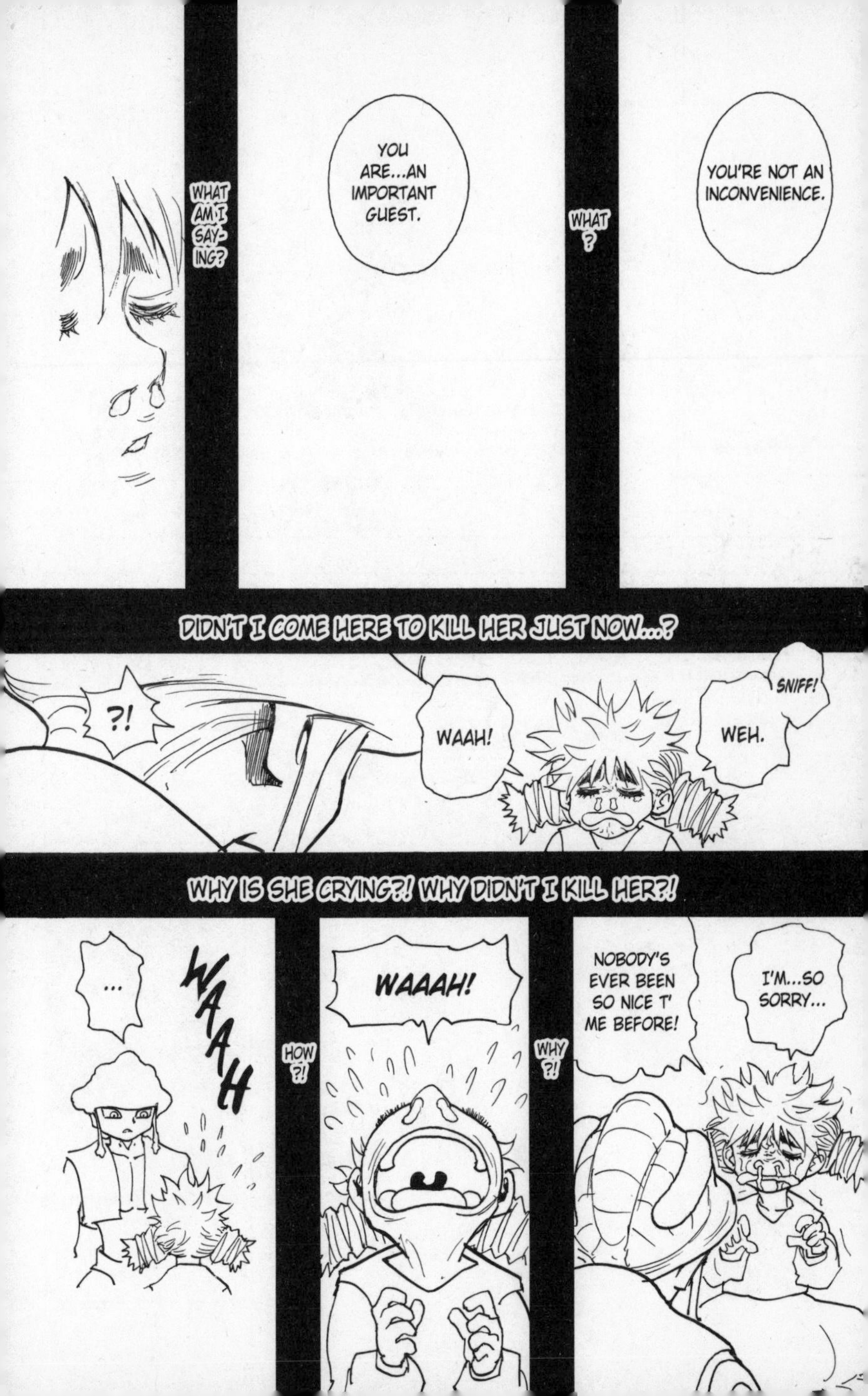
YOU'RE NOT AN INCONVENIENCE.
WHAT ?
YOU ARE...AN IMPORTANT GUEST.
WHAT AM I SAYING?
DIDN'T I COME HERE TO KILL HER JUST NOW...?
SNIFF!
WEH.
WAAH!
?!
WHY IS SHE CRYING?! WHY DIDN'T I KILL HER?!
I'M...SO SORRY...
NOBODY'S EVER BEEN SO NICE T' ME BEFORE!
WHY ?!
WAAAH!
HOW ?!
...
WAAAH

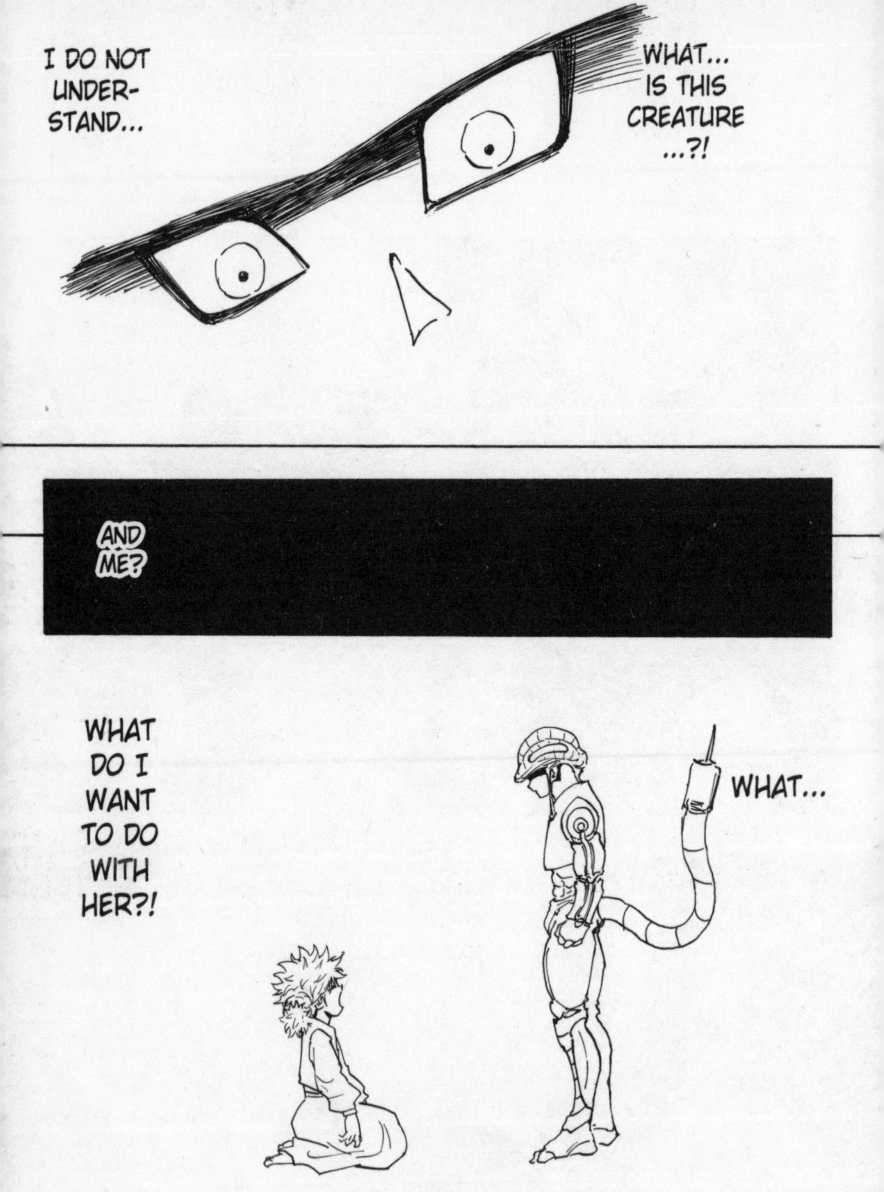
WHAT... IS THIS CREATURE ...?!
I DO NOT UNDER-STAND...
AND ME?
WHAT...
WHAT DO I WANT TO DO WITH HER?!

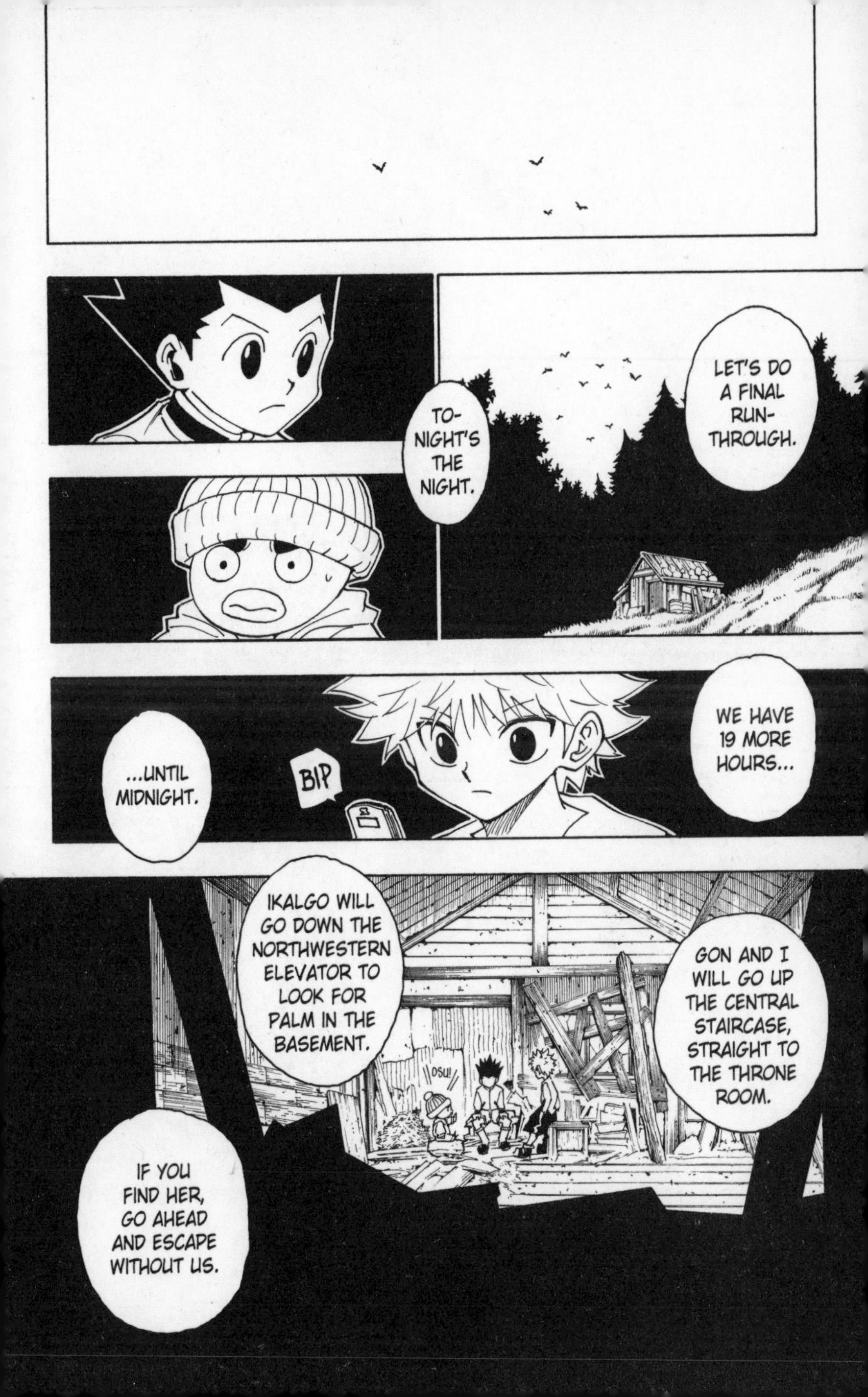
LET'S DO A FINAL RUN-THROUGH.
TO-NIGHT'S THE NIGHT.
WE HAVE 19 MORE HOURS...
BIP
...UNTIL MIDNIGHT.
GON AND I WILL GO UP THE CENTRAL STAIRCASE, STRAIGHT TO THE THRONE ROOM.
IKALGO WILL GO DOWN THE NORTHWESTERN ELEVATOR TO LOOK FOR PALM IN THE BASEMENT.
OSU!
IF YOU FIND HER, GO AHEAD AND ESCAPE WITHOUT US.

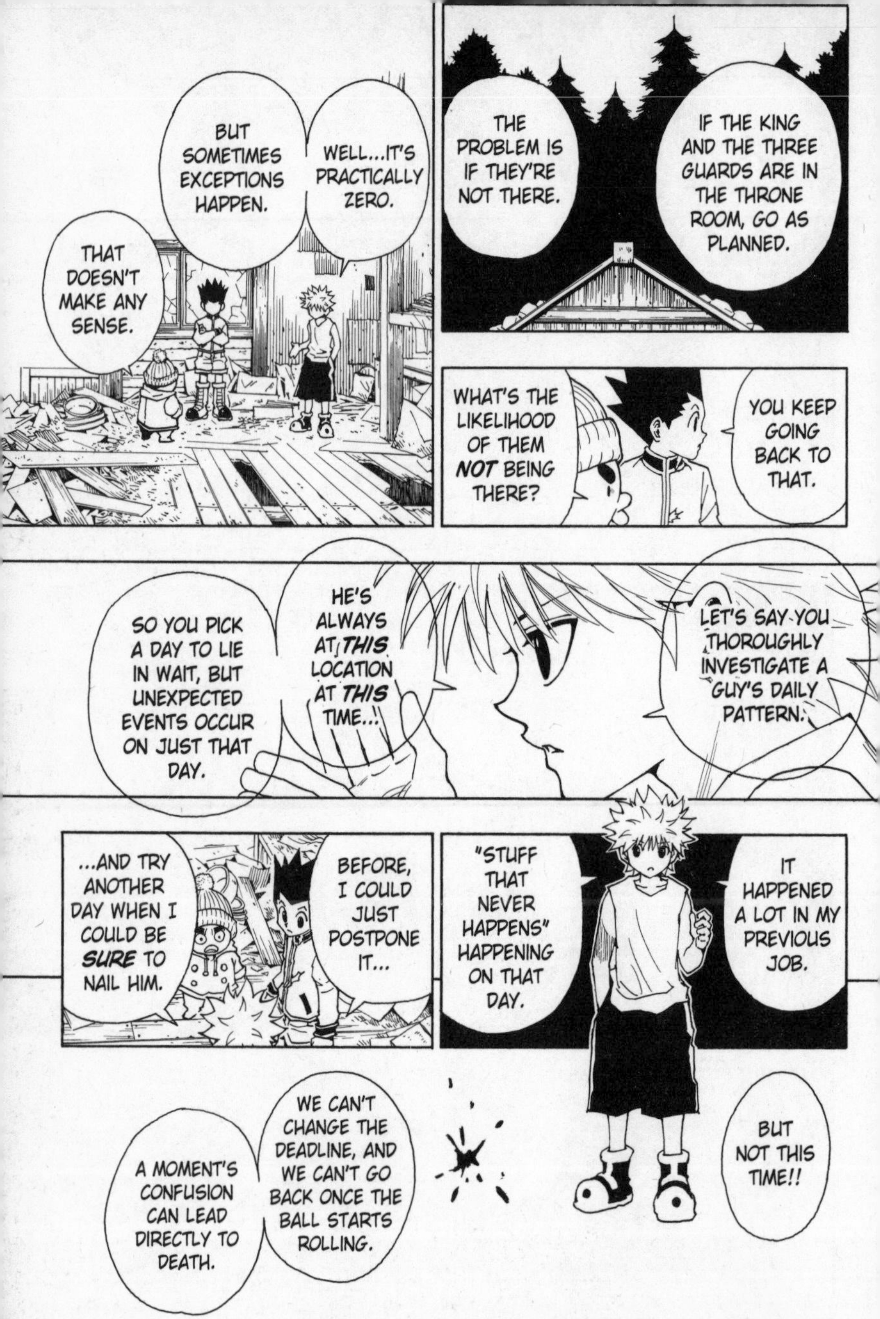
IF THE KING AND THE THREE GUARDS ARE IN THE THRONE ROOM, GO AS PLANNED.
THE PROBLEM IS IF THEY'RE NOT THERE.
YOU KEEP GOING BACK TO THAT.
WHAT'S THE LIKELIHOOD OF THEM *NOT* BEING THERE?
WELL...IT'S PRACTICALLY ZERO.
BUT SOMETIMES EXCEPTIONS HAPPEN.
THAT DOESN'T MAKE ANY SENSE.
LET'S SAY YOU THOROUGHLY INVESTIGATE A GUY'S DAILY PATTERN.
HE'S ALWAYS AT *THIS* LOCATION AT *THIS* TIME...
SO YOU PICK A DAY TO LIE IN WAIT, BUT UNEXPECTED EVENTS OCCUR ON JUST THAT DAY.
IT HAPPENED A LOT IN MY PREVIOUS JOB.
"STUFF THAT NEVER HAPPENS" HAPPENING ON THAT DAY.
BEFORE, I COULD JUST POSTPONE IT...
...AND TRY ANOTHER DAY WHEN I COULD BE *SURE* TO NAIL HIM.
BUT NOT THIS TIME!!
WE CAN'T CHANGE THE DEADLINE, AND WE CAN'T GO BACK ONCE THE BALL STARTS ROLLING.
A MOMENT'S CONFUSION CAN LEAD DIRECTLY TO DEATH.

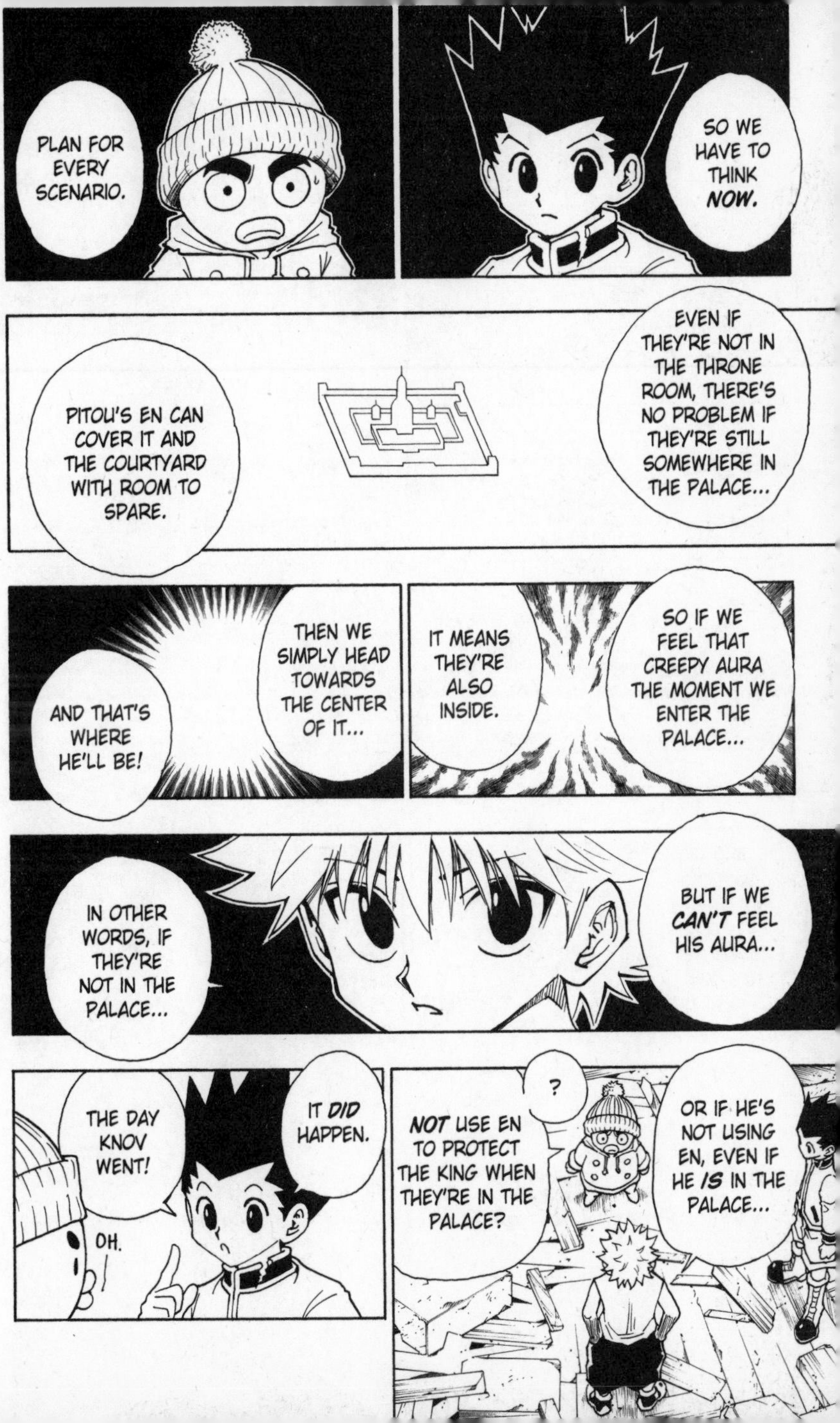
SO WE HAVE TO THINK *NOW.*
PLAN FOR EVERY SCENARIO.
EVEN IF THEY'RE NOT IN THE THRONE ROOM, THERE'S NO PROBLEM IF THEY'RE STILL SOMEWHERE IN THE PALACE...
PITOU'S EN CAN COVER IT AND THE COURTYARD WITH ROOM TO SPARE.
SO IF WE FEEL THAT CREEPY AURA THE MOMENT WE ENTER THE PALACE...
IT MEANS THEY'RE ALSO INSIDE.
THEN WE SIMPLY HEAD TOWARDS THE CENTER OF IT...
AND THAT'S WHERE HE'LL BE!
BUT IF WE *CAN'T* FEEL HIS AURA...
IN OTHER WORDS, IF THEY'RE NOT IN THE PALACE...
OR IF HE'S NOT USING EN, EVEN IF HE *IS* IN THE PALACE...
?
NOT USE EN TO PROTECT THE KING WHEN THEY'RE IN THE PALACE?
IT *DID* HAPPEN.
THE DAY KNOV WENT!
OH.

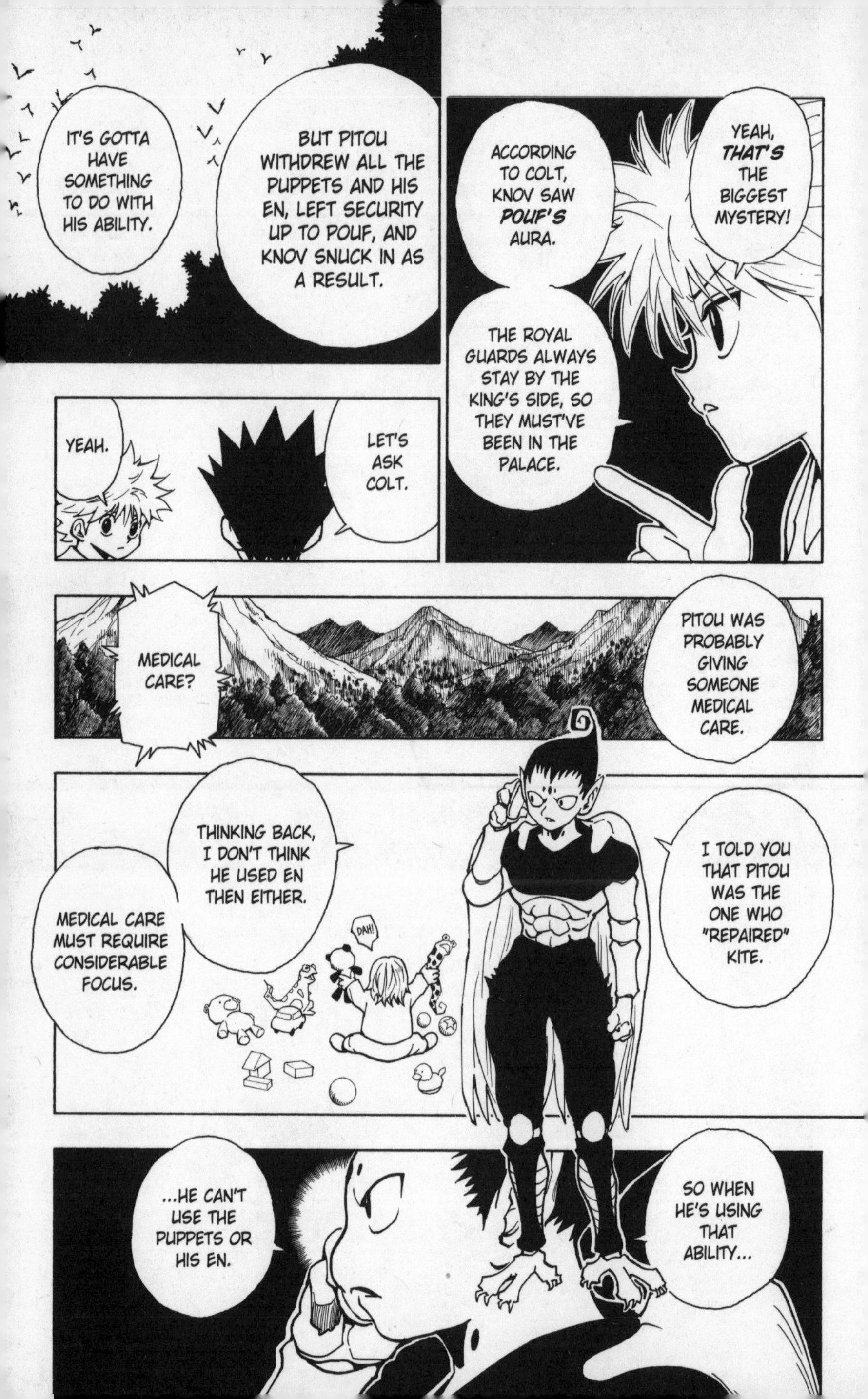
YEAH, **THAT'S** THE BIGGEST MYSTERY!
ACCORDING TO COLT, KNOV SAW **POUF'S** AURA.
THE ROYAL GUARDS ALWAYS STAY BY THE KING'S SIDE, SO THEY MUST'VE BEEN IN THE PALACE.
BUT PITOU WITHDREW ALL THE PUPPETS AND HIS EN, LEFT SECURITY UP TO POUF, AND KNOV SNUCK IN AS A RESULT.
IT'S GOTTA HAVE SOMETHING TO DO WITH HIS ABILITY.
LET'S ASK COLT.
YEAH.
PITOU WAS PROBABLY GIVING SOMEONE MEDICAL CARE.
MEDICAL CARE?
I TOLD YOU THAT PITOU WAS THE ONE WHO "REPAIRED" KITE.
THINKING BACK, I DON'T THINK HE USED EN THEN EITHER.
MEDICAL CARE MUST REQUIRE CONSIDERABLE FOCUS.
DAH!
SO WHEN HE'S USING THAT ABILITY...
...HE CAN'T USE THE PUPPETS OR HIS EN.

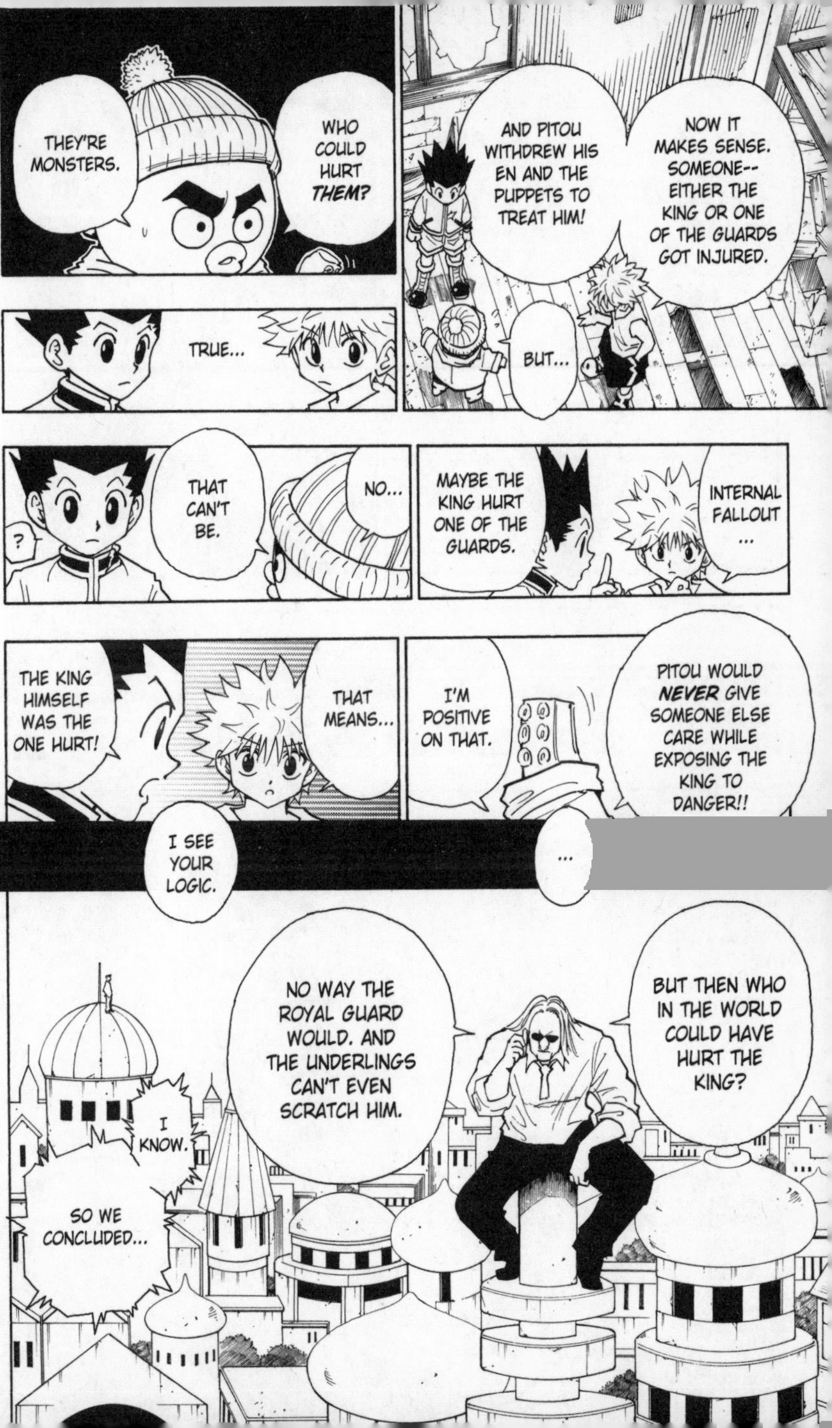
NOW IT MAKES SENSE. SOMEONE-- EITHER THE KING OR ONE OF THE GUARDS GOT INJURED.
AND PITOU WITHDREW HIS EN AND THE PUPPETS TO TREAT HIM!
BUT...
WHO COULD HURT *THEM?*
THEY'RE MONSTERS.
TRUE...
INTERNAL FALLOUT...
MAYBE THE KING HURT ONE OF THE GUARDS.
NO...
THAT CAN'T BE.
?
PITOU WOULD ***NEVER*** GIVE SOMEONE ELSE CARE WHILE EXPOSING THE KING TO DANGER!!
I'M POSITIVE ON THAT.
THAT MEANS...
THE KING HIMSELF WAS THE ONE HURT!
...
I SEE YOUR LOGIC.
BUT THEN WHO IN THE WORLD COULD HAVE HURT THE KING?
NO WAY THE ROYAL GUARD WOULD. AND THE UNDERLINGS CAN'T EVEN SCRATCH HIM.
I KNOW.
SO WE CONCLUDED...

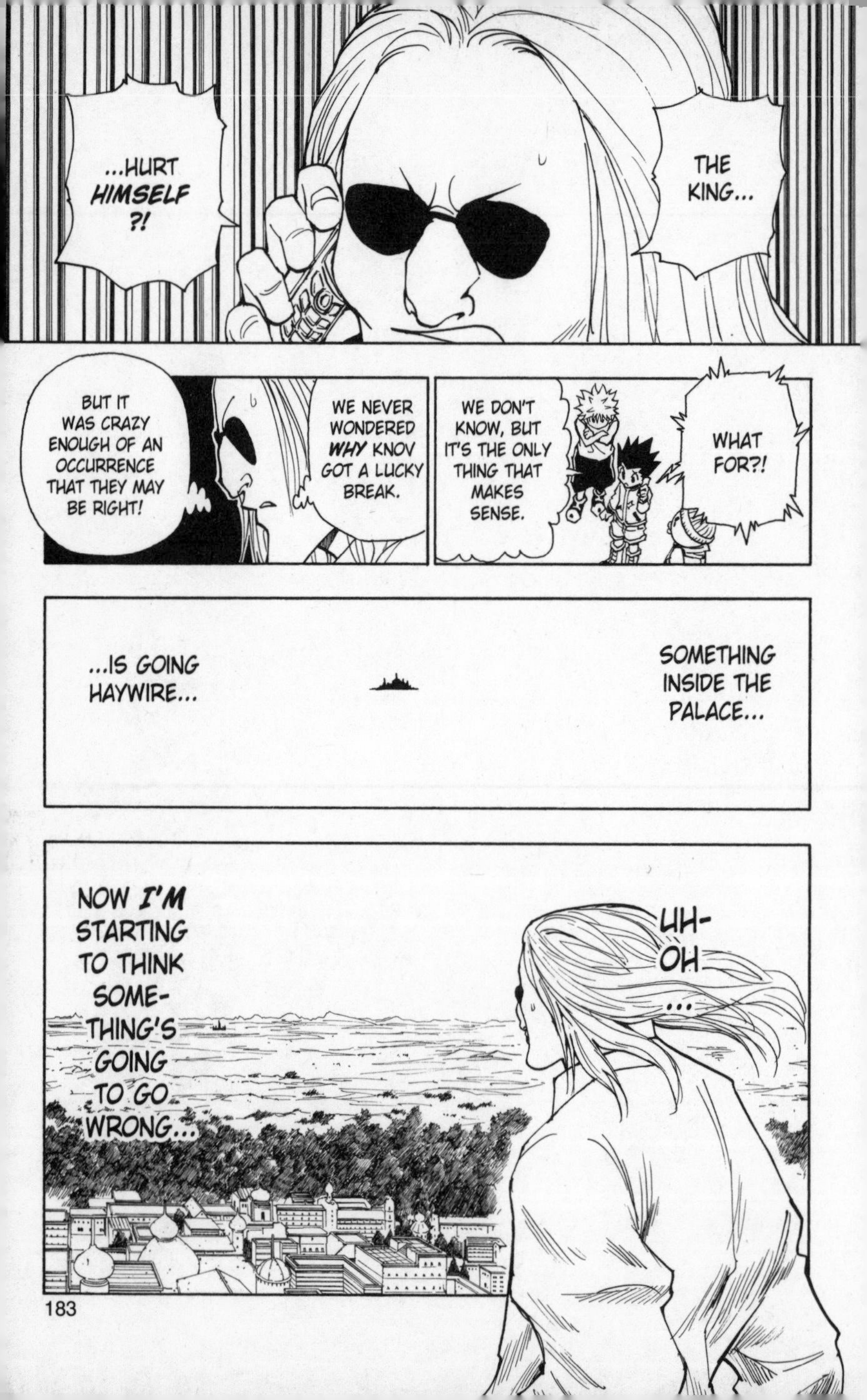
THE KING...
...HURT *HIMSELF* ?!
WHAT FOR?!
WE DON'T KNOW, BUT IT'S THE ONLY THING THAT MAKES SENSE.
WE NEVER WONDERED *WHY* KNOV GOT A LUCKY BREAK.
BUT IT WAS CRAZY ENOUGH OF AN OCCURRENCE THAT THEY MAY BE RIGHT!
SOMETHING INSIDE THE PALACE...
...IS GOING HAYWIRE...
UH-OH...
NOW *I'M* STARTING TO THINK SOME-THING'S GOING TO GO WRONG...

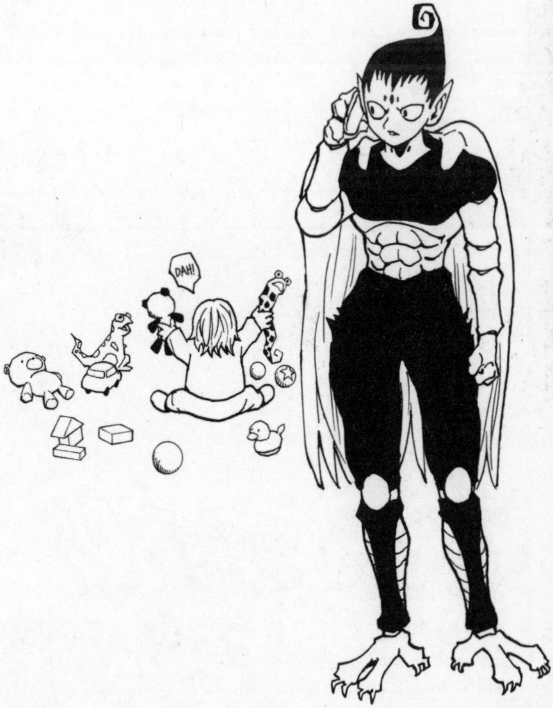
DAH!

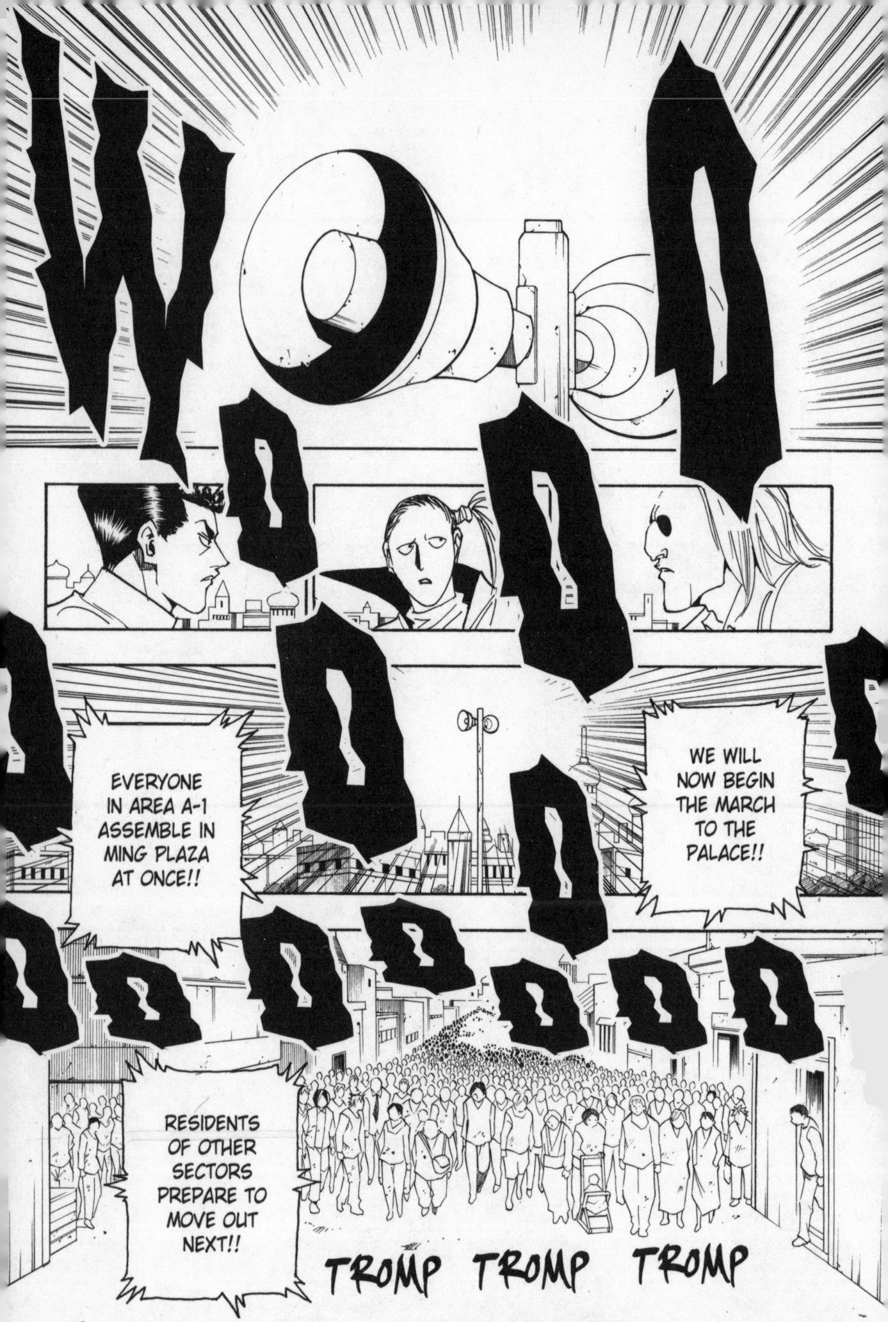
WOOOOOOOOOOOOOOO
WE WILL NOW BEGIN THE MARCH TO THE PALACE!!
EVERYONE IN AREA A-1 ASSEMBLE IN MING PLAZA AT ONCE!!
TROMP TROMP TROMP
RESIDENTS OF OTHER SECTORS PREPARE TO MOVE OUT NEXT!!

Chapter 259: 1: Part 3

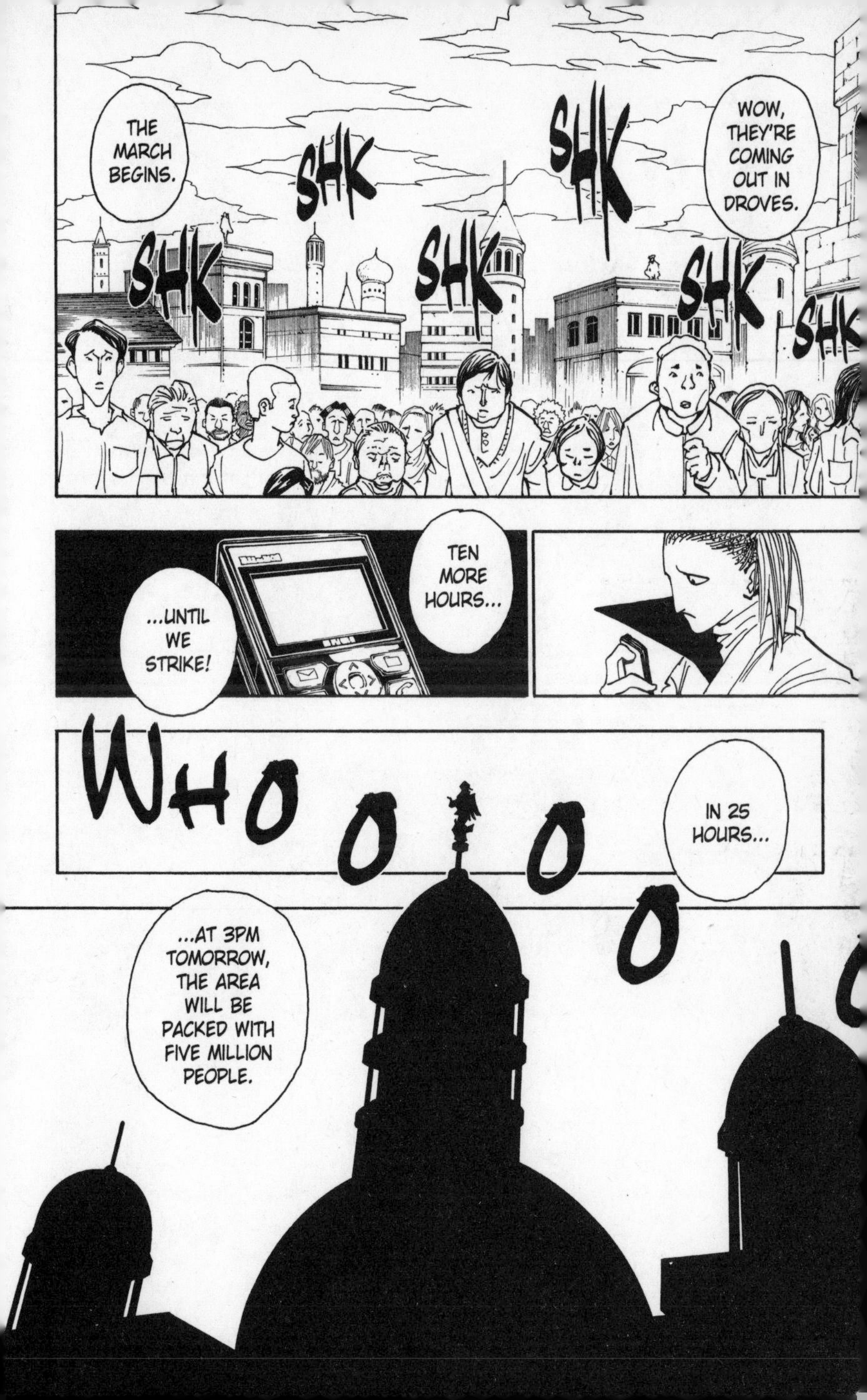
WOW, THEY'RE COMING OUT IN DROVES.
THE MARCH BEGINS.
SHK SHK SHK SHK SHK SHK
TEN MORE HOURS...
...UNTIL WE STRIKE!
WHOOOOO
IN 25 HOURS...
...AT 3PM TOMORROW, THE AREA WILL BE PACKED WITH FIVE MILLION PEOPLE.

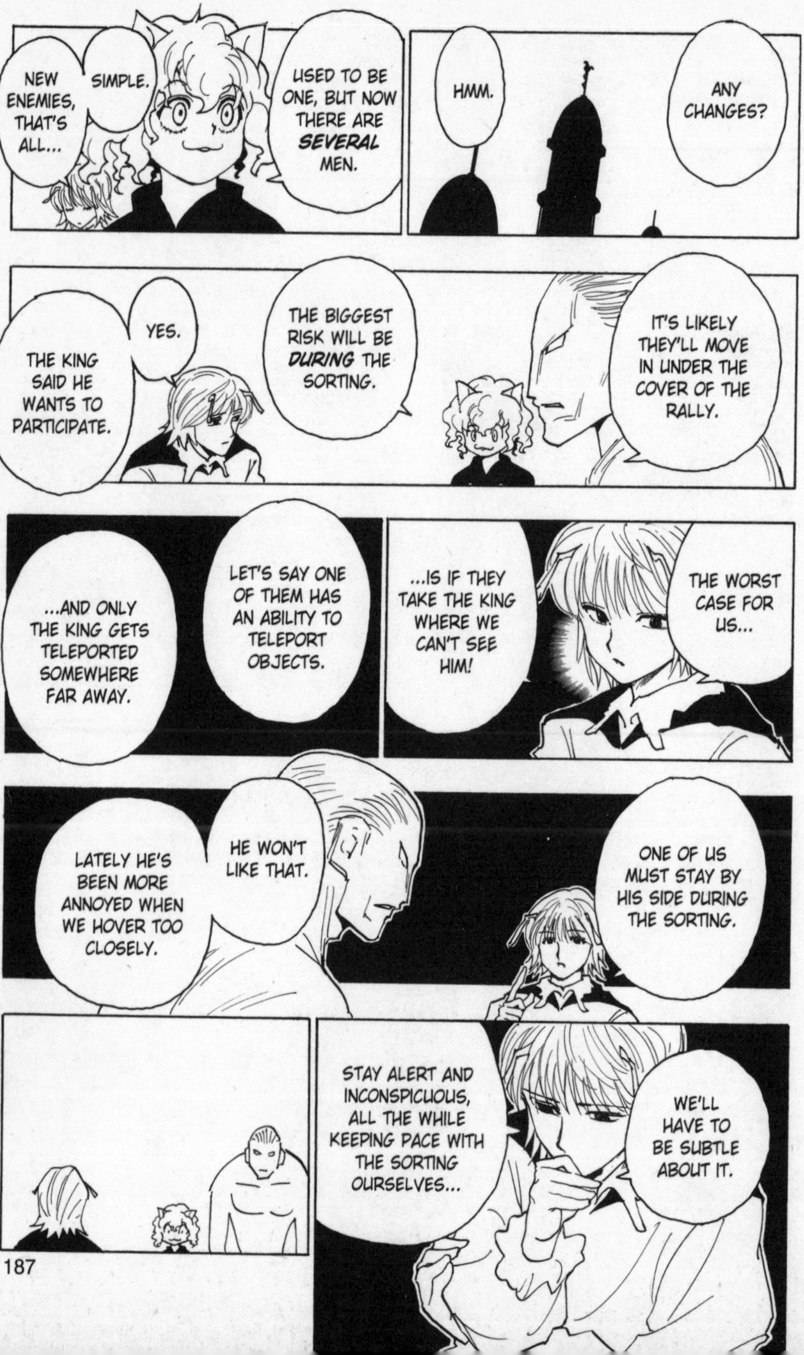
ANY CHANGES?
HMM.
USED TO BE ONE, BUT NOW THERE ARE SEVERAL MEN.
SIMPLE.
NEW ENEMIES, THAT'S ALL...
IT'S LIKELY THEY'LL MOVE IN UNDER THE COVER OF THE RALLY.
THE BIGGEST RISK WILL BE DURING THE SORTING.
YES.
THE KING SAID HE WANTS TO PARTICIPATE.
THE WORST CASE FOR US...
...IS IF THEY TAKE THE KING WHERE WE CAN'T SEE HIM!
LET'S SAY ONE OF THEM HAS AN ABILITY TO TELEPORT OBJECTS.
...AND ONLY THE KING GETS TELEPORTED SOMEWHERE FAR AWAY.
ONE OF US MUST STAY BY HIS SIDE DURING THE SORTING.
HE WON'T LIKE THAT.
LATELY HE'S BEEN MORE ANNOYED WHEN WE HOVER TOO CLOSELY.
WE'LL HAVE TO BE SUBTLE ABOUT IT.
STAY ALERT AND INCONSPICUOUS, ALL THE WHILE KEEPING PACE WITH THE SORTING OURSELVES...

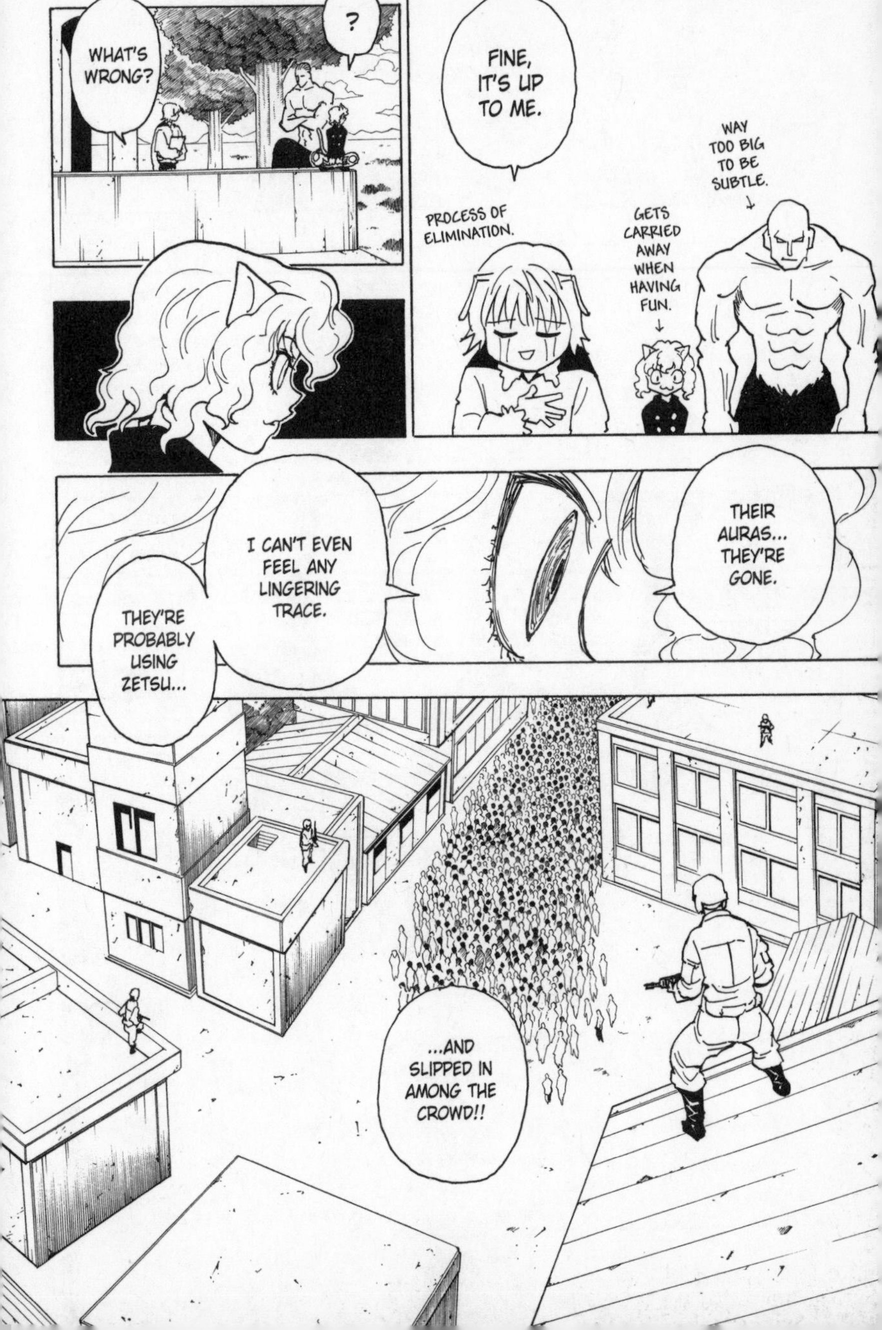
FINE, IT'S UP TO ME.
WAY TOO BIG TO BE SUBTLE.
GETS CARRIED AWAY WHEN HAVING FUN.
PROCESS OF ELIMINATION.
?
WHAT'S WRONG?
THEIR AURAS... THEY'RE GONE.
I CAN'T EVEN FEEL ANY LINGERING TRACE.
THEY'RE PROBABLY USING ZETSU...
...AND SLIPPED IN AMONG THE CROWD!!

READ THIS WAY

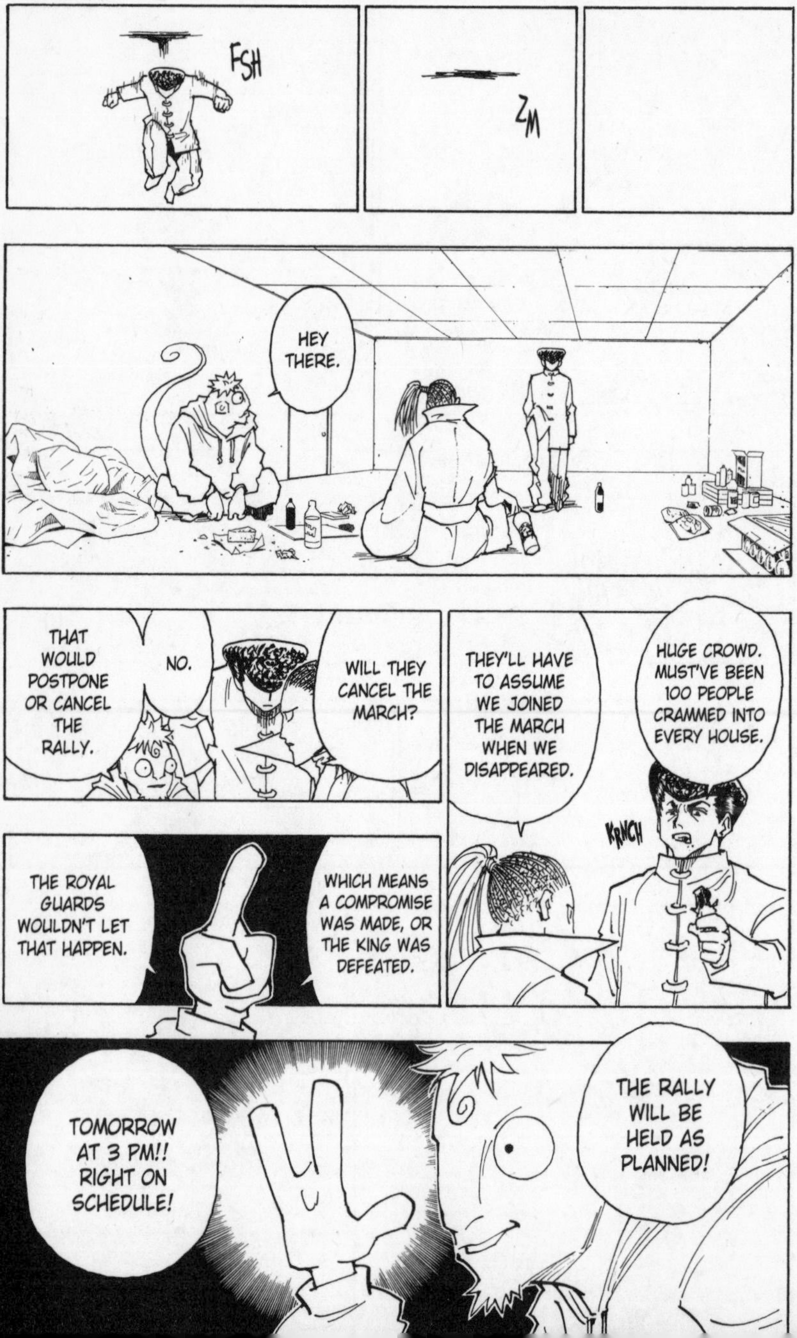
ZM
FSH
HEY THERE.
HUGE CROWD. MUST'VE BEEN 100 PEOPLE CRAMMED INTO EVERY HOUSE.
THEY'LL HAVE TO ASSUME WE JOINED THE MARCH WHEN WE DISAPPEARED.
KRNCH
WILL THEY CANCEL THE MARCH?
NO.
THAT WOULD POSTPONE OR CANCEL THE RALLY.
WHICH MEANS A COMPROMISE WAS MADE, OR THE KING WAS DEFEATED.
THE ROYAL GUARDS WOULDN'T LET THAT HAPPEN.
THE RALLY WILL BE HELD AS PLANNED!
TOMORROW AT 3 PM!! RIGHT ON SCHEDULE!

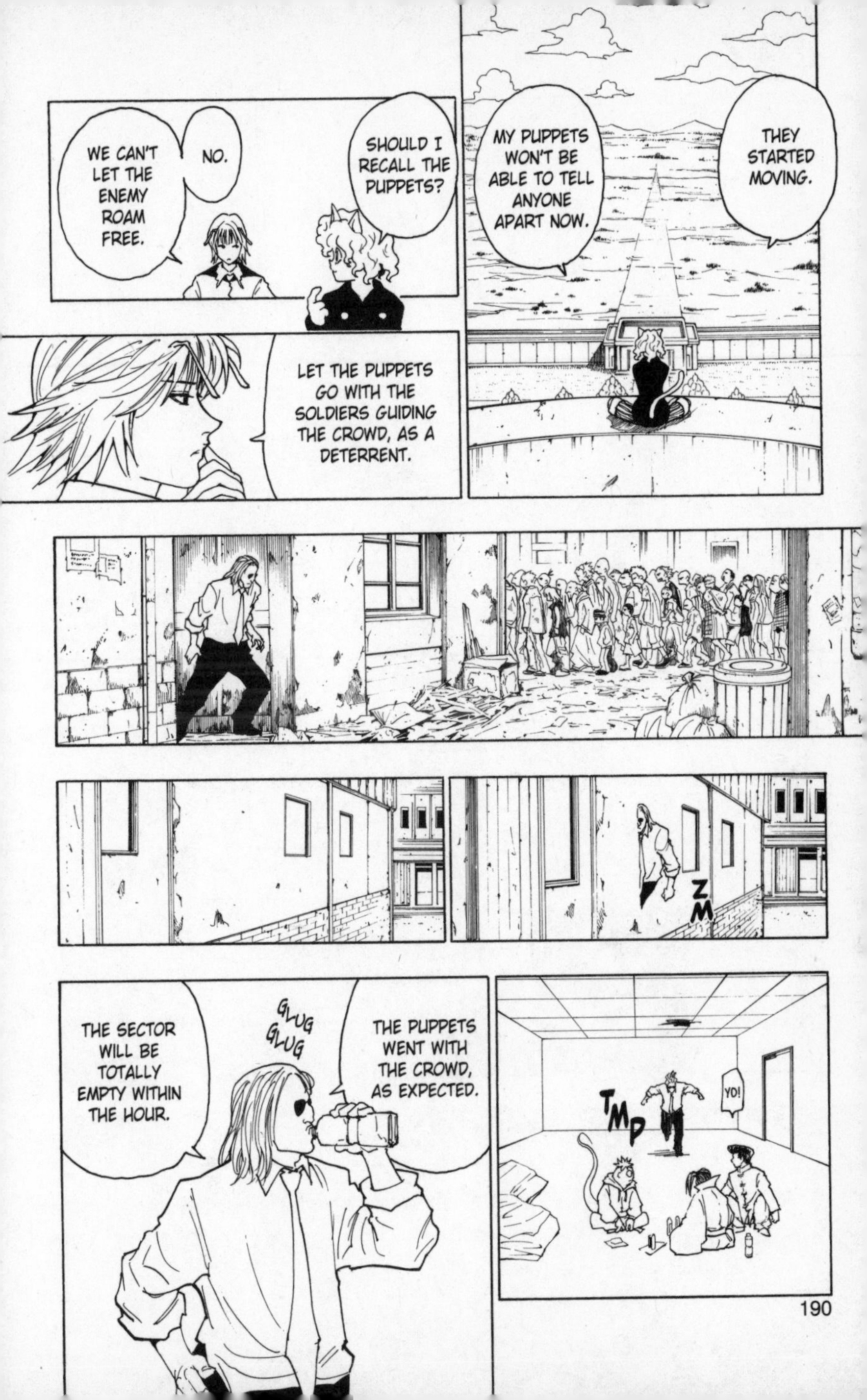
THEY STARTED MOVING.
MY PUPPETS WON'T BE ABLE TO TELL ANYONE APART NOW.
SHOULD I RECALL THE PUPPETS?
NO.
WE CAN'T LET THE ENEMY ROAM FREE.
LET THE PUPPETS GO WITH THE SOLDIERS GUIDING THE CROWD, AS A DETERRENT.
ZM
YO!
TMP
THE PUPPETS WENT WITH THE CROWD, AS EXPECTED.
GLUG GLUG
THE SECTOR WILL BE TOTALLY EMPTY WITHIN THE HOUR.

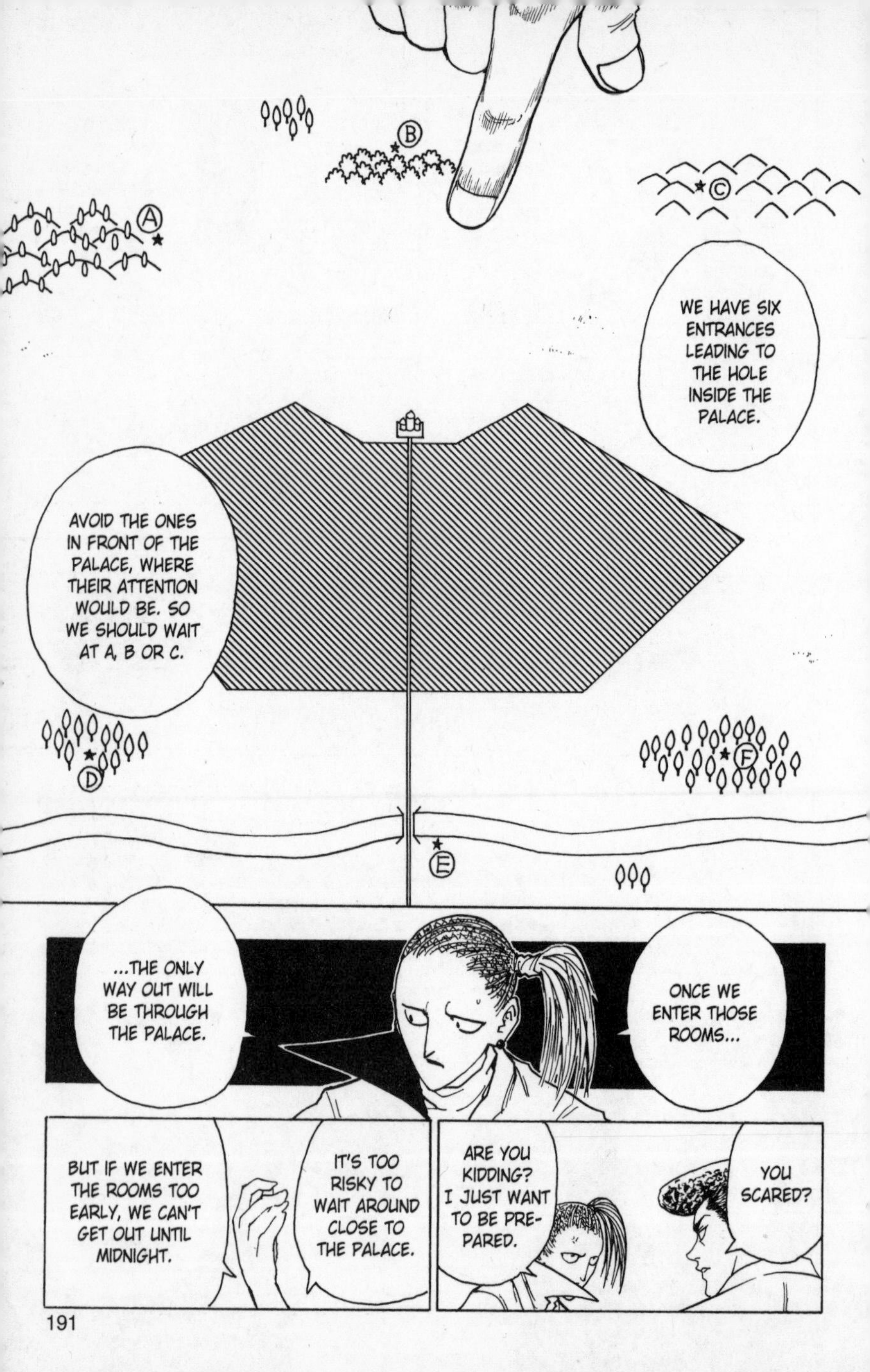
WE HAVE SIX ENTRANCES LEADING TO THE HOLE INSIDE THE PALACE.
AVOID THE ONES IN FRONT OF THE PALACE, WHERE THEIR ATTENTION WOULD BE. SO WE SHOULD WAIT AT A, B OR C.
B
C
A
D
F
E
ONCE WE ENTER THOSE ROOMS...
...THE ONLY WAY OUT WILL BE THROUGH THE PALACE.
YOU SCARED?
ARE YOU KIDDING? I JUST WANT TO BE PRE-PARED.
IT'S TOO RISKY TO WAIT AROUND CLOSE TO THE PALACE.
BUT IF WE ENTER THE ROOMS TOO EARLY, WE CAN'T GET OUT UNTIL MIDNIGHT.

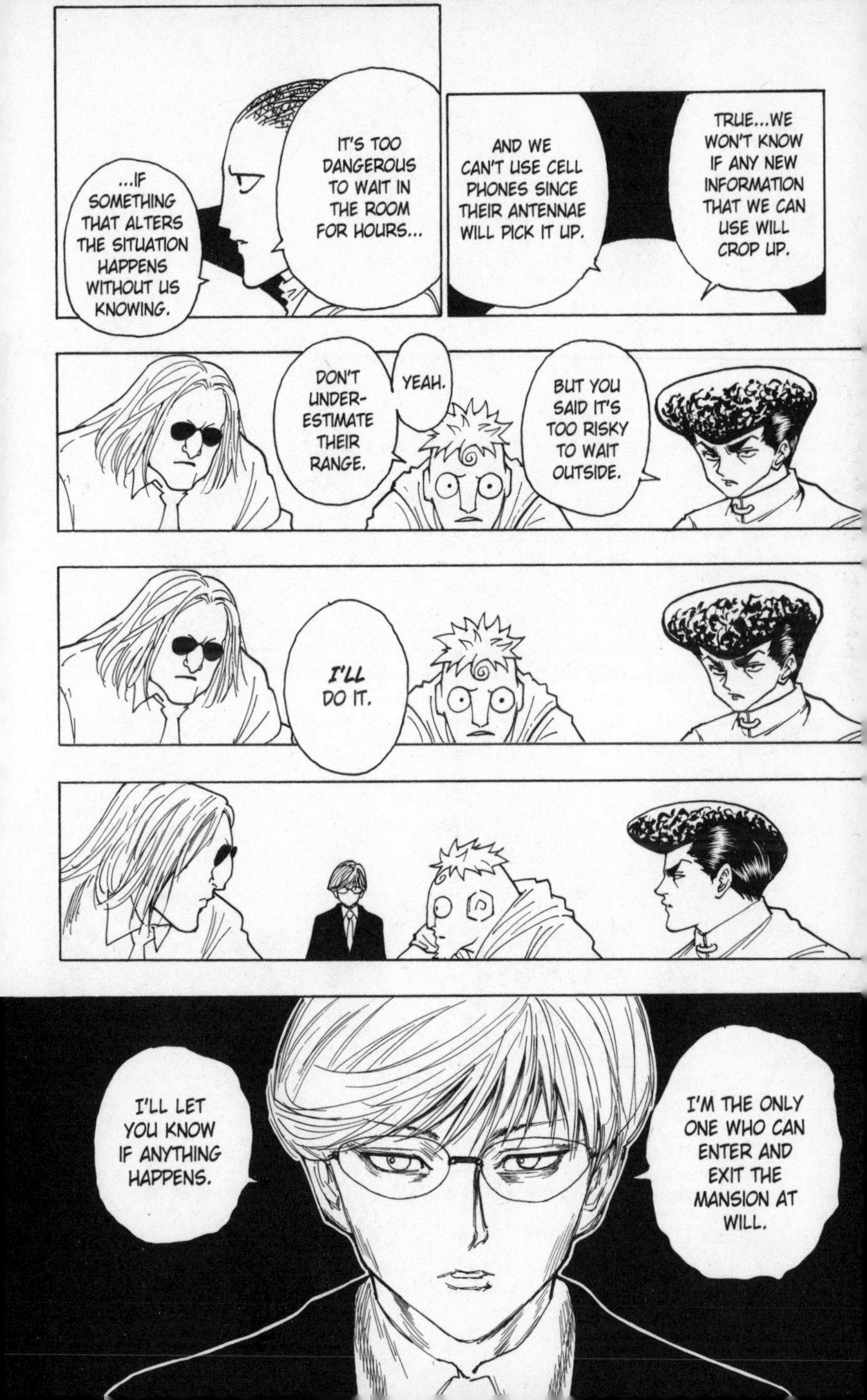
TRUE...WE WON'T KNOW IF ANY NEW INFORMATION THAT WE CAN USE WILL CROP UP.
AND WE CAN'T USE CELL PHONES SINCE THEIR ANTENNAE WILL PICK IT UP.
IT'S TOO DANGEROUS TO WAIT IN THE ROOM FOR HOURS...
...IF SOMETHING THAT ALTERS THE SITUATION HAPPENS WITHOUT US KNOWING.
BUT YOU SAID IT'S TOO RISKY TO WAIT OUTSIDE.
YEAH.
DON'T UNDER-ESTIMATE THEIR RANGE.
I'LL DO IT.
I'M THE ONLY ONE WHO CAN ENTER AND EXIT THE MANSION AT WILL.
I'LL LET YOU KNOW IF ANYTHING HAPPENS.

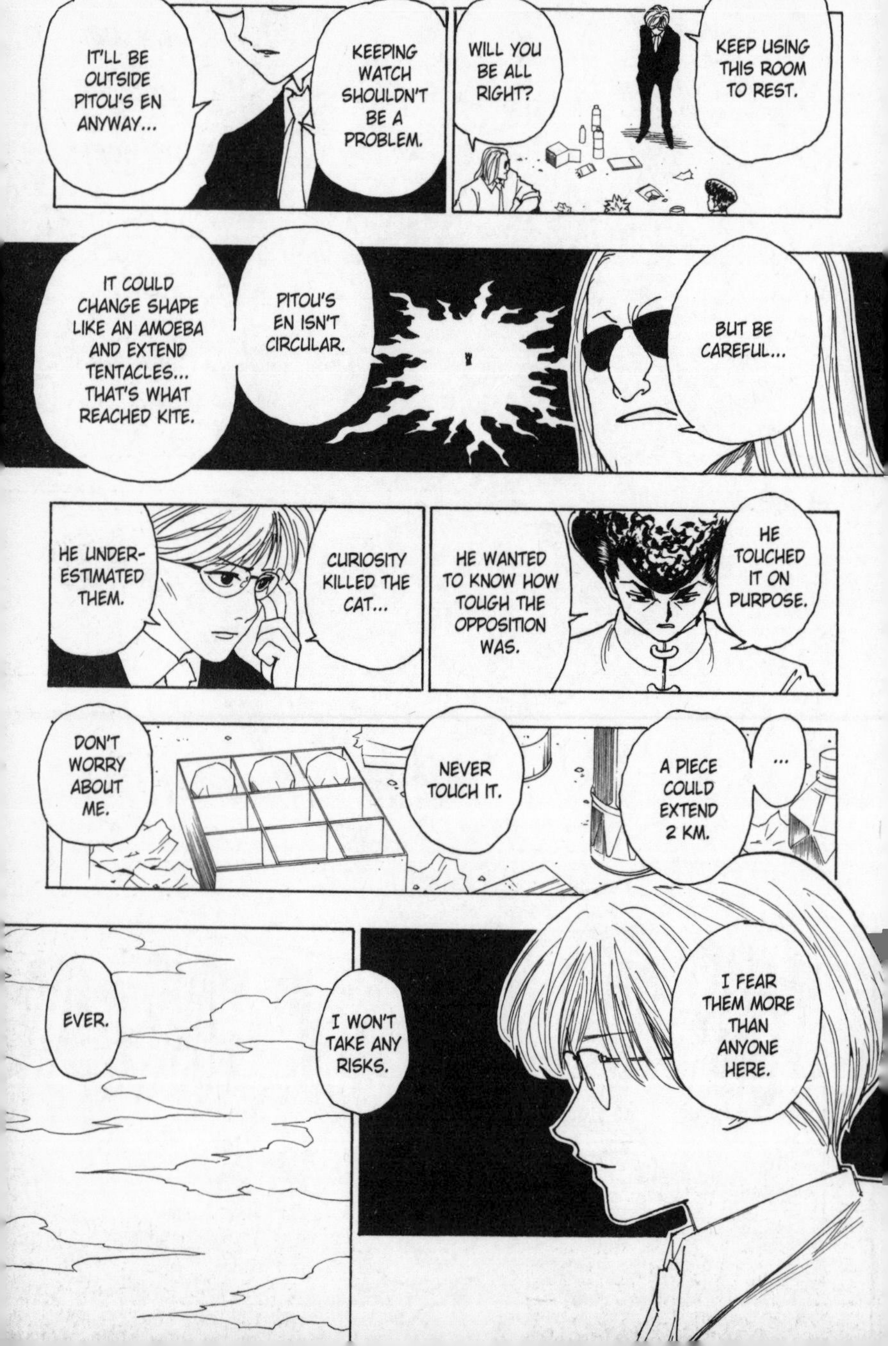
KEEP USING THIS ROOM TO REST.
WILL YOU BE ALL RIGHT?
KEEPING WATCH SHOULDN'T BE A PROBLEM.
IT'LL BE OUTSIDE PITOU'S EN ANYWAY...
BUT BE CAREFUL...
PITOU'S EN ISN'T CIRCULAR.
IT COULD CHANGE SHAPE LIKE AN AMOEBA AND EXTEND TENTACLES... THAT'S WHAT REACHED KITE.
HE TOUCHED IT ON PURPOSE.
HE WANTED TO KNOW HOW TOUGH THE OPPOSITION WAS.
CURIOSITY KILLED THE CAT...
HE UNDER-ESTIMATED THEM.
...
A PIECE COULD EXTEND 2 KM.
NEVER TOUCH IT.
DON'T WORRY ABOUT ME.
I FEAR THEM MORE THAN ANYONE HERE.
I WON'T TAKE ANY RISKS.
EVER.

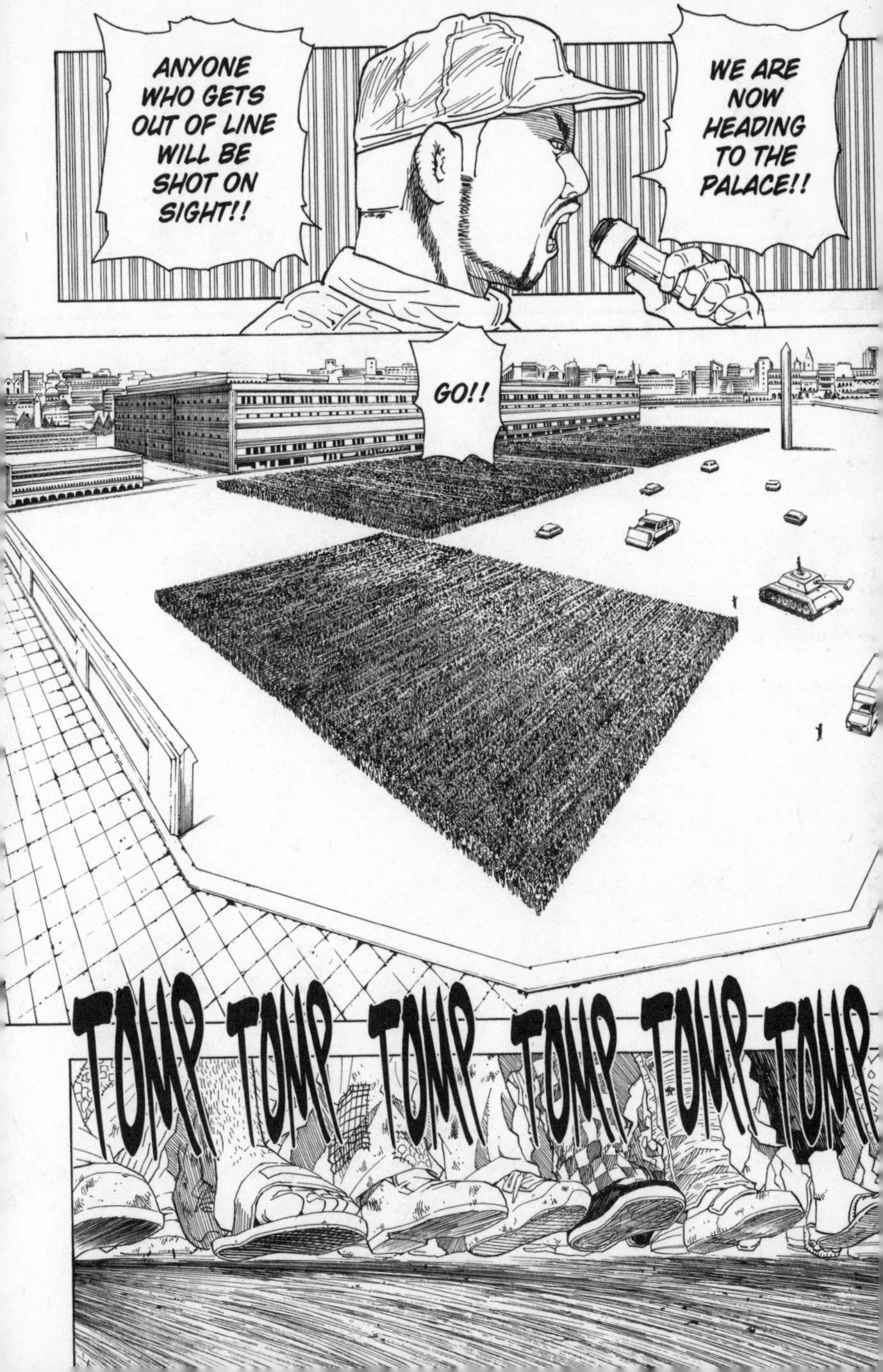

WE ARE NOW HEADING TO THE PALACE!!
ANYONE WHO GETS OUT OF LINE WILL BE SHOT ON SIGHT!!
GO!!
TOMP TOMP TOMP TOMP TOMP TOMP

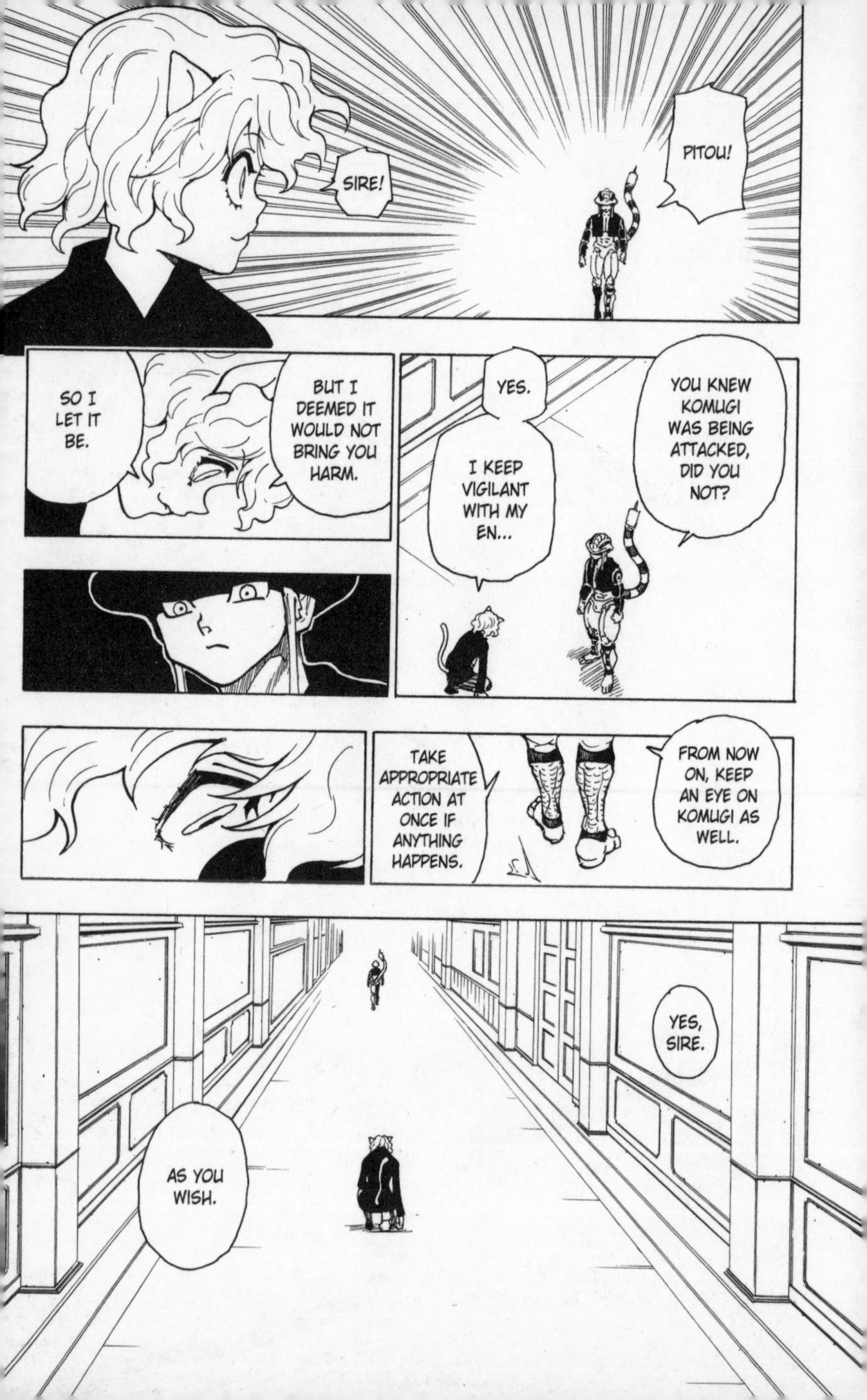
PITOU!
SIRE!
YOU KNEW KOMUGI WAS BEING ATTACKED, DID YOU NOT?
YES.
I KEEP VIGILANT WITH MY EN...
BUT I DEEMED IT WOULD NOT BRING YOU HARM.
SO I LET IT BE.
FROM NOW ON, KEEP AN EYE ON KOMUGI AS WELL.
TAKE APPROPRIATE ACTION AT ONCE IF ANYTHING HAPPENS.
YES, SIRE.
AS YOU WISH.

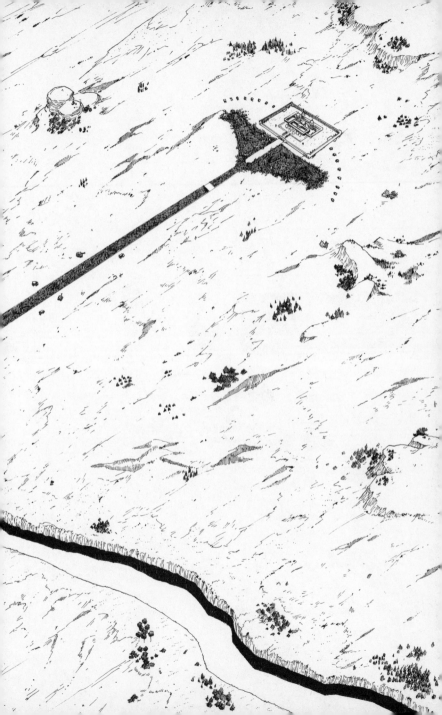

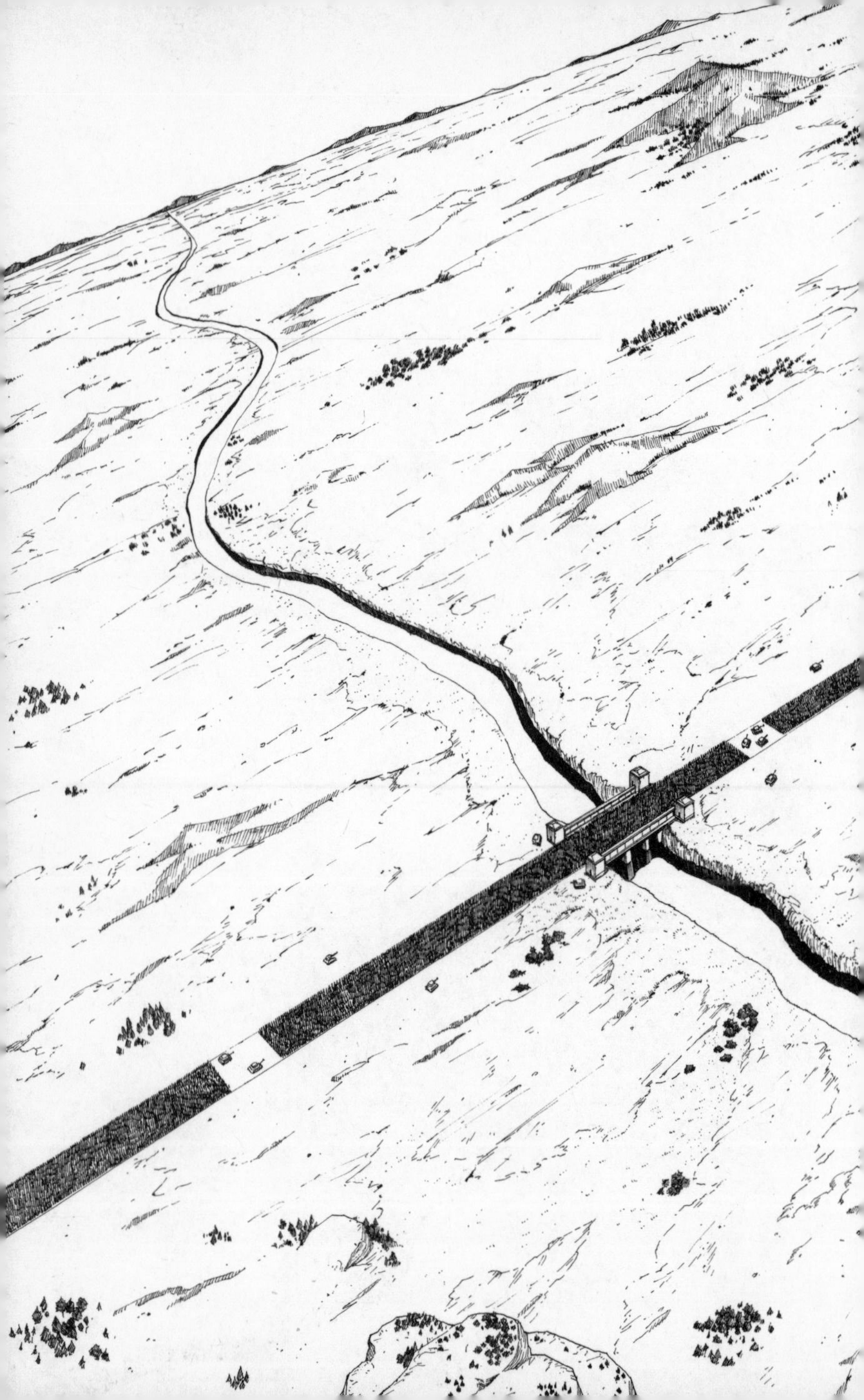

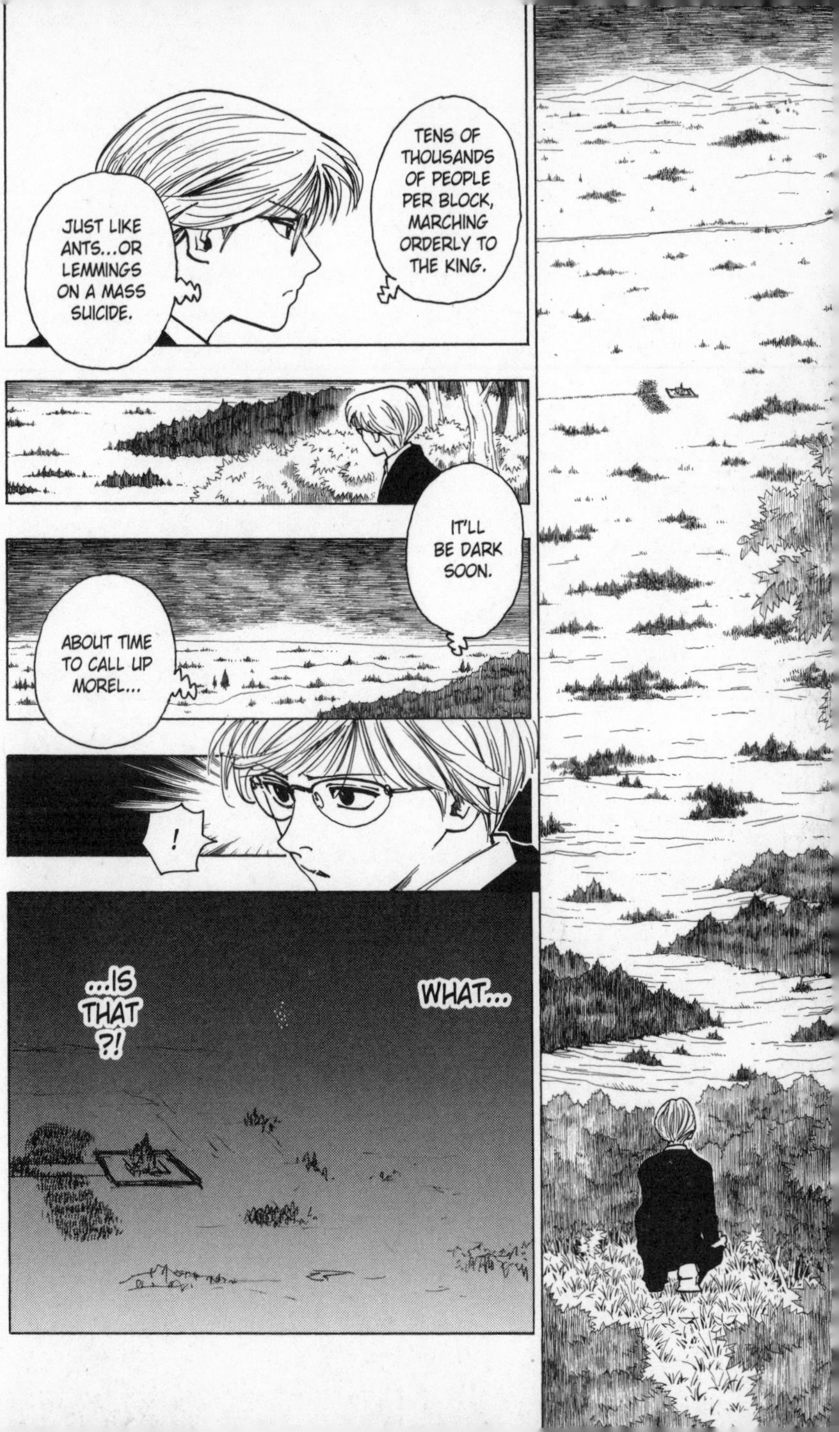
TENS OF THOUSANDS OF PEOPLE PER BLOCK, MARCHING ORDERLY TO THE KING.
JUST LIKE ANTS...OR LEMMINGS ON A MASS SUICIDE.
IT'LL BE DARK SOON.
ABOUT TIME TO CALL UP MOREL...
!
WHAT...
...IS THAT?!

READ THIS WAY

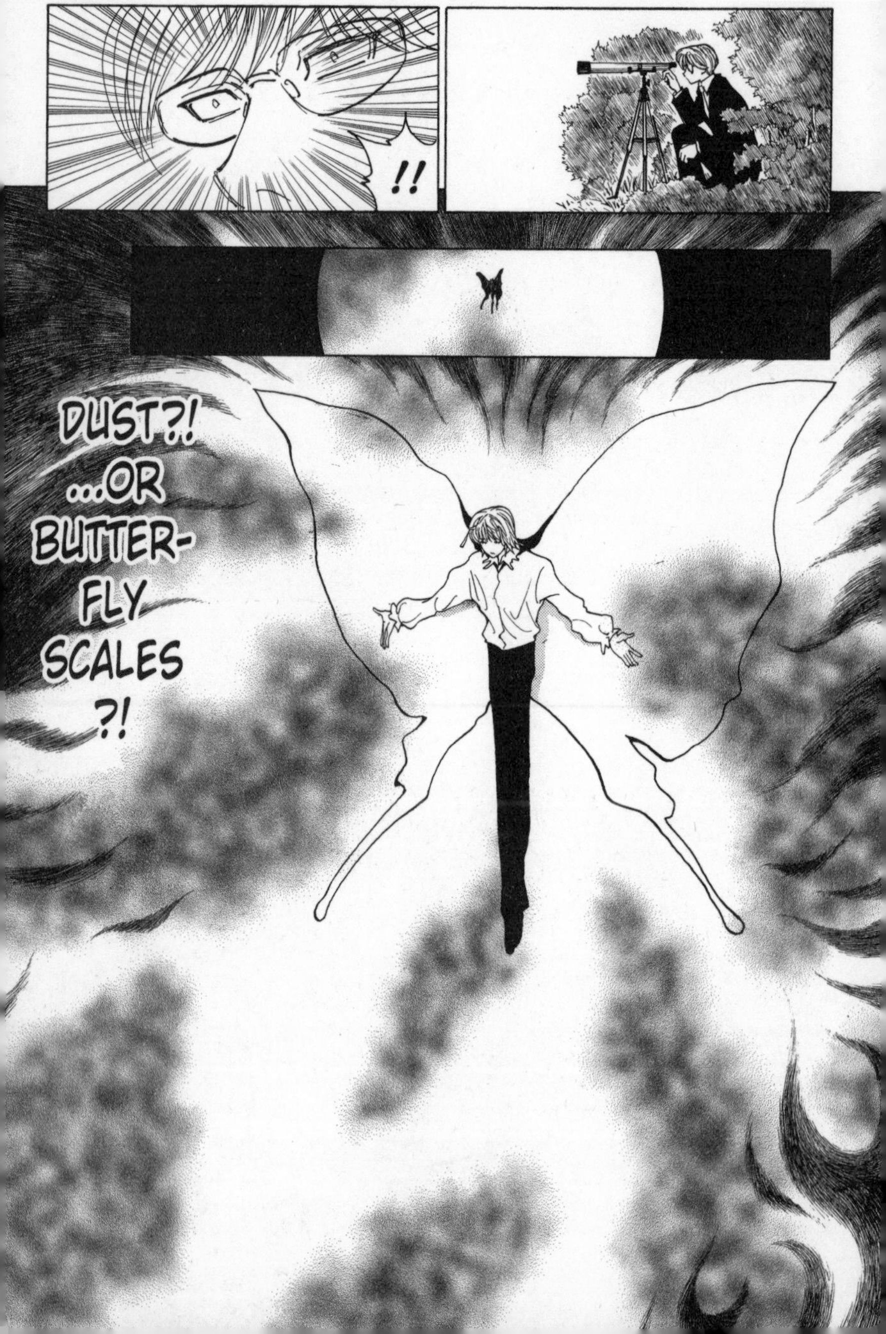
!!
DUST?! ...OR BUTTER-FLY SCALES ?!

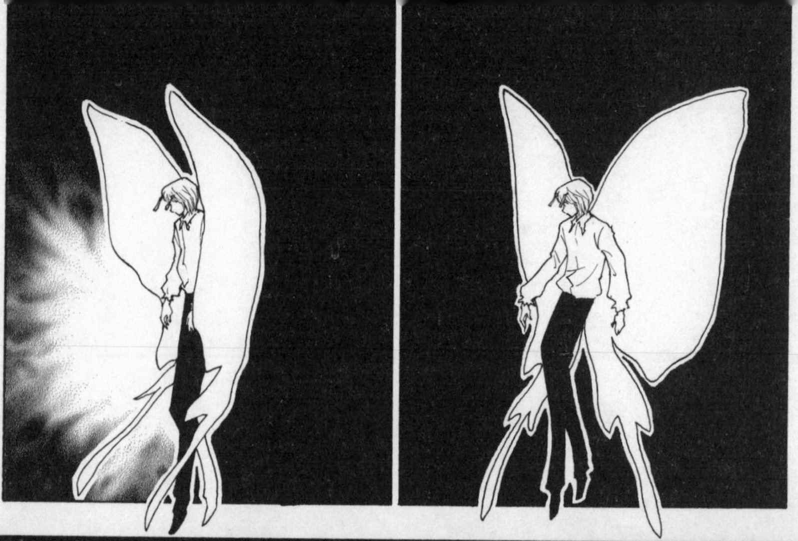

Chapter 260: 1: Part 4

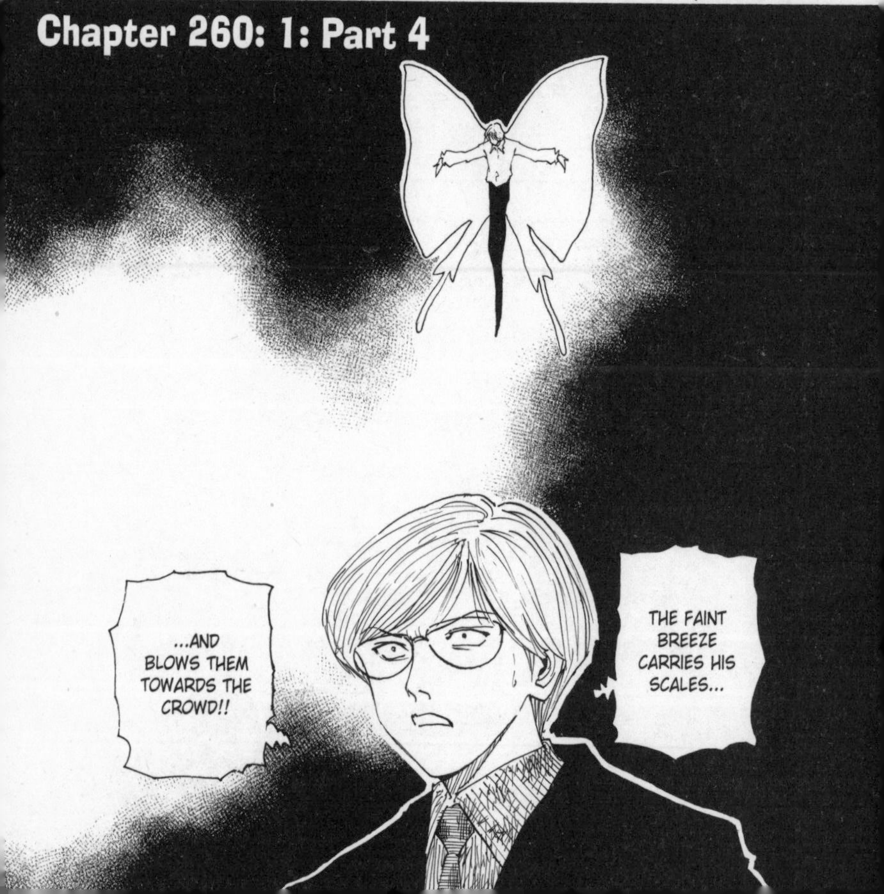
THE FAINT BREEZE CARRIES HIS SCALES...
...AND BLOWS THEM TOWARDS THE CROWD!!

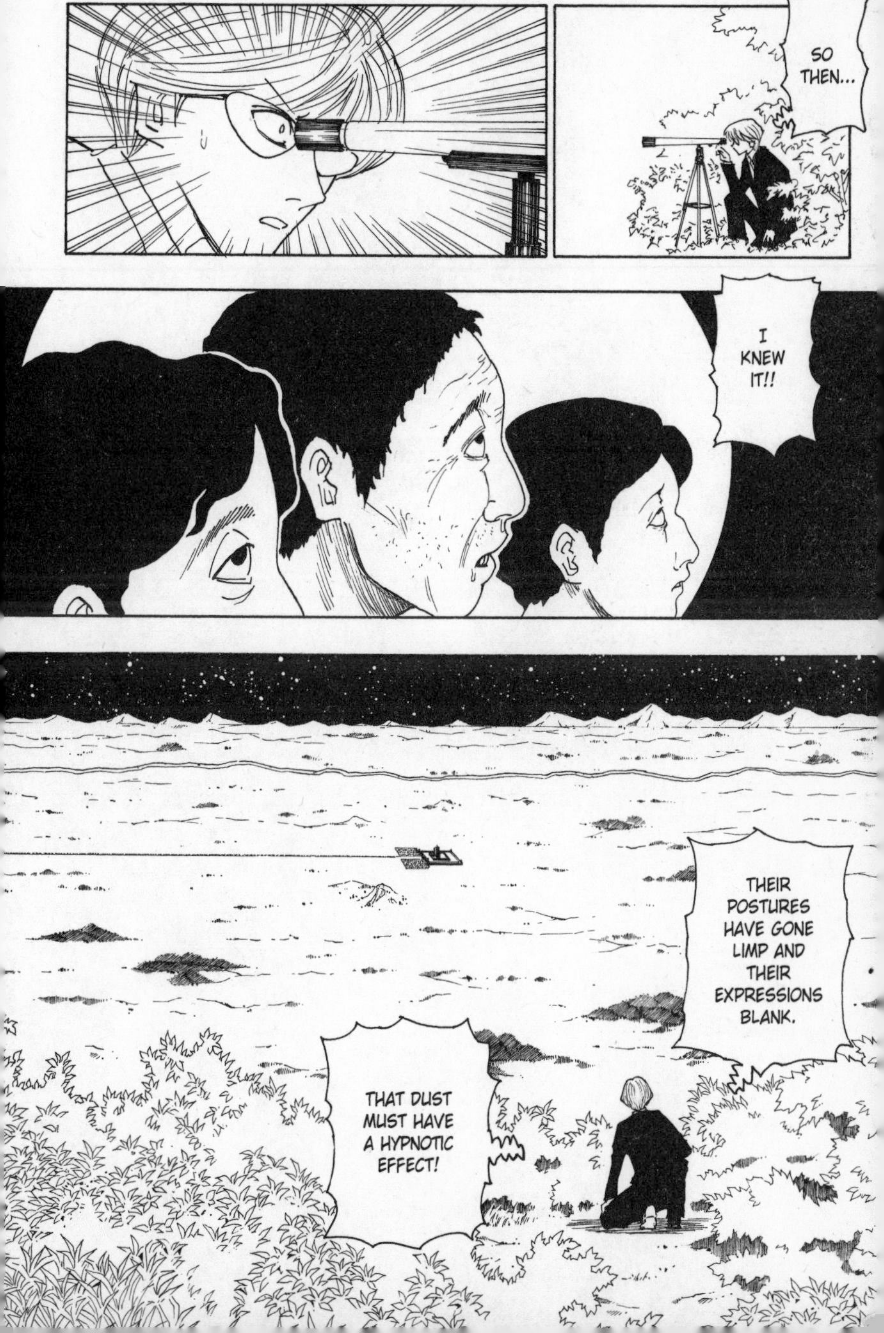
SO THEN...
I KNEW IT!!
THEIR POSTURES HAVE GONE LIMP AND THEIR EXPRESSIONS BLANK.
THAT DUST MUST HAVE A HYPNOTIC EFFECT!

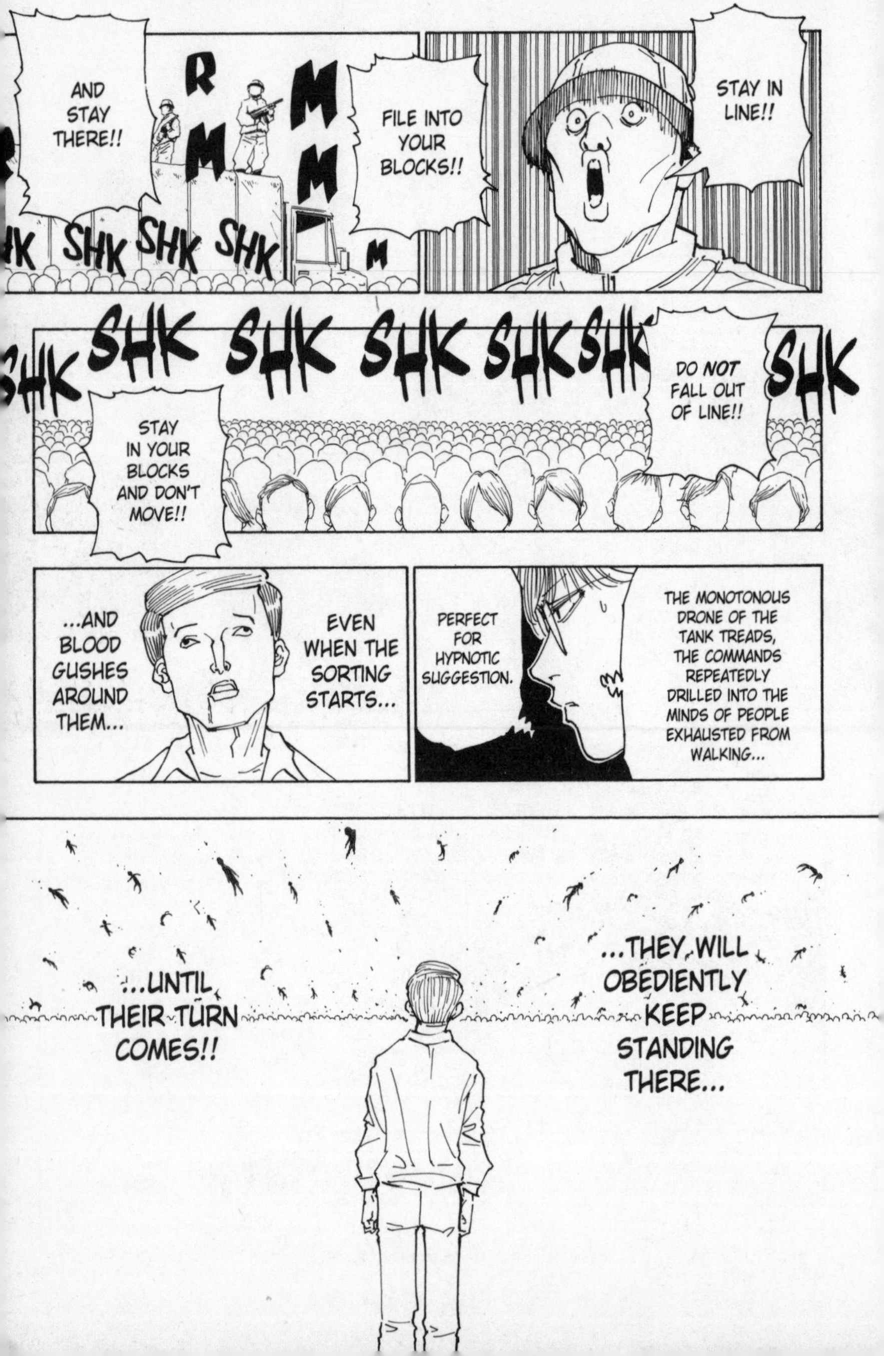
STAY IN LINE!!
FILE INTO YOUR BLOCKS!!
MMMM
RM
AND STAY THERE!!
SHK SHK SHK
DO NOT FALL OUT OF LINE!!
SHK SHK SHK SHK SHKSHK SHK
STAY IN YOUR BLOCKS AND DON'T MOVE!!
THE MONOTONOUS DRONE OF THE TANK TREADS, THE COMMANDS REPEATEDLY DRILLED INTO THE MINDS OF PEOPLE EXHAUSTED FROM WALKING...
PERFECT FOR HYPNOTIC SUGGESTION.
EVEN WHEN THE SORTING STARTS...
...AND BLOOD GUSHES AROUND THEM...
...THEY WILL OBEDIENTLY KEEP STANDING THERE...
...UNTIL THEIR TURN COMES!!

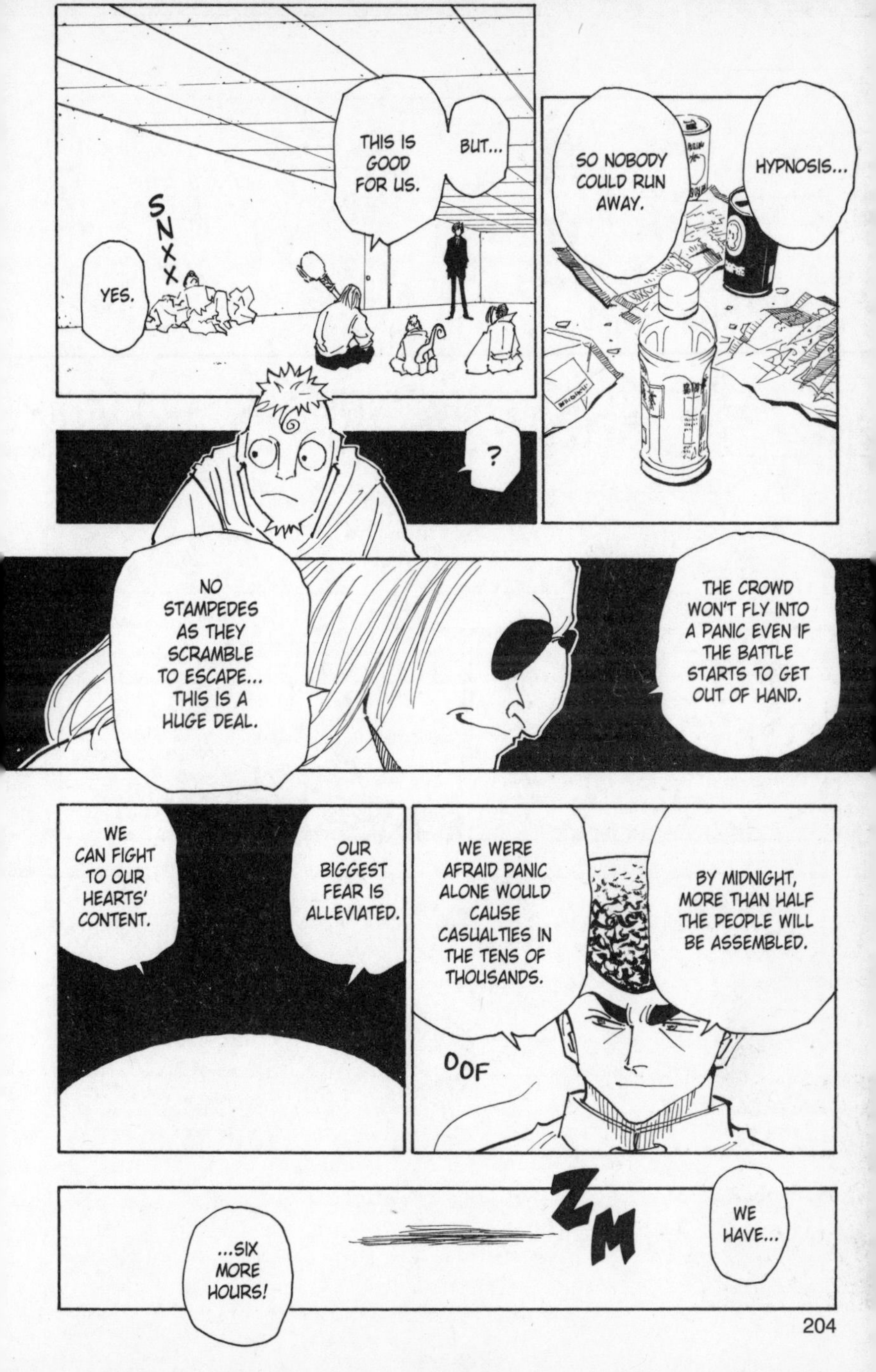
HYPNOSIS...
SO NOBODY COULD RUN AWAY.
BUT...
THIS IS GOOD FOR US.
SNXX
YES.
?
THE CROWD WON'T FLY INTO A PANIC EVEN IF THE BATTLE STARTS TO GET OUT OF HAND.
NO STAMPEDES AS THEY SCRAMBLE TO ESCAPE... THIS IS A HUGE DEAL.
BY MIDNIGHT, MORE THAN HALF THE PEOPLE WILL BE ASSEMBLED.
WE WERE AFRAID PANIC ALONE WOULD CAUSE CASUALTIES IN THE TENS OF THOUSANDS.
OOF
OUR BIGGEST FEAR IS ALLEVIATED.
WE CAN FIGHT TO OUR HEARTS' CONTENT.
WE HAVE...
ZM
...SIX MORE HOURS!

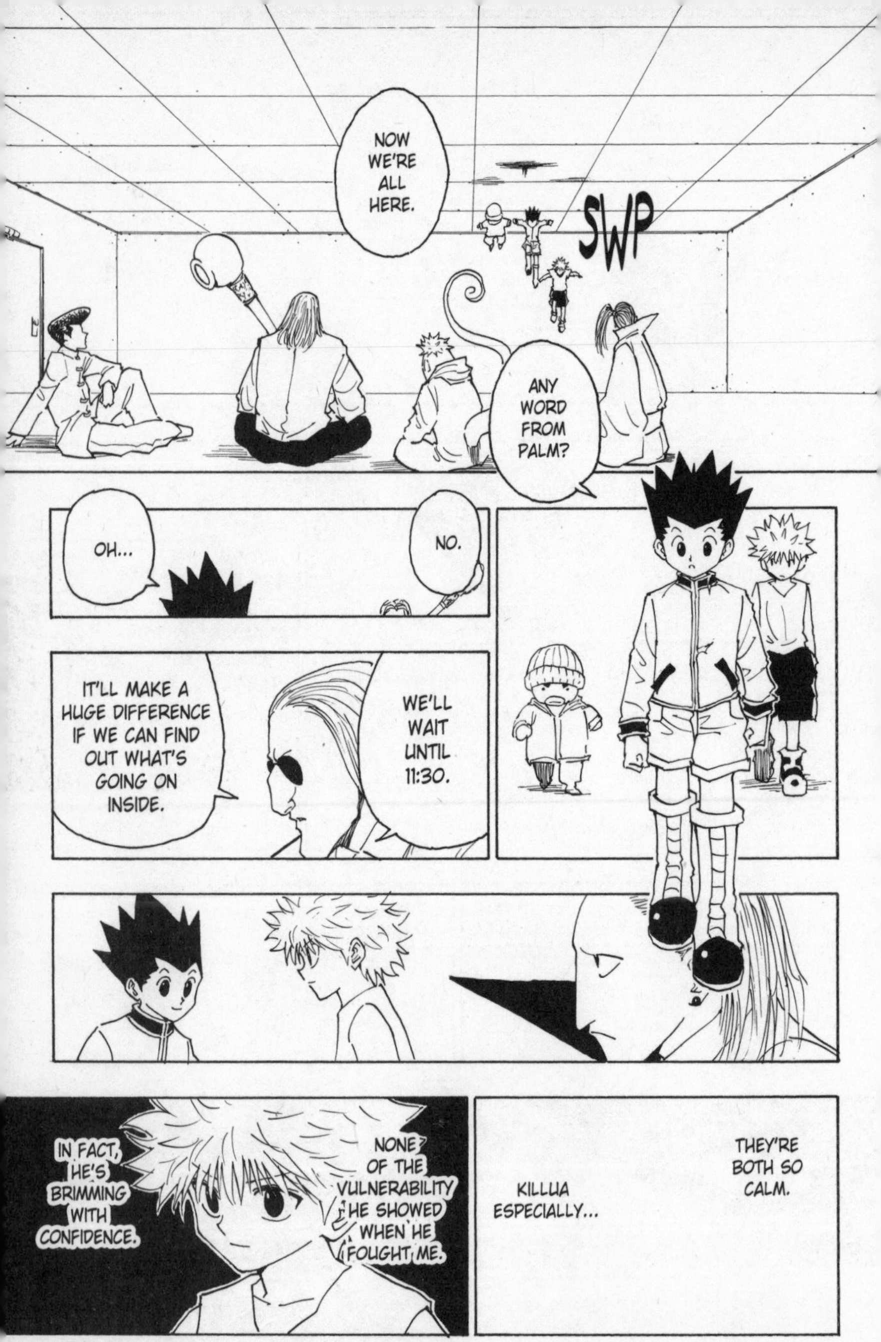
SWP
NOW WE'RE ALL HERE.
ANY WORD FROM PALM?
NO.
OH...
WE'LL WAIT UNTIL 11:30.
IT'LL MAKE A HUGE DIFFERENCE IF WE CAN FIND OUT WHAT'S GOING ON INSIDE.
THEY'RE BOTH SO CALM.
KILLUA ESPECIALLY...
NONE OF THE VULNERABILITY HE SHOWED WHEN HE FOUGHT ME.
IN FACT, HE'S BRIMMING WITH CONFIDENCE.

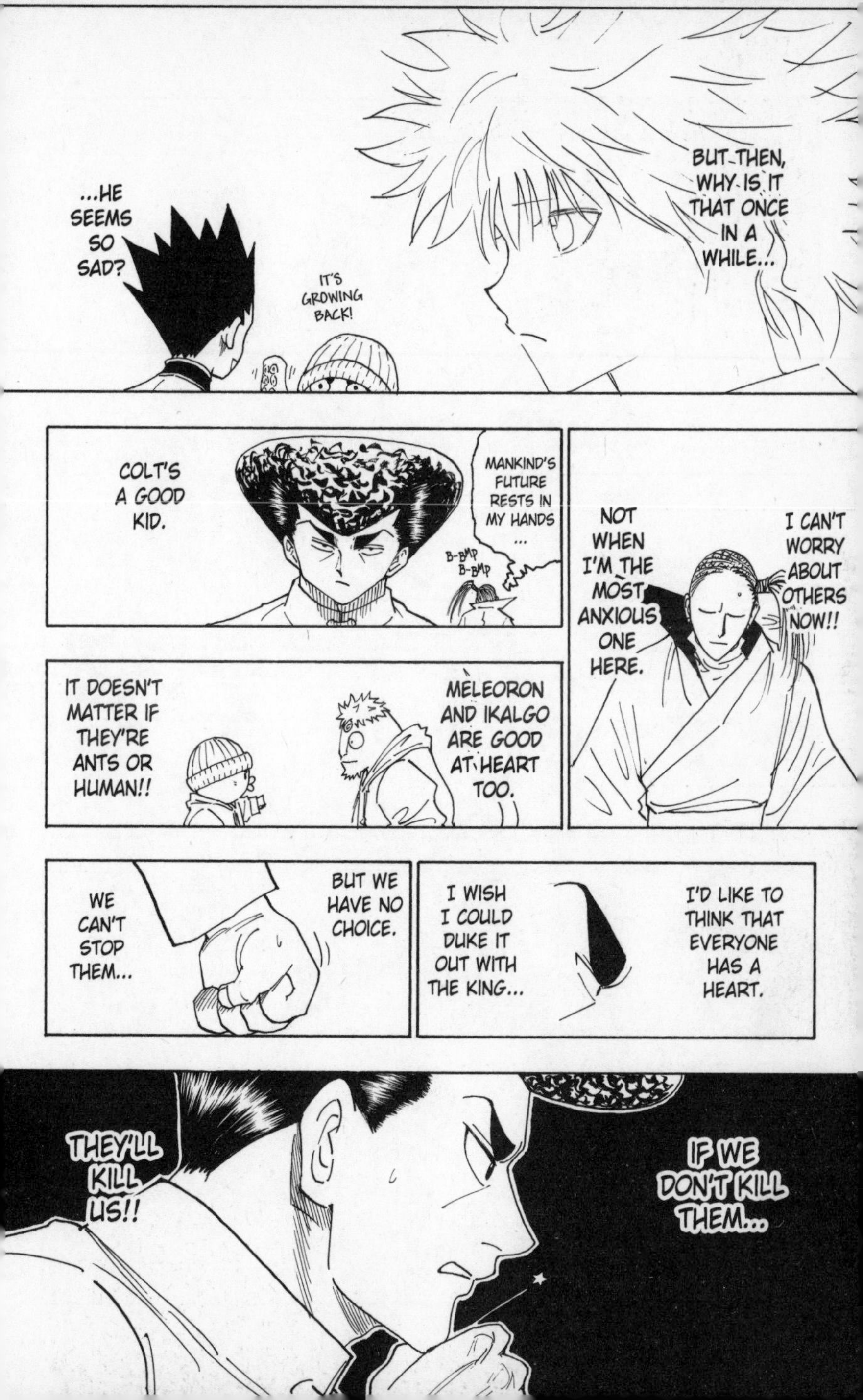
BUT THEN, WHY IS IT THAT ONCE IN A WHILE...
...HE SEEMS SO SAD?
IT'S GROWING BACK!
I CAN'T WORRY ABOUT OTHERS NOW!!
NOT WHEN I'M THE MOST ANXIOUS ONE HERE.
MANKIND'S FUTURE RESTS IN MY HANDS ...
B-BMP B-BMP
COLT'S A GOOD KID.
MELEORON AND IKALGO ARE GOOD AT HEART TOO.
IT DOESN'T MATTER IF THEY'RE ANTS OR HUMAN!!
I'D LIKE TO THINK THAT EVERYONE HAS A HEART.
I WISH I COULD DUKE IT OUT WITH THE KING...
BUT WE HAVE NO CHOICE.
WE CAN'T STOP THEM...
IF WE DON'T KILL THEM...
THEY'LL KILL US!!

READ THIS WAY

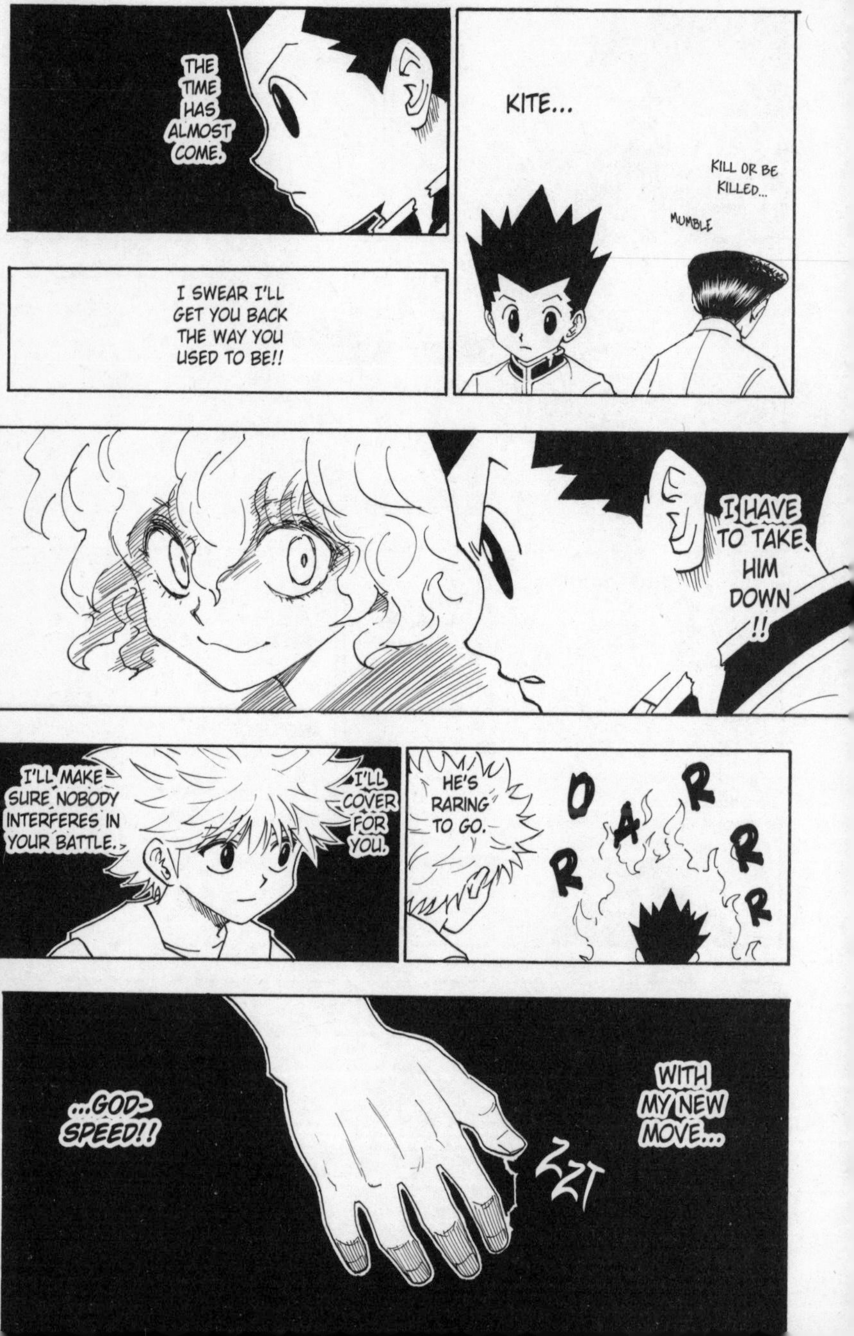
KITE...
KILL OR BE KILLED...
MUMBLE
THE TIME HAS ALMOST COME.
I SWEAR I'LL GET YOU BACK THE WAY YOU USED TO BE!!
I HAVE TO TAKE HIM DOWN!!
HE'S RARING TO GO.
ORARRR
I'LL COVER FOR YOU.
I'LL MAKE SURE NOBODY INTERFERES IN YOUR BATTLE.
WITH MY NEW MOVE...
...GOD-SPEED!!
ZZT

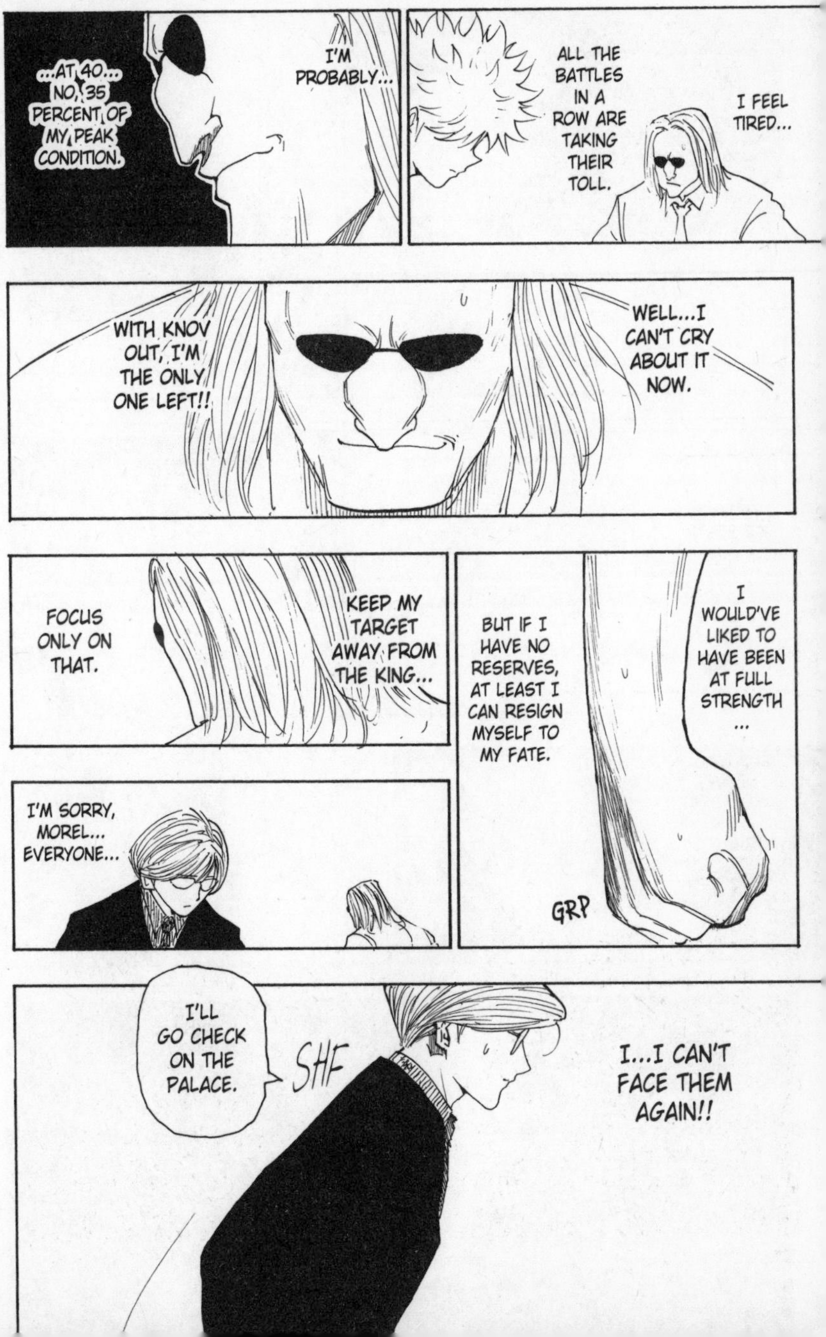
I FEEL TIRED...
ALL THE BATTLES IN A ROW ARE TAKING THEIR TOLL.
I'M PROBABLY...
...AT 40... NO, 35 PERCENT OF MY PEAK CONDITION.
WELL...I CAN'T CRY ABOUT IT NOW.
WITH KNOV OUT, I'M THE ONLY ONE LEFT!!
I WOULD'VE LIKED TO HAVE BEEN AT FULL STRENGTH ...
BUT IF I HAVE NO RESERVES, AT LEAST I CAN RESIGN MYSELF TO MY FATE.
GRP
KEEP MY TARGET AWAY FROM THE KING...
FOCUS ONLY ON THAT.
I'M SORRY, MOREL... EVERYONE...
I...I CAN'T FACE THEM AGAIN!!
SHF
I'LL GO CHECK ON THE PALACE.

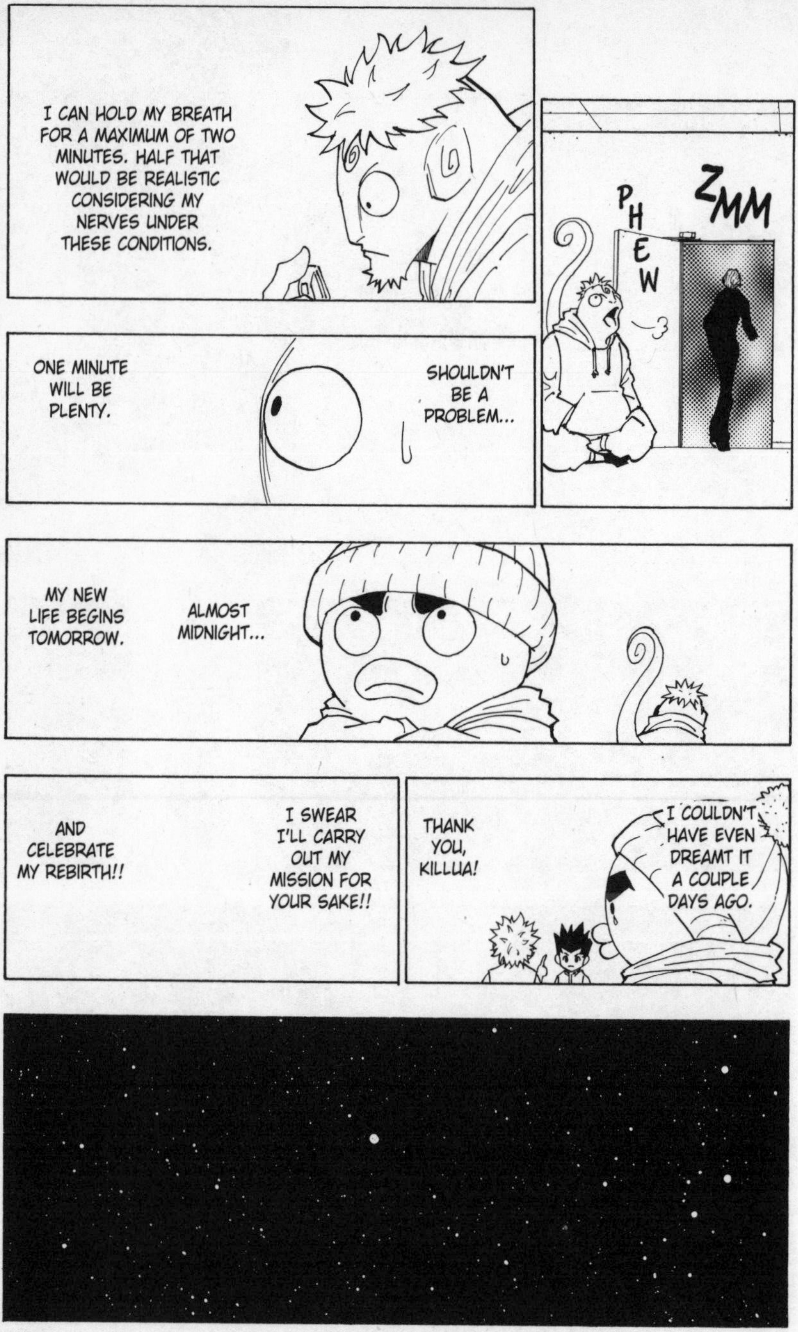
ZMM
PHEW
I CAN HOLD MY BREATH FOR A MAXIMUM OF TWO MINUTES. HALF THAT WOULD BE REALISTIC CONSIDERING MY NERVES UNDER THESE CONDITIONS.
SHOULDN'T BE A PROBLEM...
ONE MINUTE WILL BE PLENTY.
ALMOST MIDNIGHT...
MY NEW LIFE BEGINS TOMORROW.
I COULDN'T HAVE EVEN DREAMT IT A COUPLE DAYS AGO.
THANK YOU, KILLUA!
I SWEAR I'LL CARRY OUT MY MISSION FOR YOUR SAKE!!
AND CELEBRATE MY REBIRTH!!

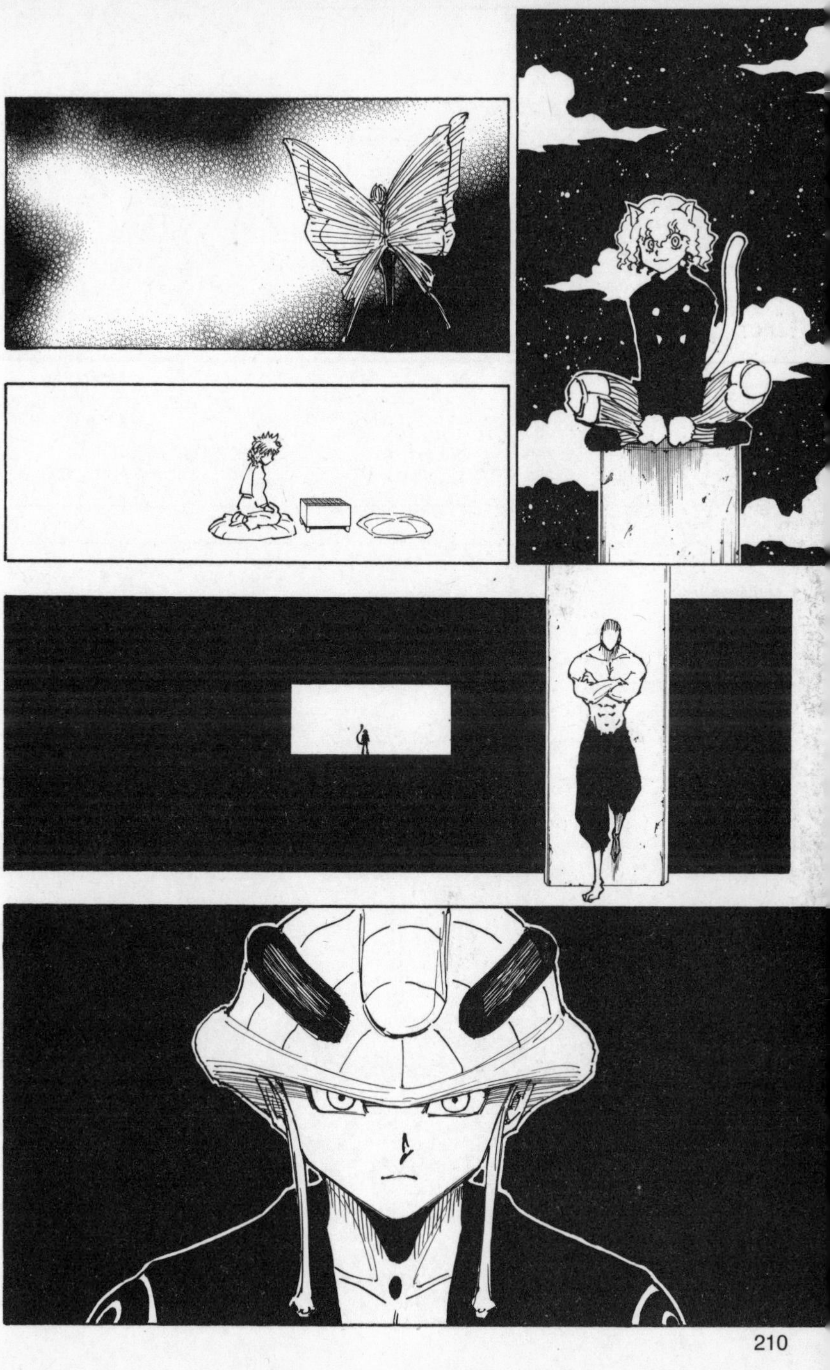

READ THIS WAY

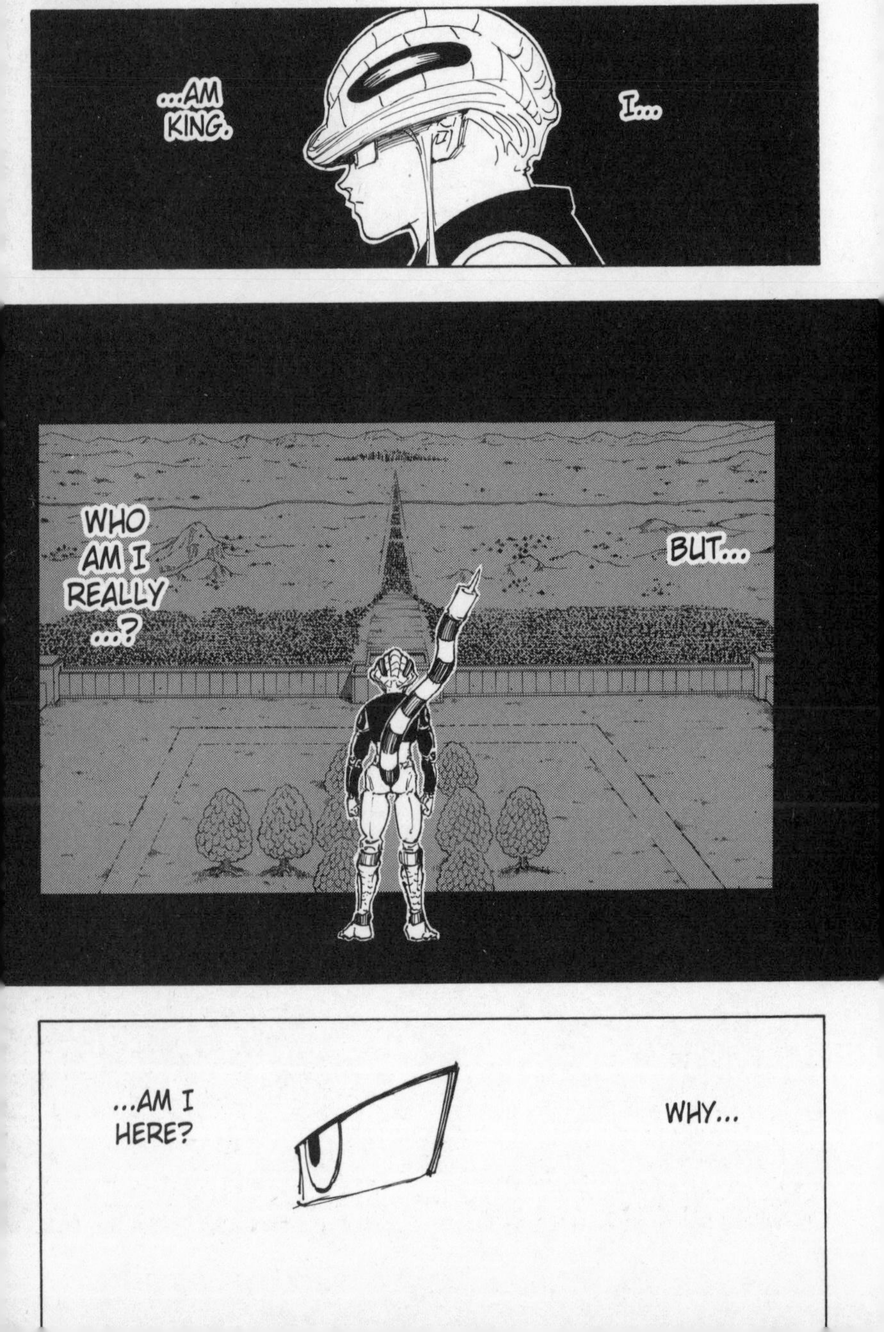
I...
...AM KING.
BUT...
WHO AM I REALLY ...?
WHY...
...AM I HERE?

FOR WHAT
REASON...

...WAS
I BORN?

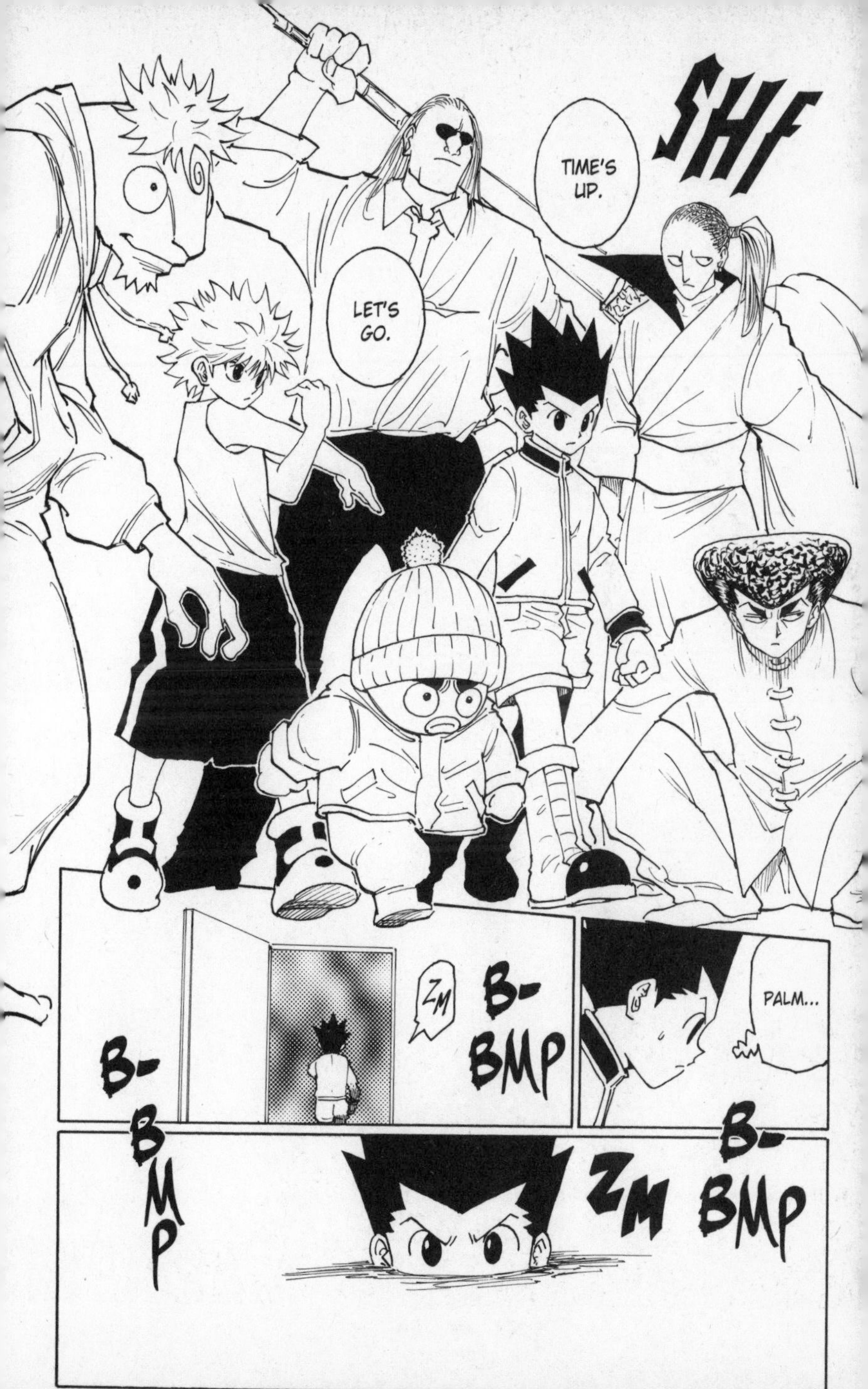
SHF
TIME'S UP.
LET'S GO.
PALM...
B-BMP
ZM
B-BMP
B-BMP
ZM
B-BMP

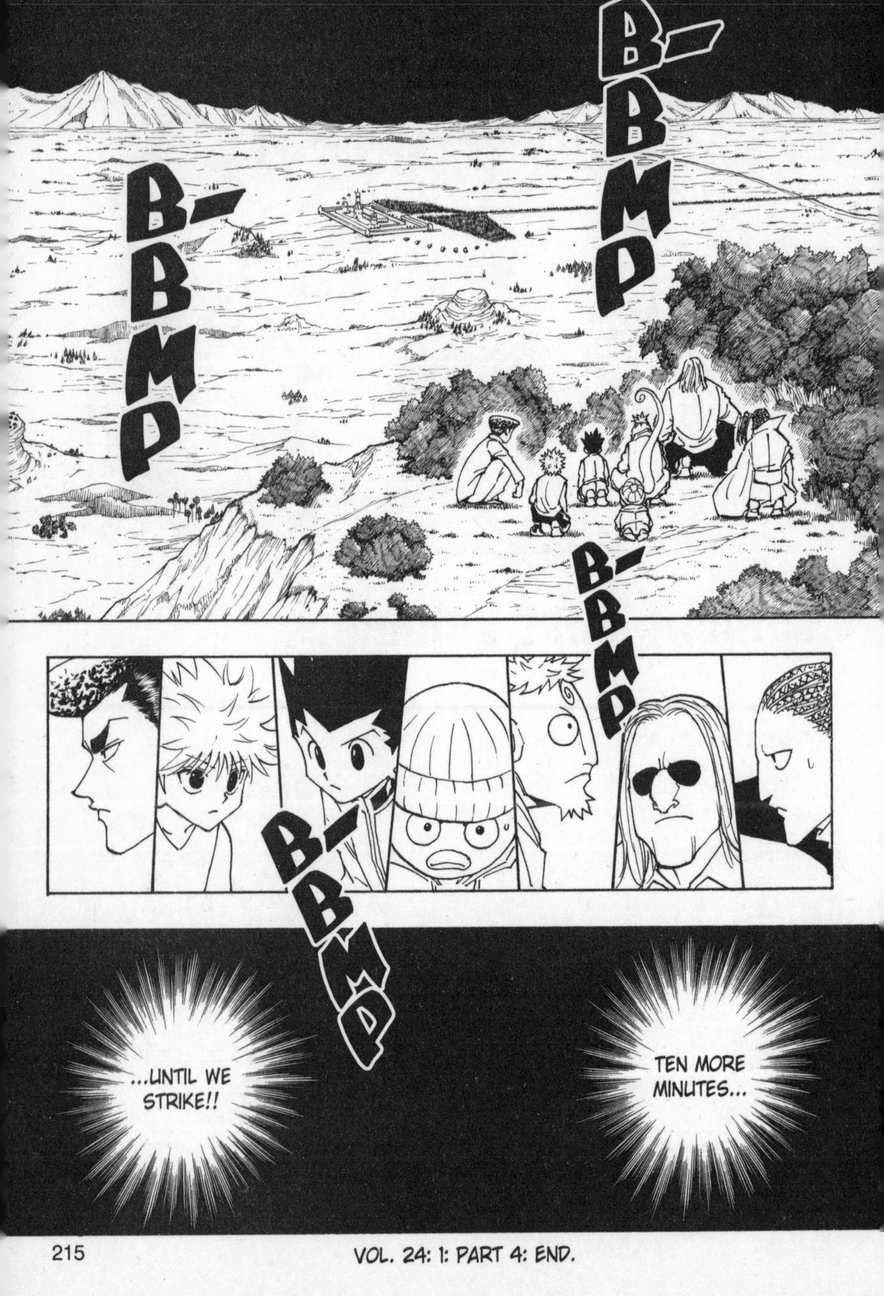
B-BMP
B-BMP
B-BMP
B-BMP
TEN MORE MINUTES...
...UNTIL WE STRIKE!!

VOL. 24: 1: PART 4: END.

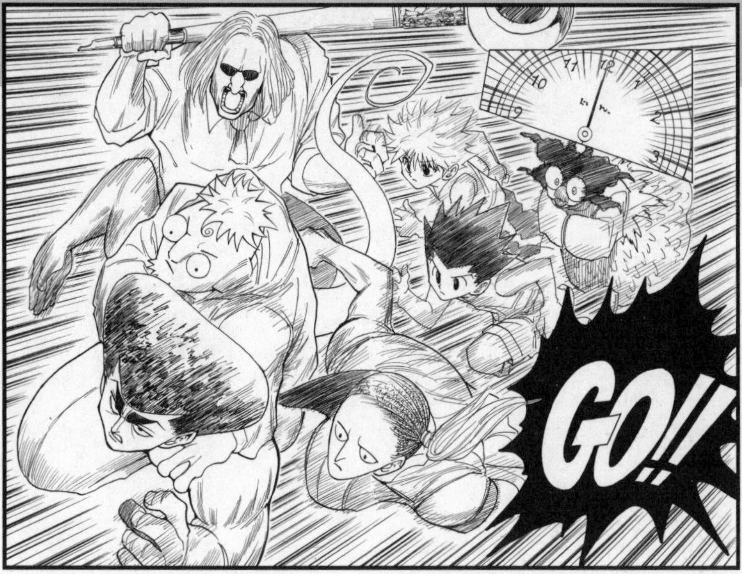
GO!!

Coming Next Volume...

Tick tock, tick tock! The final hour nears as the Hunters prepare to take on the Chimera Ant King! As they go in for the kill, they'll have some surprising allies on their side. But an unexpected turn of events may shake the Hunters' resolve when they see a side of the King that seems almost *human*...

Available now!

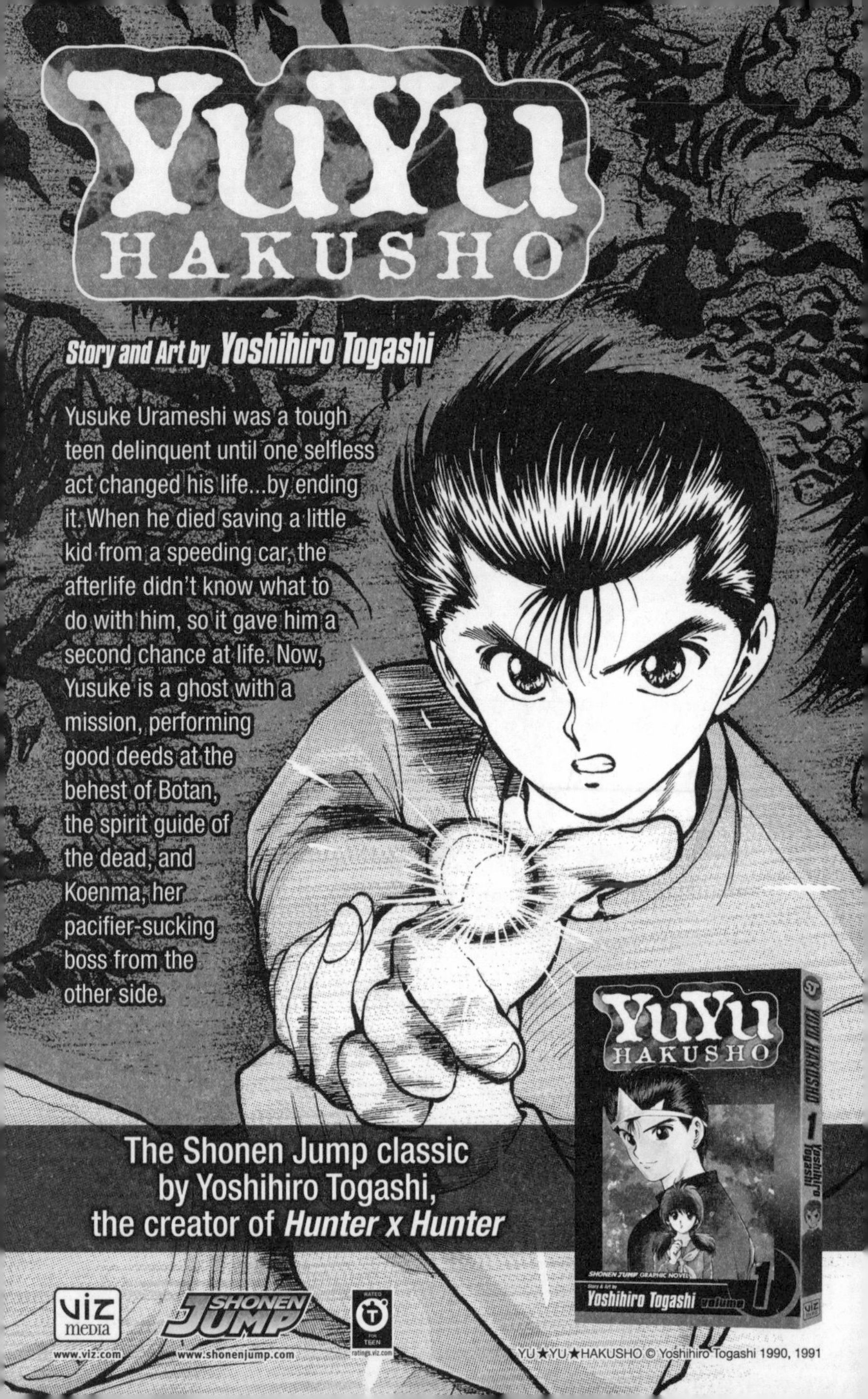
YuYu HAKUSHO
Story and Art by Yoshihiro Togashi
Yusuke Urameshi was a tough teen delinquent until one selfless act changed his life...by ending it. When he died saving a little kid from a speeding car, the afterlife didn't know what to do with him, so it gave him a second chance at life. Now, Yusuke is a ghost with a mission, performing good deeds at the behest of Botan, the spirit guide of the dead, and Koenma, her pacifier-sucking boss from the other side.
YuYu HAKUSHO
SHONEN JUMP GRAPHIC NOVEL
Story & Art by Yoshihiro Togashi volume 1
The Shonen Jump classic by Yoshihiro Togashi, the creator of *Hunter x Hunter*
www.viz.com
www.shonenjump.com
ratings.viz.com
YU★YU★HAKUSHO © Yoshihiro Togashi 1990, 1991

IN A SAVAGE WORLD RULED BY THE PURSUIT OF THE MOST DELICIOUS FOODS, IT'S EITHER EAT OR BE EATEN!

"The most bizarrely entertaining manga out there on comic shelves. *Toriko* is a great series. If you're looking for a weirdly fun book or a fighting manga with a bizarre take, this is the story for you to read."

—ComicAttack.com

TORIKO

Story and Art by **Mitsutoshi Shimabukuro**

In an era where the world's gone crazy for increasingly bizarre gourmet foods, only Gourmet Hunter Toriko can hunt down the ferocious ingredients that supply the world's best restaurants. Join Toriko as he tracks and defeats the tastiest and most dangerous animals with his bare hands.

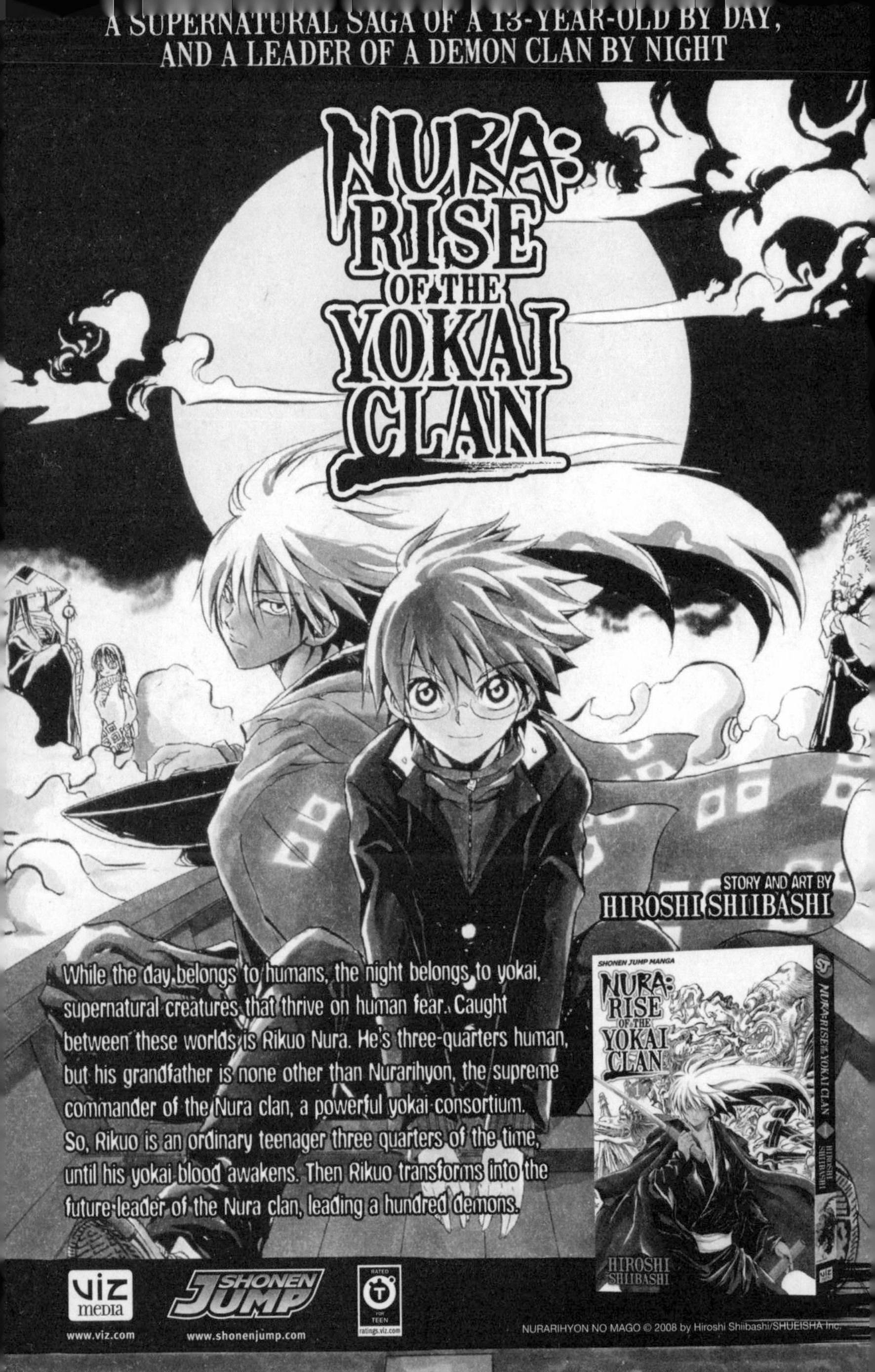
A SUPERNATURAL SAGA OF A 13-YEAR-OLD BY DAY, AND A LEADER OF A DEMON CLAN BY NIGHT
NURA: RISE OF THE YOKAI CLAN
STORY AND ART BY
HIROSHI SHIIBASHI
While the day belongs to humans, the night belongs to yokai, supernatural creatures that thrive on human fear. Caught between these worlds is Rikuo Nura. He's three-quarters human, but his grandfather is none other than Nurarihyon, the supreme commander of the Nura clan, a powerful yokai consortium. So, Rikuo is an ordinary teenager three quarters of the time, until his yokai blood awakens. Then Rikuo transforms into the future leader of the Nura clan, leading a hundred demons.
SHONEN JUMP MANGA
NURA: RISE OF THE YOKAI CLAN
HIROSHI SHIIBASHI
VIZ MEDIA
www.viz.com
SHONEN JUMP
www.shonenjump.com
RATED T FOR TEEN
ratings.viz.com
NURARIHYON NO MAGO © 2008 by Hiroshi Shiibashi/SHUEISHA Inc.

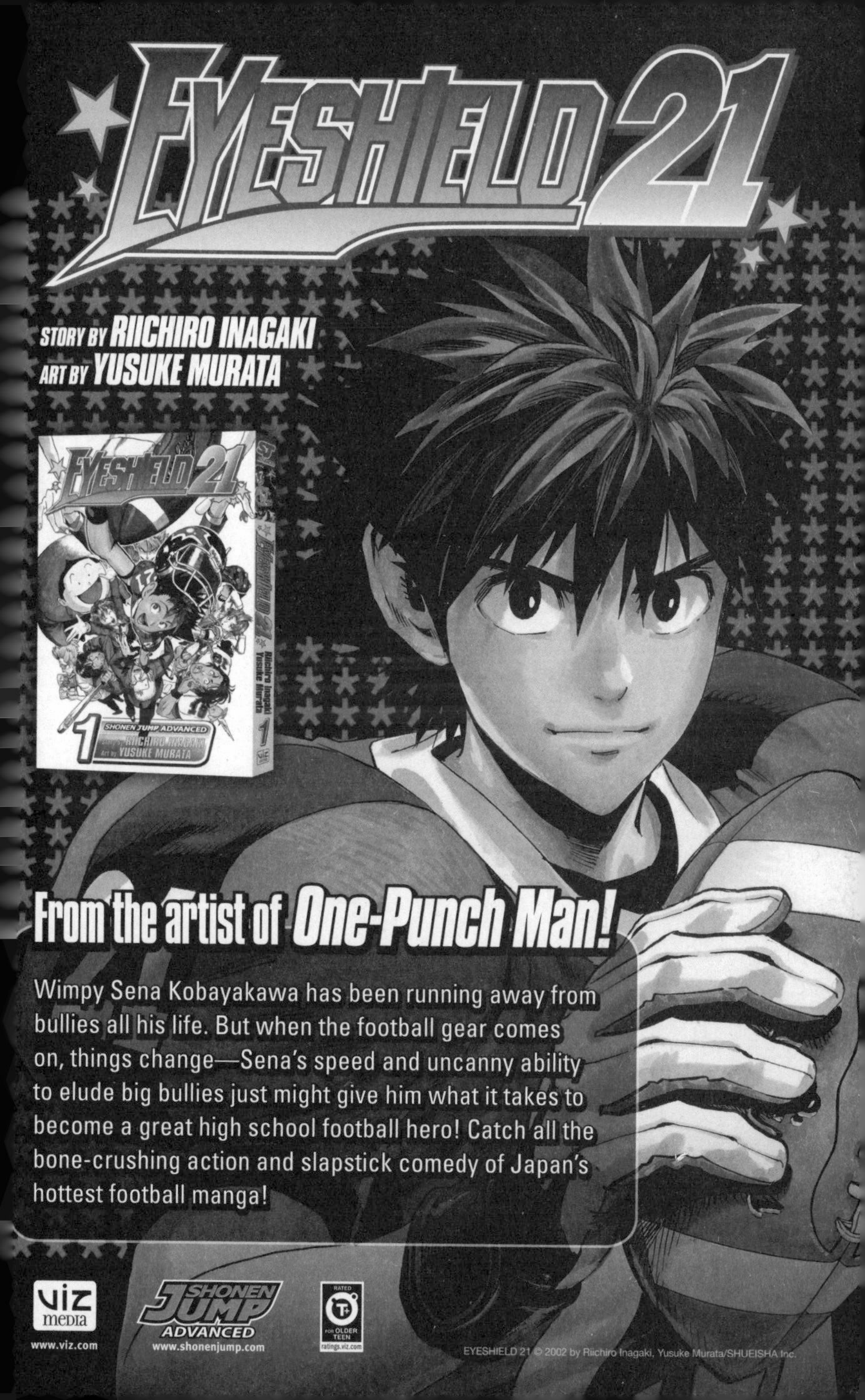
EYESHIELD 21
STORY BY RIICHIRO INAGAKI
ART BY YUSUKE MURATA
EYESHIELD 21
SHONEN JUMP ADVANCED
1
Story by RIICHIRO INAGAKI
Art by YUSUKE MURATA
Riichiro Inagaki
Yusuke Murata
From the artist of One-Punch Man!
Wimpy Sena Kobayakawa has been running away from bullies all his life. But when the football gear comes on, things change—Sena's speed and uncanny ability to elude big bullies just might give him what it takes to become a great high school football hero! Catch all the bone-crushing action and slapstick comedy of Japan's hottest football manga!
viz media
www.viz.com
SHONEN JUMP ADVANCED
www.shonenjump.com
RATED T+ FOR OLDER TEEN
ratings.viz.com
EYESHIELD 21 © 2002 by Riichiro Inagaki, Yusuke Murata/SHUEISHA Inc.

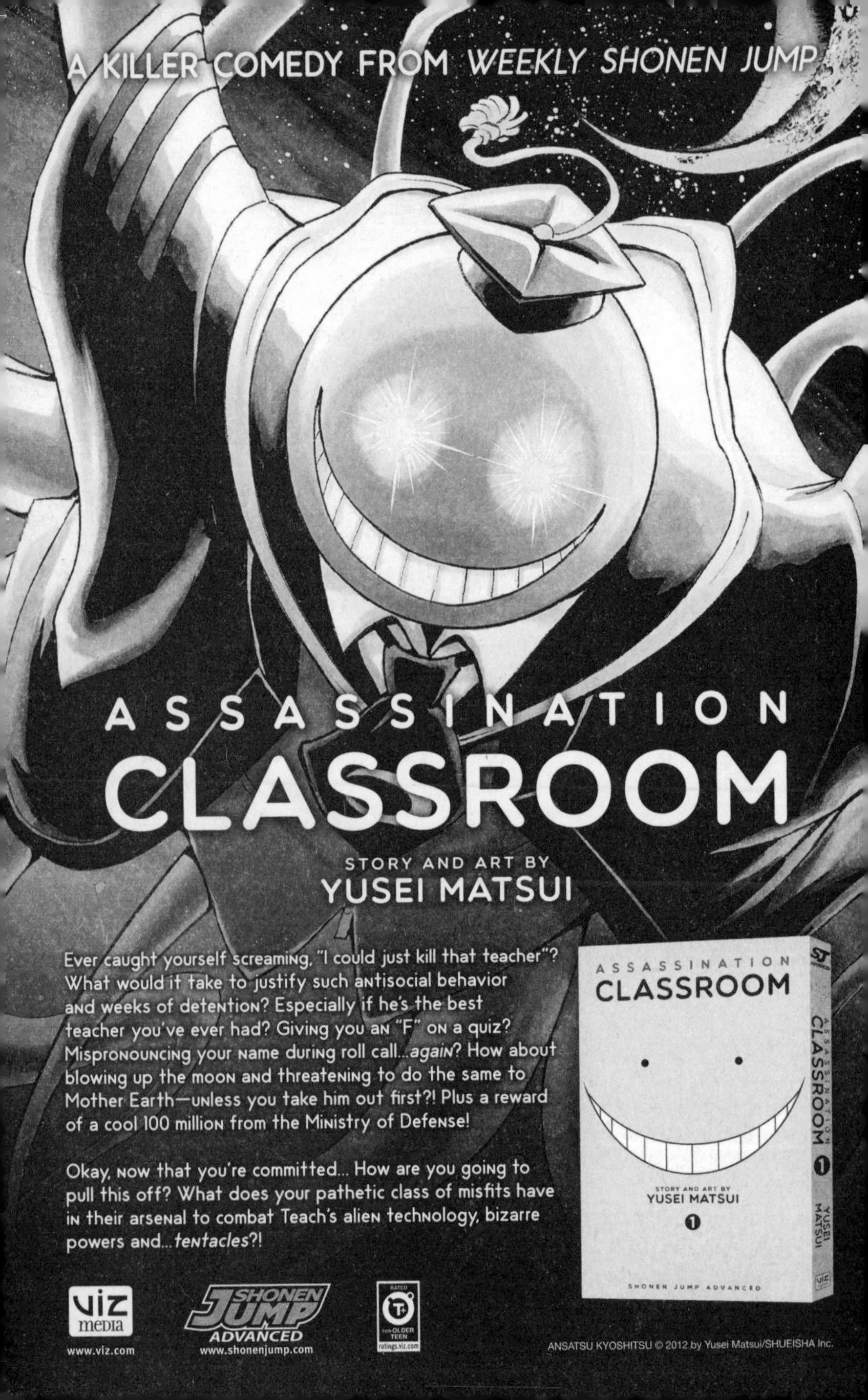
A KILLER COMEDY FROM *WEEKLY SHONEN JUMP*
ASSASSINATION
CLASSROOM
STORY AND ART BY
YUSEI MATSUI
Ever caught yourself screaming, "I could just kill that teacher"? What would it take to justify such antisocial behavior and weeks of detention? Especially if he's the best teacher you've ever had? Giving you an "F" on a quiz? Mispronouncing your name during roll call...*again*? How about blowing up the moon and threatening to do the same to Mother Earth—unless you take him out first?! Plus a reward of a cool 100 million from the Ministry of Defense!
Okay, now that you're committed... How are you going to pull this off? What does your pathetic class of misfits have in their arsenal to combat Teach's alien technology, bizarre powers and...*tentacles*?!
ASSASSINATION CLASSROOM
STORY AND ART BY
YUSEI MATSUI
1
SHONEN JUMP ADVANCED
viz media
www.viz.com
SHONEN JUMP ADVANCED
www.shonenjump.com
RATED T+ FOR OLDER TEEN
ratings.viz.com
ANSATSU KYOSHITSU © 2012 by Yusei Matsui/SHUEISHA Inc.

Seraph of the End
VAMPIRE REIGN

STORY BY Takaya Kagami ART BY Yamato Yamamoto
STORYBOARDS BY Daisuke Furuya

Vampires reign—humans revolt!

Seraph of the End
VAMPIRE REIGN
1
STORY BY Takaya Kagami
ART BY Yamato Yamamoto
Daisuke Furuya

Yuichiro's dream of killing every vampire is near-impossible, given that vampires are seven times stronger than humans, and the only way to kill them is by mastering Cursed Gear, advanced demon-possessed weaponry. Not to mention that humanity's most elite Vampire Extermination Unit, the Moon Demon Company, wants nothing to do with Yuichiro unless he can prove he's willing to work in a team—which is the last thing he wants!

THE LATEST CHAPTERS SERIALIZED IN WEEKLY SHONEN JUMP

RATED T+ FOR OLDER TEEN ratings.viz.com

SHONEN JUMP ADVANCED www.shonenjump.com

VIZ media www.viz.com

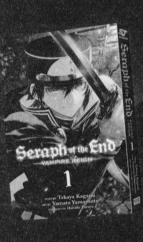

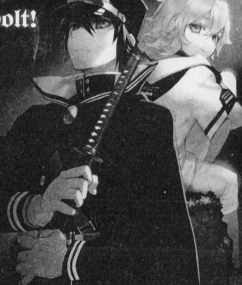

You're Reading in the Wrong Direction!!

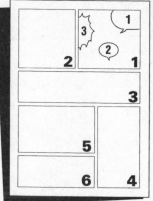

Whoops! Guess what? You're starting at the wrong end of the comic!

…It's true! In keeping with the original Japanese format, **Hunter x Hunter** is meant to be read from right to left, starting in the upper-right corner.

Unlike English, which is read from left to right, Japanese is read from right to left, meaning that action, sound effects and word-balloon order are completely reversed… something which can make readers unfamiliar with Japanese feel pretty backwards themselves. For this reason, manga or Japanese comics published in the U.S. in English have sometimes been published "flopped" – that is, printed in exact reverse order, as though seen from the other side of a mirror.

By flopping pages, U.S. publishers can avoid confusing readers, but the compromise is not without its downside. For one thing, a character in a flopped manga series who once wore in the original Japanese version a T-shirt emblazoned with "M A Y" (as in "the merry month of") now wears one which reads "Y A M"! Additionally, many manga creators in Japan are themselves unhappy with the process, as some feel the mirror-imaging of their art skews their original intentions.

We are proud to bring you Yoshihiro Togashi's **Hunter x Hunter** in the original unflopped format. For now, though, turn to the other side of the book and let the adventure begin…!

–Editor

Ceya

Hey! You're Reading in the Wrong Direction!

This is the end of this graphic novel!

To properly enjoy this VIZ graphic novel, please turn it around and begin reading from right to left. Unlike English, Japanese is read right to left, so Japanese comics are read in reverse order from the way English comics are typically read.

This book has been printed in the original Japanese format in order to preserve the orientation of the original artwork. Have fun with it!

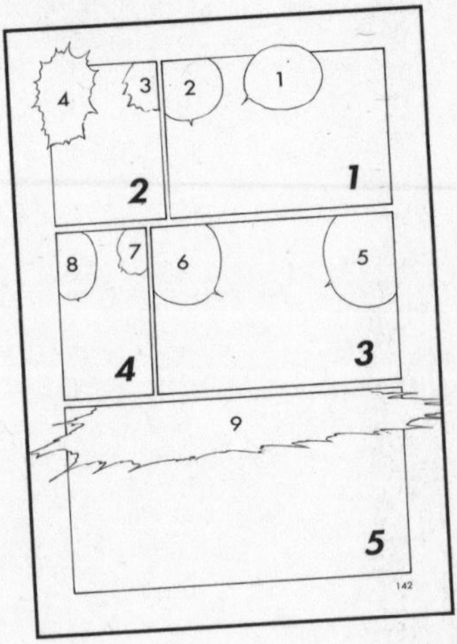

1
2
1
3
4
2
5
6
3
7
8
4
9
5
142

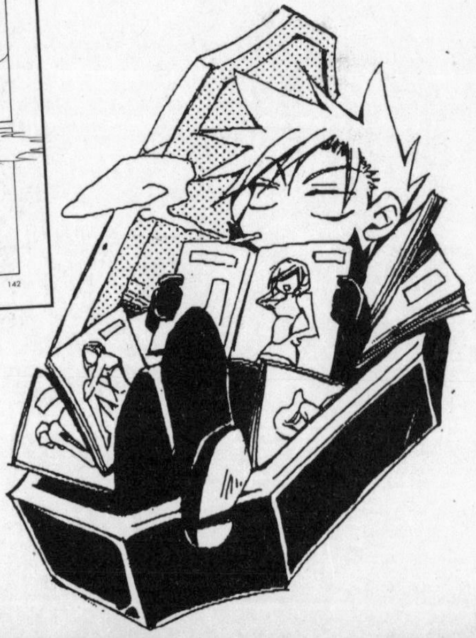

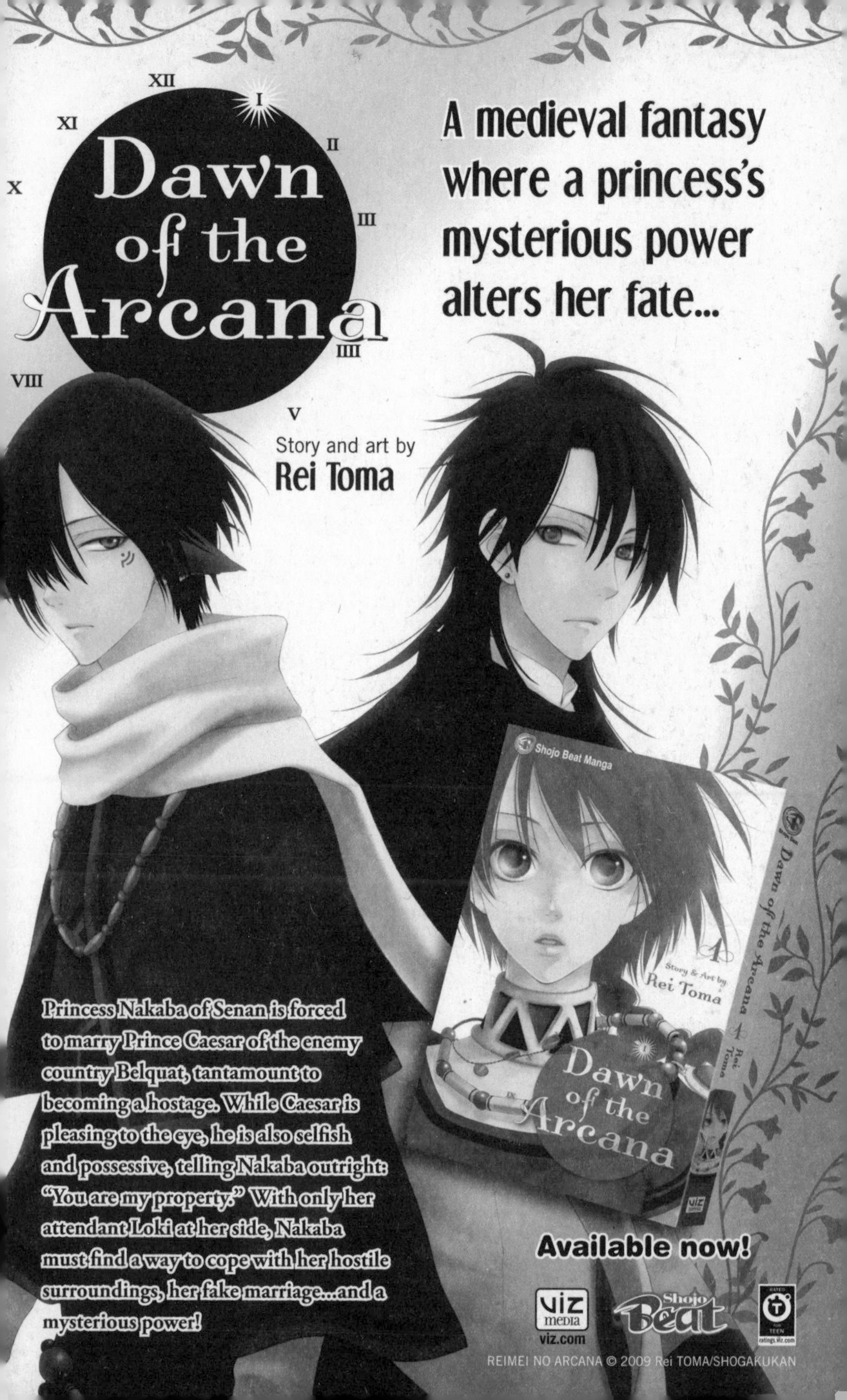
Dawn of the Arcana
A medieval fantasy where a princess's mysterious power alters her fate...
Story and art by
Rei Toma
Shojo Beat Manga
Dawn of the Arcana
Story & Art by
Rei Toma
Princess Nakaba of Senan is forced to marry Prince Caesar of the enemy country Belquat, tantamount to becoming a hostage. While Caesar is pleasing to the eye, he is also selfish and possessive, telling Nakaba outright: "You are my property." With only her attendant Loki at her side, Nakaba must find a way to cope with her hostile surroundings, her fake marriage...and a mysterious power!
Available now!
viz media
viz.com
Shojo Beat
REIMEI NO ARCANA © 2009 Rei TOMA/SHOGAKUKAN

07-GHOST

Volume 2

STORY AND ART BY
YUKI AMEMIYA and
YUKINO ICHIHARA

Translation/Satsuki Yamashita
Touch-up Art & Lettering/Vanessa Satone
Design/Yukiko Whitley
Editor/Hope Donovan

07-GHOST © 2006
by Yuki Amemiya/Yukino Ichihara
All rights reserved.
Original Japanese edition published by
ICHIJINSHA, INC., Tokyo.
English translation rights arranged with
ICHIJINSHA, INC.

Printed in Canada

Published by VIZ Media, LLC
P.O. Box 77010
San Francisco, CA 94107

10 9 8 7 6 5 4 3
First printing, January 2013
Third printing, December 2015

www.viz.com